MW01625638

The Gods of The God's Own Country: THEYYAM STORIES

Confessions of a Monkey-Trapped Prodigal Son of The God's Own Country

Tiger Rider, Santhosh Vengara, Saji Madapat

This storybook is the second part of the book: "The Gods of The God's Own Country: THEYYAM "(ASIN: B0BD3M3MJ5). Publishing it as volume II because of Amazon's file size limit (650MB). The royalties from this book will be donated to those destitute Gods of the God's Own Country for a Greater Purpose.

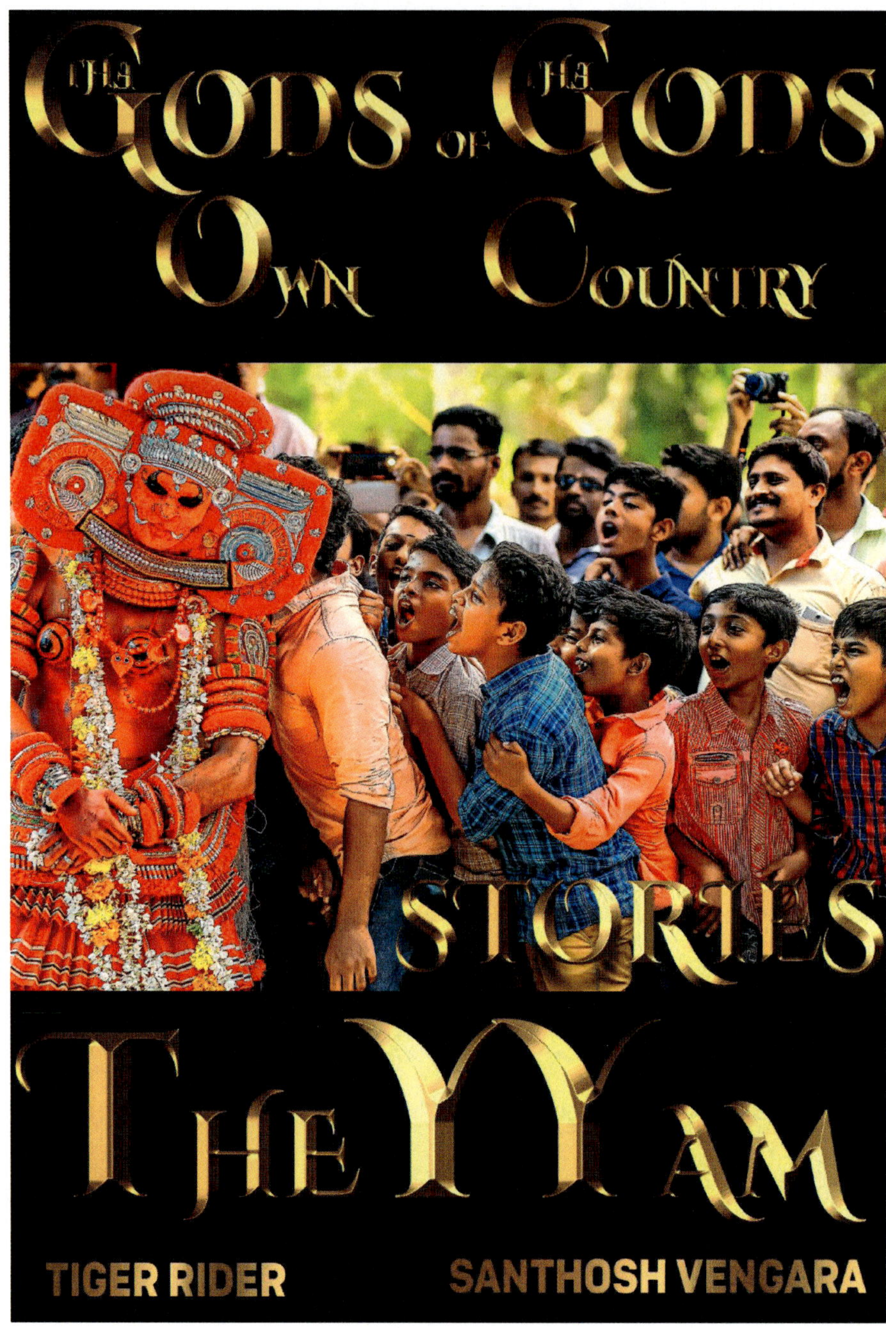

ISBN: 978-1-958260-72-2

Contents

DEDICATION

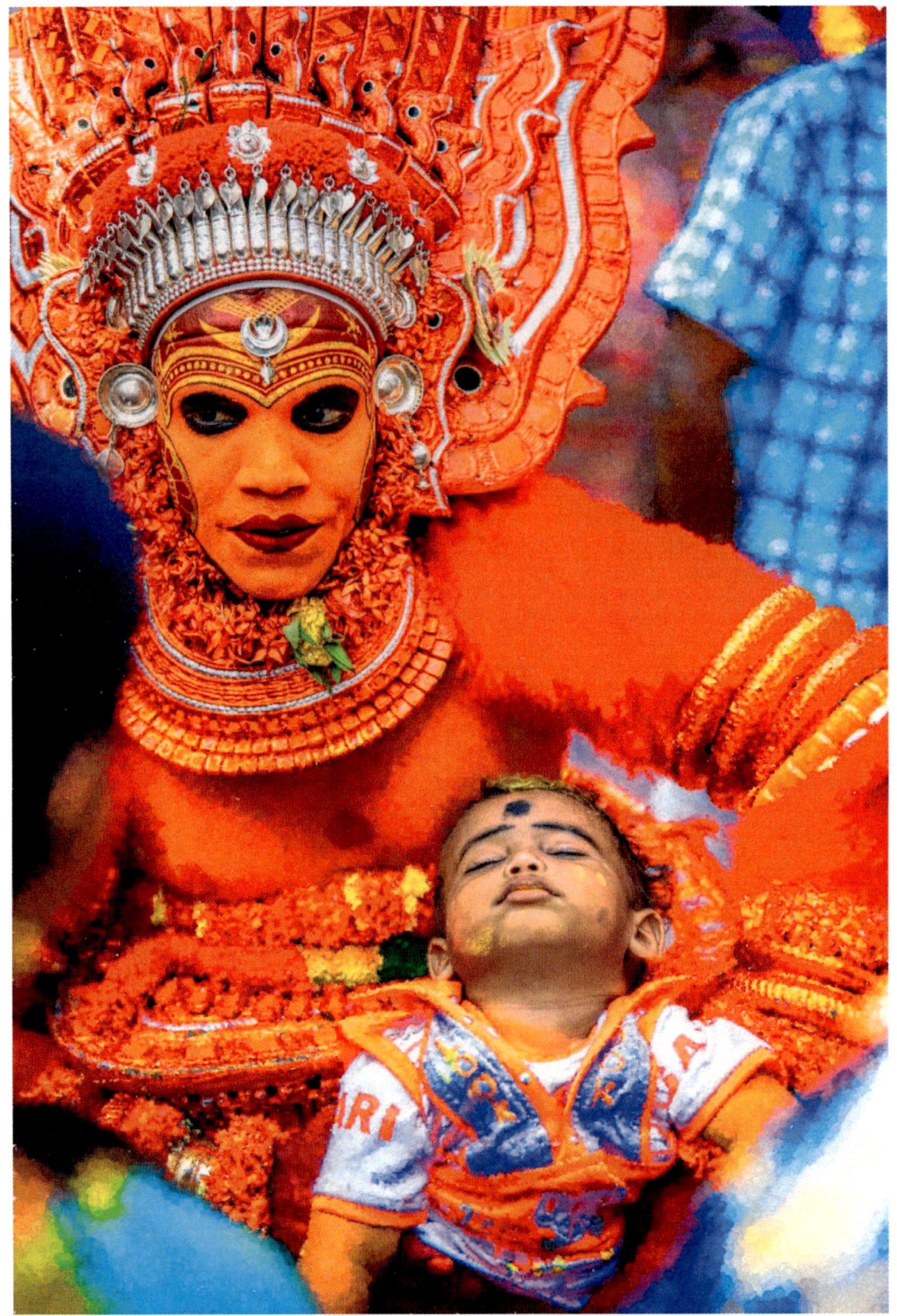

Even Jesus was poor in everything, born in a manger, yet rich in love and culture, just like the Theyyam community. This community mirrors a similar concept by being an art form of the ignored, yet rich in every inch of its existence.

I dedicate this book to the Theyyam artists, the veritable Gods "Of the People, By the People, For the People." The royalties from this book will be donated to those destitute Gods of the God's Own Country for a Greater Purpose.

Confessions of A Monkey-Trapped[1] Prodigal Son of The God's Own Country

As I turned 50 and experienced a full-blown mid-life crisis, I realized I'd become Monkey-Trapped – caught clinging to an identity I no longer recognized but which I could not break free from. I left God's Own Country 30 years ago. I have been riding a Financial Engineering Tiger like a headless chicken without knowing what the hell I am doing by distorting the distorted reality fields in the West. Three decades have flown by in the blink of an eye, and my life is trapped in the fake ivory monkey traps of the West. My guilt about drifting away from my rich culture has been walloping me more than ever.

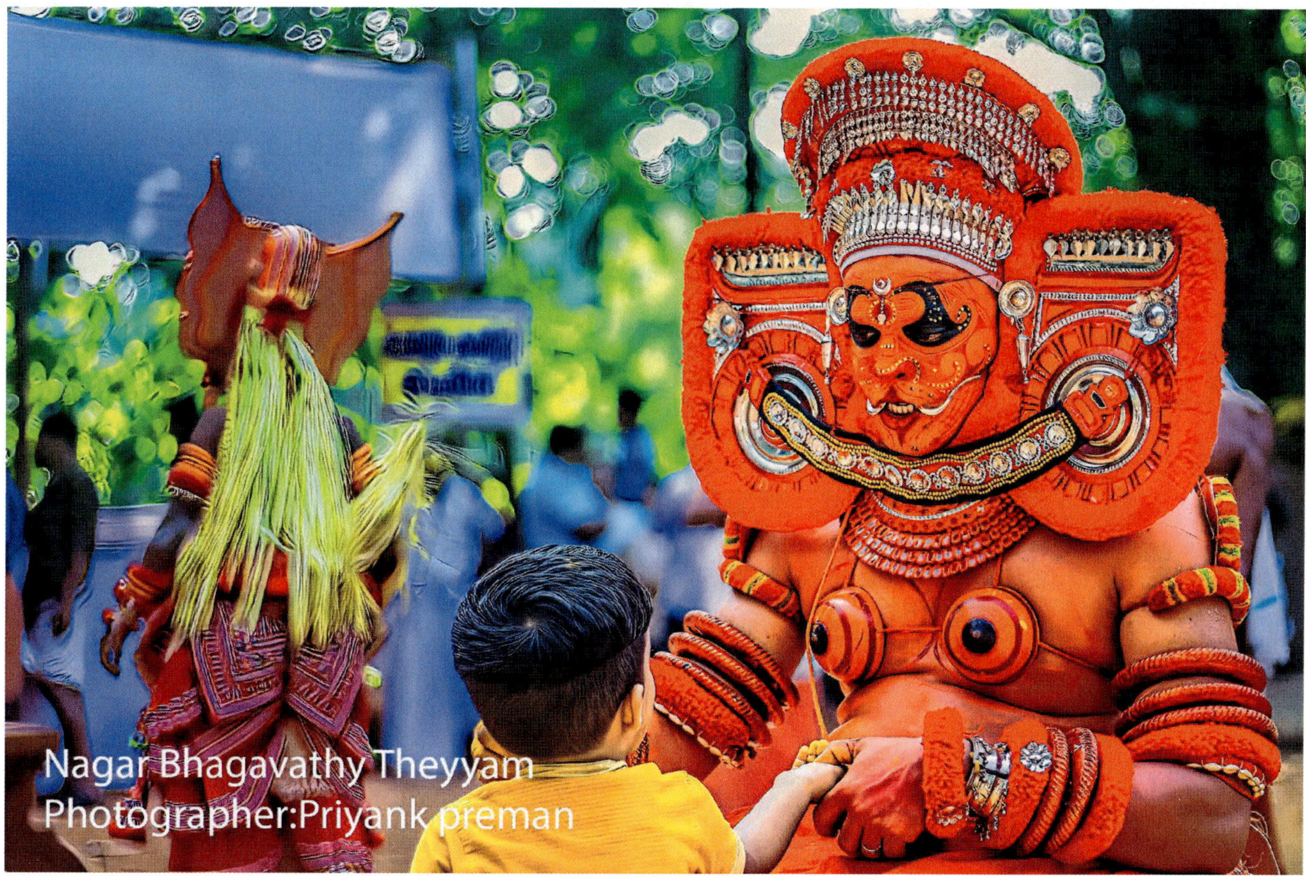

Nagar Bhagavathy Theyyam
Photographer:Priyank preman

The Covid waves and the loss of people near and dear to me amplified my identity crisis and mental jugglery. I sought answers within my roots in a globe-trotting search for my penance; it would lead me through twenty countries. My hometown, my original identity, and the only place I can curl into the comforts of 'who I am' started to cloud my head. Over the oceans, Kerala, God's own country, and my land rose in front of me. A monsoon of memories rained within me. The initial intention of this book was a consequence of this crisis, an attempt to green-wash my guilt. However, as time passed, it evolved into much more.

---

[1] A cage containing a banana with a hole large enough for a monkey's hand to fit in, but not large enough for a monkey's fist (clutching a banana) to come out; anecdotally used to catch monkeys that lack the intellect to let go of the banana and run away.

In the Beginning

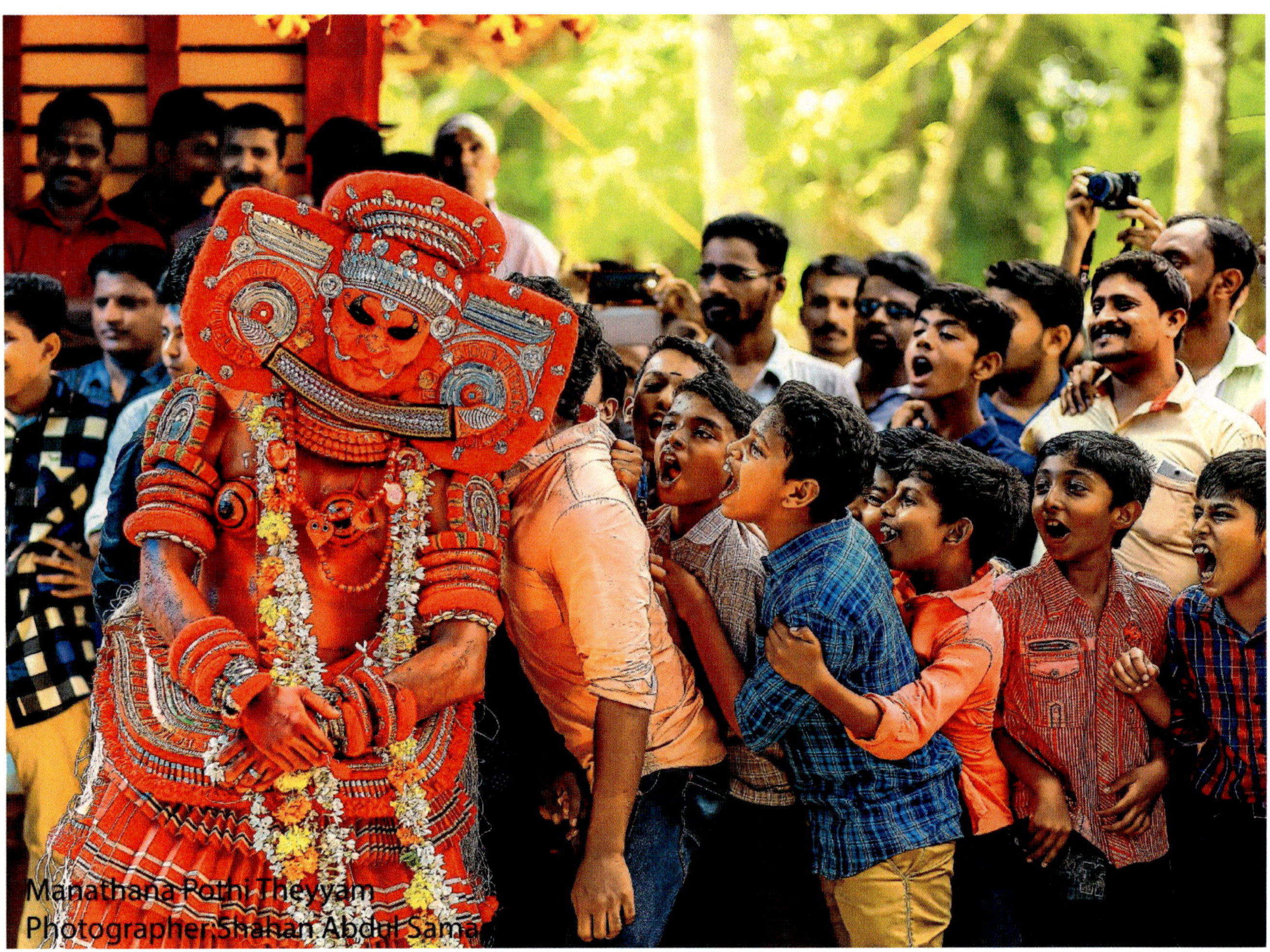

Manathana Pothi Theyyam
Photographer:Shahan Abdul Sama

As I lean back and close my eyes, the overflow of memories brings me back to the misty evening vibes of Malabar, especially during the Christmas Holidays. I contemplate bygone days and the childhood nostalgia of chasing various Theyyams from one *Theyyaparambu* or *Theyyakavu* (Places where Theyyam is performed) to the other during the seasons. I now realize there is a fathomable reason for me to lean on the Theyyam in my soul.

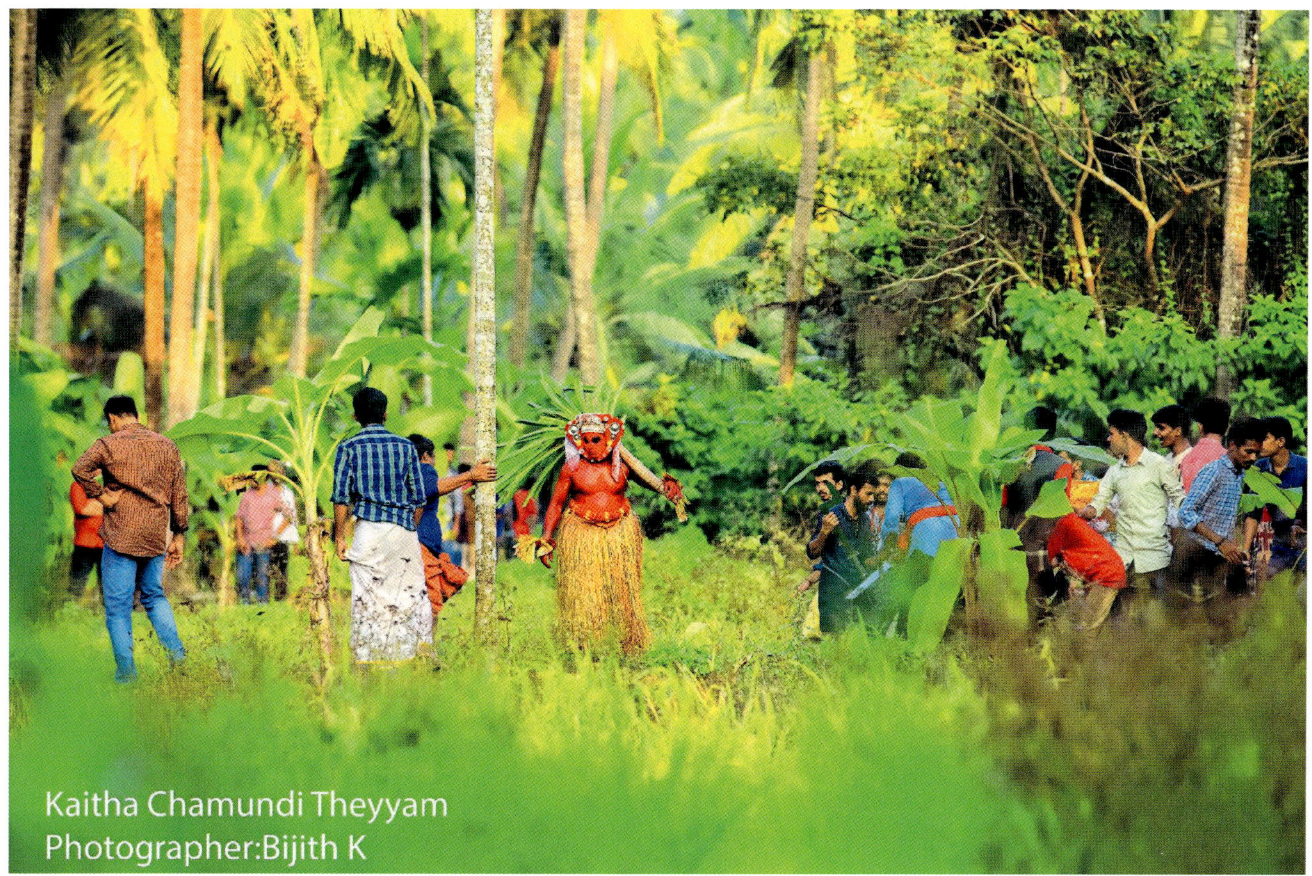

Kaitha Chamundi Theyyam
Photographer:Bijith K

I was born into a Catholic community, the followers of St. Thomas (52 AD), and educated by Christian missionaries brought by colonizers from Portugal, France, and Britain. My dad was raised in an Orthodox Catholic family and was an altar boy. After he completed his Master's in Science, he joined one of the Catholic Bishops Colleges (in Cannanore) as a professor. Following his profound reasons and logic, which are still unknown to me, he turned a rebel against the Catholic establishment. He even named me after a Hindu God (Lord Ganesha). As a result, he brought me up in a rebellious Agnostic backdrop and became more interested in Ramayana and other stories of Hindu mythology than the Holy Bible. I have been to more Kavus and temples than Catholic churches. Though many temples never allowed me inside because of my religious background, no Theyyakavu ever denied me. They embrace everyone regardless of their religion, color, and gender.

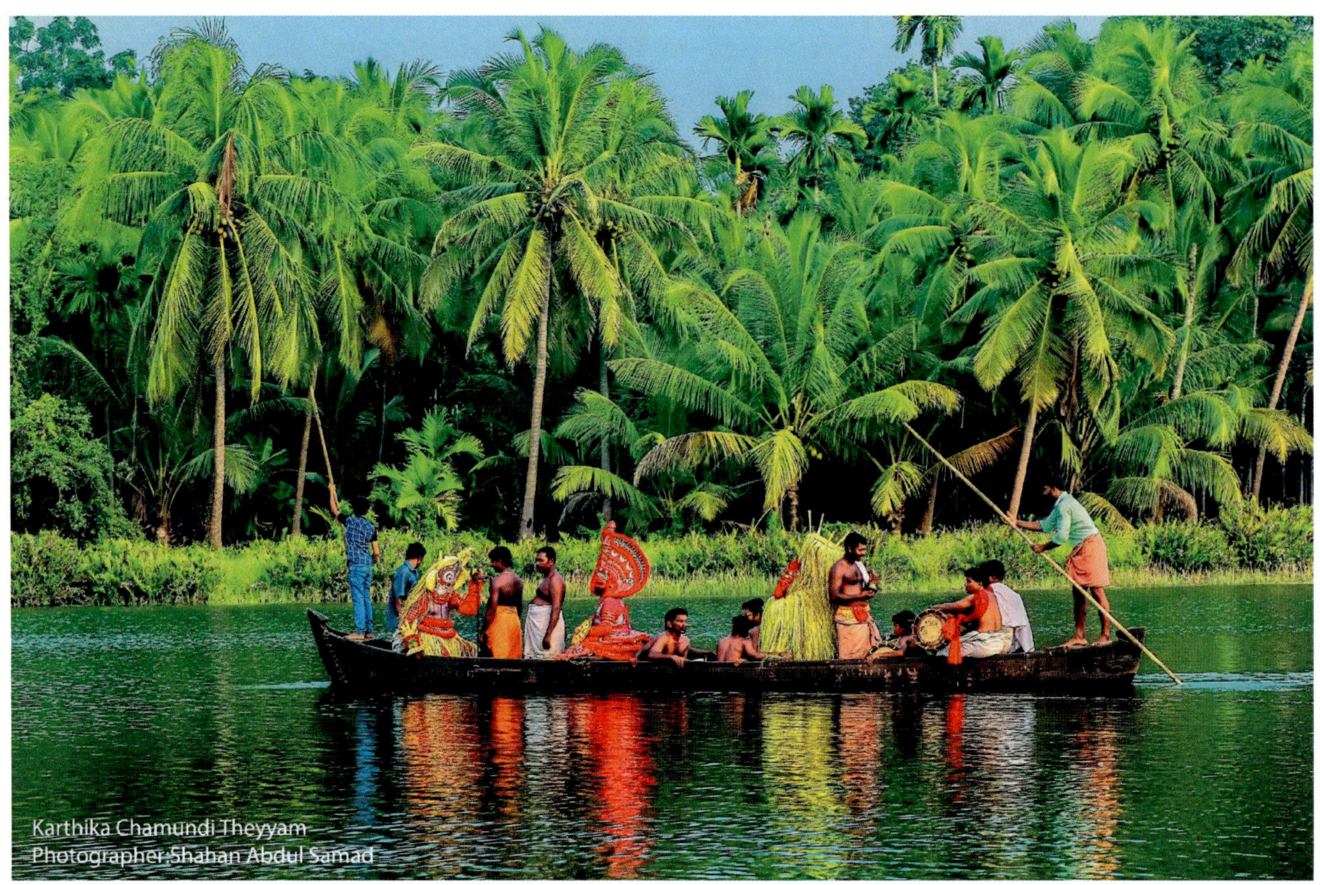
Karthika Chamundi Theyyam
Photographer:Shahan Abdul Samad

Bordered by the UNESCO World Heritage Site - the Western Ghats[2] - and carpeted by natural greenery, Malabar opens it's off-beat paths ahead of me to explore. There is still a sense of artwork created by the rust-red laterite soil beneath my feet. The same earth whirls dust in the atmosphere on festival grounds. No Keralite will forget their native festivals. They are imprinted in our souls. A reverie of my festival memories is colored with the representations of various Gods, lights, sounds, fireworks, and long nights. However, what makes Theyyam unique is the "human representation of God." The human-to-God transition is a memory that haunts you from the get-go and transforms you into a worshiper. Maybe not of God, but the Dravidian[3] traditional arts for sure.

---

2 https://whc.unesco.org/en/list/1342/ Second to the Rocky Mountains only, the Western Ghats is a mountain range that covers an area of 160,000 km² in a stretch of 1,600 km parallel to the western coast of the Indian peninsula.

3 The Dravidian peoples, or Dravidians, are a linguistic and cultural group living in South Asia who predominantly speak any of the Dravidian languages. There are around 250 million native speakers of Dravidian languages.

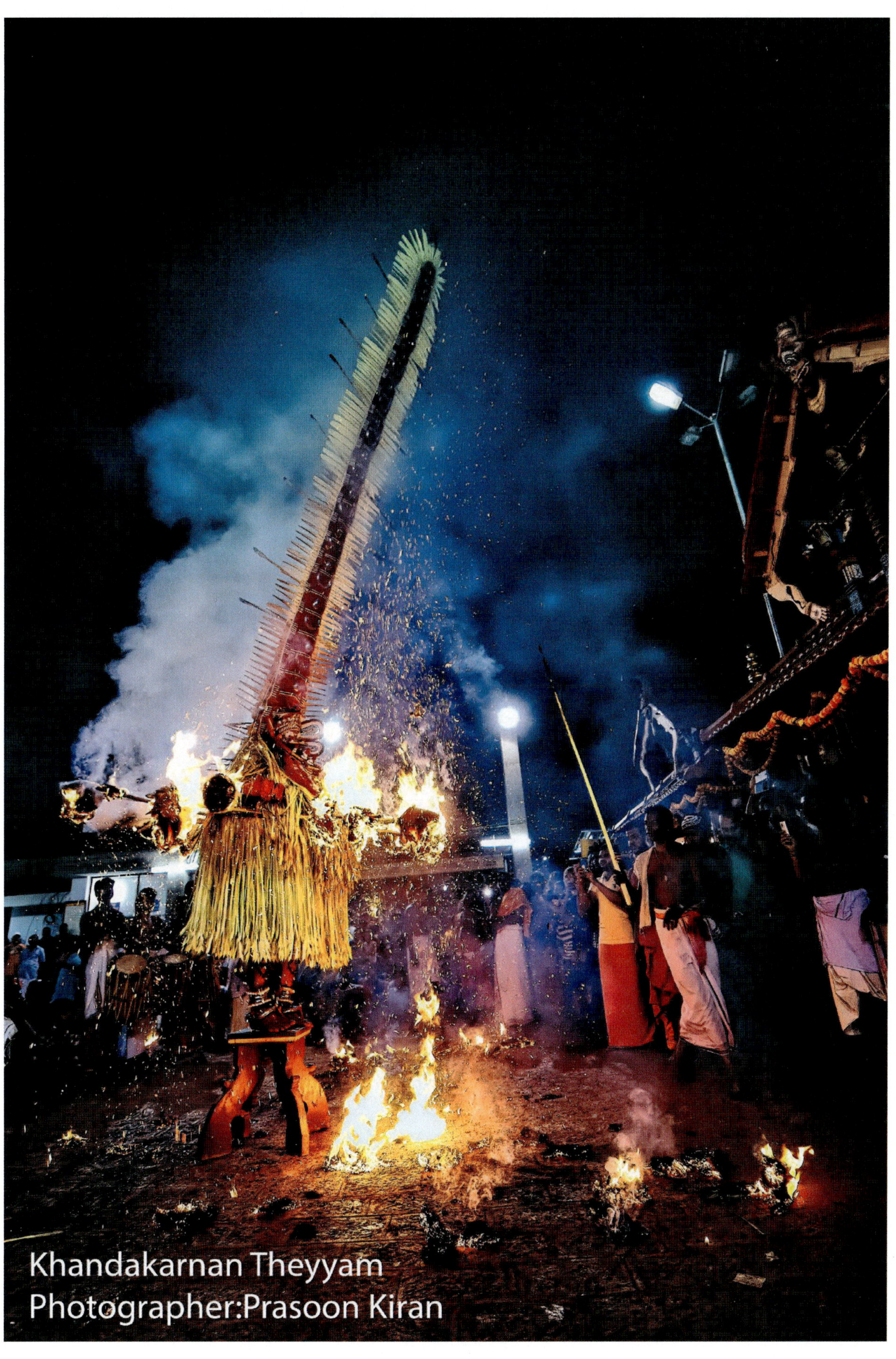

Khandakarnan Theyyam
Photographer:Prasoon Kiran

There are many deities and beliefs worldwide. Some are unique in Kerala; their underlying stories are deeply rooted in the region's incredible cultural and social history. The artists of Theyyam are versatile in their niche. They can double up as costume designers, painters, musicians, artisans, drummers, and choreographers. They evolve into a mystical human form where they can walk through the fire, carry heavy masses of costumes and headdresses, and perform other seemingly magical feats. Being a contrarian, I find myself following the footsteps of these "rebel Gods" against the mighty establishments and centuries-old systems that were forced upon us. Understanding Theyyam is an appreciation of Kerala and its history.

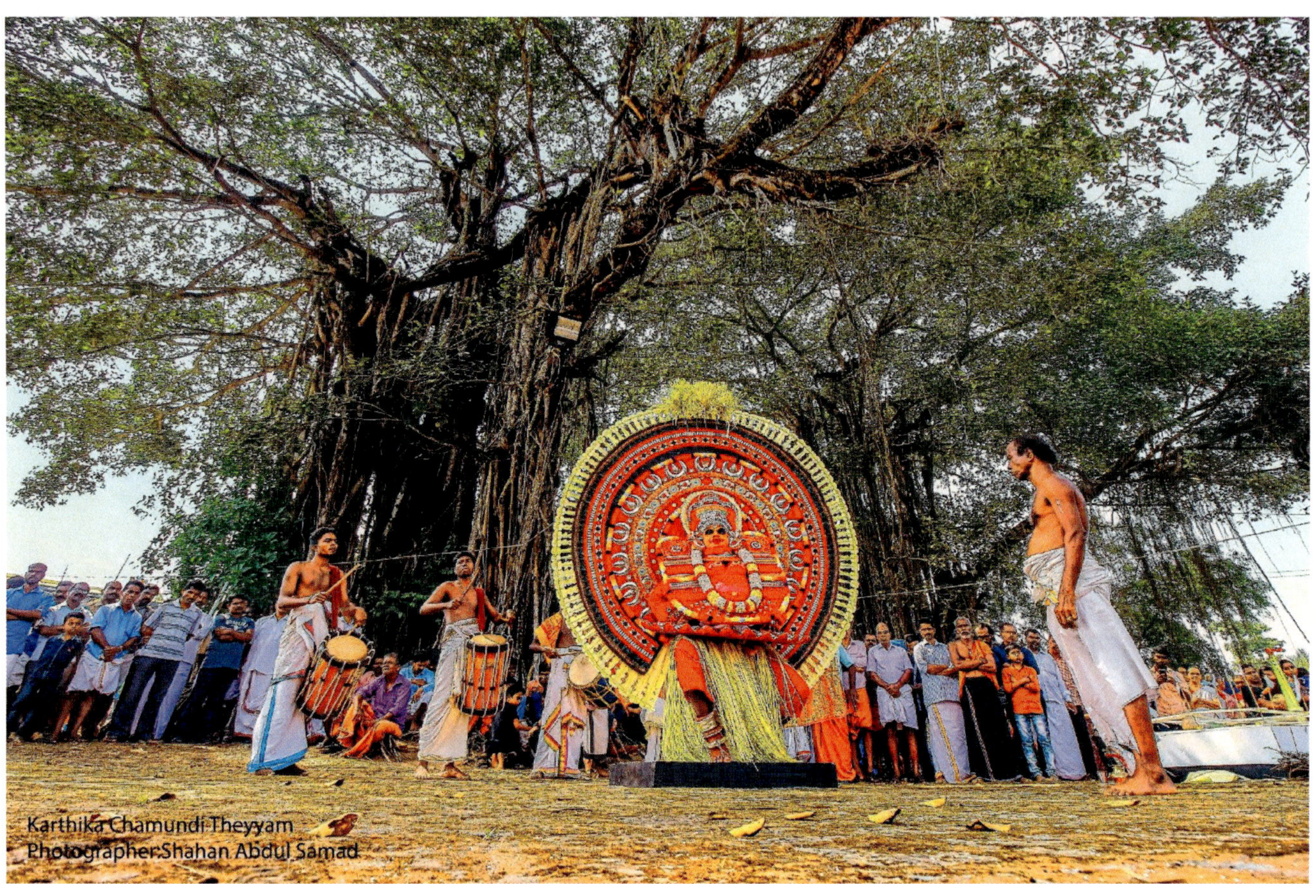
Karthika Chamundi Theyyam
Photographer:Shahan Abdul Samad

Kerala is a small but densely populated state in India with a population of around 35 million, a tropical paradise famous in the eco-tourism industry for its abundant greenery. I was born in the Kannur district, the same place where Theyyams are predominantly performed. I spent my childhood here amid the Western Ghats mountain shades and the Arabian sea's cool breeze. Most months of the year are filled with monsoon rains and cold weather. As summer approaches, the atmosphere warms and fills with dust as it throws color on the greenery. The Western Ghats and the Arabian Sea perfectly balance Kerala's climate. People here are primarily farmers. They work hard for their bread and butter. I grew up among these people when Kerala worked for their upliftment.

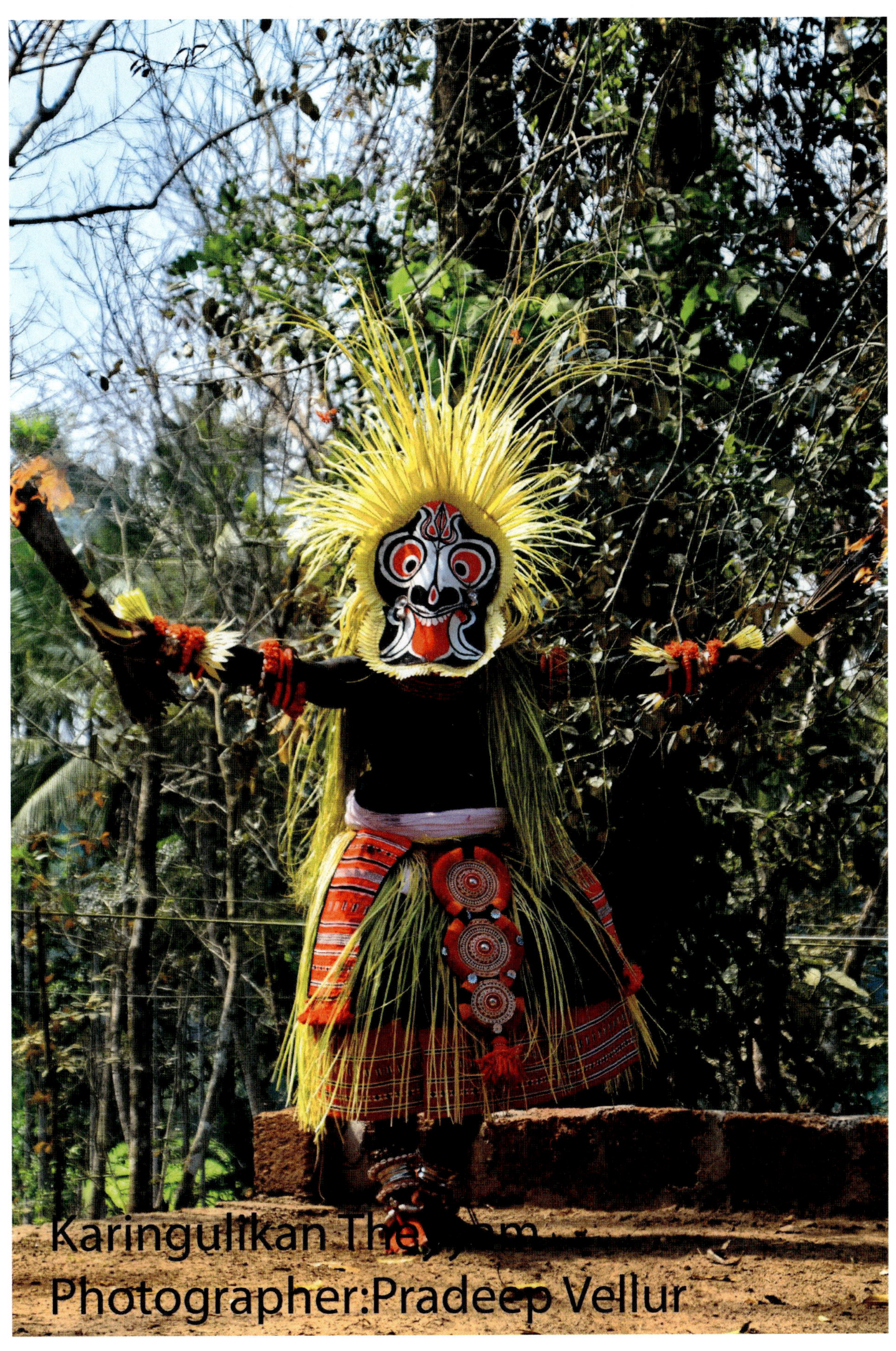

Karingulikan Theyyam
Photographer:Pradeep Vellur

India was the wealthiest country since ancient times till the British invasion in the 17th century. She faced countless incursions, including Aryans, Persians, Greek, and Mughals. Europeans, especially the Brits, were the last looters on the list. India became financially weak after surviving all these invasions. After achieving independence in 1947, India struggled to develop politically, economically, and socially. Unifying different princely states and infusing the idea of socialism into peasants were herculean tasks for the leaders.

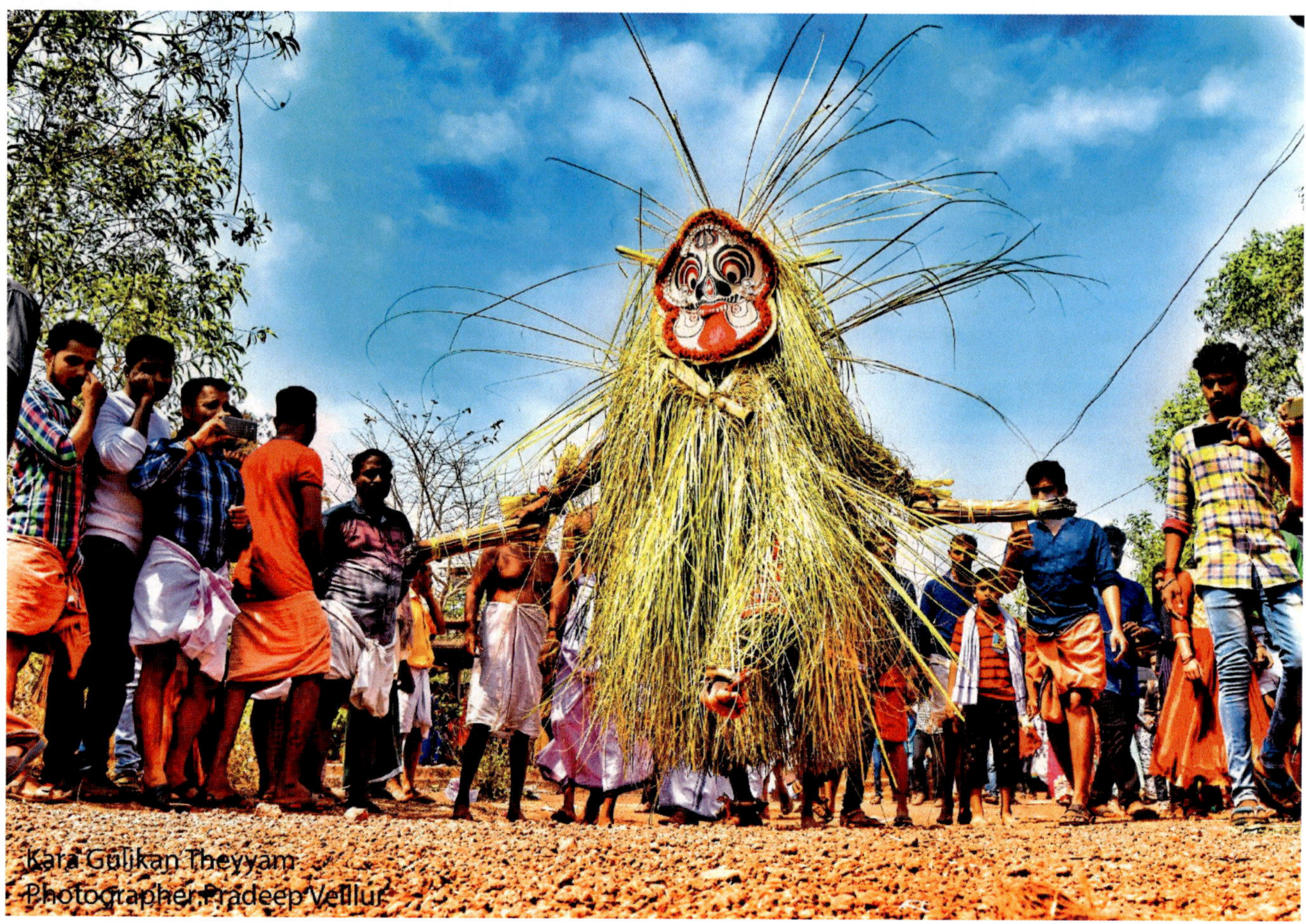

Kara Gulikan Theyyam
Photographer Pradeep Vellur

Kerala is the first place where communists became democratically elected to power in world history and have ruled since 1957. Kerala gave importance to developing social capital and many progressive movements. Catholic missionaries brought by colonizers from Europe from the 18th century onwards also helped kick-start the educational institutions in every nook and corner of the state. Hence, Kerala became the first state in India to garner complete literacy in the 1990s. The communist ideology in the minds of people acted as a double-edged sword. The resulting industrial desert brought on by Communism forced me to pack my bags after obtaining my Industrial Engineering degree and seek a job in Bombay (the commercial capital of India, now called Mumbai). Even after years of political education given to the people, the ancient caste stratification known as Chaturvarnya still conditioned their minds[4]. I soon realized my prospects beyond the factory floor were limited by my dark skin (as a lungi-wearing Kala *Madrasi*[5]).

---

4 https://ccnmtl.columbia.edu/projects/mmt/ambedkar/web/section_17.html

5 A derogatory word used in North India against the dark skin colored South Indians who wear Lungi. The Lungi is a simple, single piece of cloth best suited for the tropical weather that is worn as

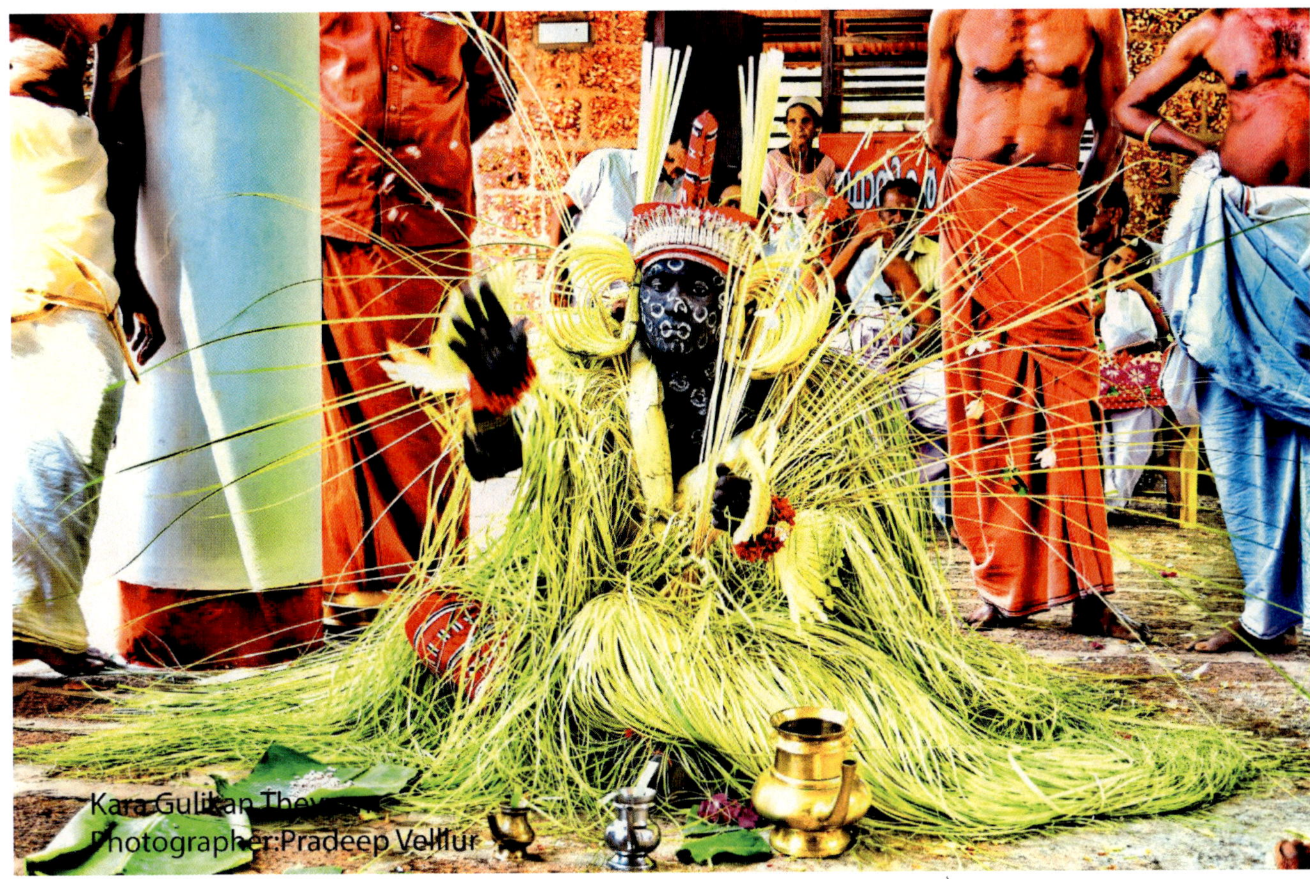
Kara Gulikan The
Photographer:Pradeep Velllur

I wanted to react, but I was scared and did not know how. Theyyam once again dominated my thoughts. Like a Theyyam, the struggle of the lower strata of society danced in front of me. I could understand the pain each performing community had endured for centuries. I wanted to dance like them, like a frenzied human being who transformed himself into God to revolt against the Chaturvarnya system. But I could not. It was next to impossible to rebel against a 5000-year-old Aryanacal system. I could not survive. Fearing for my future, I fled to the South to escape the Chaturvarnya professional ladder. I obtained my MBA in finance as a candidate for national integration.

---

casual wear, mostly by men, across south India. https://www.thenewsminute.com/article/one-size-fits-all-kerala-lungi-and-its-relevance-culture-133079

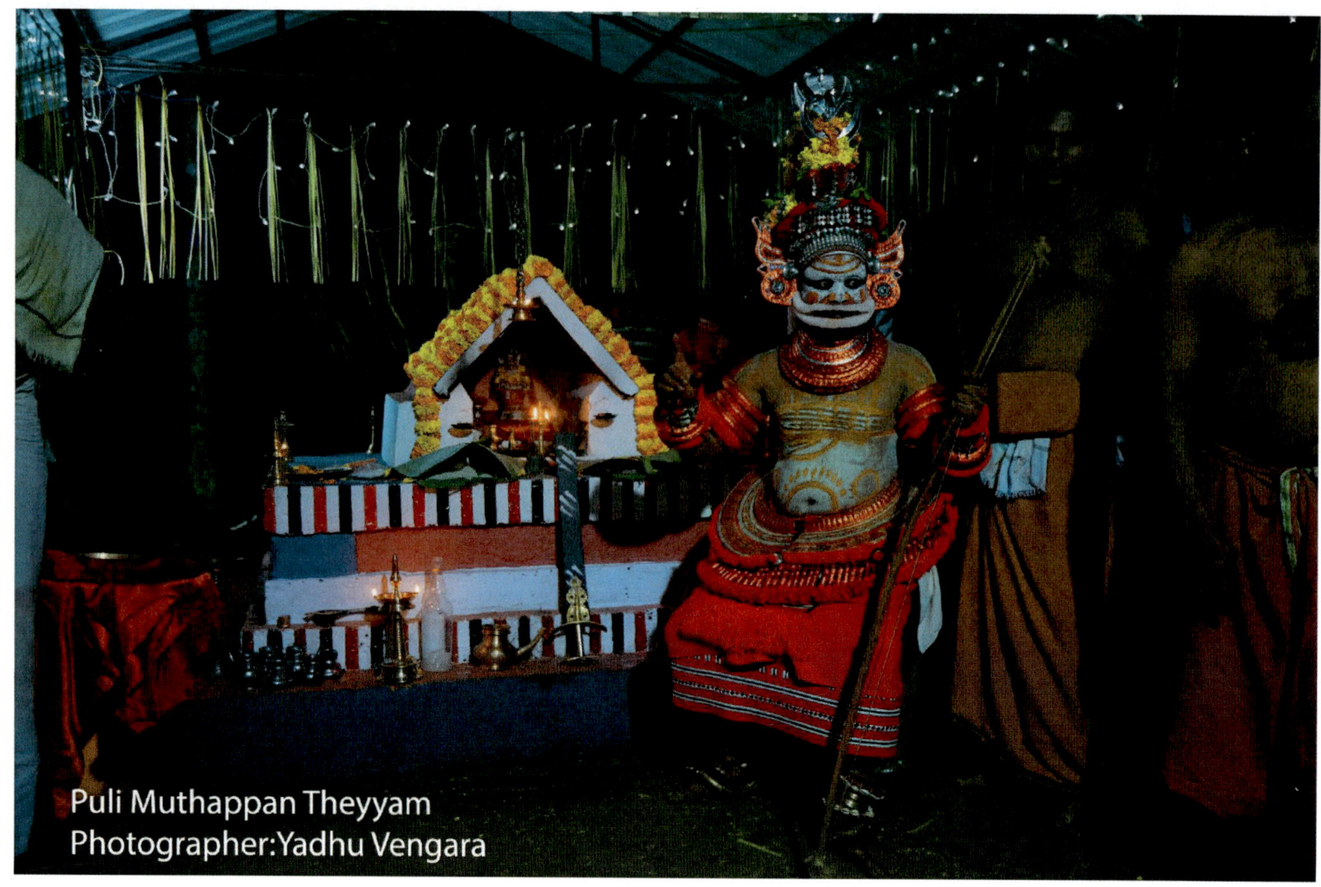
Puli Muthappan Theyyam
Photographer:Yadhu Vengara

Providentially for me, in 1990, the entire Indian economy collapsed under the weight of the half-a-century-old mighty Indian License Raj.[6] The result was a liberalized Indian economy. The timing was impeccable, as it provided me with the opportunity to start my career as an Investment Banking Analyst. Then India's 1996 stock market crash allowed me to move on from my investment banking career; fortune smiled upon me again.

[6] The License Raj or Permit Raj (rāj, meaning "rule" in Hindi) was the system of licenses, regulations, and accompanying red tape that hindered the setup and running of businesses in India between 1947 and 1990. https://en.wikipedia.org/wiki/Licence_Raj

My Prodigal Tiger Ride

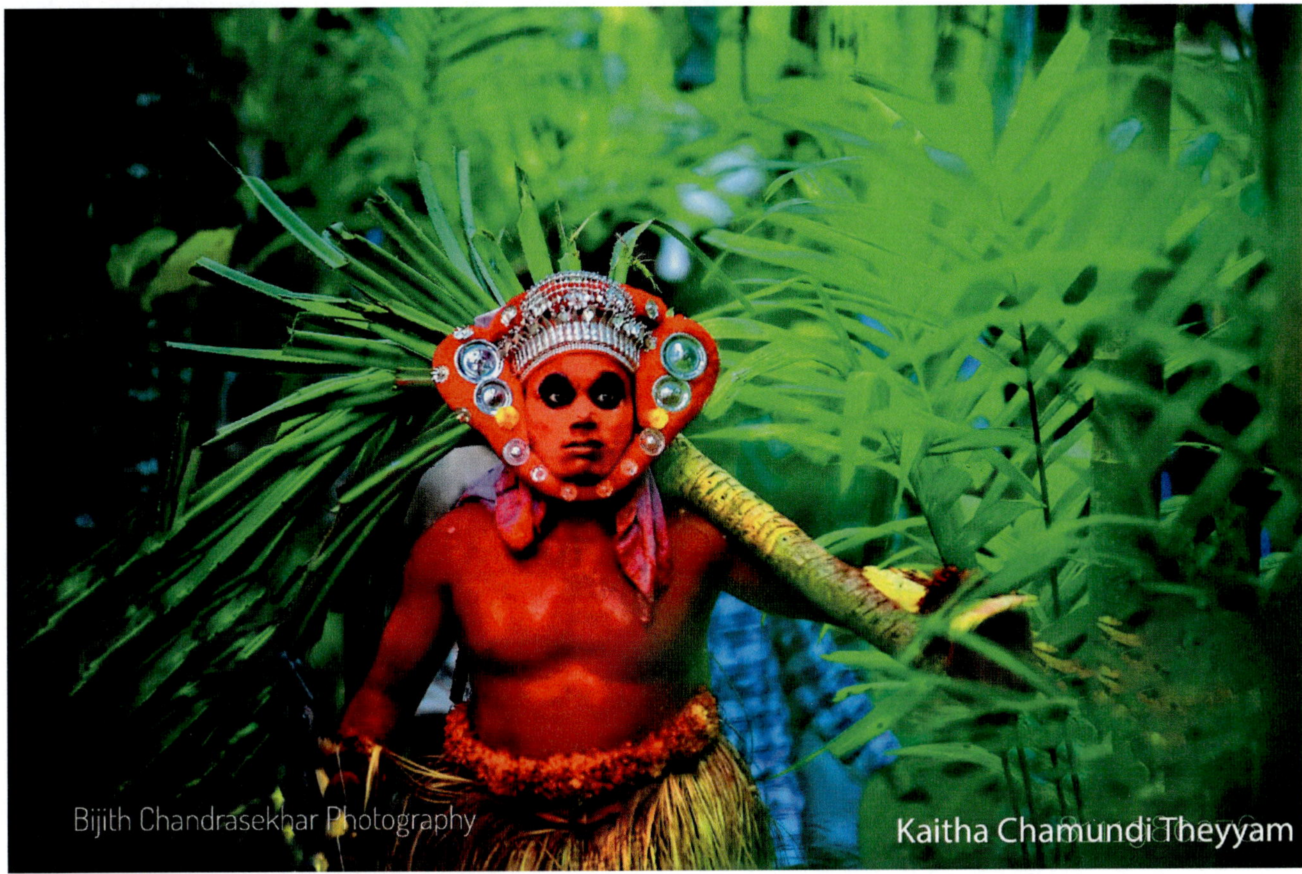

As mentioned earlier, *Nehruvian* India[7] took the socialist route and was not in the good graces of the US Superpower. During the conflict of the 1970s with Pakistan, it declared an emergency rule. Because of the war and other non-alignments, the US and India's relationship soured, and IBM and many western businesses abandoned India. Hail to the vacuum (to be filled), TCS and other Indian IT conglomerates were born out of desperation. They coded us in IT to kick-start the legacy computers and mainframes left behind by IBM. Thanks to the biggest blunder in business history (Y2K), IBM and the other western enterprises saw us 'Cyber Coolies[8]' as the thrifty solution to fix the doomsday Armageddon code. During this time, I managed to migrate from corporate finance to ERP (Enterprise Resource Planning) solutions and snatched my 'Cyber Coolie' passport to the epitome of capitalism, the USA.

---

[7] Embracing the social, political, and economic ideals of Jawahar Lal Nehru, the first Prime Minister of independent India

[8] A **coolie** (also spelled **koelie**, **kuli**, **khuli**, **khulie**, **cooli**, **cooly**, or **quli**) is a term for a low-wage laborer, typically of Indian or Chinese descent. https://en.wikipedia.org/wiki/Coolie

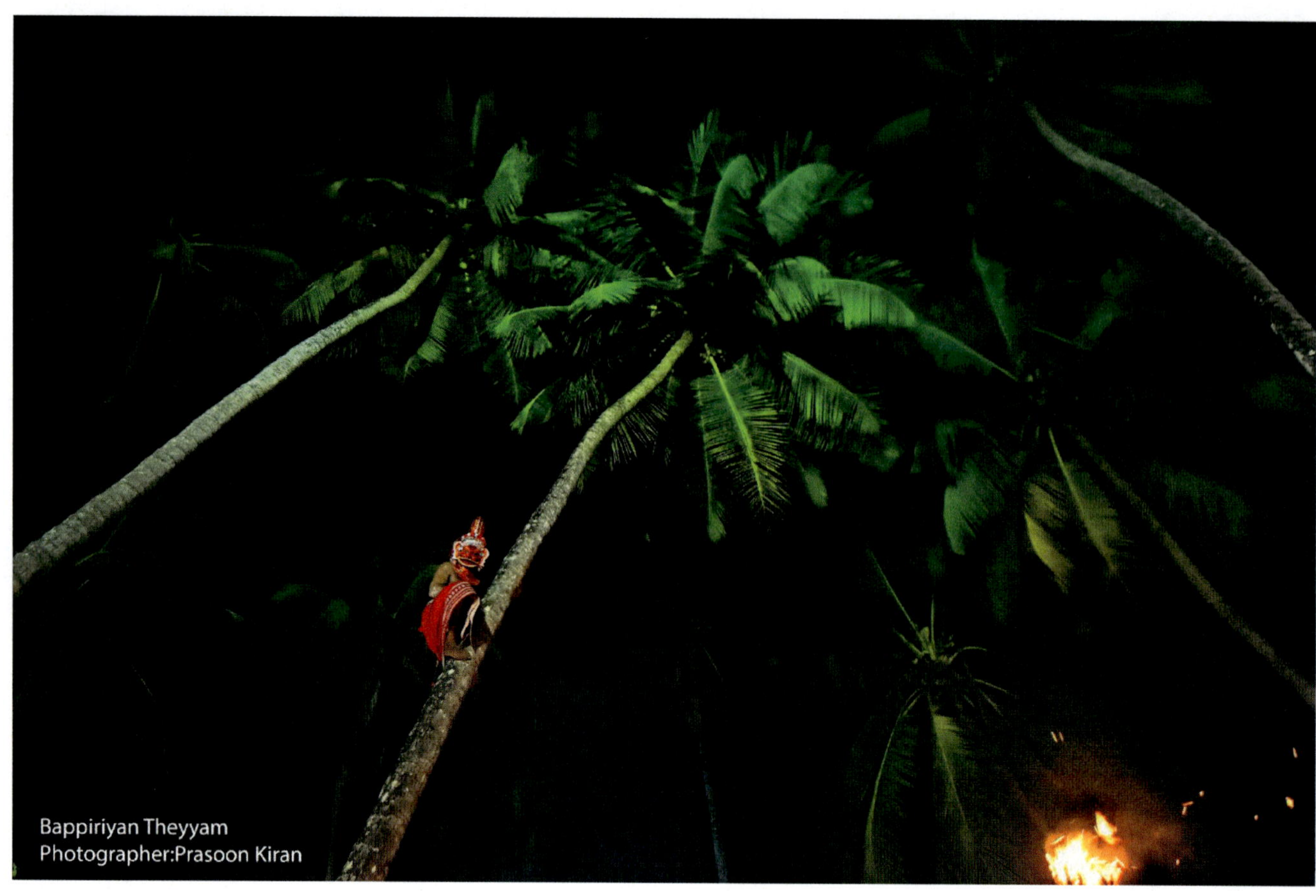
Bappiriyan Theyyam
Photographer:Prasoon Kiran

In America, I had the incredible privilege to write the global (in 20 languages) Amazon bestseller *The Gods Must Be Crazy!: Cradle of Communism to Catacomb of Capitalism* (Royalties to Mother Teresa). I have published and presented approximately 50 papers globally and contributed to all five major PMI Books/standards (PMBOK, OPM3, P&PM, and PMCD) based on experience with the ERP[9] & EPM[10] global implementations. I volunteered for the Project Management Institute globally, and I was responsible as a mentor for eight Asian countries, including India, Pakistan & China. I served as the Architect of the Team India Movement and transformed ASIA-PAC into the PMI's most strategic region forever.

---

[9] Enterprise Resource Planning (ERP) https://www.gartner.com/en/information-technology/glossary/enterprise-resource-planning-erp

[10] Enterprise Performance Planning(EPM) https://www.gartner.com/en/information-technology/glossary/epm-enterprise-performance-management

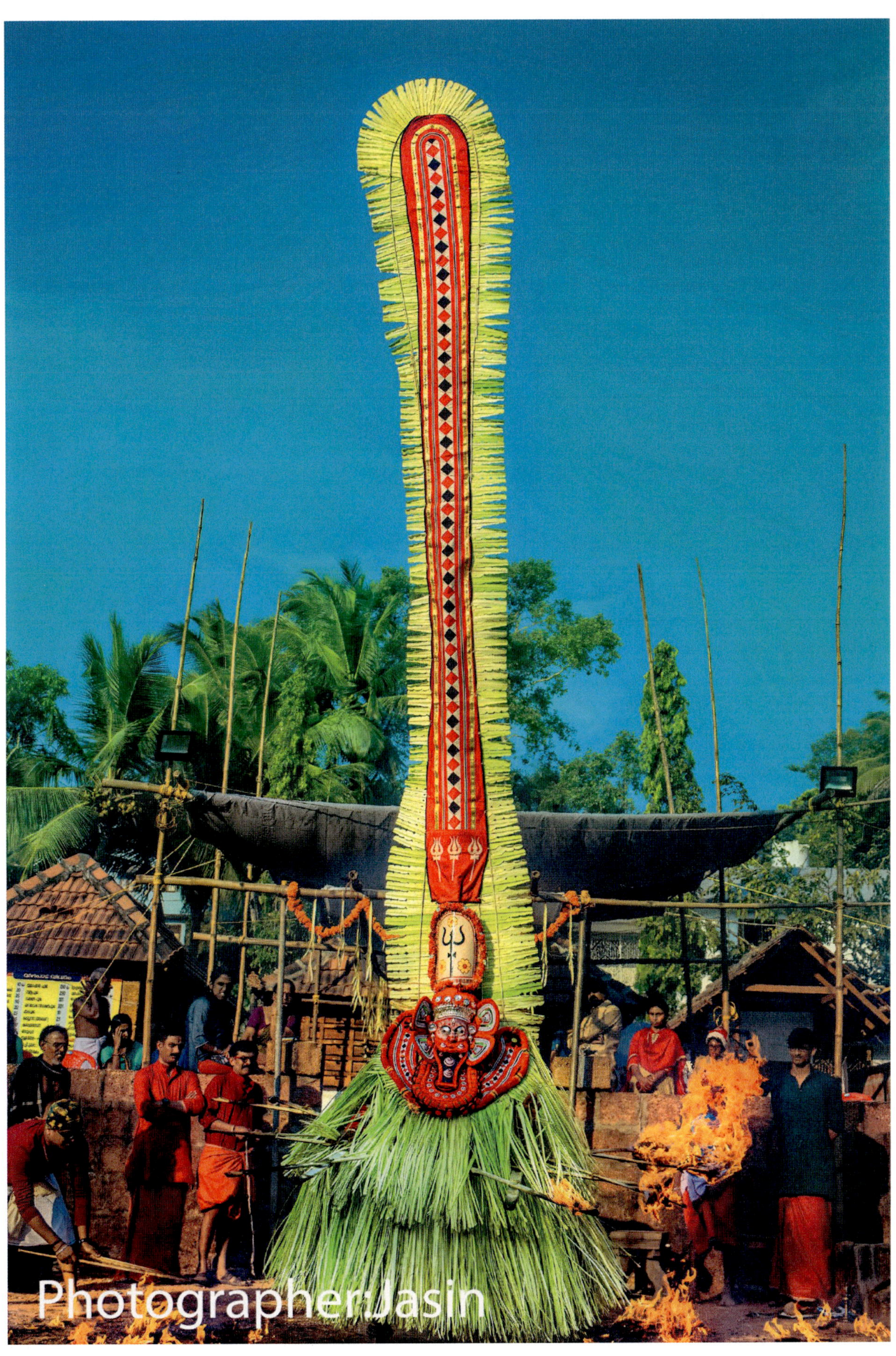
Photographer:Jasin

In 2008, amid the economic tsunami, I served as an advisor to the CFO (Chief Financial Officer), setting up the Project Portfolio Management Office for a Fortune 10 World's Most Admired Company. I saved them around half a billion dollars but became the victim (became unemployed) of my short-term financial engineering. As a result, in 2009, I packed my bags for the Cambodian Jungles in search of answers from the bottom of the pyramid through Chinese GIFT (Global Institute for Tomorrow) – a Clinton Global Young Executive Leadership Program (YLP) Graduate. After returning from the wilderness of the Cambodian killing fields, I reincarnated my career yet again, becoming an EPM (Enterprise Performance Management) consultant out of the 2008 Economic Tsunami in the BIG4[11] world.

[11] The Big 4 firms in management consulting are Deloitte Touche Tohmatsu (Deloitte), KPMG International (KPMG), PricewaterhouseCoopers (PwC), and Ernst & Young (EY).

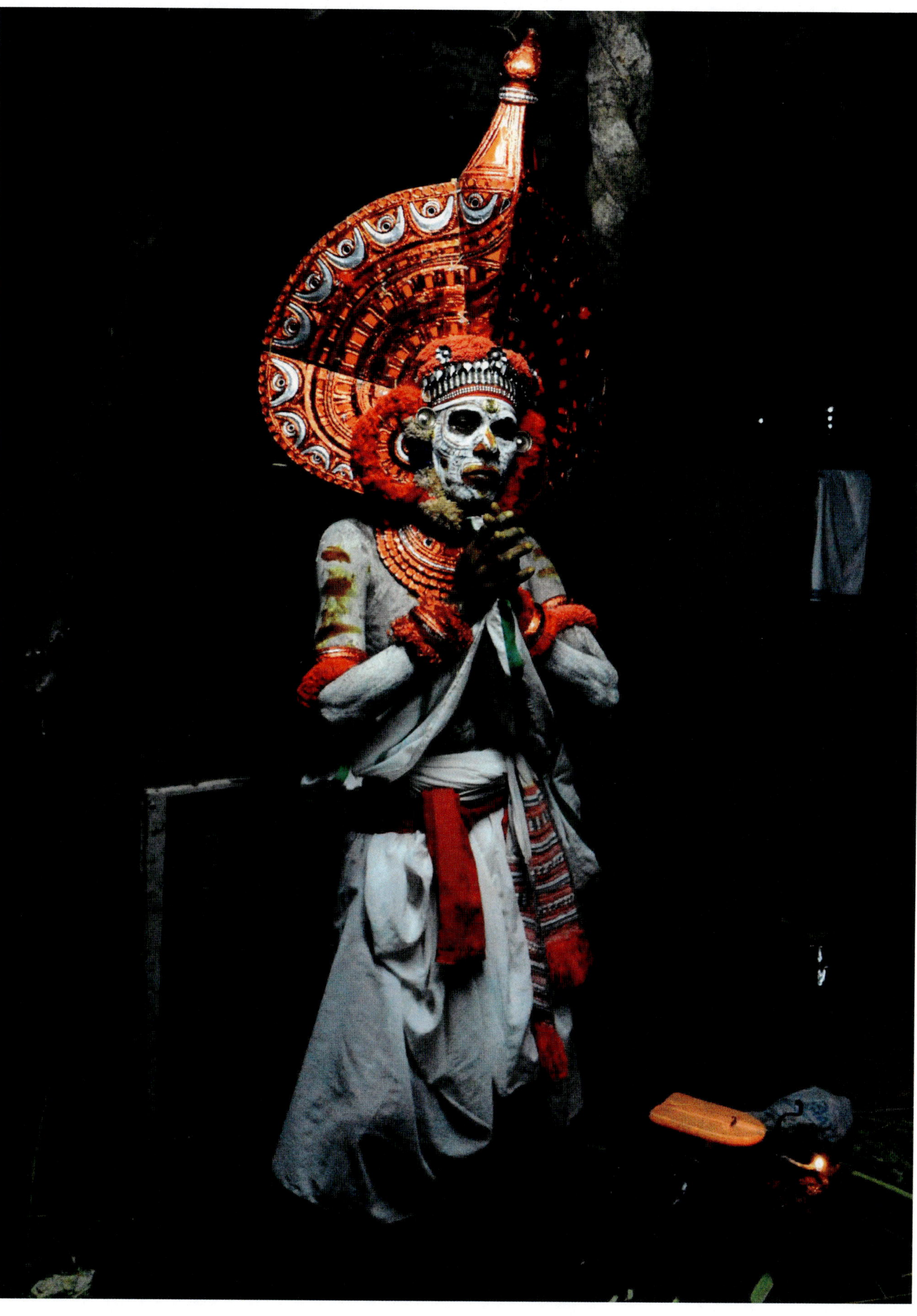

Monkey Trap

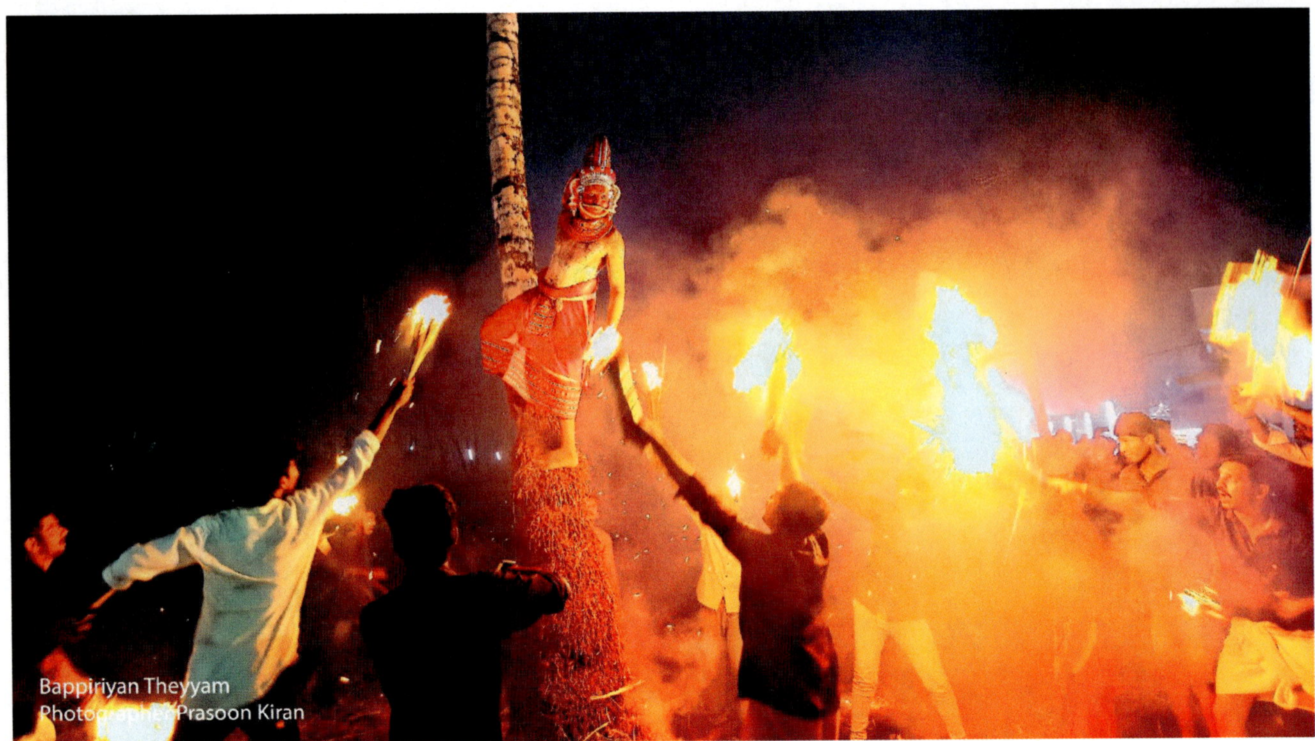

The more I examined the Western finance world, the more disillusioned I became. Thanks to the Chinese GIFT executive leadership program (https://global-inst.com/learn/) in Cambodia's killing fields, I found solace by trekking the jungles of Chiangmai-Chiangrai, Laos, and Myanmar in search of snake wine.[12] While sipping the rancorous snake wine, I wondered how these resource-cursed countries became impoverished and debt-trapped slaves of the Chinese Empire.[13] Hail to Hernando de Soto; I was born again to *The Mystery of Capital Gospel*.[14]

---

[12] Snake wine is a liquor that is prepared by putting an entire snake — sometimes while still alive — inside a jar of rice wine or some other kind of grain alcohol. https://theculturetrip.com/asia/china/hong-kong/articles/a-brief-introduction-to-snake-wine/

[13] I covered this topic in detail in my book "The Gods Must Be Crazy!: Cradle of Communism to Catacomb of Capitalism" https://www.amazon.com/Make-Enterprise-Great-Again-Capitalism-ebook/dp/B08BJ9WH65/

[14] https://www.amazon.com/Mystery-Capital-Capitalism-Triumphs-Everywhere/dp/0465016154 The Mystery of Capital: Why Capitalism Triumphs in the West and Fails Everywhere Else

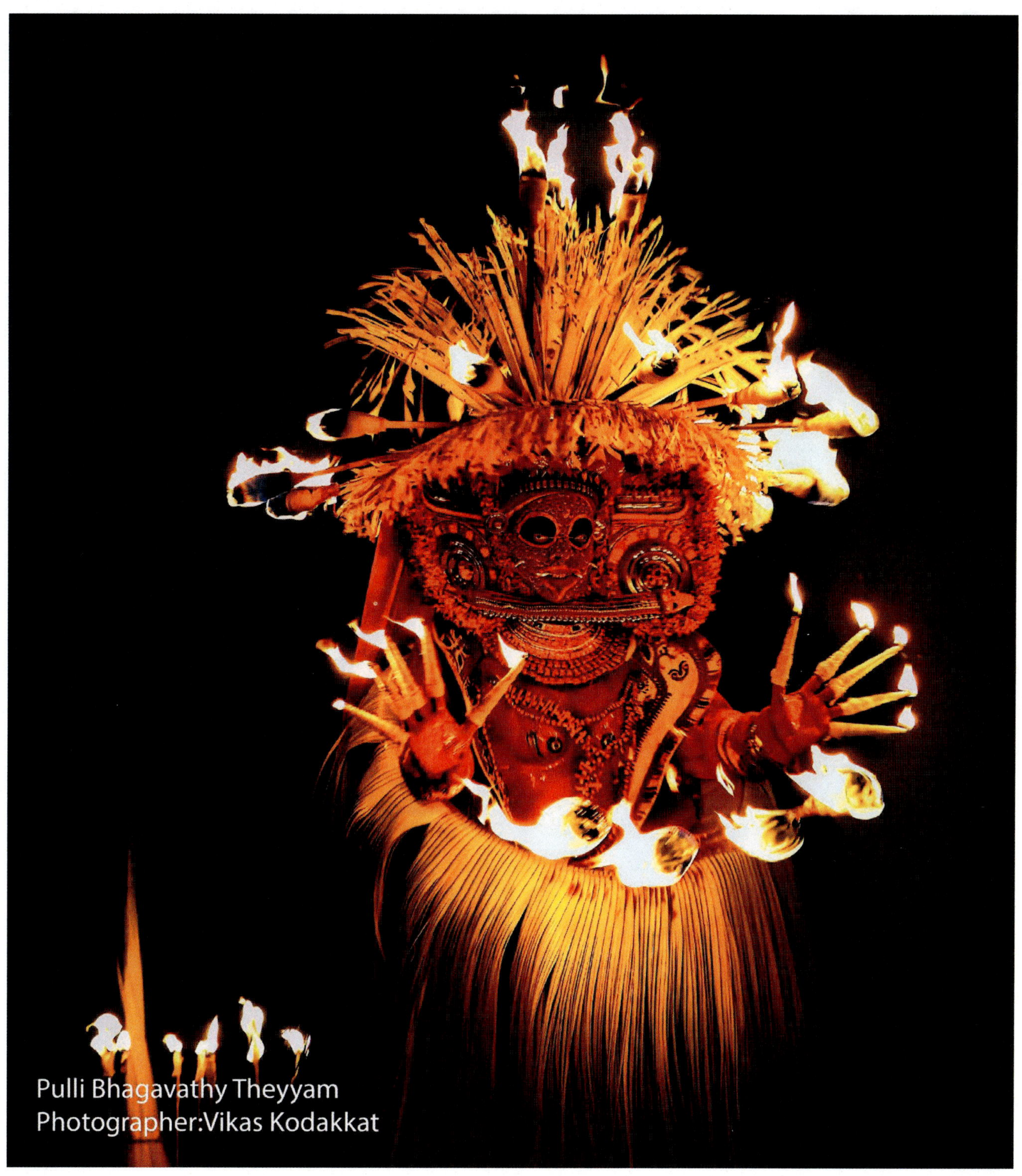
Pulli Bhagavathy Theyyam
Photographer:Vikas Kodakkat

Sadly, after over three decades, it looks like I need to ride back to God's Own Country through that Mad Max fury redemption road and climb through the apocalypse rubble of Roosevelt's capitalist nostalgic era. After all these extreme life events, I feel embarrassed about forgetting my roots. I see myself as a prodigal son of my own culture caught in a Monkey Trap.

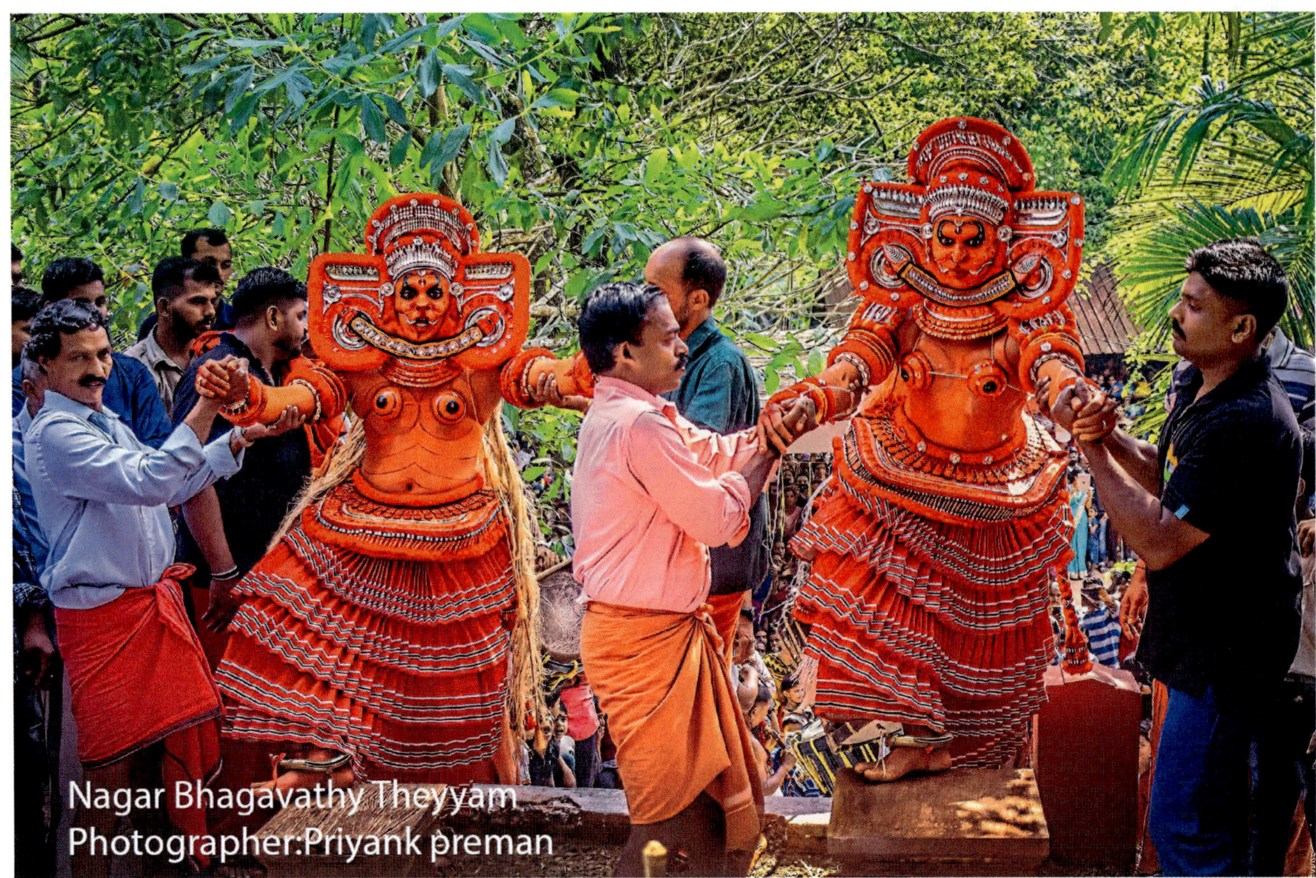

Nagar Bhagavathy Theyyam
Photographer:Priyank preman

I had the privilege to globe-trot with my camera in various professional and volunteer roles in around 20 countries. Despite all the countries and regions I visited, I still see my soul flying back to my sweet homeland, thinking there is no better place in this world than in this Malabar corner. I see the Theyyam Seasons I spent running from one Theyyakkavu to the other through the viewfinder. My parents and relatives still live in Malabar (Cannanore & Kasaragod, Theyyam region). Visiting them during the Christmas holidays was an opportunity to spend nights chasing the Theyyam movements and capturing them with utmost passion since photography has always been a passion of mine.

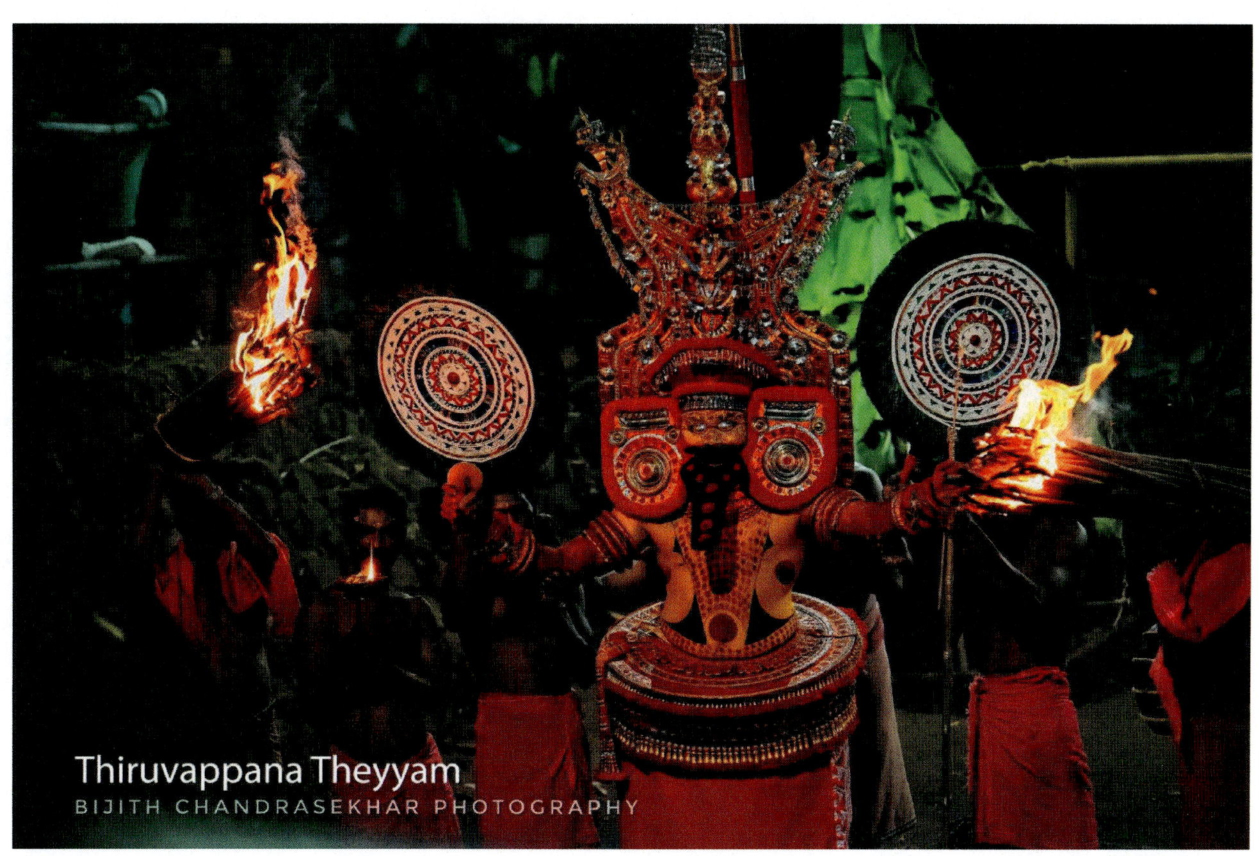

Thiruvappana Theyyam
BIJITH CHANDRASEKHAR PHOTOGRAPHY

My Penance

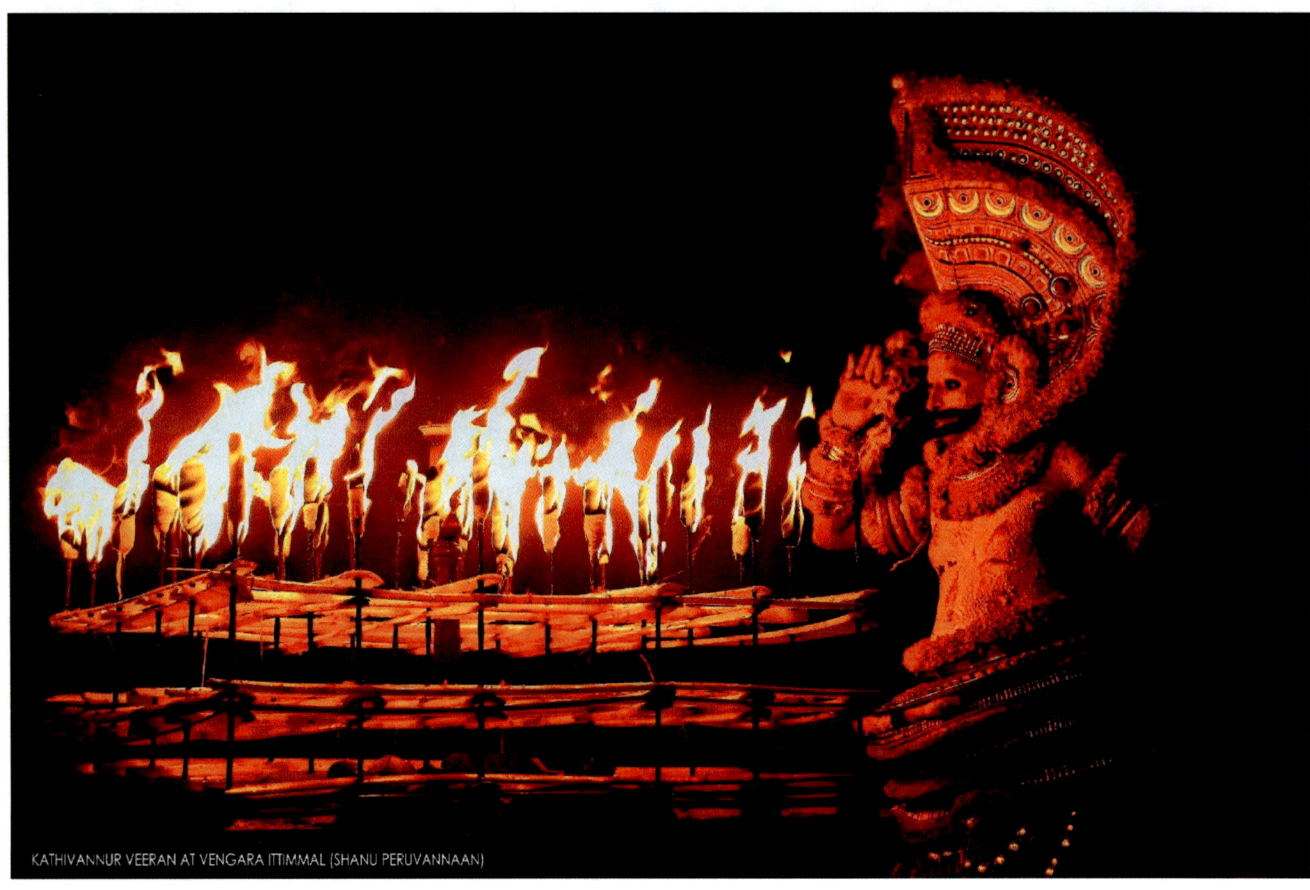
KATHIVANNUR VEERAN AT VENGARA ITTIMMAL (SHANU PERUVANNAAN)

Theyyam has always fascinated me, ever since my childhood days. I am not aware of any other ritualistic festival and artistic form as colorful, massive, and rebellious at the same time. No pilgrimage on earth will introduce you to around five hundred Gods in a single season. Sadly, these Theyyams are underappreciated and unexplored even within Kerala, God's Own Country. Unlike Kathakali[15] and other aristocratic art forms promoted by Kalamandalam Deemed University, there is hardly any research or promotional effort on underprivileged Theyyams. While writing this book, I looked into over fifty reference books. Sadly, most are out of print, and the books available touch only the peripherals of these massive Theyyam Gods. The Theyyam artists are one of the most destitute communities in the world. I documented their aesthetics to create a positive impact on their real life. I have ideas for documentaries, movies, and collaborations with various academia, professionals, and businesspeople to promote and develop eco-cultural tourism in God's own country. I finally decided to start writing as a stepping stone to test my hypothesis.

---

[15] Kathakali, the 300-year-old classical dance form of Kerala, has combined facets of ballet, opera, masque, and pantomime. https://www.kalamandalam.ac.in/arts/kathakali

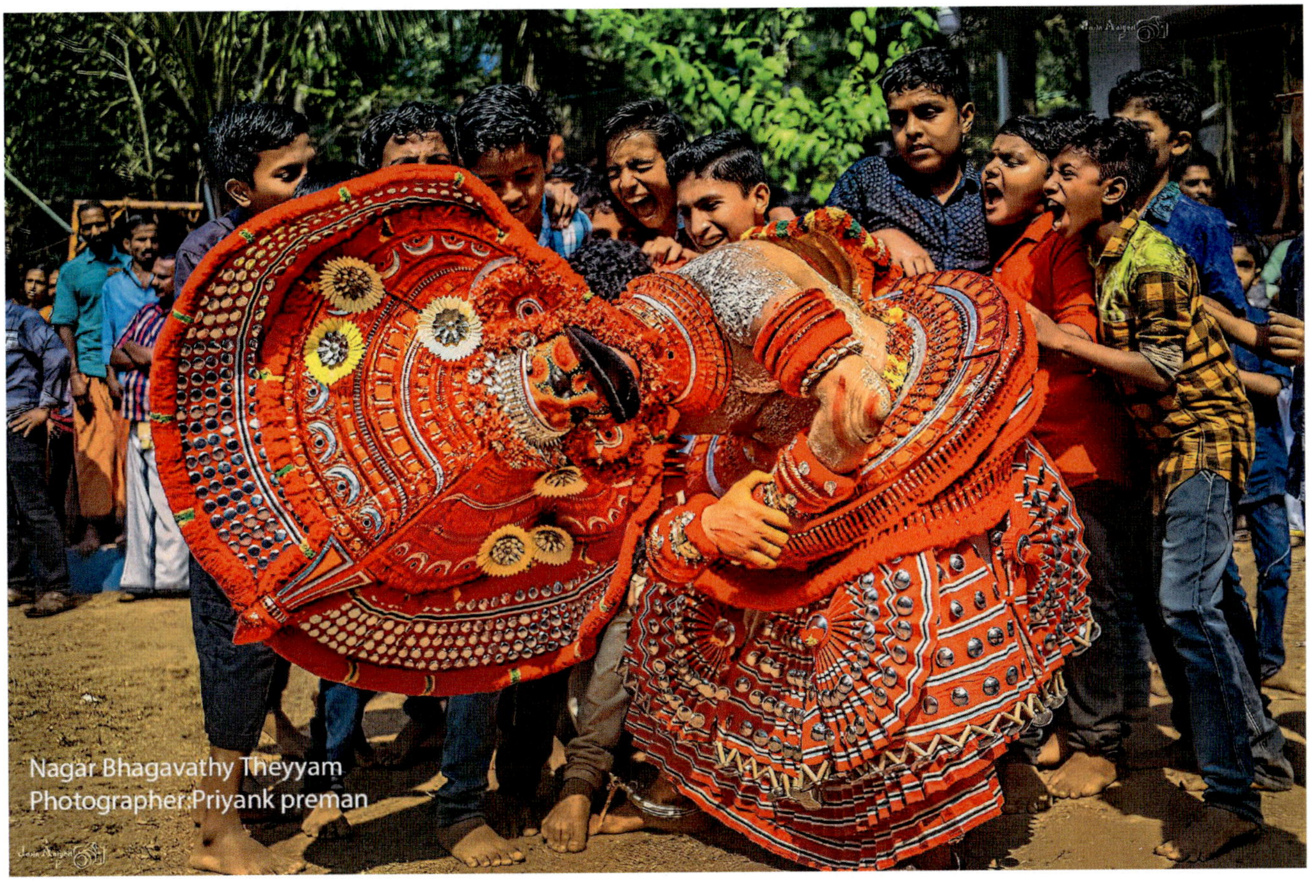

Nagar Bhagavathy Theyyam
Photographer:Priyank preman

The aim of this work is not just to green-wash my "Prodigal Son" guilt but also to uplift my homeland - "God's Own Country" - and its Gods. I believe that the thirty years of my professional and volunteer Monkey-Trap roles have finally given me enough strength to be a rebel. I dedicate this Greater Purpose to the Theyyam rebel Gods of the long-gone past. And I hope beyond the few dollars of royalty profit; these seeds will help the destitute Gods of God's Own Country: Theyyam Artists. I hope the book and subsequent efforts will turn the eyes of the EAST and WEST towards this precious tradition.

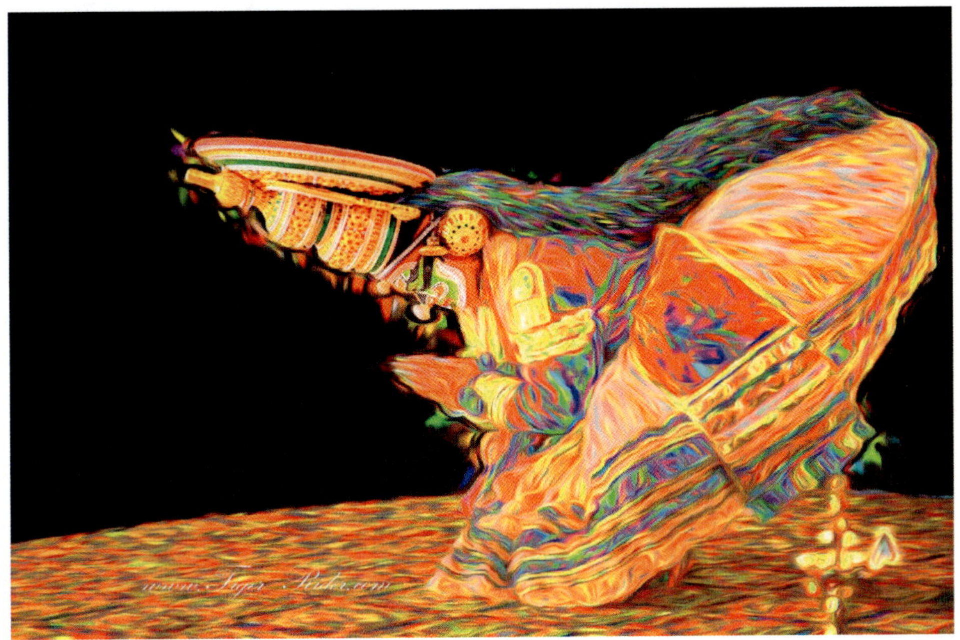

Karim Chamundi Theyyam

It was late at night when Ali woke up hearing the cries of his dear wife, who was pregnant. They were residents of Payyath hill. After noticing her going through unbearable pain, Ali knew she was going into labor. Ali thought it was all happening fast and felt unprepared to welcome his child. After consoling his wife, he quickly rubbed away his tiredness and set out in search of a midwife. He walked past many houses enquiring, but all in vain. Soon, he met a beautiful woman in the valley who introduced herself as a midwife and agreed to assist. She accompanied him back to his house. Once they reached, the midwife entered his wife's room and asked Ali to stay outside. After a long time, Ali heard his wife crying loudly, almost as if she was about to die. He prayed for it to be over soon but suddenly noticed blood oozing out through the steps of the room. In a panic, Ali banged on the door, only to realize that it would not open. After trying for a while, he broke open the door and entered the room at the sight of a demon sucking blood from his wife's abdomen, which was now ripped apart. To his horror, Ali realized it was a demon who had come with him in the disguise of a midwife. He attacked the demon with full might and released her grip on his wife. The demon screamed piercingly and ran out of the room. Ali chased her and struck her head with an iron pestle. The entire village shuddered as the demon screamed in pain. She furiously turned around and took hold of Ali. She hauled him to the top of a Blackboard tree, where she sucked his blood, crumbled his skeleton, and finally dropped his mortal remains to the ground.

After this incident, many tragedies occurred in the village, and the devastated villagers approached the local ruler to find the reason for these unfortunate events. With the help of an astrologer, the ruler performed a Prasna, a ritual of problem-solving in Hindu astrology. The Prasna discovered that the demon was causing these tragedies because of her unavenged anger. The importance of pleasing the demon was also revealed in the Prasna. It can only be done by giving her a *Kaavu* (shrine) and a highly regarded title. This turned into the Theyyam, known as *Karim Chamundi*. While this legend is popular in the *Pulaya* community, the abodes (*Maatams*) of the Nambiar community believe Karim Chamundi to be *Mahadevi*, a form of *Parvati*, who fought the evil *Asuras* of *Sumbha* and *Nisumbha* on the spot.

Karim Chamundi is a Theyyam of the Vaa Devata sect (Goddess of forests or the Indian counterpart of the Roman rustic Goddess Fauna). They are primarily performed in the Kavus (shrines) of North Malabar. The face of a *Karim Chamundi Theyyam* is painted with rice powder and carbon paste. Its hair and body are decorated with tender coconut fronds. Because of their ferocious and wild appearance, devotees worship the Theyyam with the utmost fear and respect. The name '*Karim Chamundi*' originated from its dark visage and appearance. According to ancient Malayalam legends, Karim Chamundi belongs to one of the evil sects *Yakshi* (Spirits), who seduces men and drinks their blood. Although fierce in appearance, the motive of this Goddess is to let peace prevail in her region and save her citizens from the wicked powers of evil forces such as the *Asuras*.

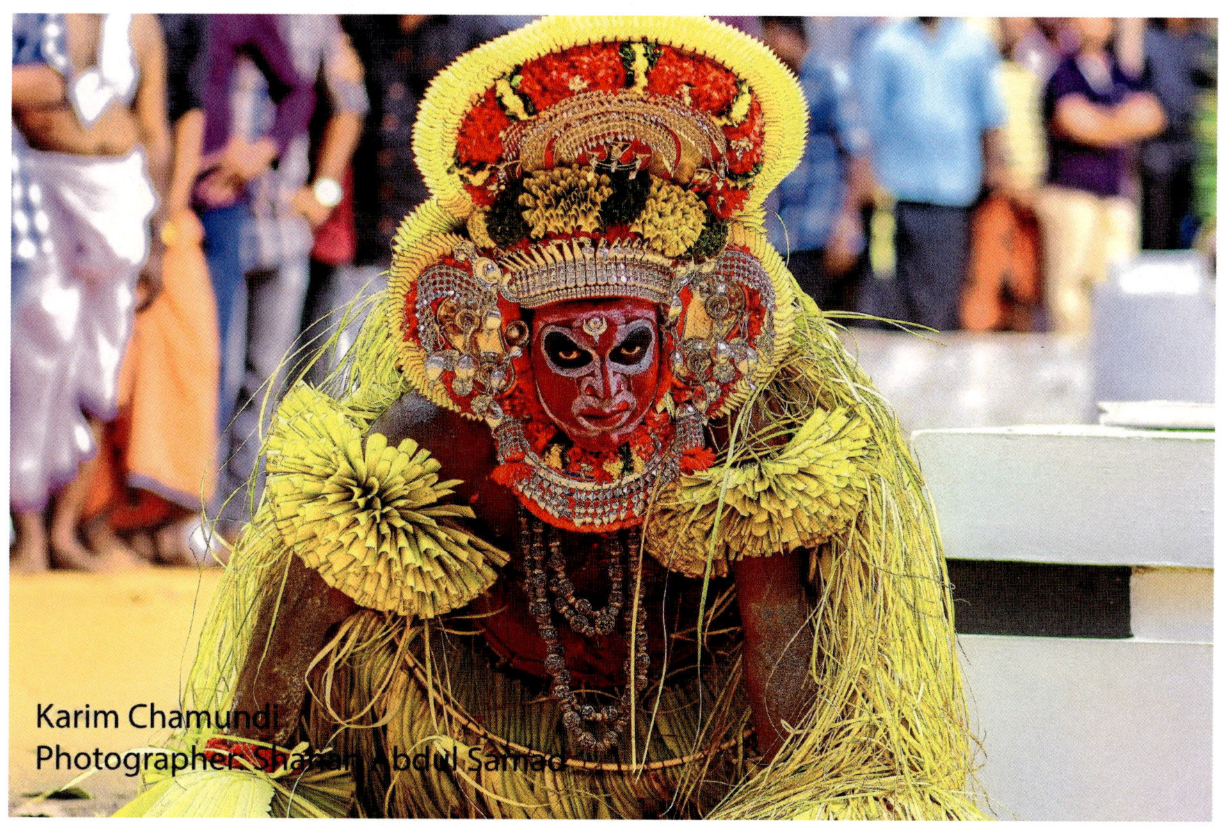
Karim Chamundi
Photographer: Shahan Abdul Samad

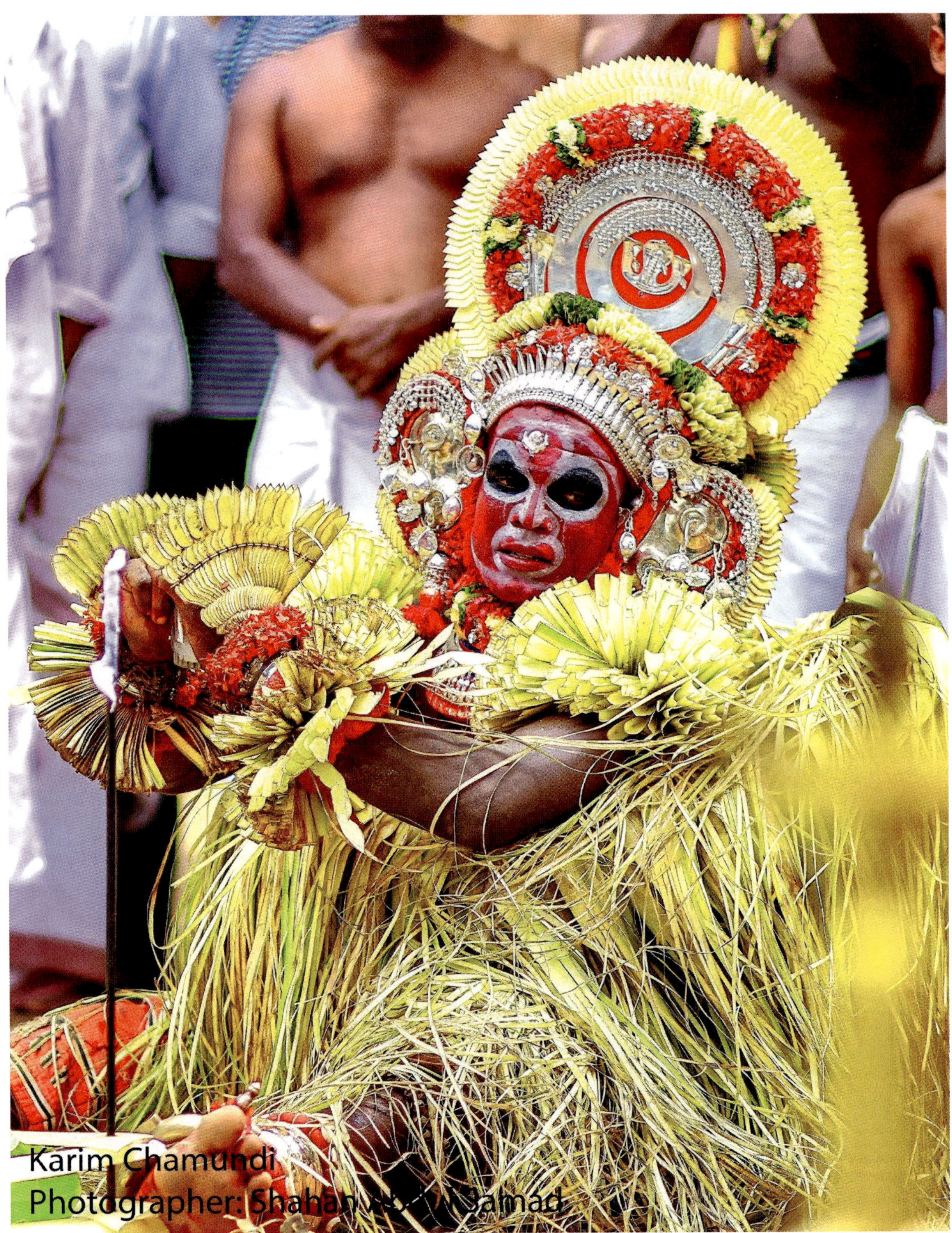

Karim Chamundi
Photographer: Shahan Ab[illegible] Samad

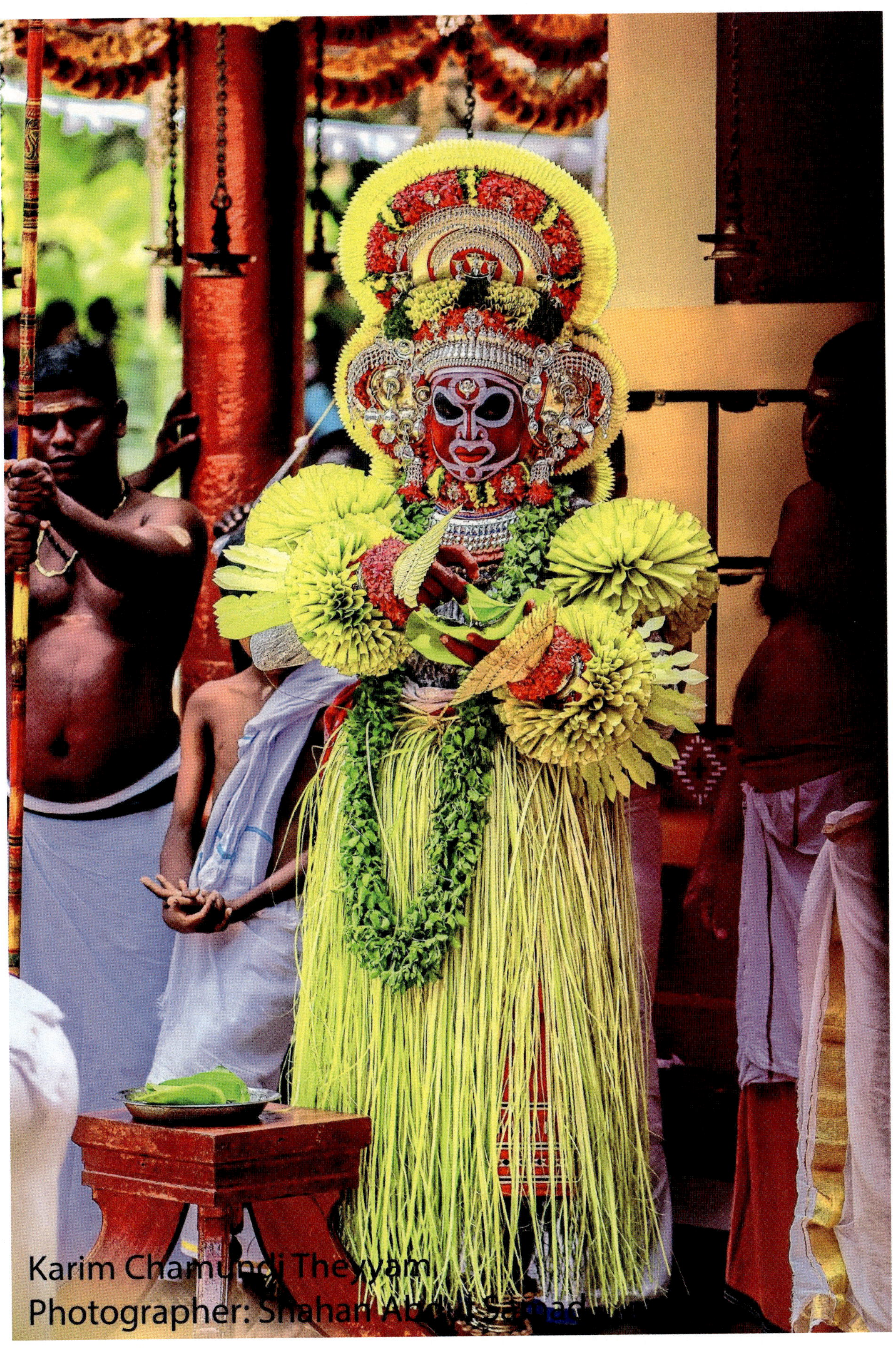

Karim Chamundi Theyyam
Photographer: Shahan Abdul Samad

Raktha Chamundi Theyyam

Rakthabeejasura is the son of *Krodhavathi, an Asura (Demon)*. While fighting a war for the *Asura* brothers *Sumbha* and *Nisumbha, Rakthabeejasura* fought against the Goddess *Chandika*. From every drop of Rakthabeejasura's blood that fell on the battlefield, several *Asuras* emerged. The Goddess was enraged with this rapid procreation, and she unfurled a tongue undulating on a dark, horrifying face. It came from her forehead and sucked every drop of Asura's blood without letting it fall to the ground. This prevented the creation of multiple Asuras on earth. Thus, she is named after *Rakthabeejeswari* as *Raktha Chamundi* (Blood Goddess). She is the protector of the *Moovari* community, which isolated itself from the Brahmin community long ago.

The Malayan community also performs Raktha Chamundi Theyyam, also called *Aayiramthengu Chamundi*. When the entire Kolathiri region was affected by flood and famine, the wards pleaded to the *Kolathiri King,* who prayed to Goddess *Annapoorneshwari*. The Goddess and her accompanying Bhagavathis entered the region on a wooden vessel. Goddess Annapoorneshwari brought paddy seeds for their relief. Her wooden ship was halted at the ford at *Aayiramthengu*. The King received her and offered her tender coconuts. The Goddess threw away the husk of the coconuts, which started to move. She demanded an abode for her at the area where the husk was hurled. The King built a temple for her, and the accompanying Bhagavathis turned into favorites of the *Moovaaris* (the ones who collect or scoop flower petals after the pooja).

Apart from Raktha Chamundi and Ayiramthengu Chamundi, this Goddess has several other names, including *Neelamkai Chamundi, Raktheshvari, Kuppol Chamundi, Kuttikkara Chamundi, Kizhakkekara Chamundi, Kuthirakaali, Periyaatt Chamundi, Kaarel Chamundi, Chalayil Chamundi, Plavadukka Chamundi, Edappara Chamundi, and Veera Chamundi.* For all these different names and forms, *Aayiramthengu Chamundi* is the principal deity.

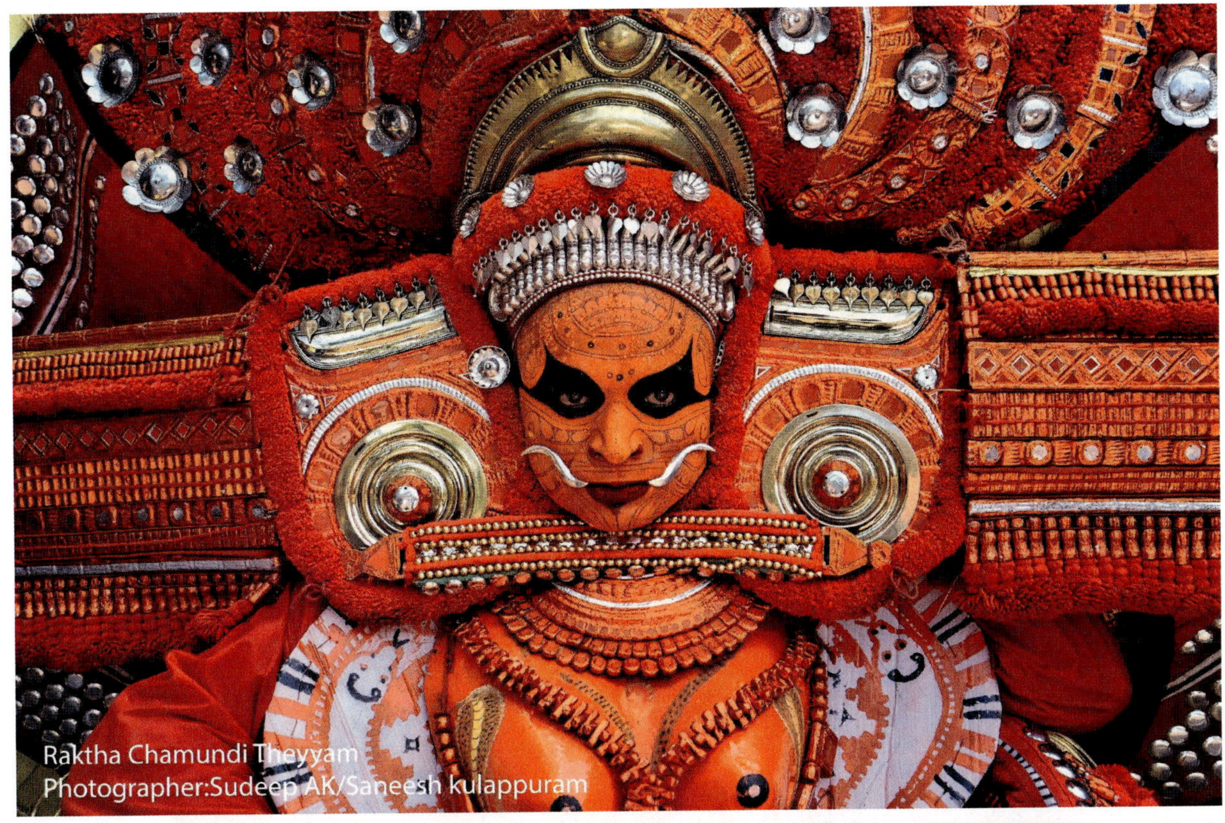

Raktha Chamundi Theyyam
Photographer:Sudeep AK/Saneesh kulappuram

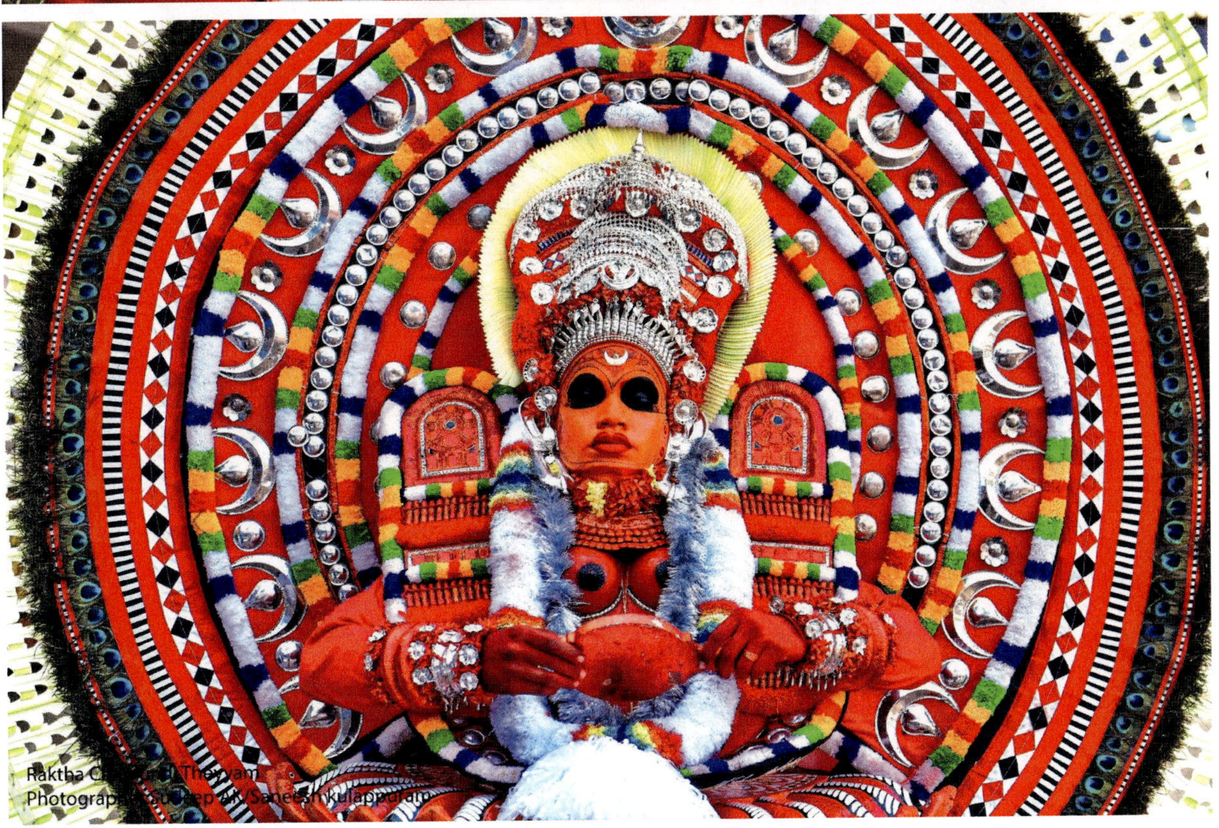

Raktha Chamundi Theyyam
Photographer:Sudeep AK/Saneesh kulappuram

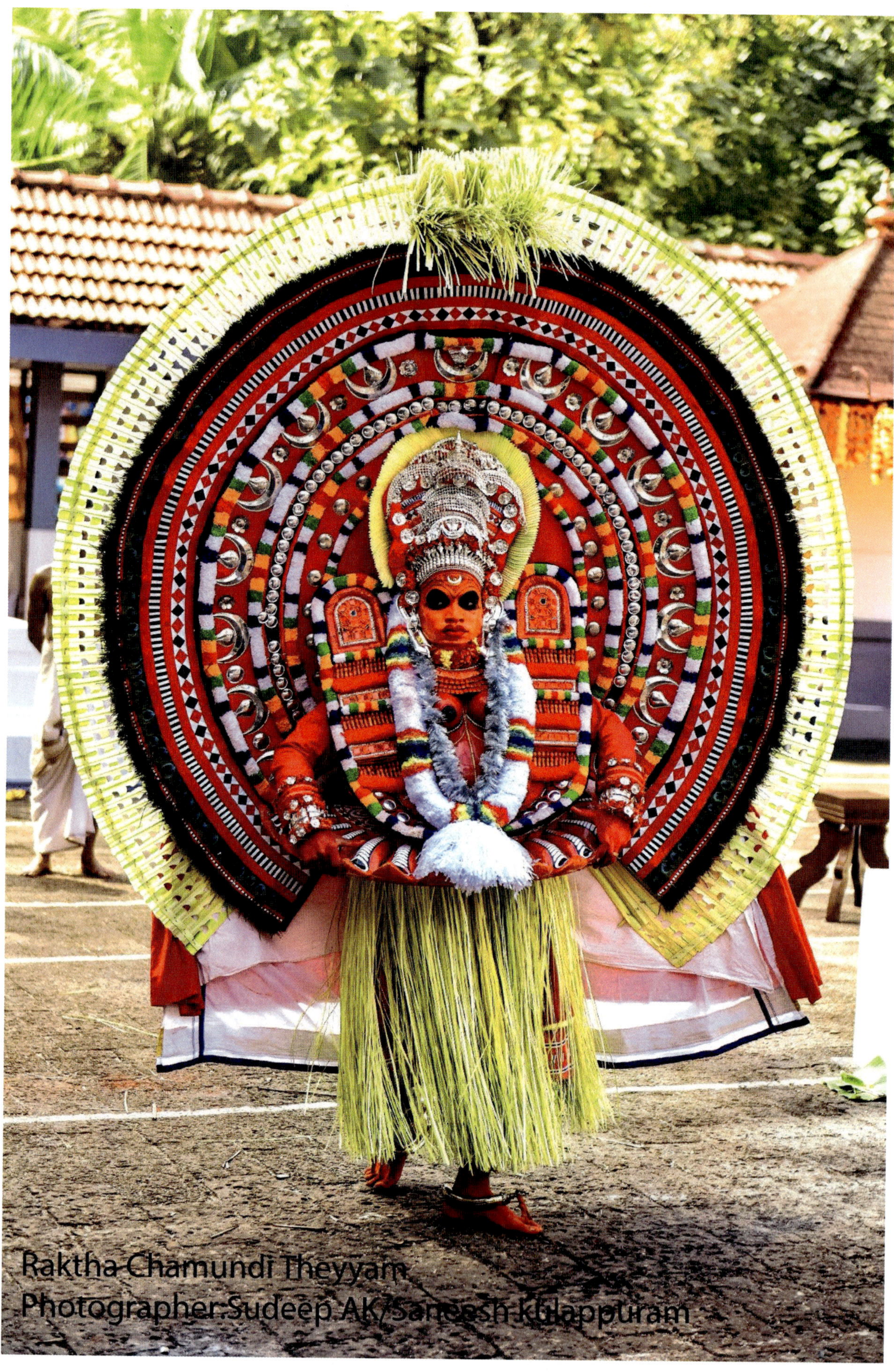

Raktha Chamundi Theyyam
Photographer:Sudeep AK/Saneesh Kulappuram

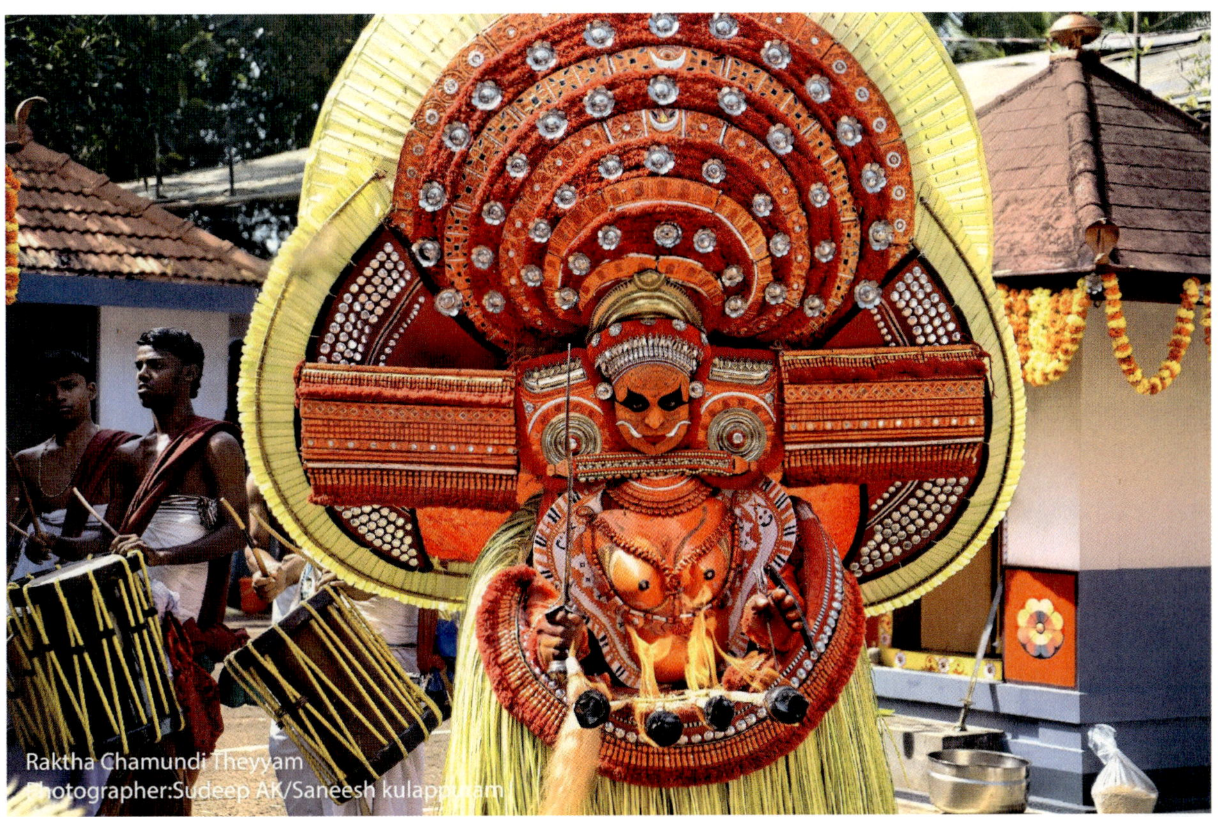
Raktha Chamundi Theyyam
Photographer:Sudeep AK/Saneesh kulappuram

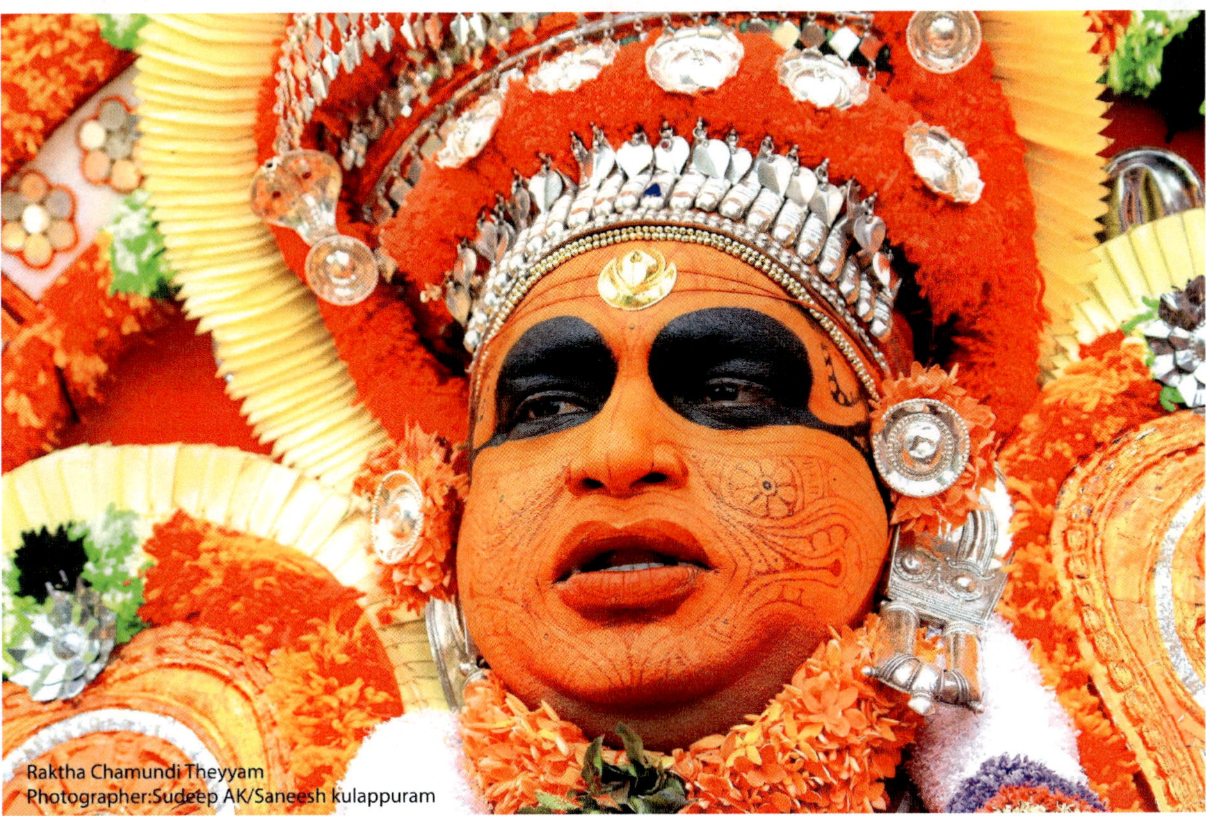
Raktha Chamundi Theyyam
Photographer:Sudeep AK/Saneesh kulappuram

Muthappan Theyyam

The Thiruvan river flowed serenely. Padikutty Amma, the wife of an Iyengar Brahmin (a high caste Tamil-speaking Brahmin society), walked by its banks, lost in her own thoughts. The grief of not having a child had overtaken her a long time back, and she had constantly been praying to Lord Shiva to grant her a child. Suddenly, she was awakened from her deep thoughts by a faint cry from somewhere in the distance. To her amazement, she found an infant lying on the banks of the river, and she knew that her prayers had been answered.

Padikutty Amma and her husband raised the child as their own. But, to their dismay, the child showed interest in eating meat and fish, which was against the Brahmin tradition. He hunted many animals and roasted and consumed them. Iyengar despised his routines. They admonished him, but his eyes would turn red with anger instead of realizing his mistakes. His scorching gaze burned everything he looked at into ashes. His parents could not afford to raise him anymore, and *Padikutty* asked him to leave the house and go his own way.

The boy walked left the house. He went to *Parassinikadavu,* where he saw a palm tree, drank the toddy on top of it, and enjoyed the intoxication. Chandan, a toddy tapper, saw this and tried to shoot him with an arrow. But because of the strange power of the boy's anger, Chandan became petrified. Chakki, Chandan's wife, came in search of Chandan and saw the boy on top of the palm tree, recognizing him as God. She repented for Chandan's mistake; hence, Chandan was reinstated in a human form. It is said that an angler who was fishing near the palm forest saw the exchange between Muttappan, Chandan, and Chakki. He told his friend from the 'Theeya' community about his mystical experience. They both built a shrine for the boy hailed as *Muthappan* at *Parassinikadavu* and started worshipping him.

Muthappan Daivam traveled to places like *Maniparambu, Onaparambu, Punnadu, Aanjilattukunnu, Moozhakunnu,* etc. *Kunnathoor Padi* is this God's place of rest. There is also a story about Muthappan going to the Kunnathoor Padi hill and gaining his powers there. Another tale describes his journey to *Puralimala* (*Purali hill*), where he resided for a long time, engaging in farming and hunting. During this time, he was close friends with the tribes and resisted the feudal system. *Muthappan* and *Thiruvappan* are the same deities. He is also referred to as *Puralimala Muthappan or Nanmala Muthappan* because of the places he resides.

Muthappan Theyyam always performs as *Thiruvappana* and *Vellattam*. In this, *Vellattam* is the assistant to the main body, *Thiruvappana*. Some believe that this assistant *Vellattam* is Chandan, who Muthappan petrified. Others believe this Vellattam is *Nambola* Muthappan, Muthappan's companion when he left for Puralimalaa.

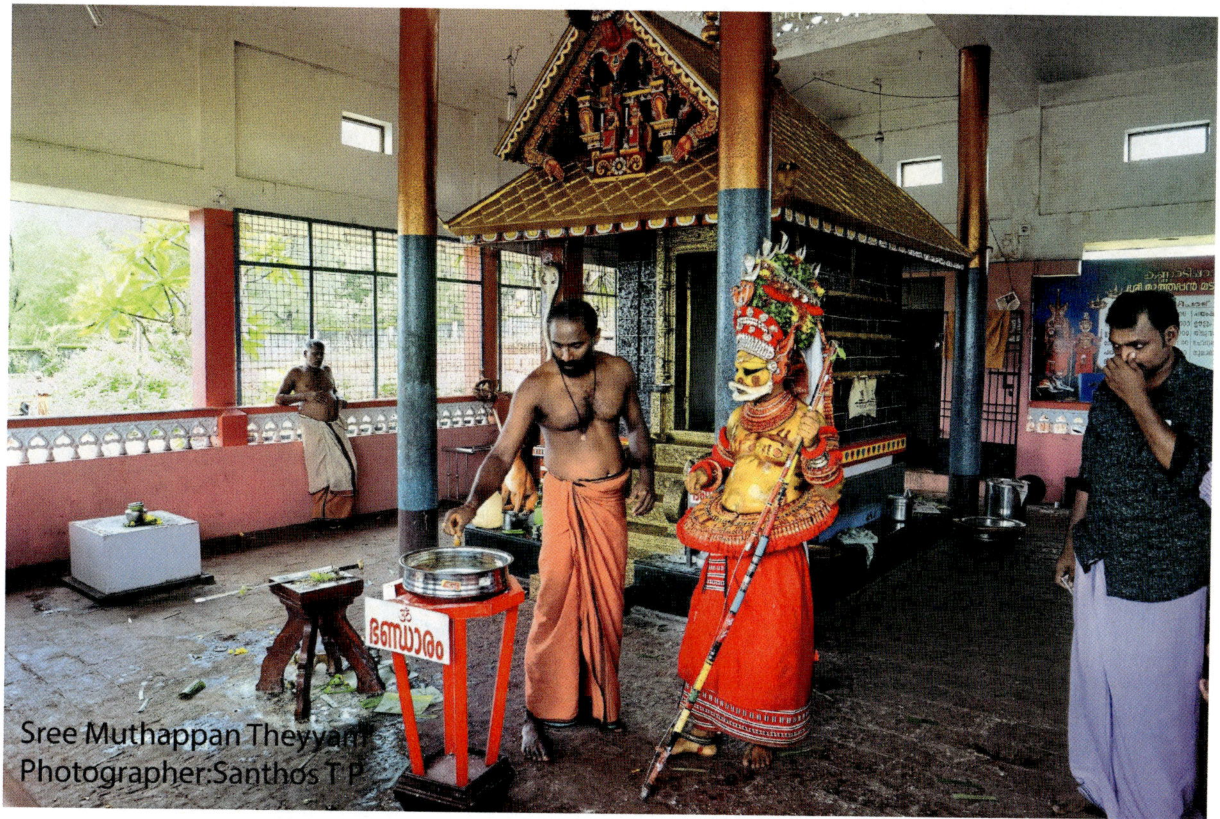

Sree Muthappan Theyyam
Photographer:Santhos T P

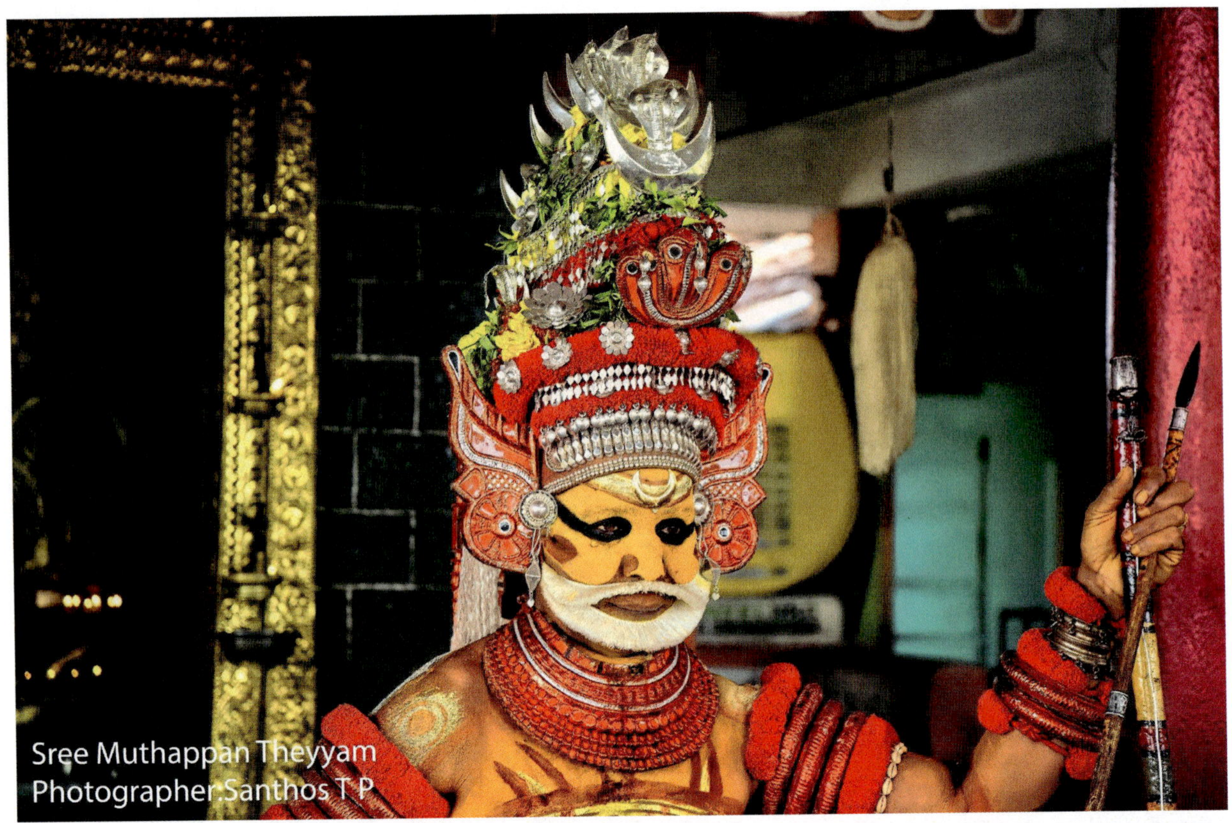

Sree Muthappan Theyyam
Photographer:Santhos T P

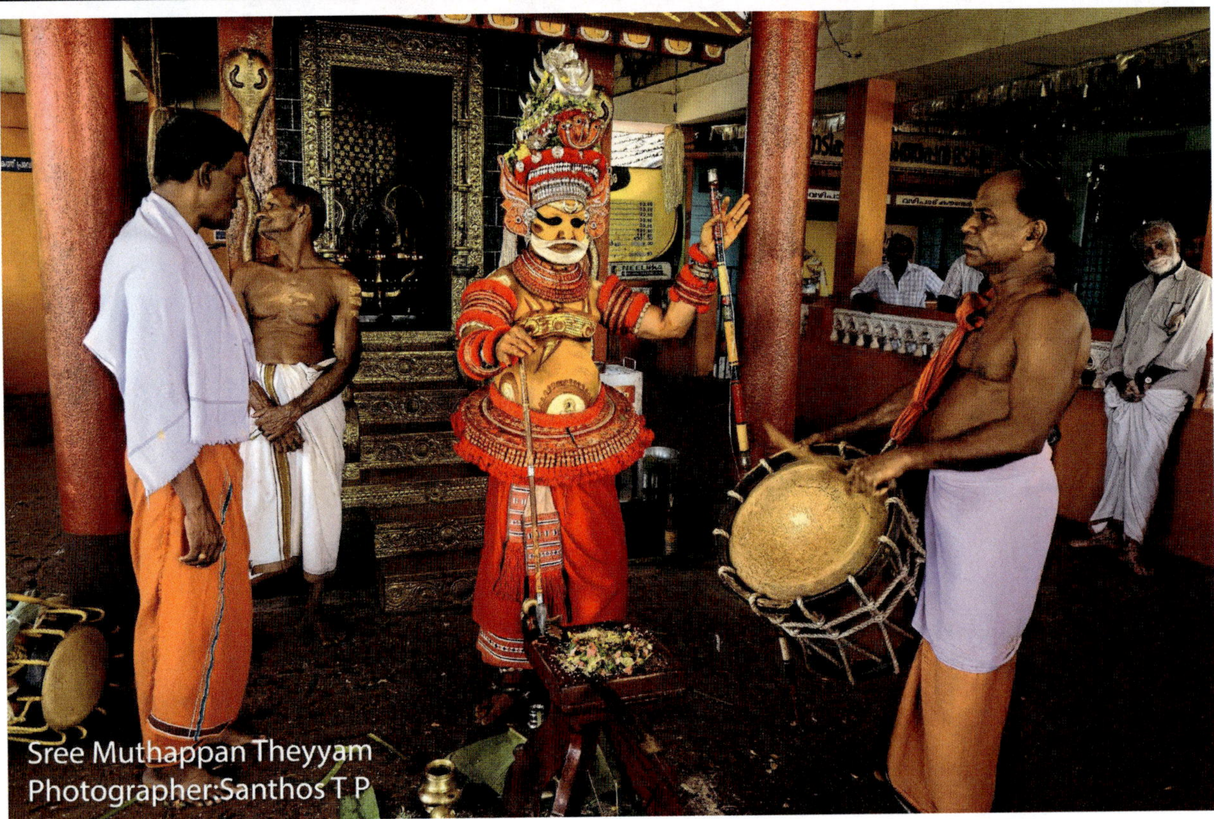

Sree Muthappan Theyyam
Photographer:Santhos T P

Madayil Chamundi Theyyam

The eldest *Poduval (temple-dwelling caste in Kerala)* of *Vannad Tharavadu* (joint family) went hunting along with his assistant, Kuruvadan Nair. They heard a rustling in the winds and assumed the presence of wild goats nearby in the forest. Determining the position of the creatures, *Poduval* aimed and released the arrow from the bow. They ran towards the spot where the wild goat should have been, but there was no sign of their prey. They both grew tired of searching for the wounded or killed goat and sat under the trees to rest.

Suddenly, they heard an ear-piercing scream from the bushes. They raced towards the sound source and discovered a Mada or den entrance. Out of the *mada*, a strange and terrifying being appeared and began chasing them. It was the Pathala Bhairavi *(*similar to Hades in Greek mythology, Pathala Bhairavi was the Goddess of the netherworld). The chiming of anklets and waistbands followed them, along with deafening screams and raucous laughter. *Poduval* sought refuge in the *Palliyara (*The temple of the Thiyya community is called a Palliyara) of Goddess *Kanakkara Bhagavathi*.

Goddess *Kanakkara* stopped the enraged *Pathala Bhairavi* and said, "I have given shelter to my beloved, the eldest *Poduval*. Suppress your anger and return from here." However, the Goddess of the netherworld could not help her fury and killed the assistant, Kuruvadan Nair. She tore his stomach apart, chewed his bowels, and kicked his body. Once she calmed down, *Poduval* threw rice grain to welcome her, assigned an abode, and installed her as *Madayil Chamundi* (*Chamundi* of the den). She is also called *Alanthatta Madavathilkkal Bhagavathi* because she appeared from a cave in the forests in the *Alanthatta* area.

According to legends, *Madayil Chamundi* is also called *Pathala Moorthy* because she went to *Pathala* or the netherworld. Another version of this story says *Chamundi* killed the eldest *Poduval* and not his assistant, Nair, as depicted in the other versions.

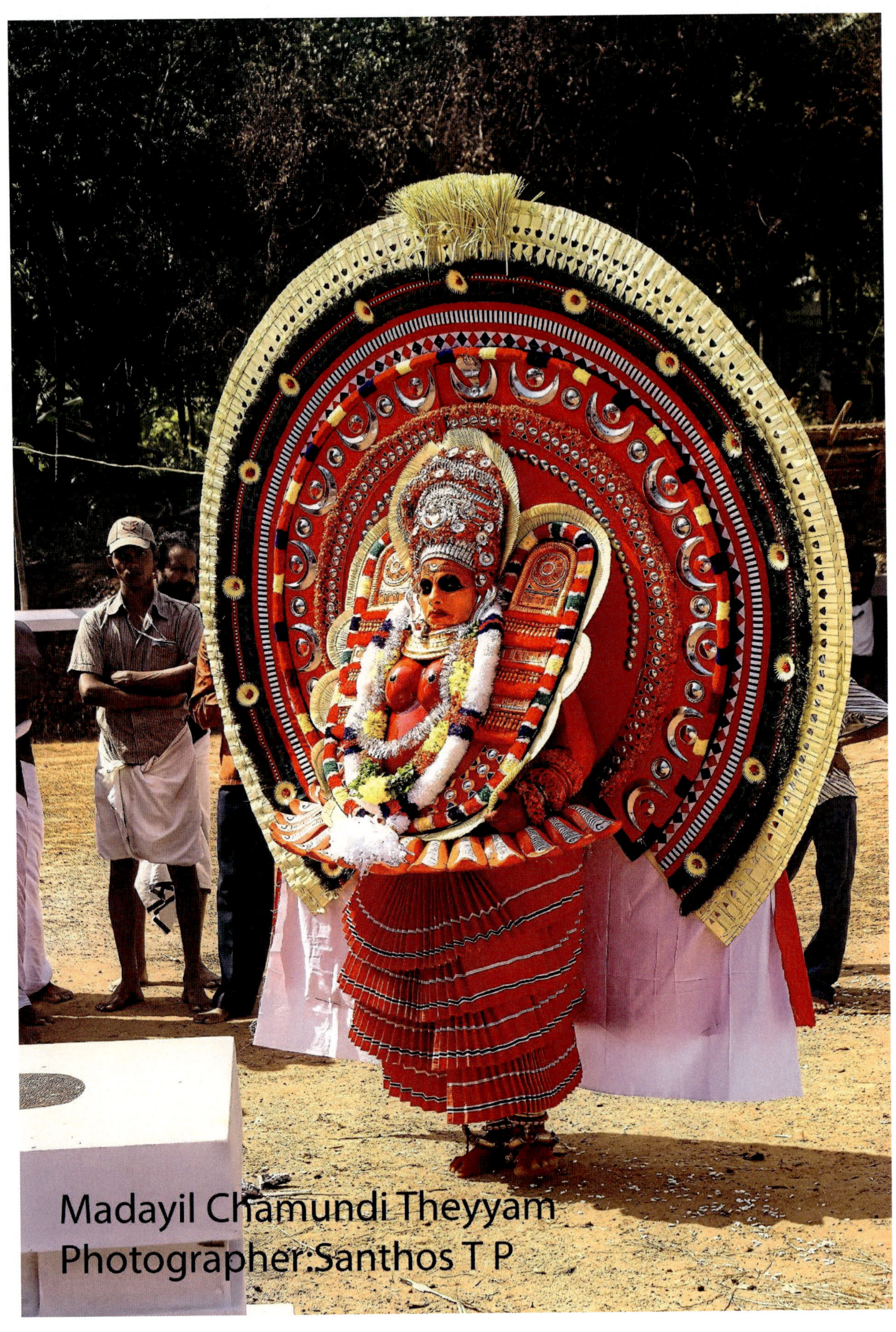

Madayil Chamundi Theyyam
Photographer:Santhos T P

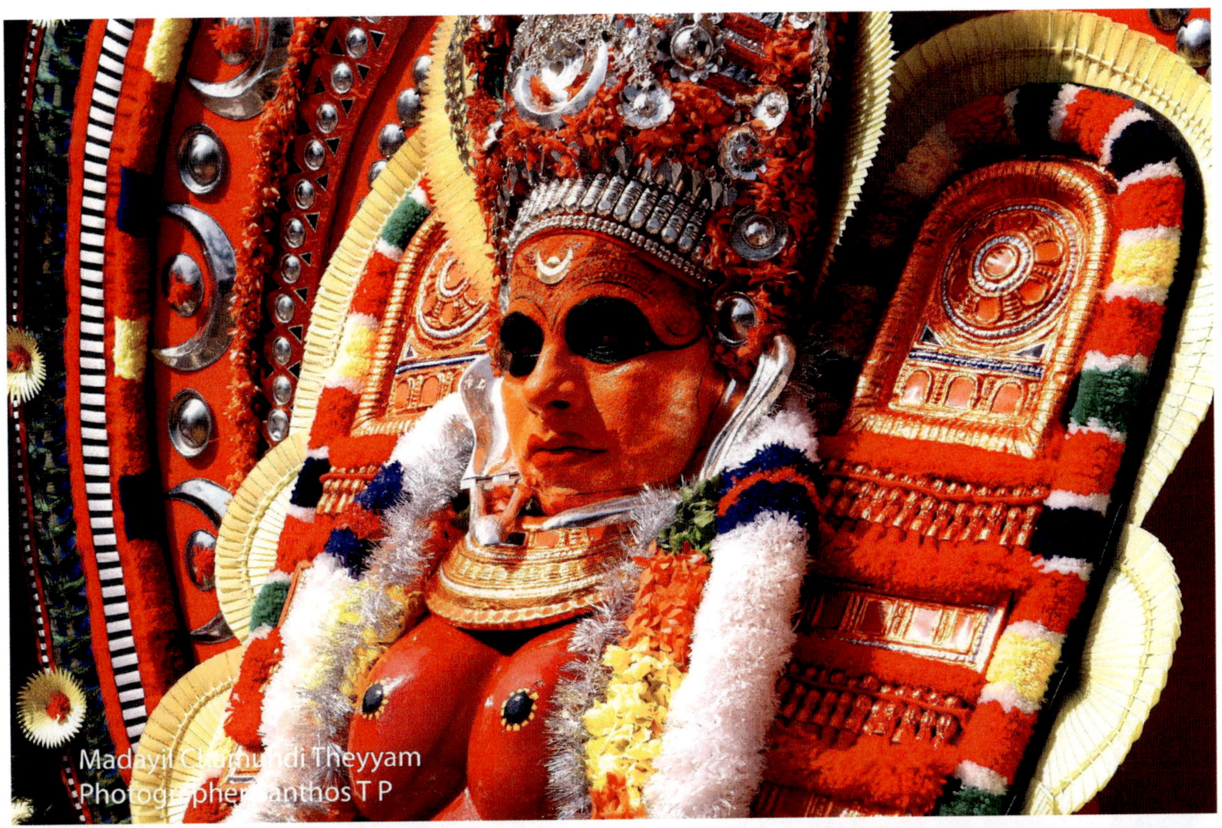

Madayil Chamundi Theyyam
Photographer Santhos T P

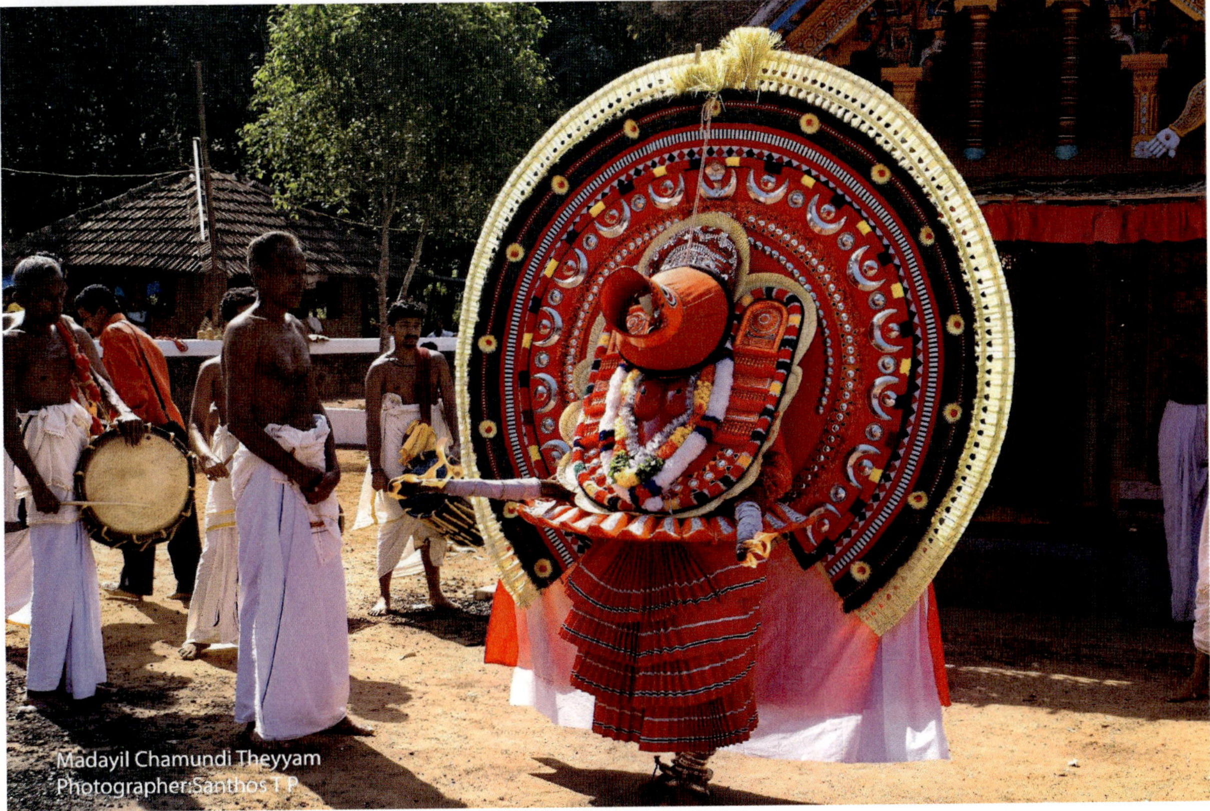

Madayil Chamundi Theyyam
Photographer Santhos T P

Neeliyar Bhagavathy Theyyam

The *Manathana Illam* (Brahmin residence) is at *Kottiyoor* near *Kannur*. When travelers reached the pond in the courtyard of this *Illam*, Goddess *Neeliyar Bhagavathy* appeared before them as a beautiful woman. She lured them to her by asking if they needed oil or shampoo to take a bath in the lagoon. Those who dared to go near her were killed, and their blood was sucked by her. Those who attempted to bathe at that pond have never returned.

Once, a *Namboodiri* scholar reached the spot and prepared to take a bath before eating. He saw the beautiful *Neeli* standing at the other bank of the lagoon. He enquired who she was, and she replied she was *Kaali*. As usual, she gave him the oil and shampoo. Rather than bathing, the *Namboodiri* drank the oil and shampoo, saying it was an elixir given by Mother. As he addressed her as a mother, she did not kill him; instead, she got into his palm-leaf umbrella and traveled with him. She asked the *Namboodiri* to install her abode at a place where cows and tigers live in harmony. Legends say that cows and tigers were living in harmony at *Mangattuparamba,* and the *Namboodiri placed a palm leaf* umbrella there to install an abode for *Neeliyar Bhagavathy*.

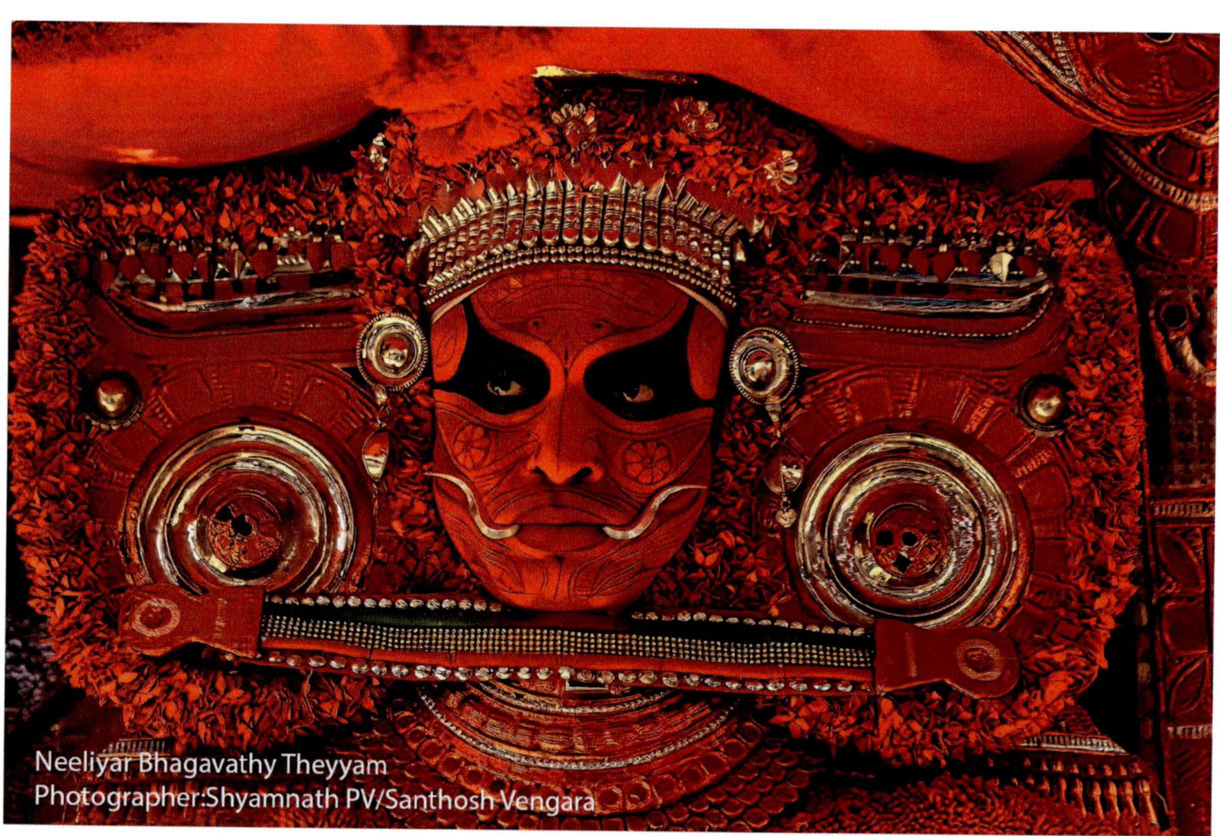

Neeliyar Bhagavathy Theyyam
Photographer:Shyamnath PV/Santhosh Vengara

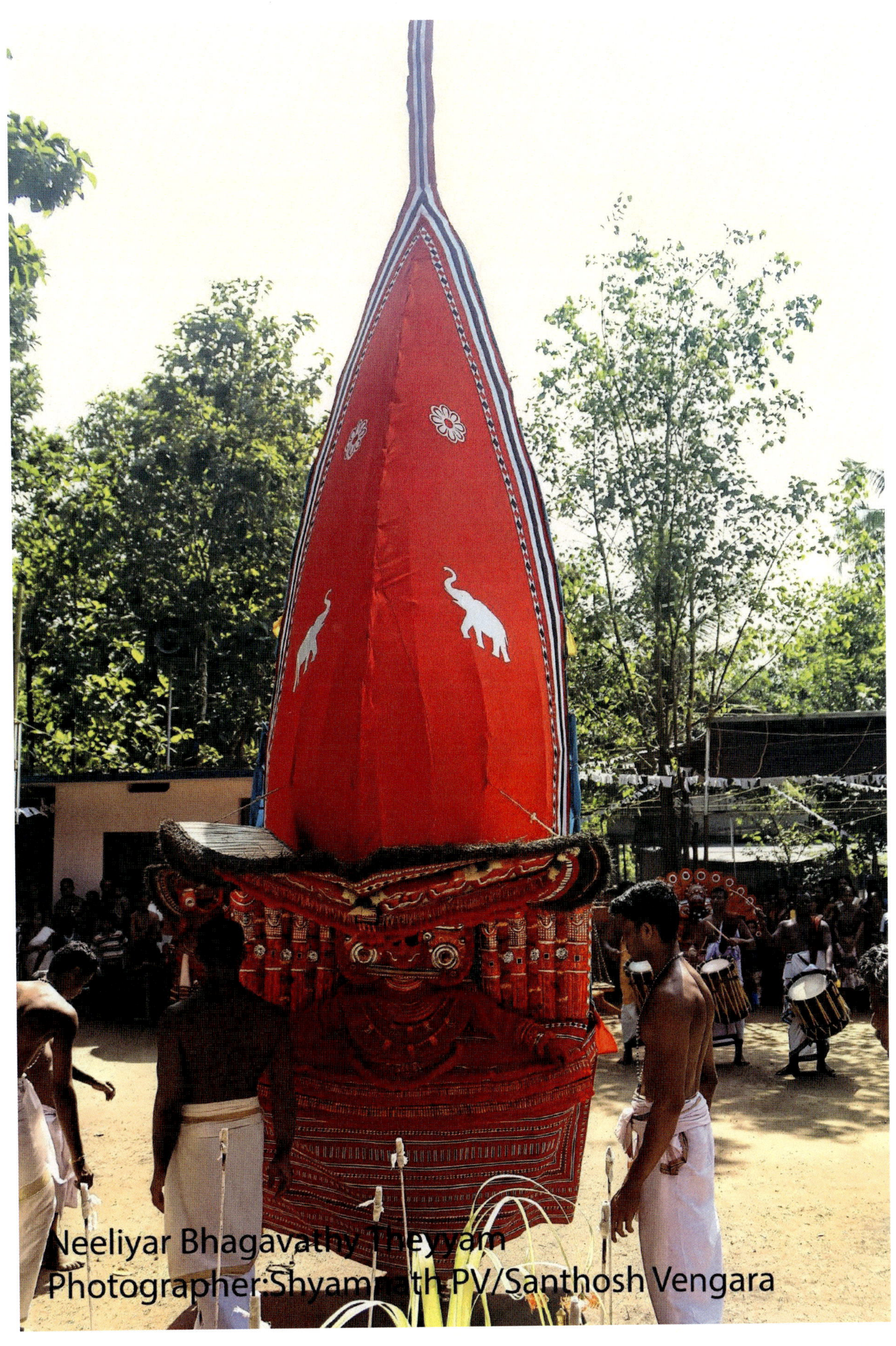

Neeliyar Bhagavathy Theyyam
Photographer:Shyamnath PV/Santhosh Vengara

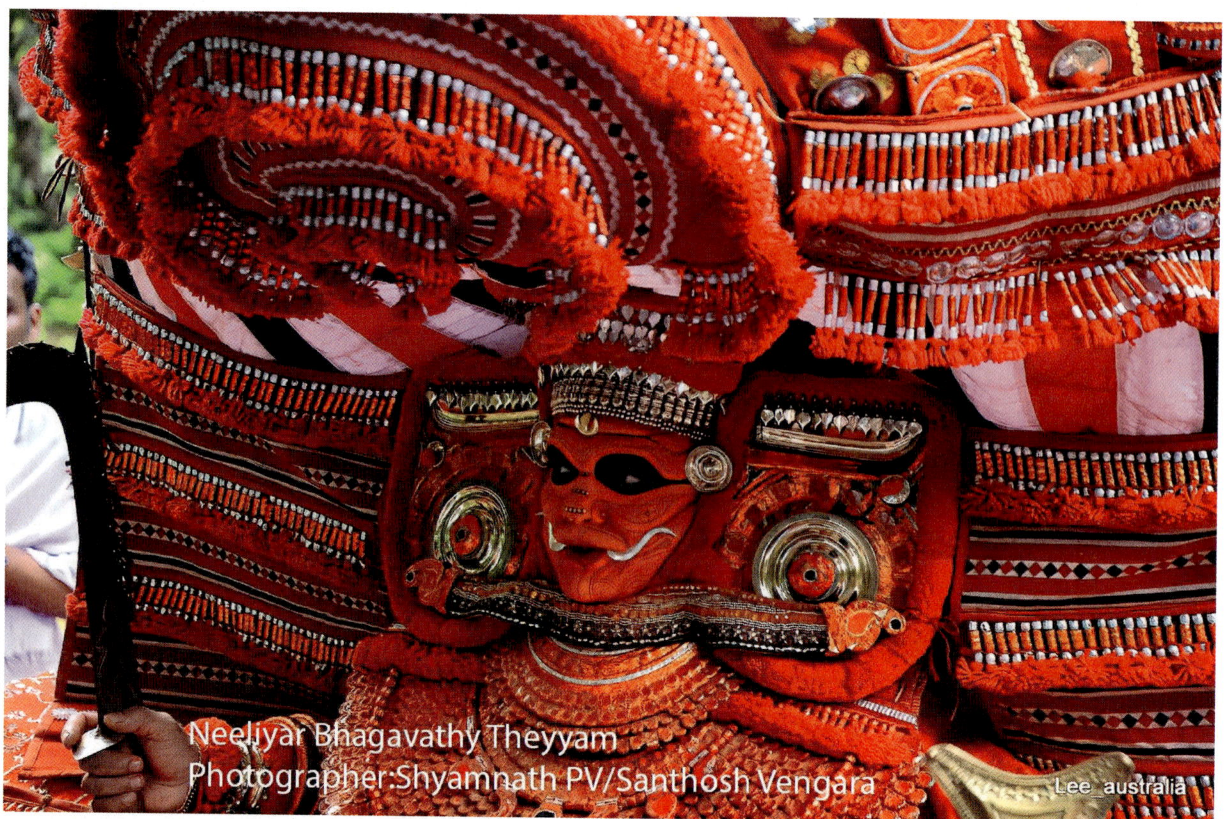
Neeliyar Bhagavathy Theyyam
Photographer:Shyamnath PV/Santhosh Vengara
Lee_australia

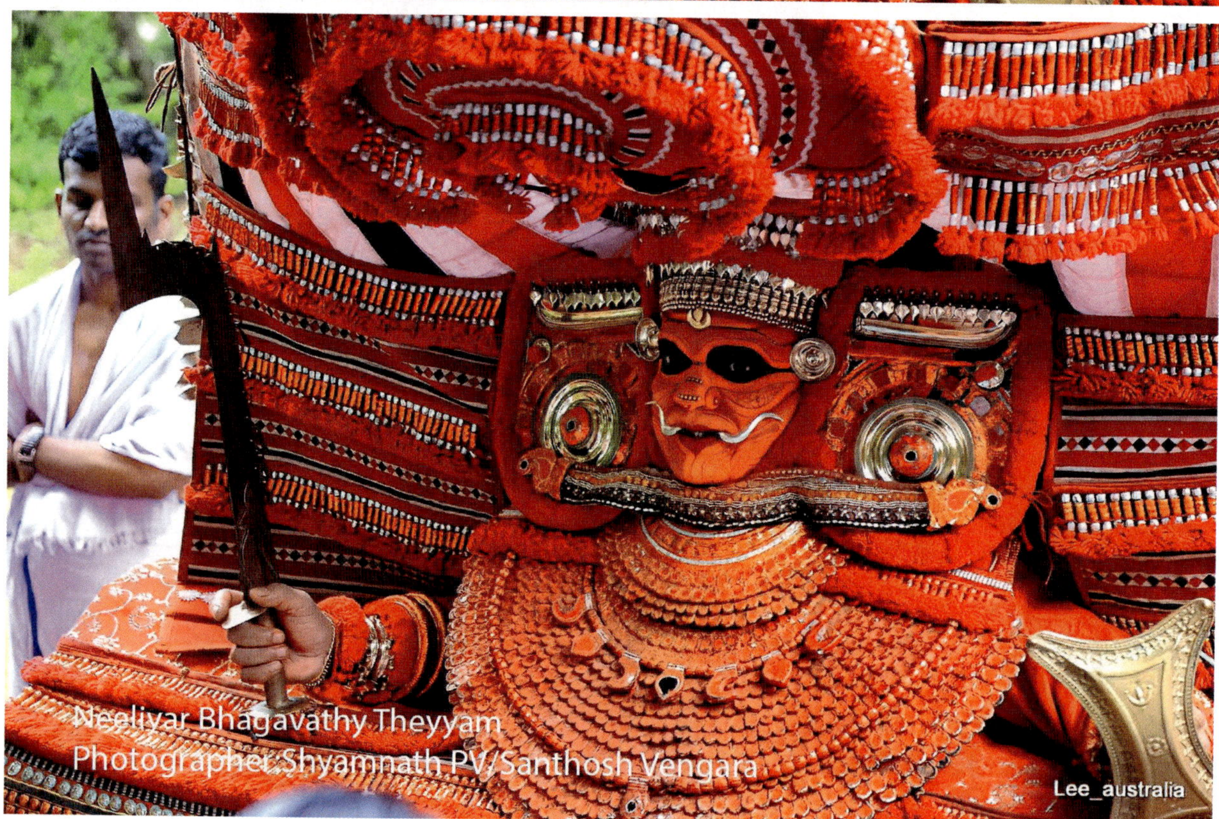
Neeliyar Bhagavathy Theyyam
Photographer:Shyamnath PV/Santhosh Vengara
Lee_australia

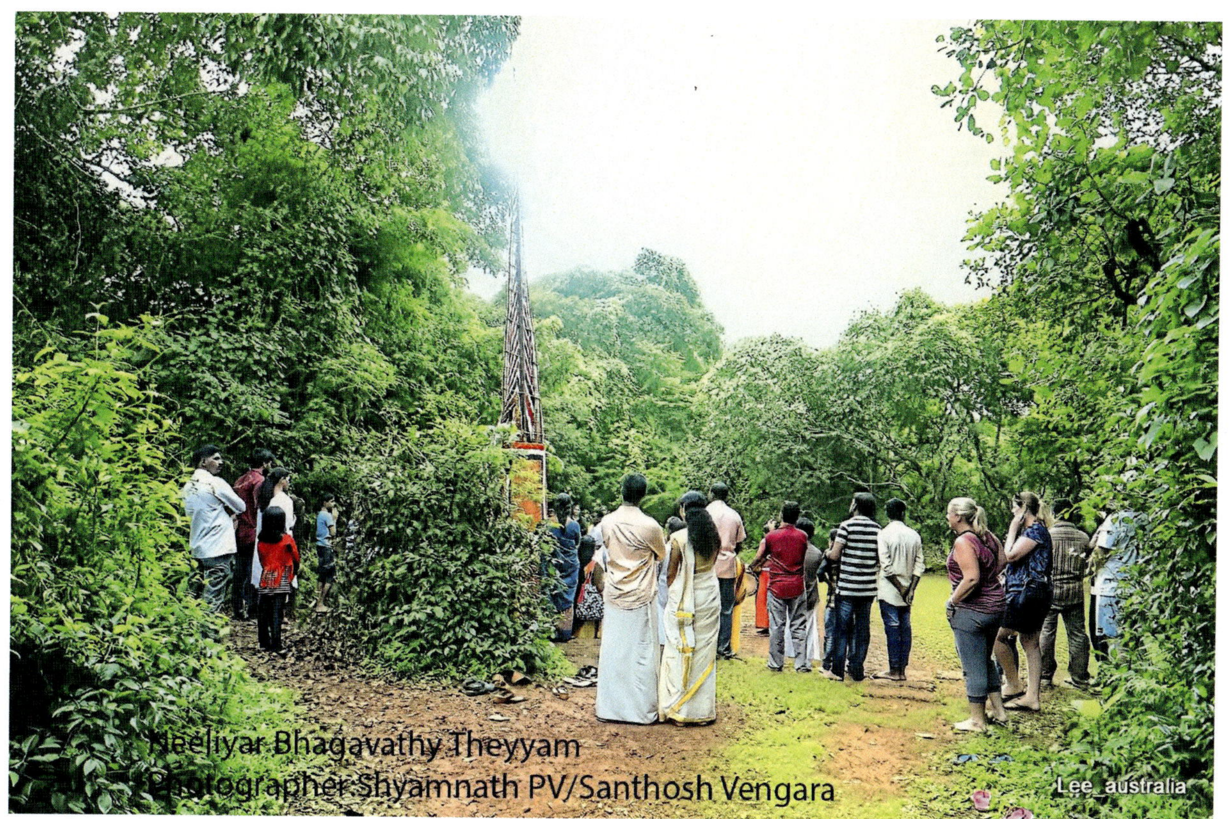
Neeliyar Bhagavathy Theyyam
Photographer Shyamnath PV/Santhosh Vengara
Lee_australia

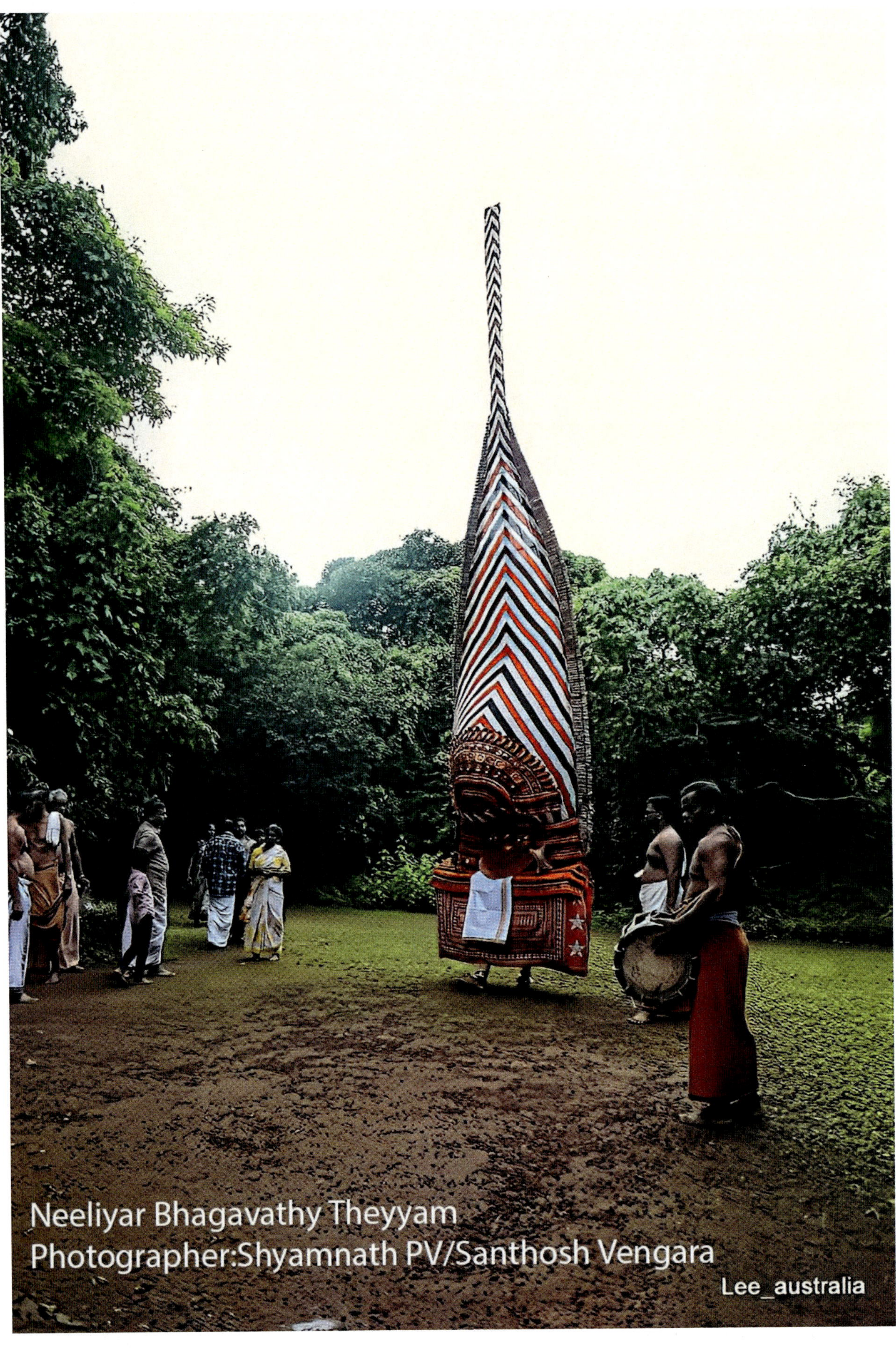

Neeliyar Bhagavathy Theyyam
Photographer:Shyamnath PV/Santhosh Vengara

Kadavath Bhagavathy Theyyam

Kalakkatt, an eminent *Tantri* (priest), was intensely focused on his tantra mantra (sacred rituals) practices when the cry of a child annoyed him. He casually wished that someone would pacify the child. The Goddess he worshiped instantly killed that child at his wish. It enraged the priest that the Goddess had murdered the child instead of soothing him. The infuriated Tantri threw away the wooden plank and stool where the Goddess was invoked, which fell in the woods inside the premises of *Palayil Idamana Tantri,* another priest. *Idamana Tantri* recognized the Goddess and installed her at his residence. He threw the wooden plank and stool in the *Arayi River*. These artifacts were whisked along by the river until, one day, they touched the body of *Arayi Thiyya,* a lower caste person. Thus, the austerity in those artifacts shifted to the courtyards of *Arayi Thiyya*, and this Bhagavathy came to be known as *Kadavath Bhagavathy* in the *Arayi* region in Kanhangad. The same Goddess is known as *Kanakkara Bhagavathy* in the Cheemeni Alanthatta region. The legend of the *Kanakkara Bhagavathy* is also similar. They performed mainly *Kadavath Bhagavathy or Kanakkara Bhagavathy Theyyam* at the Mundya shrine at *Arayi Erath* in Kanhangad.

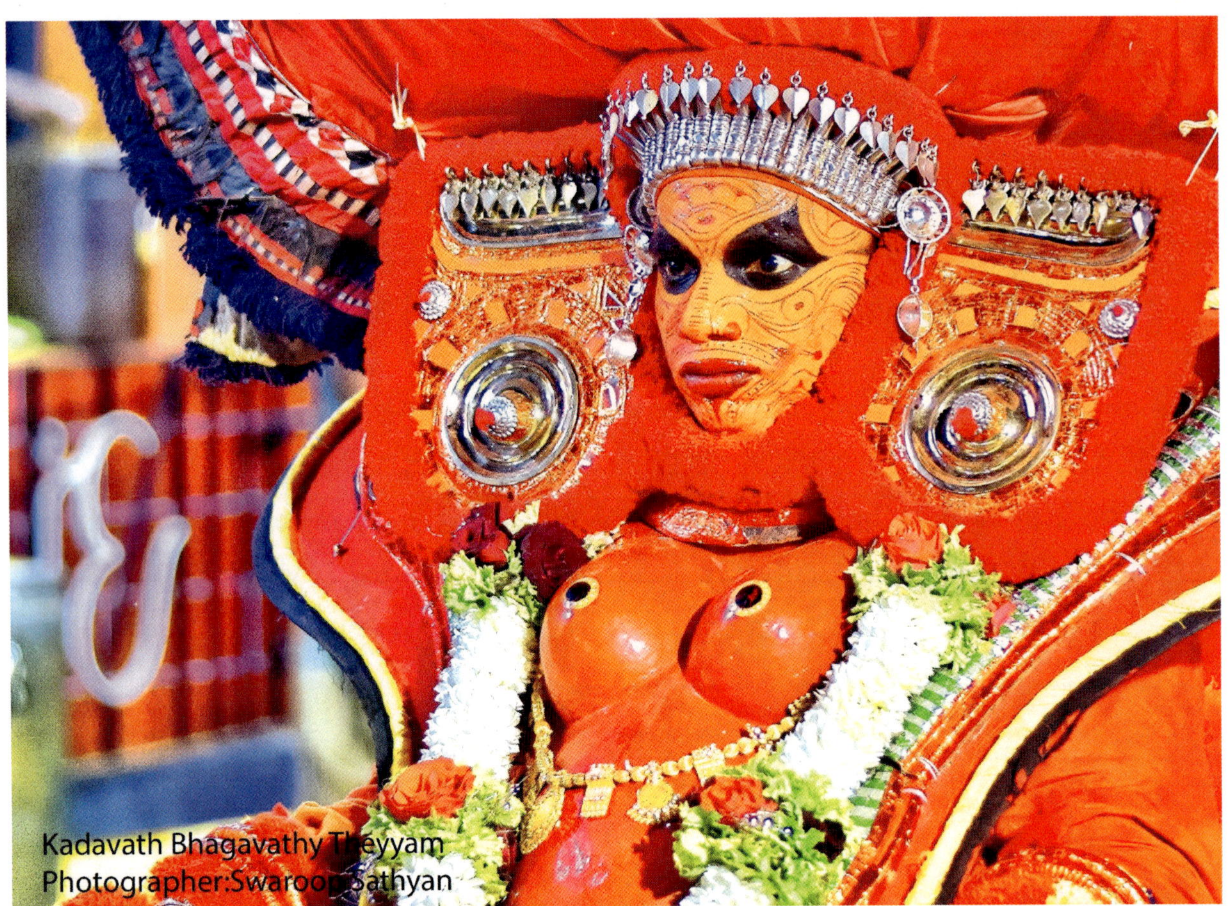

Kadavath Bhagavathy Theyyam
Photographer:Swaroop Sathyan

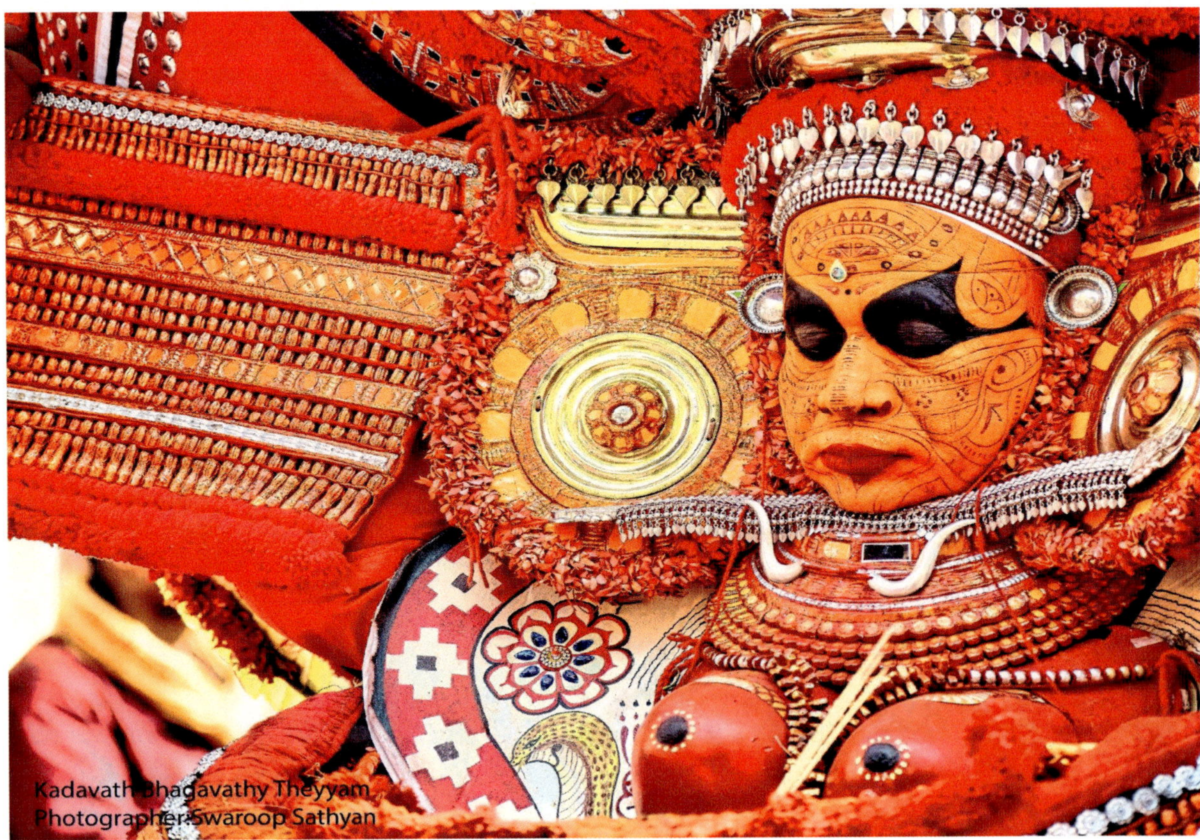

Kadavath Bhagavathy Theyyam
Photographer:Swaroop Sathyan

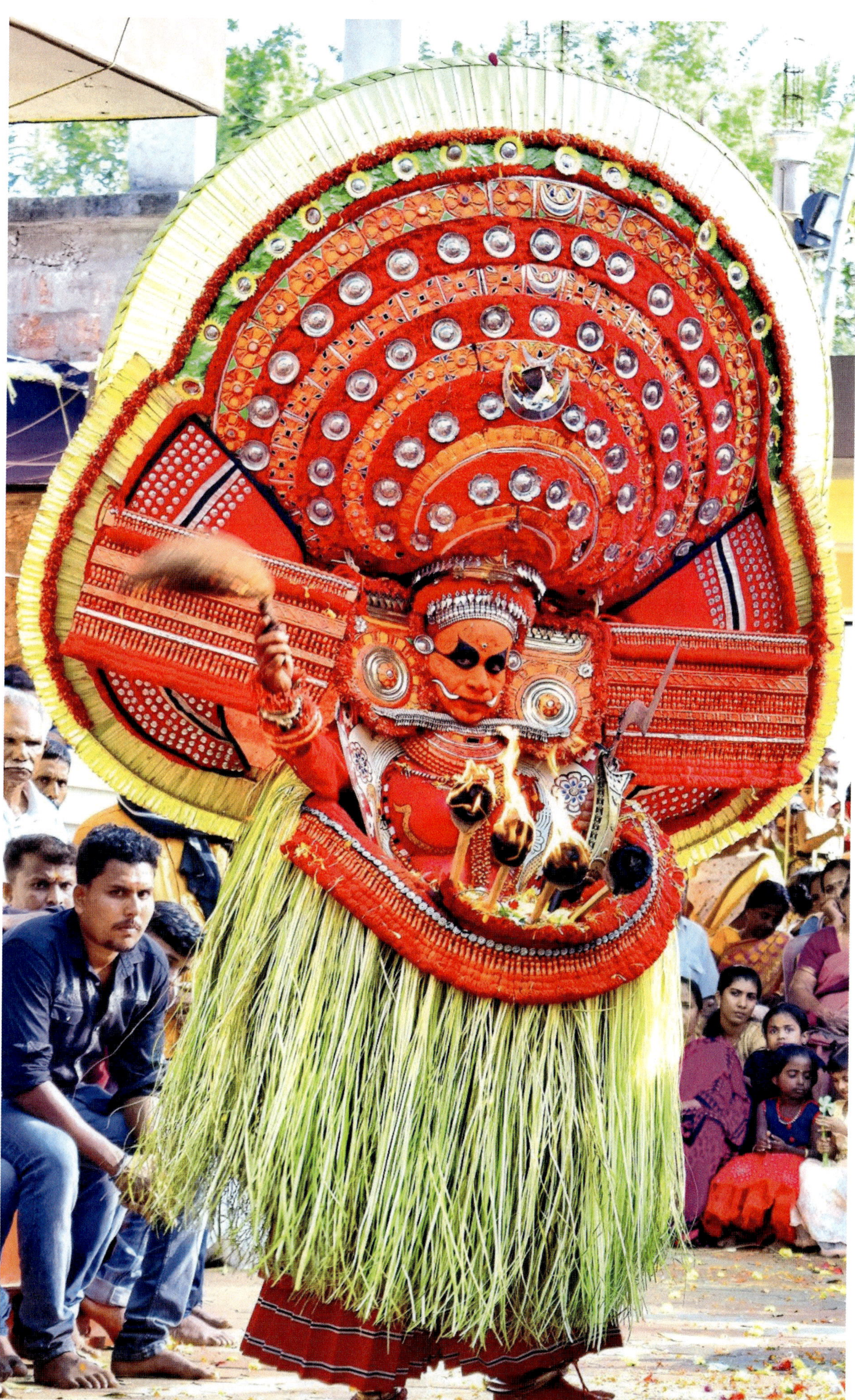

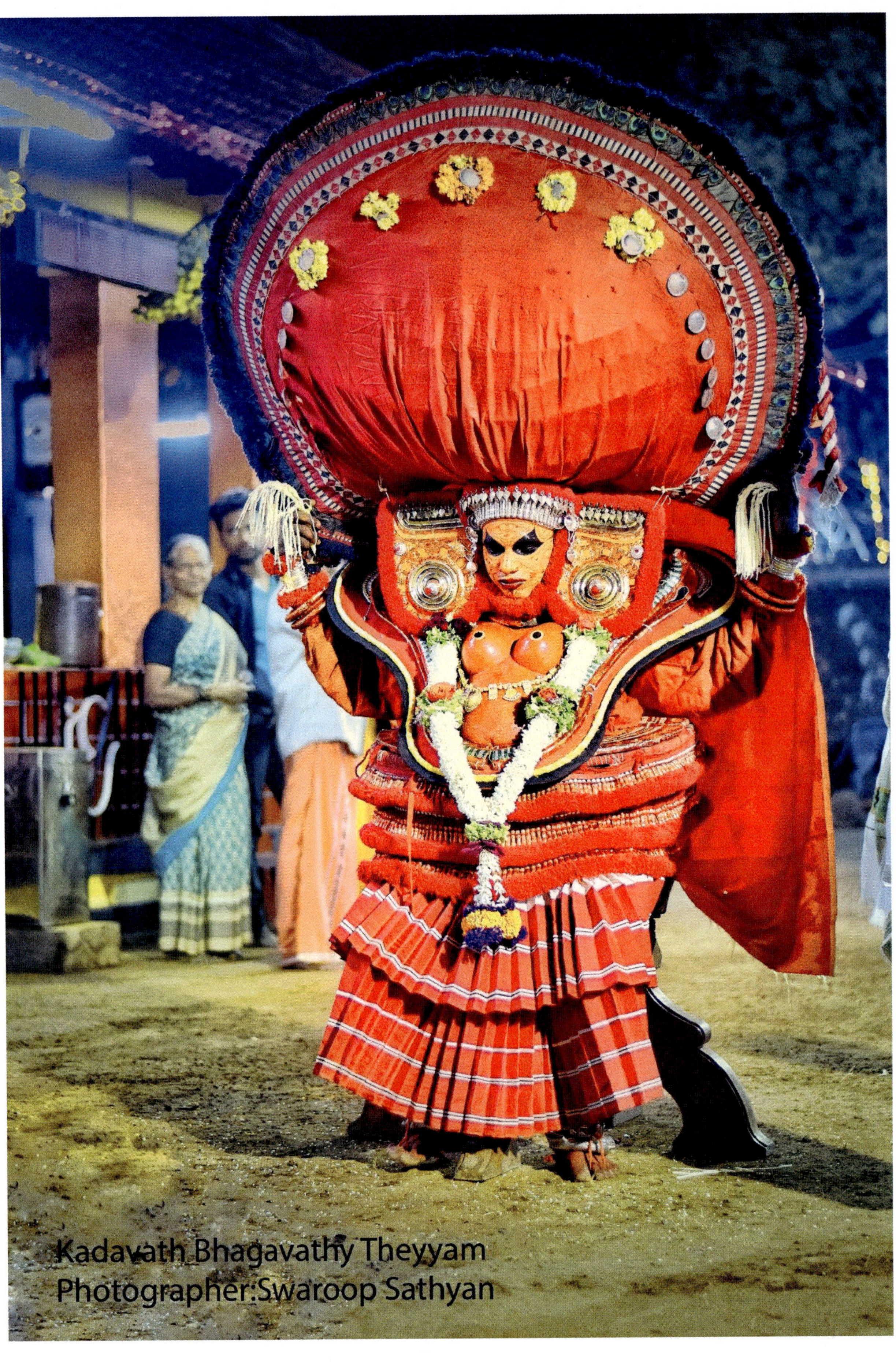

Kadavath Bhagavathy Theyyam
Photographer:Swaroop Sathyan

Thondachan Theyyam

Lord Shiva and Goddess Parvati, disguised as tigers and tigresses (*Pulikandan* and *Puli Karinkali Theyyam* concepts), gave birth to six children who became tiger Gods. They were the male tigers *Kandappuli, Marappuli, Pulimaruthan, Kaalappuli, and Puliyur Kannan,* and one female offspring-*Puliyur Kali*, who lived in the Thulu forests. One night while prowling, the tigers entered the cattle shed of Kurumbranthiri Vanavar and slaughtered the cattle. Though a firm believer, this incident highly dismayed Kurumbranthiri Vanavar. Kurumbranthiri Vanavar and friend Kannan Nair decided to destroy the little tigers and hide on top of a tree house. But that night, the tigers pounced on him before he could use the bow and arrow against them and killed him. Eventually, Kurumbranthiri Vanavar came to be revered as a Godly Theyyam called the *Thondachan Theyyam* performed at *Cheemeni Kariyappil Bhagavathi Kavu* (shrine) and shares the legend of the *Pulikandan Theyyam*.

Once Kariyath *Thandan* (the title given to the headman of the Thiyya community) from Ramaramath went to watch a Theyyam performance in the Thulu forests. The tiger Gods followed the *Thandan,* and he installed them at Ramaramath. Apart from this place, the tiger gods also dwelled in the house of Panayanthatta Nair. But soon, the atrocities of the tiger Gods became unbearable. So, during the festival season, Nair complained to the Goddess *Muchilott Bhagavathy* about it. *Bhagavathy* removed the lamp upon which the tiger gods were installed at the house of Nair and shifted it to the left corner of *Muchilottu Kavu* (shrine). Thus, *Puliyur Kannan* established his presence at *Muchilottu Kavu* as well. *Puliyur Kannan Theyyam* belongs to the *Vaniya* caste. *Puliyur Kannan* is worshipped, especially in the oil mills. Temples, where tiger God Theyyams are performed are known as *Aivar Paradevata* Temples (the Penta clan deity temples).

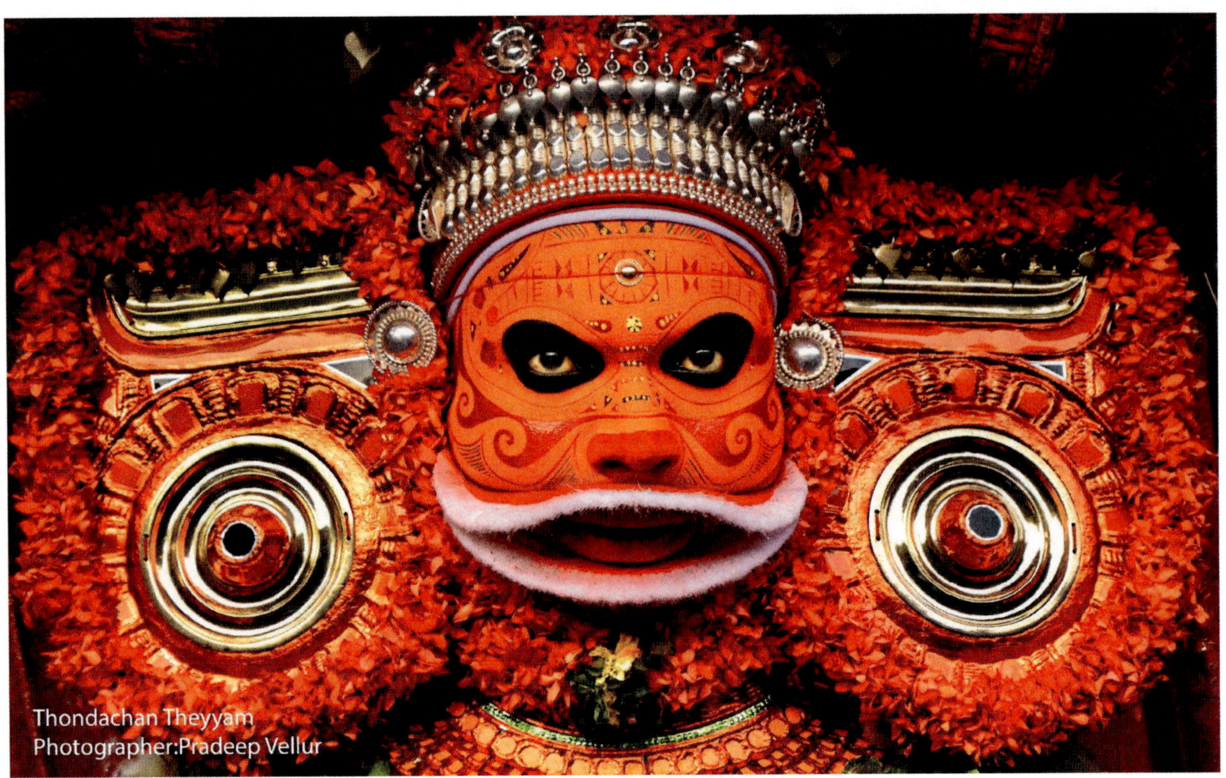
Thondachan Theyyam
Photographer:Pradeep Vellur

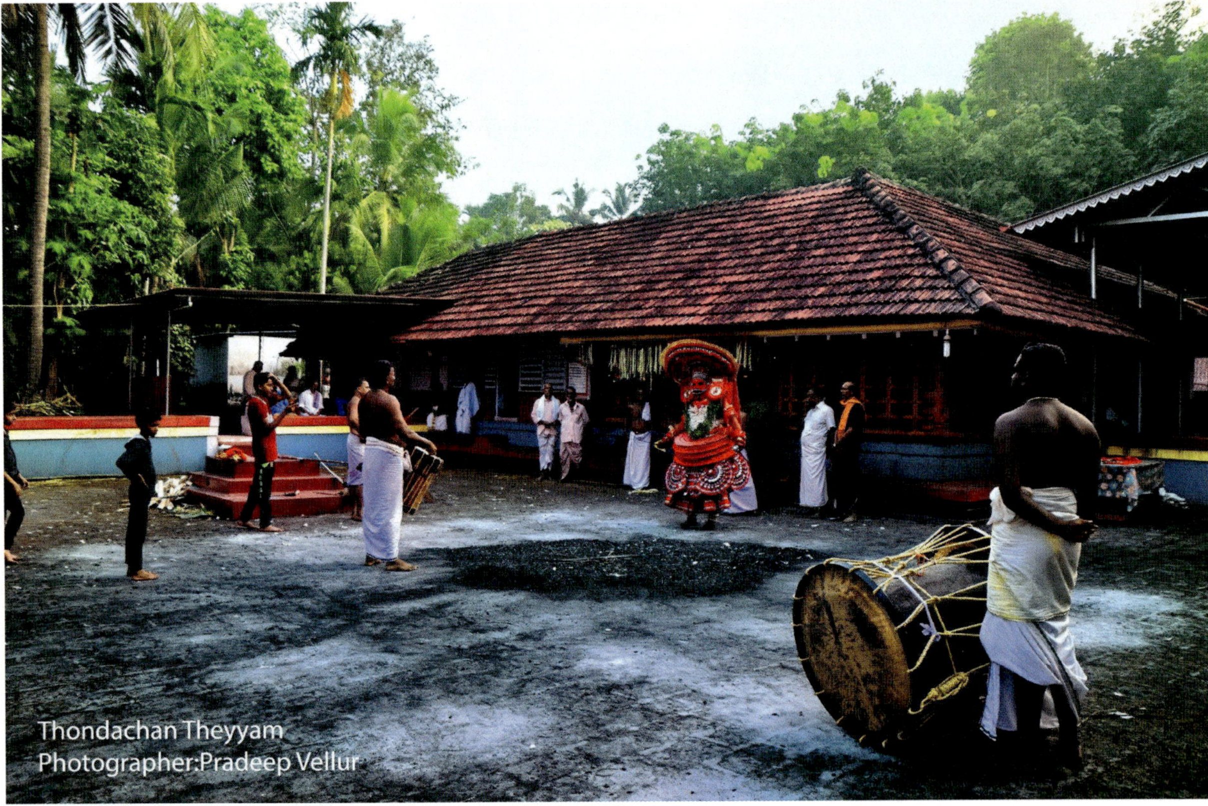
Thondachan Theyyam
Photographer:Pradeep Vellur

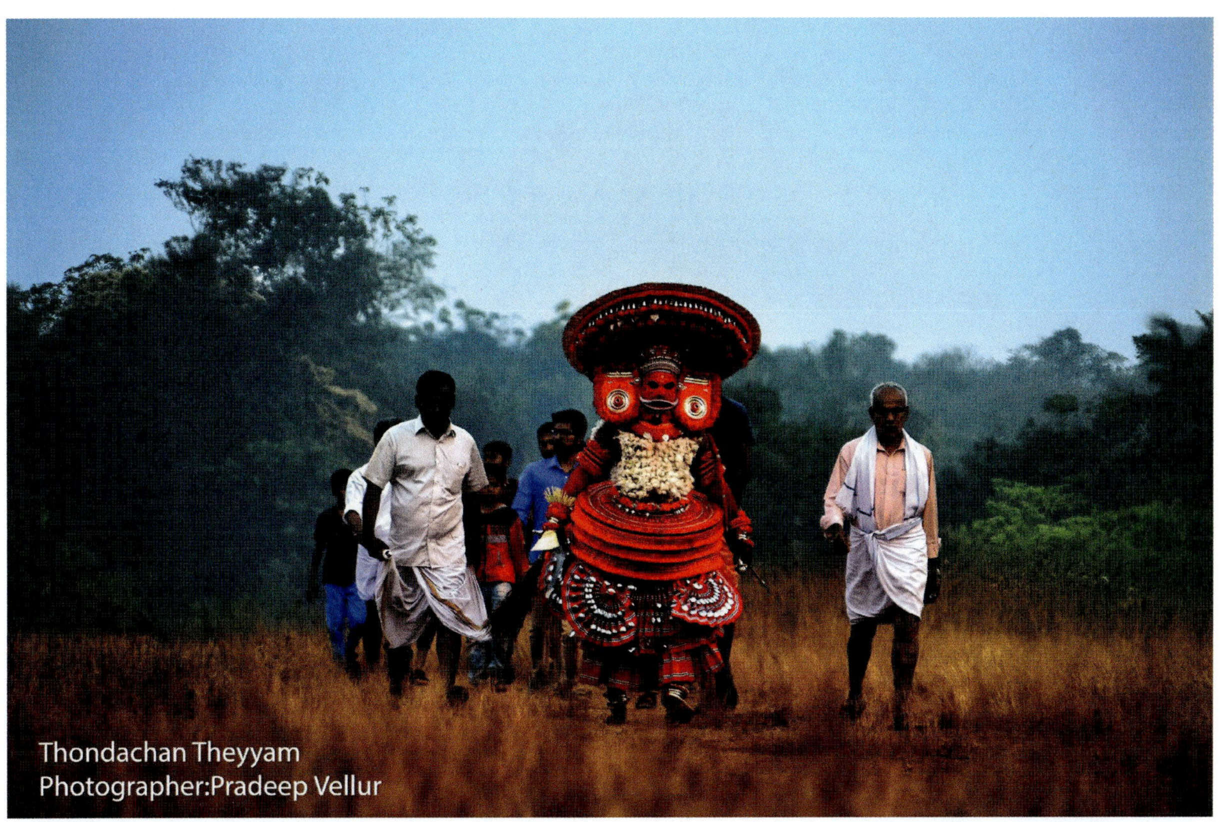

Thondachan Theyyam
Photographer:Pradeep Vellur

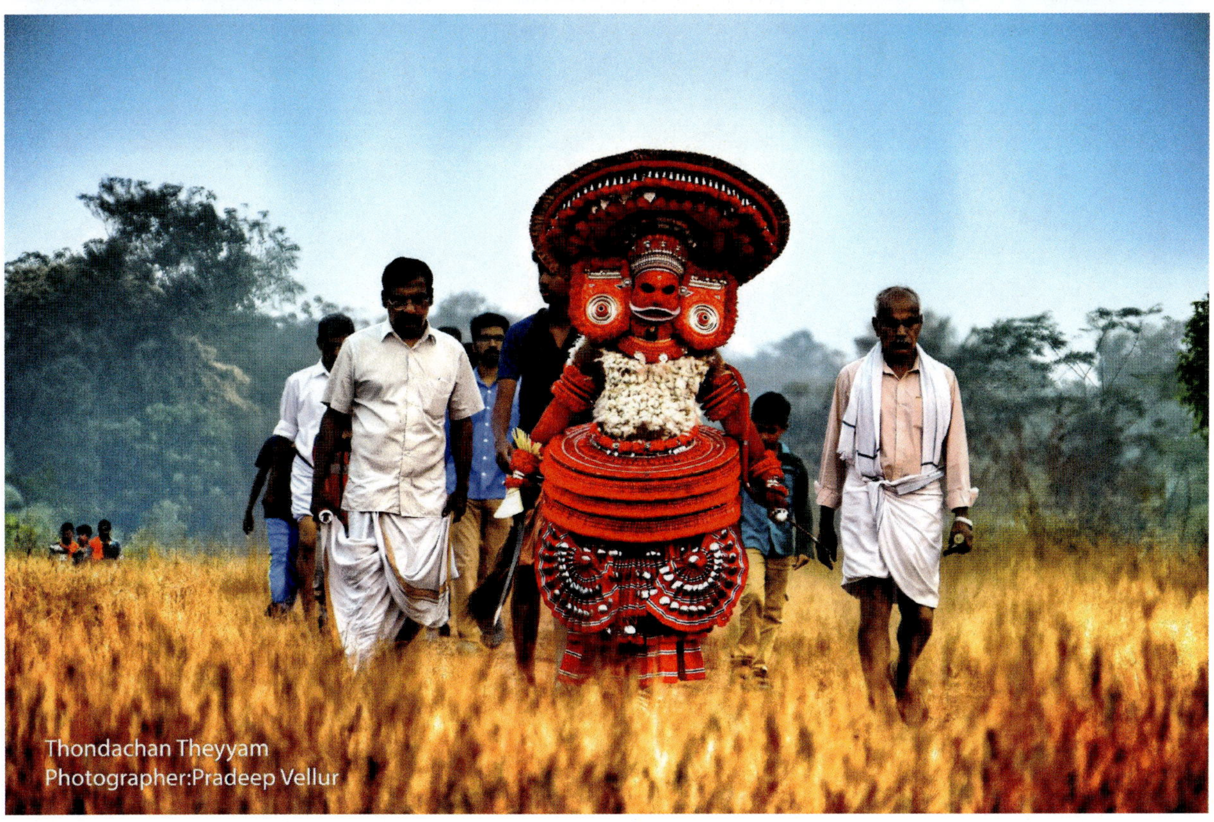

Thondachan Theyyam
Photographer:Pradeep Vellur

Kurathi Theyyam

Kuravar in Tamil stands for hill-dweller or hunter. The male members of the *Kuravar* community are called Kurava, and the females as *Kurathi*. According to the legend of *Kurathi Theyyam*, *Kurathi* is the Goddess of *Kanni Rashi* (the Virgo Sign according to western astrology). She belonged to *Thulunattambalam Thulu Thiyya* house and was incarnated as the hill's daughter with a broom, dagger, and a winnowing tray.

It is believed that Kurathi is Goddess Parvathi herself, who started from the *Thulu* region and visited Malanadu, or the hilly areas, where she met several rulers to establish her abode. During this visit, she also instituted her presence at *Kannamangalam Kazhagam*. Kurathi is the first Theyyam that commences from a shrine where they are performed.

Kurathi is the favorite Goddess of mothers and girls, who revere her the same way they respect their own mothers. *Kurathi Theyyam* is performed by the *Velar, Koppalan,* and *Pulaya* community members. *Kunjar Kurathi, Pullikurathi, Malankurathi, Thekkan Kurathi,* and *Sevakkari* are the prominent *Kurathis*.

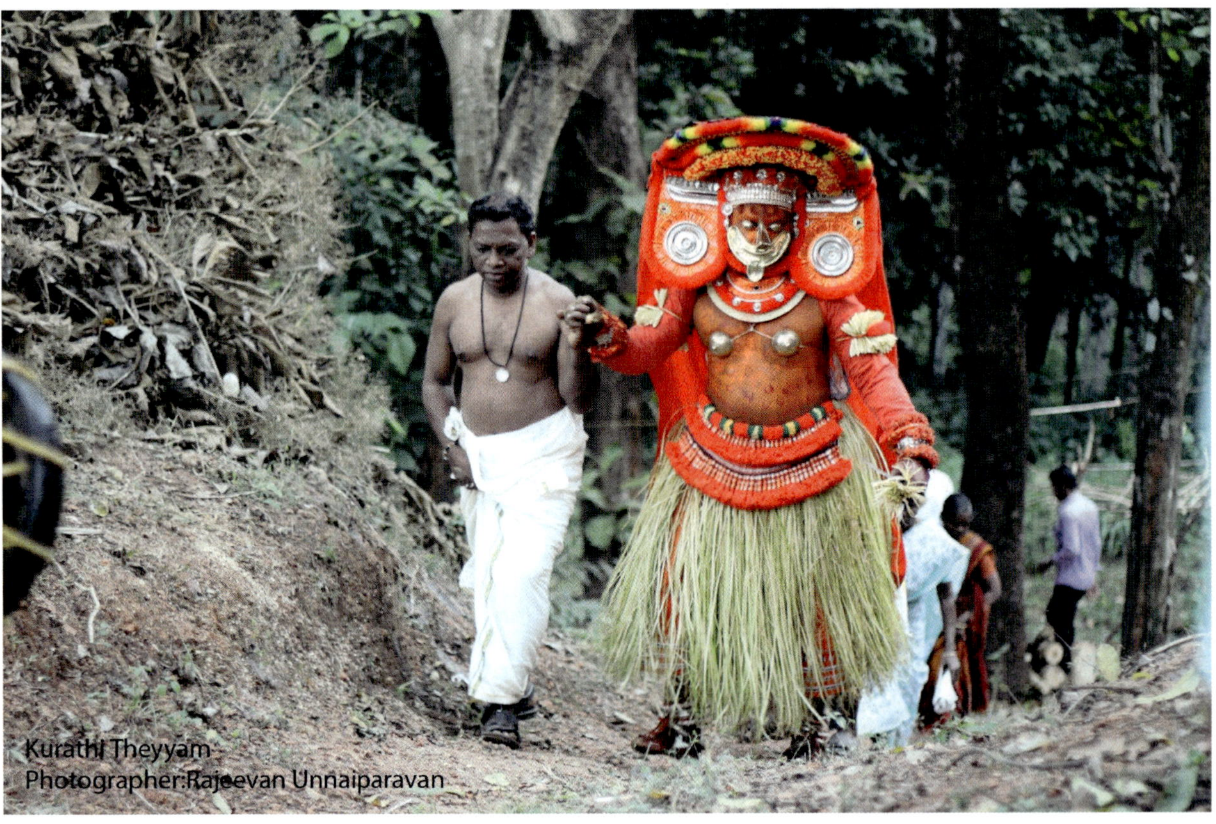
Kurathi Theyyam
Photographer:Rajeevan Unnaiparavan

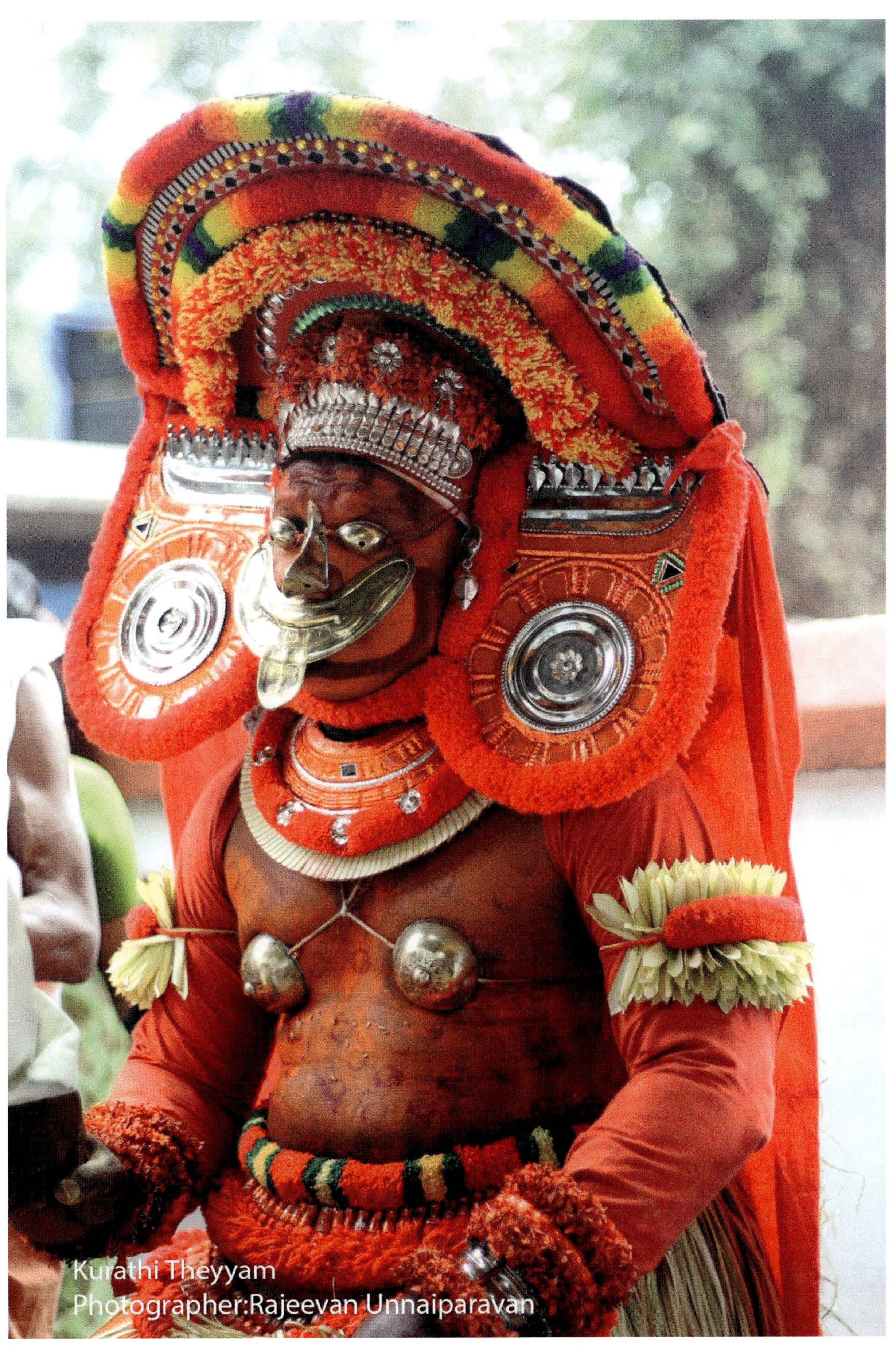

Kurathi Theyyam
Photographer:Rajeevan Unnaiparavan

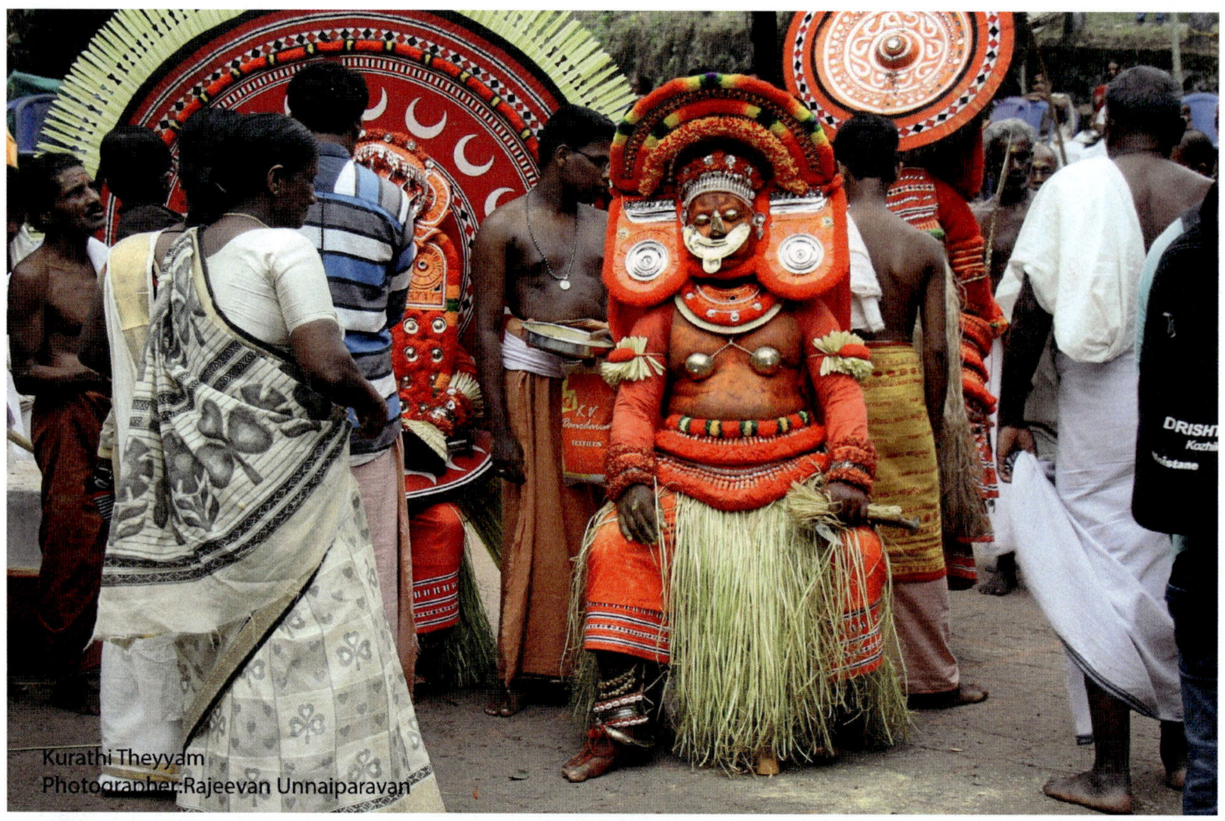
Kurathi Theyyam
Photographer:Rajeevan Unnaiparavan

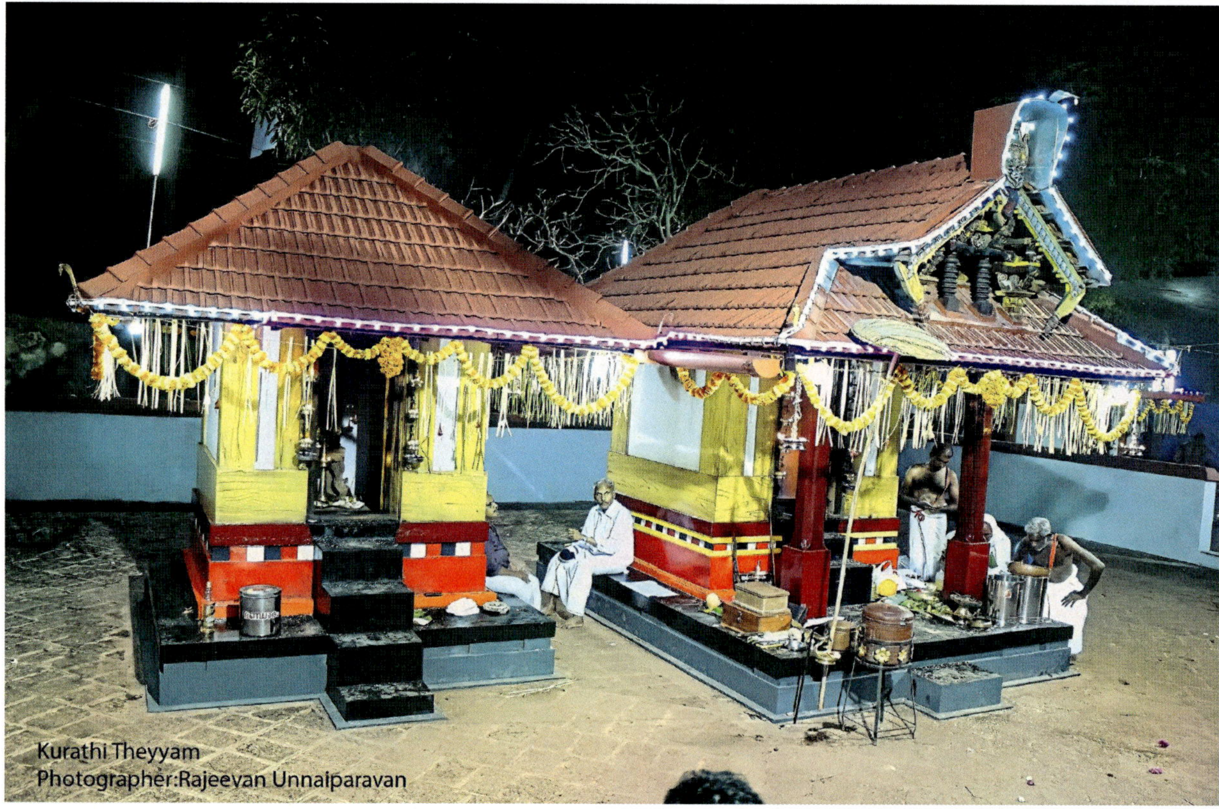
Kurathi Theyyam
Photographer:Rajeevan Unnaiparavan

Kathivanoor Veeran (Mandappan) Theyyam

Kumarappan of *Mangad Methaliyillam* house and his wife Chakki Amma of *Parakayillam* house grieved their childlessness for many years. Finally, a boy was born to them, and they named him Mandappan. He grew up as a lazy and lethargic boy who only liked to wander aimlessly. His father was worried and advised him not to be irresponsible. Before the father resorted to harsh punishments, the furious Mandappan left his house with his weapons and headed to Kodagu (present-day Coorg) with his friends. His friends, who knew his laid-back nature, wanted to filter him out of the group and gave him alcohol. Mandappan loses consciousness. When he woke up, he realized his friends had betrayed him. He also recognized that no one was there to give him company, so he started by following the footsteps of the bullocks towards Kodagu and reached his uncle's house in *Kathivanoor*. His loving aunt received him and pampered him just like her own son, and his uncle sent him to learn Kalari (Kalaripayattu, or Kalari in short, is an Indian martial art originating in Kerala).

Once he met a girl called Chembarathi and fell in love with her. His uncle arranged for them to marry. Later, It was only that Chembarathi realized that Mandappan was a lazy man and disliked employment of any form. Though they loved each other, his sluggishness often triggered arguments between them. To help motivate him, one day, she asked him to take some sesame seeds to the oil mill and bring the oil for her. Mandappan returned with the oil after roaming aimlessly and was late. Chebmarathi was doubtful and scolded him while falsely accusing him of spending time with another pretty girl. Mandappan, although hurt, decided not to fight with Chembarathi and sat down to eat.

At first, he got a strand of hair in the rice, which was considered a bad omen. He threw that handful of rice and scooped up a second, but he heard the rappel, another bad omen, which was a battle cry. The locals of Kodagu were about to attack Malayalathans (Keralites or the people whose first language is Malayalam). He knew that sitting calmly and eating food was unfair when the Malayalathans, the community to which he belonged, were in trouble. He decides to join the battle and sets out. While he was walking out, his head hit the door frame and started to bleed, yet another bad omen. Chembarathi, seeing all the bad omens, continues to address her concerns that he will die in the battle because of these bad omens.

Mandappan did not defend her accusations about spending time with a girl and also about the bad omen of seeing blood on the way to a battle. Let it be so; Mandappan smiled and started with his weapons. Along the way, he met his brother-in-law and bid goodbye saying that if he died on the battlefield, all the banana trees in that area would bear fruit instantly. Malayalathans, with the help of Mandappan, defeated the locals of Kodagu. They considered Mandappan as their savior. At home, Chembarathi felt guilty about her curses on Mandappan and was glad her husband had won the battle.

Meanwhile, Mandappan lost his wedding ring and index finger in the battle. The guilt of losing the ring that Chembarathi had given him and the fear of the harshness of Chembarathi stop him from returning to his house. As an alternative to committing suicide, he returns to the battlefield without arms and ammunition. Enemy soldiers see him as an easy target and sever him into pieces.

All the banana trees Mandappan planted at his uncle's house instantly bore fruits as Mandappan had promised, signaling Chembarathi of his death. Chembarathi, saddened by her acts, jumped into the pyre of Mandappan and self-immolated. Each piece of Mandappan's body, mutilated by the enemy soldiers, started moving, and people realized his divinity. They installed Mandappan at *Kathivanoor Padinjattu* and worshipped him.

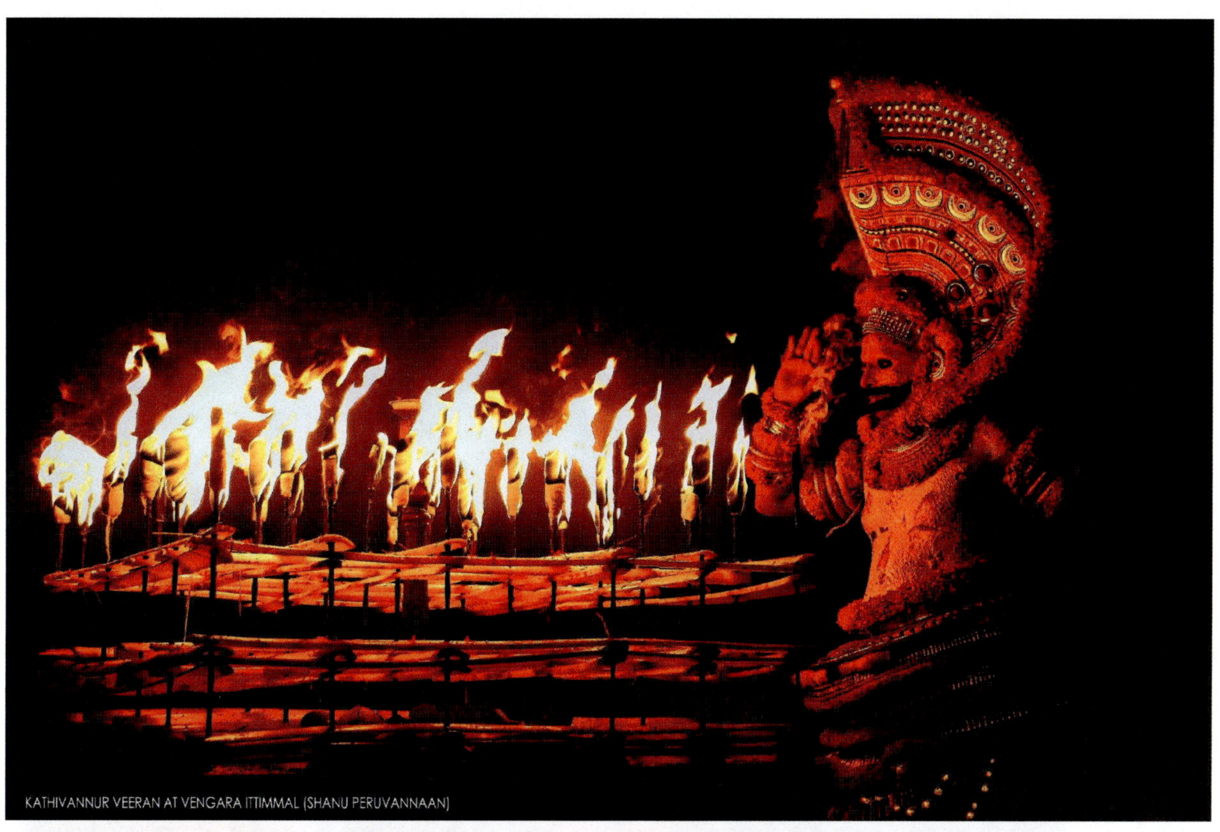

KATHIVANNUR VEERAN AT VENGARA ITTIMMAL (SHANU PERUVANNAAN)

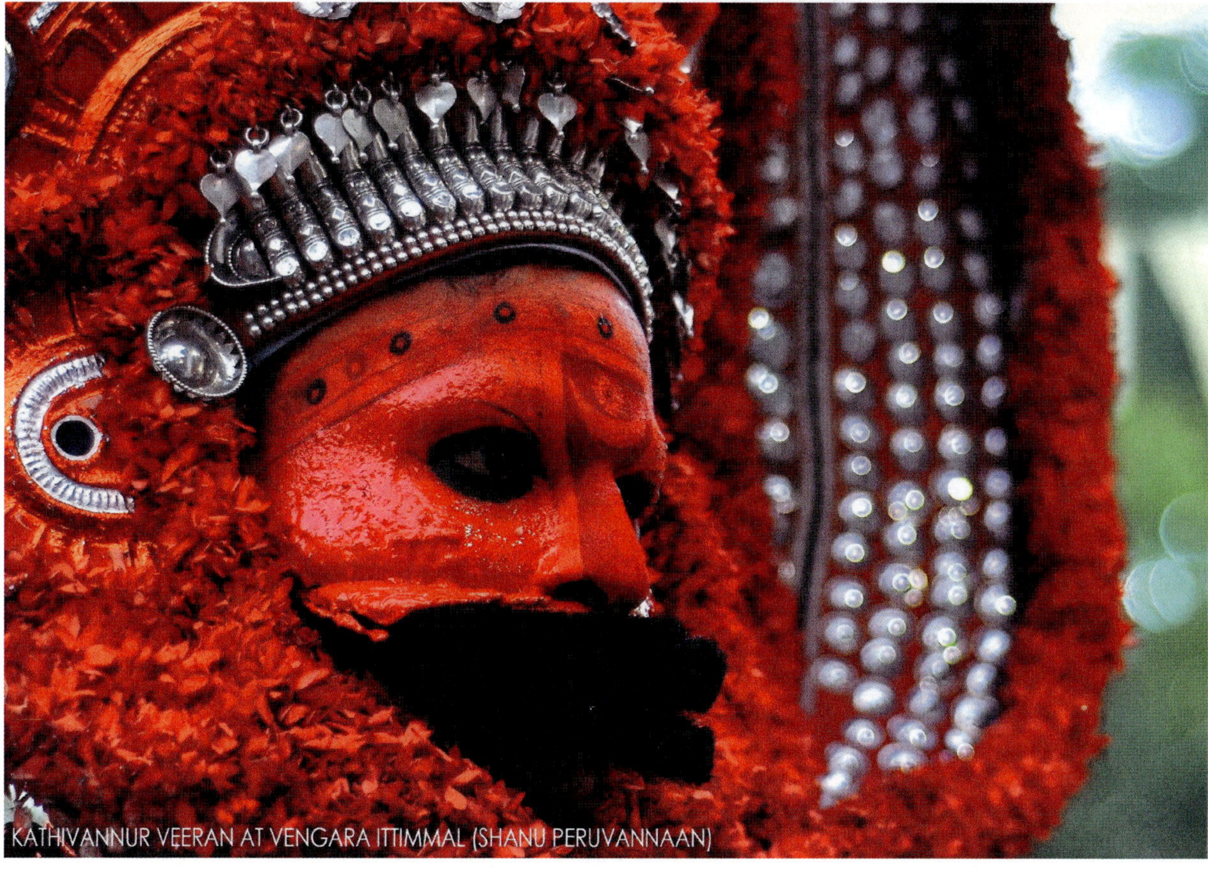

KATHIVANNUR VEERAN AT VENGARA ITTIMMAL (SHANU PERUVANNAAN)

Uchitta Theyyam

An ember dropped from the aura of Agni, the fire god, fell onto the Lotus flower, the abode of Lord Brahma. From there, a Goddess with impeccable beauty and a bright aura was born. Lord Brahma gifted the Goddess to Lord Shiva via Kama Deva(Indian equivalent of Cupid), the God of love and lust. Eventually, at the request of the Earth God, the Goddess was sent to earth as a human known as Uchitta to look after devotees. Uchitta is the most beautiful and foremost Goddess of Manthramoorti and Panchamoorti deities.

Since she is the daughter of Agni, the fire god, she sits and plays with fire. Her speech is similar to humans, and she has a playful personality and is loved by female devotees dearly. She is known as *Adiyeri Madathil Uchitta Bhagavthi* and is especially revered in houses with a tradition of sorcery.

Another story states that Uchitta is the sister of Lord Krishna. Prominent families with the tradition of sorcery, like *Kaladu, Kattumadam, Poothilla, Poonthottam,* etc., are where this Theyyam is performed. Worshiping Uchitta is believed to result in easy delivery of a child without complications. She is also an image of Goddess Parvathi. The Goddess amazed Lord Shiva by enduring the fire generated by his anger. Since she laughed loudly at the flames, her name 'Uchitta' (or loud) was derived from it.

There is also a story that she is the Goddess that loudly declared that Kamsan's killer had arrived on earth. (From Lord Krishna's birth story)

Malayan and Velan communities perform this Theyyam.

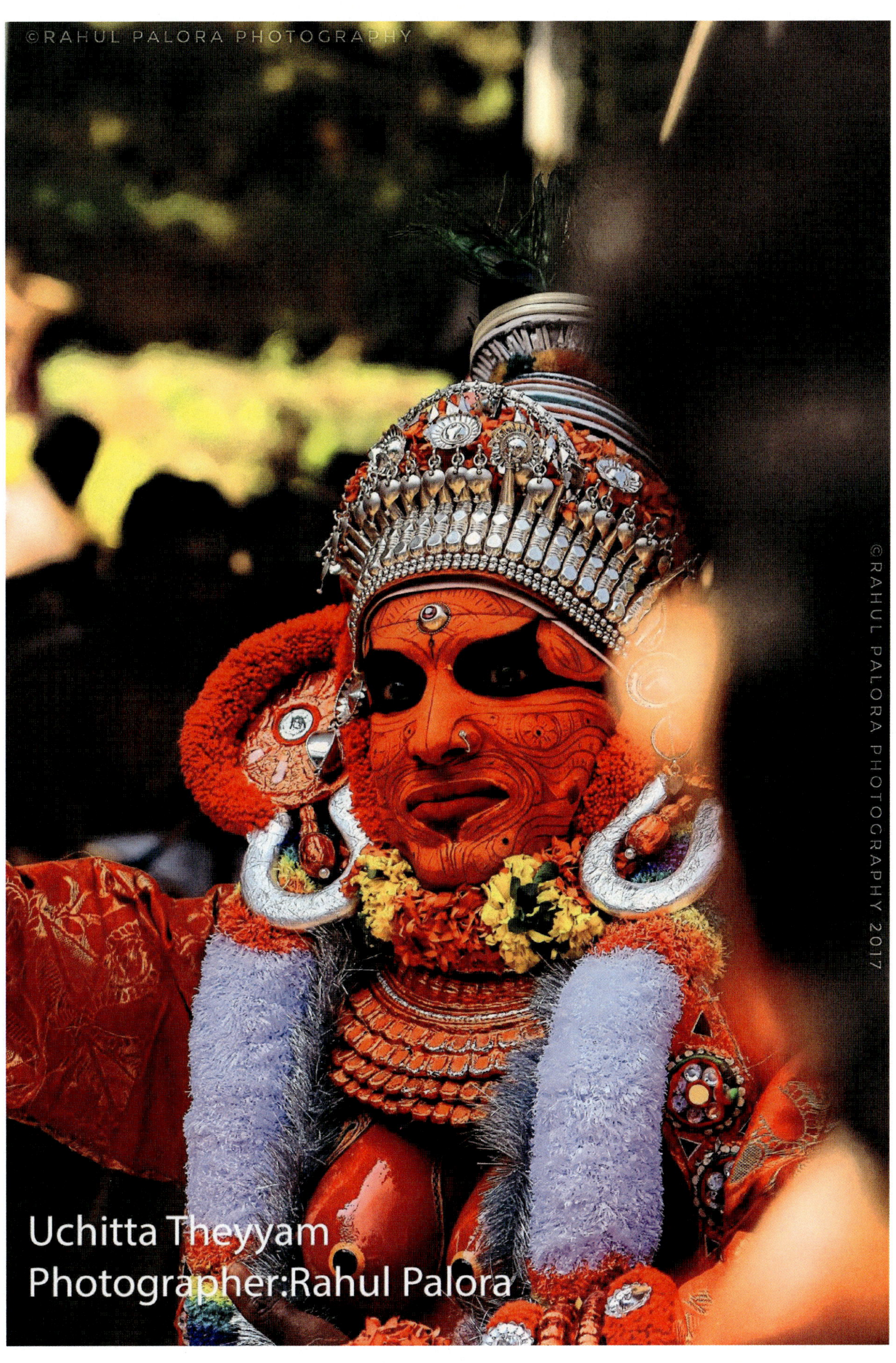
©RAHUL PALORA PHOTOGRAPHY
©RAHUL PALORA PHOTOGRAPHY 2017
Uchitta Theyyam
Photographer:Rahul Palora

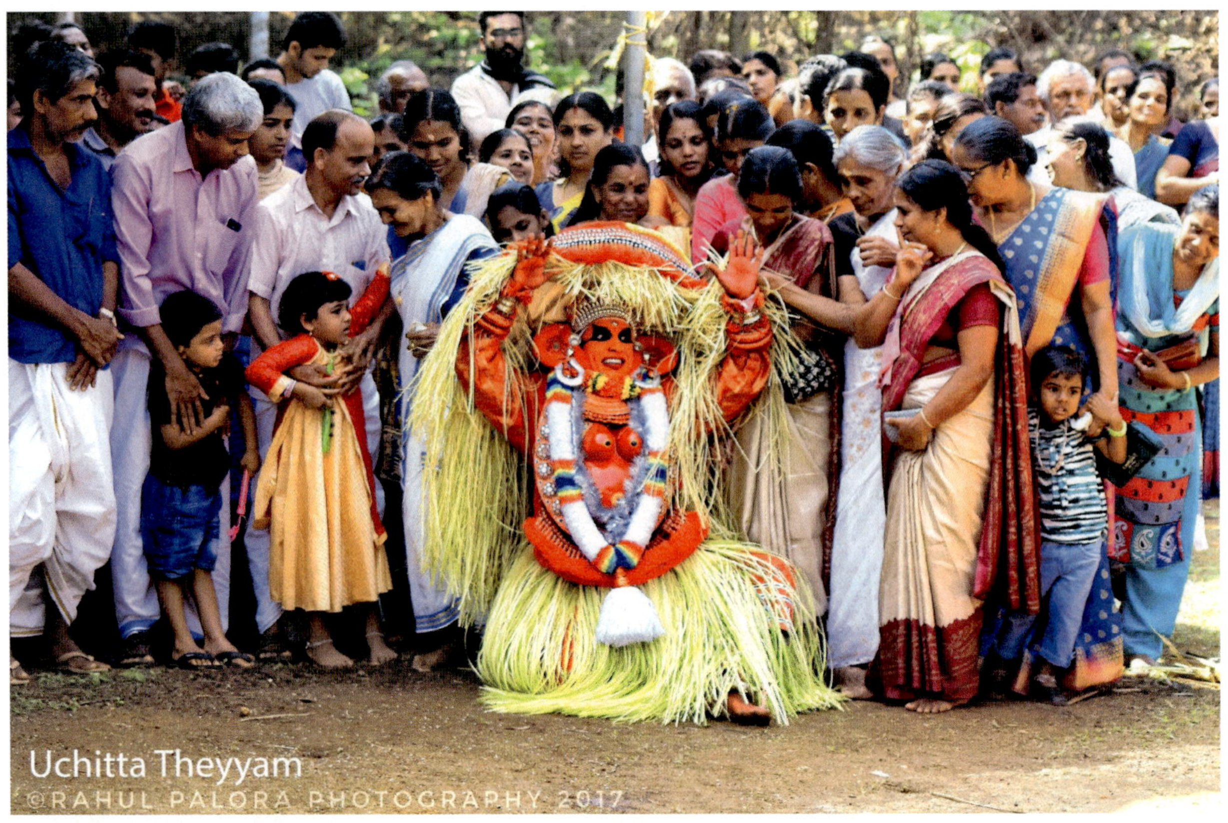

Uchitta Theyyam

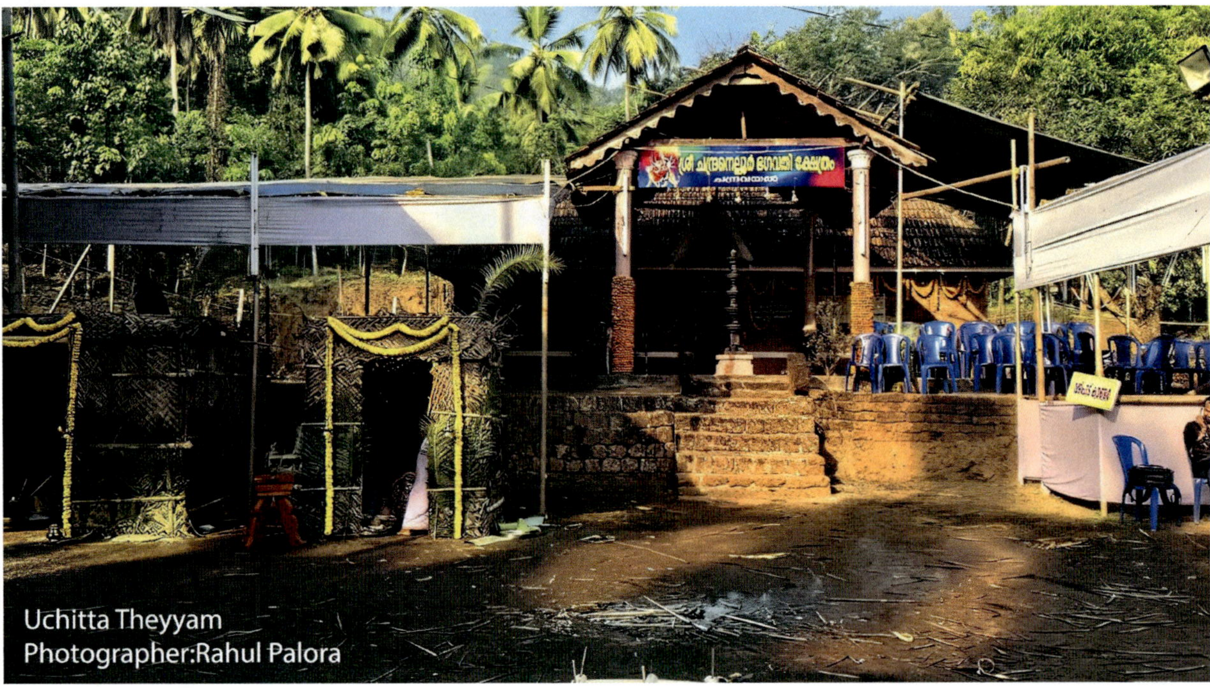
Uchitta Theyyam
Photographer:Rahul Palora

Vadakkathi (Padakkathi) Bhagavathy Theyyam

The divine Palmyra Palm tree that grew near the Velliman rocks in the sacred Milk Ocean was known to have seven stems and eight tender leaves. On the eighth leaf were seven golden eggs, six of which were broken. The six eggshells transformed into six mountains, from which six people incarnated, and from the seventh egg emerged a Godly virgin.

When the virgin maiden had her first menstrual phase at twelve, her brothers decided to celebrate the menarche. All six of them set out for a hunt in *Kariyoor Kalvalavu* to garner enough meat for the celebratory party. But upon returning with a deer they had slain, all of them were detained by their uncle's children. According to the cousins, it was their exclusive right to hunt on the mountain, and the brothers were asked to hand over the head and legs of the deer to them. The petty disagreement ended in a grave battle that resulted in the deaths of the six brothers. The Goddess became furious with grief and avenged them by annihilating her cousins and evolving into a war Goddess.

After that, she traveled to various places and acquired eighteen different weapons. She defeated Airavata, the deity Indra's white elephant, and captured its trunk. Then, she traveled to the Tulu region (present-day districts of Dakshina Kannada and Udupi in Karnataka and Kasaragod in Kerala). She is also said to have defeated the *Chekavar* (a martial caste of Kerala). Acquiring a Tulu-style beard and mustache, she confiscated weapons and tools while roaming the land. After visiting many places, she expressed her desire to go to *Kolathunadu* (one of the four kingdoms in Kerala) to see *Vishvakarma* (the divine architect of the Gods), who she asked to make her a *marakkalam* (wooden vessel). She traveled all over the *Kolathunadu* region in that vessel and stopped at *Idathoor* when *Vishvakarma* requested her to make it her abode.

Goddess Vadakkathi Bhagavathy/ Padakkathi Bhagavathy is considered the daughter of Lord Shiva. She is the supreme deity of the community of craftsmen, especially of the carpenters. The word *Pada in Malayalam* means battle, and according to another legend, this Goddess came along with Lord Parashurama to kill Asuras (demons), hence the name Pada-kkathi Bhagavathy. Once she descended to earth, she was in a dilemma about her purpose and ultimate destination. Finally, she went in the *Vadakk* (north) direction. Thus, she is known as *Vadakkaththi Bhagavathi* as well.

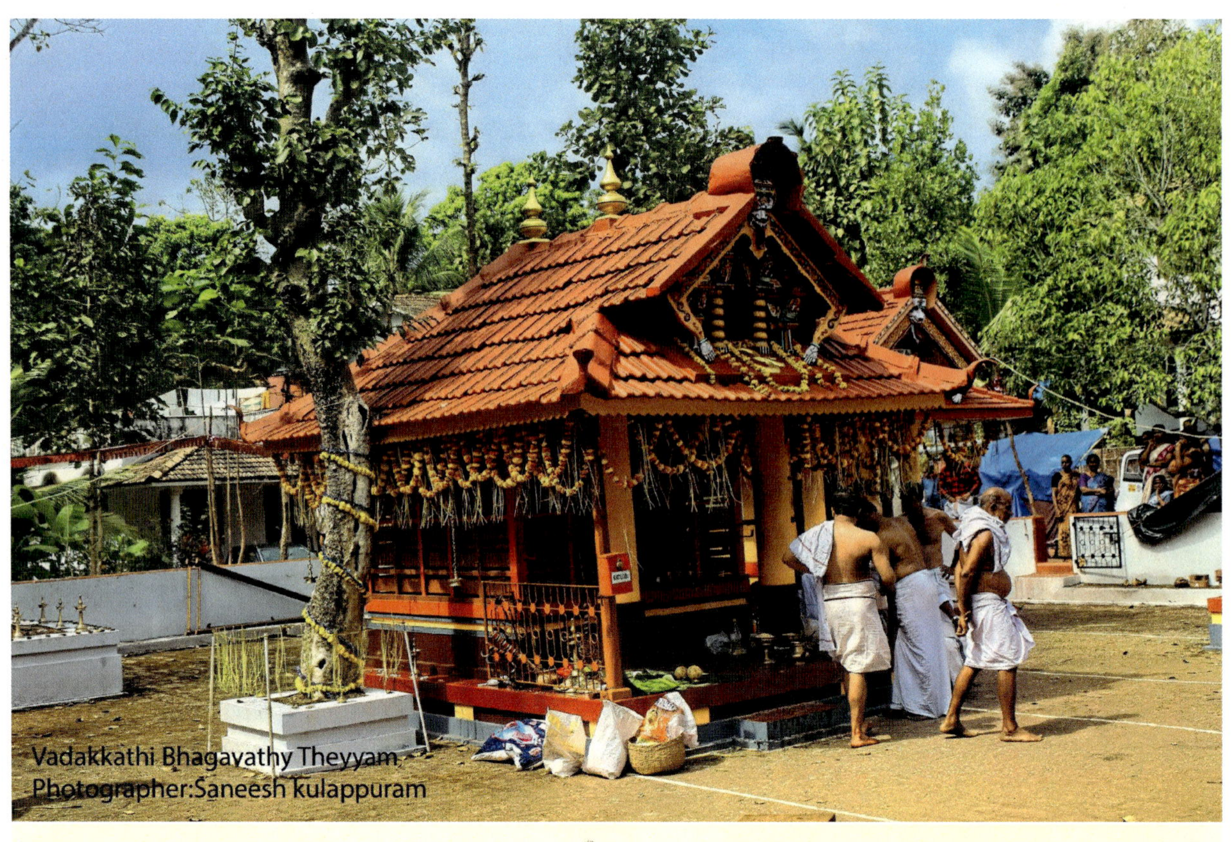

Vadakkathi Bhagavathy Theyyam
Photographer:Saneesh kulappuram

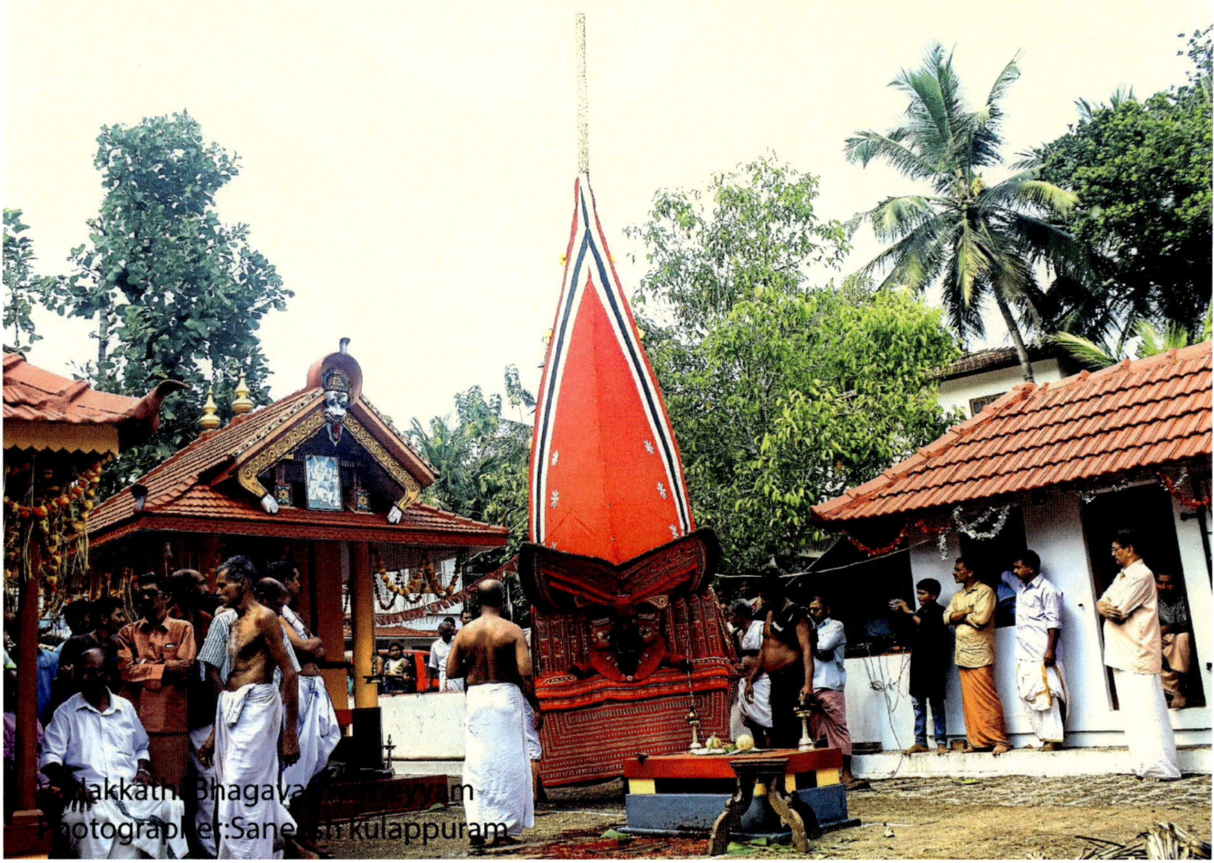

Vadakkathi Bhagavathy Theyyam
Photographer:Saneesh kulappuram

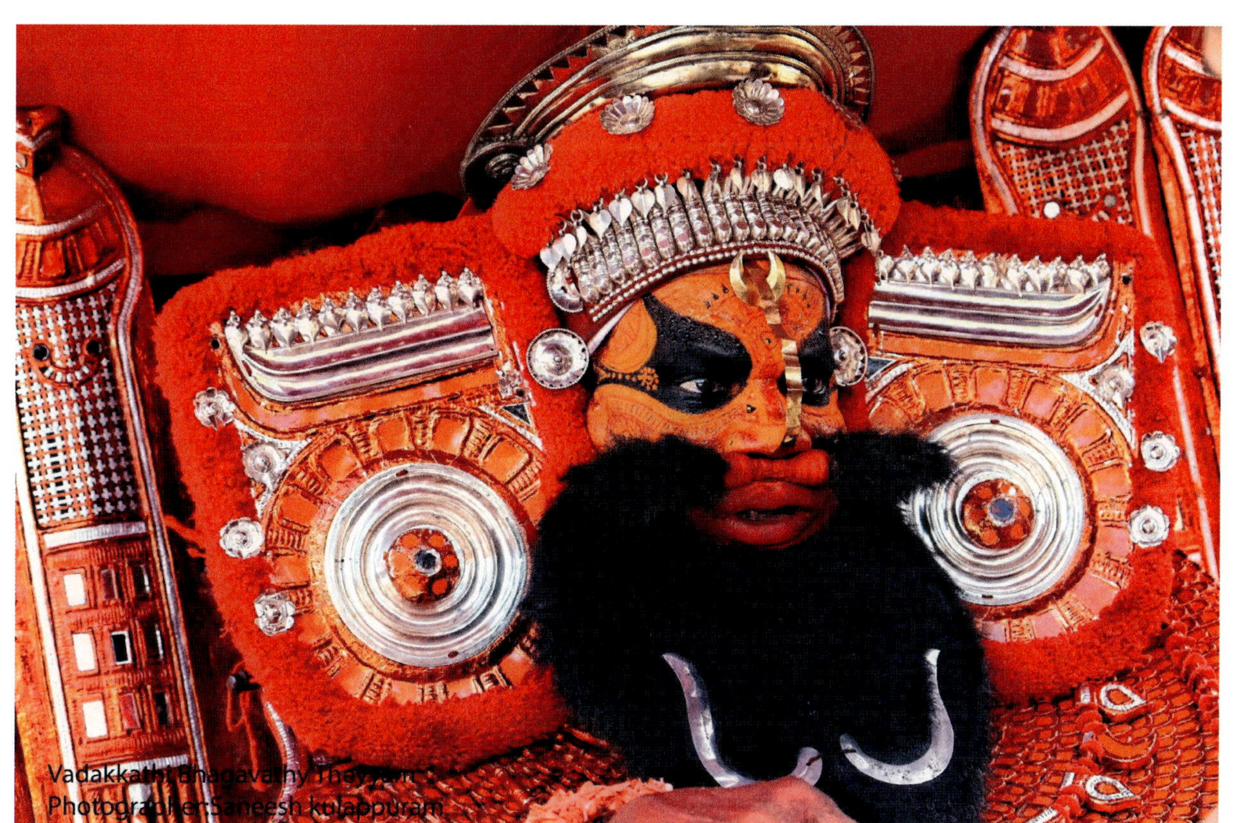
Vadakkathi Bhagavathy Theyyam
Photographer:Saneesh kulappuram

Thoovakkari Theyyam

Chandika is a powerful form of Goddess *Mahadevi,* who manifested to destroy evil. *Thoovakkari,* or *Thoovakkali,* is believed to be the companion of the Goddess Chandika. In ancient times, a disease with symptoms such as fever, red rashes, itching, and irritation was prevalent. The symptoms resembled Scarlet Fever and were common among children. To cure this disease, people worshiped the Goddess Chandika. They prepared an effigy of her with a haystack, affixed dry coconut kernels, and burned it on the third day at twilight. They believed that praying before this inflorescence of coconuts would heal skin diseases by the grace of *Thoovakkari* or *Thoovakkali.*

The members of the Mavilan community perform this Theyyam and have different *Kolams* (a figure made for worship) at different *Kavus* or shrines. The legend of the *Thoovakkaran* Theyyam is the same, except that *Thoovakkaran* is the masculine counterpart.

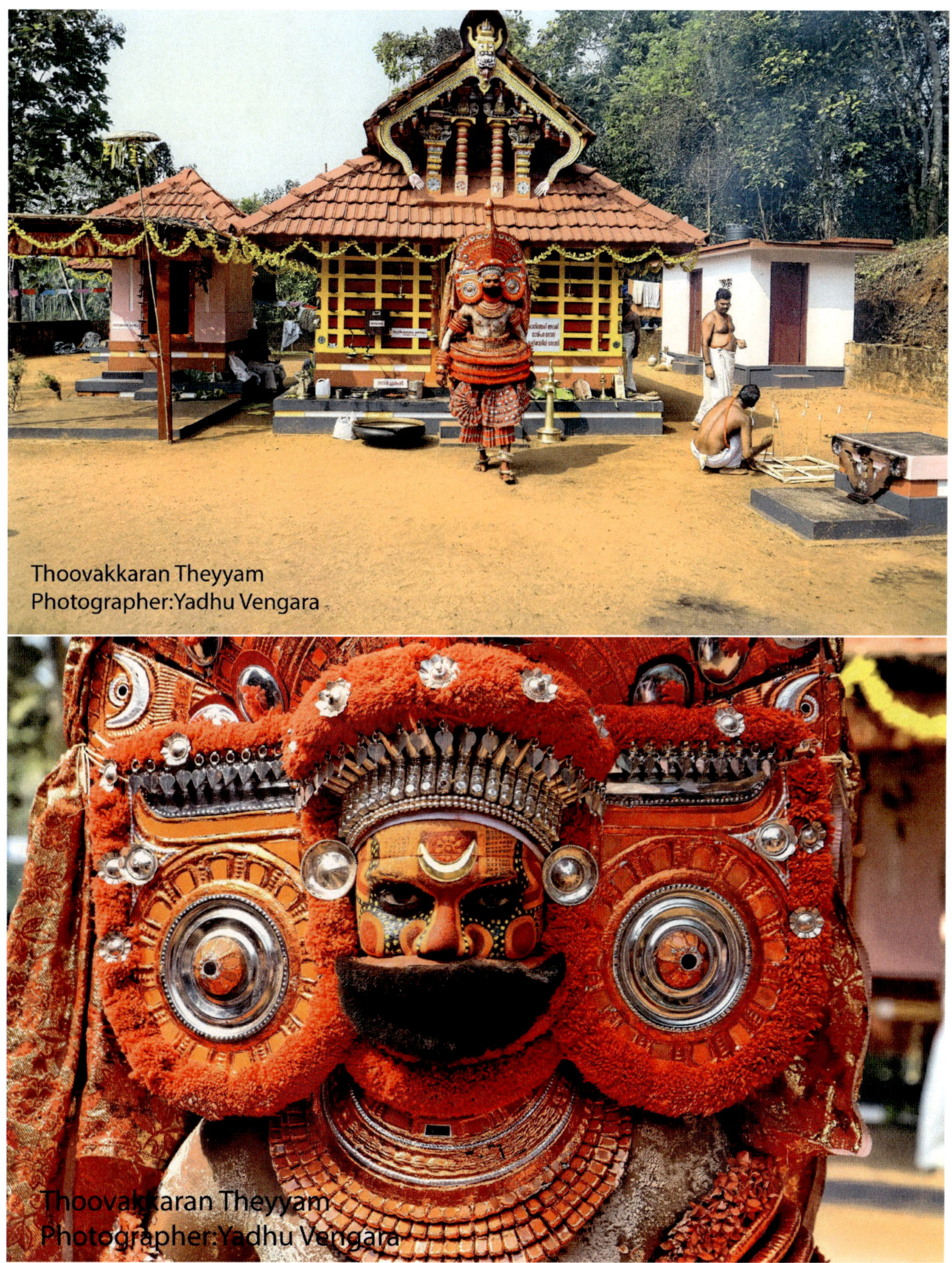

Thoovakkaran Theyyam
Photographer:Yadhu Vengara

Thoovakkaran Theyyam
Photographer:Yadhu Vengara

Chekkichery Bhagavathi Theyyam

(Similar to Kadavath Bhagavathy story)

The eminent *Tantri* (priest) of *Kalakkatt Illam* was entirely focused on his tantra mantra practices (the mantra is a sacred utterance. It is an inevitable part of tantra, which means technique and also an esoteric tradition). He was annoyed by the cry of a child and aimlessly uttered, "Won't anyone contain this child?" Though he intended for someone to 'control' the child, he happened to use the word 'contain.' Thus, the child passed away shortly after. The child's death saddened him, and he accused the Goddess of a murder he had worshipped and revered until then. Enraged by the child's demise, he threw the Goddess *Pallivaal* (the holy sword) into the river. A man called *Poonthottam Nampoothiri* found this sword in the river and installed it at the *Kakkara Kavu*. As it was kept there under the concept of *Bhadrakali*, she began to be referred to as *Kakkara Bhagavathi*. This Goddess is also known as *Mambally Bhagavathi, Arumbally Bhagavathi, Chekkichery Bhagavathi, Karat Bhagavathi, Kozhikulangara Bhagavathi, Dhuliyanga Bhagavathi, Kurumbilott Bhagavathi, Kaya Bhagavathi, Kalkkura Bhagavathi*, and *Poyil Bhagavathi*. All these Theyyams share a similar face makeup.

Kakkara Bhagavathi is based on the concept of the Goddess *Bhadrakali*. The abode of *Kakkara Bhagavathi* is sanctified with flaming torches on her dress. She dances to the tune of the *Asura Vadya* (the background instruments), and her face is adorned with a makeup style (*Mukhathezhuthu*) known as *Bhadrachotta*. Though known by different names in different places, the ritualistic song or *Thottam Pattu* denotes her original name as *Kalkkurangara Bhagavathi* and her abode as *Kalkkura Kavu*.

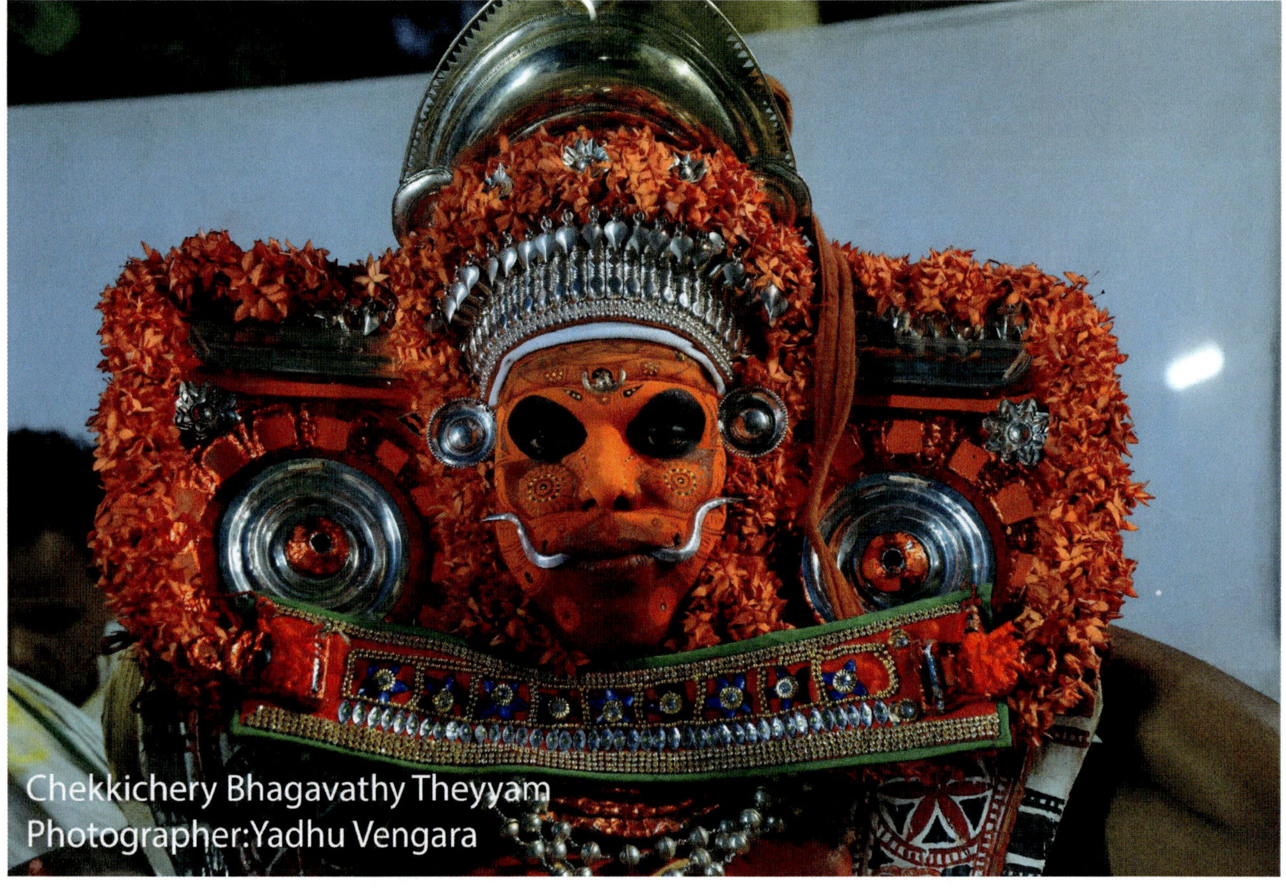
Chekkichery Bhagavathy Theyyam
Photographer:Yadhu Vengara

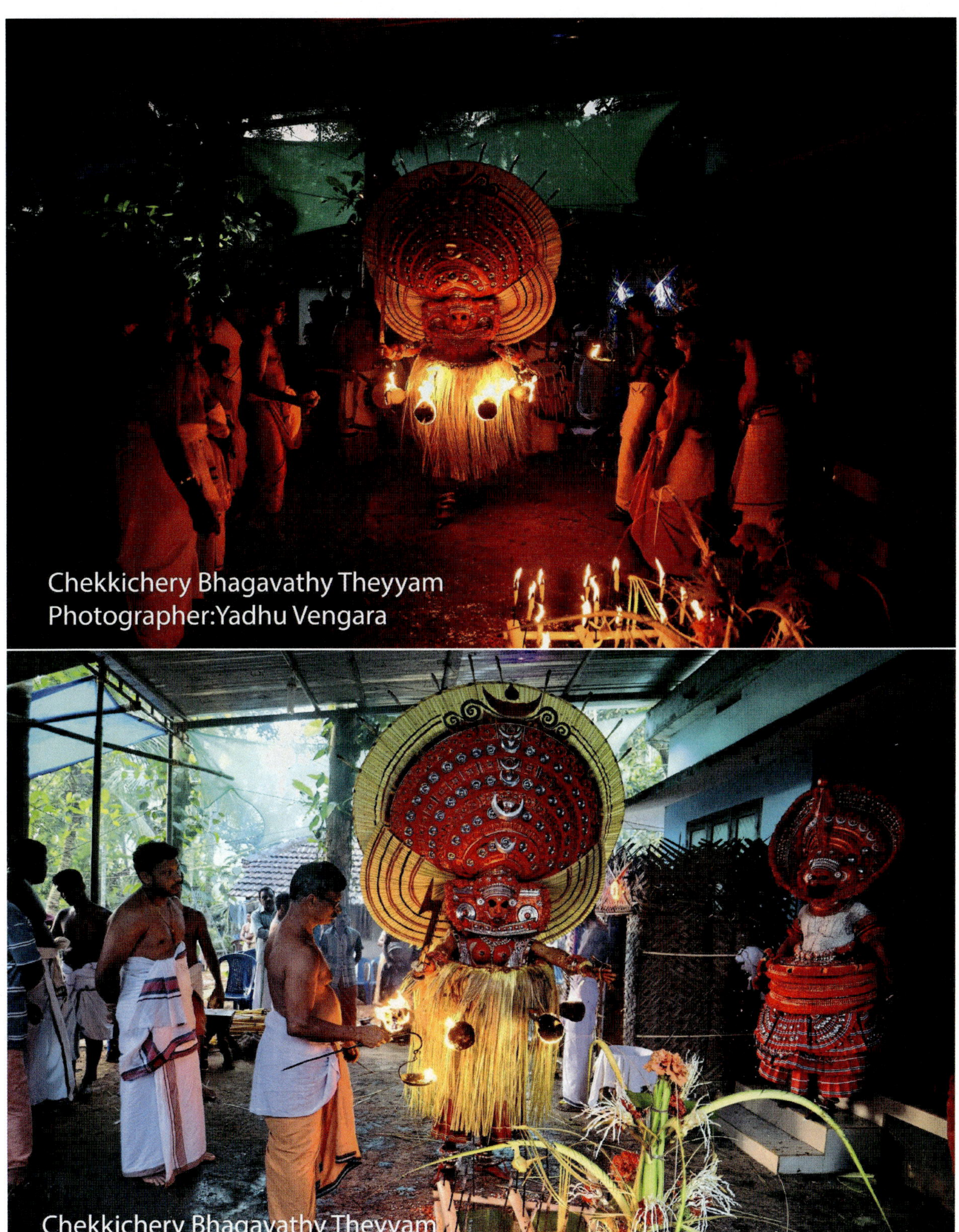
Chekkichery Bhagavathy Theyyam
Photographer:Yadhu Vengara

Chekkichery Bhagavathy Theyyam
Photographer:Yadhu Vengara

Bali Theyyam

According to *Ramayana*, the dispute between the brothers Bali and Sugriva ended in the death of Bali, who was deceived by Lord Rama and died. In this ritual dance, Bali is glorified as a hero who managed to reach the sun and bow before it by crossing seven seas. The headgear used in this Theyyam resembles the crown in the popular art of Kathakali.

When Bali visited the holy waters of Vaduvakkotta, he met the divine architect, Vishwakarma. Bali was astounded to see his disciplined attitude and decided to accompany him on his journey. Bali escorted him to Eramam Mannunmmal and was later assigned several honors at Morazha, Kurunthazha, and Vadakkan Kovval. Bali remains the community deity of the Vishwakarma caste (comprising carpenters, blacksmiths, bronzesmiths, goldsmiths, and stonemasons.)

This Theyyam portrays the story of the heroic character Bali, also known as Vali, from the Hindu epic *Ramayana*. In this Theyyam, *Sree Bali* is known as God *Netu-Baliyan*. Hanuman's (Lord Rama's companion) eye makeup is the specialty. Unlike the eye makeup of other Theyyams, this face art is unique.

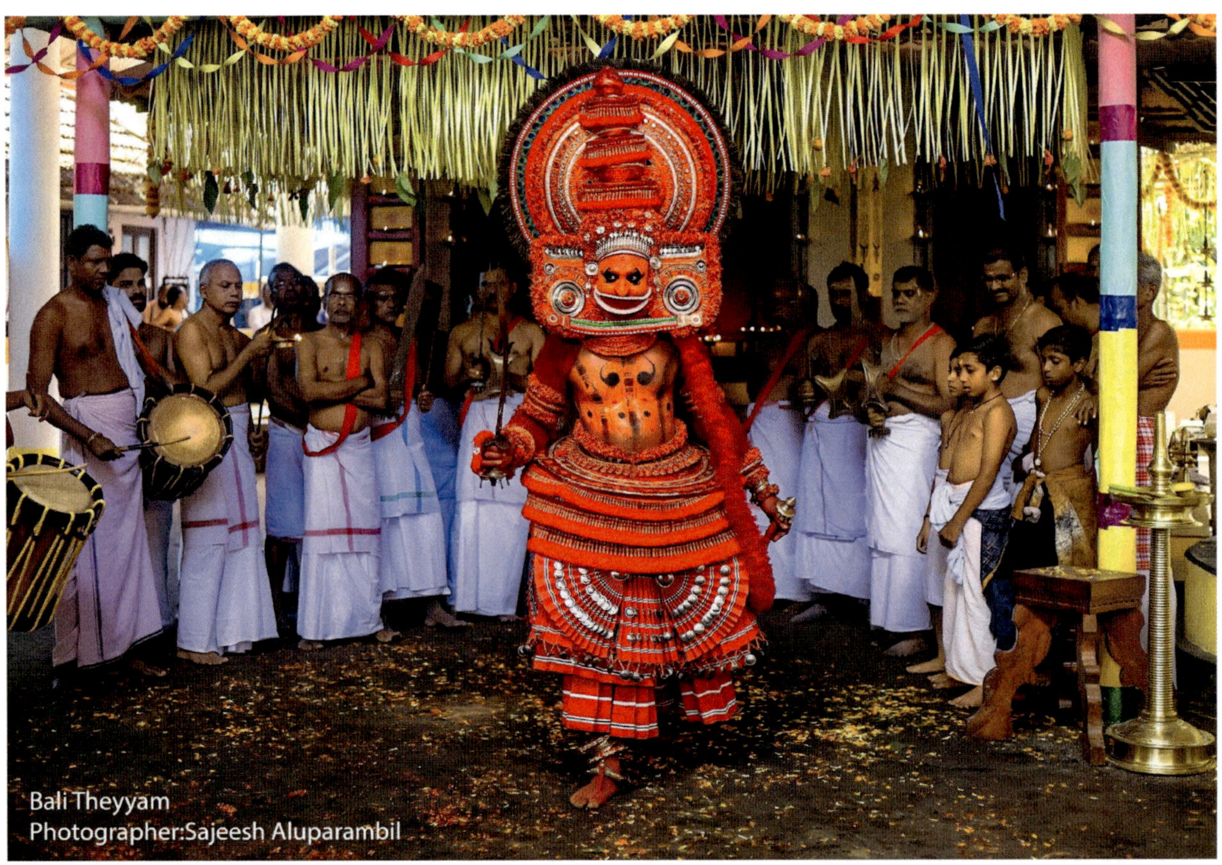

Bali Theyyam
Photographer:Sajeesh Aluparambil

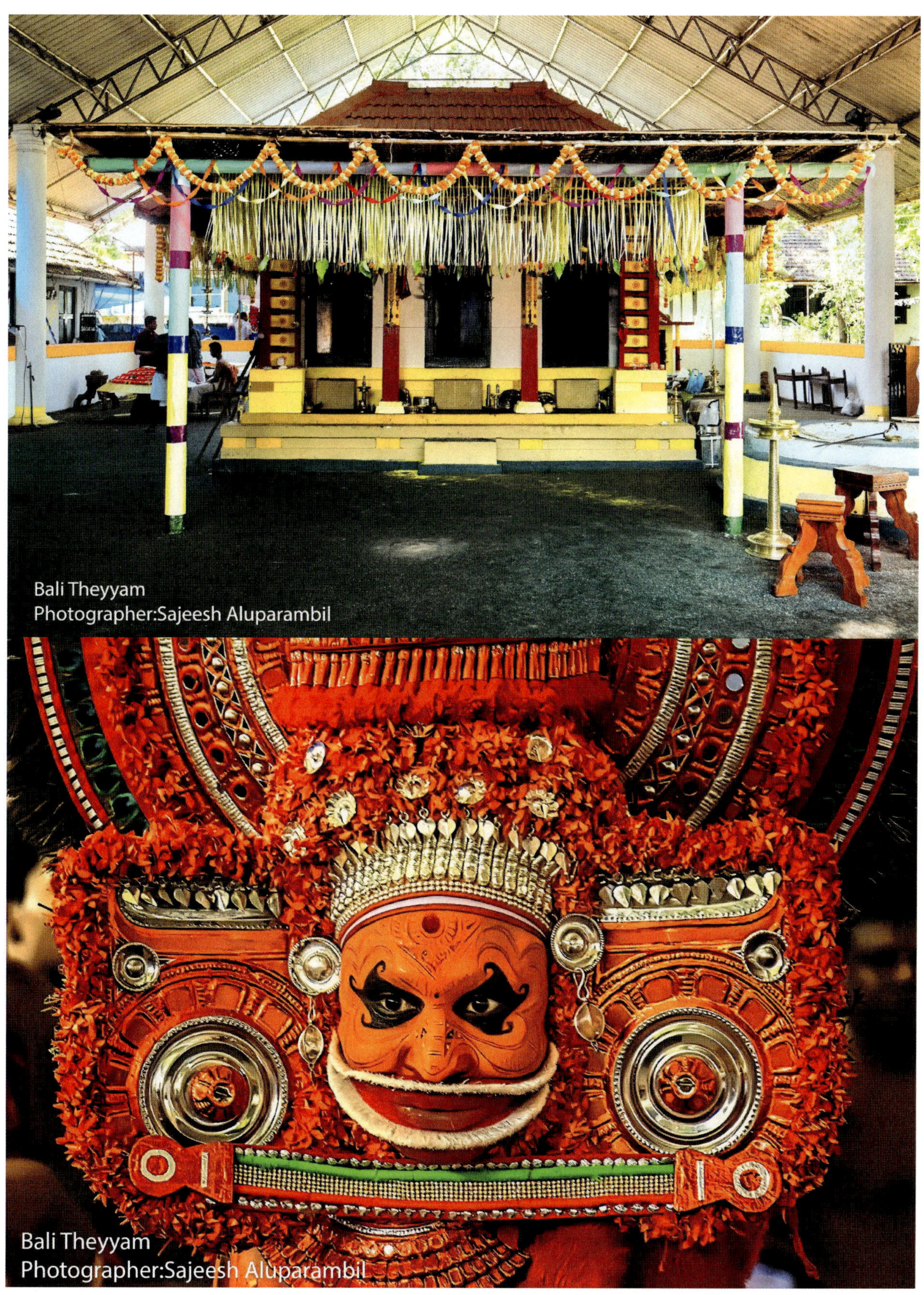

Bali Theyyam
Photographer:Sajeesh Aluparambil

Bali Theyyam
Photographer:Sajeesh Aluparambil

Kaitha Chamundi

Once upon a time, two demonic brothers lived: *Chandan* and *Mundan*. They pleased Brahma, the God of creation, and thus were granted a boon. This boon, bestowed upon only the most blessed, protected them from being killed by men and women. The brothers soon started to misuse their newfound immortality by pestering others and pushing their limits. Eventually, people were fed up and complained to Brahma about the atrocities the duo committed. Since it was impossible for any man or woman to annihilate the brothers, Brahma consulted Mahadevi, who was neither a man nor a woman, and she promised to resolve this issue. The brothers learned about the threat and were shaken with fear. Chandan and Mundan decided to hide by disguising themselves as a plant known as *Kaitha* (a type of pine).

Mahadevi set out in search of them and realized that they might be masquerading after not finding them. While searching for them in the pine fields, she noticed that two of the plants were not moving in the winds. She identified the two plants as Chandan and Mundan. She took out her sword and cut the two plants down. This is symbolized in Theyyam by the act of cutting a Kaitha plant during the frenzied dance of the Kaitha Chamundi performance. Since the act narrates bloodshed and death, a fowl's blood is used to stain the attire of Theyyam during the performance.

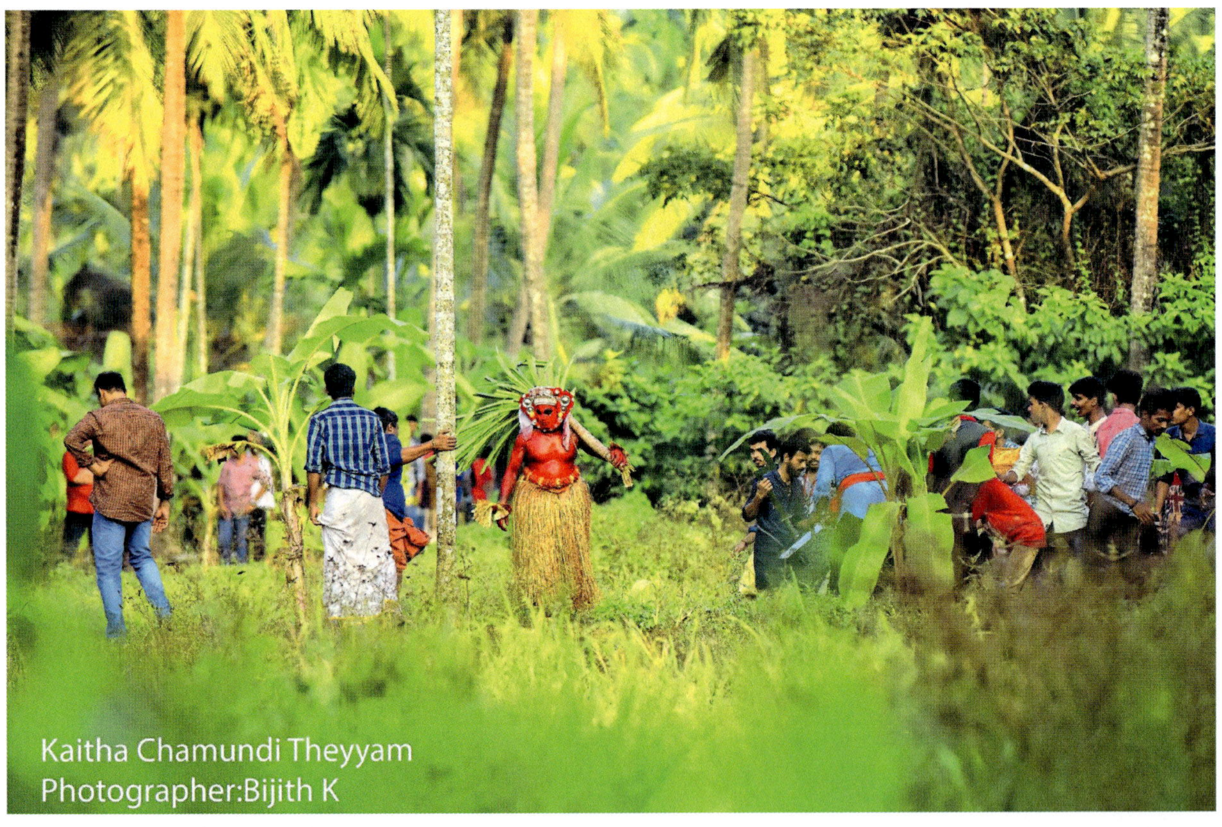

Kaitha Chamundi Theyyam
Photographer:Bijith K

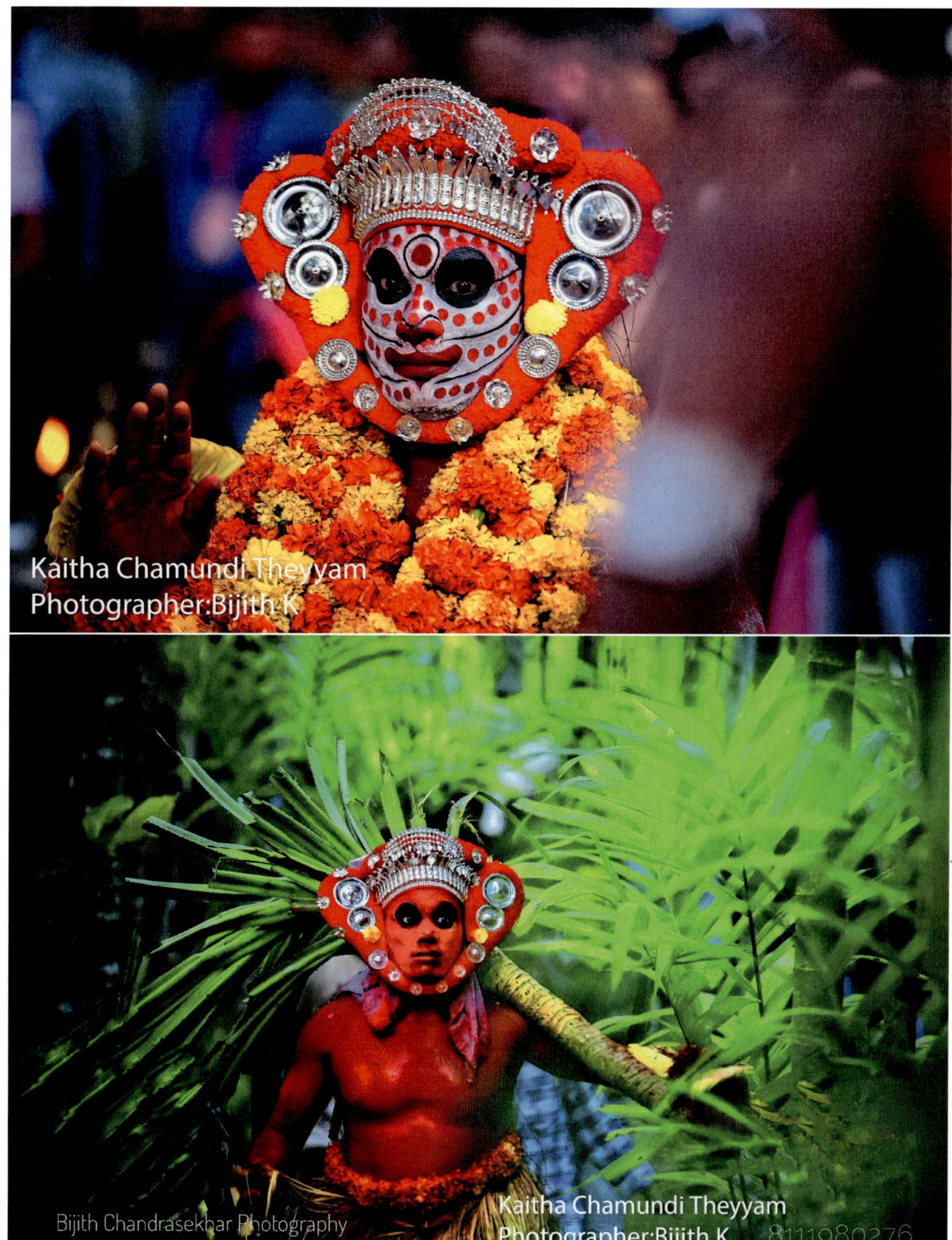
Kaitha Chamundi Theyyam
Photographer:Bijith K
Bijith Chandrasekhar Photography
Kaitha Chamundi Theyyam
Photographer:Bijith K
8111980276

Thottinkara Bhagavathy

Once again, Theyyam speaks for those oppressed and devastated through Thottinakara Bhagavathy. A few centuries back, when Chaturvarnya (four divisions of caste in the social order) was prominent in society, the lower caste were not allowed to recite epics like Ramayana and Mahabharata. The upper caste always controlled this through strict penalties.

The manager of Chirakkal Thamburan (the ruler) learned about a Thiyya (a lower caste) woman who recited Ramayana and summoned her to the Thamburan. Upon questioning her, she confessed that she recited Ramayana to overcome the pain of the death of her fourteen children. Reciting the holy book gave her peace and relieved her of the unbearable fire in her chest, although she was aware of the restrictions. Her pleading for forgiveness was met with mockery from the Thamburan, who decided to test her. He ordered his guards to lay her on her back and place some paddy on her chest to see whether or not it would become fried. To his amazement, Thamburan noticed the paddy frying and was furious with insult. He ordered the guards to stab her in the head with a lighted torch and throw her into the canal for her arrogance. She escaped before they could throw her in the river. The poor lady fled the land in agonizing pain. Once she reached the place known as Kakkathodu, she extinguished the torch on her head by getting into the stream. She walked towards a light shining in the distance, coming from a *tharavadu* (ancestral home). The *tharavattamma* (godmother of the house) took her in and gave her protection.

The Thiyya lady died there soon after. The people of the house cremated her, even though she was unknown to them. This act of kindness and humanity brought good fortune to the Tharavadu while evil providence settled in the residence of the Thamburan. Upon realizing his mistake and seeking repentance, the Thamburan started to worship the Thiyya lady, following the instructions of an astrologer. The Vannan community performs this Theyyam.

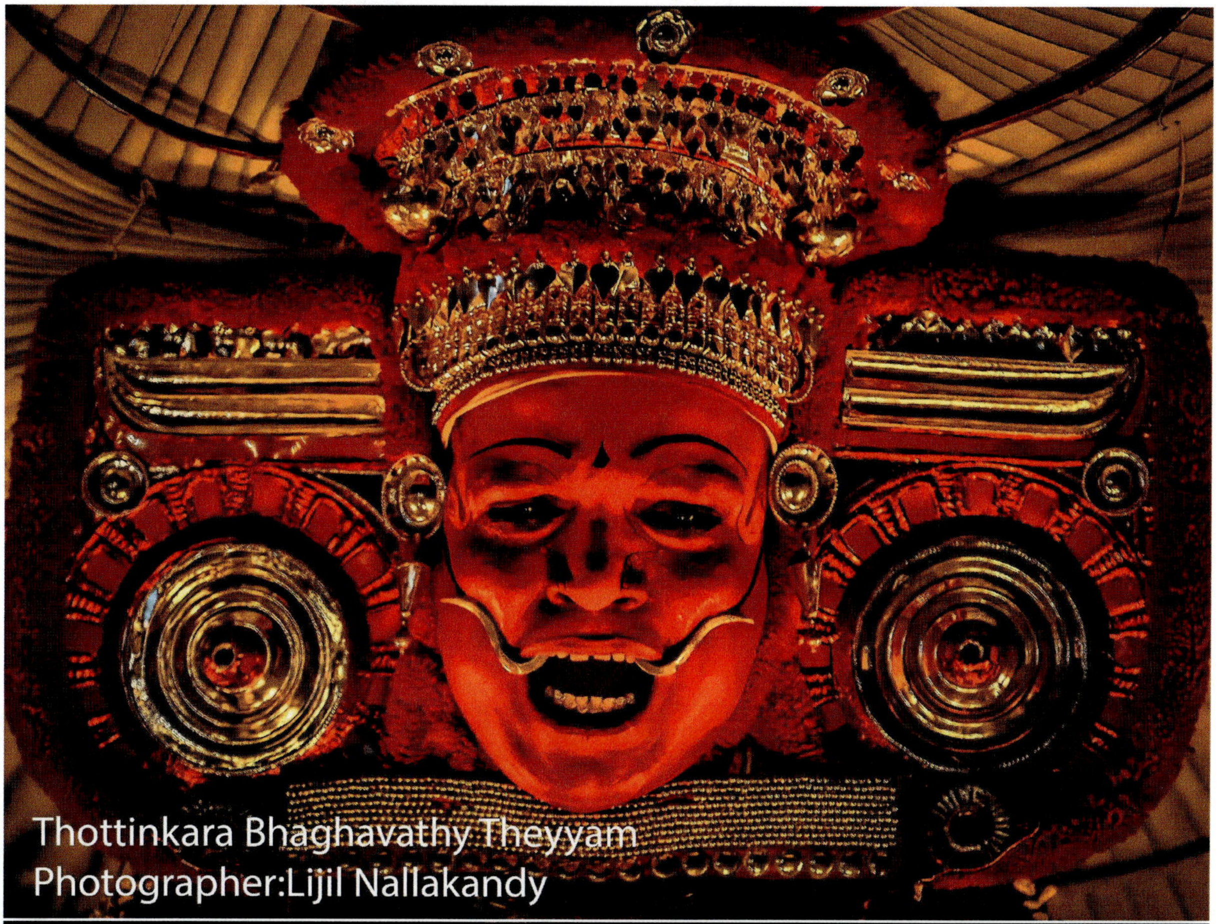

Thottinkara Bhaghavathy Theyyam
Photographer:Lijil Nallakandy

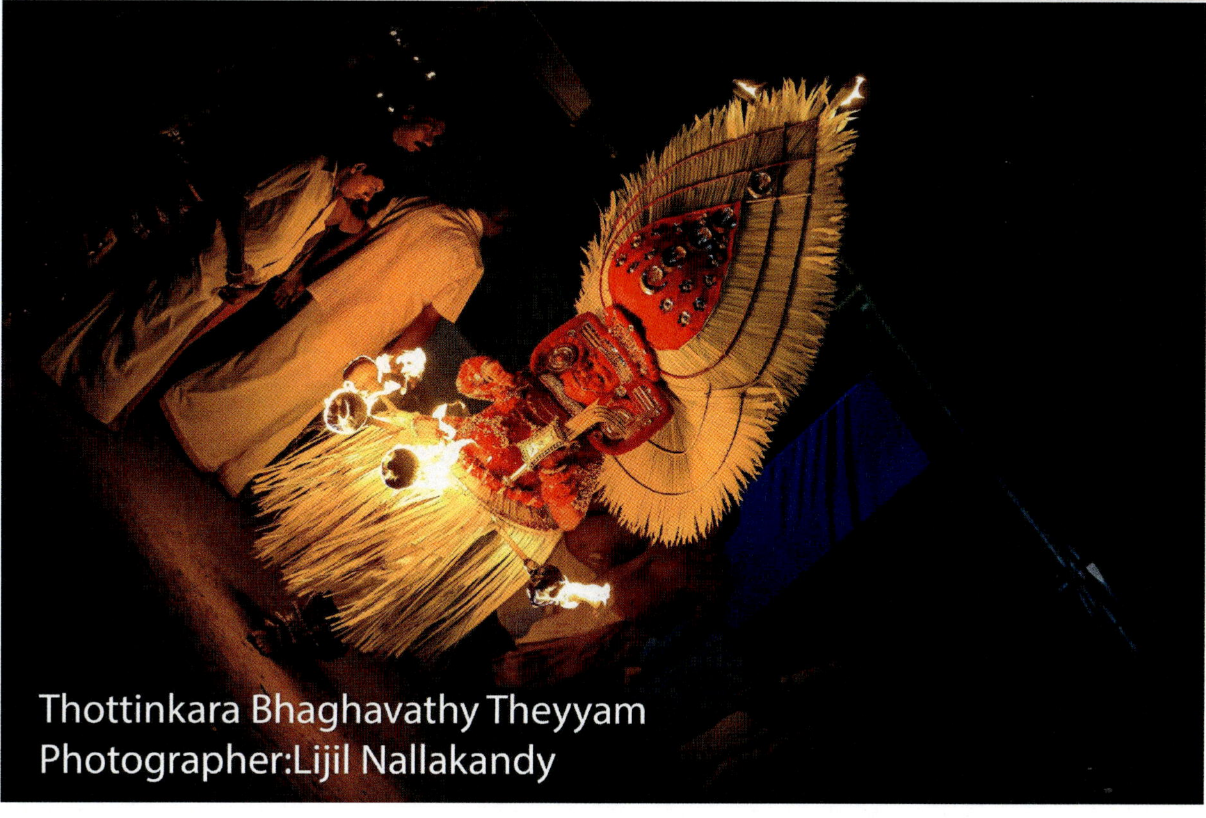

Thottinkara Bhaghavathy Theyyam
Photographer:Lijil Nallakandy

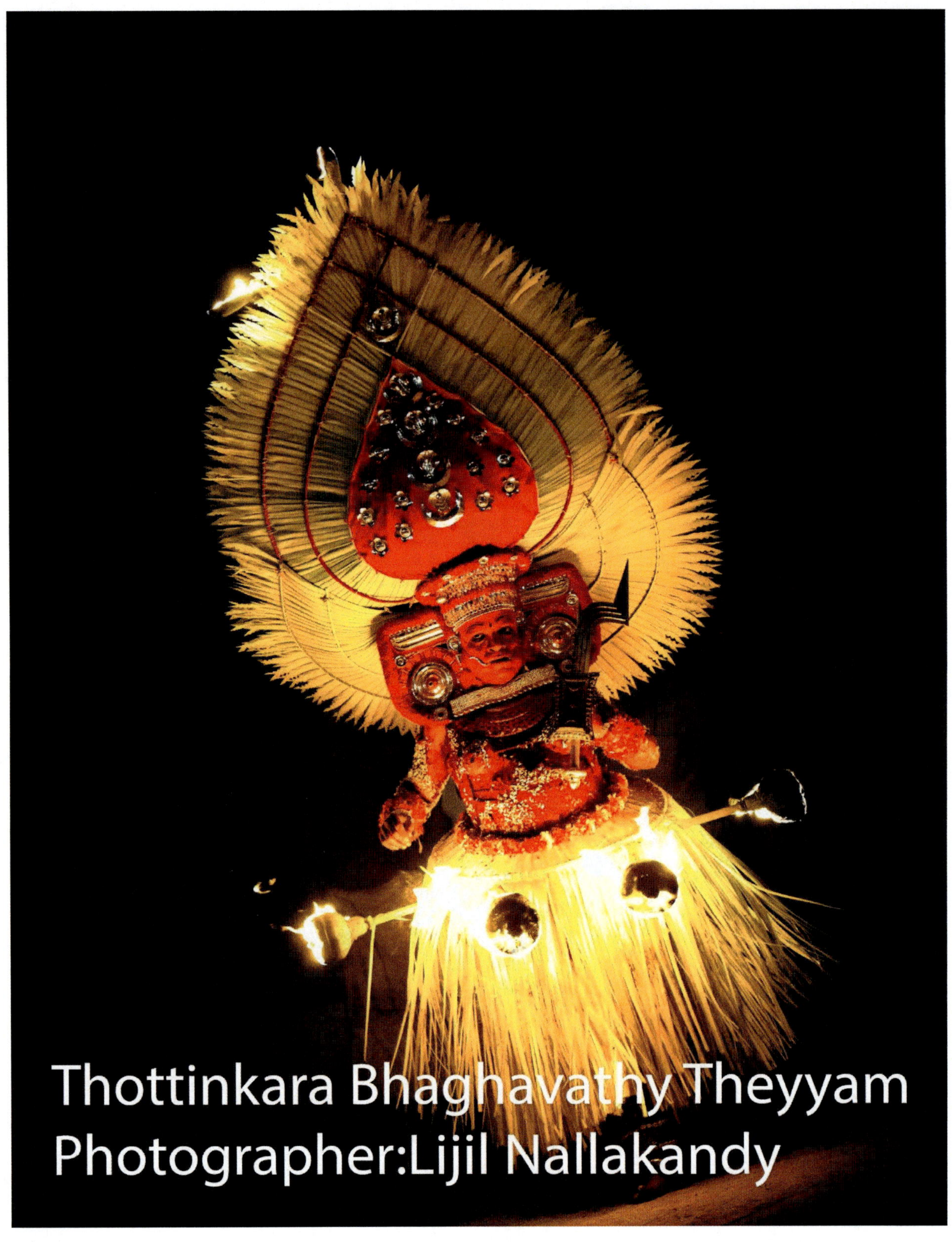

Thottinkara Bhaghavathy Theyyam
Photographer:Lijil Nallakandy

Thaiparadevatha

Darika, the monster, was as strong as seven elephants. Despite this, Goddess Bhadrakali grabbed him with seven of her hands and severed his head with one of her left hands. (According to Hindu mythology, Bhadrakali has three eyes and sixteen or eighteen hands. She carries many weapons, with flames flowing from her head and a tusk protruding from her mouth.). He was a demon that the world wanted to get rid of, so when Goddess Kali beheaded him, the entire universe was stunned. She held his head in one of her ten hands and performed a frenzied dance. The planet split apart; the tri-ocular God Shiva bore the weight, and Goddess Kali danced vigorously on his chest. This is the form of *Kolasvaroopathingal Thai Paradevatha* (mother clan deity), with which she blesses her worshippers.

Legends say that when the Goddess accomplished her purpose of incarnation, Lord Shiva sent her to earth and granted her four sectors by dividing the Kolathunadu region into four parts; Thiruvarkkad (Madayi Kavu) in the north, Kalarivathukkal in the south, Mamanikunnu in the east, and Cherukkunnu Annapoorneswari temple in the west. Ultimately, Goddess Bhadrakali became the primary deity of worship in the Kolathunadu region. Thiruvarkkattu Bhagavathy is known as Thai Paradevatha. The villagers fondly call her Madayi Kaavil Achi. This Goddess was the principal worshipping Goddess of the king of the Kolathiri dynasty. Therefore, she is prominent among the mother Goddesses.

The mudi (holistic headgear) of Thiruvarkkadu Bhagavathi is special. Made with bamboo sticks, up to fifty meters high and fourteen meters wide, the whole headgear is clad with red and black color fabric. This is the tallest headgear of all the Bhagavathy Theyyams. Performed by members of the Vannan community, about seventy different Goddesses are parallel to that of Thai Paradevatha.

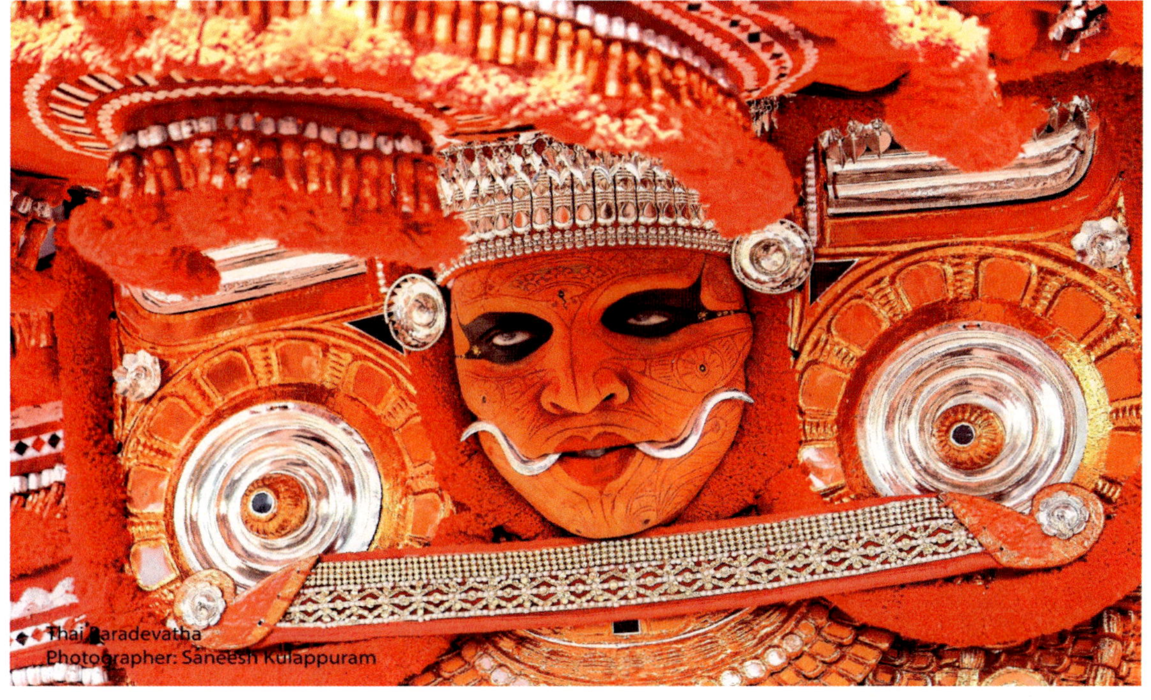

Thai Paradevatha
Photographer: Saneesh Kulappuram

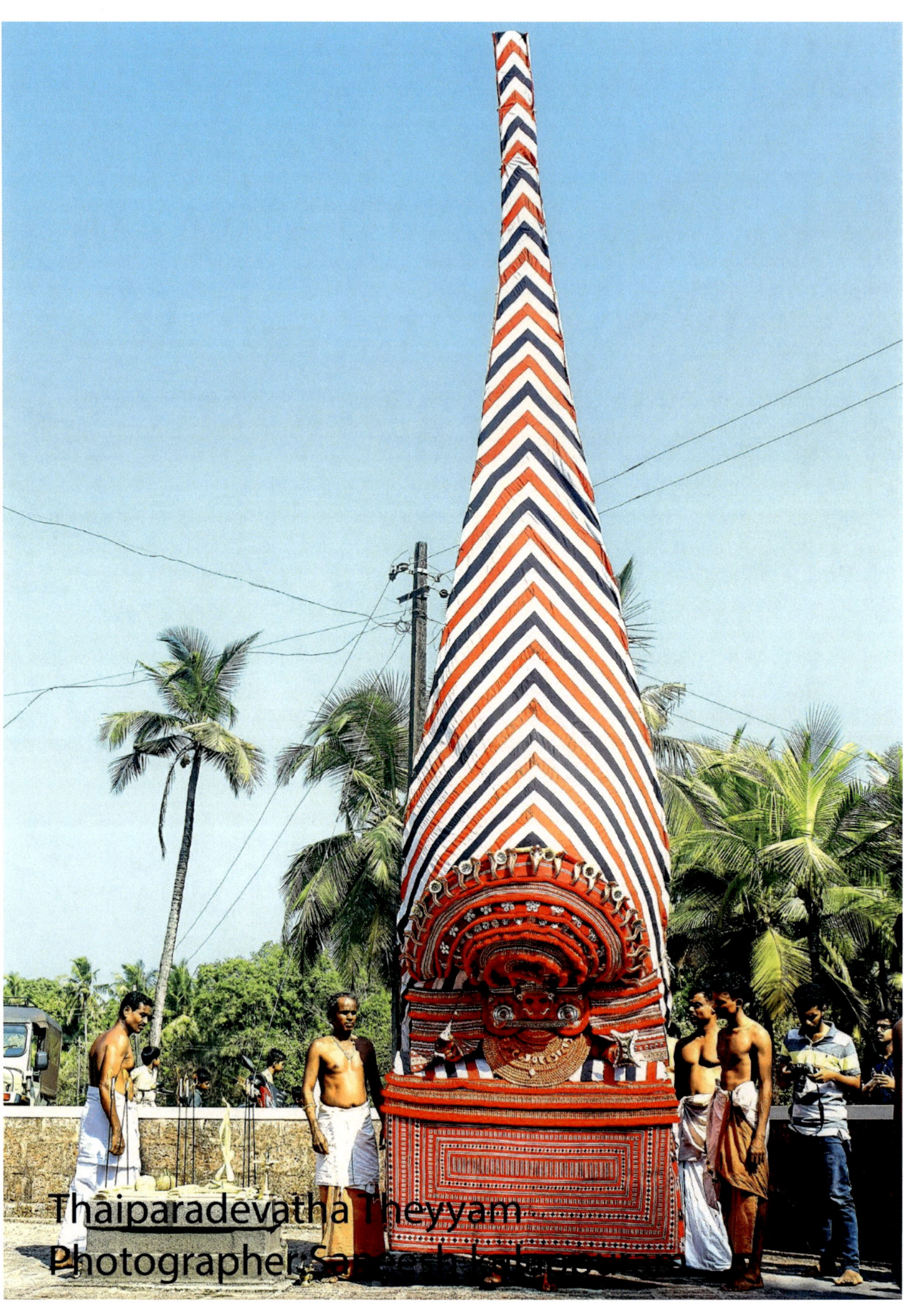

Thaiparadevatha Theyyam
Photographer:

Bappiriyan Theyyam

Bappiriyan Theyyam is performed in the shrines of *Azhikode Muchiriyan Vayanattu Kulavan Kaavu* and *Cherikal Bhagavathy Kaavu*. The legend of Bappiriyan Theyyam is related to the monkey God Hanuman from the epic of Ramayana. When Hanuman reached the seashore in search of Goddess Sita, the consort of Rama, he climbed a coconut tree for aerial surveillance. He not only did the reconnaissance but also destroyed the coconuts and their sprouts in a fit of rage, as he could not see Sita anywhere.

This Theyyam appears with a lot of humorous actions. The dance form *Vellattam* takes place at midnight, and the *Kolam* (figure) is displayed early in the morning. The Theyyam runs across the agricultural fields with a flaming torch made of dry palm leaves. During this sprint, the Theyyam interacts with the worshippers, especially the youngsters, by laughing at them and even shouting to frighten them. The Theyyam climbs on a tall coconut tree, smiling or mockingly sneering at onlookers. Once the Theyyam reaches the top of the tree, he plucks all the coconuts and hurls them away from the tree. Bappiriyan Theyyam has diverse legends and forms in Thalassery in Kannur, Kerala.

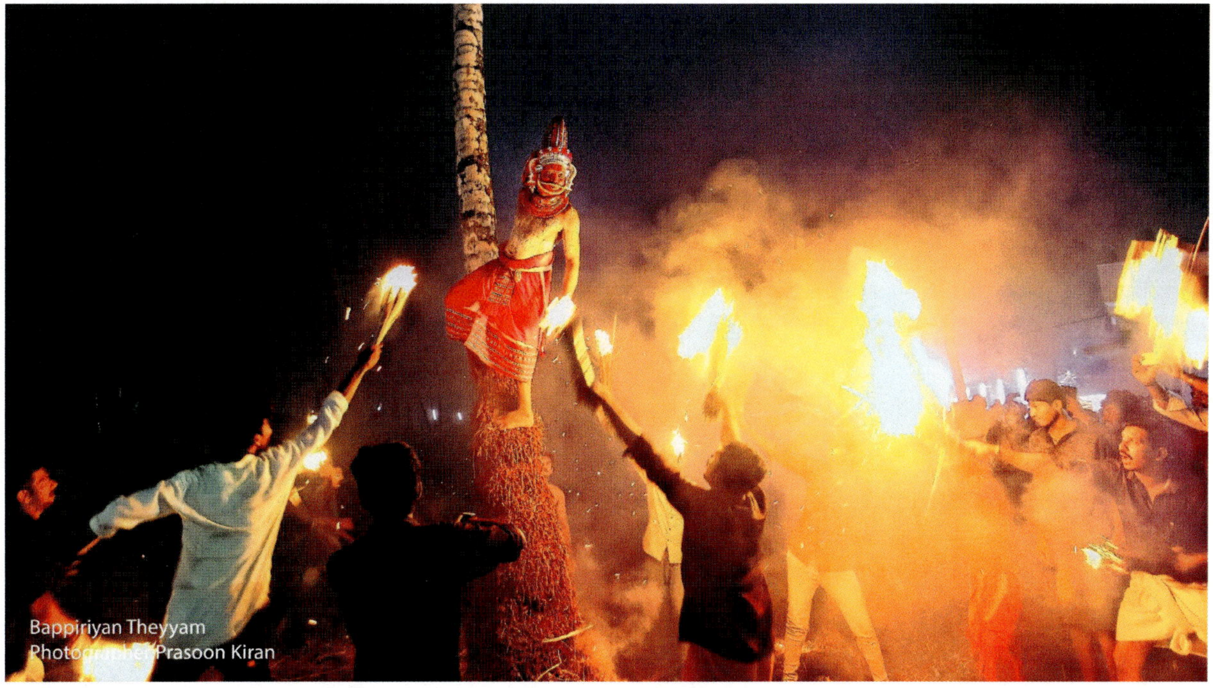

Bappiriyan Theyyam
Photographer Prasoon Kiran

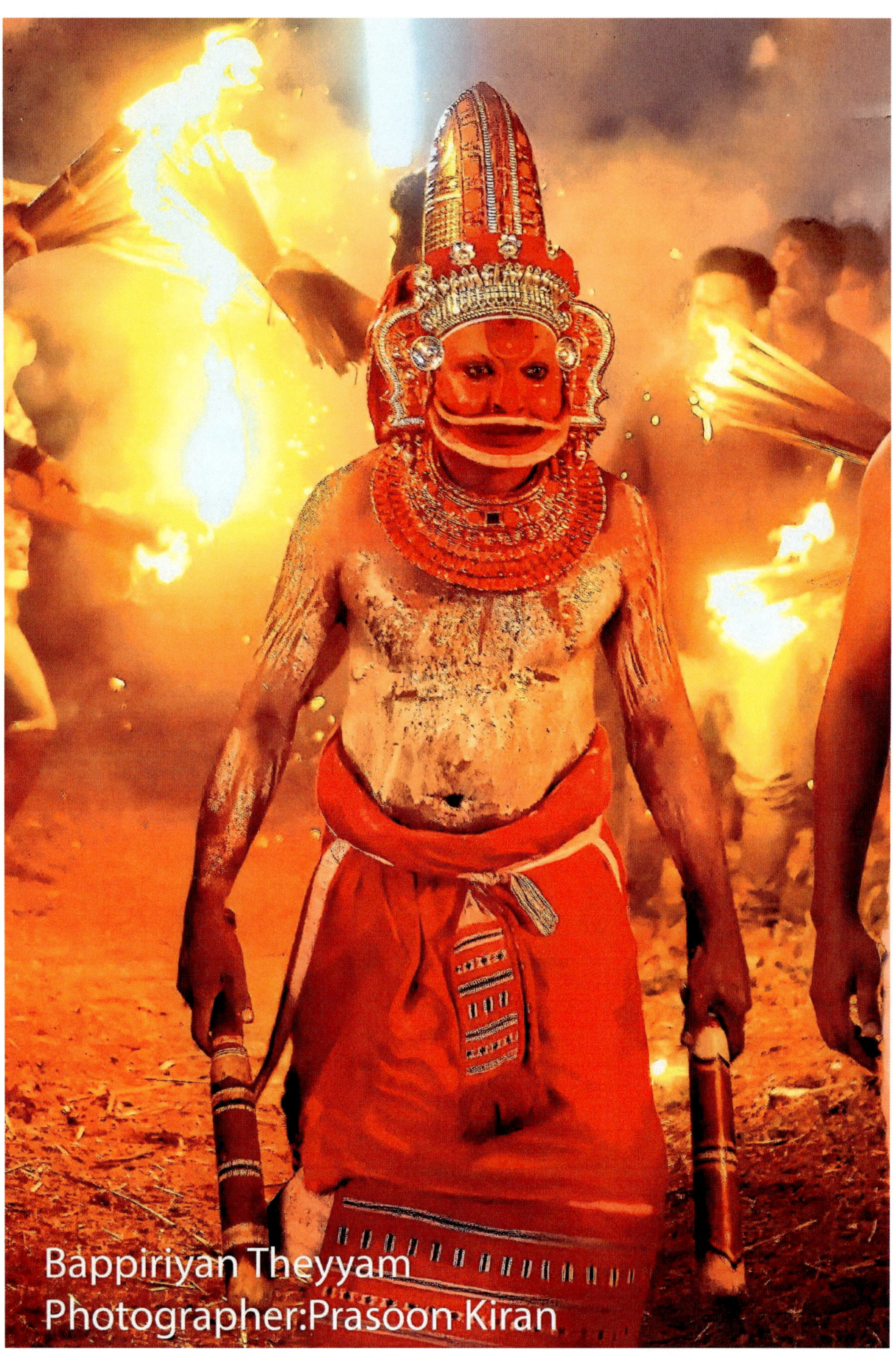

Bappiriyan Theyyam
Photographer:Prasoon Kiran

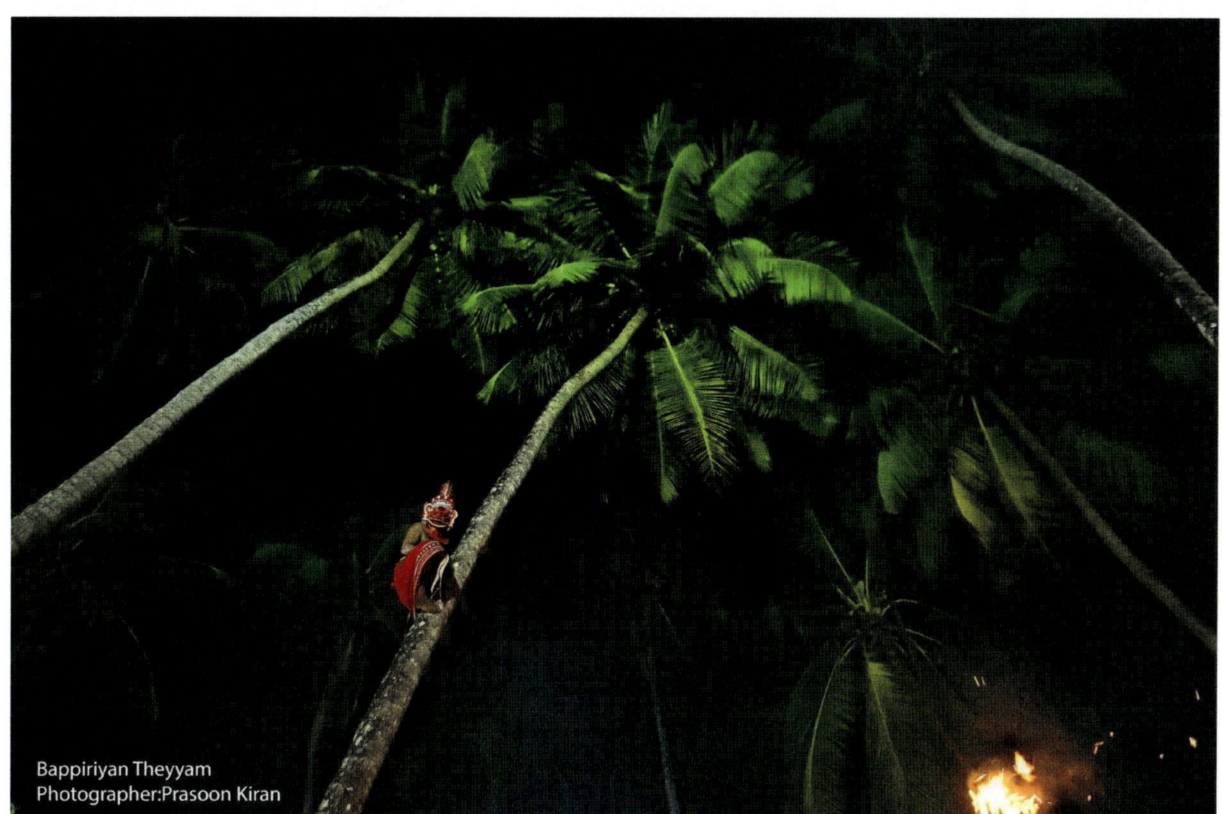

Bappiriyan Theyyam
Photographer:Prasoon Kiran

Thee Chamundi (Ottakolam or Single form)

In ancient times, people could not endure the Asura (demon) known as Hiranyakashipu. He had a boon that prevented humans or animals from killing him inside or outside any residence, day or night. To overcome this tricky boon, the principal deity Vishnu incarnated as a half-lion, half-human creature known as Narasimha Moorthy. This incarnation killed Hiranyakashipu at twilight by sitting at the door, tearing apart his body using his claws, and sucking his blood. All the fourteen worlds were delighted to see the annihilation of that Asura. (These 14 worlds are the seven lower ones or Patala (Hell), and seven higher worlds called heaven.) All Gods praised Vishnu for the timely help, and the Apsaras (the female spirits of the clouds and waters) danced jubilantly. The sages, including Narada, chanted the Narayana Mantra, and the entire world was jubilant and praised Vishnu. However, Agni, the God of fire, wasn't happy. He avoided these celebrations, saying it was a silly matter to slay Hiranyakashipu, and anyone could have killed him easily. Vishnu was angry when he heard Agni, the God of fire, had criticized him. Vishnu decided to suppress Agni's arrogance. He jumped into Agni's fierce flames and started beating the God of fire. Finally, the fire pit was nothing but a heap of ash. This form of Vishnu that expelled the arrogance of the God of fire is called Thee Chamundi (Fire Chamundi) or Ottakkolam (meaning only a single form of Theyyam).

Another version of the myth says that the Hiranyakashipu was hidden at Agni's palace, and Narasimhamoorthy started searching in the palace. Hence, it is said that the Thee Chamundi Theyyam symbolizes the search in the palace of God of fire.

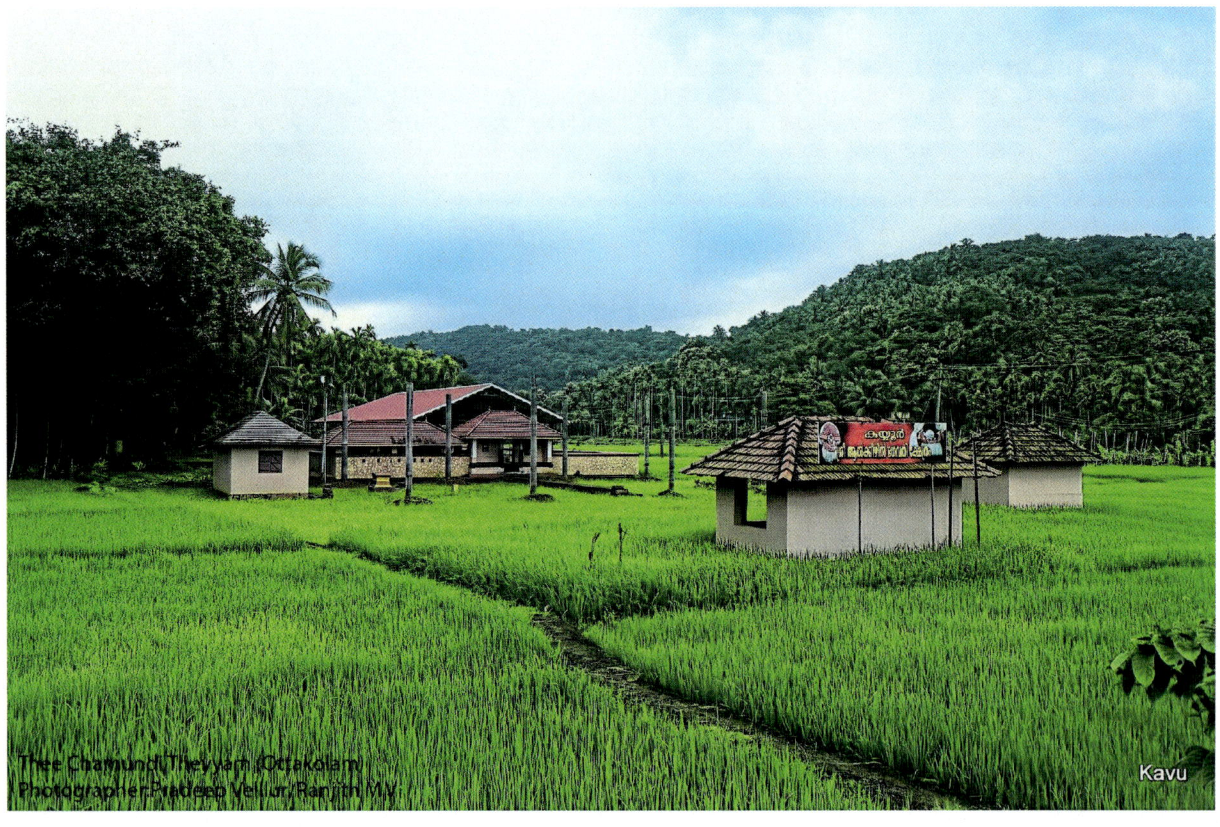

Thee Chamundi Theyyam (Ottakolam)
Photographer: Pradeep Vellur/Ranjith M.V.

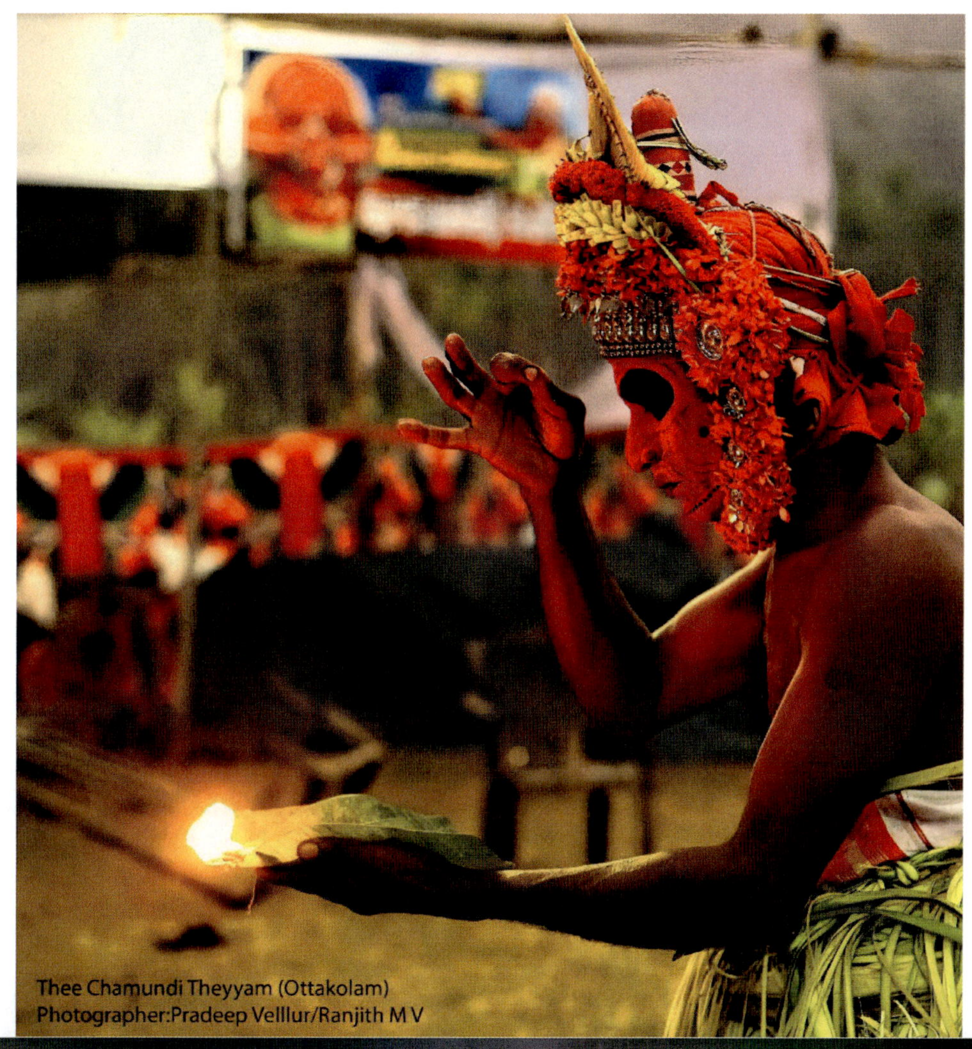

Thee Chamundi Theyyam (Ottakolam)
Photographer:Pradeep Velllur/Ranjith M V

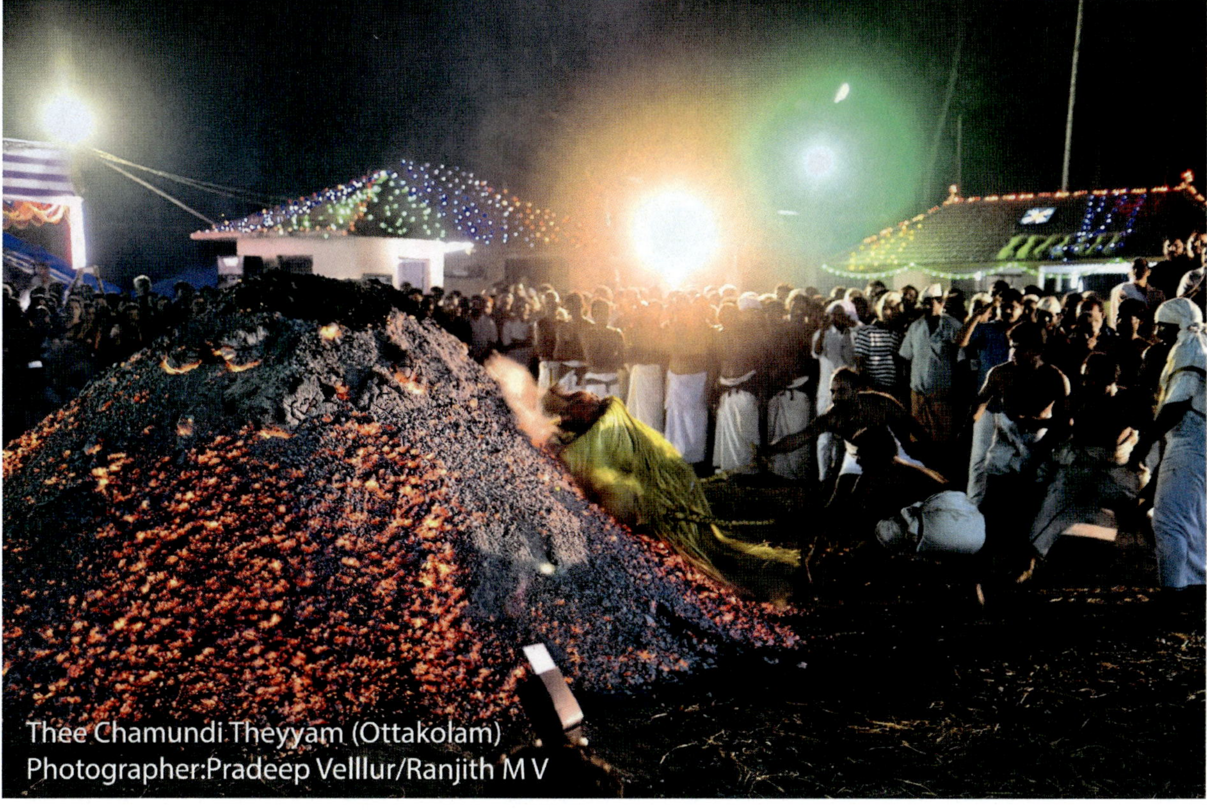

Thee Chamundi Theyyam (Ottakolam)
Photographer:Pradeep Velllur/Ranjith M V

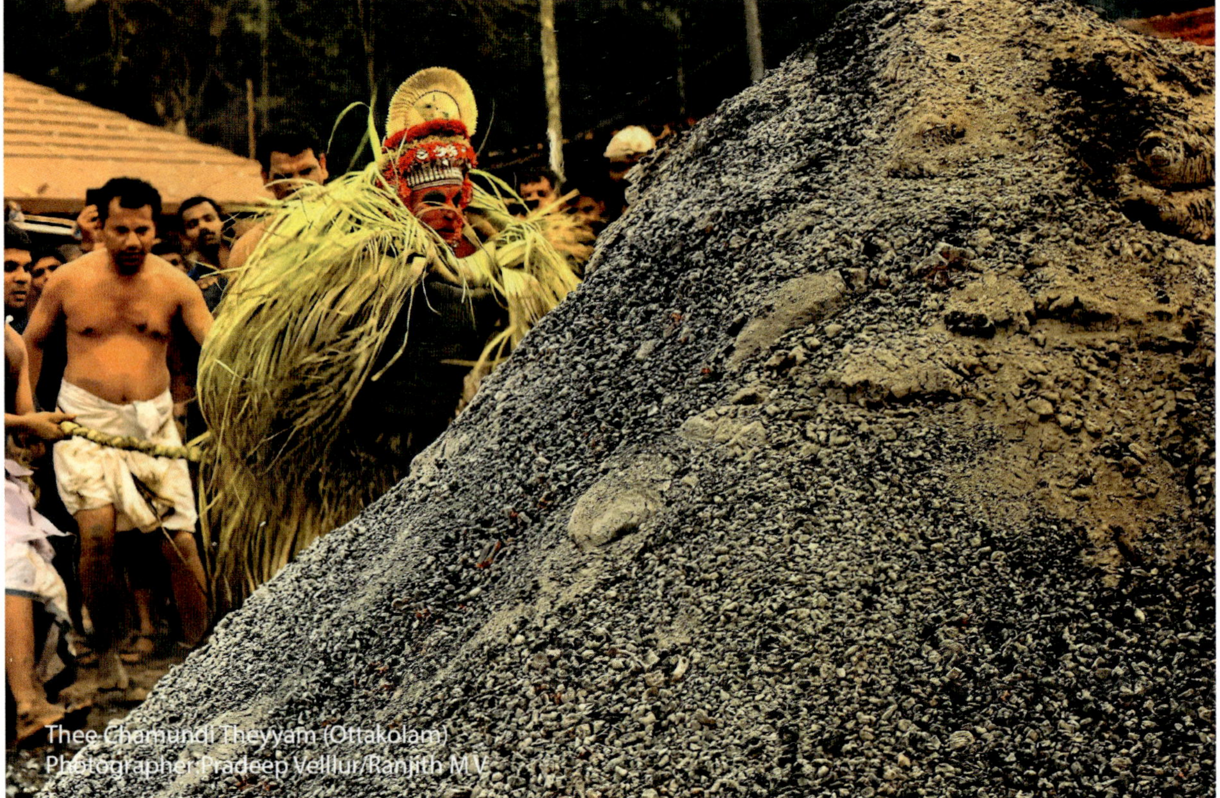

Thee Chamundi Theyyam (Ottakolam)
Photographer:Pradeep Velllur/Ranjith M V

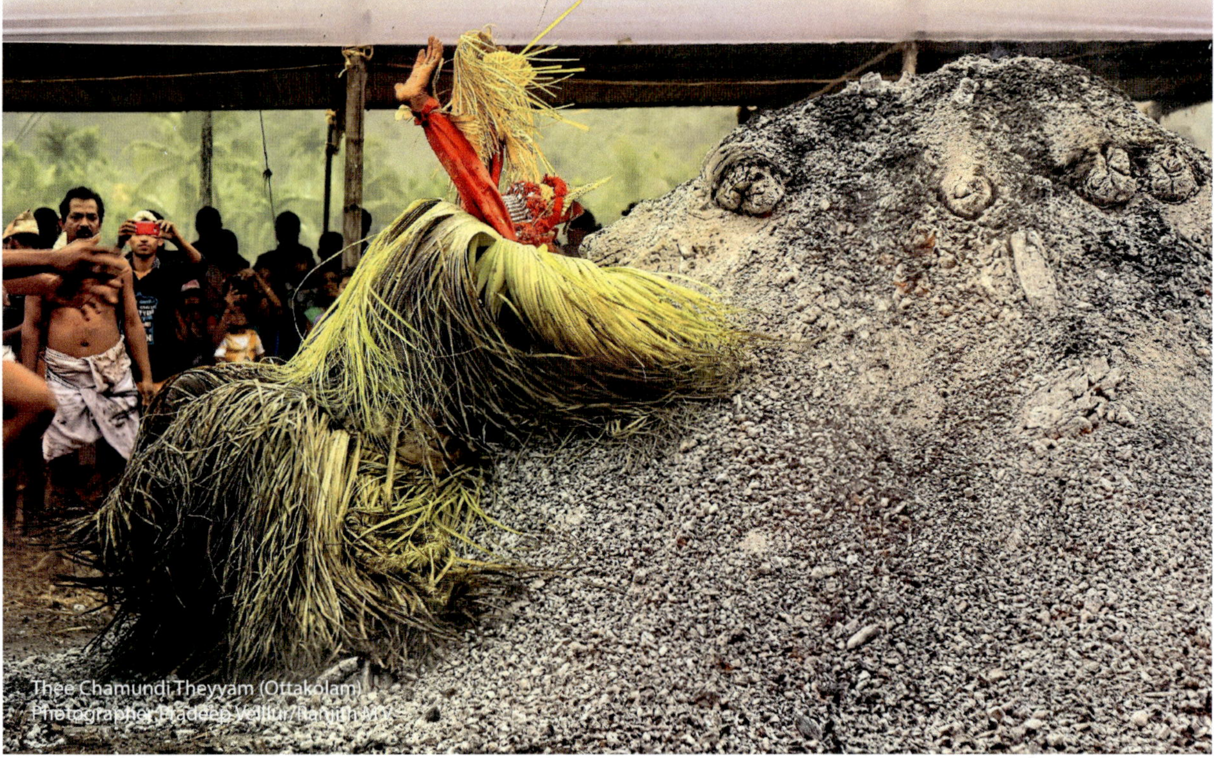

Thee Chamundi Theyyam (Ottakolam)
Photographer:Pradeep Velllur/Ranjith M V

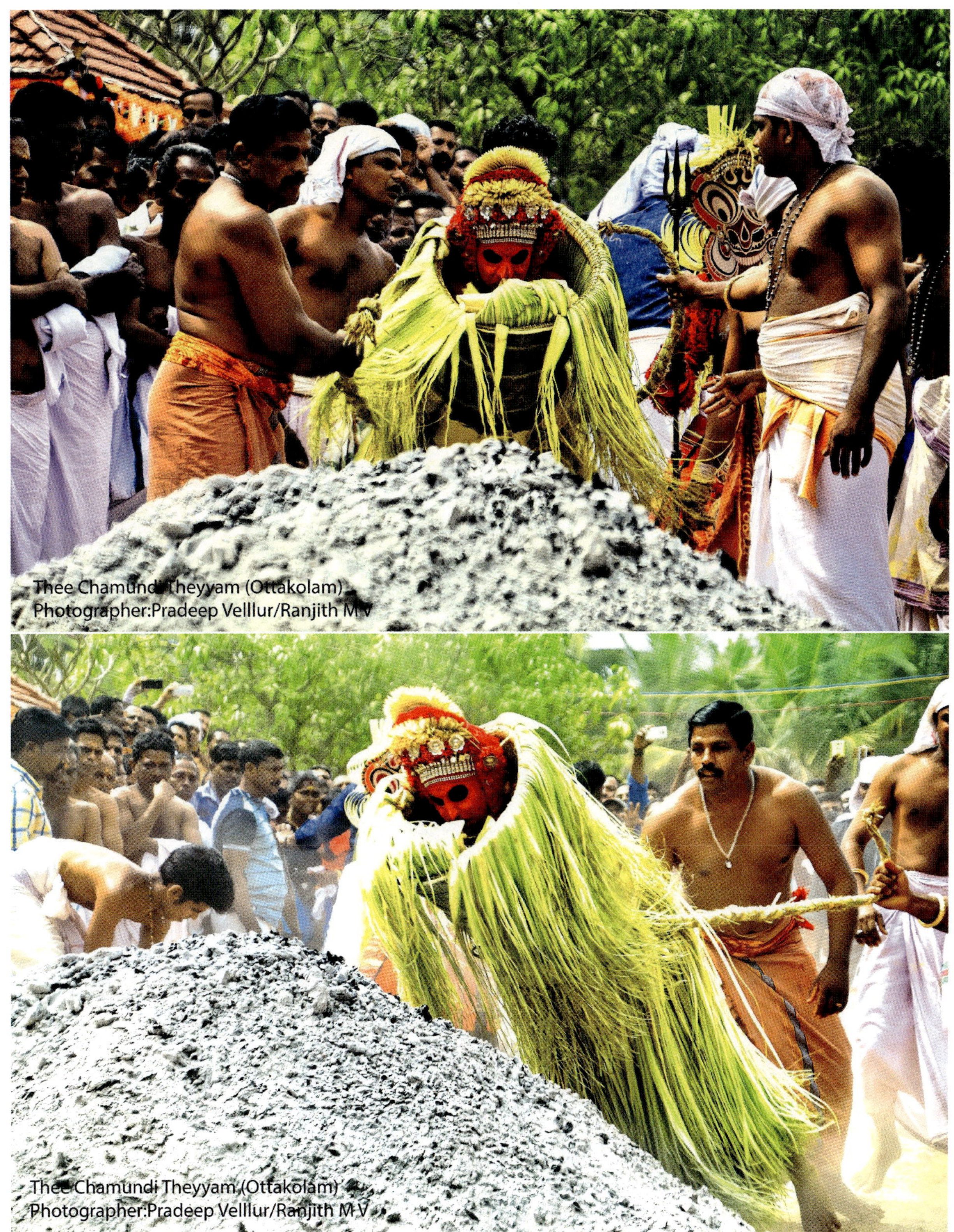
Thee Chamundi Theyyam (Ottakolam)
Photographer:Pradeep Velllur/Ranjith M V
Thee Chamundi Theyyam (Ottakolam)
Photographer:Pradeep Velllur/Ranjith M V

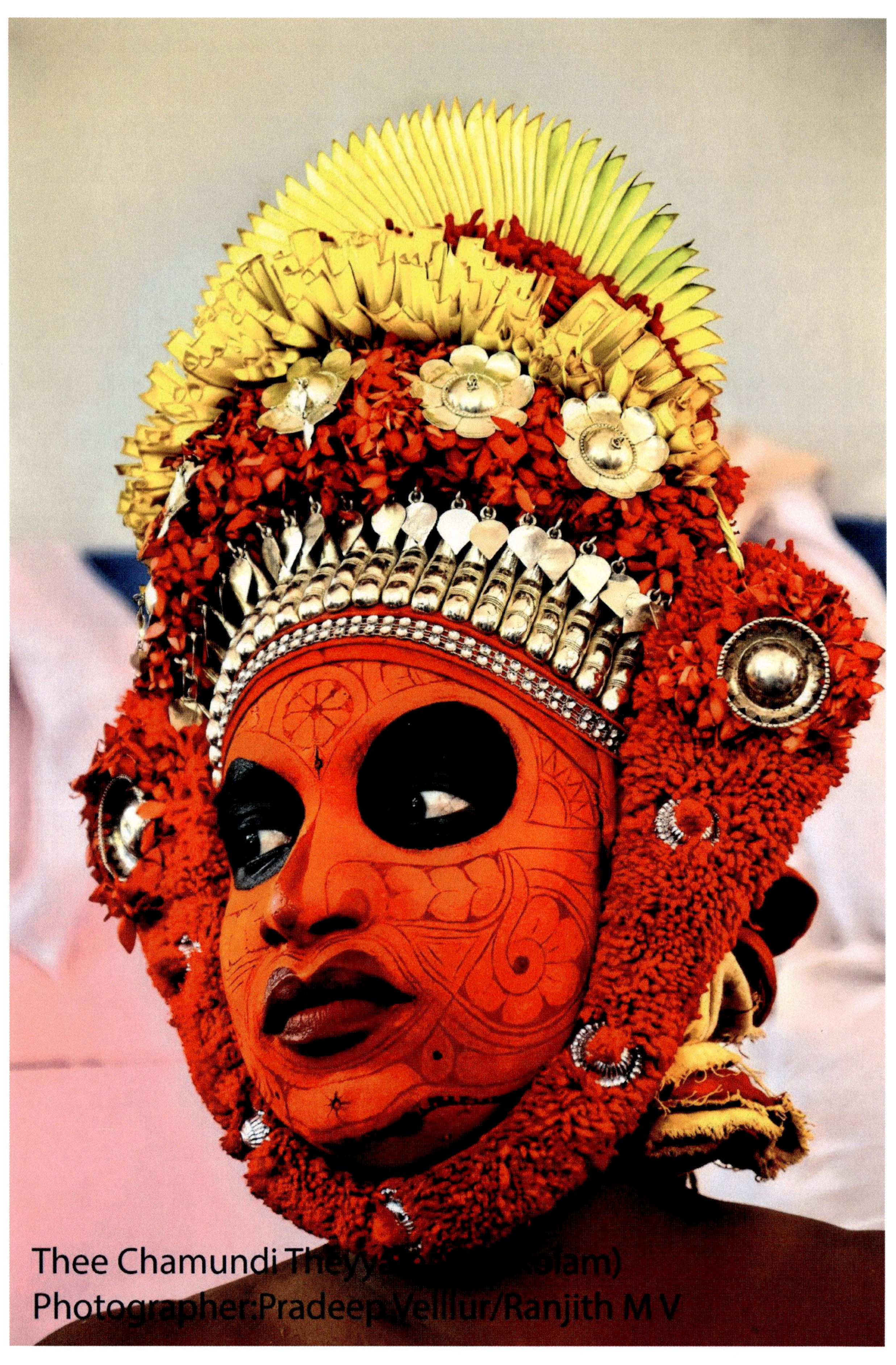

Thee Chamundi Theyy[illegible]slam)
Photographer:Pradeep Vellur/Ranjith M V

Theyyathkari Theyyam

Theyyathkari Theyyam and Karthika Chamundi Theyyam are the protectors of paddy fields and farming. Karthika Chamundi is believed to be the deity who sowed *ari* (rice), which resulted in the abundance of the paddy field and hence is known as '*Arayi Chamundi*.' The Theyyam of these Goddesses are performed in *Arayi Karthika Kavu* of *Kanhangad* by people belonging to the Pulaya community.

It is peculiar that the Karthika Chamundi Theyyam, Theyyathu Kari Theyyam, and Gulikan Theyyam travel on a rowboat to the Kalichan kavu. When they arrive, they are welcomed by the Kalichan Daivam. The Theyyams who come have conversations with Kalichan Daivam. They also bless the devotees by giving them holy turmeric powder. These Theyyams visit nearby houses of Kalichan kavu and give blessings before returning to their own kavu (Shrine). The meeting of the deities of these two kavus is a symbol of nature's engagement with the Gods. It is also a reminder of a time when farming was impossible without farm animals. Previously, agriculture in these villages commenced only after this theyyam performance.

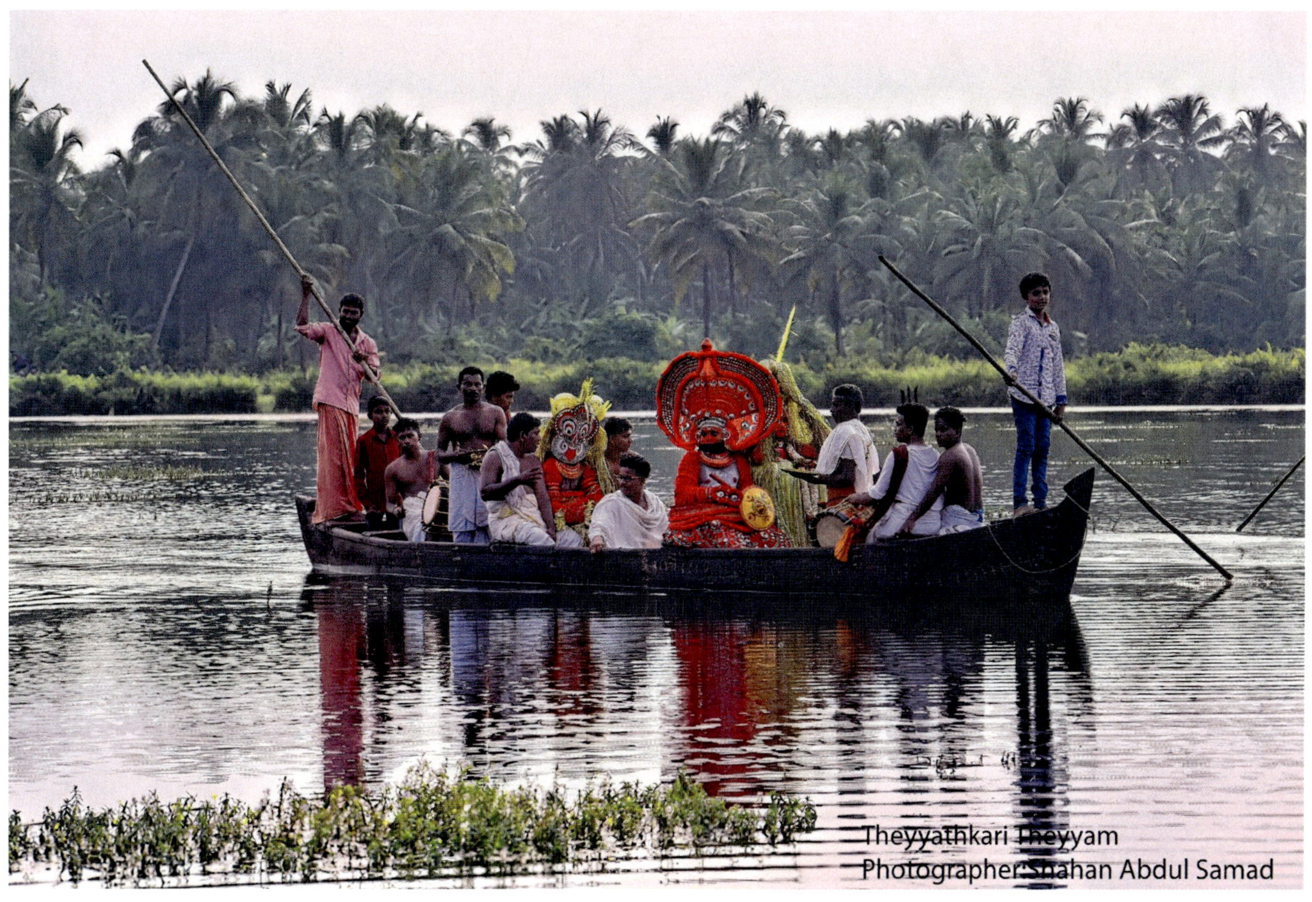

Theyyathkari Theyyam
Photographer: Shahan Abdul Samad

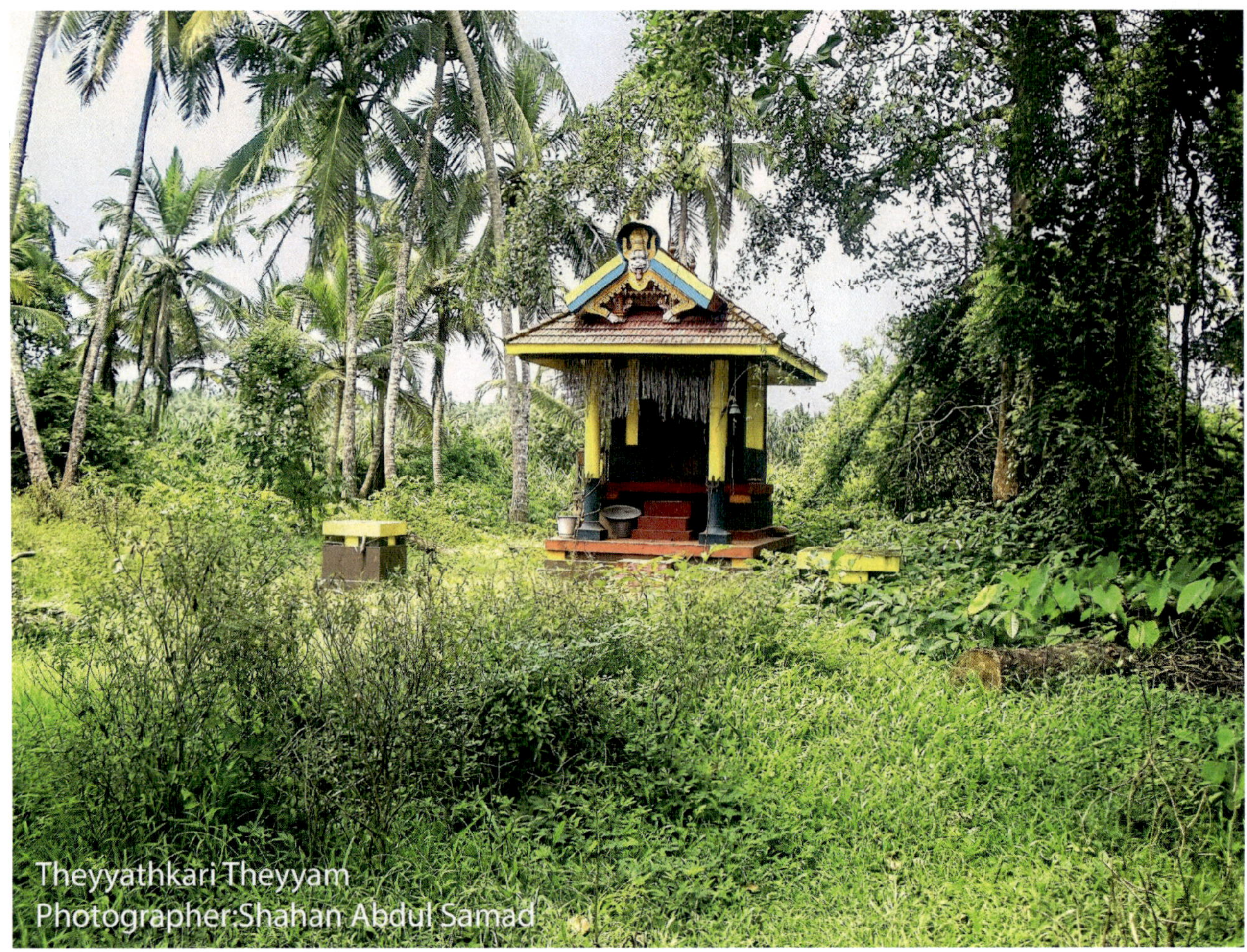
Theyyathkari Theyyam
Photographer:Shahan Abdul Samad

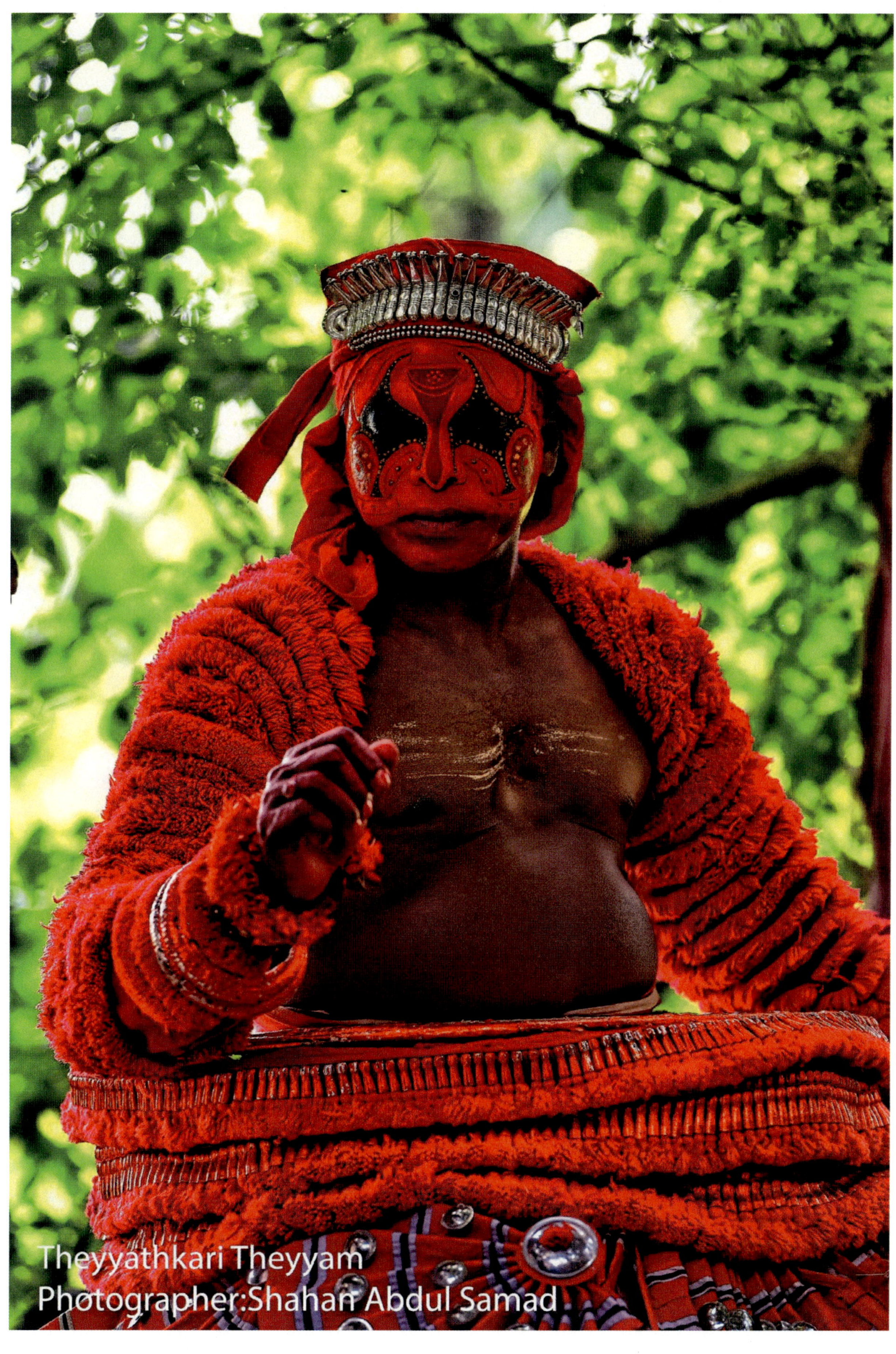

Theyyathkari Theyyam
Photographer:Shahan Abdul Samad

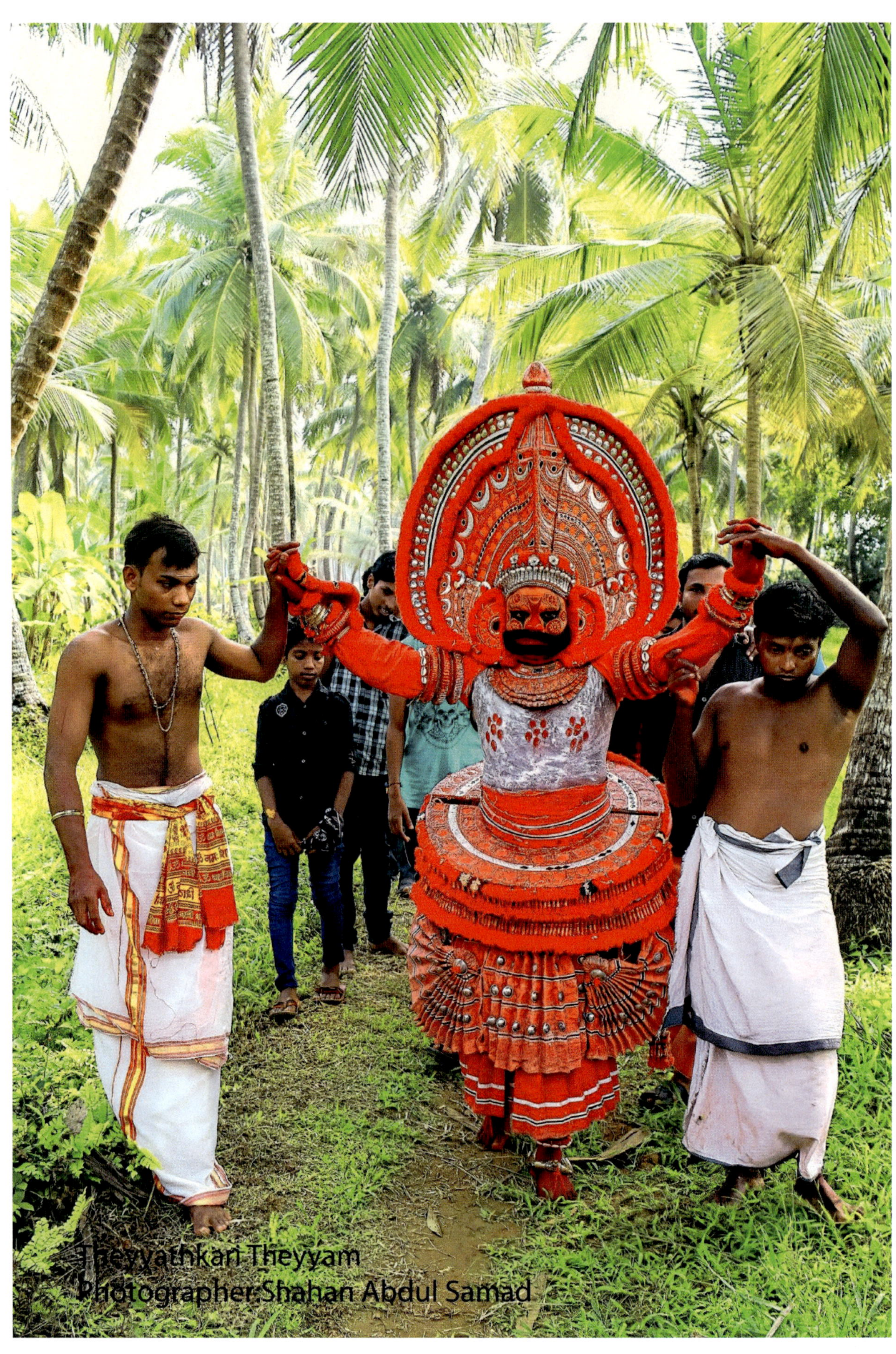

Theyyathkari Theyyam
Photographer:Shahan Abdul Samad

Nagakanni

In most *Kavus* (Shrines) of Kerala, a separate abode for snake Gods is typical. Theyyams such as *Nagakanni, Nagarajan, Nagathan, Nagappothi,* etc., are very auspicious among the different theyyams performed in reverence of these snake Gods. Such Theyyam performances are held in snake sanctorium such as the *Kayyath Nagam, Muyyath Nagam, Erumbal Nagam, Karippal Nagam, Edatt Nagam,* and some houses. It is believed that these Gods were born out of the *Maninagaputtu* (an abode of snakes) near the *Maninaga Manipavizham* on the *Velliman* stone situated in the middle of the holy ocean of Milk (*Palkadal*).

Naga (snake) figures are essential in the costumes and other adornments of these Theyyams. The hair of the Theyyam, known as *Nagapothi,* is called *Nagamudi*. Naga motifs can also be found in the ornaments of several other Theyyams. It is customary to draw Nagas on their *Kuruthodis* and face plates. It is said that there is an exclusive style of face makeup called *Nagam Thathezhuth*.

While the Vannan community performs Theyyams such as Nagakandan and Nagakanni, the Munnuttan and the Paanan communities perform *Nagakali* and *Nagabhagavathy* Theyyams. Additionally, the Vannan community also practices performances on a deity known as *Nagathin Daivam* at the Ramavilyam Kazhakam. *Kurunthiri Bhagavathy* and *Kurunthinikaman* (also known as *Nagakaman*) are Naga (snake) deities who dance to the *Kurunthini* song. On the day of the Theyyam performance, a ceremony called *Sarpathbali* is also conducted. These Goddesses are believed to grant the boon of a child to the childless and are worshipped as the Asclepius (Greek god of medicine).

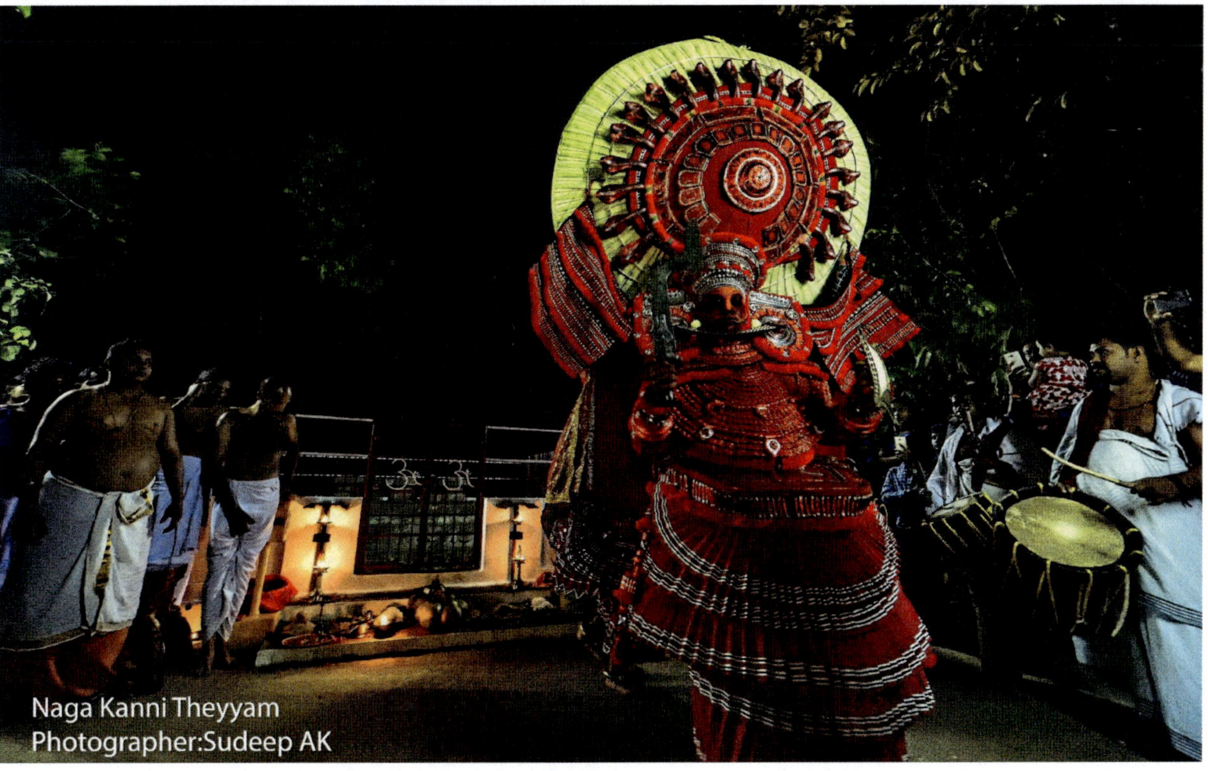

Naga Kanni Theyyam
Photographer:Sudeep AK

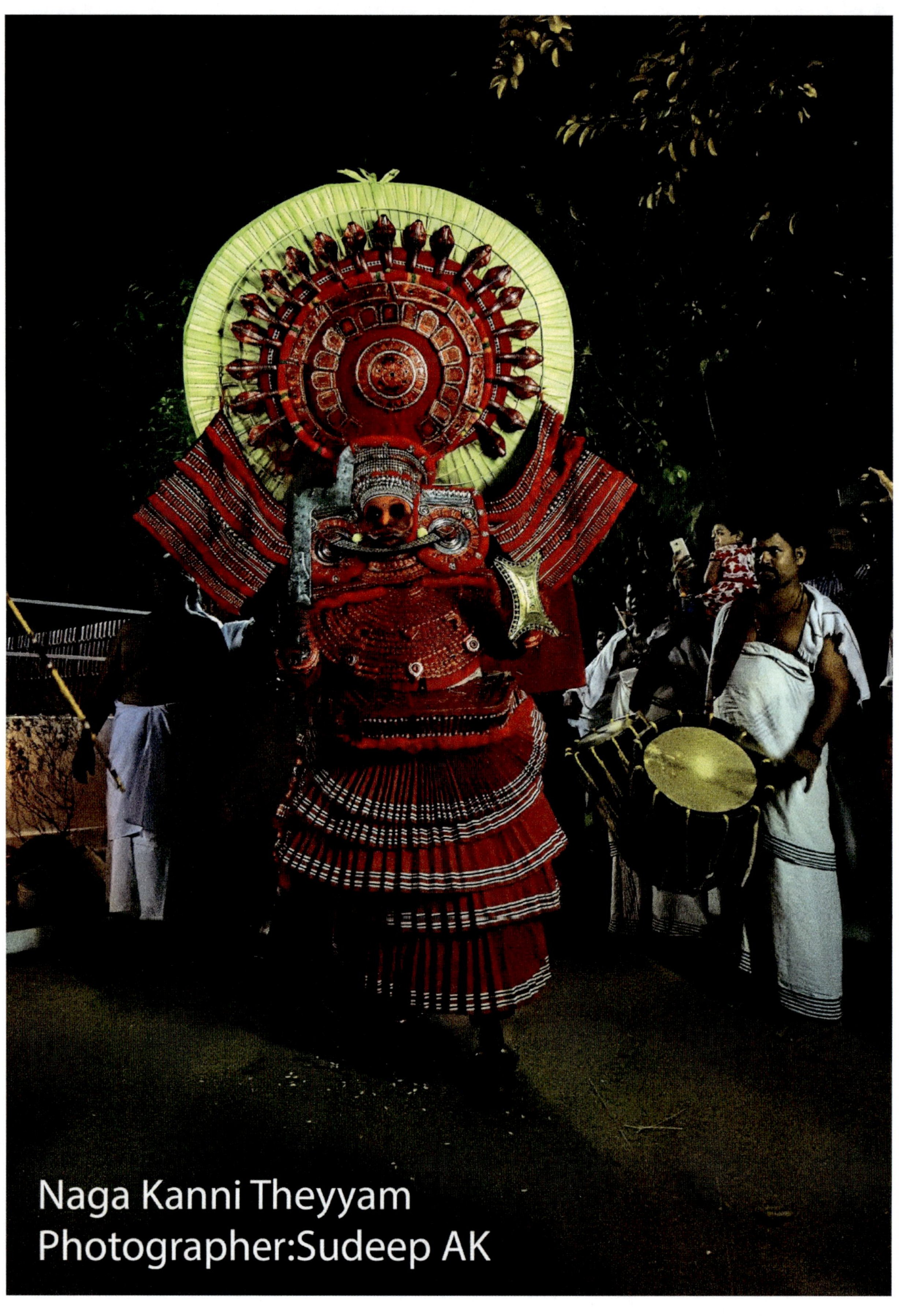

Naga Kanni Theyyam
Photographer:Sudeep AK

Kammiyamma

Paraliyamma is a mute Goddess in the concept of Parvati, for whom others speak on her behalf. The Goddess, who is the protector of Thiruvarkadu Kavu, killed and consumed a Brahmin. An infuriated Thiruvarkadu Bhagavathi pulled out Paraliyamma's tongue and threw her out of Madayi Kavu, which landed at Arippamba. Later, she was given a seat there. She is one of the Vanadevathas (forest deities) and is performed by the Chingathanmar community. Goddess Kammiyamma was accused of the same crime as Paraliyamma. Legend has it that Kammiyamma was thrown out of her abode and landed at Eruvatti.

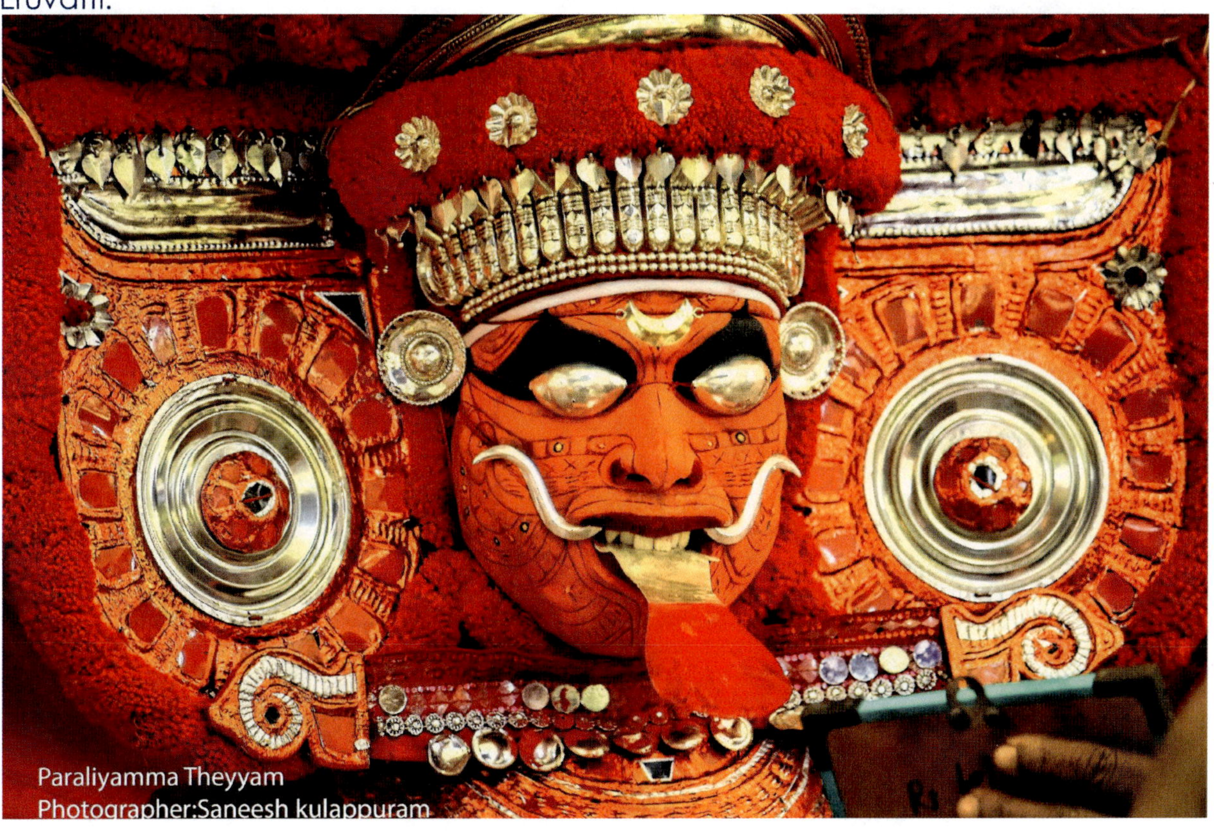

Paraliyamma Theyyam
Photographer:Saneesh kulappuram

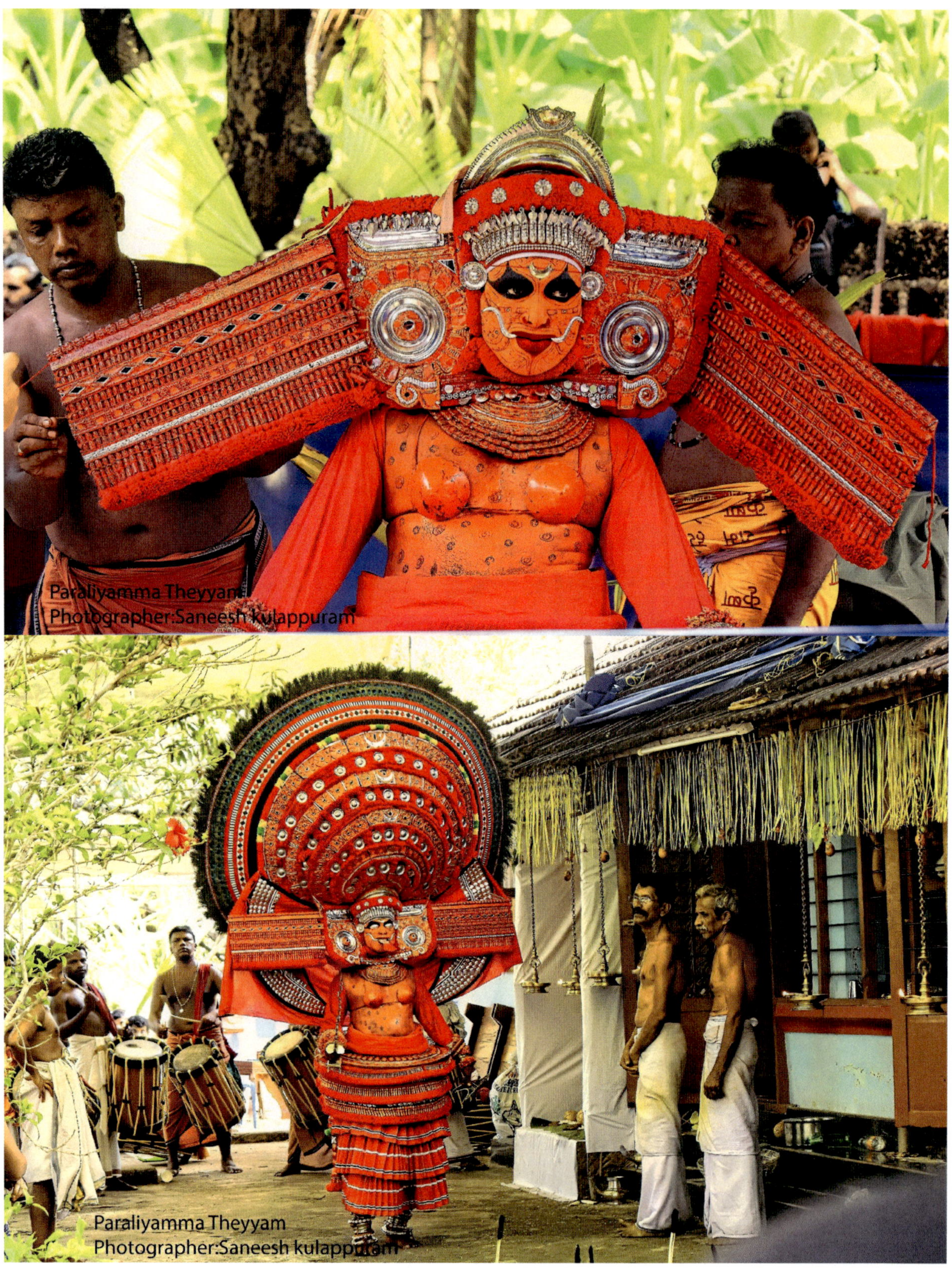
Paraliyamma Theyyam
Photographer:Saneesh kulappuram

Paraliyamma Theyyam
Photographer:Saneesh kulappuram

Malakkari

This Theyyam is performed as the commemoration of a tribal hero. Hero worship is the foundation of this worship, and the celebration of the tribal hero is embedded in it. During the initiation of the performance, Malakkari Theyyam has the same costume as any other *Veeran* (Hero) form of Theyyam. They smear their entire bodies with Arichand. The hair of this Theyyam is similar to Kathivanoor Veeran Theyyam. People from the Vannan community perform this Theyyam at Andalur Kavu in Dharmadam village of Kannur, Kerala. Malakkari Theyyam usually starts during the mornings between 8:00 am-10:00 am. Adivasis (Tribal groups) and people of the Thiyya community worship this deity.

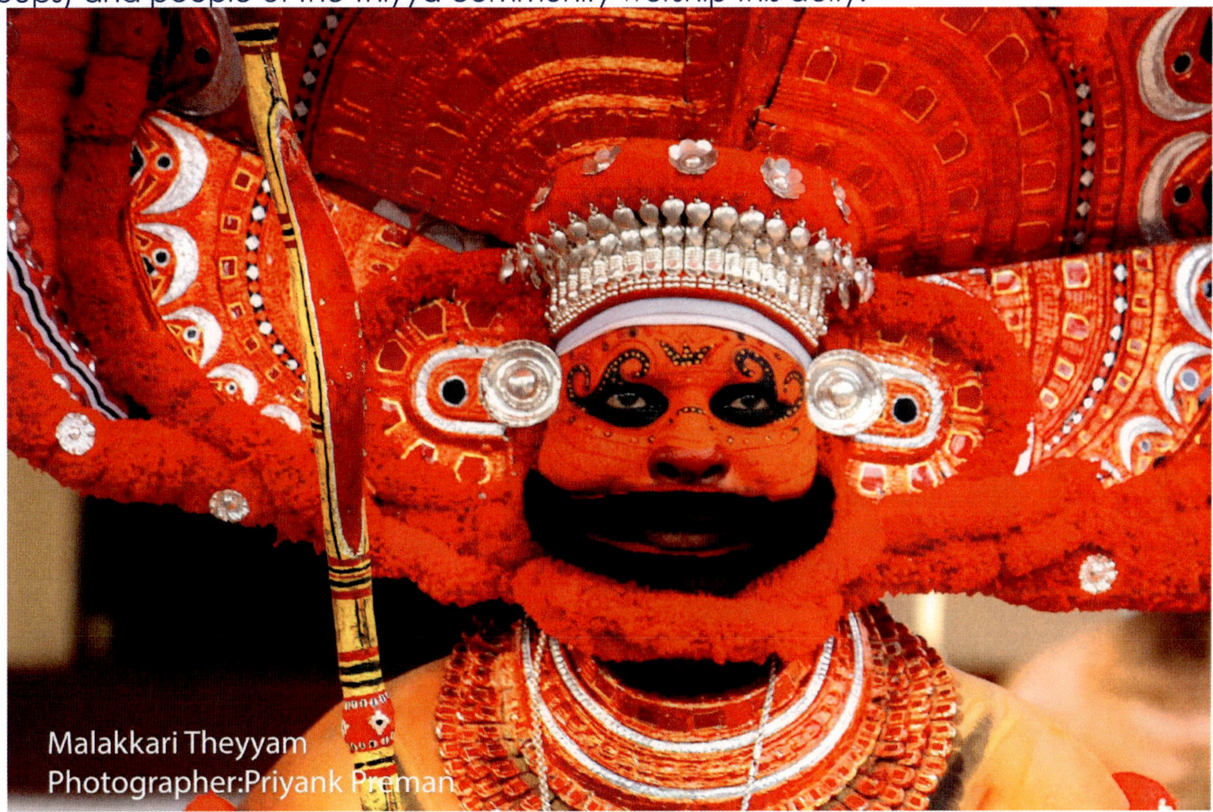

Malakkari Theyyam
Photographer:Priyank Preman

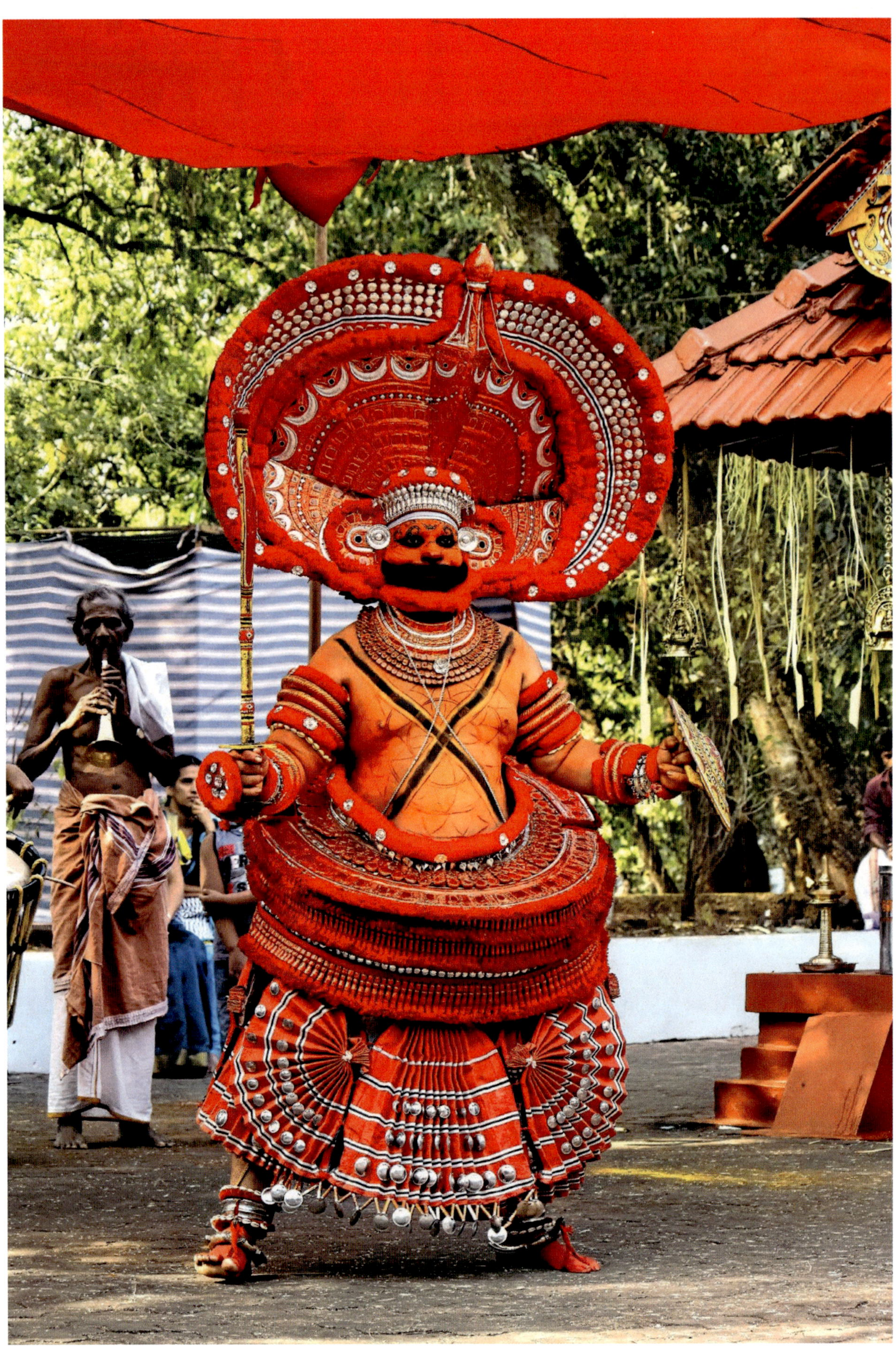

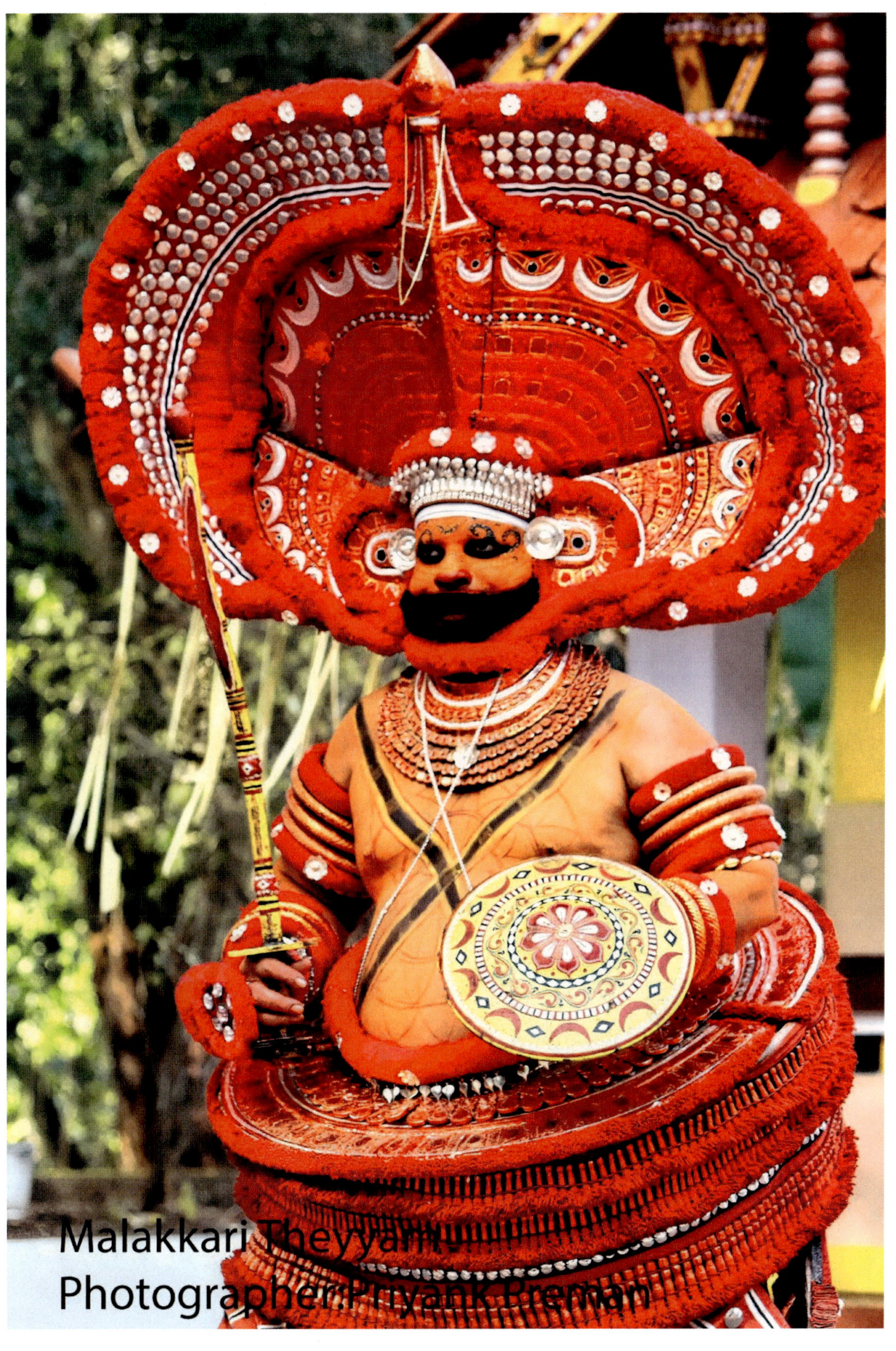

Malakkari Theyyam -
Photographer:Priyank Preman

Kelan Kulangara Bhagavathy

Kelan Kulangara Bhagavathy is an exclusively localized 'Amma Daivam' (mother Goddess). It is primarily performed in places such as Cheruthazham, Edattu, Kunhimangalam, and Vellur.

A Cherikkall comprises an area that includes a field, the dwellings, and the population living in and around it. The *Kolathunad* region of Kerala has many such Cherikkalls. One among these is the Cheruthazhathe Periyattucherikkallu, which is situated in the fields and surrounding area on the west side of Pilathara, in Payyannur in Kannur, Kerala. The Nairs (a community) of Periyatt were once the chiefs of this Cherikkall. The legend behind the Kelam Kulangara Theyyam is that of the transformation of a virgin Nair maiden from this Tharavdu (ancestral house) into a Theyyam.

The oldest male member of the ancestral house partitioned the entirety of his properties to his elder daughters. He did not give any of the property to his younger daughter, Mani, who was crippled and thus could not walk well. However, the girl was well-learned and had mastered sorcery as well. She questioned her father about the partiality he displayed. He consoled her and said, "May all the land you set foot on be yours." However, Mani felt he mocked her about her disability. In a fury, she walked out of Periyatt and vanished.

Kelan, a local toddy tapper, was doing his daily chores on a coconut tree near a pond in the region of Kelangara when he caught sight of a divine girl near the river banks. However, she was gone by the time he climbed down the tree. A person named Edadan Maniyani passed that way, and Kelan shared what he saw. Just then, people from the Periyatt Nair Tharavadu came searching for the lost girl. They were shocked that a crippled girl had traveled from her house to Kelangara in such a short time! They arranged a prasna (branch of Hindu astrology), revealing that she had transformed into a Godly form. Legends say that since she turned into a Goddess at Kelangara, she was thus named Kelan Kulangara Bhagavathy.

The local deity of the Edatt region, Kundora Chamundi, along with Kelan Kulangara Bhagavathy, are said to have been in charge of the punishments and protection of the province. Most grievances were settled in the courts of these mother Goddesses.

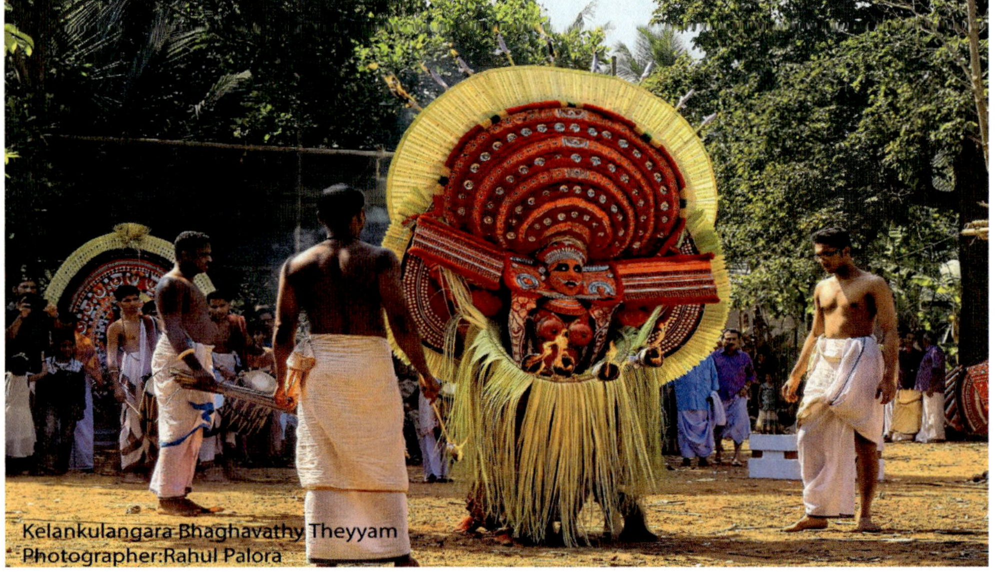

Kelankulangara Bhaghavathy Theyyam
Photographer:Rahul Palora

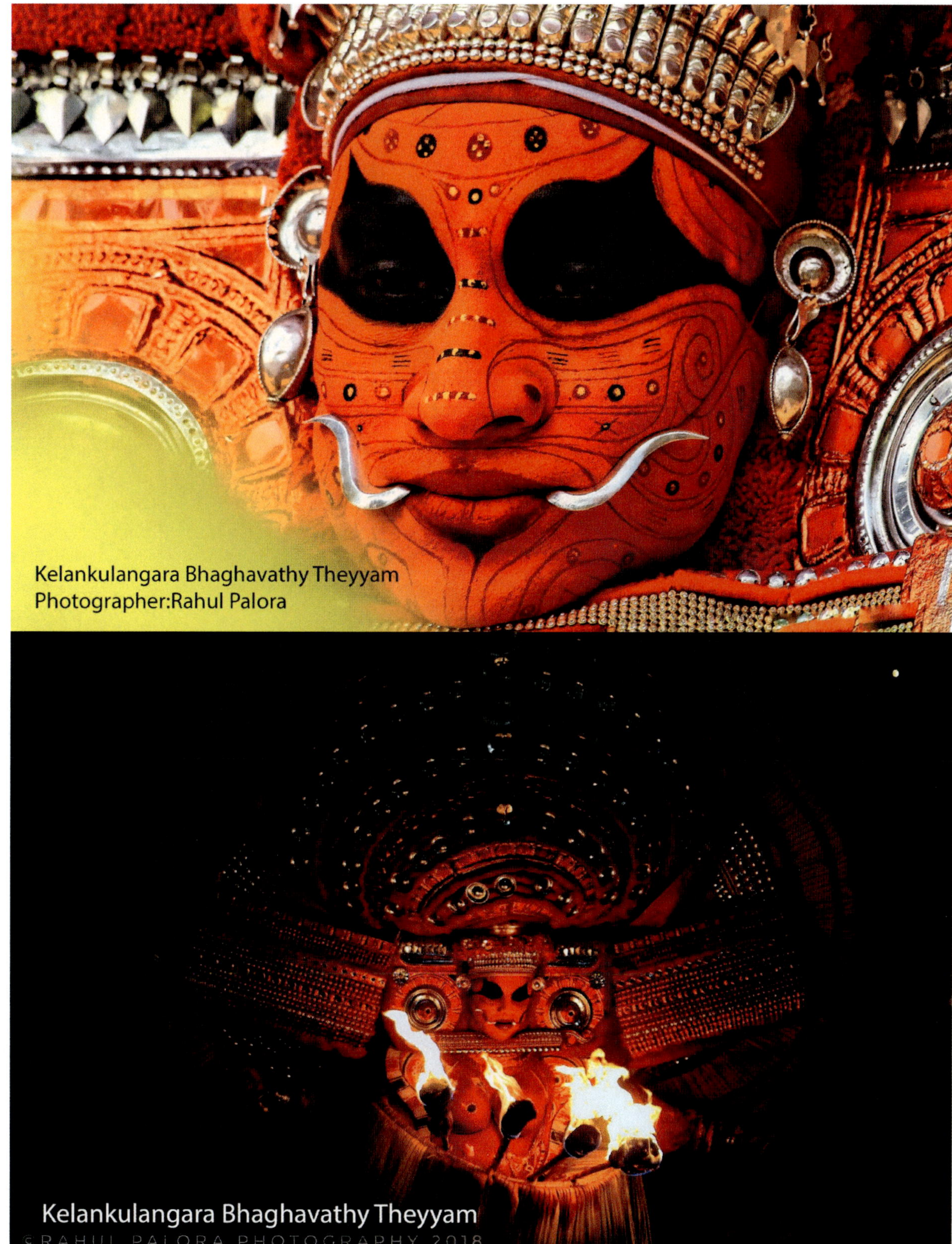

Kelankulangara Bhaghavathy Theyyam
Photographer:Rahul Palora

Kelankulangara Bhaghavathy Theyyam

Panayakkatt Bhagavathy and Kanangattu Bhagavathy Theyyam

Panayakkaattu Bhagavathy is the beloved Goddess of the Yadavas. She wore a burning torch and had elaborate makeup on her face. This story is similar to Kannangattu Bhagavathy.

The legend behind Panayakkattu Bhagavathy is related to the birth of Lord Krishna. Devaki was the sister of King Kamsa of Mathura. It was predicted that one of the sons of Devaki would kill Kamsa. Hence, the king jailed both Devaki and her husband, Vasudeva. Kamsa killed seven of her children, and to save their eighth, Vasudeva carried the child to Ambadi and pawned his son Krishna for Nandagopans and Yashoda's daughter. Nature helped him to accomplish this exchange of kids through many celestial incidents. Kamsa tried to kill the child despite knowing it was a girl. But when he tried to smash the child by holding its legs, the baby slipped from his hand, and Sri Bhagavathy appeared before him. The deity also revealed that the slayer of Kamsa was already born at Ambadi. This Goddess, who divulged the whereabouts of Krishna, came to be known as *Kanangattu Bhagavathy*. The name is believed to be a shortened form of '*Kannane Kaatiya Bhagavathy*,' which means the Goddess who showed Krishna. When exchanged with Krishna at Ambadi, the Goddess's form is known as Panayangattu Bhagavathy. This name reminds us that the girl child was a pawn (Panayam).

Some scholars suggest that the very concept of Panayakkatt Bhagavathy is that of Kannaki, a legendary Tamil woman who forms the central character of the Tamil epic Silapathikaram, which is very popular in South India. The male character Kovalan left Pandya Street after pledging the anklets of Kannaki to Kavanthitiyal of Ayambadi. The deity's name, 'Panaya,' which means 'to pledge,' is derived from that pledge. Another legend is that the form of Goddess Kali, which jumped out of the third eye of Lord Shiva to annihilate the evil Asuras, is what turned the Bhagavathy here.

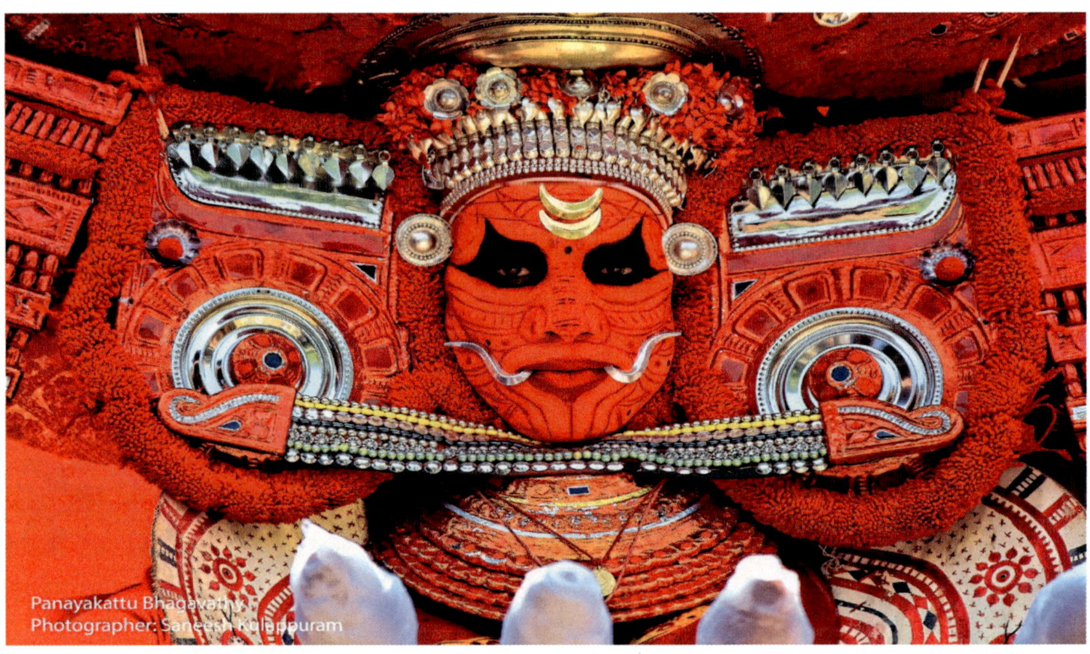
Panayakattu Bhagavathy
Photographer: Saneesh Kulappuram

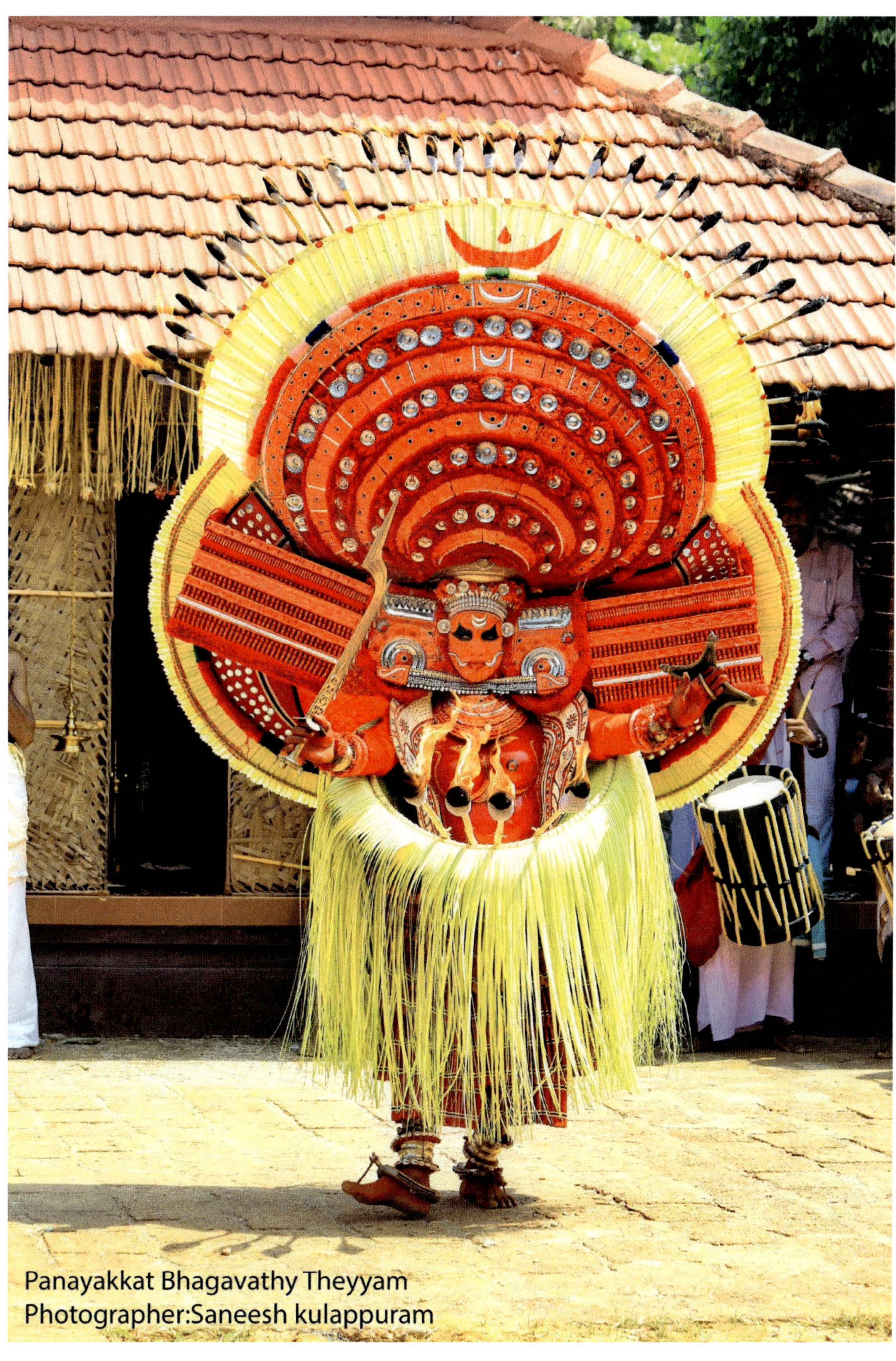
Panayakkat Bhagavathy Theyyam
Photographer:Saneesh kulappuram

Chooliyar Bhagavathy Theyyam

Chooliyar Bhagavathy Theyyam, also known as *Shuliyar Bhagavathy,* is a form of the Goddess who appeared from the third eye of Lord Shiva, yielding the spear to kill the demon *Karthaveerasuran,* who attempted to set fire to the granaries of *Thrukkanyalappan*.

The primordial Goddess Adi Parashakti was attracted to Mahad Guru, a devotee of Goddess Mookambika, and she accompanied him. When she reached this location, the Goddess was stunned by the serene village and expressed her desire to be invoked and settled there. The Goddess was self-begotten as a stone idol close to where her devotee was meditating. Therefore, Chooliyar Bhagavathy is considered another form of the self-begotten Goddess Durga. She is the protector of 96 towns sprawling across the west to east. Chooliyar Bhagavathy bears flambeau on her waist belt. Chooliyar Bhagavathy is worshipped using ashes and is considered the family deity of *Padmavedankar*. Her hair is adorned with ghee lamps and flambeau on her waist belt, and she has several expressions and names in different regions.

Chooliyar Bhagavathi came to this world to ease all grievances, the Goddess of all arts and learning and mother of the three *gunas* (Qualities): *Tamas* (apathy), *Rajas* (passion), and *Sattva* (harmony), and is one of the trinity of supreme divinity. According to ancient legend, Lord *Parameshvara* fired a flower arrow to point to the spot when the Goddess requested an abode. Chooliyar Bhagavathy is the sixth of the six *Paradevathas*.

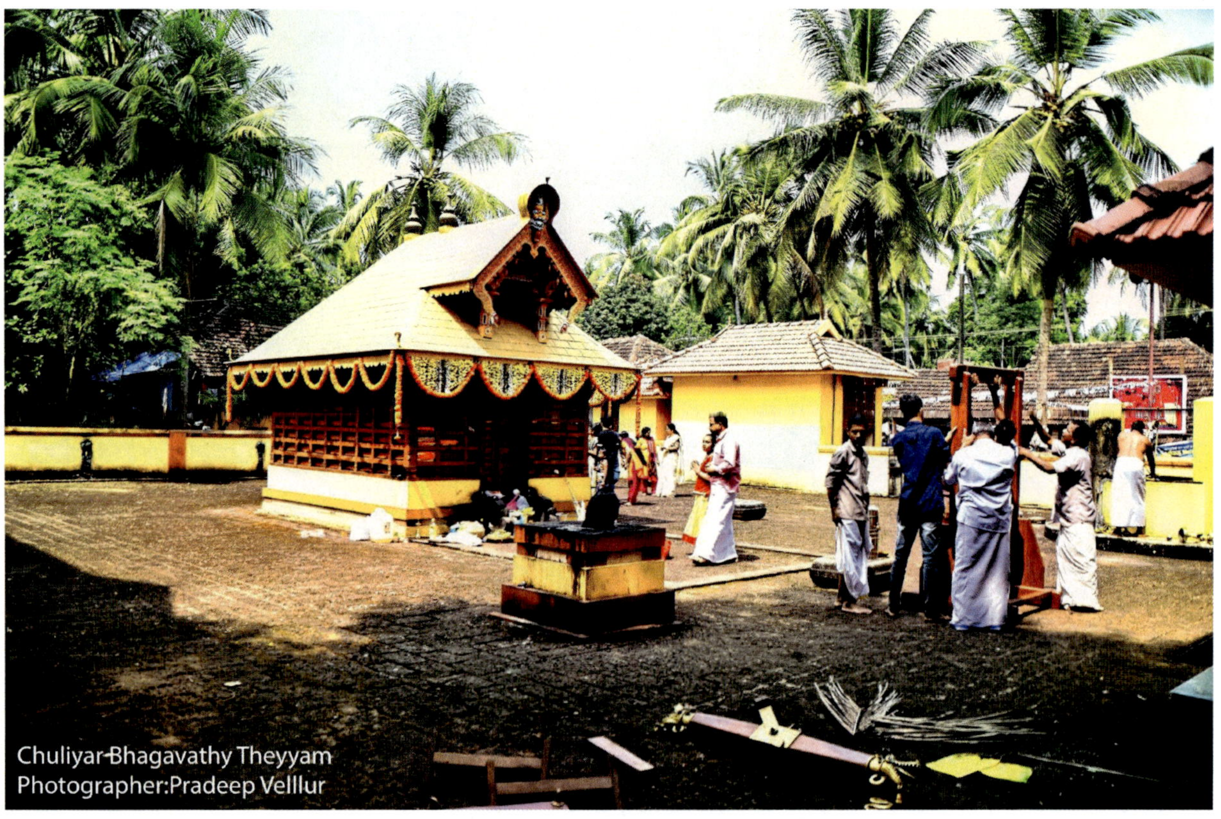

Chuliyar-Bhagavathy Theyyam
Photographer:Pradeep Vellur

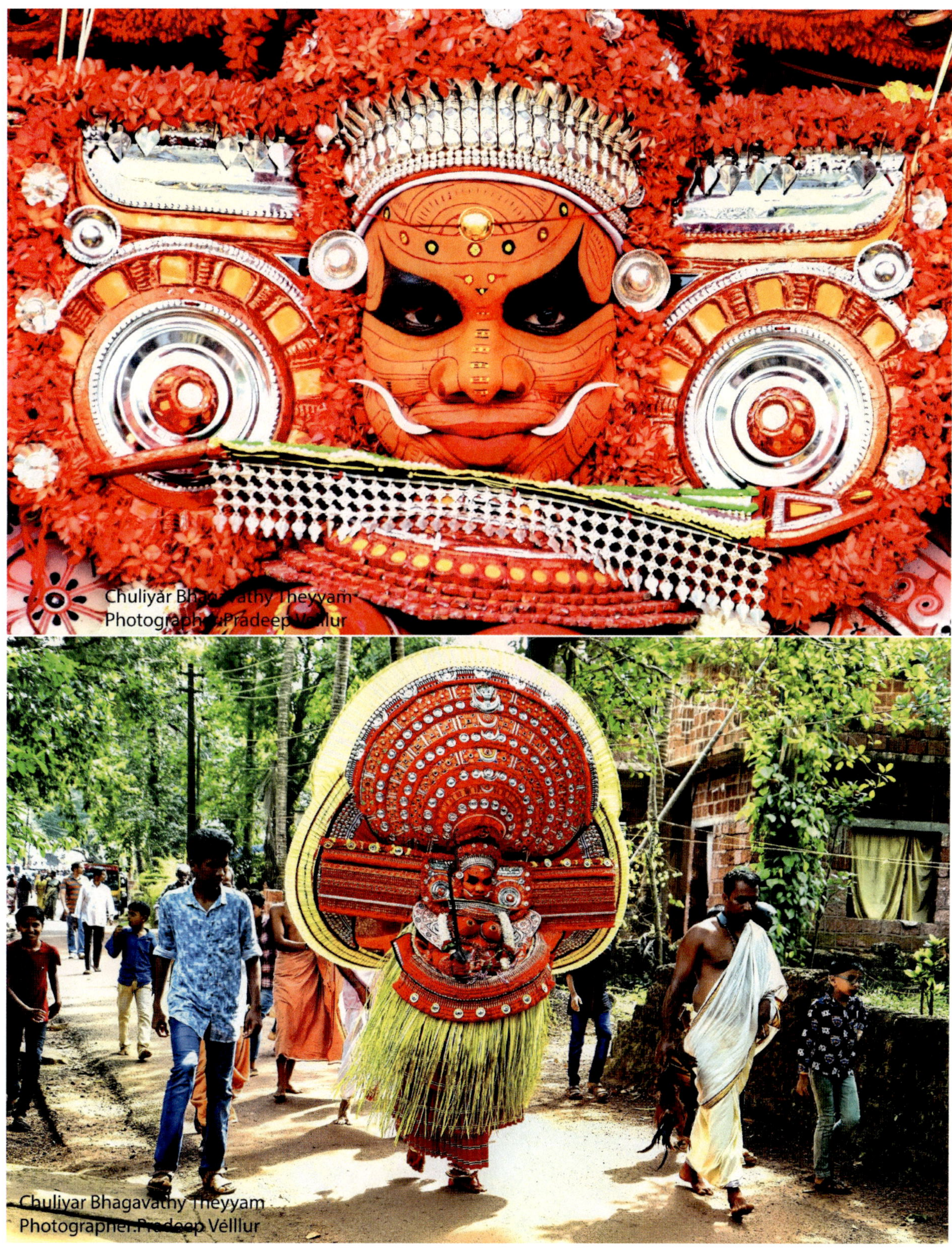

Chuliyar Bhagavathy Theyyam
Photographer:Pradeep Vellur

Chuliyar Bhagavathy Theyyam
Photographer:Pradeep Vellur

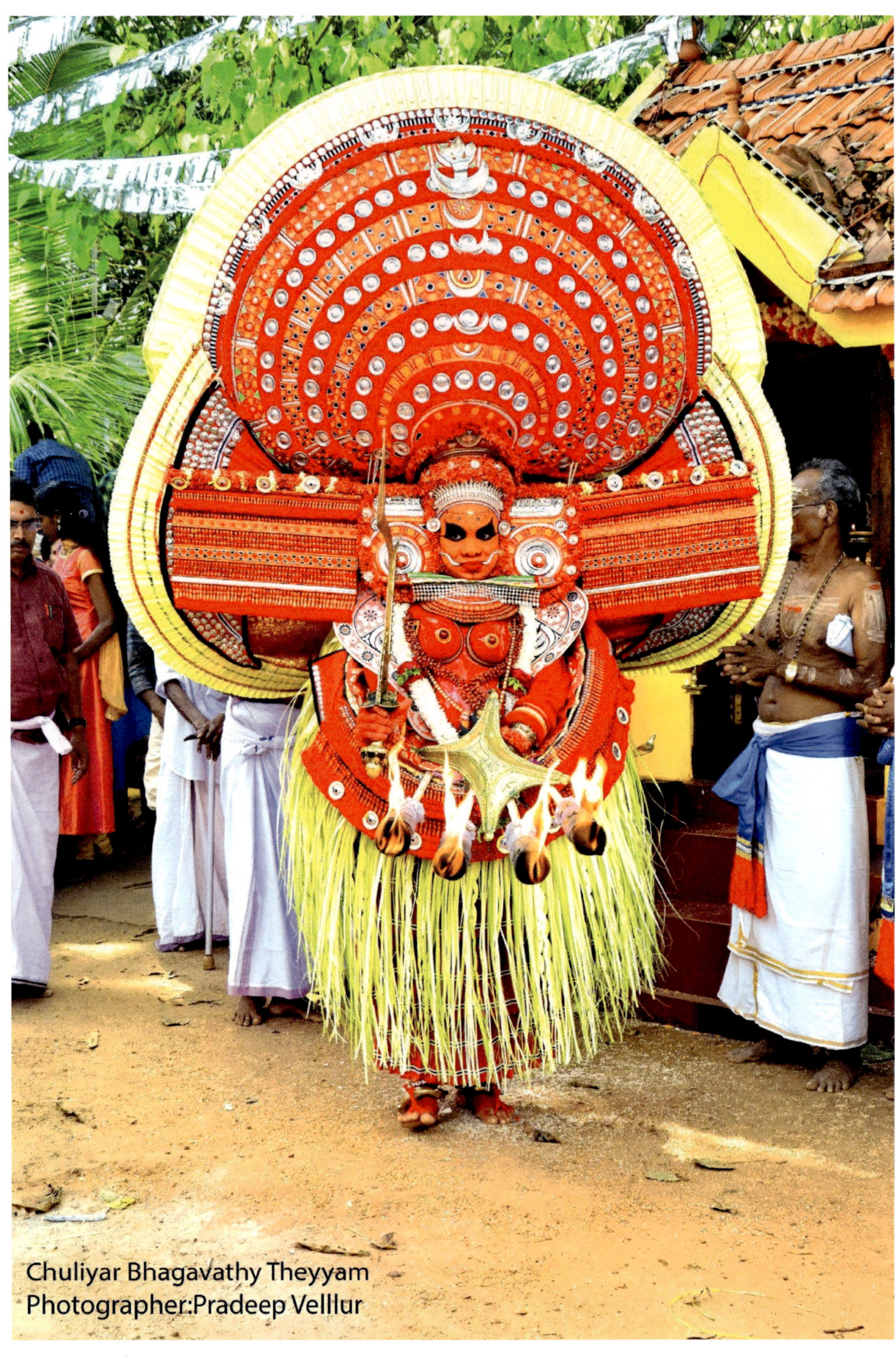

Chuliyar Bhagavathy Theyyam
Photographer:Pradeep Velllur

Padarkulangara Bhagavathy and Cheralath Bhagavathy Theyyam

Amrita, or the elixir of eternal life, appeared when the *Devas* uprooted Mount *Mandara* and used it as the churning rod to stir the *palazhi* (Ocean of Milk). The devilish Asuras grabbed the elixir, frightening the Devas. Drinking the elixir would give the Asuras an upper hand over the Devas. Hence, Devas sought help from *Mahavishnu*. He decided to take the form of a beautiful damsel called *Mohini*. The form of Mohini is the *Padarkulangara Bhagavathy* Theyyam. The enchanting beauty deceived the Asuras and brought the elixir back to the hands of Devas. When Mohini tricked the Asuras and snatched the elixir from them, the Asuras realized it and started to chase her towards heaven. Suddenly Mohini changed her enticing expression and turned into the fierce Maha Kali. Mohini, with the ferocious look of Maha Kali, became *Cheralath Bhagavathy* and resided at *Kaniyada Cheralath Kaavu*. The ascended location of this Bhagavathy is at *Kinavoor Cheralath Kaavu* and worshipped as *Kandathilamma* of *Aalinkeezhil Bhagavathy Kaavu*.

The Vannan community performs Cheralath Bhagavathy Theyyam. They believed she listened to their very first prayer and gave them answers. There are tales of Cheralath Bhagavathy resurrecting a dead elephant and moving it to a sanctuary.

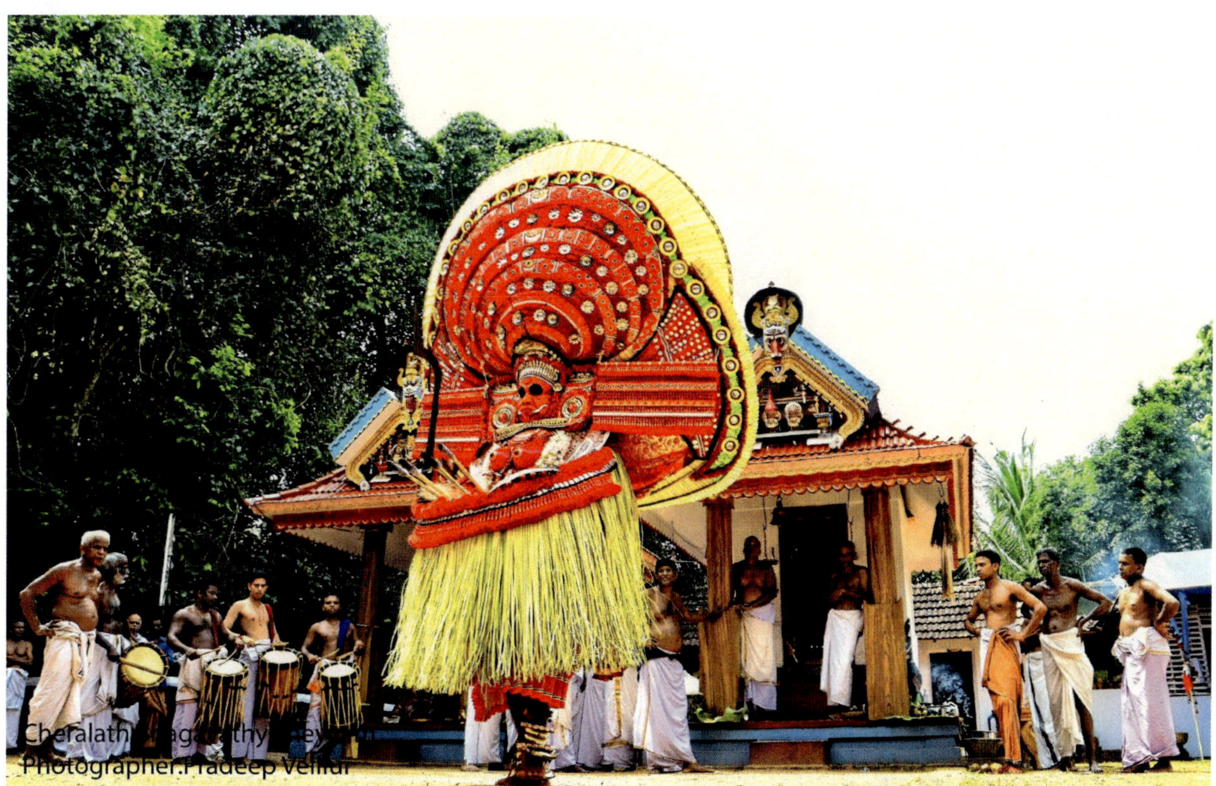

Cheralath Bhagavathy Theyyam
Photographer:Pradeep Vellur

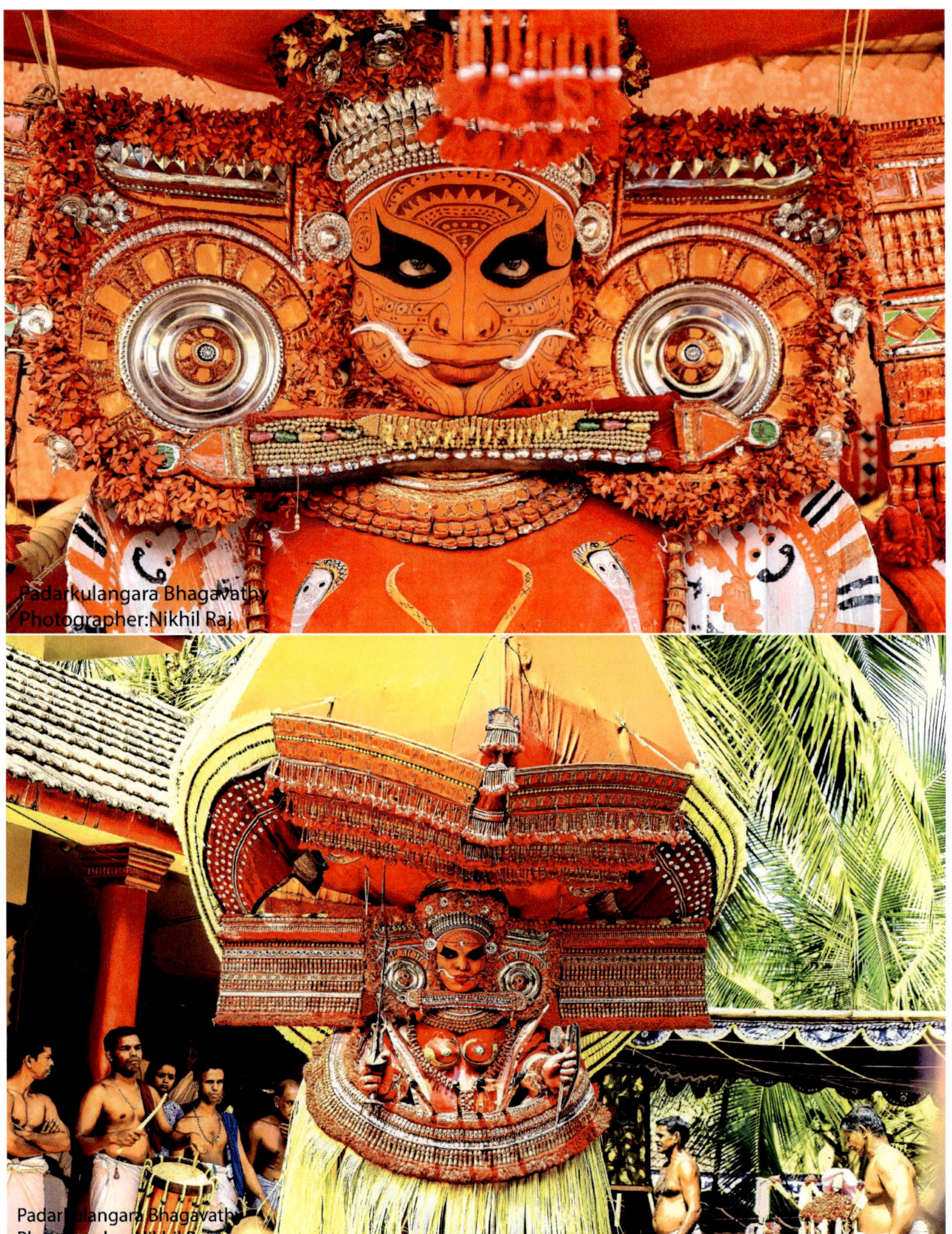

Padarkulangara Bhagavathy
Photographer:Nikhil Raj

Padarkulangara Bhagavathy
Photographer:Nikhil Raj

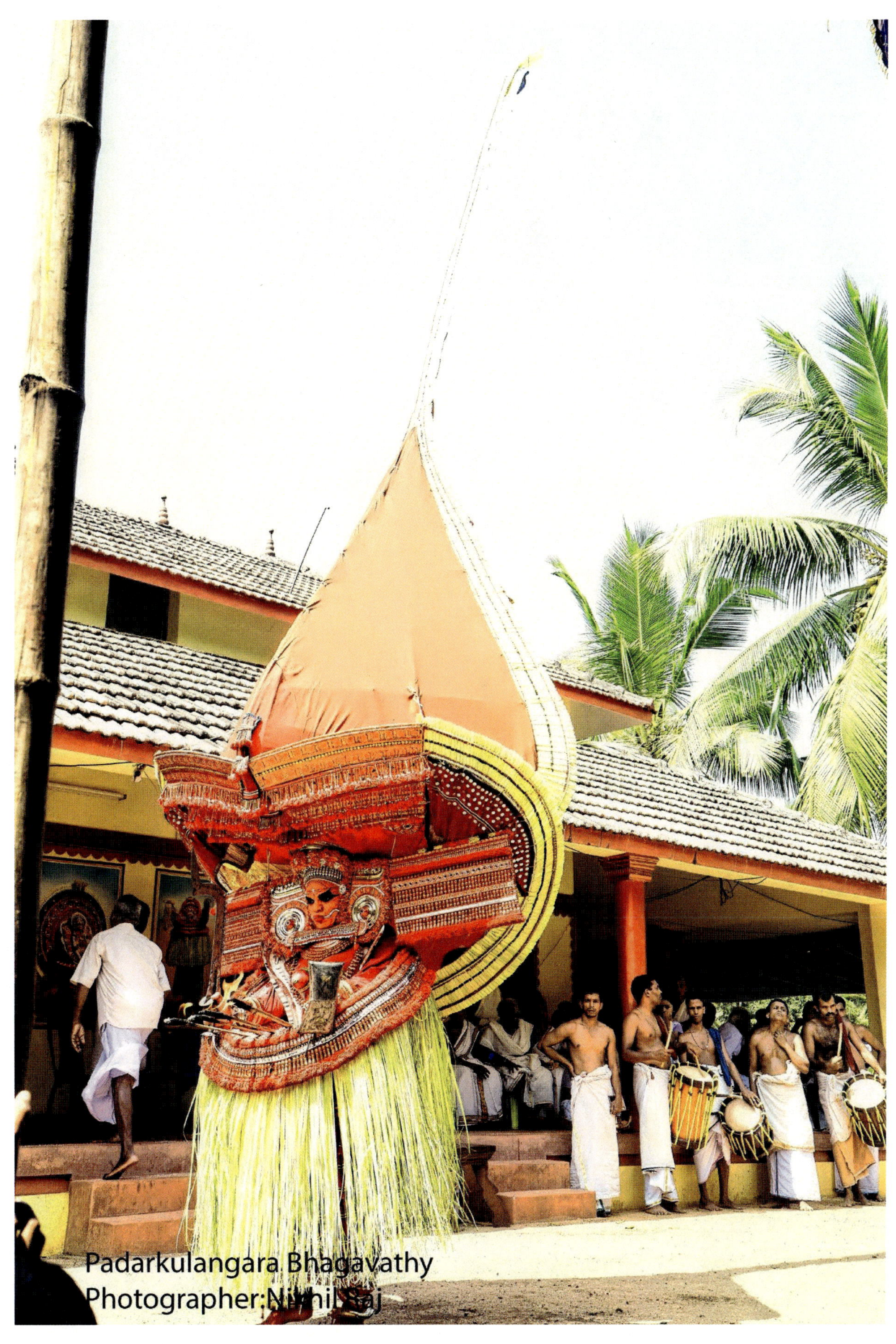

Padarkulangara Bhagavathy
Photographer:Nikhil Raj

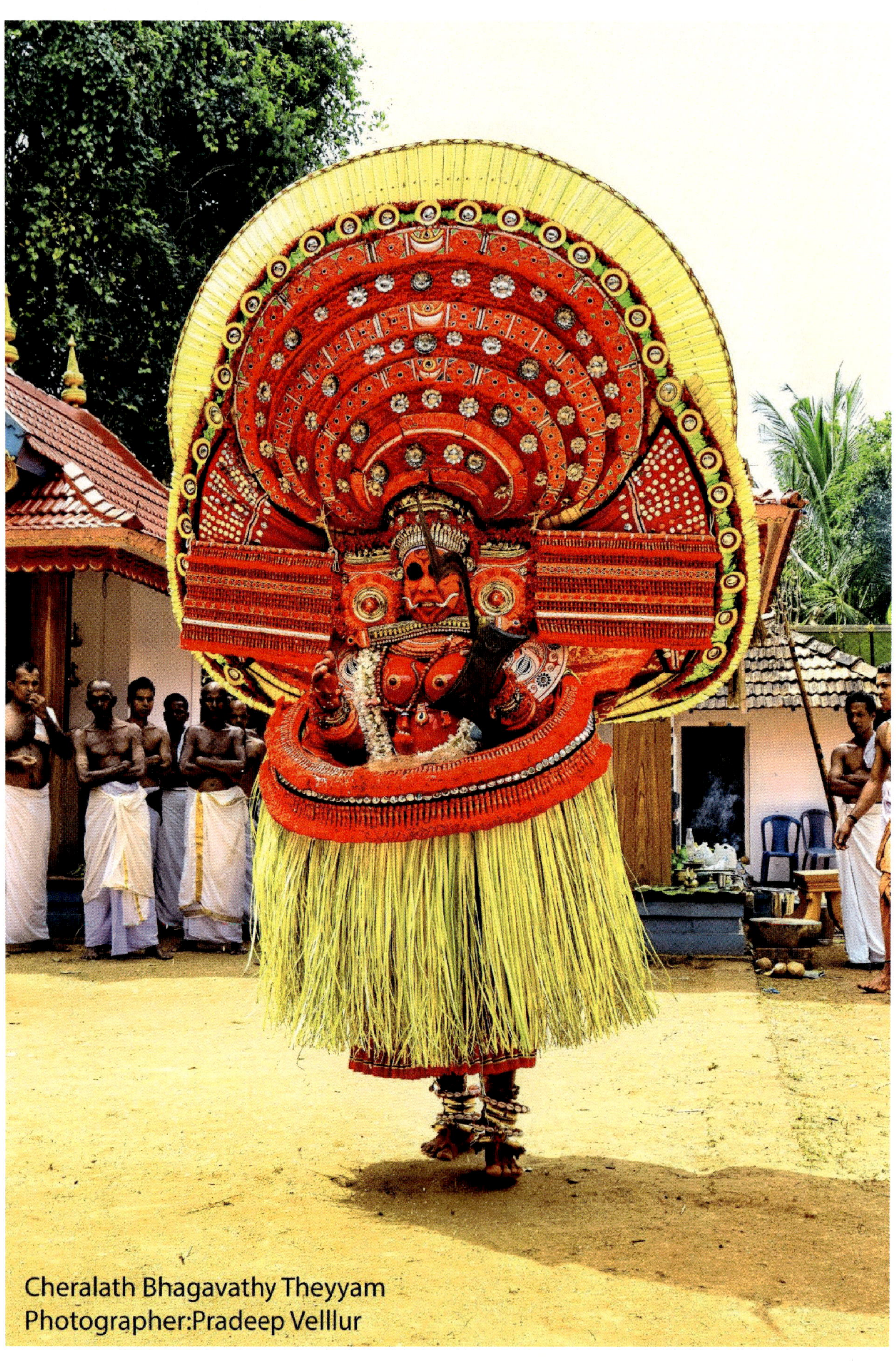
Cheralath Bhagavathy Theyyam
Photographer:Pradeep Velllur

Manathana Kali Theyyam

Kali and Chamundi are two deities associated with blood and death. They are also known as 'Rana-Devatas.' Usually, the Goddesses who took part in the ongoing war between the Devas and Asuras (Gods and demons) are portrayed in the Theyyams. Though they are responsible for maintaining other *Dharmas* (duties), they are more concentrated on war affairs. Most of the mother Goddesses are based on the concept of Kali.

The legend of Goddess Kali is related to the fierce Asura called Darika. After a long penance to Brahma, this Asura obtained immunity from death by anyone. Darika turned arrogant after getting this boon from Brahma. He started to ridicule the Devas and prominent hermits. Finally, the Devas appealed to Lord Shiva, who created Kali from his third eye. Lord Shiva armed Kali with eighteen special weapons and also assigned *Adi Kailasa,* the *Betala* or the phantom, to be her vehicle. The war between Kali and the Asura lasted seven days and seven nights. It is said that the Darika had strength that equaled that of many elephants. But Darika began losing his power on the first day, which diminished until the seventh day. On the eighth day, Kali sucked the blood out of the Asura at twilight. She was enraged even after killing Darika. Lord Shiva consoled her and sent her to earth. Her abode is located at the northern side of the entrance of *Nidumbram Madappura* under sacred trees. Madappura is the abode of the deity Sree Muthappan. Kali Theyyam is also performed at Madappuras.

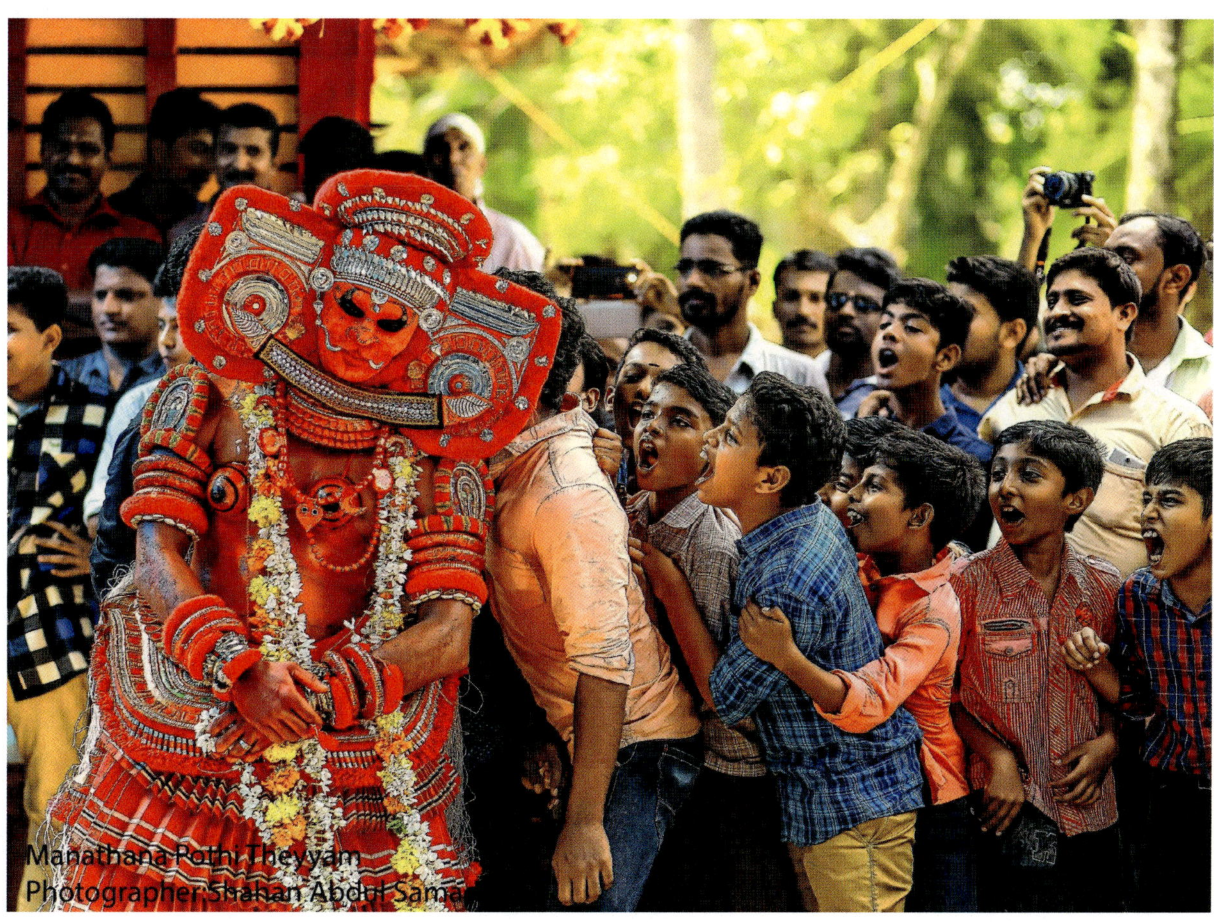

Manathana Pothi Theyyam
Photographer:Shahan Abdul Sama

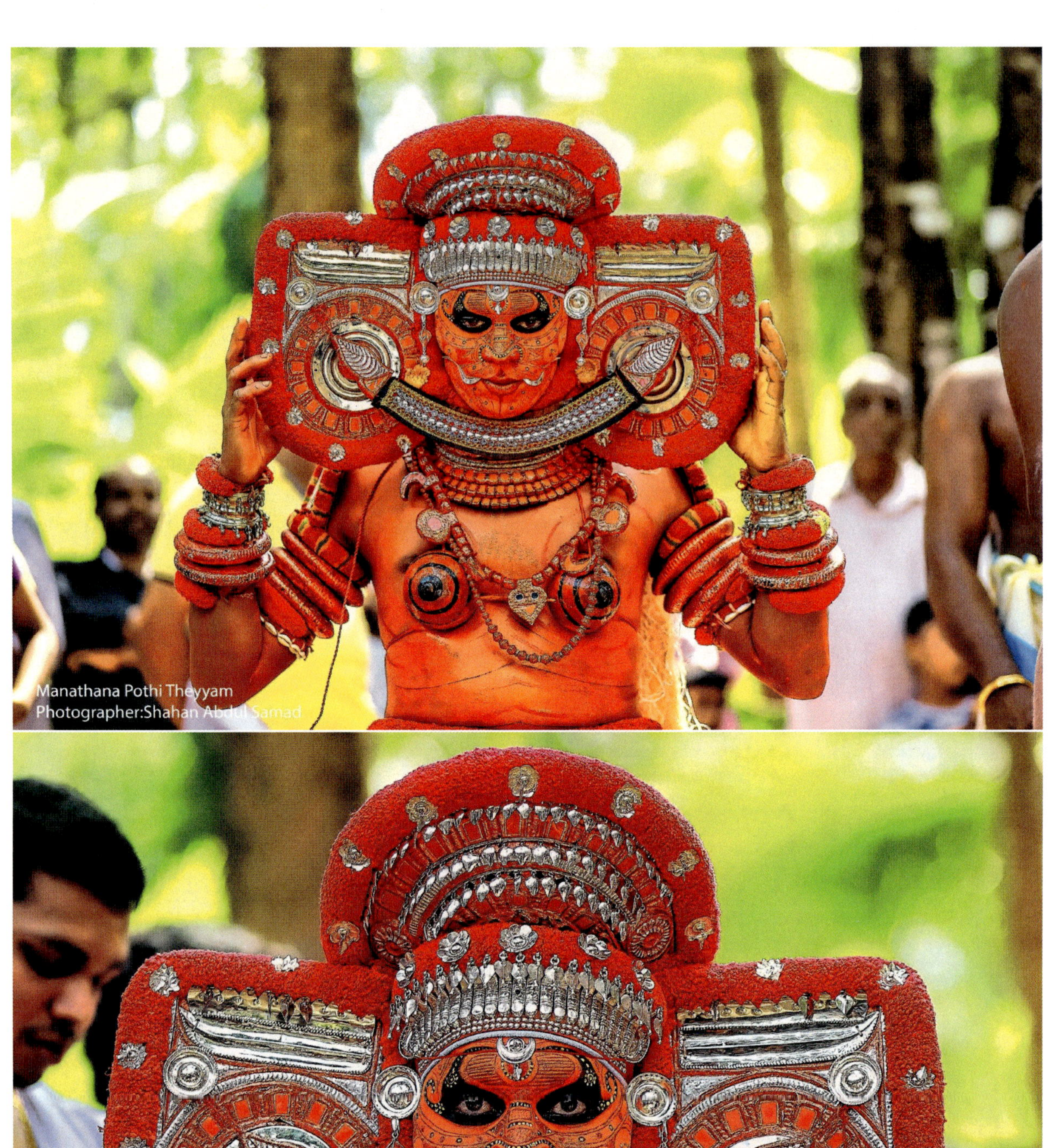

Manathana Pothi Theyyam
Photographer:Shahan Abdul Samad

Manathana Pothi Theyyam
Photographer:Shahan Abdul Samad

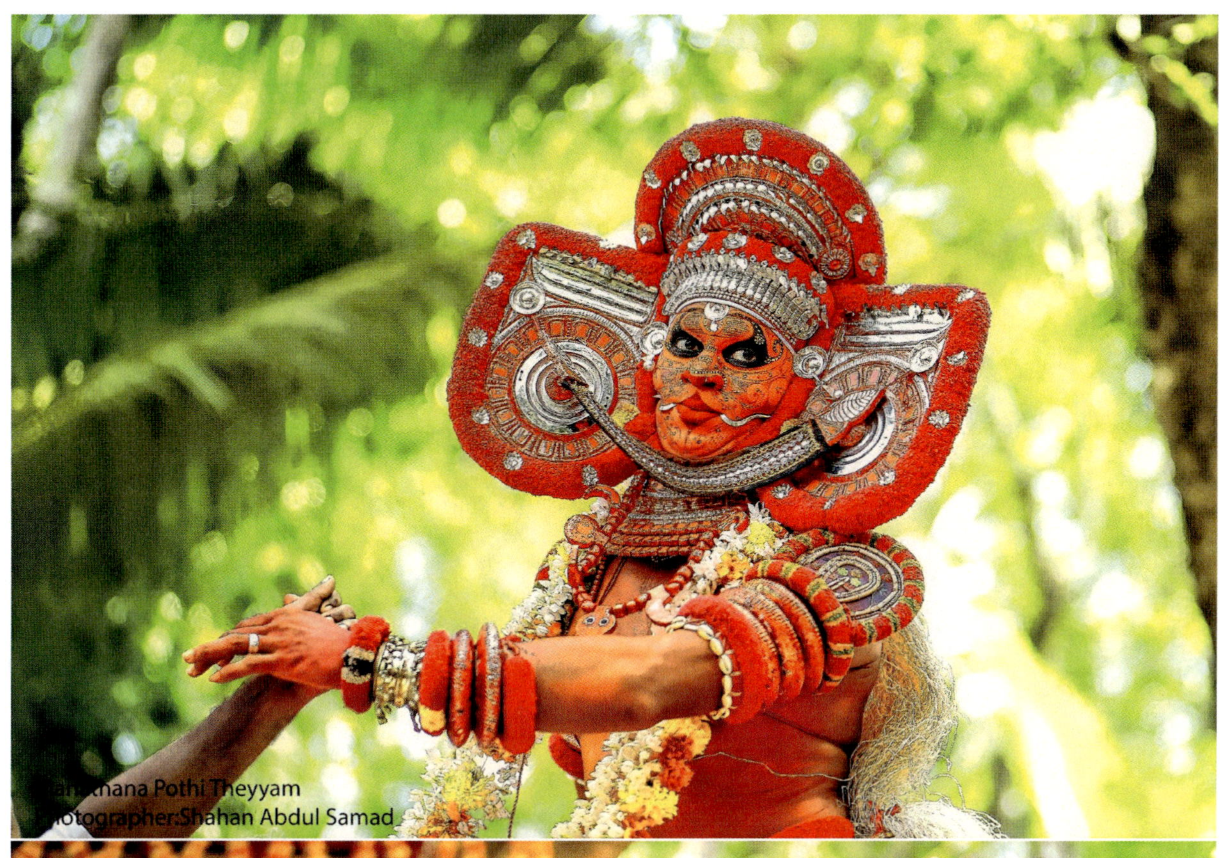

Manathana Pothi Theyyam
Photographer:Shahan Abdul Samad

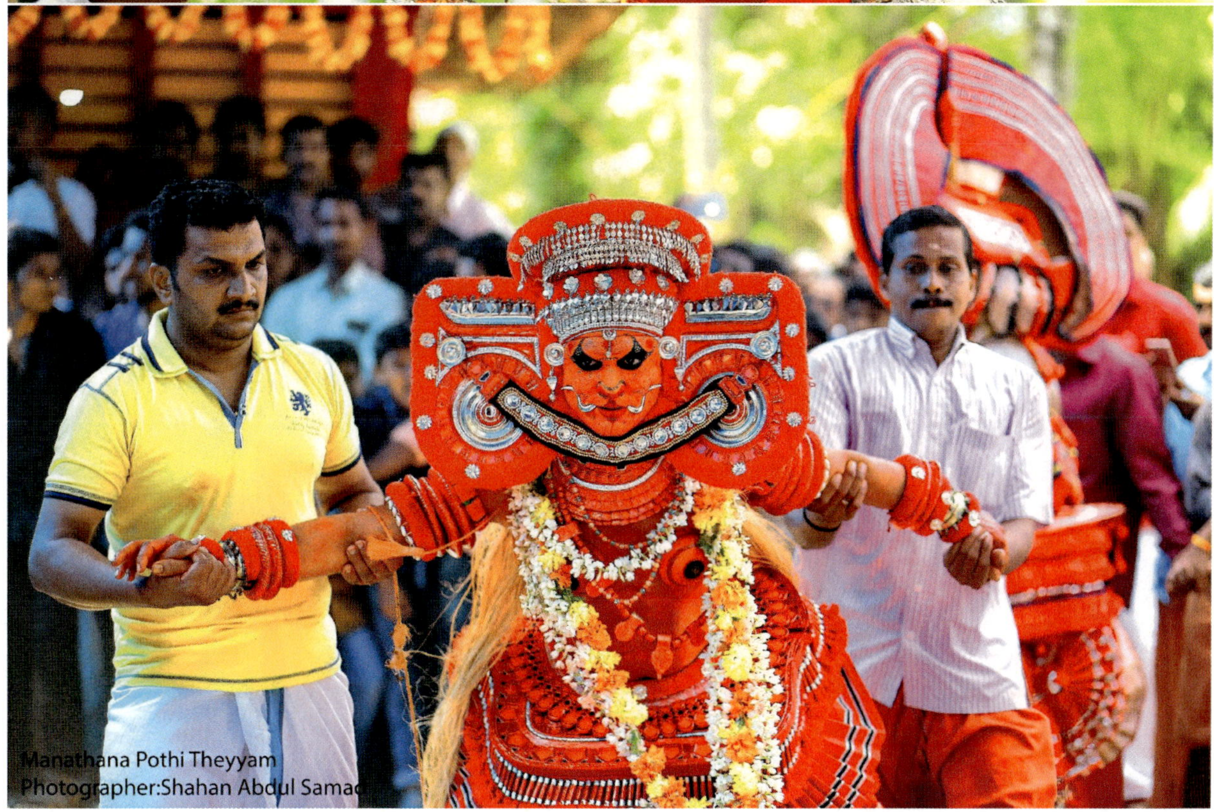

Manathana Pothi Theyyam
Photographer:Shahan Abdul Samad

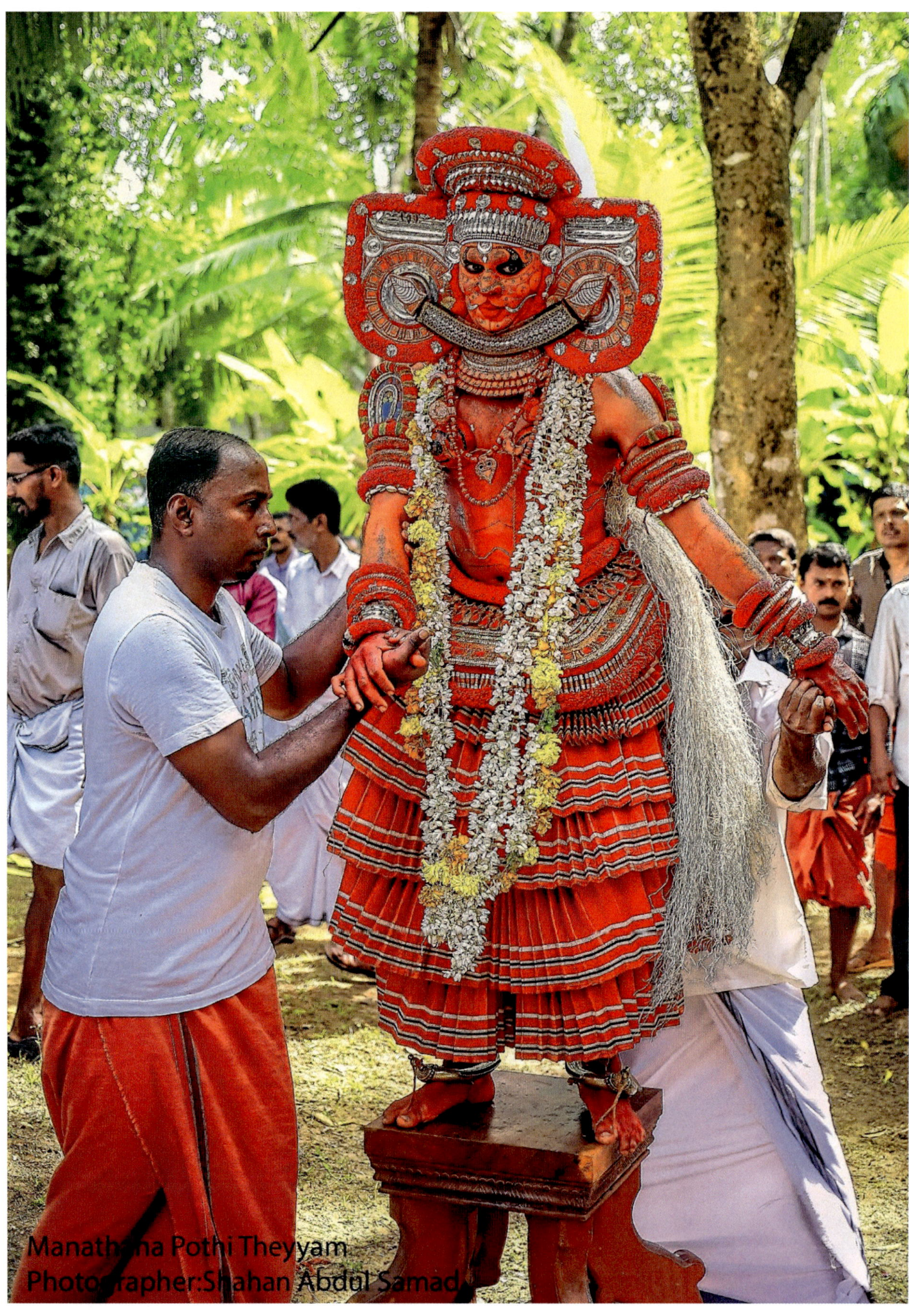

Manathana Pothi Theyyam
Photographer:Shahan Abdul Samad

Mecheri Chamundi Theyyam

(Similar story to Raktha Chamundi)

Mecheri Chamundi is another form of the deity known as *Rakthabeejeswari.* It is believed that she is the daughter of *Kallankara Chamundi*. The myth is associated with the bloodshed that occurred in the ancient wars.

Rakthabeejasura is the son of *Krodhavathi*. During the war between the Asura brothers *Sumbha* and *Nisumbha*, and *Rakthabeejasura* fought with the Goddess *Chandika*. Several Asuras started to originate from each drop of his blood, which got shed in the fight. This multiplication trick enraged the Goddess, and a figure emerged from her forehead. The figure had an undulating tongue and a horrific black face. It sucked every drop of blood from the Asura and prevented them from replicating. Therefore, she is named after *Rakthabeejeswari* or *Raktha Chamundi* (literally Bloody Chamundi).

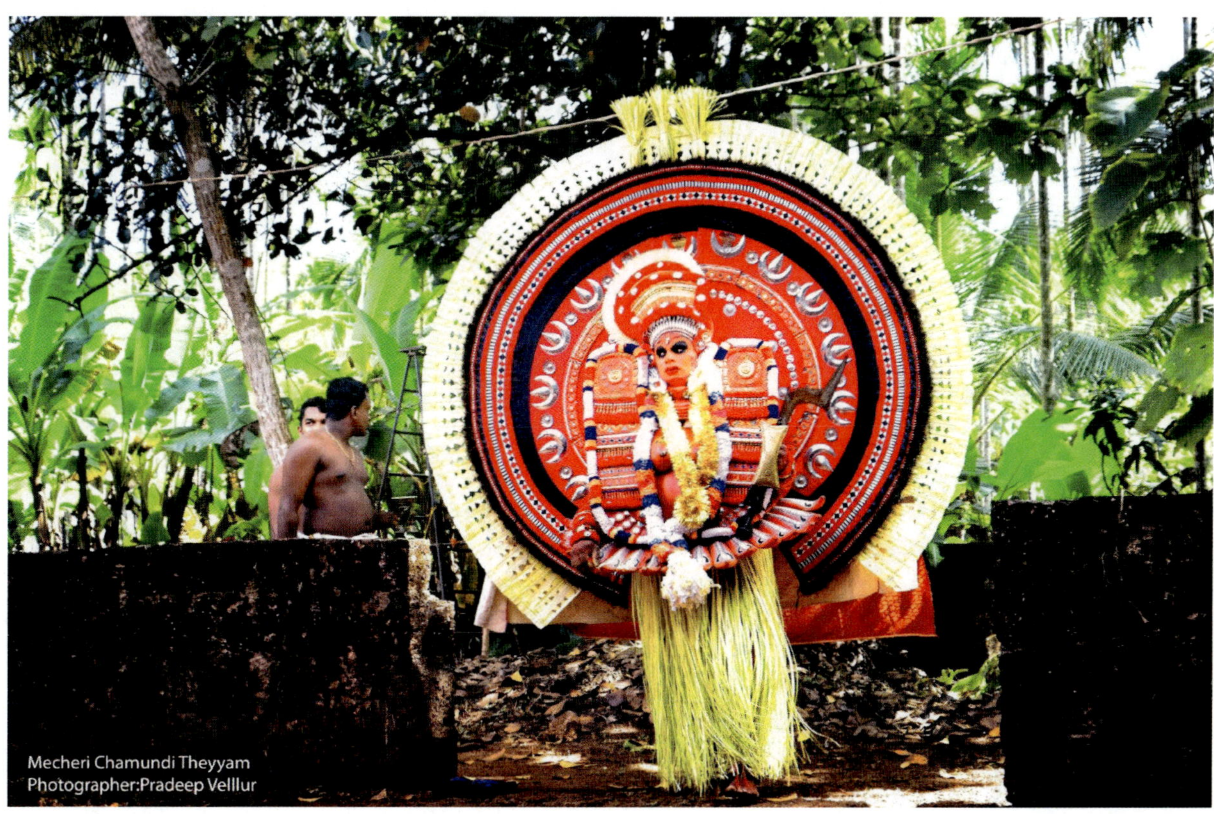

Mecheri Chamundi Theyyam
Photographer:Pradeep Velllur

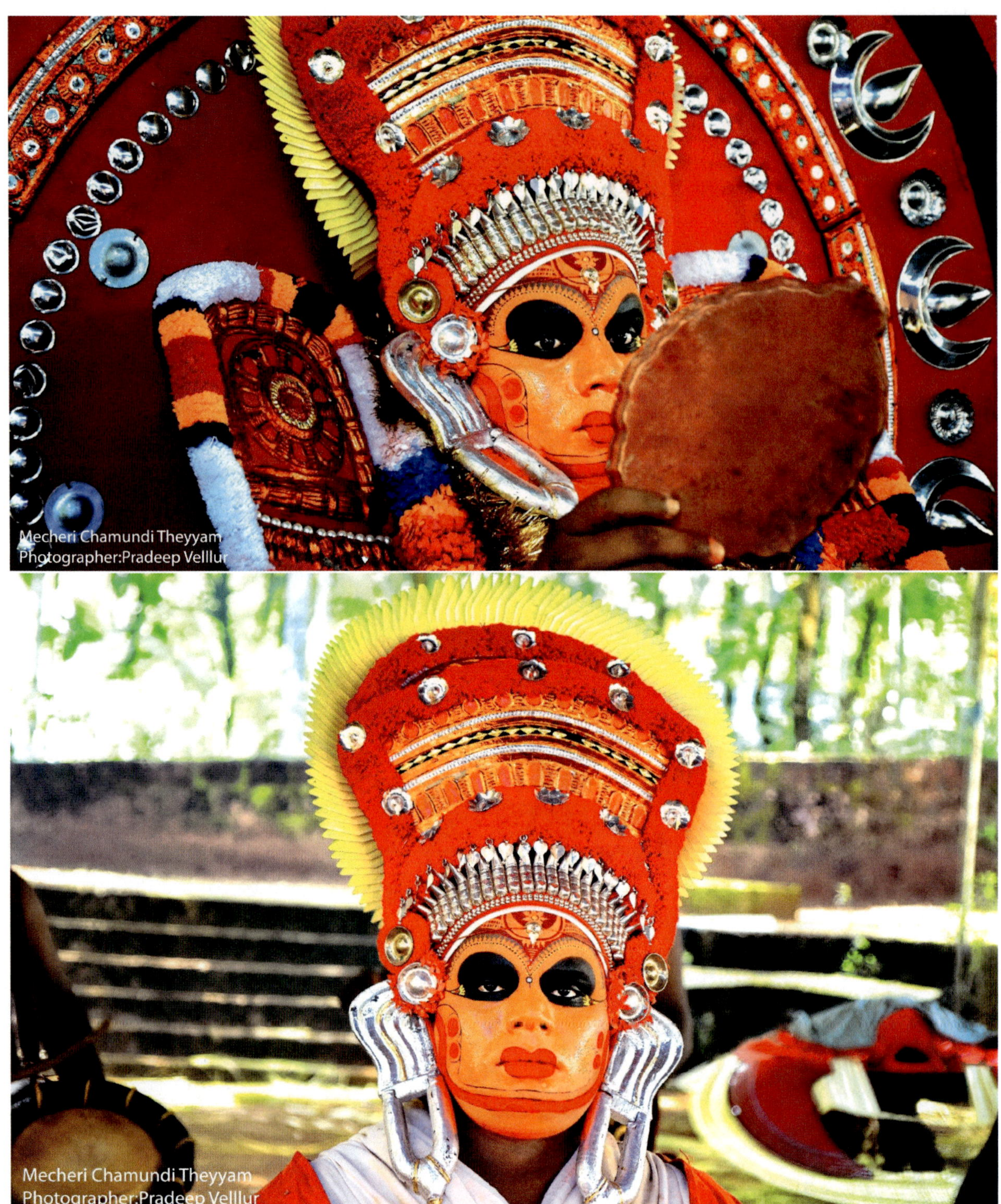

Mecheri Chamundi Theyyam
Photographer:Pradeep Velllur

Mecheri Chamundi Theyyam
Photographer:Pradeep Velllur

Kammadam Bhagavathi Theyyam

Kammadam kavu is the largest kavu (shrine) in North Kerala, surrounded by a semi-evergreen forest of around 56 Acres. This sacred forest is rich in biodiversity. The supreme deity *Dhandyanganath Bhagavathy* is also known as *Kammadath-Amma,* literally the mother of Kammadam.

As per the legends, the Goddess was resting on top of a large rock in the woods. Meethaladukkam Narayanan Namboodiri, who belonged to the Madhuram Kaipathillam (a higher caste family of priests), tried to invoke her. The Goddess started to descend beneath the earth, and Namboodiri couldn't stop her. Hence, only a part of the Goddess is elevated.

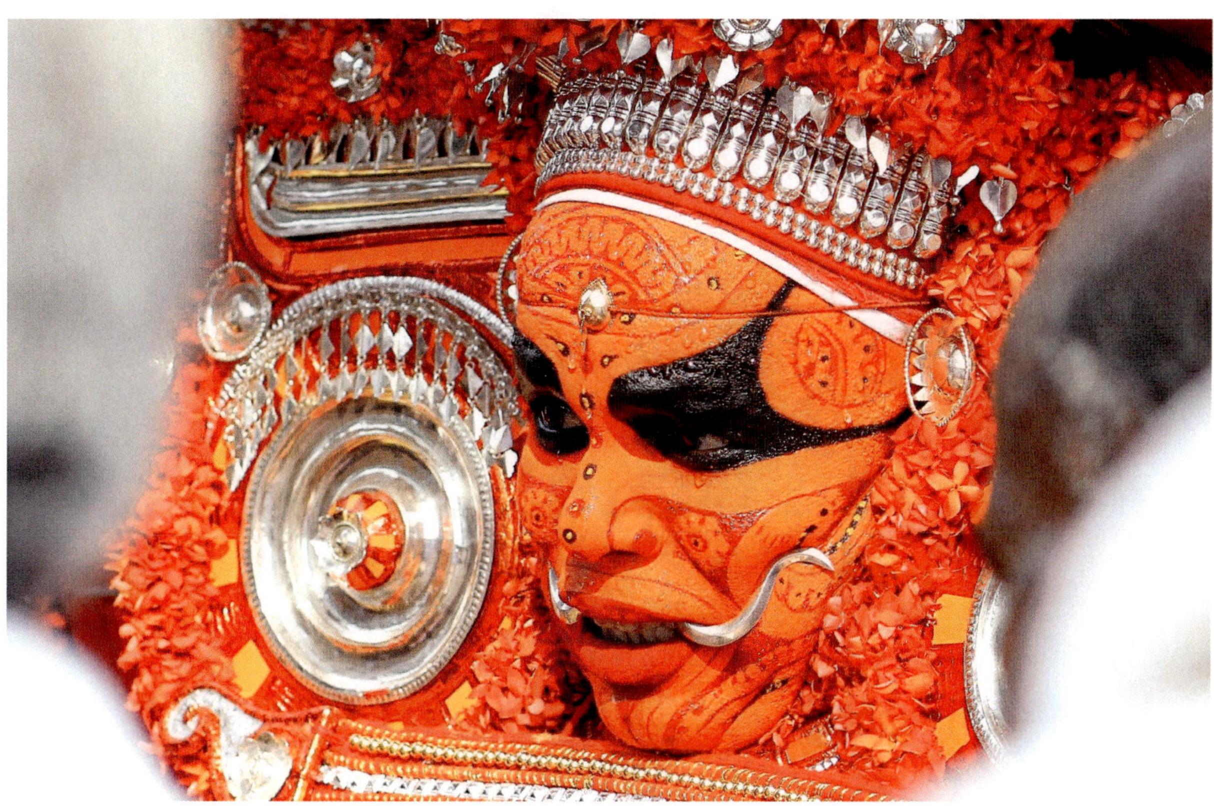

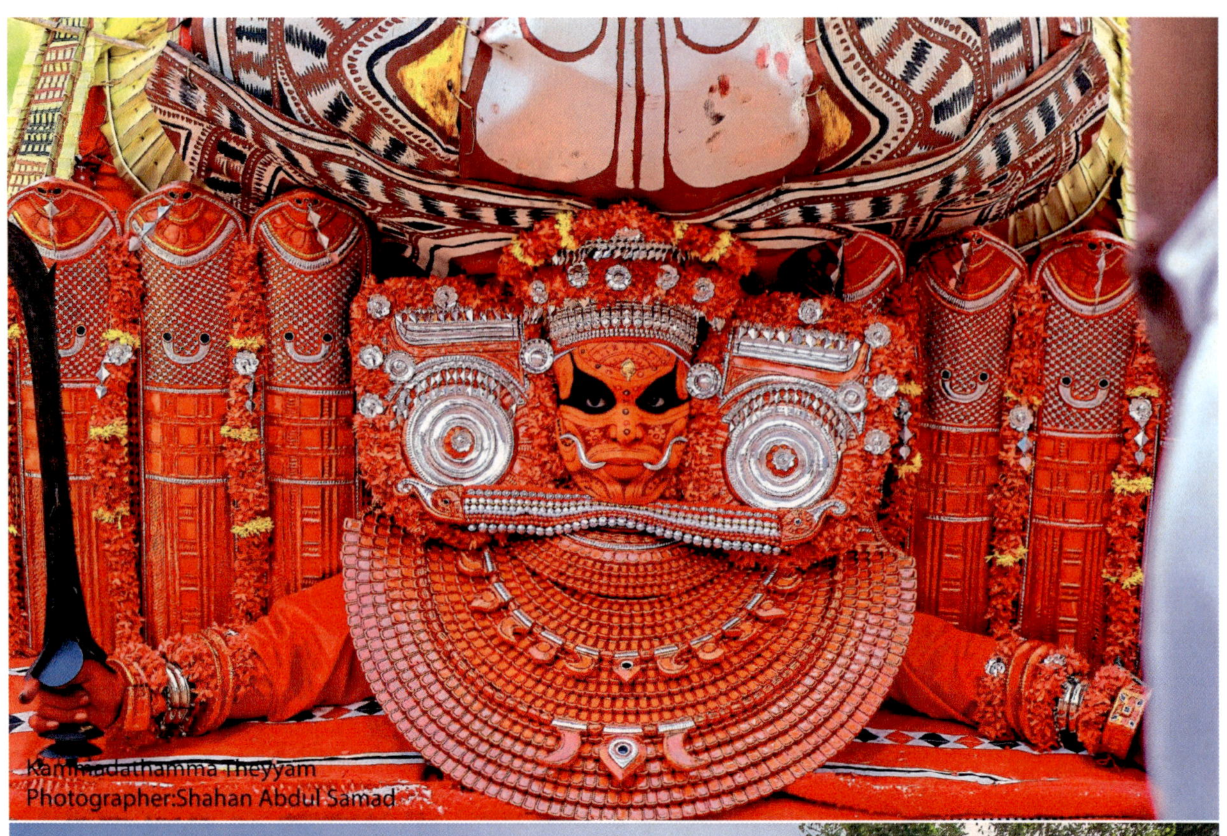

Kammadathamma Theyyam
Photographer:Shahan Abdul Samad

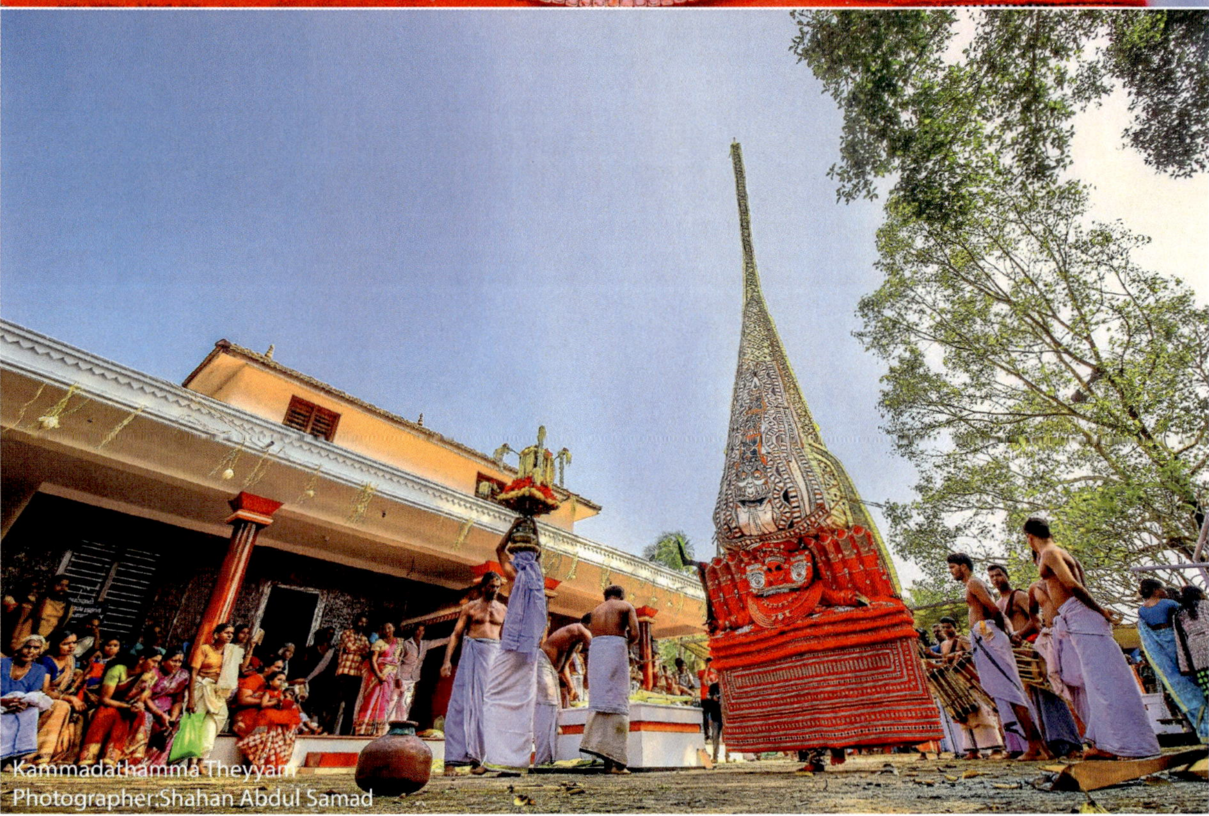

Kammadathamma Theyyam
Photographer:Shahan Abdul Samad

Chuzhali Bhagavathi Theyyam

Chuzhali Bhagavathi is the tutelary deity of Chuzhali Swaroopam (dynasty). Chuzhali Bhagavathi is believed to have come to the highlands accompanying Goddess *Annapoorna* in a *Marakalam* (a small boat made of wood). Chuzhali happens to be the principal abode of this Goddess; therefore, she is named after Chuzhali.

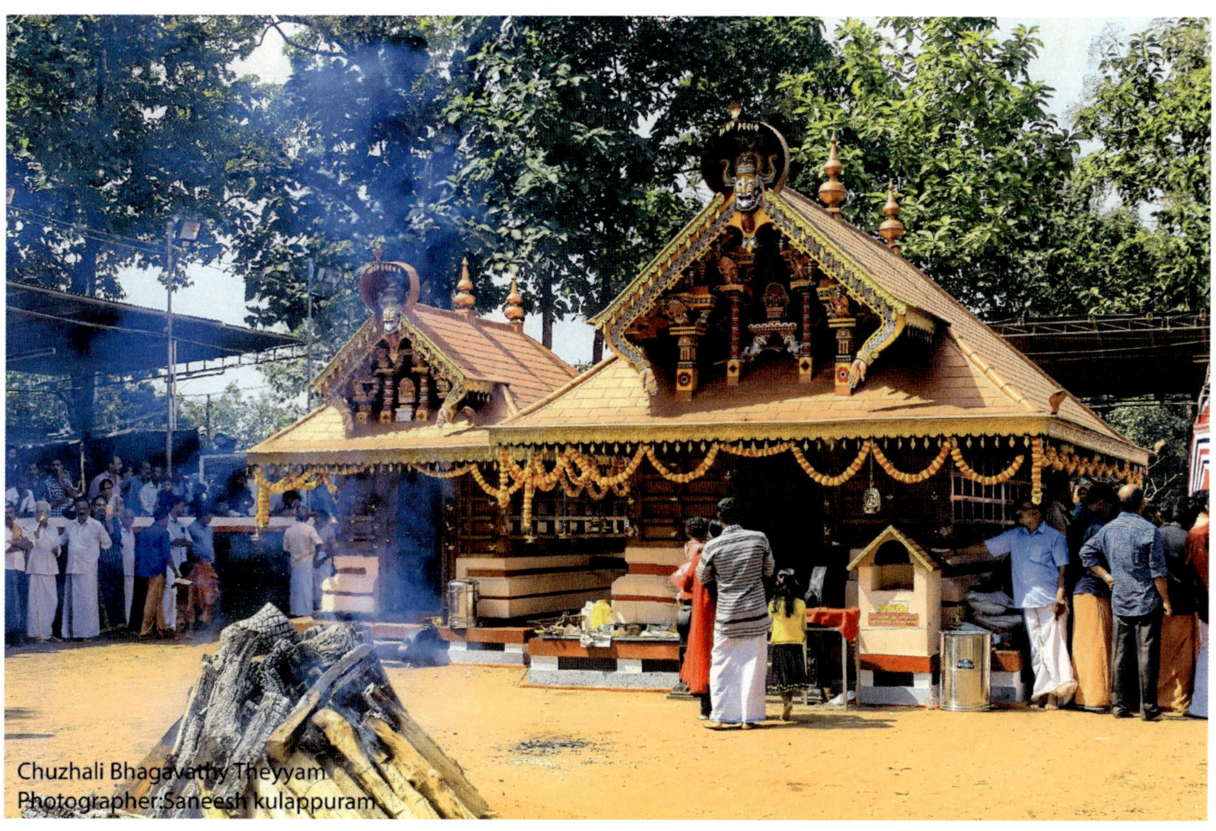

Chuzhali Bhagavathy Theyyam
Photographer:Saneesh kulappuram

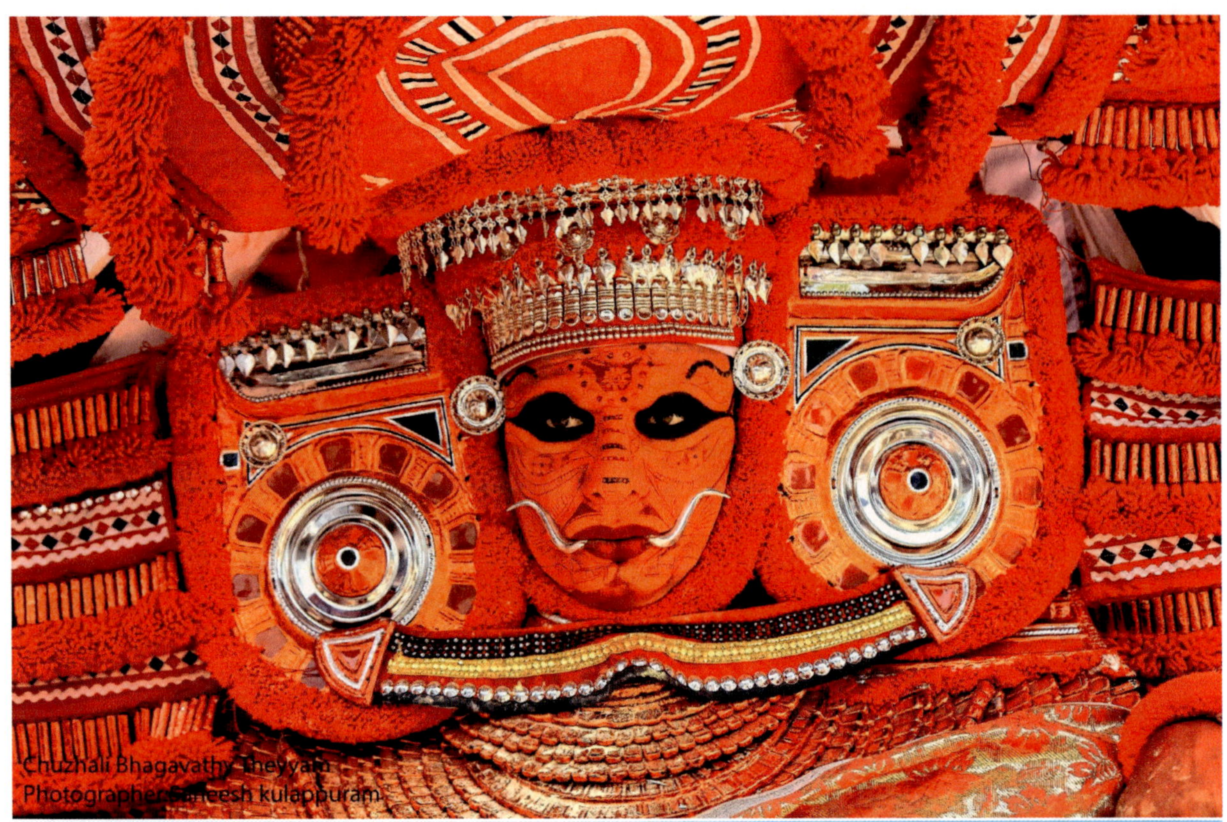

Chuzhali Bhagavathy Theyyam
Photographer:Saneesh kulappuram

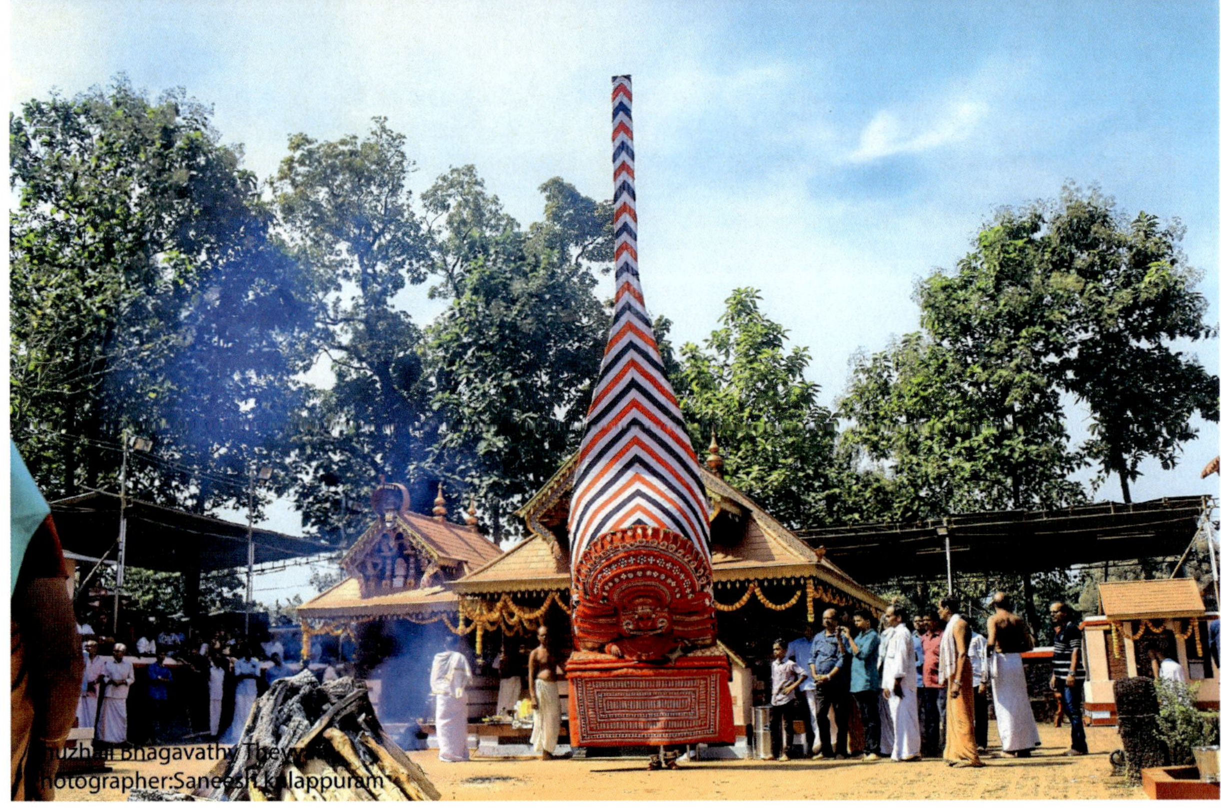

uzhali Bhagavathy Theyy
hotographer:Saneesh kulappuram

Vayanattu Kulavan Theyyam

Goddess Parvathi was concerned about Lord Shiva's alcoholism. She wanted to know the source of the liquor Lord Shiva was getting every day. She identified the place as *Madhuvana* near the *Kailasa* Mountains (the abode of Shiva). To prevent Shiva from getting drunk, she sought the black coconut trees from which the liquor was dripped. She managed to massage and lift the toddy content towards the head of the trees using her mystical power. The next day, the Lord was enraged to see the toddy content streamed towards the tops of the trees. Lord Shiva angrily removed his *jata,* or top knot hair bun, and slashed it on his left thigh. A holy son named *'Divyan'* was born from his thigh and was assigned to take care of the toddy tapping from those coconut trees.

While collecting the toddy regularly, his son started to drink it. Lord Shiva restricted him not to hunt at *Kadali-Vana* (banana grove) and not to imbibe toddy. The son ignored his restriction and opened up the toddy pot, resulting in the wrath of the Lord. His eyes fell to the vessel. When he apologized to Lord Shiva, he forgave him and sent him to earth with false eyes, a bamboo torch, a thorn archery arrow, a bowl of seeds, and a bow made of bamboo. When the smoke from the bamboo torch obscured his vision, the son threw away the false eyes, seeds bowl, and bamboo torch. They fell at the courtyard of *Kannan* of *Adi Parambu* in the Wayanad district of Kerala. Kannan was frightened to see the wiggling eyes and torch. Divyan consoled him and asked him to keep these items at his home.

He was called Vayanattu Kulavan since he visited Wayanad. The recital of this Theyyam is very engaging; even serious matters are expressed humorously.

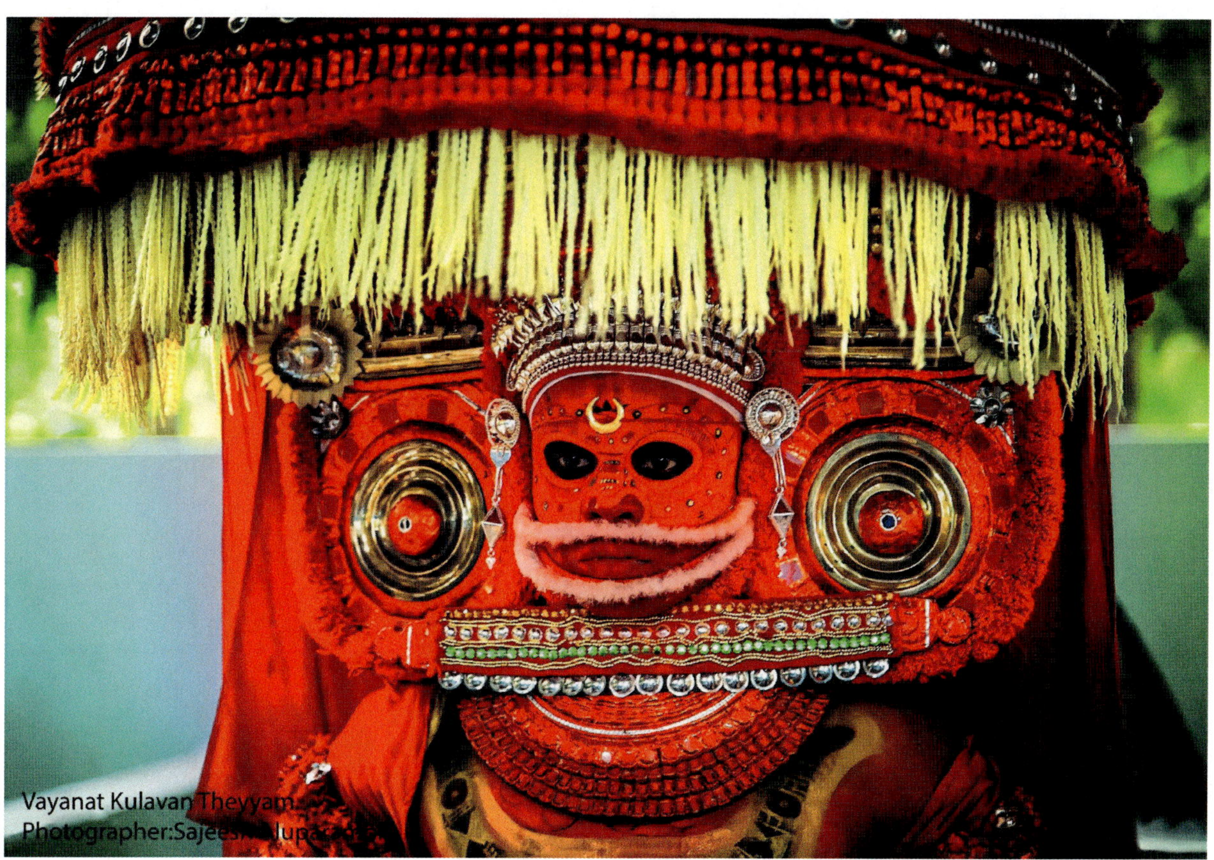

Vayanat Kulavan Theyyam
Photographer:Sajeesh ...lupa...

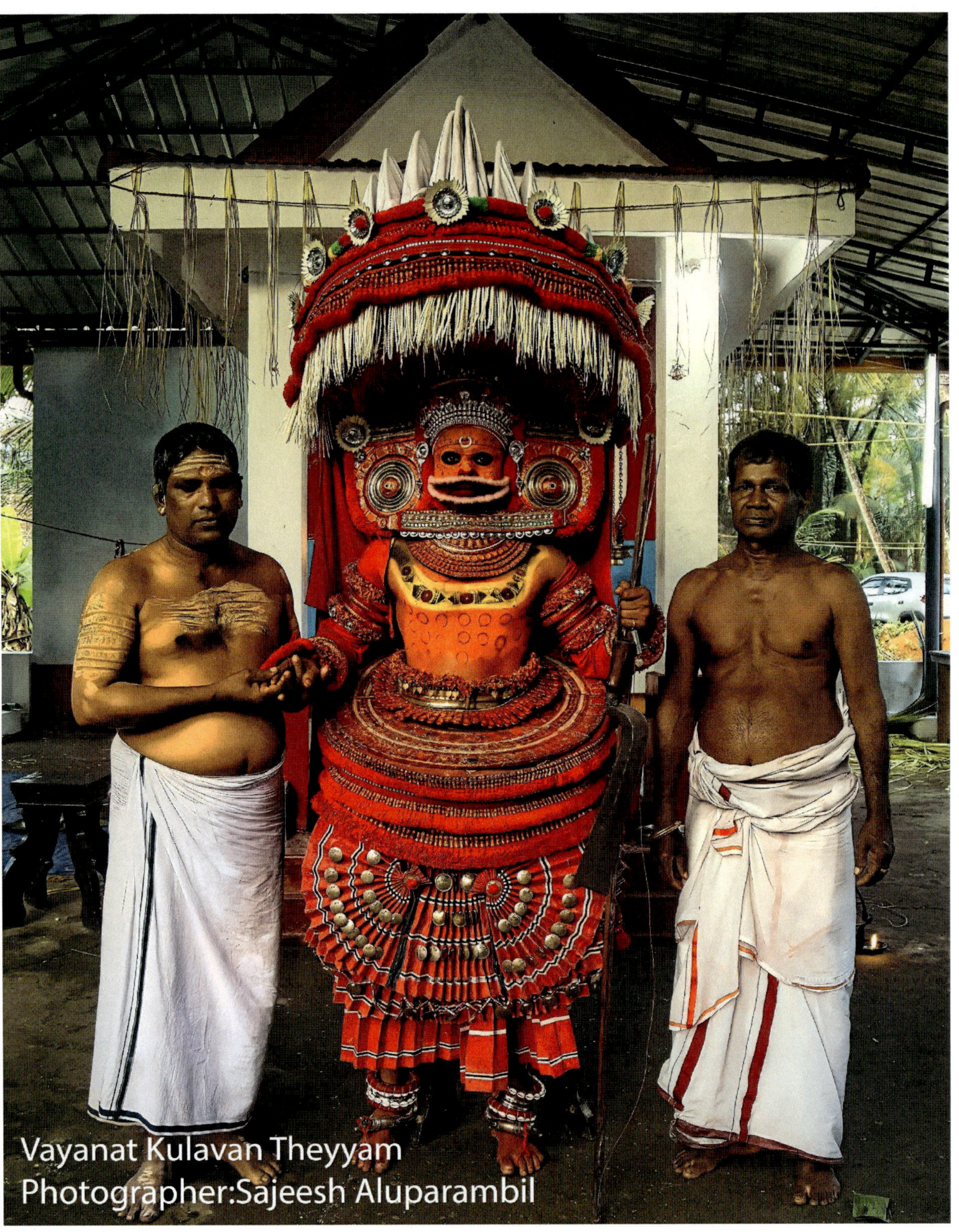
Vayanat Kulavan Theyyam
Photographer:Sajeesh Aluparambil

Moovalamkuzhi Chamundi

Eminent priests Oliyath Thanthri and Edamana Thanthri were competing to prove their prominence in the field of Mantra and their ability to expel evil spirits. They used their invoked spirits or Mantra Moorthys to fight each other. During this fighting, the Oliyath Thanthri used his favorable Parasakthi to annihilate enemies. Edamana Thanthri managed to invoke Parasakthi, the ultimate form of Goddess Parvati, closed it in a shell, and buried it. Suddenly, the pot broke apart, and Parasakthi chased him away.

Again he managed to capture and bury Parasakthi in a copper pot. And once again, Parasakthi was released from that pot. Since he buried the copper pot at a depth of three men's height and kept it there for nearly three-quarters of an hour, Parasakthi was called Moovaalamkuzhi (literally the pit of three men's height) Chamundi and was installed at the western tower of Thrikkannad. Thottam songs suggest that Parasakthi came out of the copper pot with three swords (Vaal in vernacular), and that's why Parasakthi is called Moovalam.

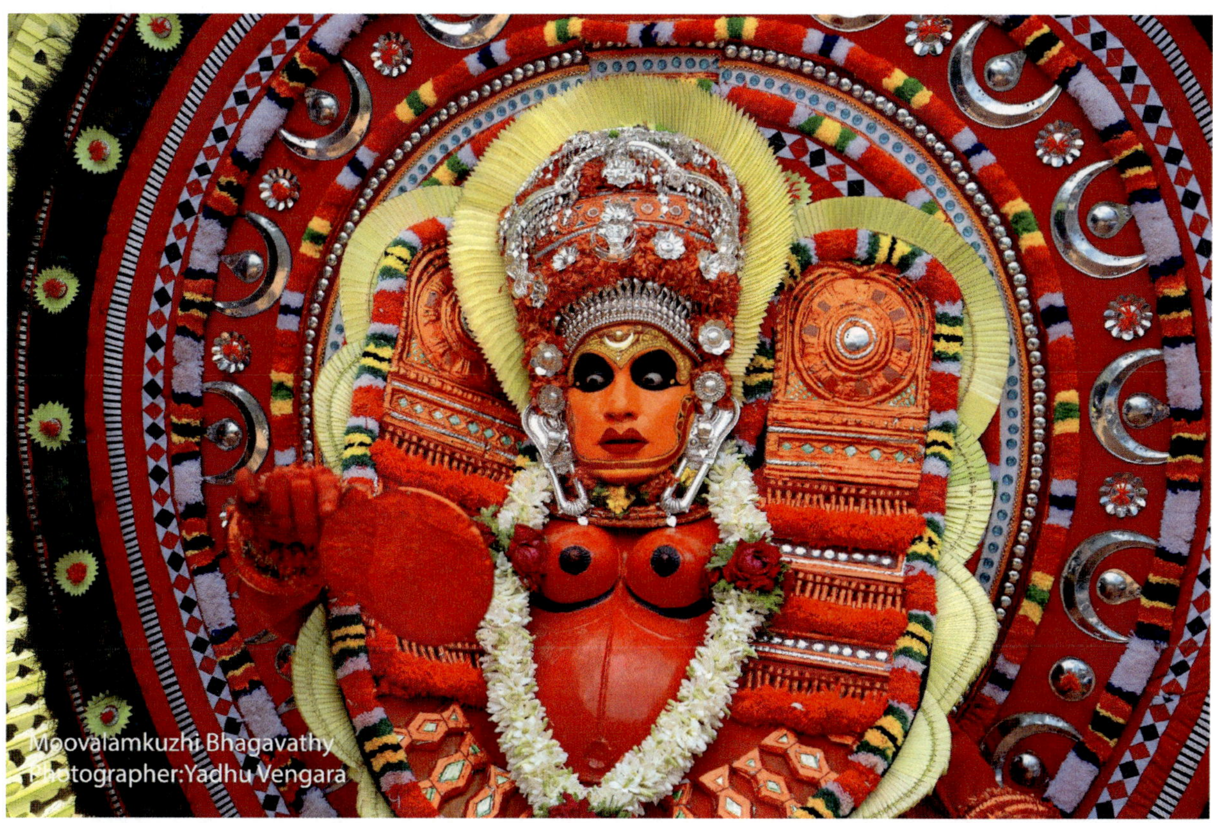

Moovalamkuzhi Bhagavathy
Photographer:Yadhu Vengara

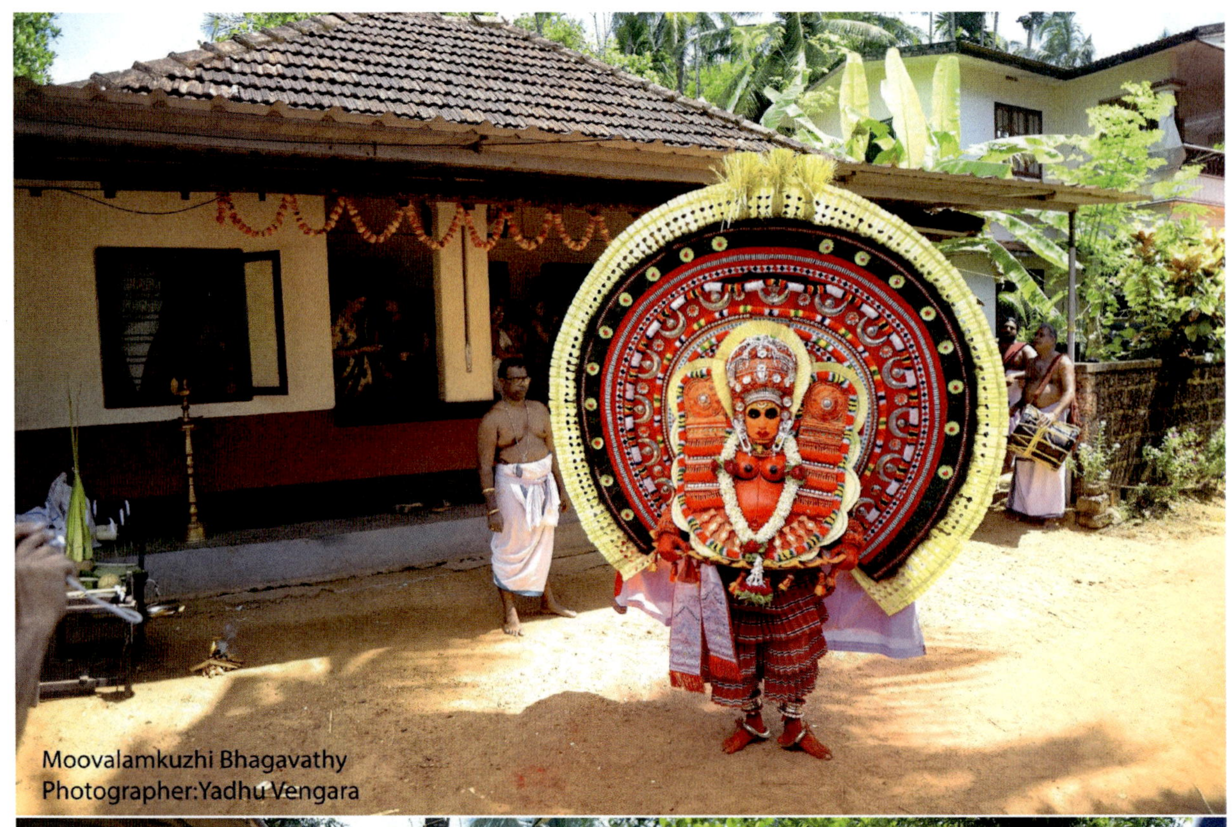
Moovalamkuzhi Bhagavathy
Photographer:Yadhu Vengara

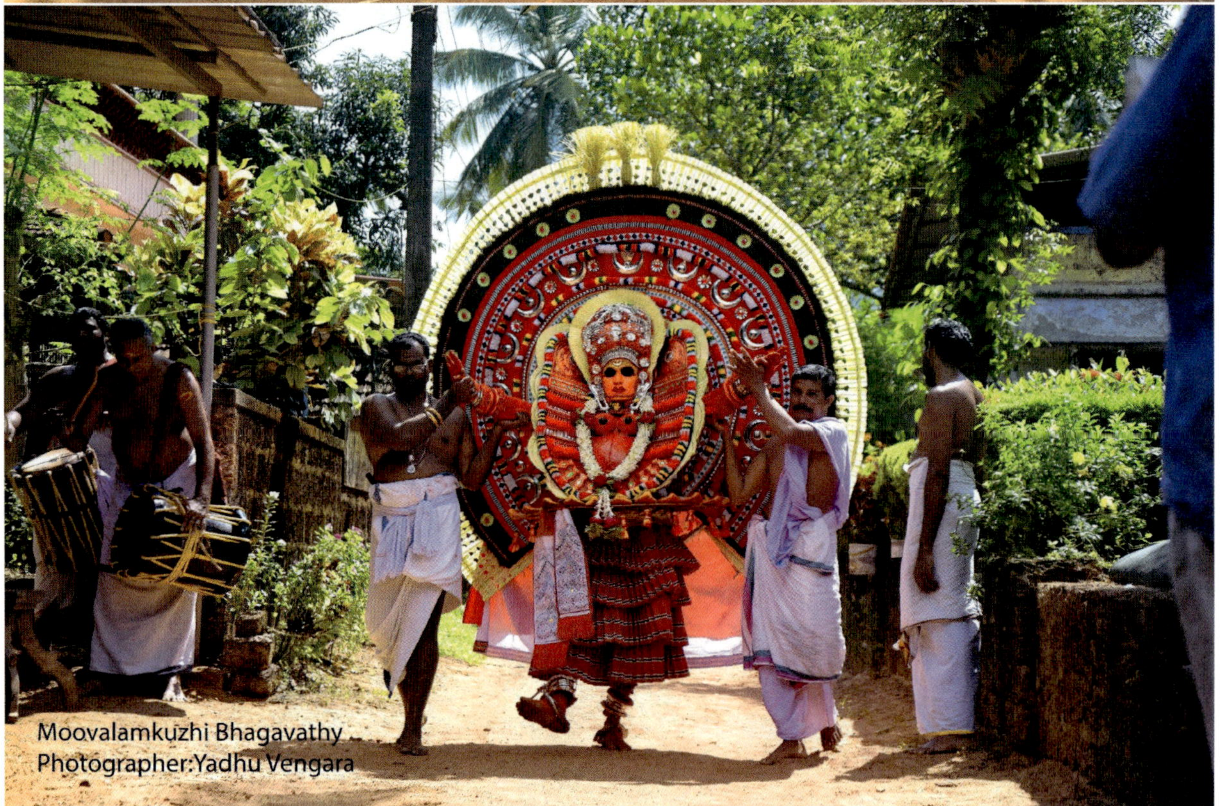
Moovalamkuzhi Bhagavathy
Photographer:Yadhu Vengara

Vellarangara Bhagavathy

A *'parashakthi'* is the ultimate form of Goddess *Parvathi*. Vellarangara Bhagavathy is one of the different forms of parashakthi. This Theyyam is performed in the *Payyanoor Thaineri Vellanrangara kavu*. Vellarangara Bhagavthy has the same myth as that of the Kolathingal Thaiparadevatha, the mother of all Goddesses. The Goddess Bhadrakali, who was born from the third eye of Lord Shiva to kill Darika, is the main deity and is known through different incarnations in different parts of Malabar. Vellarangara Bhagavthy is one of them. The previous name of the Payyanoor Vellarangara kavu was mooshari kavu. Mooshari in Malayalam means brazier. Recently, this kavu had a grand Theyyam festival known as *'perumkaliyattam'* for the first time in 95 years.

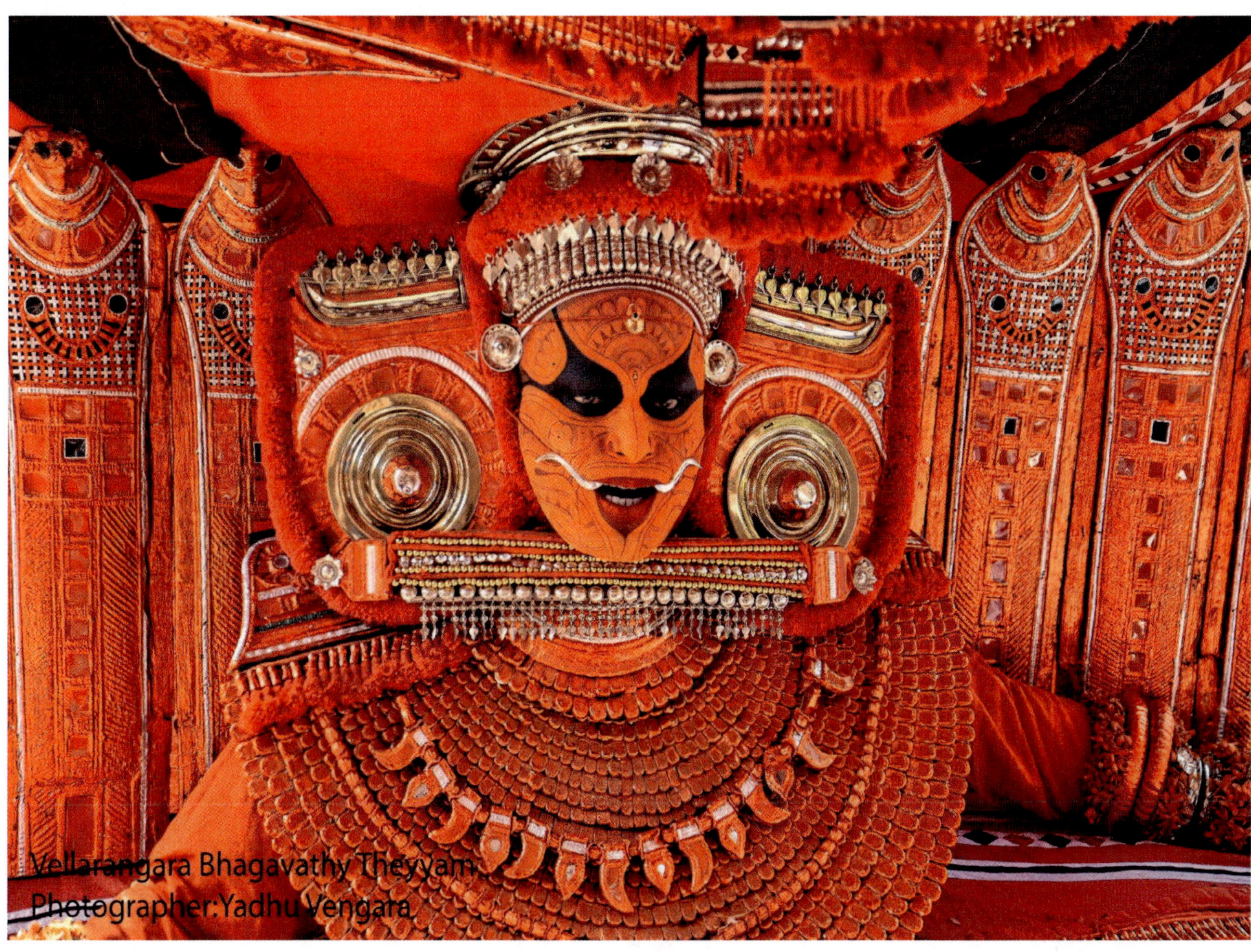

Vellarangara Bhagavathy Theyyam
Photographer:Yadhu Vengara

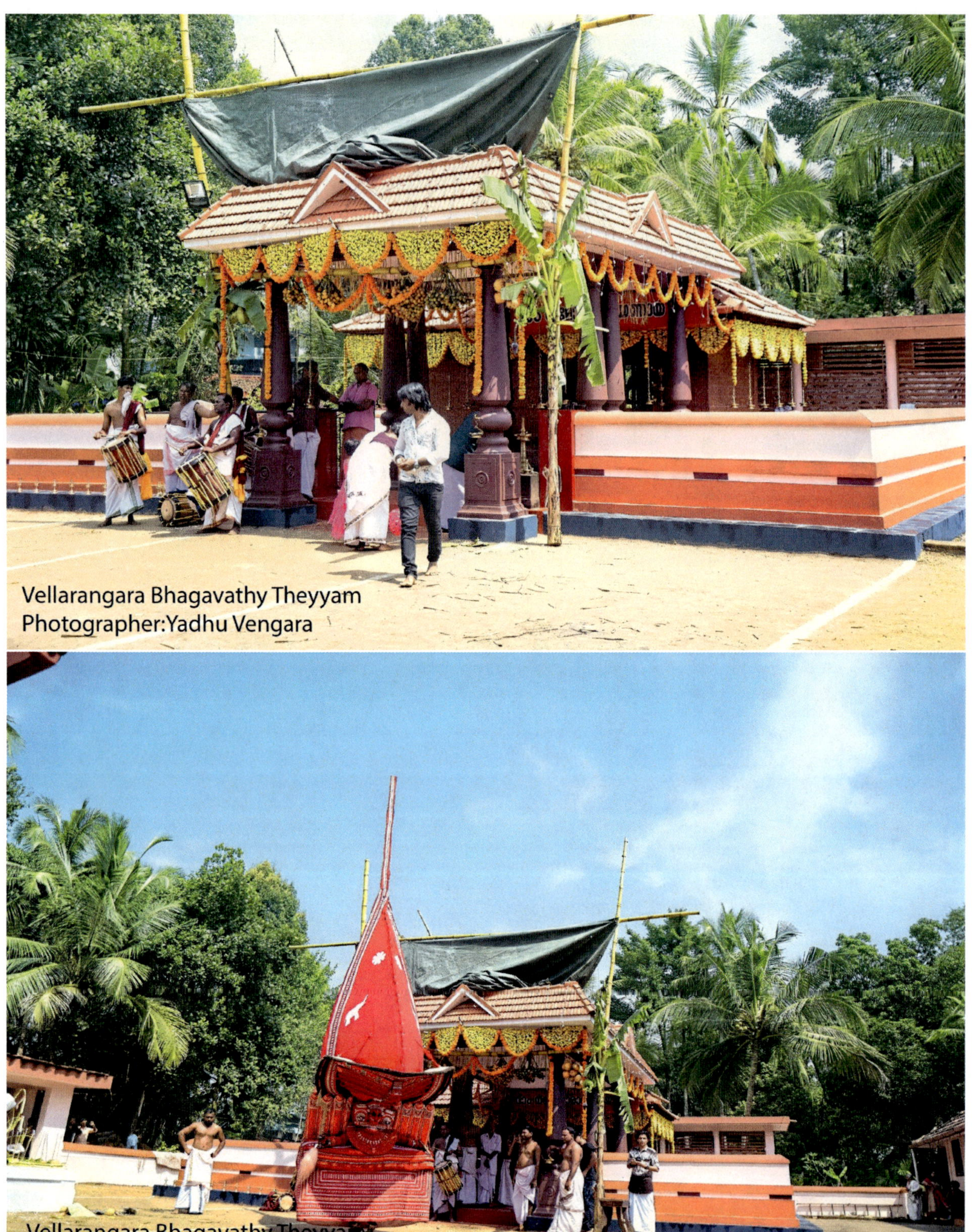

Vellarangara Bhagavathy Theyyam
Photographer:Yadhu Vengara

Vellarangara Bhagavathy Theyyam
Photographer:Yadhu Vengara

Kandanar Kelan Theyyam

Meledath Chakki was a landlady who lived at *Kunnaru* village near Ramanthali in Kerala. Once, she found a boy on her land at *Poompunam* in the present-day Wayanad district of Kerala. She named him *Kelan* and raised him like her own son. She was delighted to see he was quite intelligent and grew up with valor. Under his supervision, her land at Kunnaru was cherished, and she decided to send him to her agricultural land in the hilly regions of Wayanad.

Kelan accepted his stepmother's order and prepared metal agricultural tools and equipment for cutting down the trees of Poompunam, where four forests merged. He was intoxicated before leaving with tools and weapons. He also took a bamboo stem filled with toddy (coconut wine) in his hand and another one on his rug. He managed to clear the woods but decided not to cut down a gooseberry tree in the middle of the fourth punam (a piece of land) since it was the dwelling place of two snakes called *Kali* and *Karali*.

Then Kelan started to set fire to the grass in all four forest lands. He burned the grass and cleverly escaped from the engulfing flames. He was thrilled when he managed to evade the raging fire in three of the forest lands. Finally, he reached the fourth plot where the gooseberry tree was located. As usual, he set fire to the grass, but both *Agni* (fire) and *Vayu* (air) were enraged. The flames raised towards the sky, and Kelan couldn't run away from there as he had before. He realized climbing the gooseberry tree was the only option left for him. He scrambled to the top of that gooseberry tree, but the startled snakes bit him on both sides of his chest. He cried aloud, uttering his stepmother's name. Finally, Kelan and those snakes fell into the raging fire and turned into a heap of ash.

At this juncture, Wayanad Kulavan was returning after hunting. He found Kelan lying there with two snakes on his chest. Kulavan touched the scorched Kelan with an arrow made of bamboo. Kelan woke up and grabbed Kulavan's feet. He then reincarnated with the two snakes and became Godly. Wayanad Kulavan blessed Kelan and said Kelan would become famous because he happened to "see" (Kandu) him, and he will be known as "Kandanaru Kelan." He also gave him a place to sit beside him on the left side and armed him with instructions for the Pooja (worship ceremony) procedure.

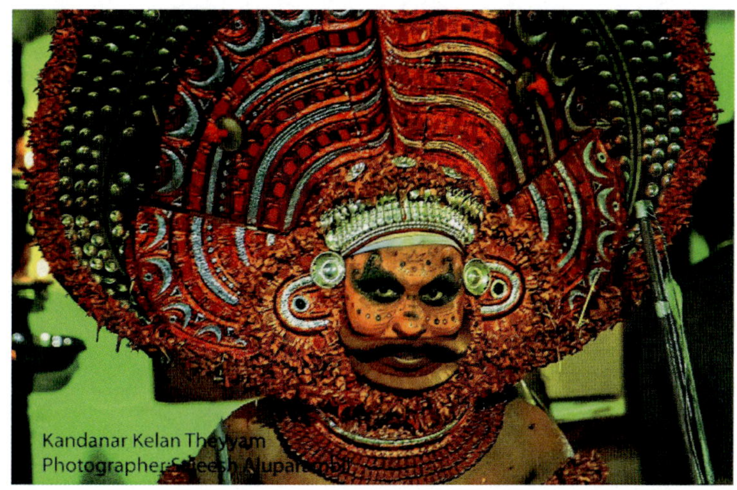

Kandanar Kelan Theyyam
Photographer:S[illegible]eesh Alupar[illegible]mbil

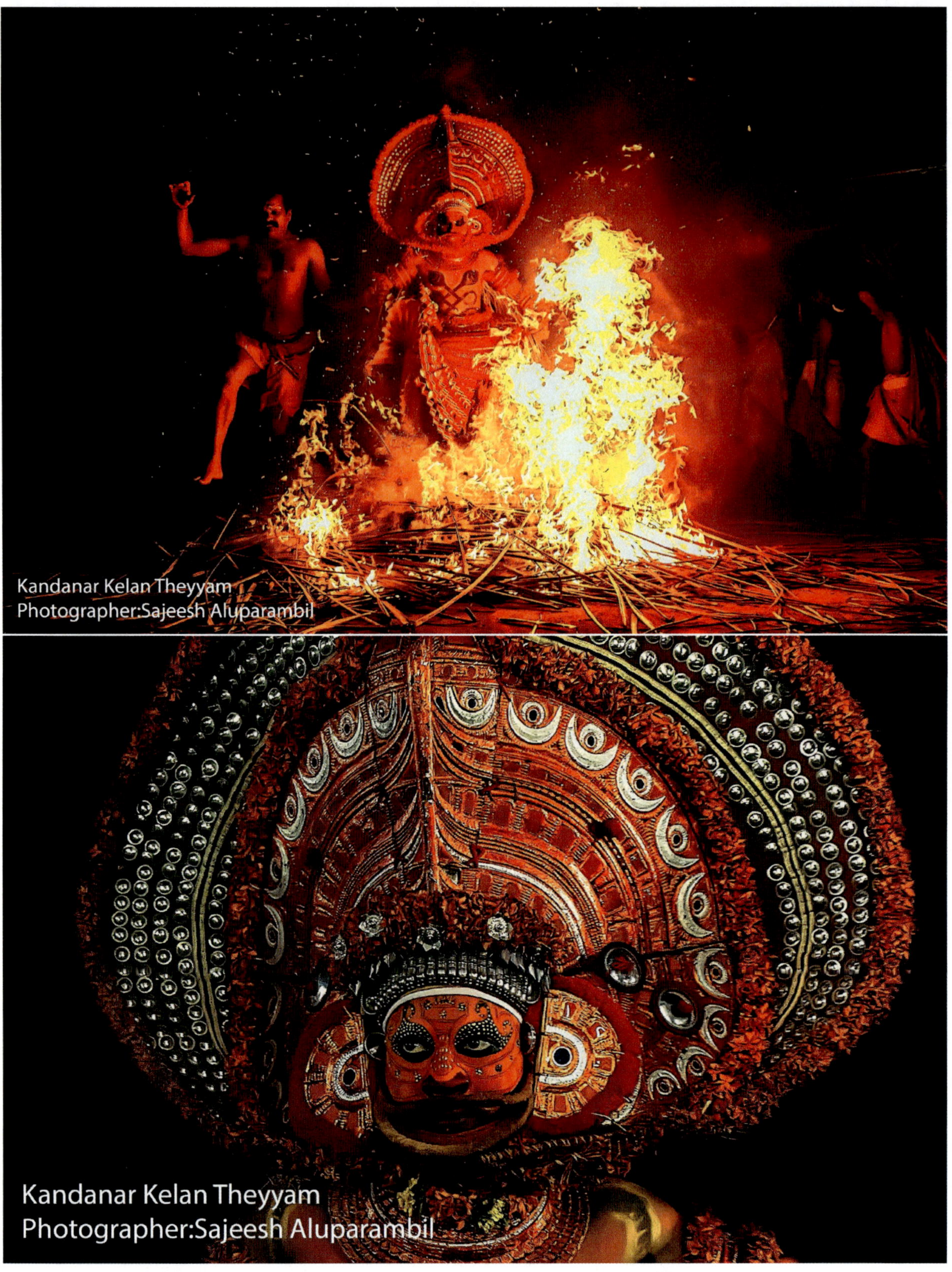

Kandanar Kelan Theyyam
Photographer:Sajeesh Aluparambil

Kandanar Kelan Theyyam
Photographer:Sajeesh Aluparambil

Kara Gulikan Theyyam

Lord Shiva once killed Yama or Kala (God of death and justice) by opening his third eye to rescue his worshipper, sage *Bhargava Markandeya*. Kala was burned to a heap of ash by the fierce rays of energy that flew from the Lord's third eye. As he had killed the God of death, there were no deaths on the earth, and the population was increasing steadily. Planet earth complained to all the Gods and Goddesses about it. Lord Shiva pressed his left toe deep into the earth, and his toe was torn apart, and *Gulikan* incarnated. Lord Shiva provided a trident to Gulikan and assigned him to do what Kala had been doing. There are over a hundred Gulikans; however, Southern Gulikan, Kara Gulikan, and Northern Gulikan are the major Gulikan Theyyams. The southern Gulikan is quite intense, but the other two Gulikans are rather humorous.

This Theyyam is performed by the Malaya community members, who worship Gulikan, and the deity is pleased only when being worshipped by them. The presence of Gulikan will prolong one's life from birth to death. Supposedly, Gulikan is present in every ritual, including fireworks, smoke, and even ashes. There are Theyyam forms for Gulikan, Mari Gulikan, Northern Gulikan, Pula Gulikan, Japa Gulikan, Karim Gulikan, Kara Gulikan, Jathaka Gulikan, Unmatha Gulikan, Red Gulikan and Southern Gulikan. The rituals of Kara Gulikan include running into the sharp thorns and then laying on them.

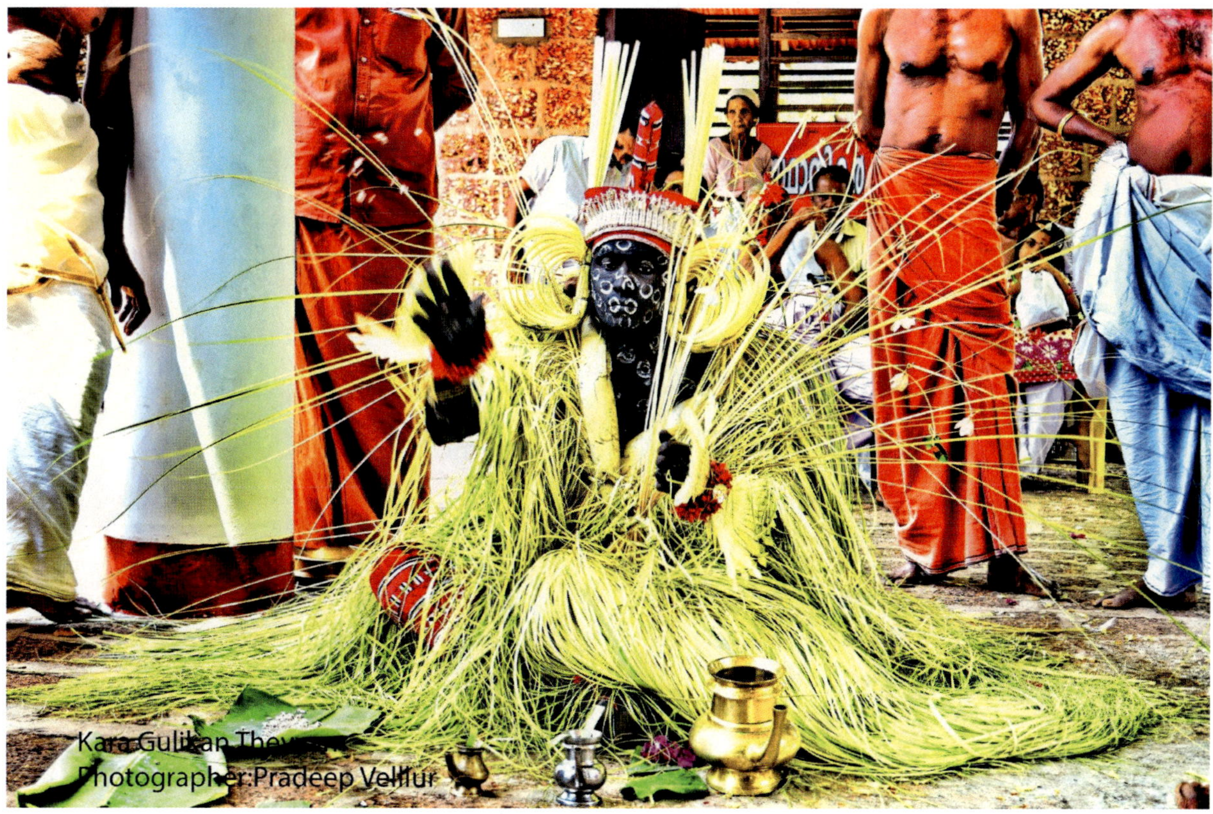

Kara Gulikan They
Photographer:Pradeep Vellur

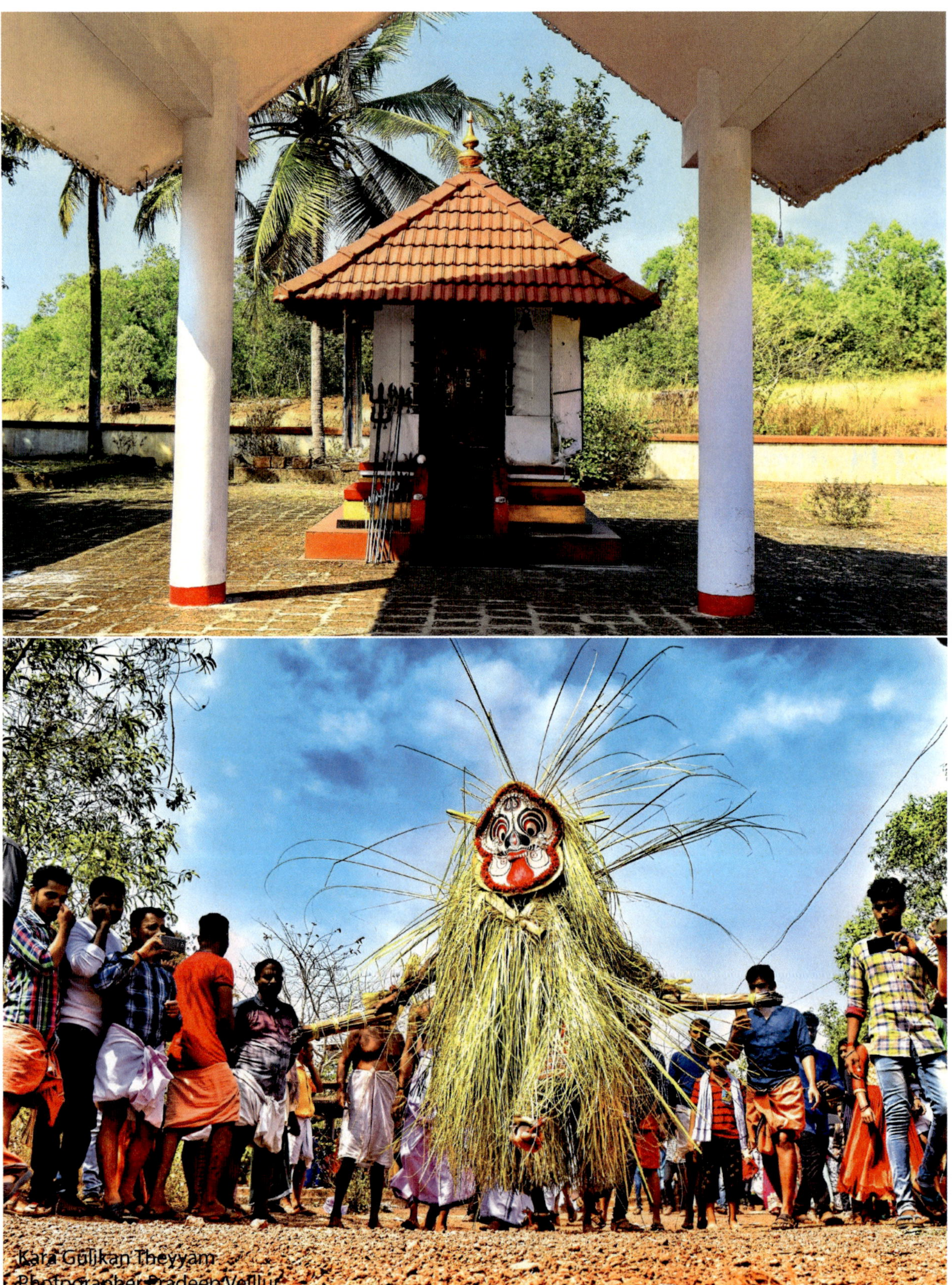

Kara Gulikan Theyyam
Photographer Pradeep Vellur

Pulli Vettakkorumakan Theyyam

(Story similar to Vettakkorumakan Theyyam)

Vettakkoru Makan deity is believed to be the son of Lord Shiva with his wife Parvathy when they are incarnated as forest dwellers. Since this form of Vettakkoru Makan lived in Pullimana after descending on earth, he is also called 'Pullivettakkuorumakan.' It is also believed that Pulivettakkorumakan is an angry form of the Vettakkorumakan God. He is the deity of the *Kushava* Community, primarily focused on pottery.

The myth is that Lord Shiva sent his son Vettakkorumakan to earth to protect the people. He came to Kerala and engaged in a relationship with a young lady from the Karakoora Mana (A prominent family of that period). They had a son who was valiant like his father. There was a fort of the Karakoora family, which Karumbranthiri forcefully ruled. Vetttakkorumakan requested Karumbranthiri to give the fort back. Karumbranthiri, aware of the fighting skills of Vetttakkorumakan, would engage in no physical battle. Instead, he set a condition that the son of Vettakkorumakan must de-husk 20600 coconuts. The child did so within a short duration. Scared by this, Karumbranthiri relinquished the fort, and Vettakkorumakan became its protector.

The Pulli Vettakorumakan Theyyam is considered a regional variation of Vettakorumakan Theyyam.

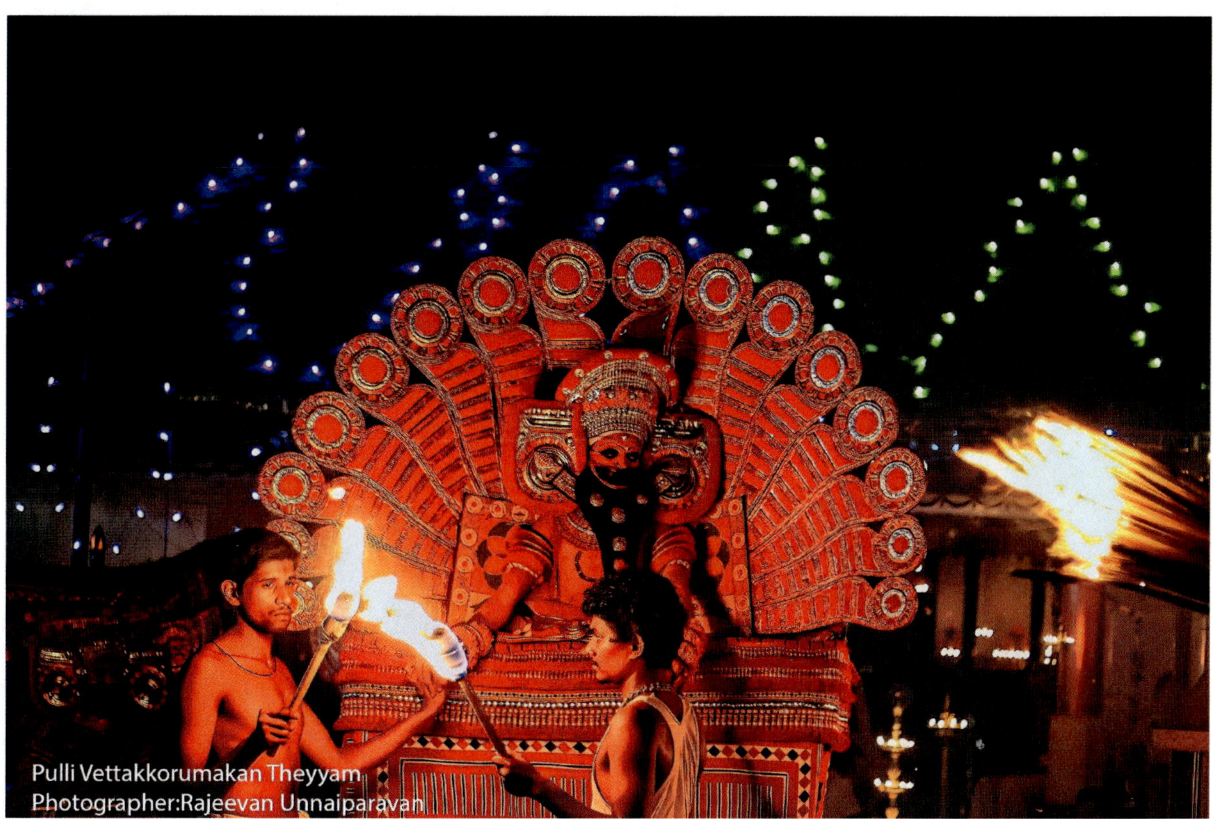
Pulli Vettakkorumakan Theyyam
Photographer:Rajeevan Unnaiparavan

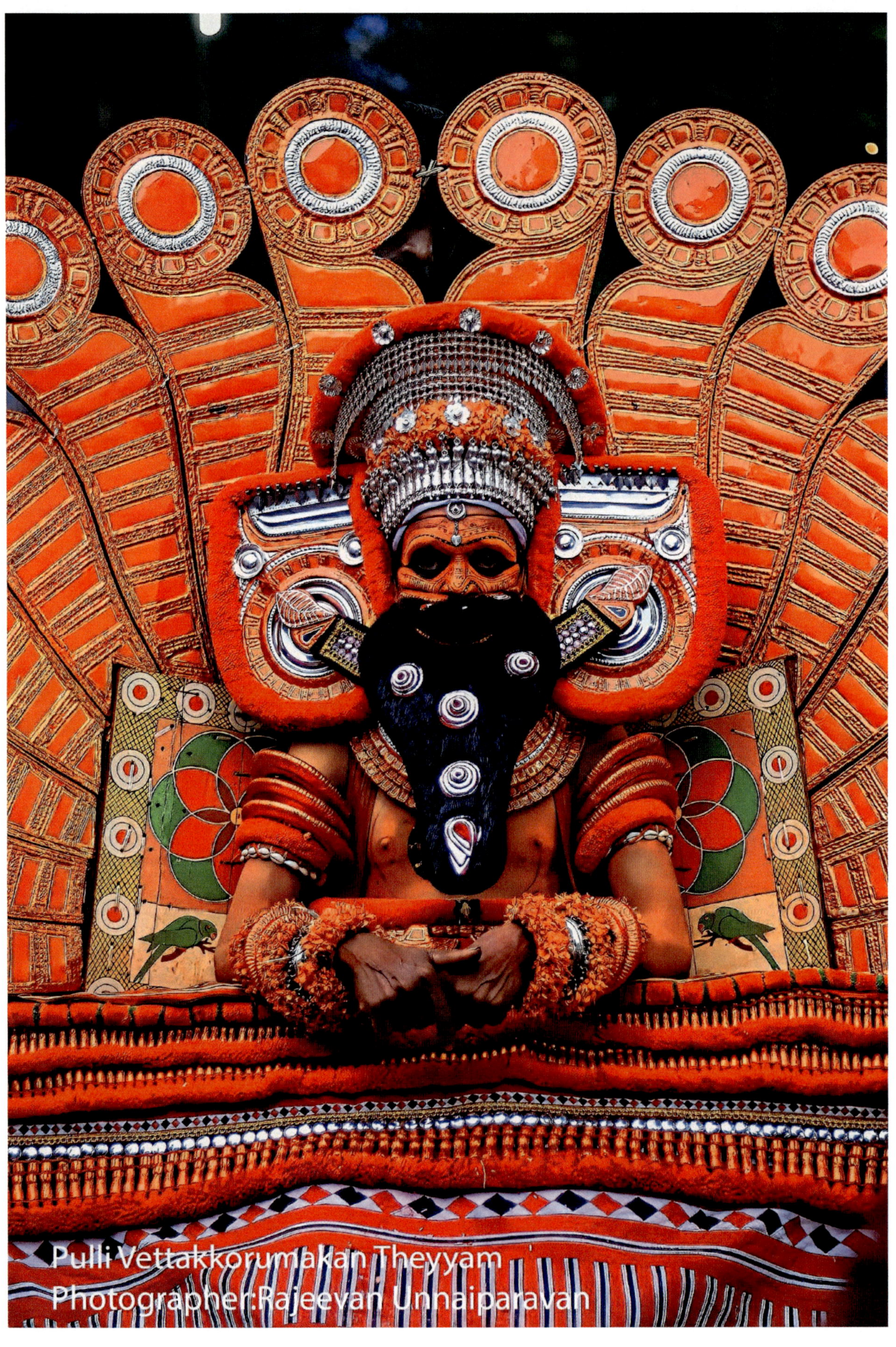

Pulli Vettakkorumakan Theyyam
Photographer:Rajeevan Unnaiparavan

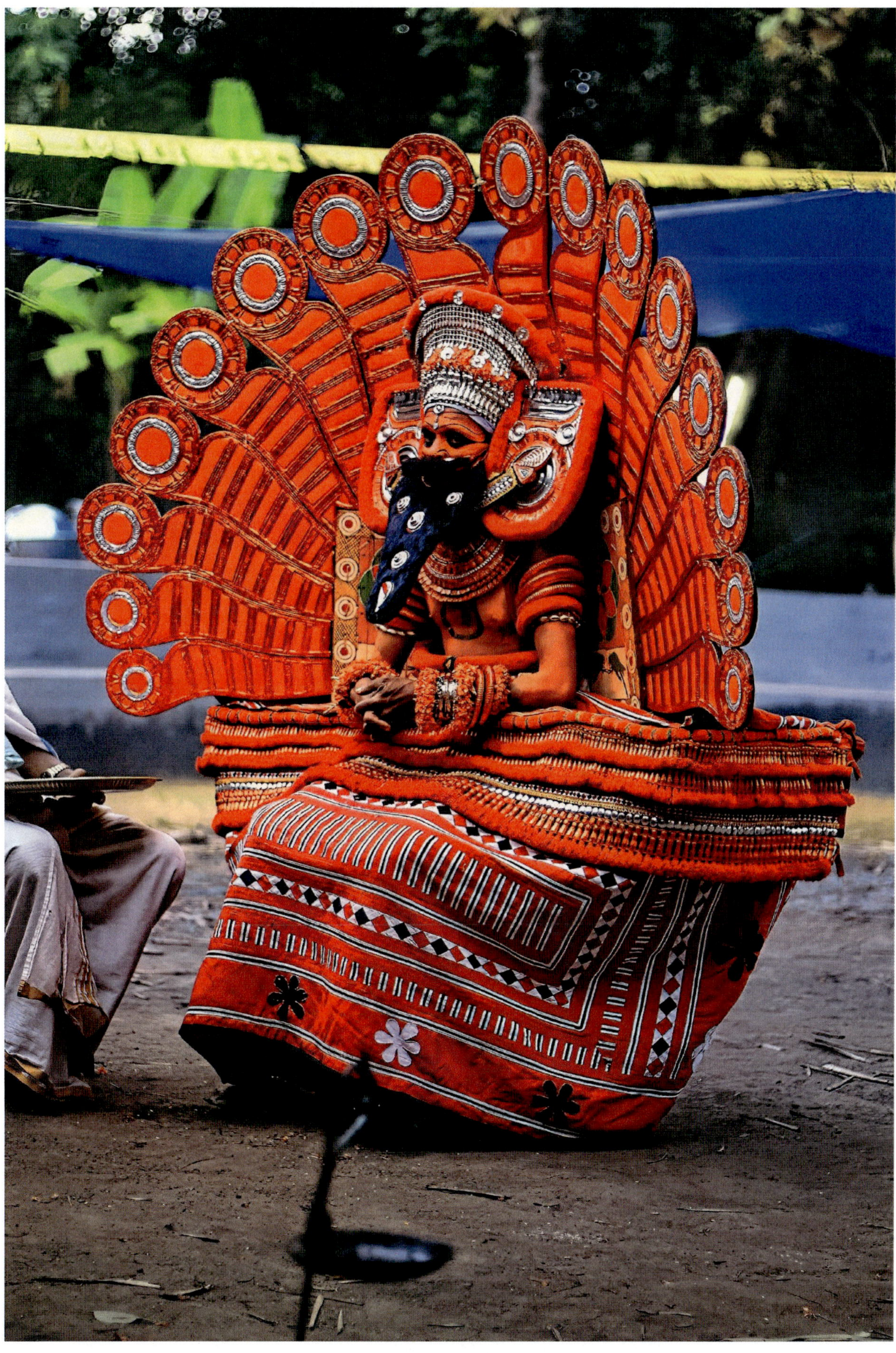

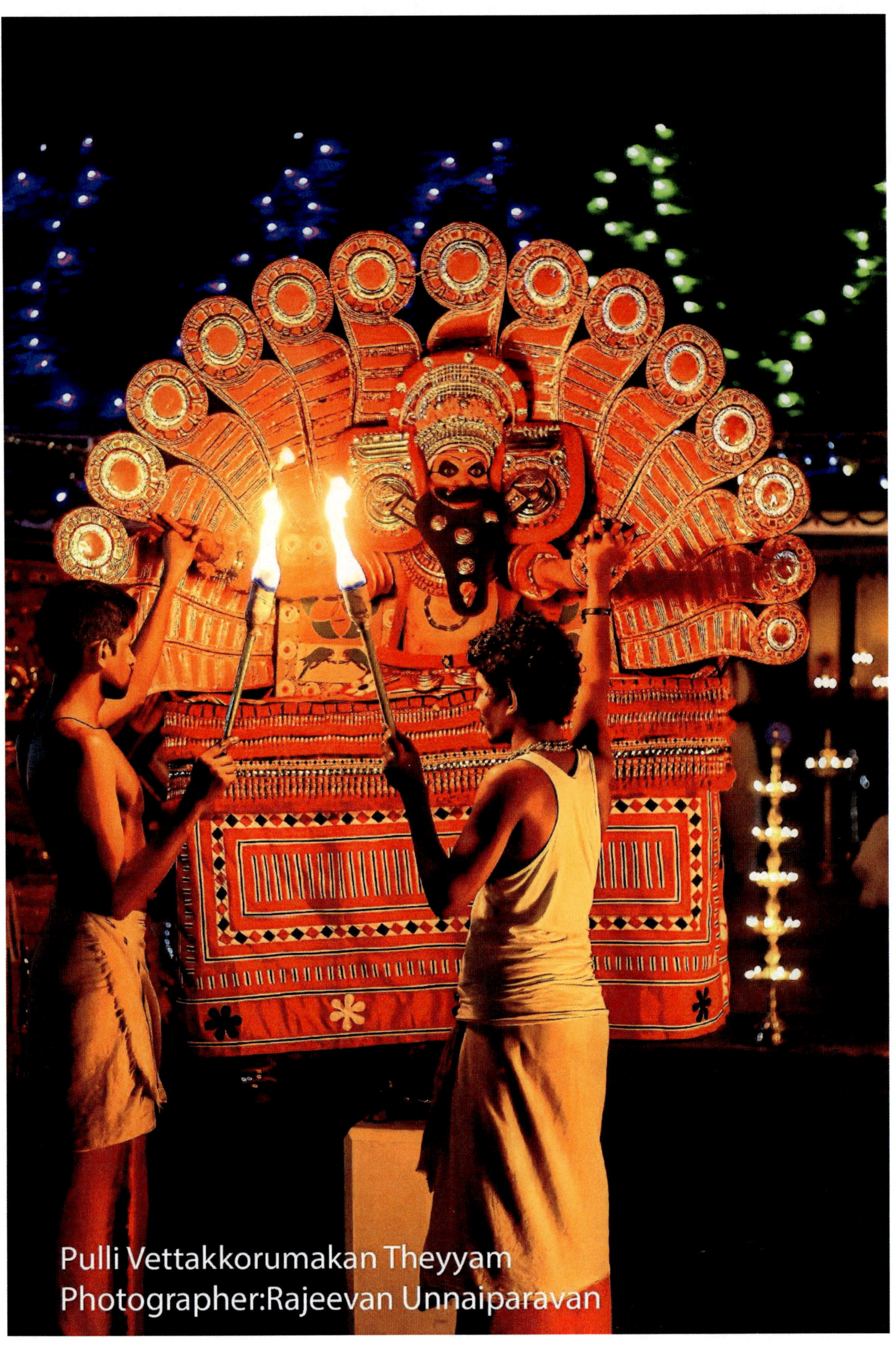

Pulli Vettakkorumakan Theyyam
Photographer:Rajeevan Unnaiparavan

Uchabali Theyyam

In the old times, feudal lords' houses and upper caste family homes had a ritual called '*Kanneru pattu.*' This was conducted in *Karkidaka* Month of Malayalam Calender and used to be a ritual of wading off evil. In some *tharavadu* (ancestral homes), this ritual is conducted before the Theyyam performance. The ritual '*Kanneru pattu,*' which includes singing and playing the drums, is believed to wade off the evil eye and the evil spells the family is affected by. After *Kanneru pattu,* The Theyyam will come to perform in the afternoon. The Theyyam will have an *ezhuthani* (stylus) used for writing on the palm leaves. They thrust this into their palm and give the blood as a sacrifice to the deity, which is why it is called Uchabali Theyyam, as it offers blood sacrifice in the afternoon.

This Theyyam is performed in *Karamel Vellora Tharavadu Devasthanam, Chutta Valiyaveedu tharavadu,* and *Panayakkattu Bhagavathi Kavu,* which are some of the important shrines of Kerala.

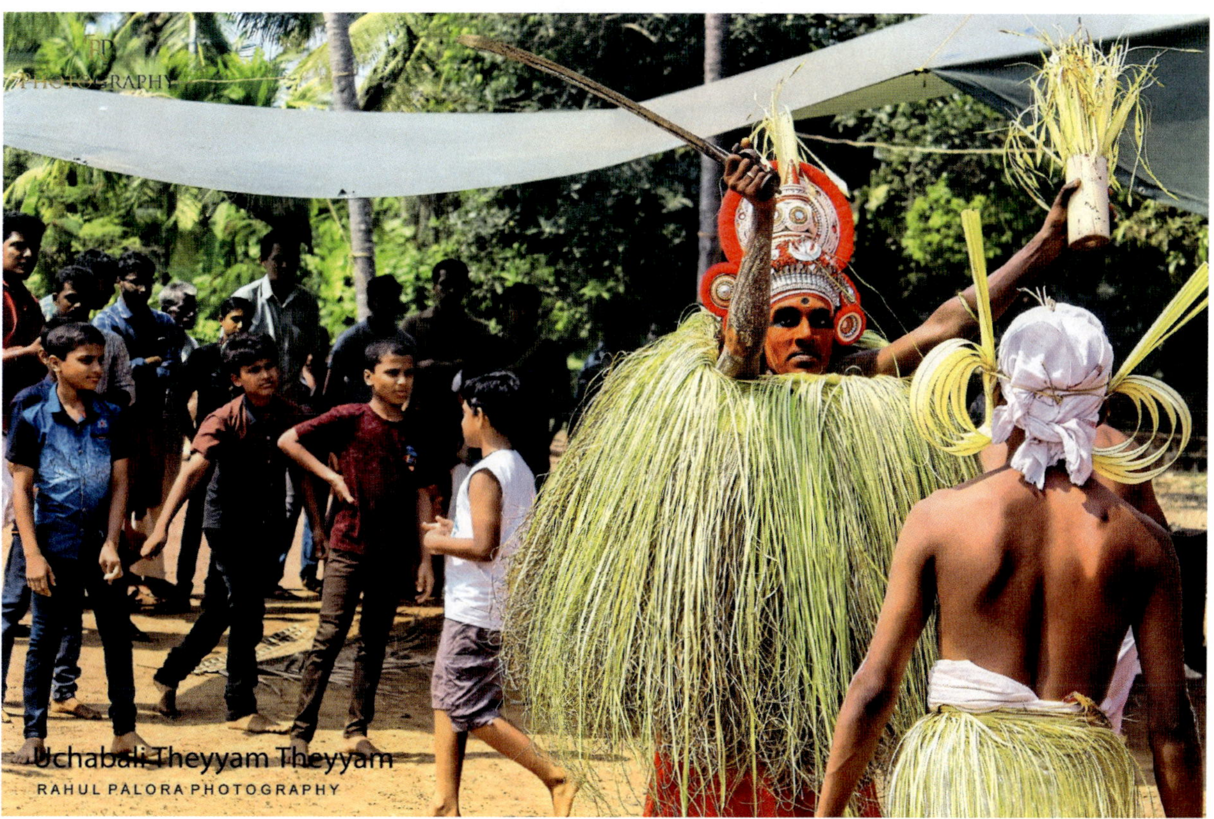

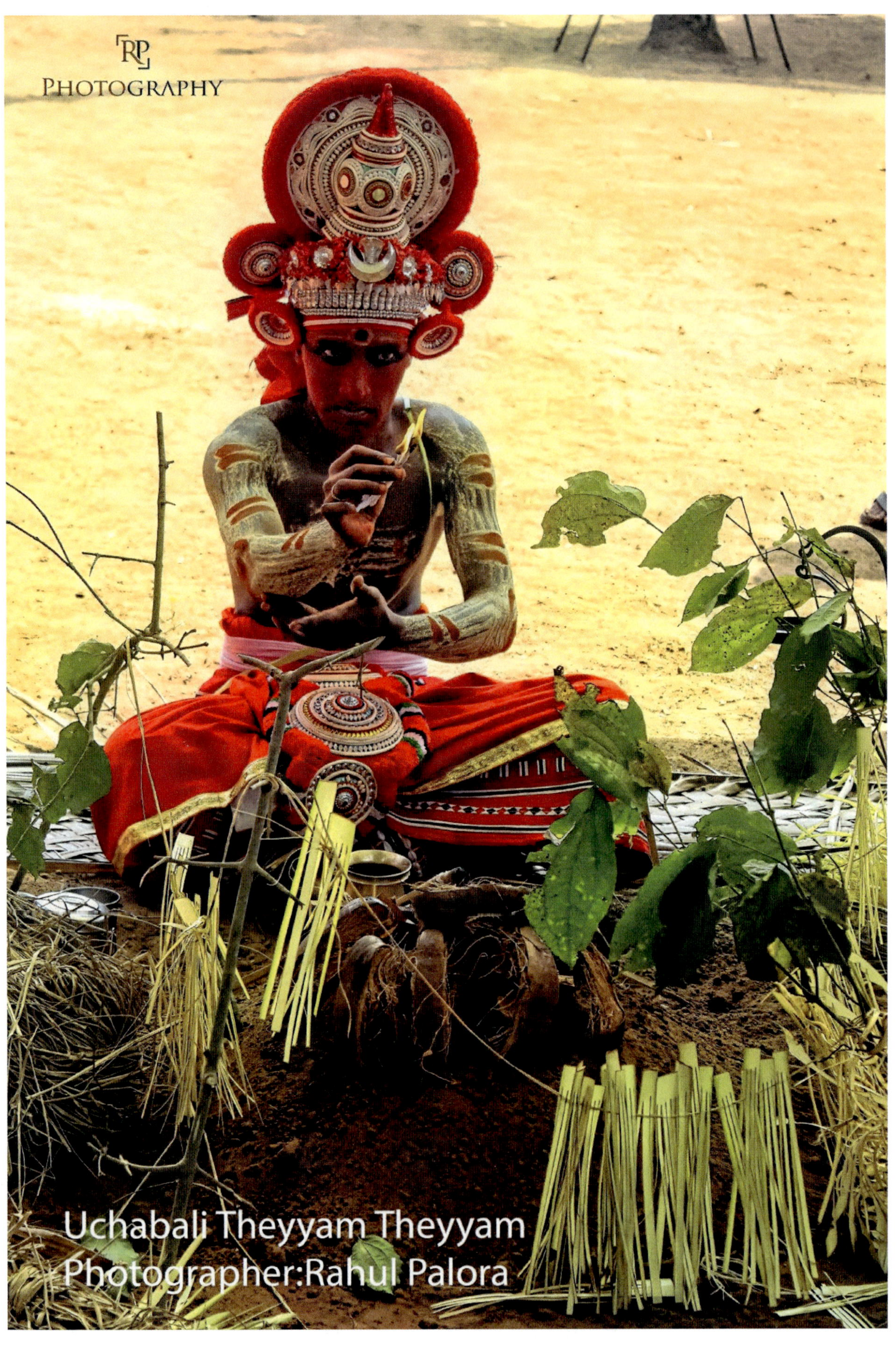
RP
PHOTOGRAPHY
Uchabali Theyyam Theyyam
Photographer:Rahul Palora

Shasthaveeshwaran Theyyam

Shasta could mean teacher, guide, lord, ruler, etc. Eeswaran is the Malayalam word for God. Hence, the term Shasthaveeshwaran denotes the God who is incarnated as a guide, teacher, etc.

Shasta came to the present shrine while Kunnummal Karanavar (Head of the Kunnummal family) was returning from *Kodagu* (Present day Coorg) with all his earnings. Thieves spotted him on the way, and *Karanavar* ran away from them. While running, the Karanavar came to the bank of a river where the current was strong. Expecting his death either at the hands of the thieves or by jumping into the river, Karanavar closed his eyes and prayed to Vana Shastha (Lord of the woods). Suddenly, a soldier on horseback appeared and rescued him. It is believed that it was Shasta who came to the rescue. The legend says Shasta accepted the Naduvalath Tharavadu (ancestral home) as his abode since the prayers of Kunnummal Karanavar pleased him.

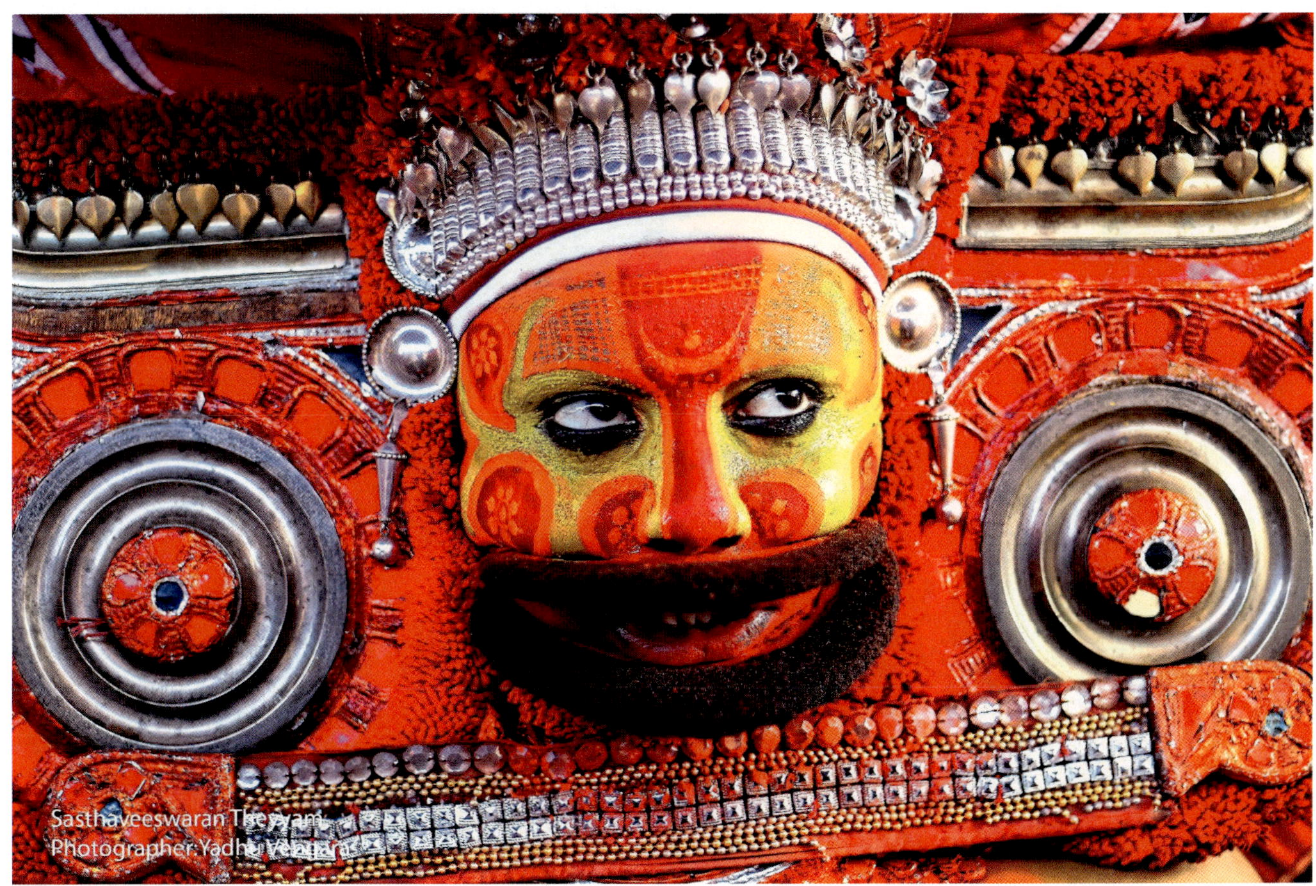

Sasthaveeswaran Theyyam
Photographer:Yadhu Vengara

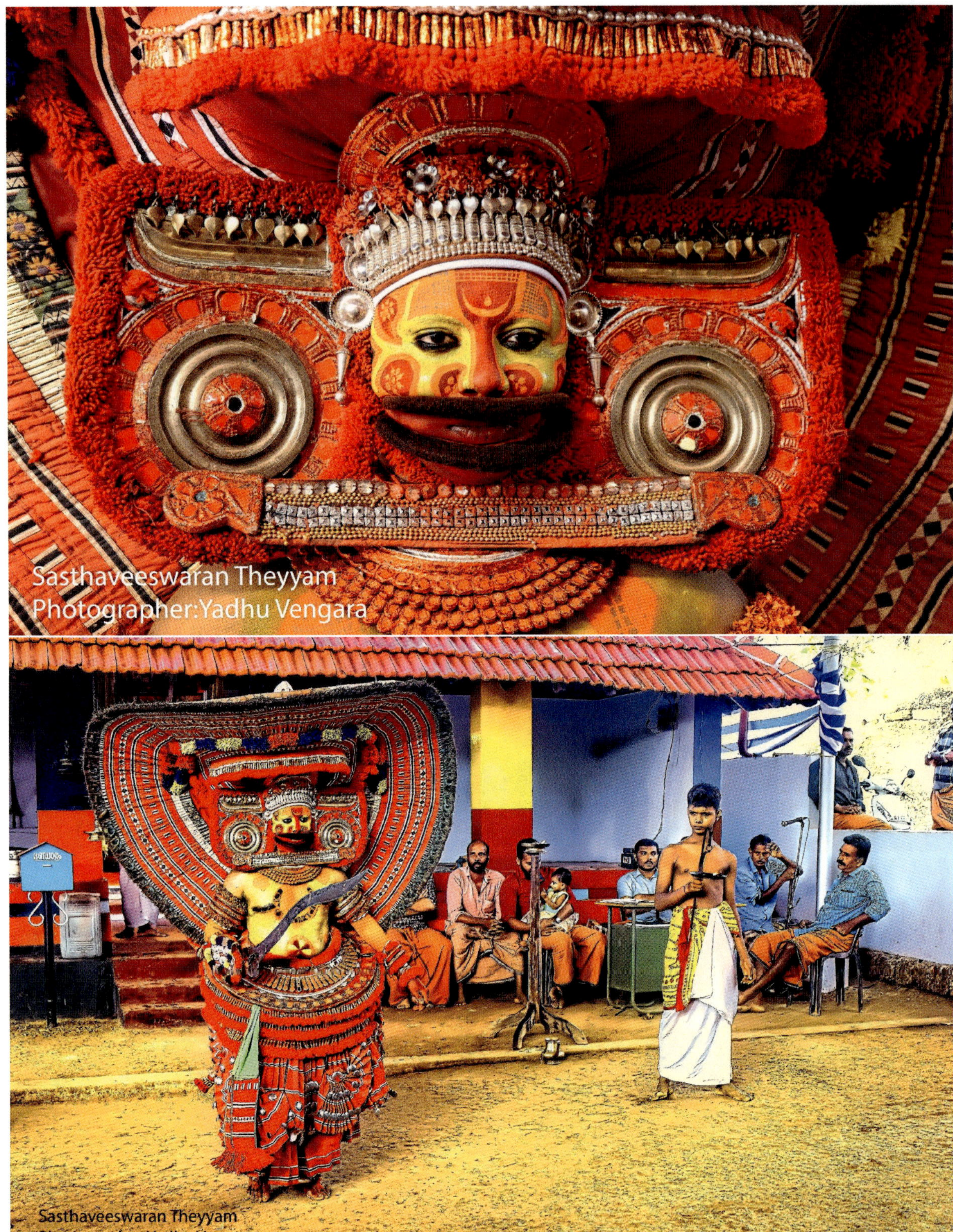

Sasthaveeswaran Theyyam
Photographer:Yadhu Vengara

Sasthaveeswaran Theyyam
Photographer:Yadhu Vengara

Karinthiri Nair Theyyam

Kurumbranthiri Vaanavar was regularly annoyed by tigers killing his calves. So Karinthiri Kannan Nair went to the forest to hunt down the tigers, but he went missing. Bewildered, the ruler prayed to his deity Rajarajesvari Bhagavathy of the Thuloor forest area when Karinthiri Nair failed to return from the woods after the mission. The Goddess appeared in his dreams and revealed that the tigers were none other than Lord Parameswara (Shiva) and Karinthiri Kannan Nair died in a Godly manner. She mentioned that Karinthiri Kannan Nair's soul could be invoked and placed beside her to expel the harm forever. Ruler Kurumbranthiri Vaanavar agreed and built a Kaavu (Shrine) for him. Since then, Karinthiri Nair Theyyam has been performed, along with other Tiger-based Theyyams.

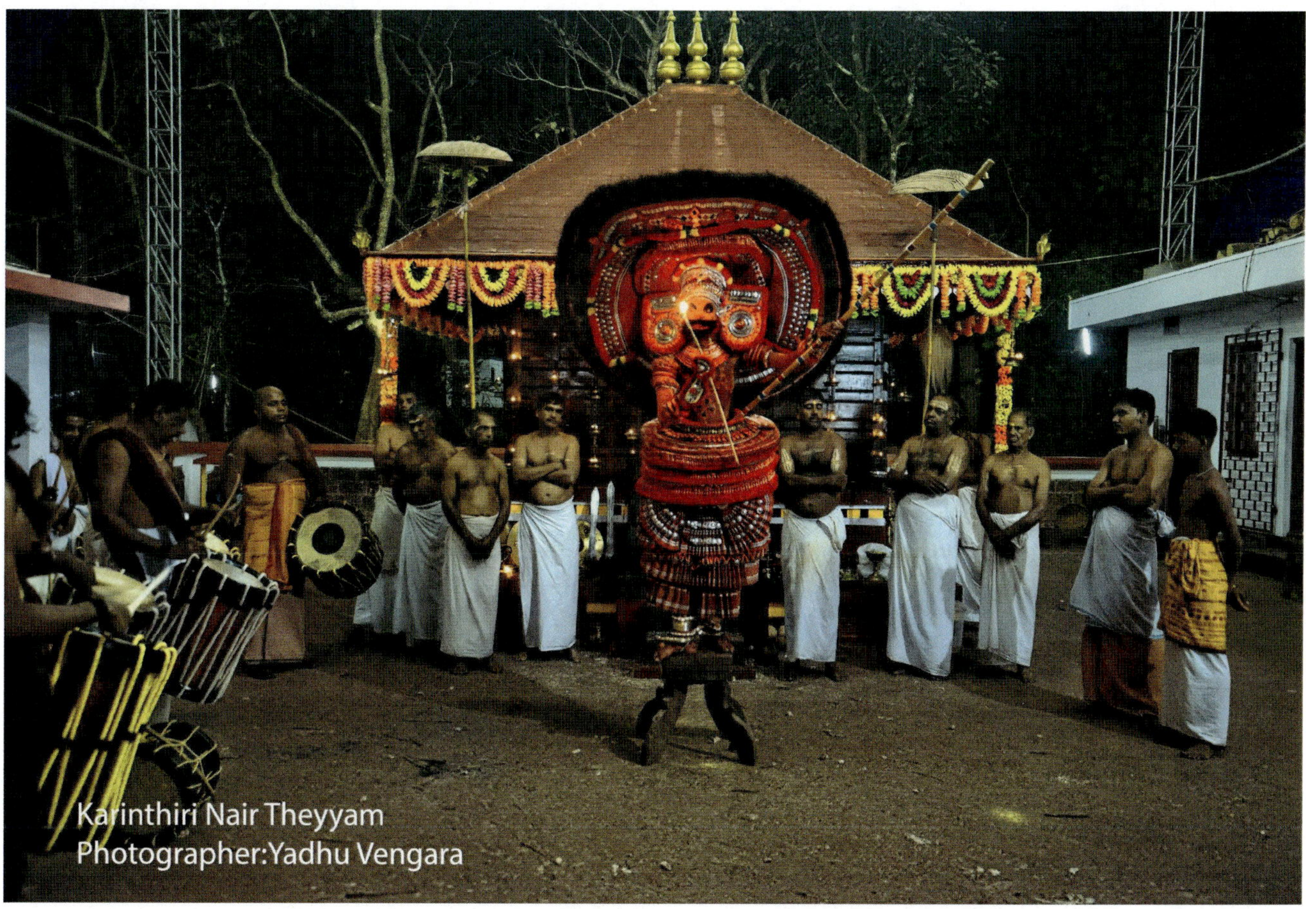
Karinthiri Nair Theyyam
Photographer:Yadhu Vengara

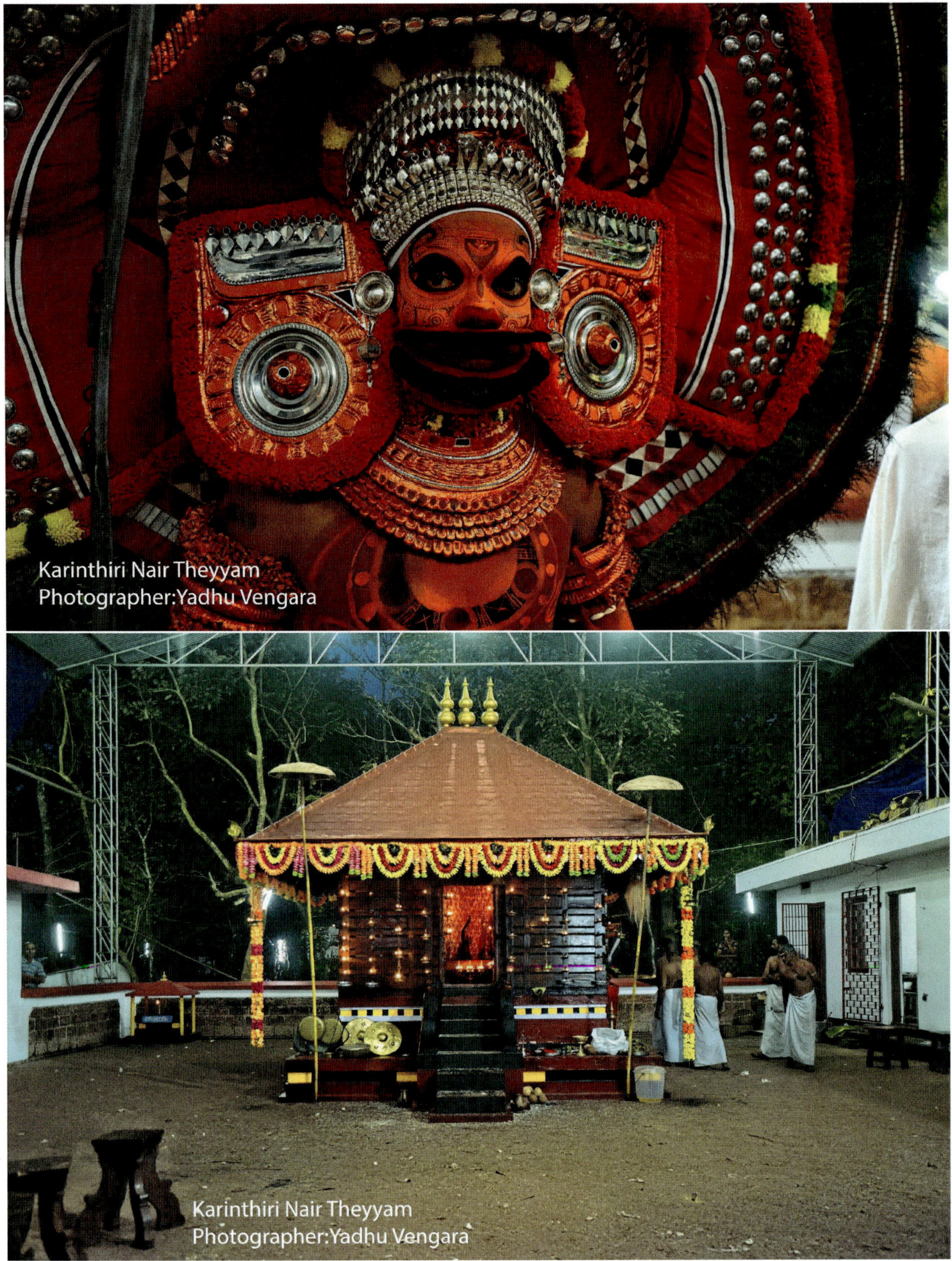

Karinthiri Nair Theyyam
Photographer:Yadhu Vengara

Karinthiri Nair Theyyam
Photographer:Yadhu Vengara

Kubera Moorthy Theyyam (The Mountainous Gods)

The God of wealth, Kubera, will attend prayers instantly and give boons to worshippers lavishly. He is believed to be the provider. Believers pray to Kubera to ease their financial difficulties. Kubera Moorthy Theyyam is rarely performed, and one of the few such venues is Karuvachery Kuttiyatt Thondachan Devasthanam of Payyannur.

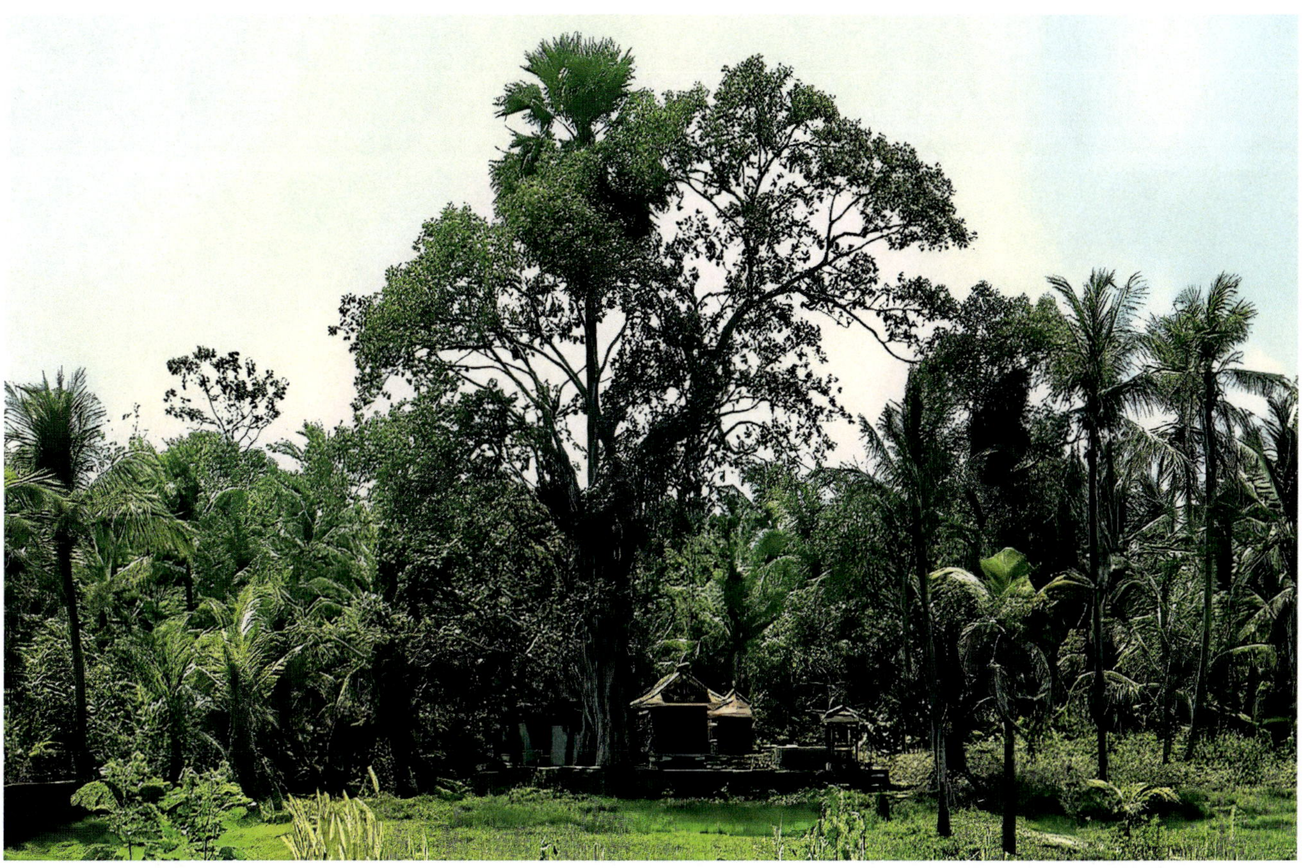

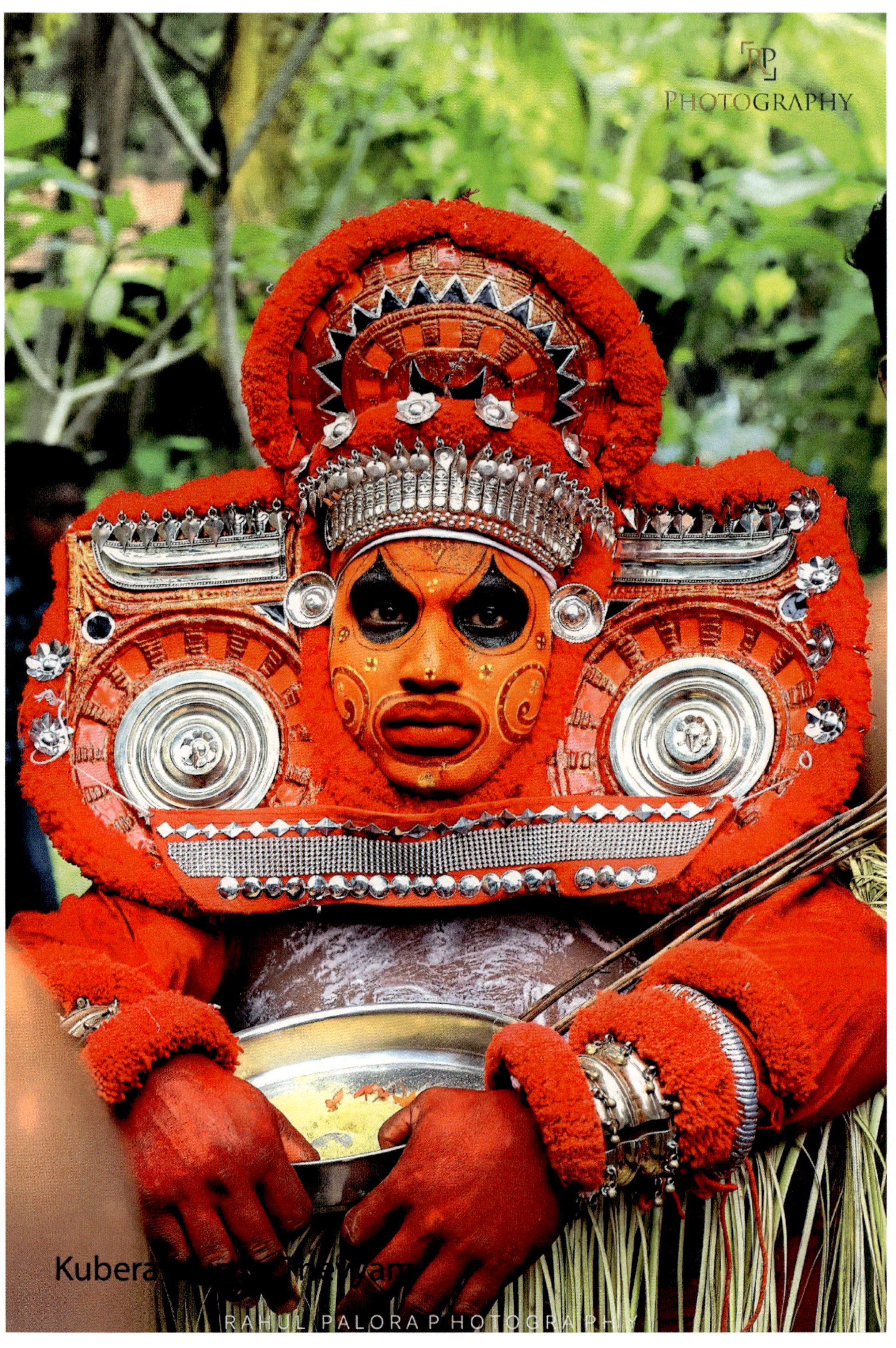

Kubera [illegible]

Munnayeeswaran Theyyam

Kattoor Nair was the ultimate devotee of Tuluvanathil Bhagavathi. It is believed that he used to bring the Goddess to him with his prayers. When he passed away, he was buried in the temple. He became Munayareshvaran Theyyam after his death. When the Pulidaivangal set their journey to Kerala, Munnayar of the Kerala-Karnataka border is said to have joined them. And so, in certain temples where Pulidaivangal is revered, Munayareshvaran is also performed.

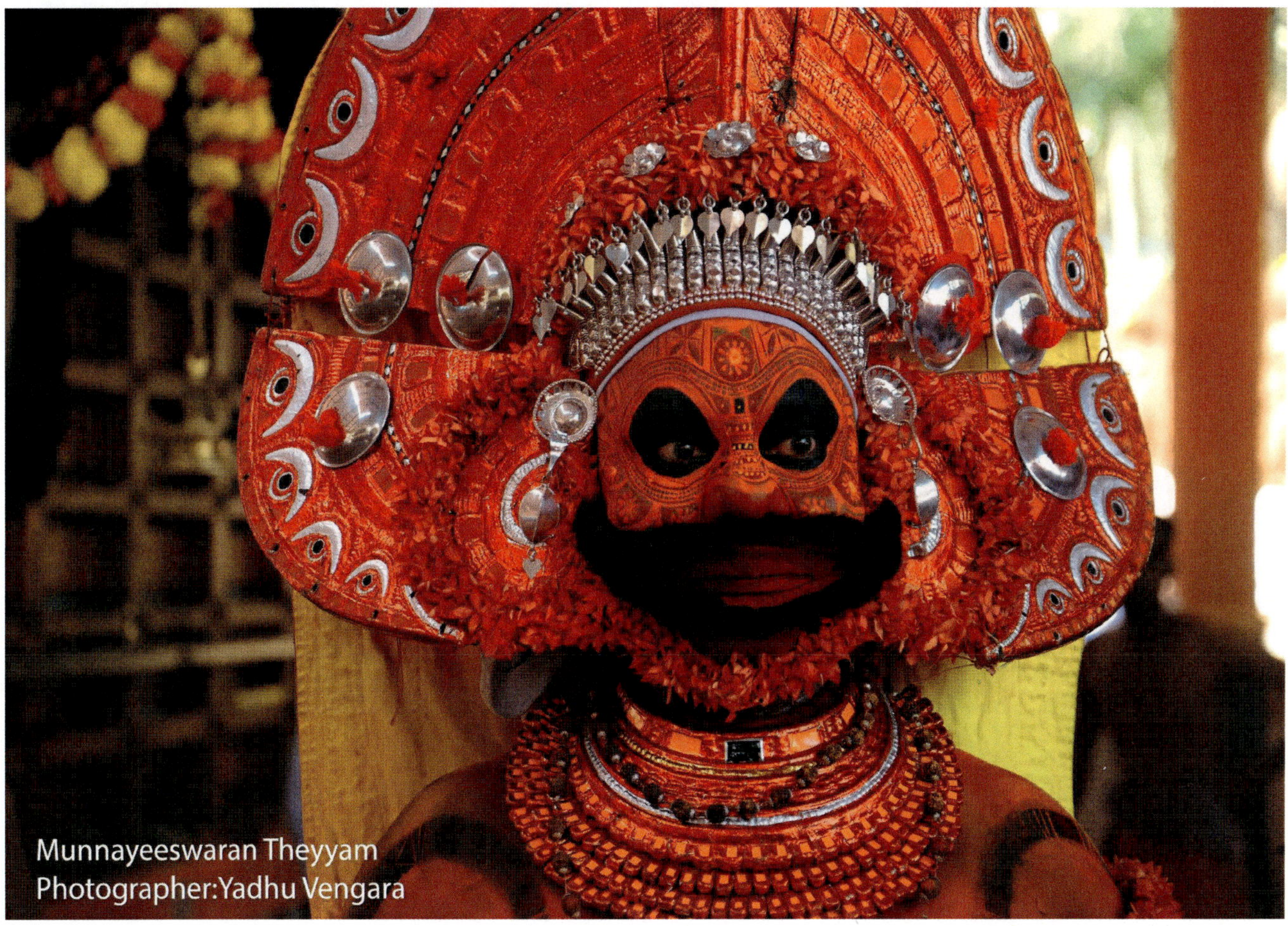

Munnayeeswaran Theyyam
Photographer:Yadhu Vengara

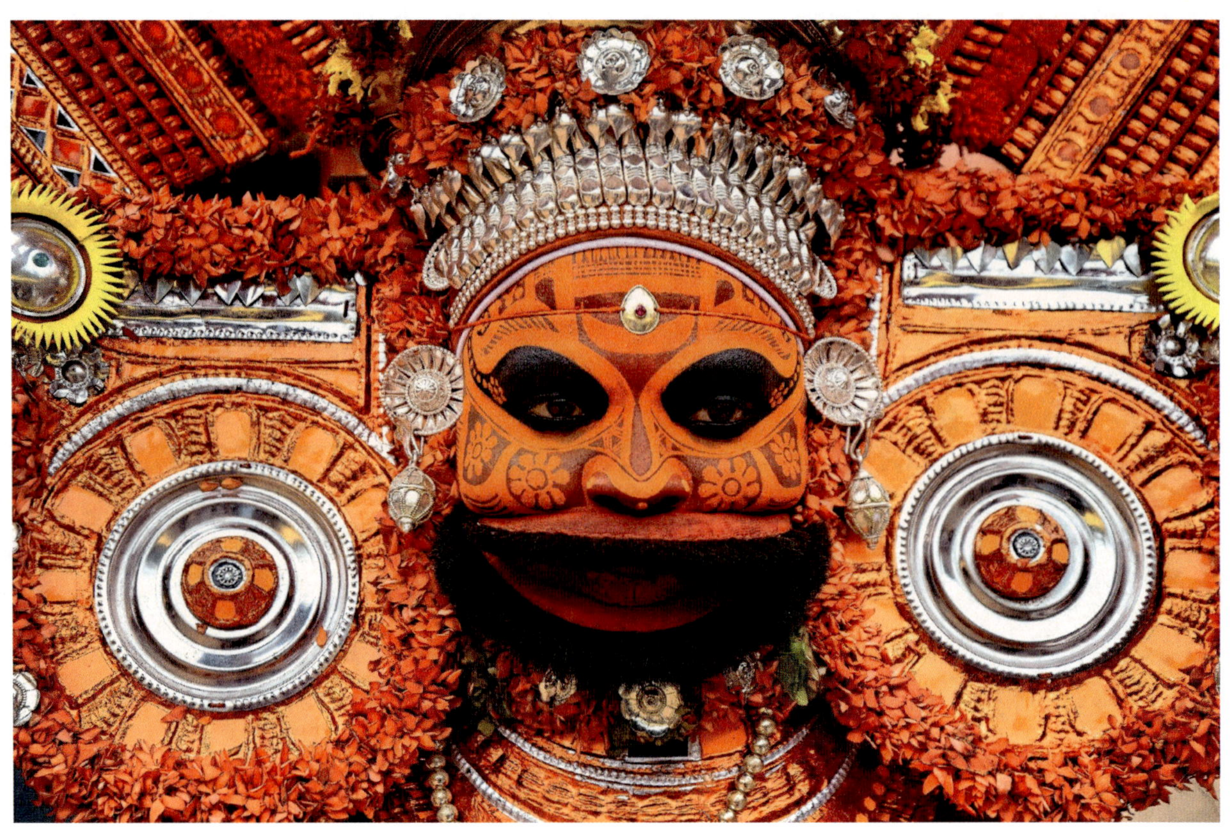

Kariyappil Bhagavathy Theyyam and Thiruvakkattu Bhagavathy Theyyam

Kariyappil Bhagavathy Theyyam shares the same legend as Thiruvarkkattu Bhagavathy Theyyam. *Kammoth Nair* of Kunnumbram tharavadu (joint family) and his aides went to *Pilikkod Rayaramangalam* to take a holy bath and worship. The Goddess accompanied them to the shrine at *Kariyapp* near Cheemeni and decided to make Cheemeni Appan's temple her abode. Legend says, later, she came to *Kunnumbram tharavadu*.

Villagers fondly call Thiruvarkkattu Bhagavathy Thaiparadevata (the mother clan deity). She was the primary Goddess worshipped by the Kolathiri dynasty. She has over seventy different names in different *desams* (places). Out of the six Theyyams that were incarnated from the third eye of Lord Shiva, this Thai (mother) is a fierce-looking annihilator of Darika, the demon. Goddess Parvati, the wife of Lord Shiva, is said to have incarnated as Bhadrakali. After killing Darika, Lord Shiva sent the Goddess to earth to take care of her worshippers; when Bhadrakali reached earth, she was given abode in the north at Thiruvarkkad (Madayi Kaavu), in the south (Kalarivathilkkal), east (Mamanikunnu), west (Cherukunnu Annapoornneswari Temple). As she was given abode in four directions by dividing the Kolathiri kingdom, she became the worshipping Goddess of Kolathnadu.

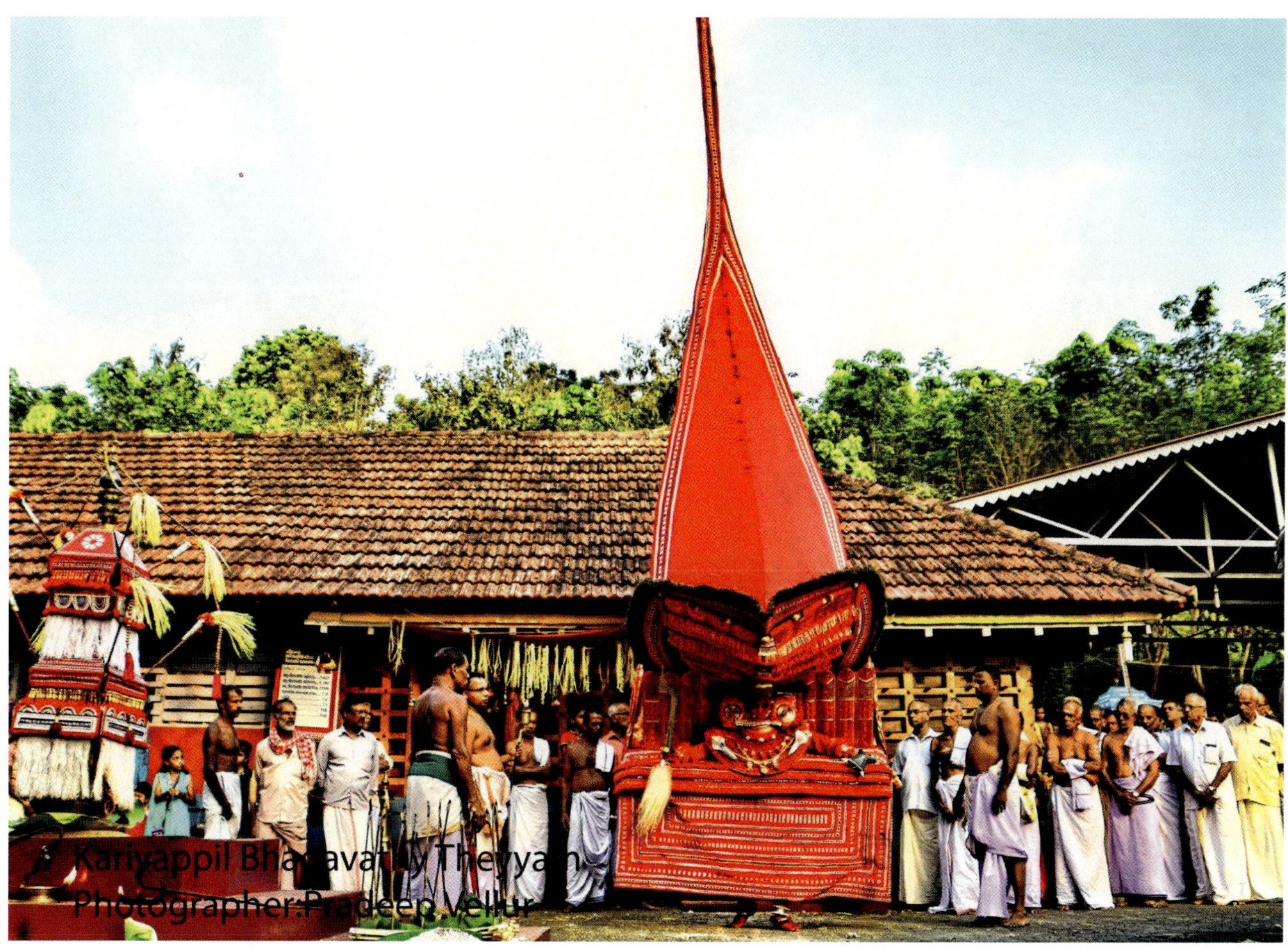

Kariyappil Bhagavathy Theyyam
Photographer:Pradeep Vellur

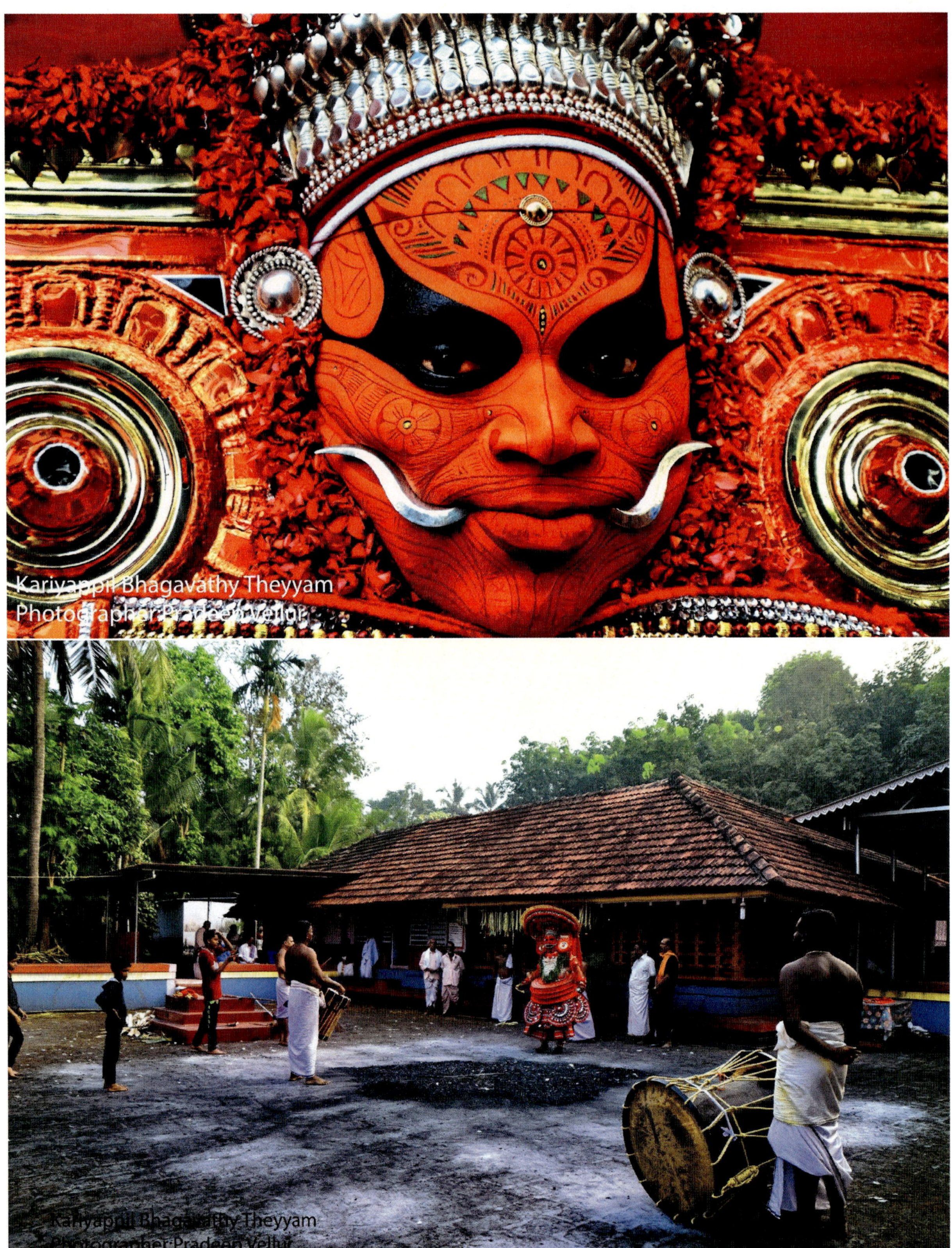

Kariyappil Bhagavathy Theyyam
Photographer:Pradeep Velur

Kariyappil Bhagavathy Theyyam
Photographer:Pradeep Velur

Pulli Pothi (Pulli Bhagavathy) Theyyam

Pothi is a vernacular contraction of Bhagavathy which means Goddess. Pulli Pothi is known as Pulli bhagavathy in some parts of *Kerala's Karivellur- Cheruvathur regions*.

The legend of Pulli Pothi is the story of worshipper Paimbaran Koppalan, who used to fill four *Uruli* (traditional cookware made of clay, copper, and bronze) with blood for his forest nymph deity of Pulli Pothi. One day the deity was enraged to see her worshipper had failed to fill the urulis with blood. She beheaded him and sucked his blood instead. Later, she abandoned her abode on the hilltop and descended. This fierce-looking deity is in the form of *Chuzhali*, and her Theyyam is performed as *Kolam* (figure). Once the God known as *Chengalad* has performed, the same performer will also bear the kolam of Pulli Pothi.

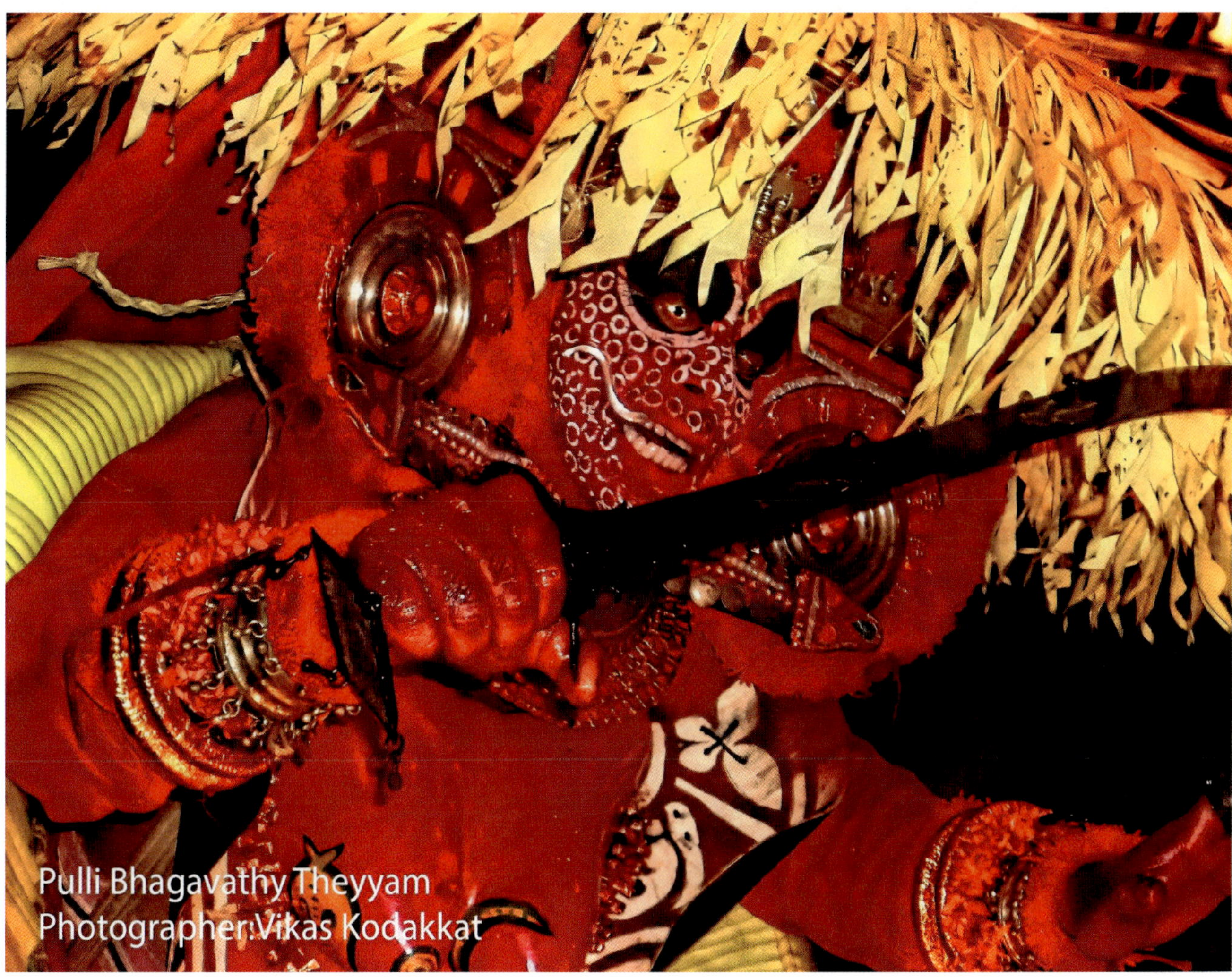

Pulli Bhagavathy Theyyam
Photographer:Vikas Kodakkat

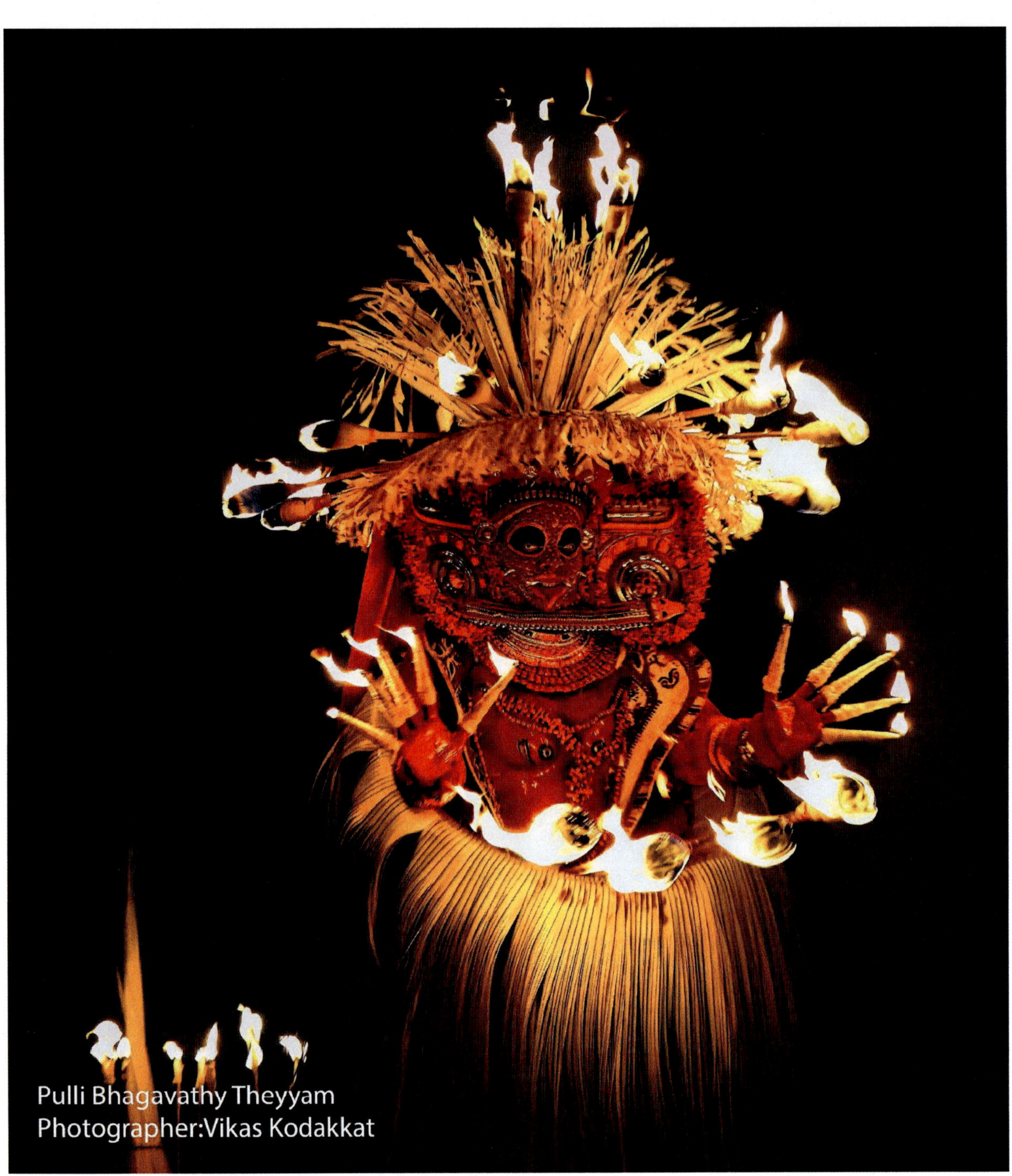

Pulli Bhagavathy Theyyam
Photographer:Vikas Kodakkat

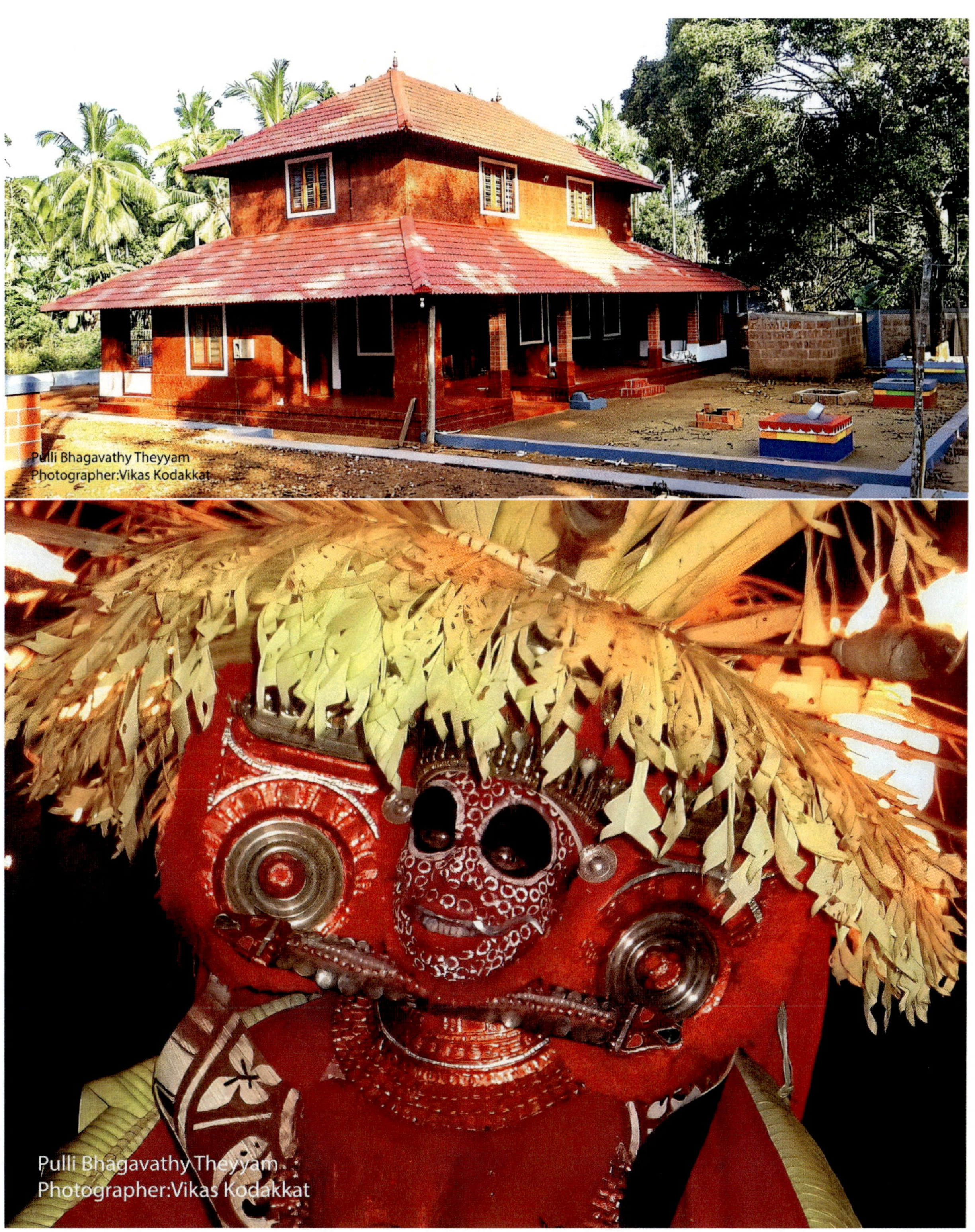

Pulli Bhagavathy Theyyam
Photographer:Vikas Kodakkat

Pulli Bhagavathy Theyyam
Photographer:Vikas Kodakkat

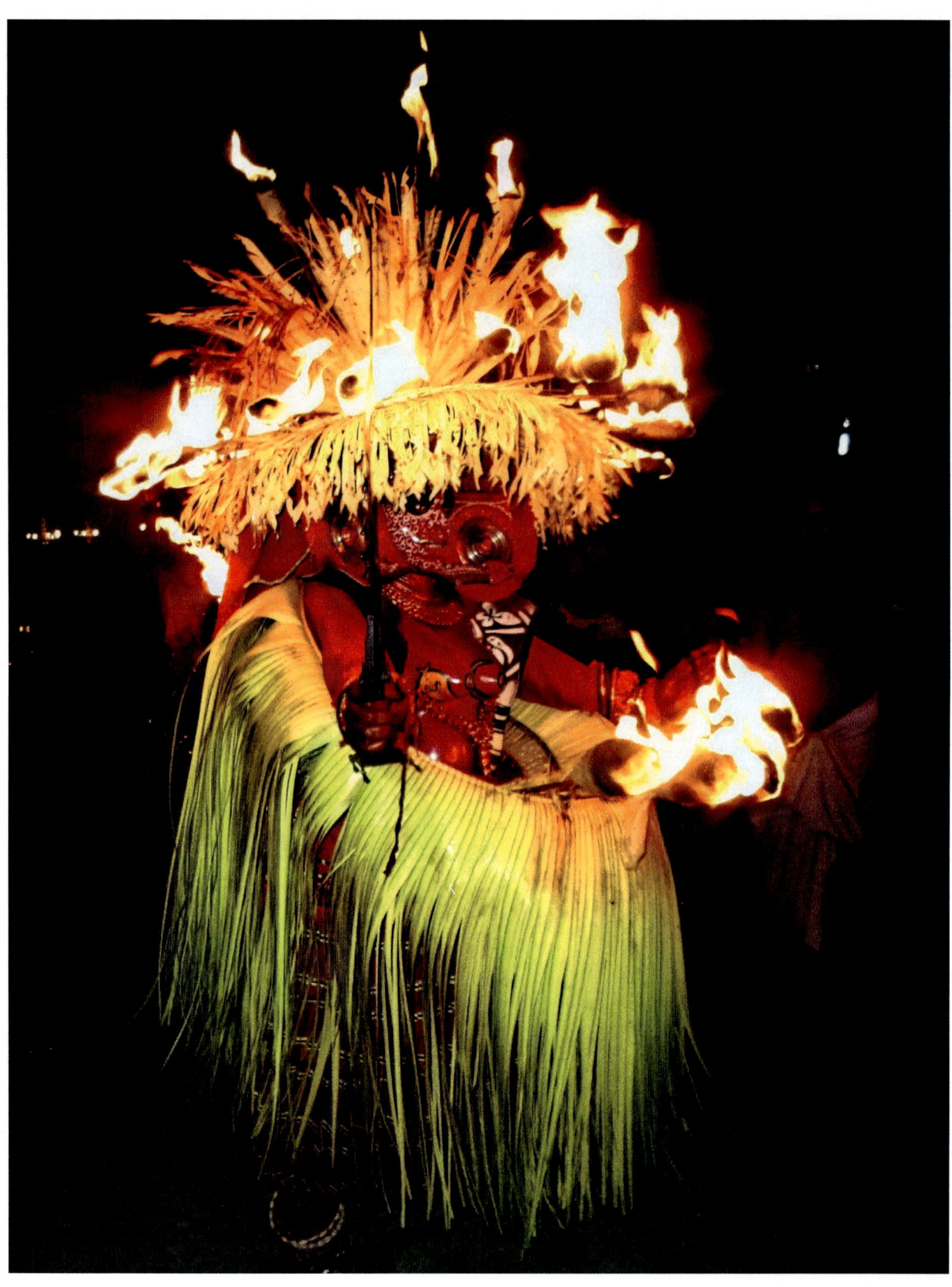

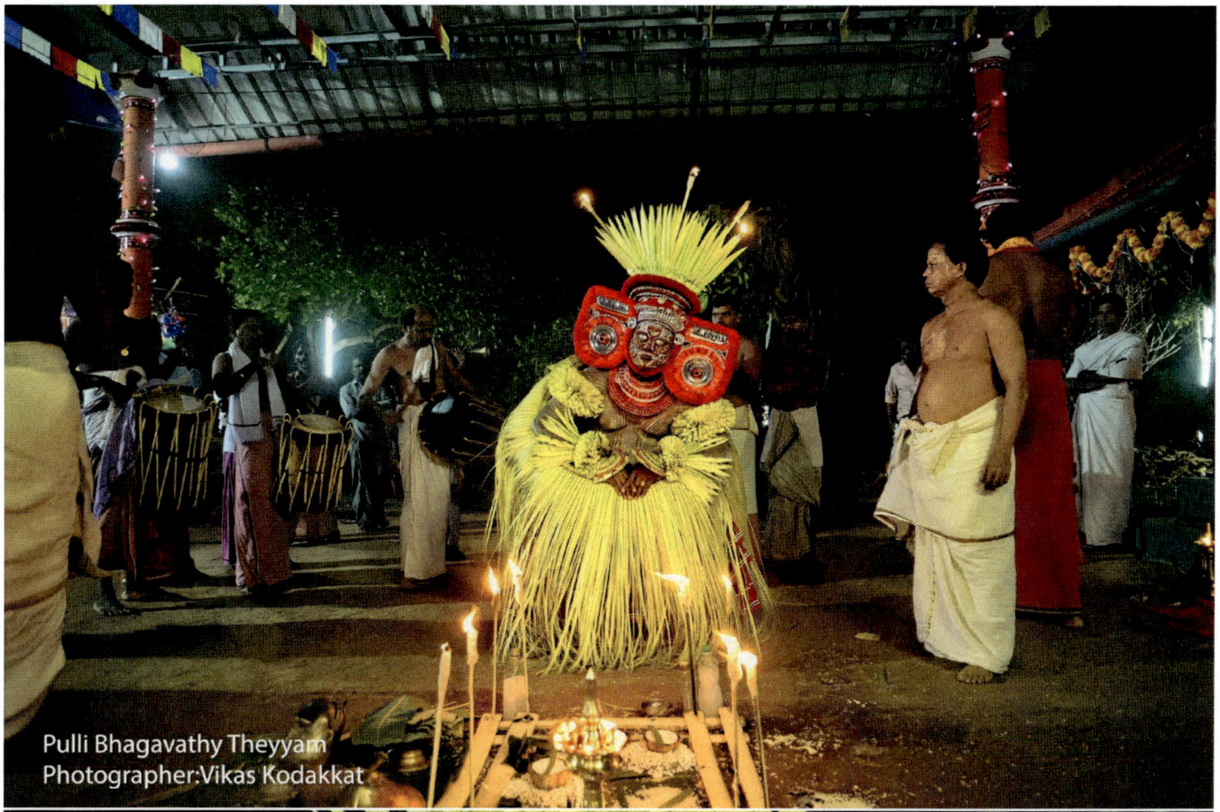

Pulli Bhagavathy Theyyam
Photographer:Vikas Kodakkat

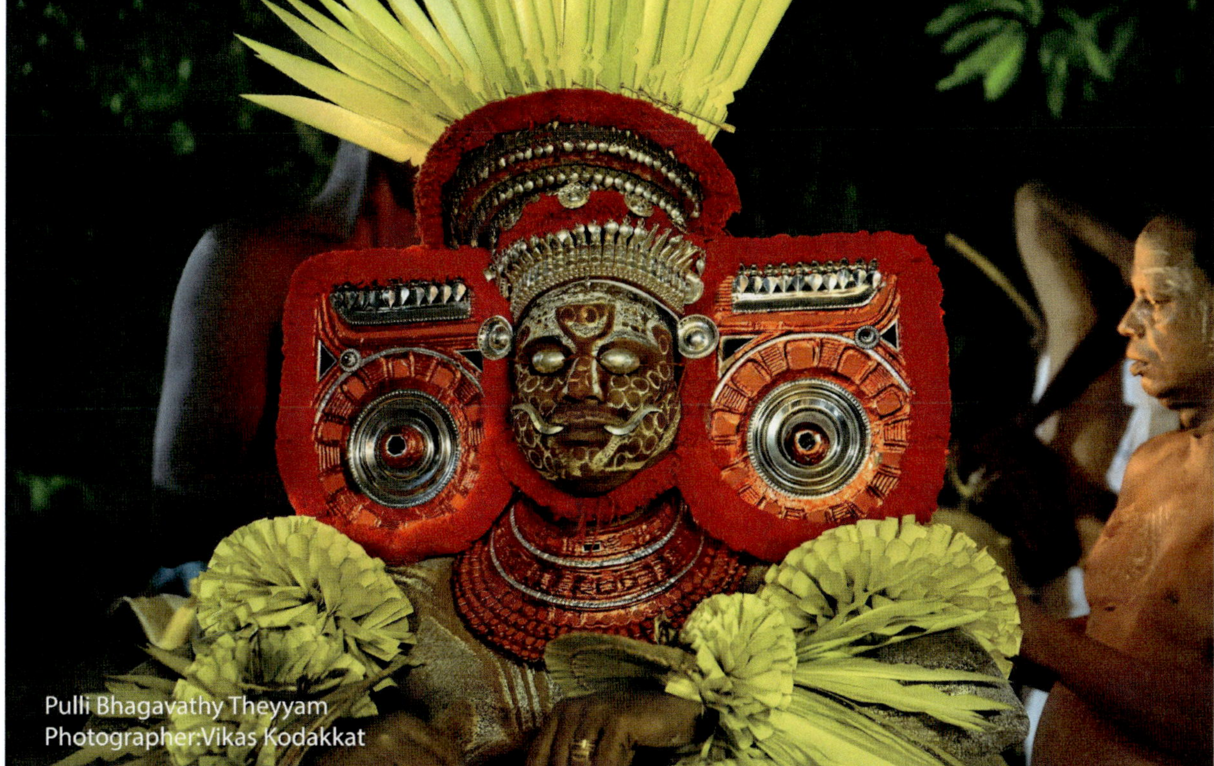

Pulli Bhagavathy Theyyam
Photographer:Vikas Kodakkat

Kaliyar Bhagavathy / Padayil Bhagavathy

Centuries ago, there was a war between the Devas and Asuras. The Devas faced difficulties in defeating the Asuras. Hence, they approached Lord Shiva, seeking a solution to the problem. Lord Shiva got angry, and his eyes turned red. He performed the frantic and violent dance called Thandava. This shook thousands of *jada magudam* (matted locks adorned by the moon). All four directions trembled. A divine soul came from the sacrificial fire pit, one hundred and eight feet in depth. This divine soul took the form of a Goddess and won the war against the Asuras. She is later known as Padayil bhagavathy. She has other names such as Kaliyar bhagavathy, Sree bhagavathy, etc.

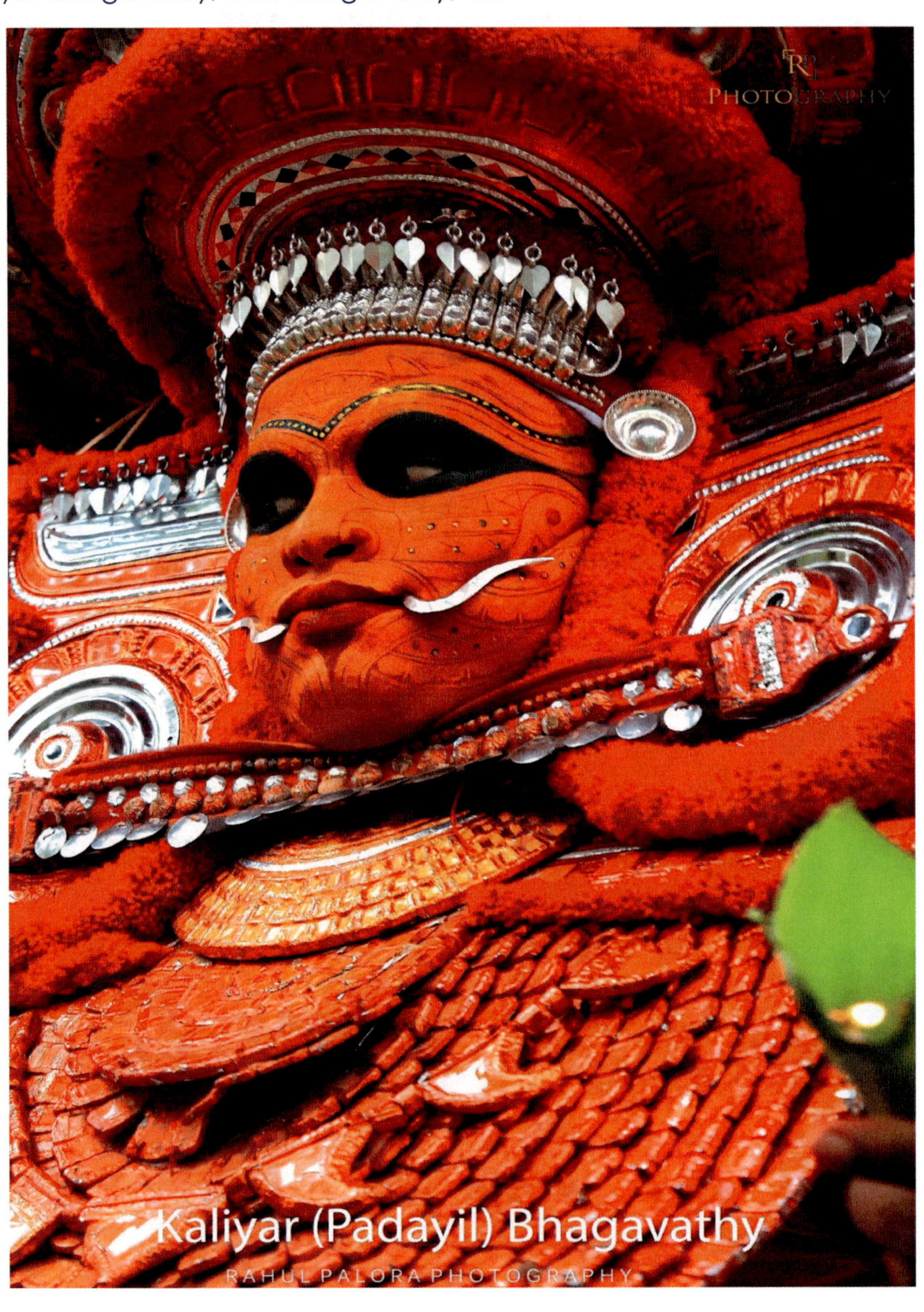

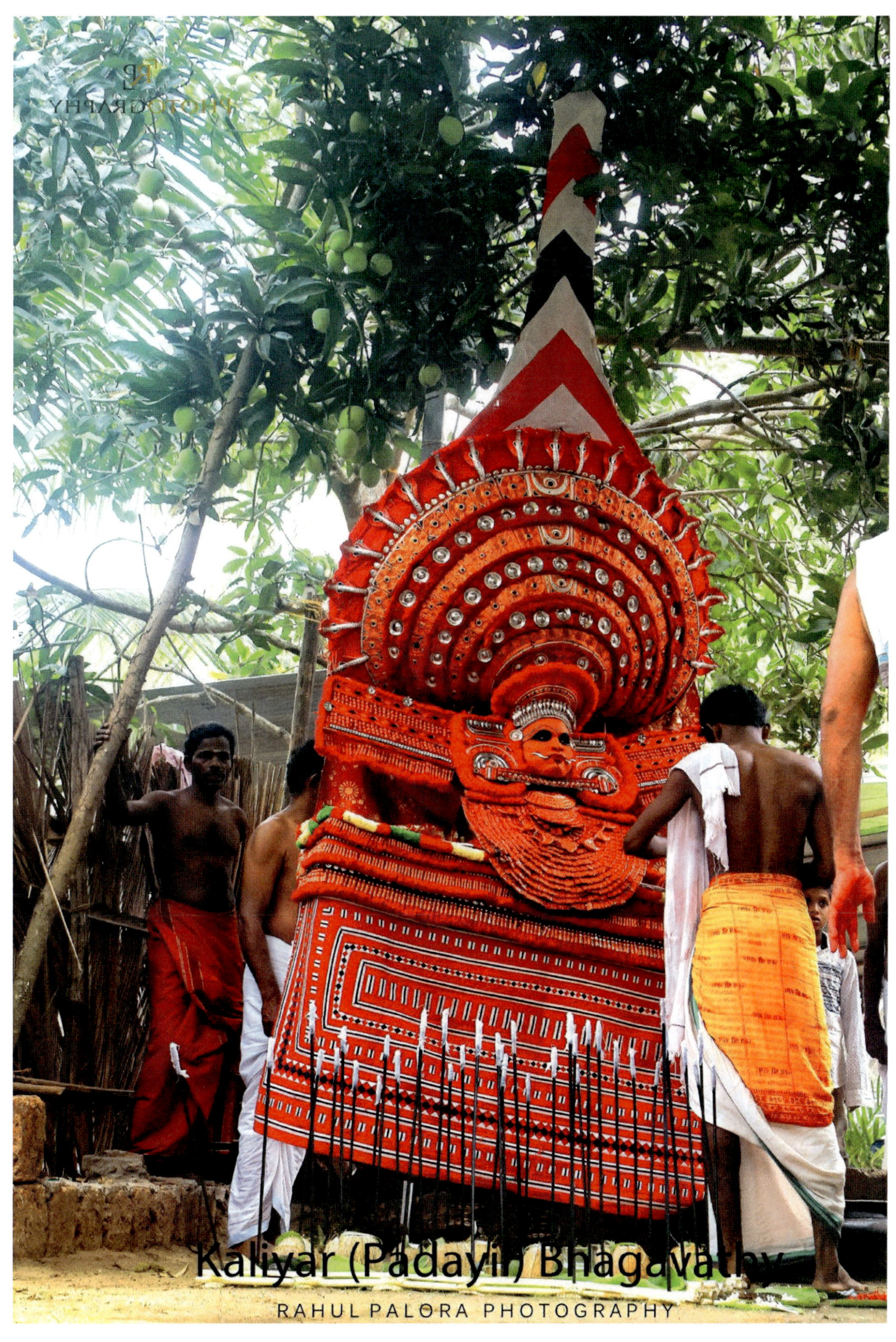

Kaliyar (Padayil) Bhagavathy

Chukannamma (Chonnamma) Theyyam

The Vannan community performs Chukannamma Theyyam. This Goddess is also called *Chonnamma* (*Chukanna* means reddish, and *Chonna* is the vernacular usage). Though this Theyyam looks similar to the *Thampuratti* Theyyam, the mudi (hair) is comparatively shorter.

Legend says women of *Eravalli Mathilakam* were suffering from infertility; therefore, a miraculous medicine was prepared for them. The ingredients were mainly rice and flowers. Unfortunately, a doe (female deer) consumed the medication, giving birth to a human child. The hunters found this baby girl in the forest. They picked her up and handed her over to the Eravally Mathilakam. The Brahmin couples called her '*Vaanaar Paithal*,' and her characteristics were unique to other children her age.

Once, her parents scolded the child for playing in the soil. The girl was angry and stormed off. She met some carpenters on the way and asked them about the road. The carpenters ignored her query, but later, they felt the girl they encountered must have some divine power. When the carpenters spotted her, she demanded an 'Aarudam' (a sacred seat). They built the foundation for her, and she made it her abode.

Later, when she had her menarche, she forgot about the rituals and stayed there as usual. Her parents heard of this and rushed to her abode with the traditional *Paal Pungan* (stew prepared with milk and rice, this ritual is part of the Samskara (Culture), i.e., rites of passage in a human being's life described in ancient Sanskrit texts. Pungan is the second ritual of Samskara and one of the three rituals for the unborn child). Despite the pleading of her parents, she refused to meet them, so the parents left the Pungan there and returned home. As she was angry with her parents, she kicked away the sacred pungan, which landed at the paddy field in Kuttanadu. It is believed that the pungan grew as red rice in that field. Later she said she would not stay at the place where her parents had burst into tears. She ran away from there and made the top of an Asian Palmyra palm her abode.

Eventually, people from the Nambiar community came to cut down that palm tree. They planned to make a bow and arrow with the Palmyra palm trunk. When they started to cut the palm with an axe, the girl's cry lingered in the atmosphere. The palm tree did not fall because of the girl's presence, so they talked with the tree and agreed to arrange a temple and regular rituals on her behalf. The girl went with them. Later, they installed the girl as Chukannamma (literally a red mother) and organized for a priest to conduct the rituals there.

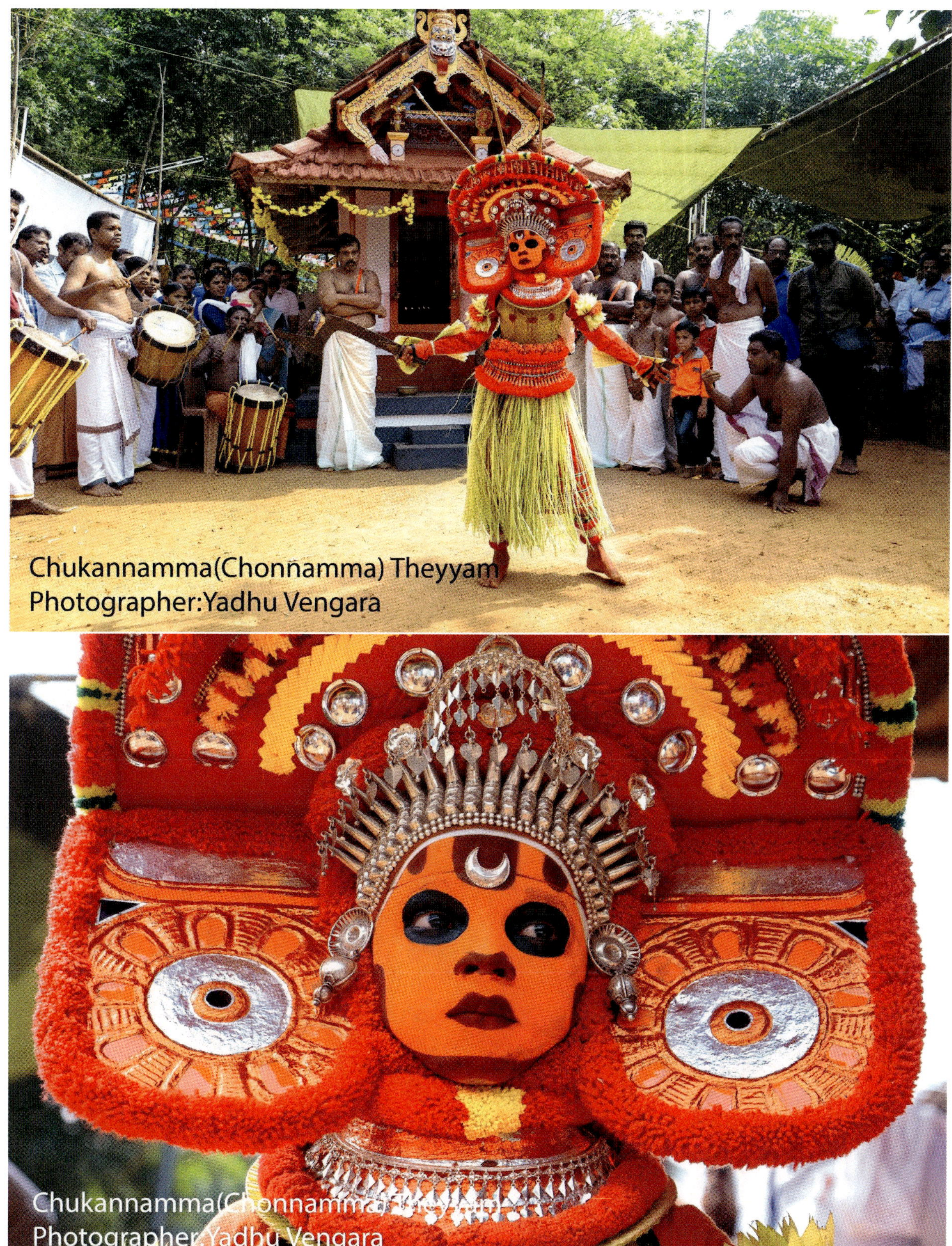

Chukannamma(Chonnamma) Theyyam
Photographer:Yadhu Vengara

Chukannamma(Chonnamma) Theyyam
Photographer:Yadhu Vengara

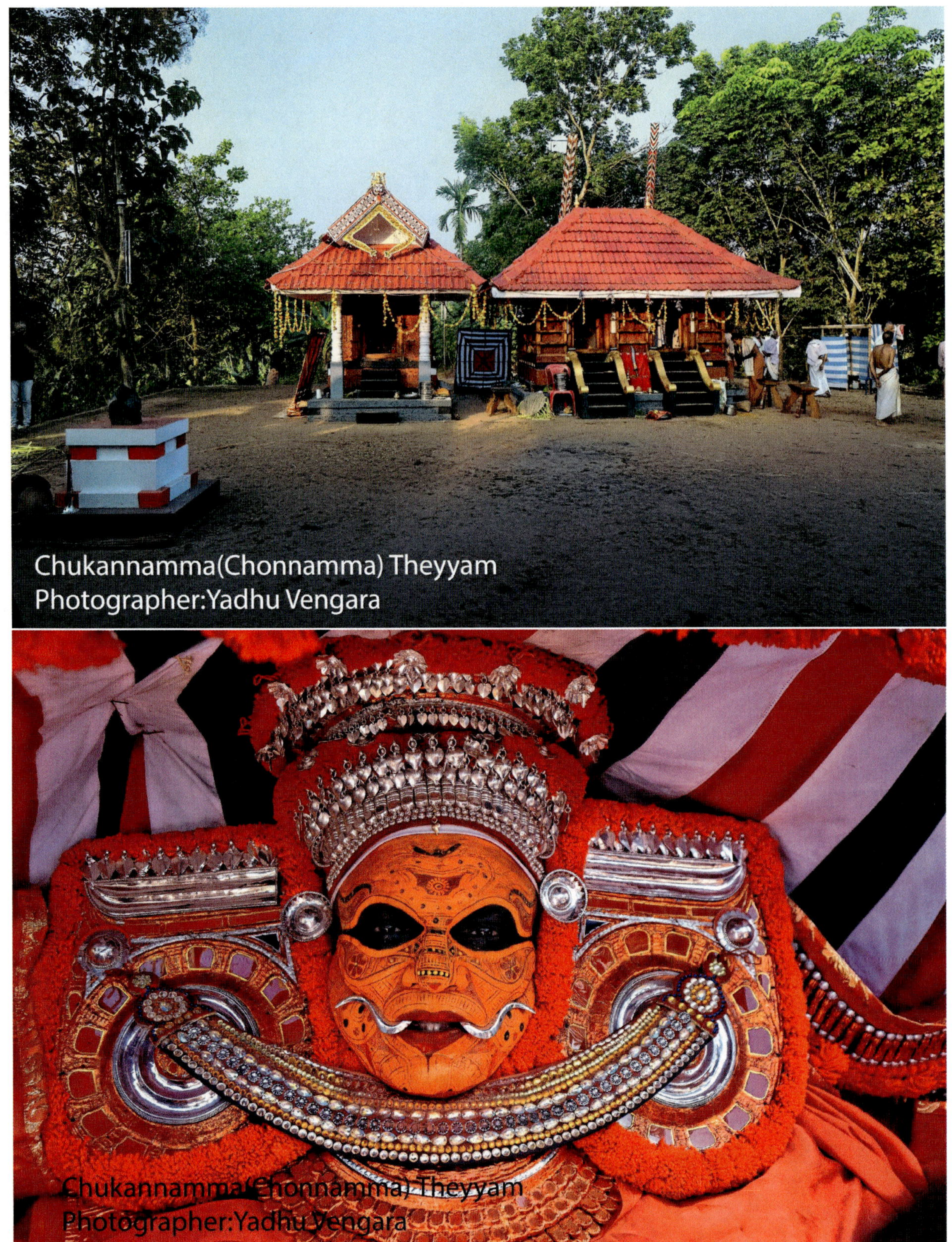

Chukannamma(Chonnamma) Theyyam
Photographer:Yadhu Vengara

Chukannamma(Chonnamma) Theyyam
Photographer:Yadhu Vengara

Thekkan Kariyathan

Pada Nair of *Palar* house and *Kelachandra Nair* of *Palakkunnath* house went hunting and fishing. The hunting failed, as they couldn't find any animals. Tired and thirsty from their attempts, they went to the residence of *Karinkulakkandathamma*. The host compelled them to dine there. They agreed and bathed at the *Karinchilatan Chira* (a reservoir nearby), where they found strange fish species but couldn't catch them. They found the same peculiar fish in the well when they returned home. They placed a bunch of plantains in a bucket made of areca nut spathe and lowered it with the help of the pulley and rope. When the bucket reached the water's surface, the fish reduced its size to fit into the bucket. But when they tried to cut the fish into pieces, the fish showed them its real self-form. They were startled and begged for pardon. Also, they decided to make atonement for all the wrongdoings. They swore if two golden boys took birth on either side of the granite gatehouse of Mathilakam, they would train them in the combat sport of fencing, prepare real-size replicas of them in gold, and take them to the fortress in Kunjimangalam. There, the two golden boys, *Thekkan Komappan* and *Thekkan Chathu,* were incarnated on either side of the granite gatehouse.

They were taught traditional martial arts, and when they grew older and were ready to take hold of the rapier and accept the status of Chekavar, they received the blades from the Tamil king Pandi Perumal and received their status names. Thekkan Chathu became 'Thekkan Kiriyathan,' and Thekkan Komappan became 'Theykkan Karumakan.' They cut down a large palm tree and prepared bows for archery. Later in their lives, several miracles occurred. They inflicted mental disorders on Chanthan Thandan and Thirunellur Thandathi (a Thiyya couple), for they had refused to give them alcohol. Their mental ailments were cured only after giving a warm reception to both of them. Kariathan wasn't reluctant to sever the hand of a boy who teased him, but later the hand was returned when the boy begged for pardon. That boy decided to be their servant. The 'Kaikkolan Theyyam' performed along with 'Kariathan Theyyam' is based on this boy who lost a hand.

With white color on the body and yellow on the face, the overall make-up for this Theyyam is comparatively simple. This Theyyam uses a short hair called the *Kozhupattam mudi*. Kariathan is the supreme deity at two temples, one at Thazheppalliyath Kottath in Blathur, Kannur district, and the other at Arimbur Shree Kariathan temple in Purakkad village in Thikkodi Panchayath of Kozhikode district.

The traditional professions of certain castes like that of *Nathian* (also called Naavu Theeyar and Valanchiyar), *Nadyan,* and *Vilakkithala Nair* are hair-cutting and shaving services for the upper castes. *Thekkan Kariathan* is one of their clan deities. They have Theyyam shrines (kavus) at *Kannapuram*, *Kandakkai*, *Kundayam Kovval,* and *Pariyaram*.

Another legend is that an ancestor of Chenicheri tharavadu (a noble family) went to battle at Ambalappuzha and Thekkan Kriathan helped him momentously. He brought Thekkan Kariathan and installed him at the abode there. Aroli Shree Melchira Kottam of Kannur is one of the main shrines where Thekkan Kariathan Theyyam is performed.

It is believed that Thekkan Kariathan is the energy of Lord Shiva, and Thekkan Karumakan is the energy of Lord Vishnu. Kariathan means Param Shiva. Kariathan is also known as

Thekkan Chaathu, but more popularly, by the name Thekkan Kariathan. Usually, another Theyyam called Kaikkolan also is performed along with this Theyyam.

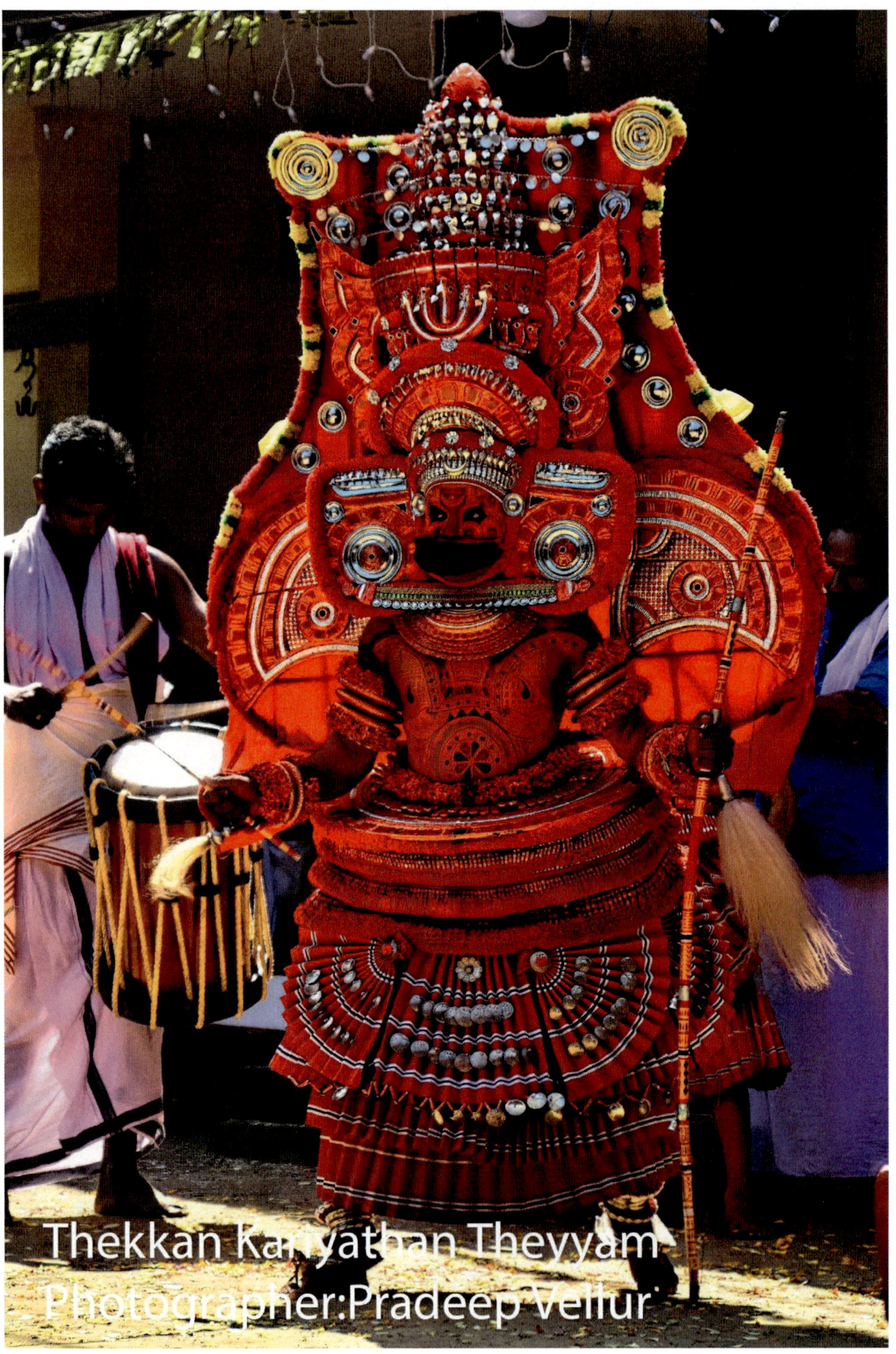

Thekkan Kariyathan Theyyam
Photographer:Pradeep Vellur

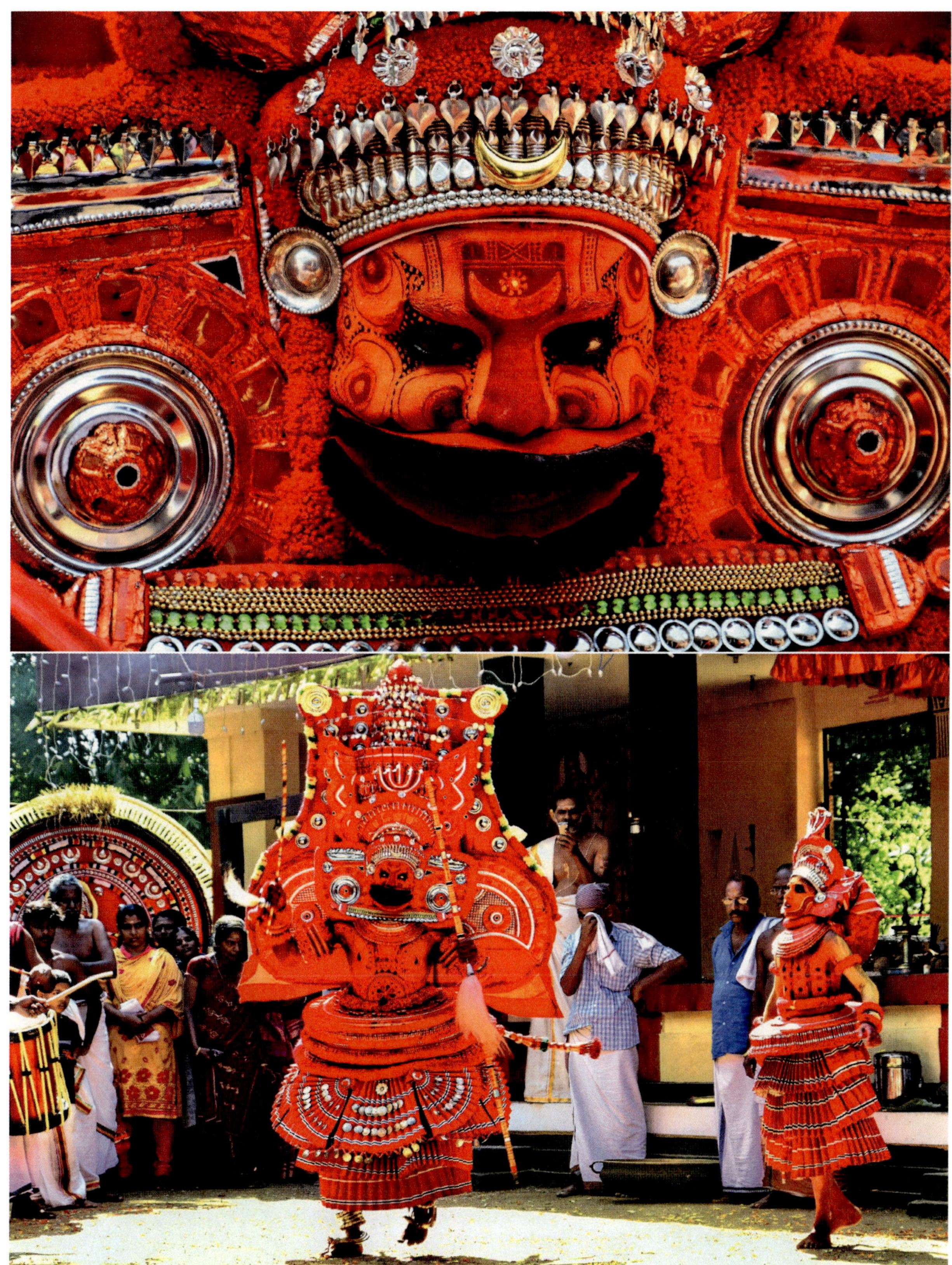

Puli Muthappan Theyyam

Puli Muthappan and Puli Muthachi are Theyyams based on the Parameshvara-Parvathi concept, with installations at Puli Daivam shrines at Kilalur and Iriveri at Thalassery in the Kannur district.

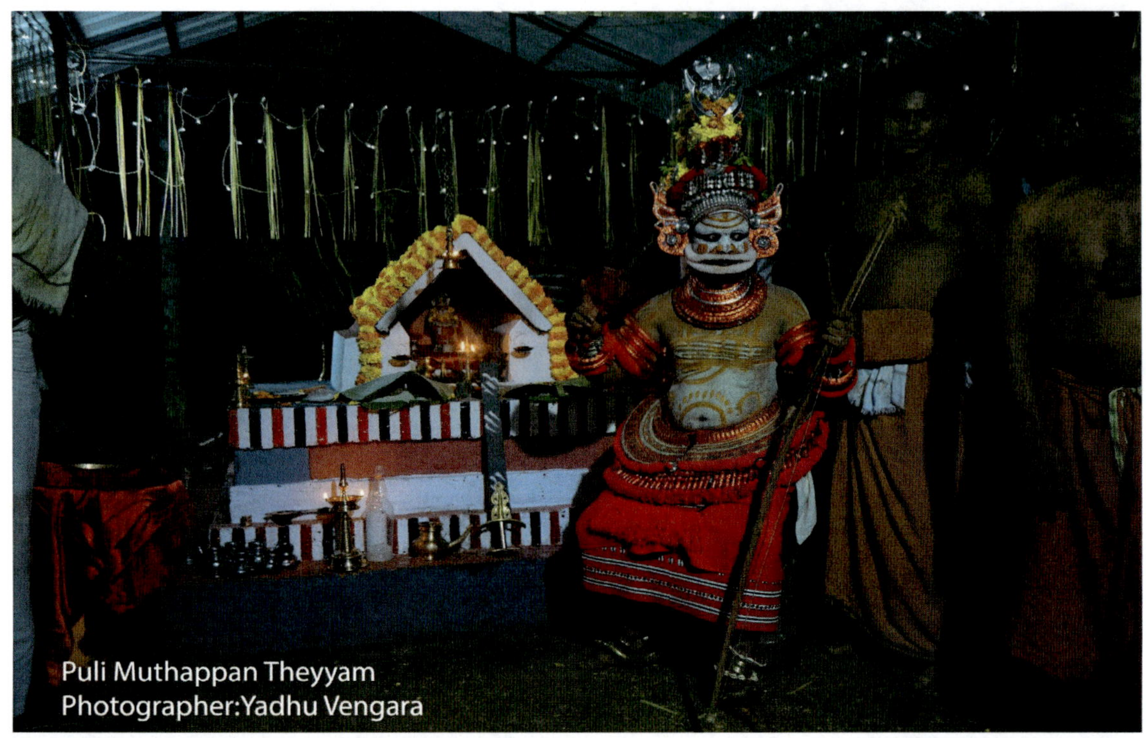

Puli Muthappan Theyyam
Photographer:Yadhu Vengara

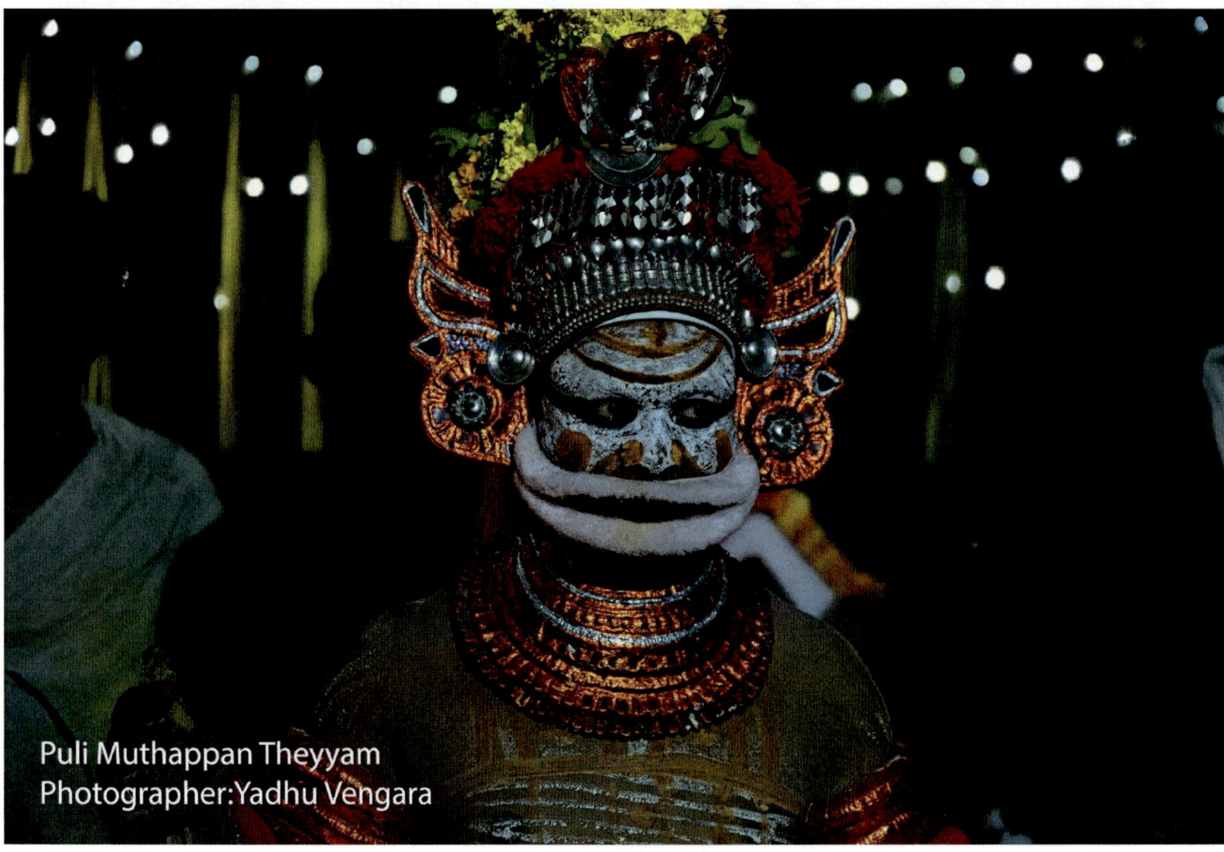

Puli Muthappan Theyyam
Photographer:Yadhu Vengara

Vannathi Pothi Theyyam

Peruvannathi was the wife of a Theyyam artist from the Peruvannan community. According to ancient customs, women take a ritualistic bath on the fourth day of their menstrual cycle. Peruvannathi was responsible for replenishing clean, fresh clothes for these women. A dark-skinned girl spotted Peruvannathi on her travel from her house to the nearby river. She asked Peruvannathi for clean garments, as she had completed the ritualistic bath on the third day. However, Peruvannathi rejected her request as it was getting late. But the girl obstructed her path, so Peruvannathi mocked the girl asking why a girl from the forest needed clothes. Infuriated, the girl murdered her by hitting her with a rock. After her demise, Peruvannathi became the Theyyam in the form of Vannathi Pothi.

The legend behind the Vannathi Pothi Theyyam is shared by the Bhadrakali Theyyam.

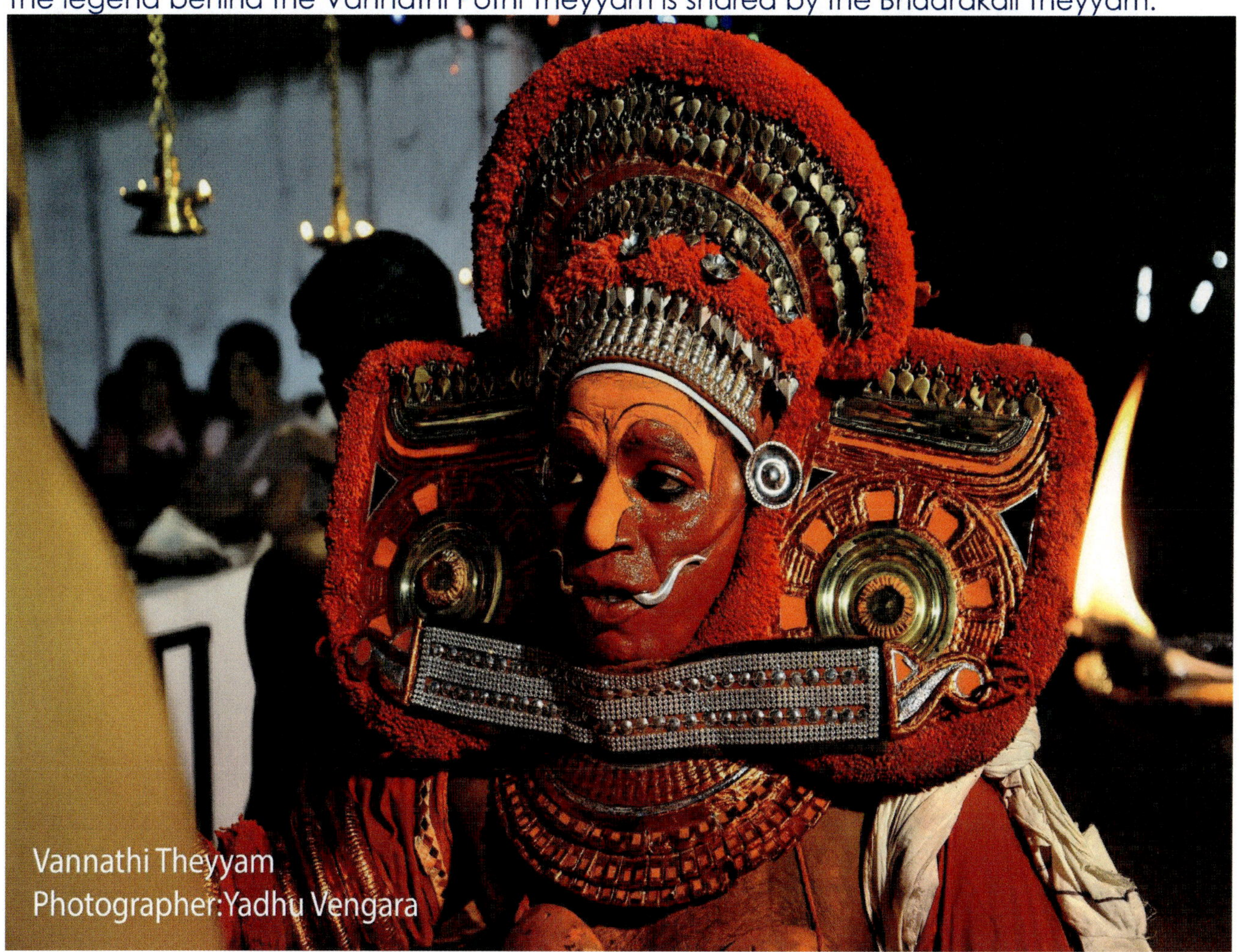

Vannathi Theyyam
Photographer:Yadhu Vengara

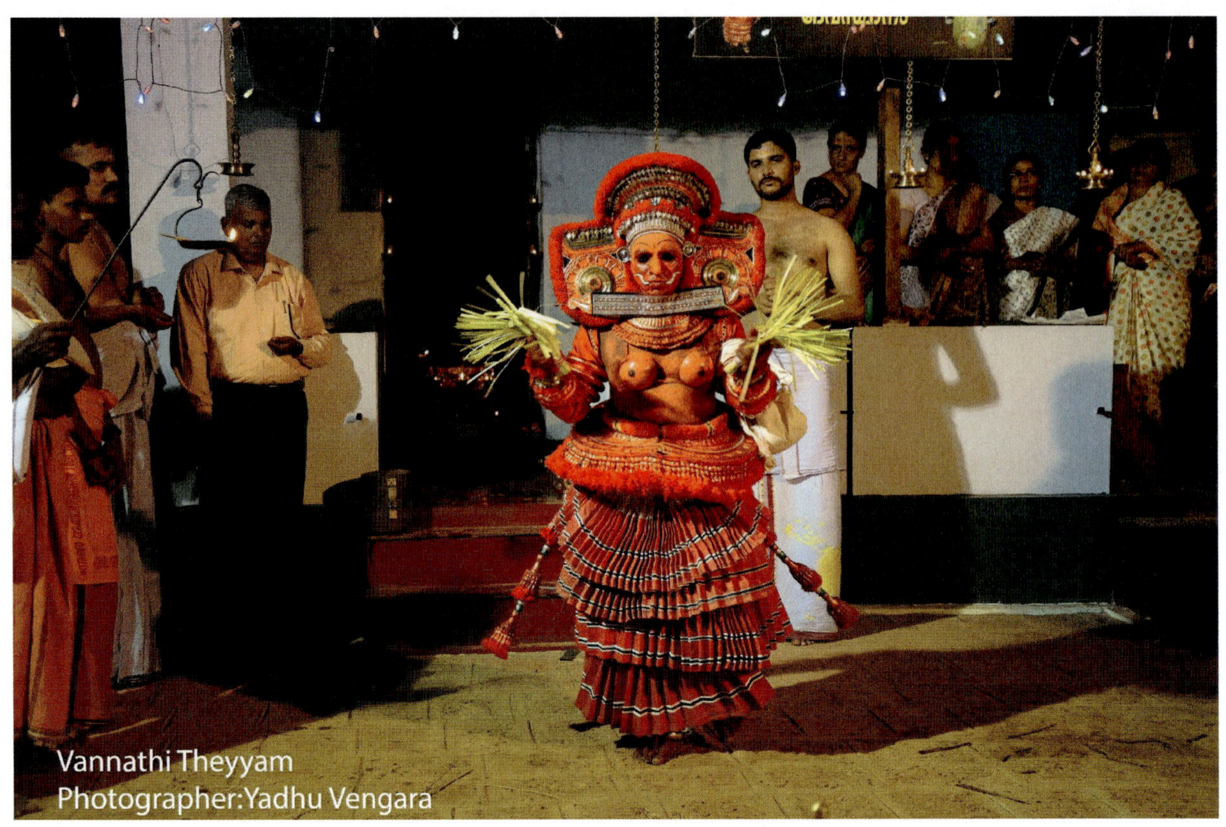

Vannathi Theyyam
Photographer:Yadhu Vengara

Kaikkolan Theyyam

Kariyathan refers to Lord Shiva. He is also known as Thekkann Chathu. However, he is legendarily known as Thekkan Kariyathan. It is common to spot a Theyyam by the name of Kaikkolan along with the Thekkan Kariyathan Theyyam. They share the same legend.

The Pada Nair of Palar House and Kelendra Nair of Palakunnam House ventured forth, climbing the mighty mountains to hunt and explore the vast seas to catch fish. However, since their efforts at hunting were futile, the tired duo arrived at the house of Karingulakandathakkamma, asking for water. She invited them to stay for lunch, to which they agreed. Before eating, they went to the Karinchiladan River for a bath, where they saw mystical varieties of fish. But all their efforts to catch these fishes were in vain. Upon returning to the house of *Karingulakandathakkamma*, they spotted the same fishes in the house's well. The duo kept one banana on a silver plate and lowered it into the well to attract the fish. The fishes shrunk their size and got onto the plates. Rejoicing their success, they decided to cut these fish into pieces to prepare a dish from them. But as soon as they attempted this, the mystical fishes revealed their true forms, disclosing the divinity of Lord Shiva and Vishnu in them. Scared and guilty about their actions, the duo begged forgiveness for their unintentional mistakes. They decided to do penance for their wrong actions by agreeing to train two children, who were due to be born on the seventh day on either side of the river, in martial arts and erect their gold statues in Kunhimangalam.

On the seventh day, Thekkan Komappan and Thekkan Chathu were born on either side of the river. When it was time for them to be warriors after undergoing training in martial arts by taking the sword from Pandi Perumal, Thekkan Chathu came to be known as Thekkan Kariyathan, and Thekkan Komappan came to be known as Thekkan Karumakan. One day, they chopped a palm tree and made bows out of it, resulting in many surprises in their lives. Chandan Thandan and Thirunellur Thandathi, who denied giving alcohol to them, became angry. Only after they treated the warriors well were they cured of the mental instability. A child once mocked Thekkan Kariyathan, and he chopped off the child's hand. But when the child pled guilty, his hand was restored. The child later became their ardent subject. The Kaikkolan Theyyam that is performed along with Kariyathan Theyyam depicts the concept of this child who lost his hand. This Theyyam adorns a simple costume with white color all over the body and a yellow painted face. It also features a short hair wig known as Kozhupattam. They are the significant deities at the Blathur Thazhepalli Kottam in Kannur, Kerala as well as at the Arimbur Sri Kariyathan Kshethram in Kozhikode, Kerala. These deities also have shrines at Kannapuram, Kandakai, Kundayam Kovval, and Pariyaram. The Theyyam hails the deities as 'Aruvar Karanonmare!'

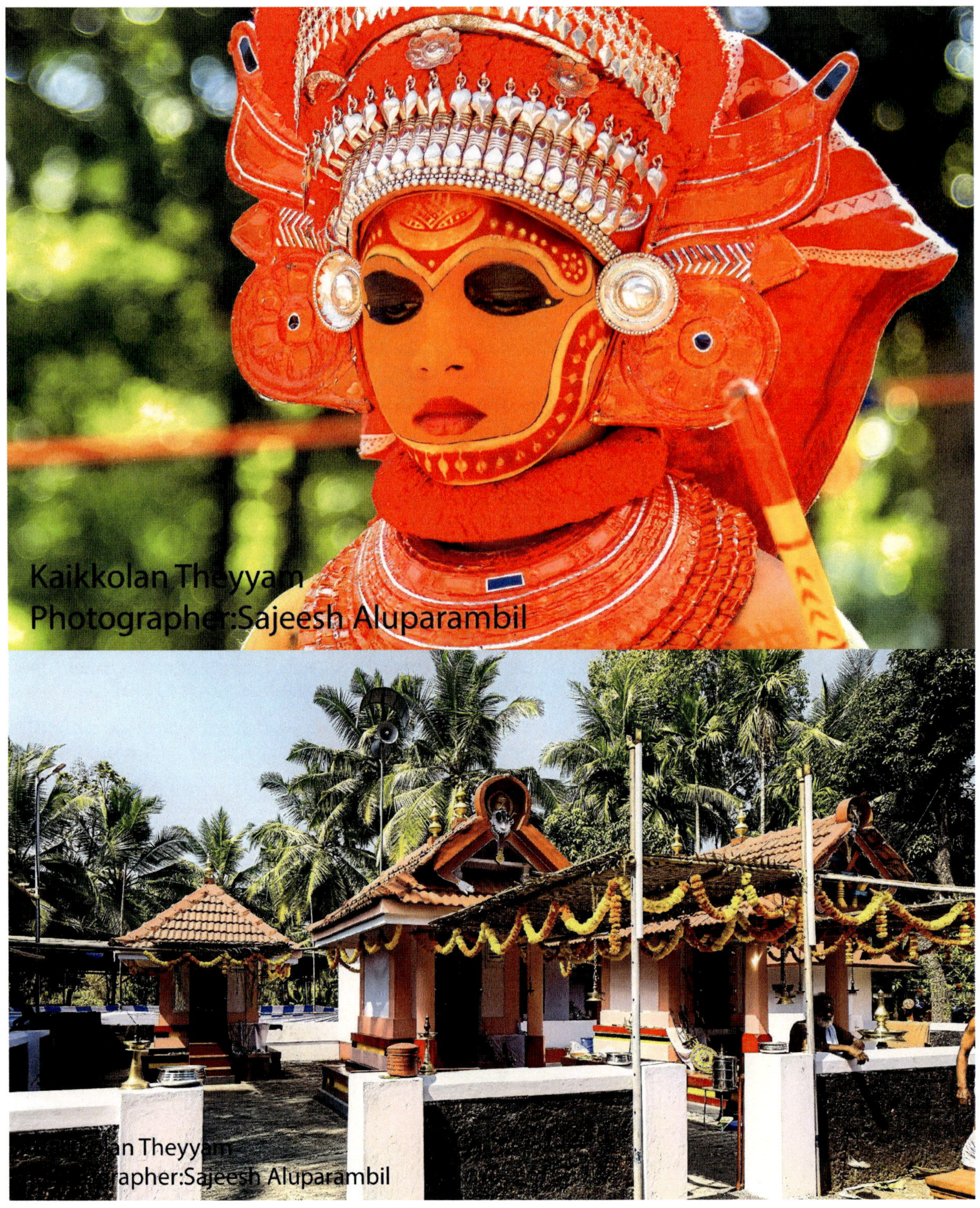

Kaikkolan Theyyam
Photographer:Sajeesh Aluparambil

an Theyyam
rapher:Sajeesh Aluparambil

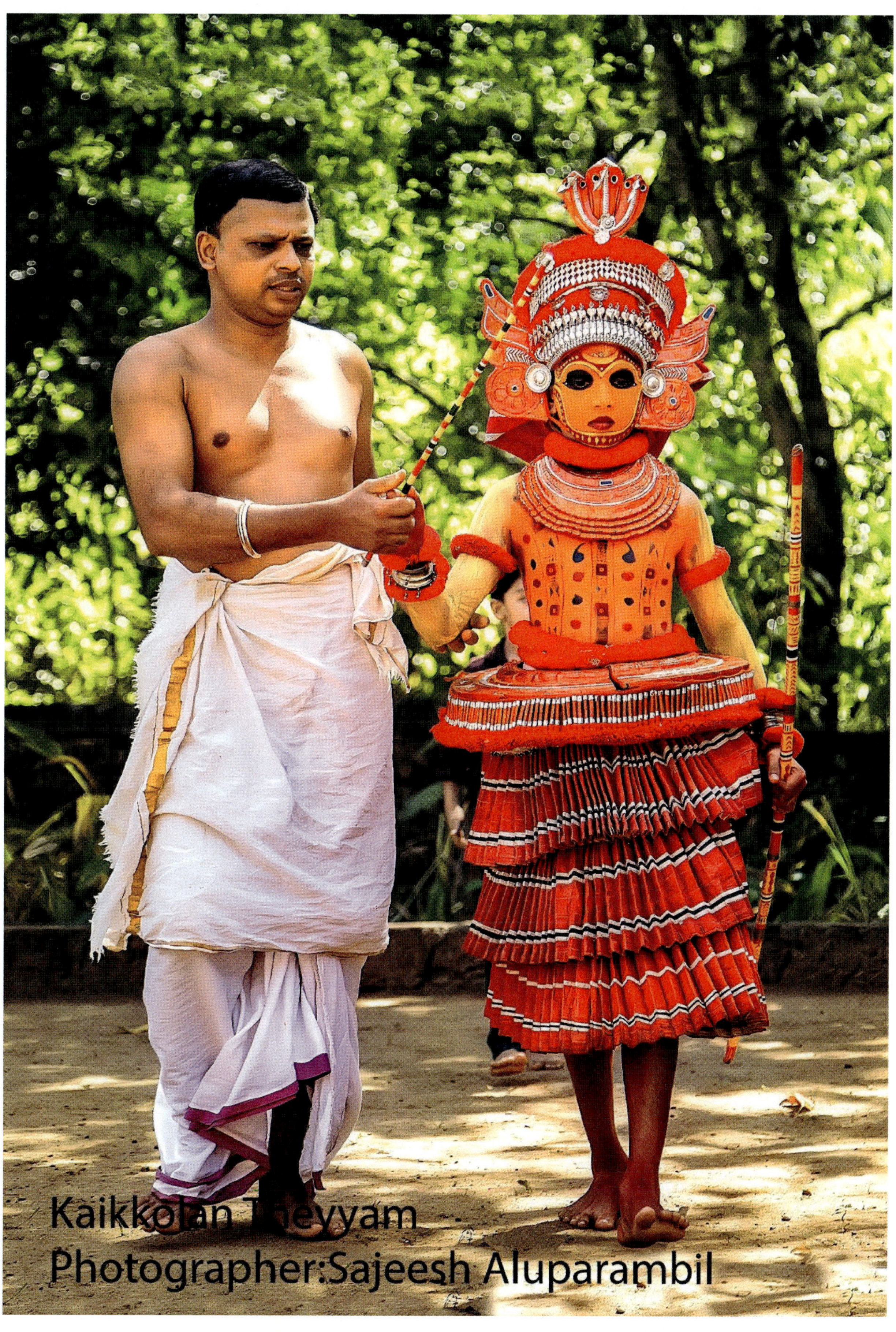

Kaikkolan Theyyam
Photographer:Sajeesh Aluparambil

Korachan Theyyam

Kottapuram Kunhikoran was an ardent believer and highly religious. He faithfully lit the lamps of the Vettakorumakan deity at all auspicious times and, as a fanatic, pierced his own body with the bamboo arrows, which is the weapon of Thondachan, thus sacrificing his own life for Vettakkorumakan. After that, Kottappara Kunhikoran was hailed as the deity Korachan after Vayanattukulavan was appeased by the divine consciousness he spotted in him, thus bringing glory to the entire Thiyya community to which Kottapuram Kunhikoran belonged.

Korachan Theyyam shines brightly to date and escorts Vayanattukulavan and Kandanar Kelan Theyyams to ancestral houses where Theyyam is performed.

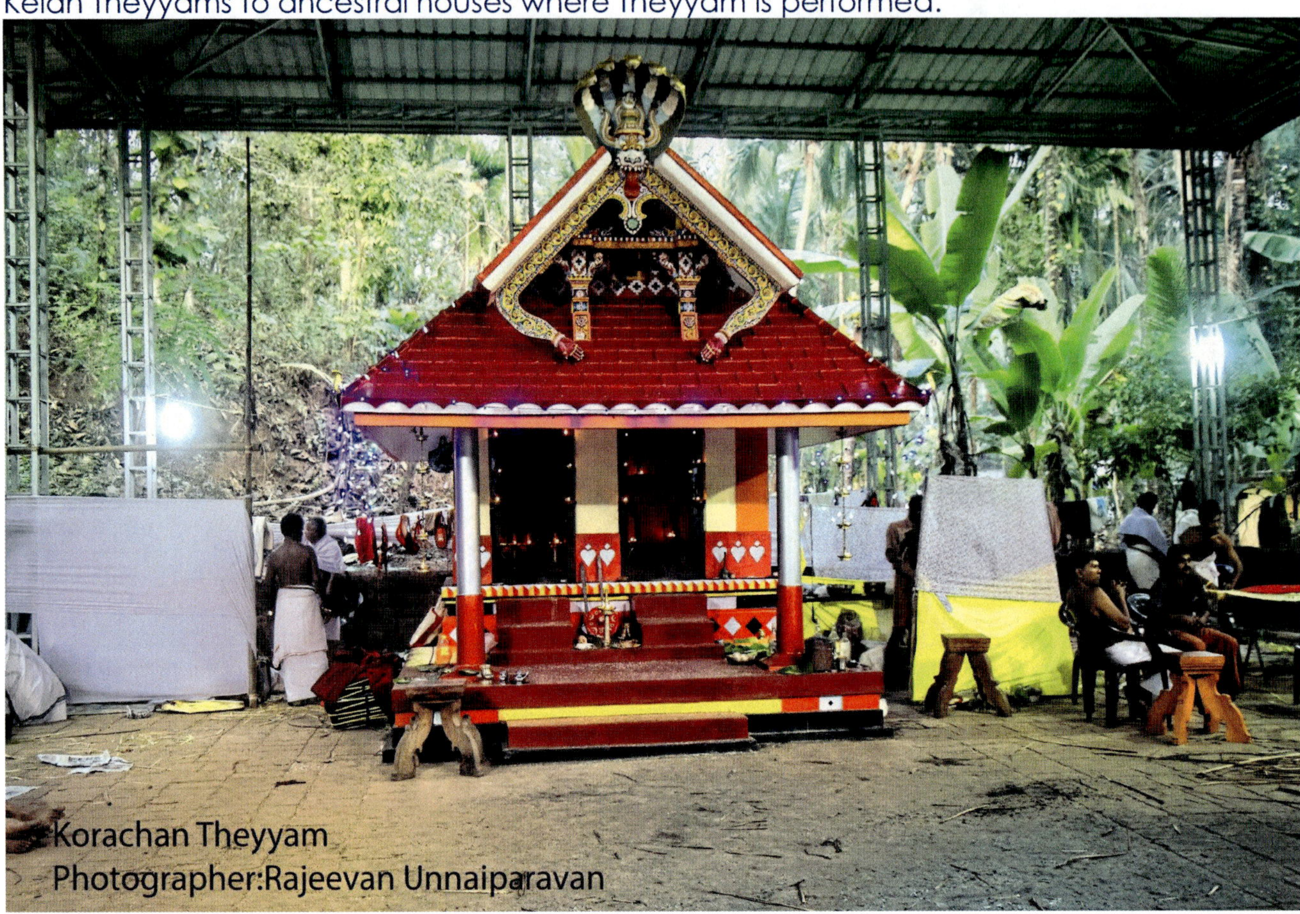

Korachan Theyyam
Photographer:Rajeevan Unnaiparavan

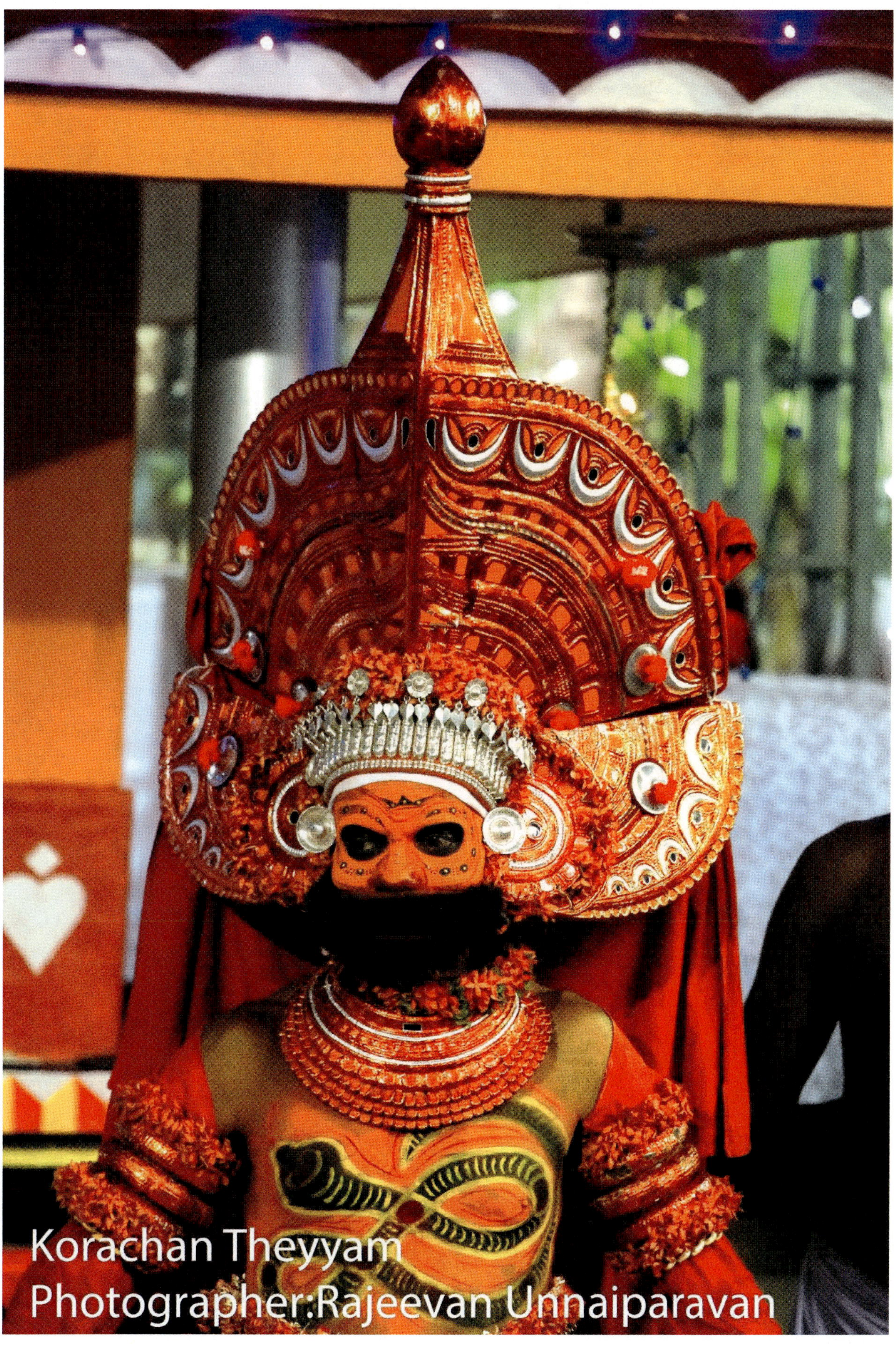
Korachan Theyyam
Photographer:Rajeevan Unnaiparavan

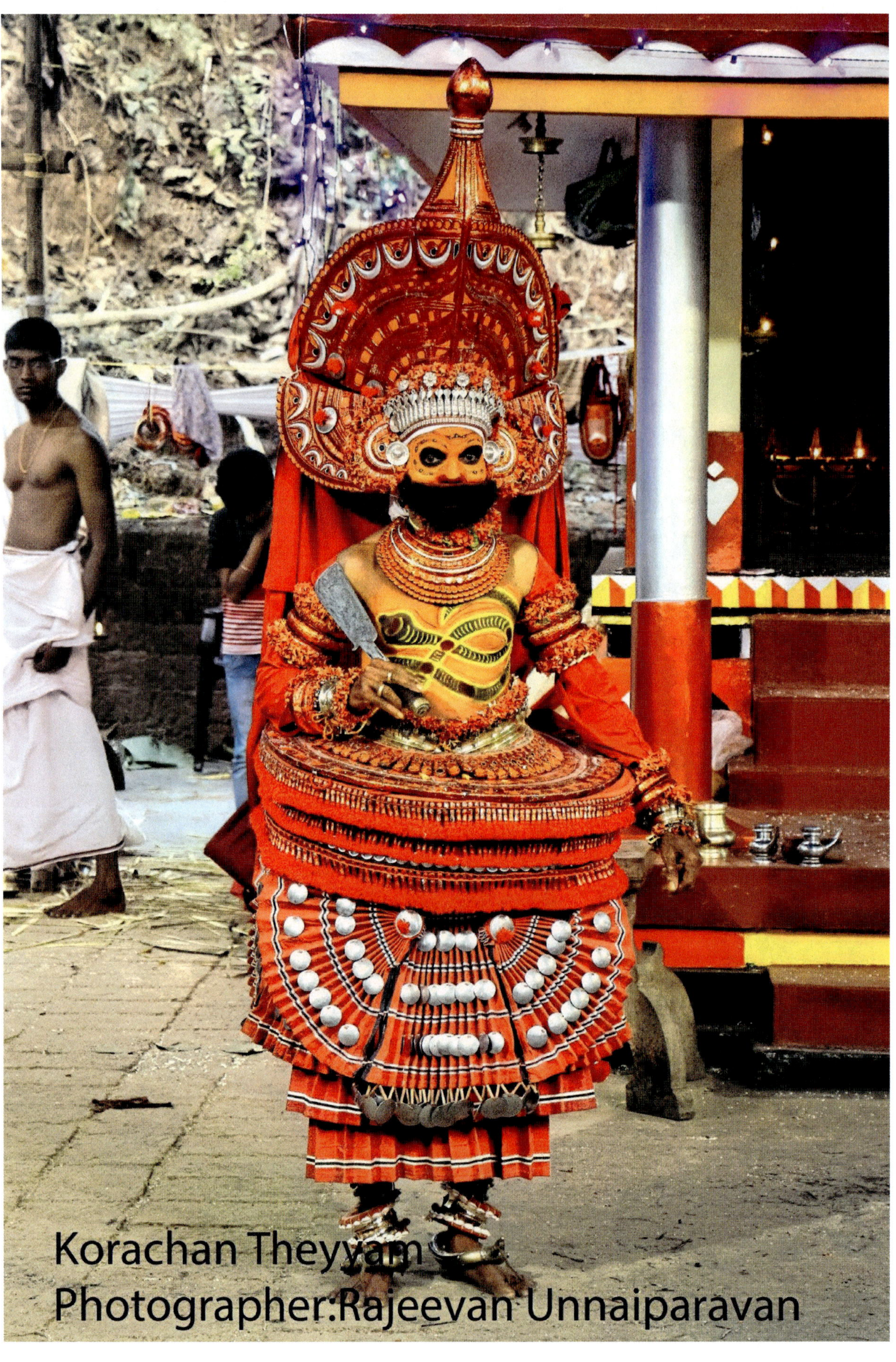

Korachan Theyyam
Photographer:Rajeevan Unnaiparavan

Valiyavalappil Chamundi Theyyam

Valiyavalappil Chamundi Theyyam is performed at the *Cheruvathoor Thimiri Kottumburam Valiyavalappil Devasthanam*. Folks in and around Thimiri consider *Valiyavalappil Chamundi Theyyam* or *Mother Valiyavalappil* as the Goddess of farmlands, similar to Demeter in Greek mythology. The peasants wait to plant until the Theyyam initiates the seed sowing process. Earlier, the Thimiri region was owned by the *Thazhakkattu Mana*. *Valiyavalappil Chamundi* was responsible for protecting the cultivations in the vast paddy fields sprawled across *Naalilamkandam* and *Njaanankai*. It is believed that the Goddess *Madayil Chamundi* entrusted this responsibility to *Valiyavalappil Chamundi*.

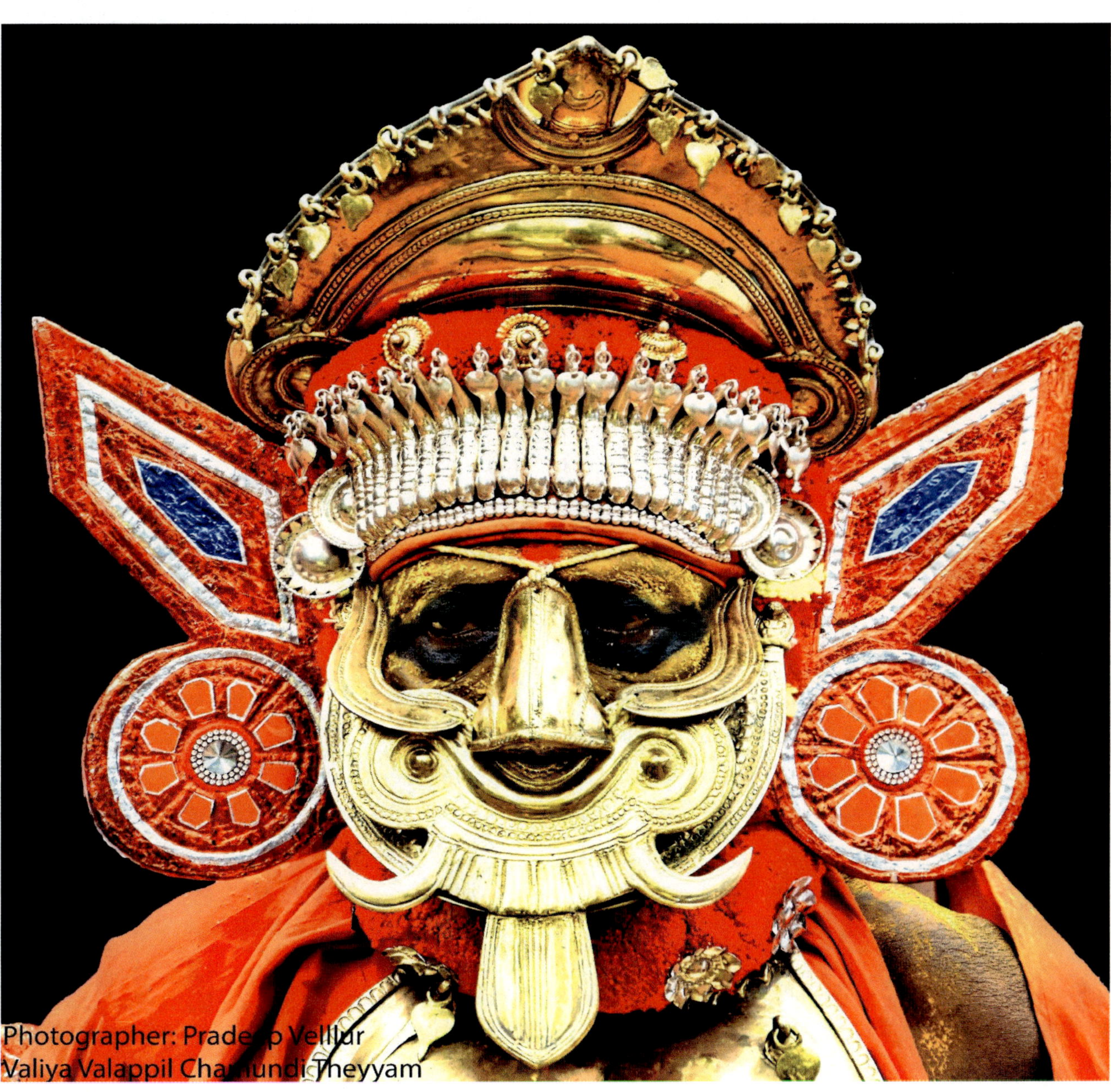

Photographer: Pradeep Vellur
Valiya Valappil Chamundi Theyyam

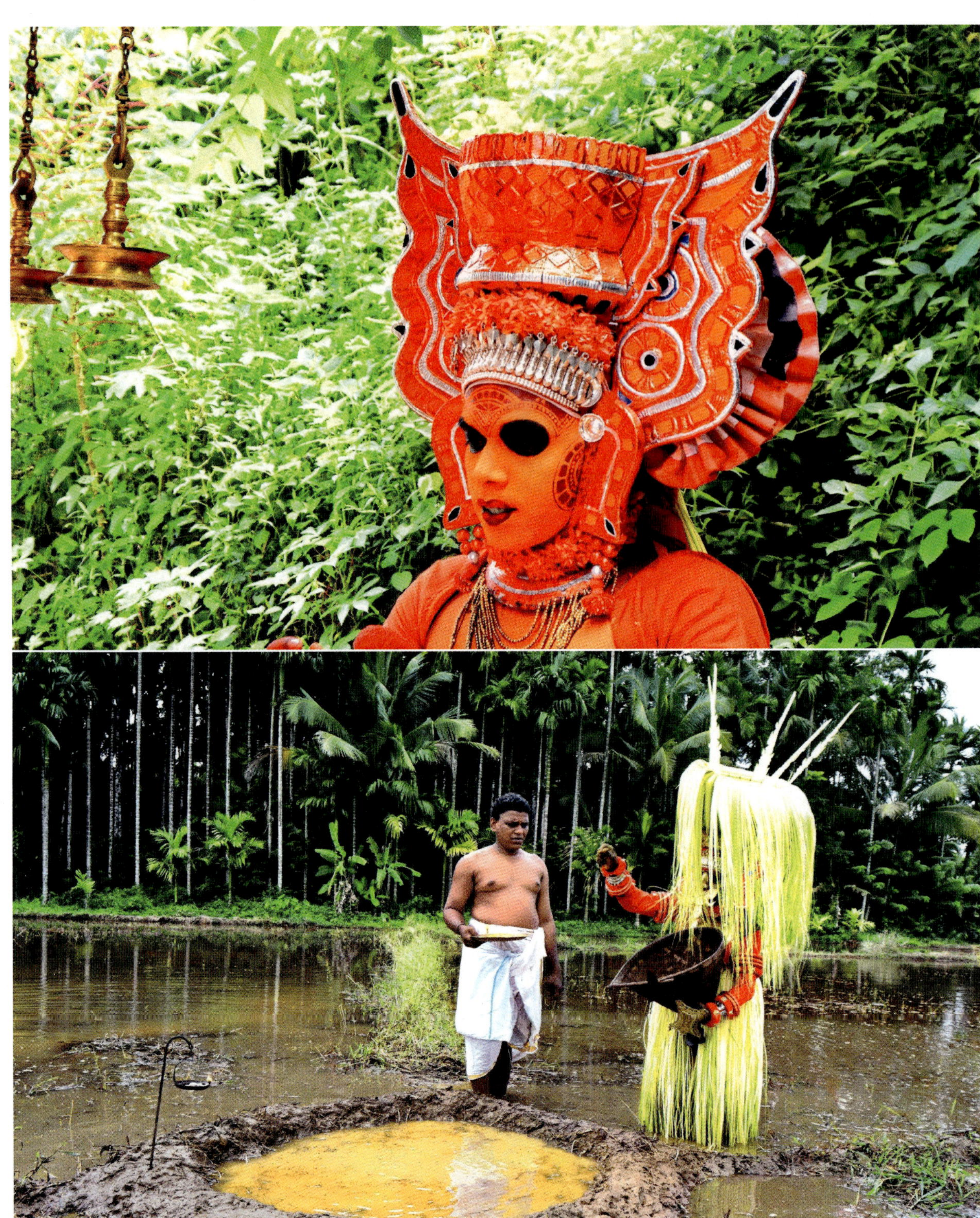

Photographer: Pradeep Vellur
Valiya Valappil Chamundi Theyyam

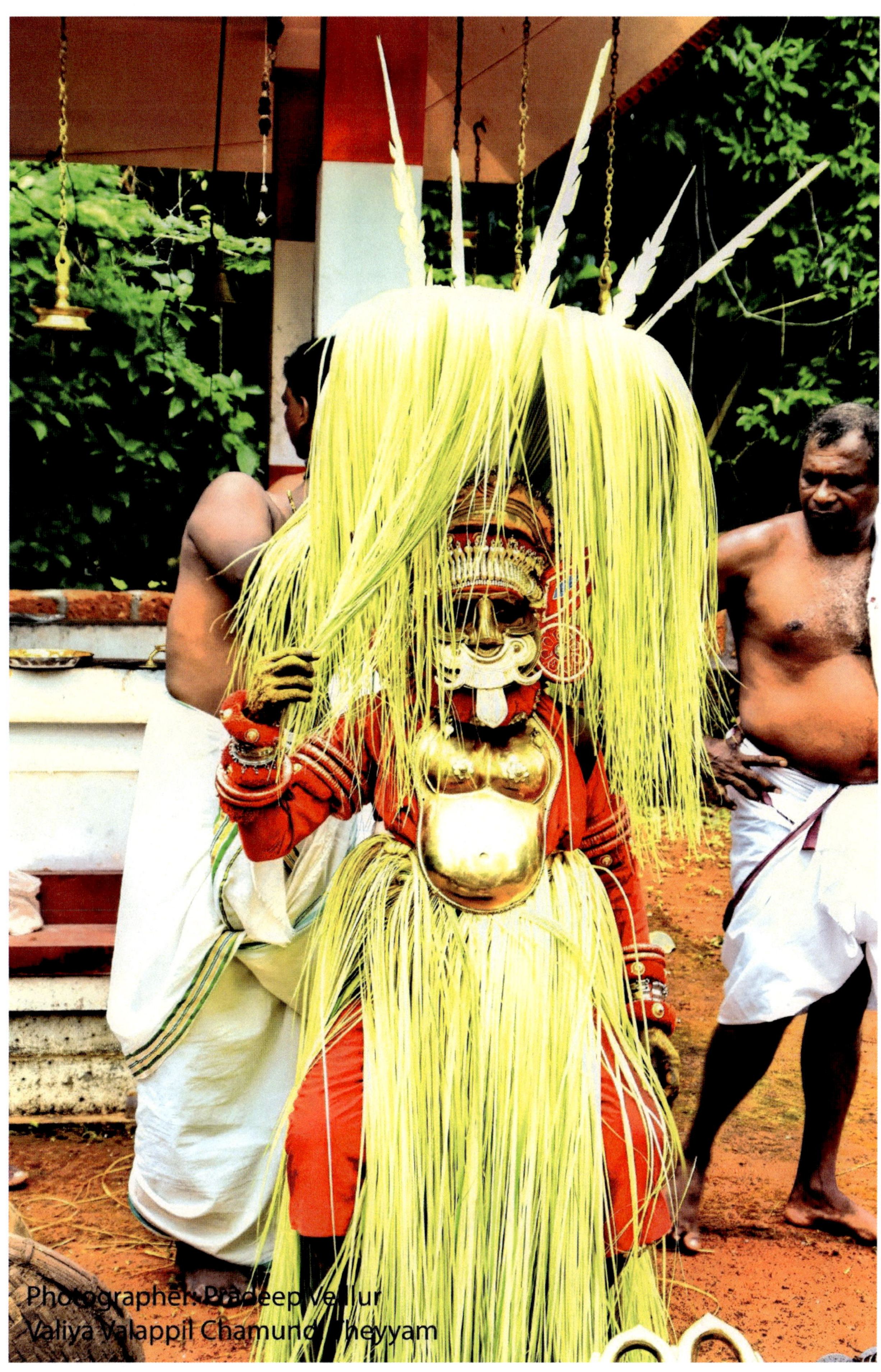

Photographer: Pradeep Vellur
Valiya Valappil Chamundi Theyyam

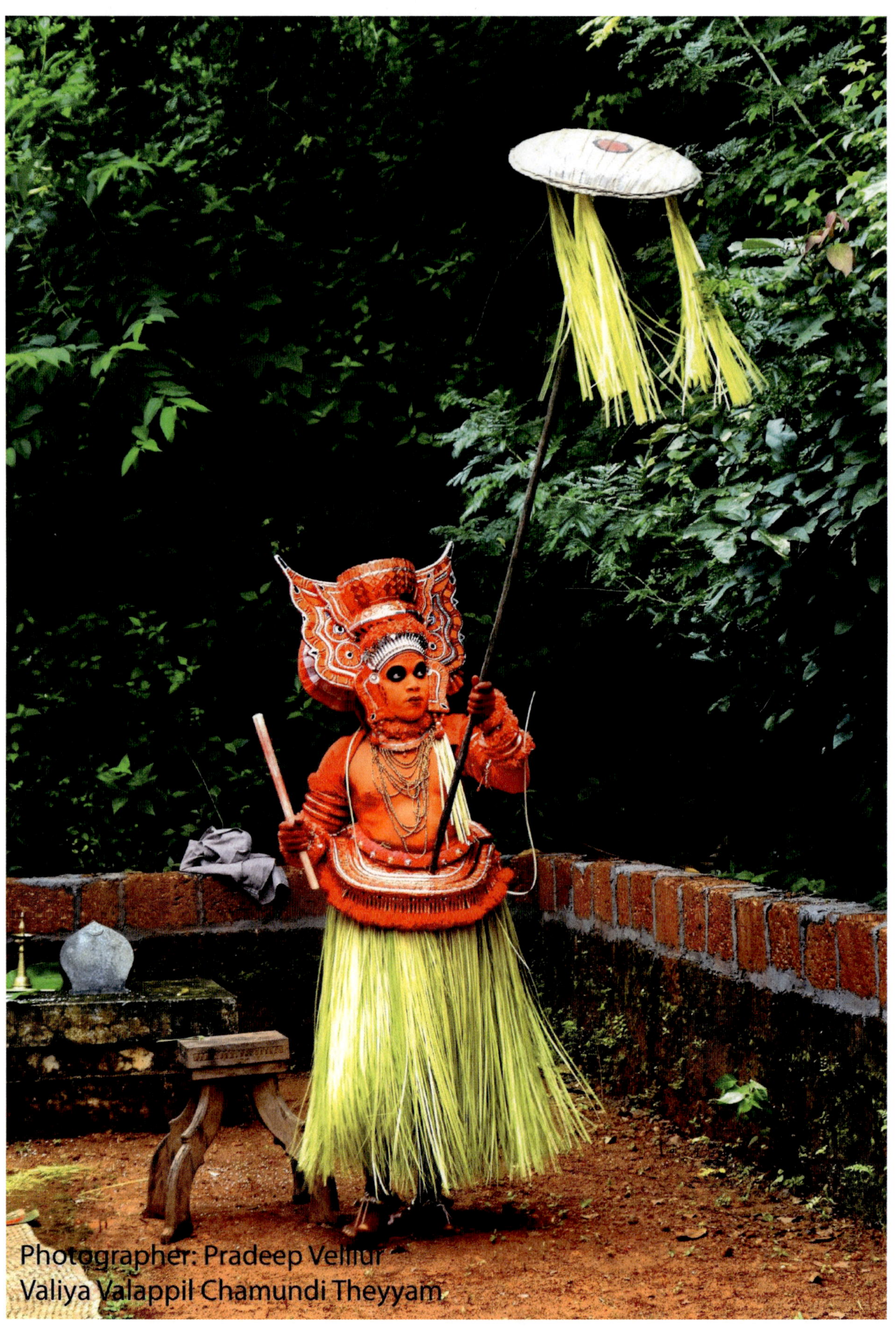
Photographer: Pradeep Vellur
Valiya Valappil Chamundi Theyyam

Kalichan or Kalichekon Theyyam

Kalichan or *Kalichekon Theyyam* is the savior of livestock, such as cattle. Kalichan Theyyam appears holding a palm umbrella and dances around with ringing anklets. It blesses the calves and the shepherds and is believed to have descended on earth along with the sun on *Pathamudayam* (the tenth sunrise or the autumnal equinox) when the sun's disk crosses the earth's horizon directly in the east at dawn. This Theyyam is also believed to be the savior of hunter-gatherer societies. Their worship centers are called *Kalichan Kaavus* or *Kalichamaras*. The *Kalichan* is generally worshipped for bountiful harvests and the protection of cattle, and the *Kalichan Theyyam* is believed to reside on strychnine trees. Believers offer a sweet dish called payasam (rice pudding) under this tree as an offering to the Kalichan when their cattle go missing. Ancestors chose the *Pathamudayam* to worship the *Kalichan*, so this day is also considered auspicious to sow seeds and initiate hunting.

One story behind Kalichan Theyyam describes him as the son of Lord Shiva. After a long day of hunting, Shiva sought abode in Asthamanakkotta with Paadikkuttiyamma. She gave birth to a boy, and he was sent to his father, Shiva, for a few days. One day he unknowingly drank a potion made especially for Lord Shiva, who cursed his son in a sudden rage. The innocent child apologized, but the curse had to be carried out, and he was sent to the human world. But before sending him off, Shiva offered him a silver eye and a false eye. From then on, Kalichan Theyyam became a Chekon (Chekavan, friend) of Kaali (cattle), therefore going by the name Kalichekon.

Some believe that Kalichekon/ Kalichan Theyyam is an embodiment of Lord Krishna, who belonged to the shepherd community.

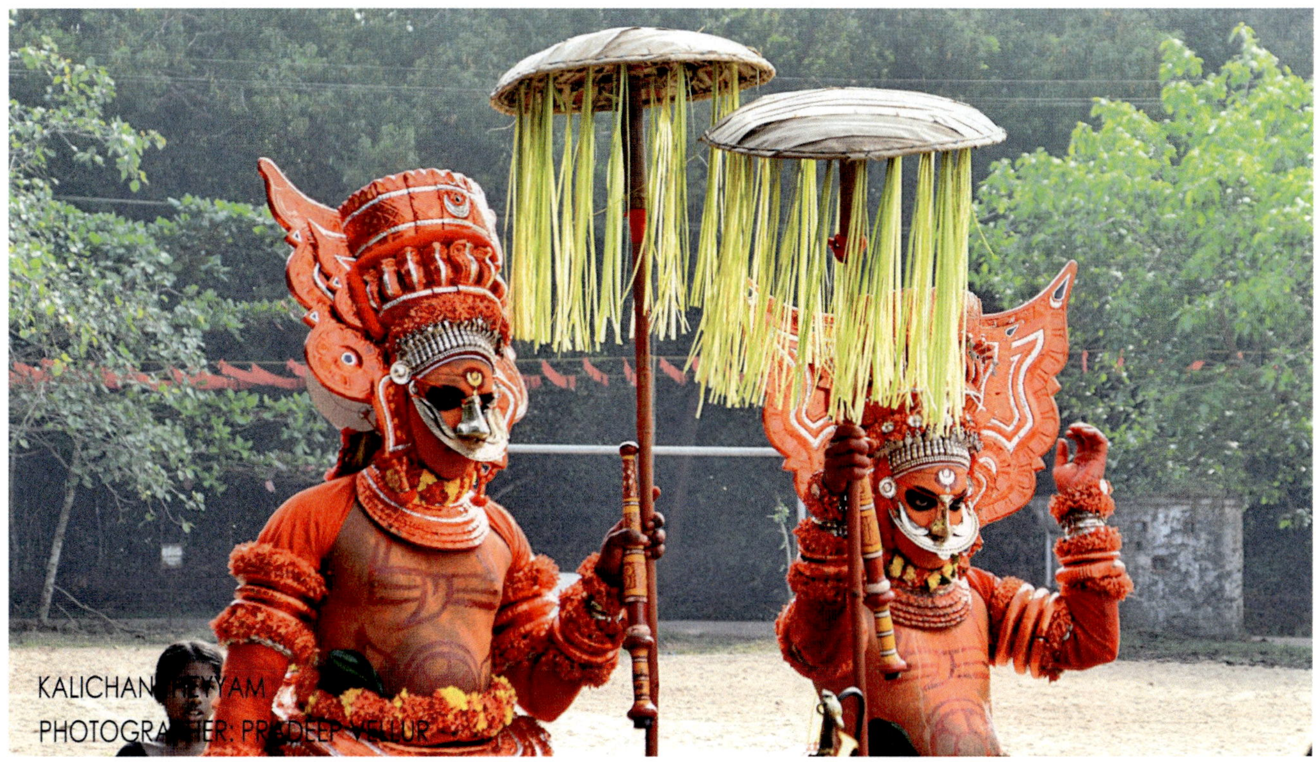

KALICHAN THEYYAM
PHOTOGRAPHER: PRADEEP VELLUR

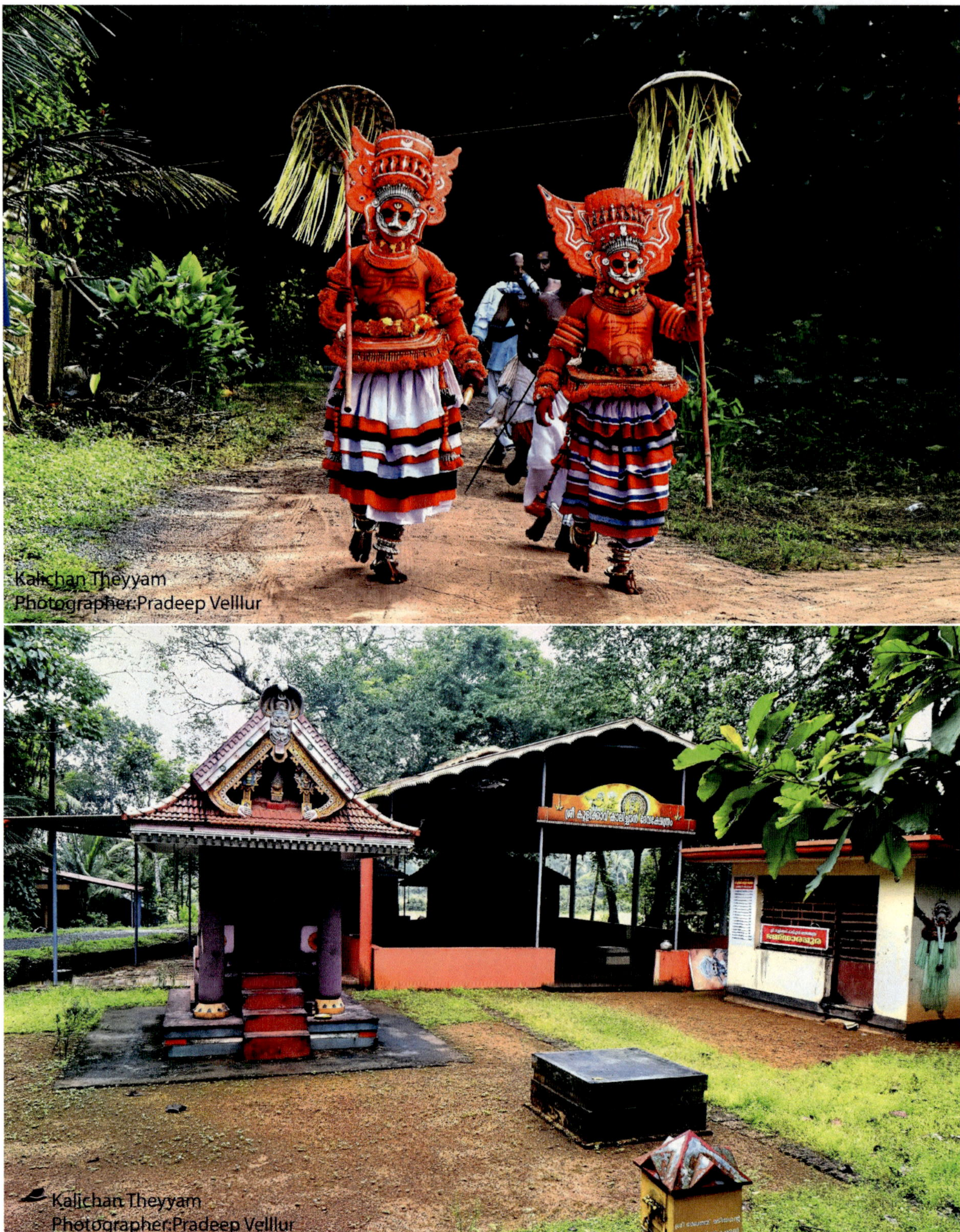

Kalichan Theyyam
Photographer:Pradeep Velllur

Kalichan Theyyam
Photographer:Pradeep Velllur

Ayitti Bhagavathy

(Punnakkal Bhagavathi, Uchulikadavath Bhagavathi, and Mekkot Bhagavathi have the same story)

Aayitti Bhagavathi is one of the Goddesses who arrived in Malabar on a ship. *Aayitti Bhagavathi and Uchoolikkadavathu Bhagavathi* both traveled on their vessels. After *Uchoolikkadavathu Bhagavathi*'s ship sank, Aayitti Bhagavathi gave her an abode, and they traveled together. She crossed *Gangakkara* (banks of Ganga) and *Arabikkara* (banks of Arabia) and passed by places like Ponnani, Vadiveeswaram, Kayakodi, and others. The ship docked in the harbor of Edathooramazhi, where the Bhagavathi lived for 12 years. She later met *Nellikkatheeyan* and traveled with him before settling down in *Aayitti Kavu*. Hence, she came to be known as *Aayitti Bhagavathi*. She shares her legend with *Uchoolikkadavath Bhagavathi and* is known by other names like *Punnakkal Bhagavthi, Mekkattu Bhagavathi, etc*.

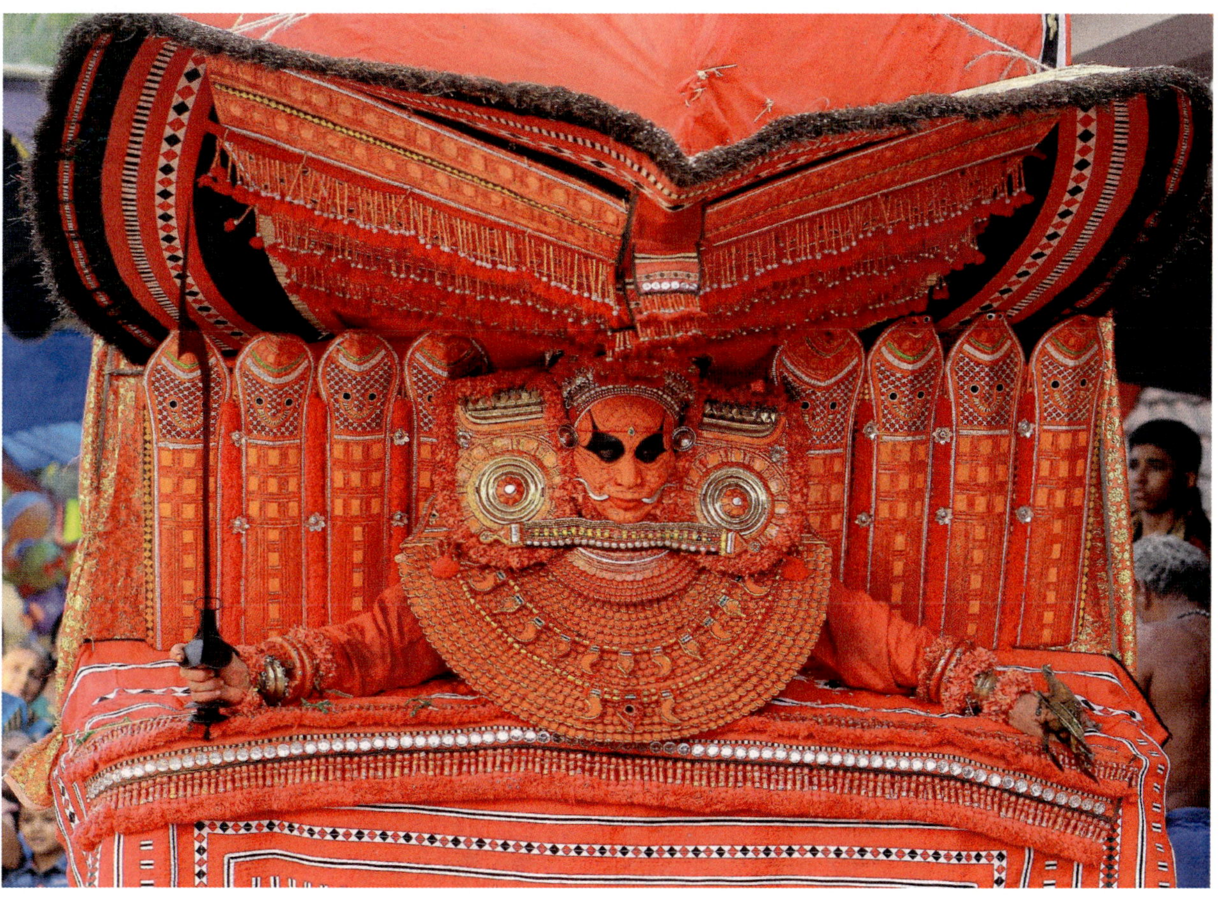

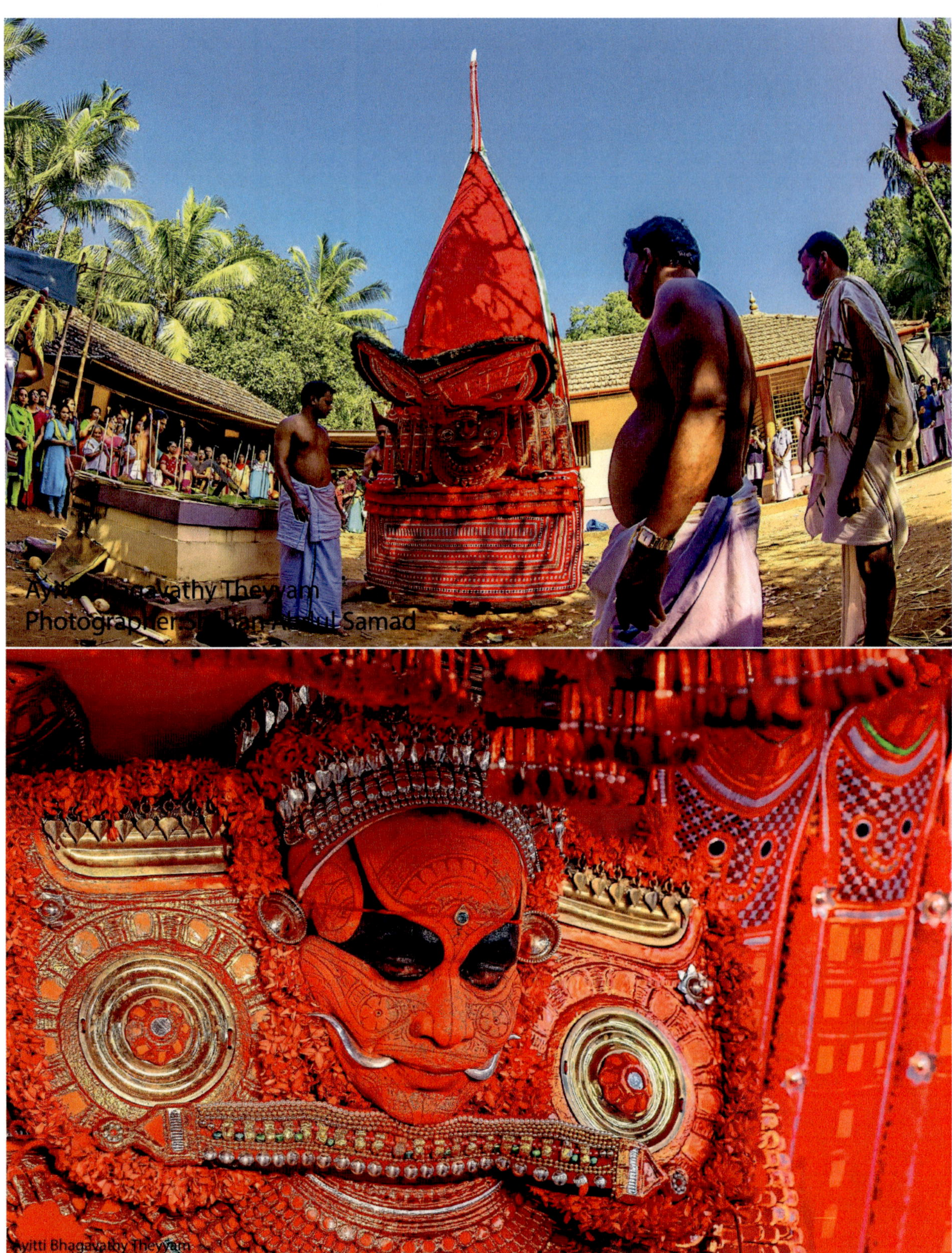

Ayitti Bhagavathy Theyyam
Photographer:Shahan Abdul Samad

Ayitti Bhagavathy Theyyam
Photographer:Shahan Abdul Samad

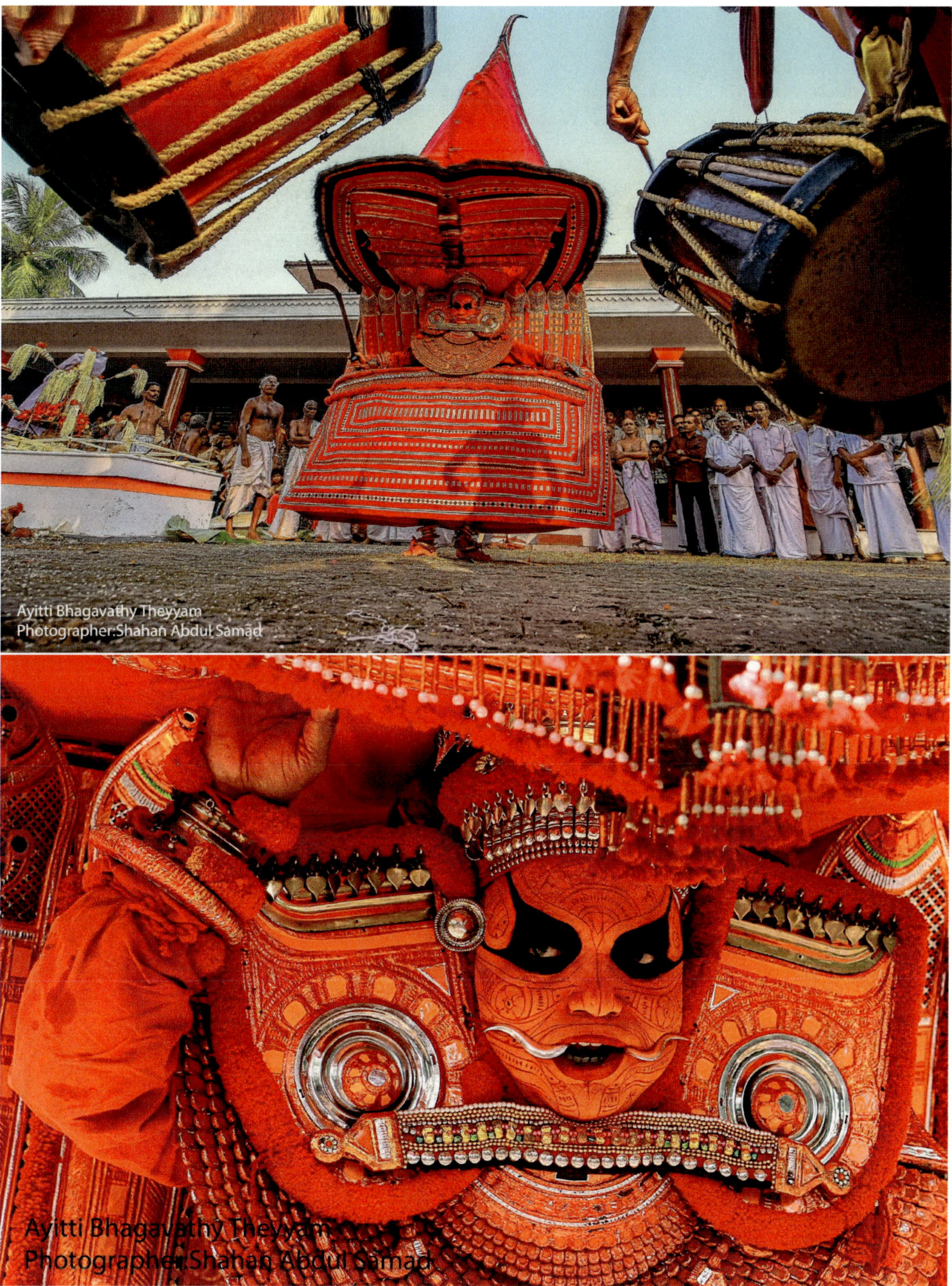

Ayitti Bhagavathy Theyyam
Photographer:Shahan Abdul Samad

Ayitti Bhagavathy Theyyam
Photographer:Shahan Abdul Samad

Karthika Chamundi

Karthika Chamundi Theyyam and *Theyyathukari Theyyam* are the protectors of paddy fields and farming. Since they sow rice (ari) and provide a good harvest, *Karthika Chamundi* is also known as *Arayi Chamundi*. The Theyyam of these Goddesses is performed in *Arayi Karthika Kavu* in Kanhangadu by people of the Pulaya community. *Karthika Chamundi* is accompanied by *Gulikan* and *Kalichan* (two other types of Theyyam). *Karthika Chamundi, Theyyathukari,* and *Gulikan* Theyyams travel on row boats to reach the *Kalichan Kavu*, which is a peculiar sight. When they arrive, they are welcomed by *Kalichan Daivam* (God of Kalichan) of *Kalichan Kavu*. The Theyyams who arrive at the *Kalichan Kavu* will have conversations with the *Kalichan Daivam*. They also bless devotees by distributing the holy turmeric powder and return to their own Kavus only after visiting the nearby houses and blessing them. The rendezvous of the deities of these two Kavus is symbolic of the meeting of nature and God. It is also a reminder of a time when farming was impossible without farm animals. Previously, cultivation in these villages commenced only after this Theyyam performance.

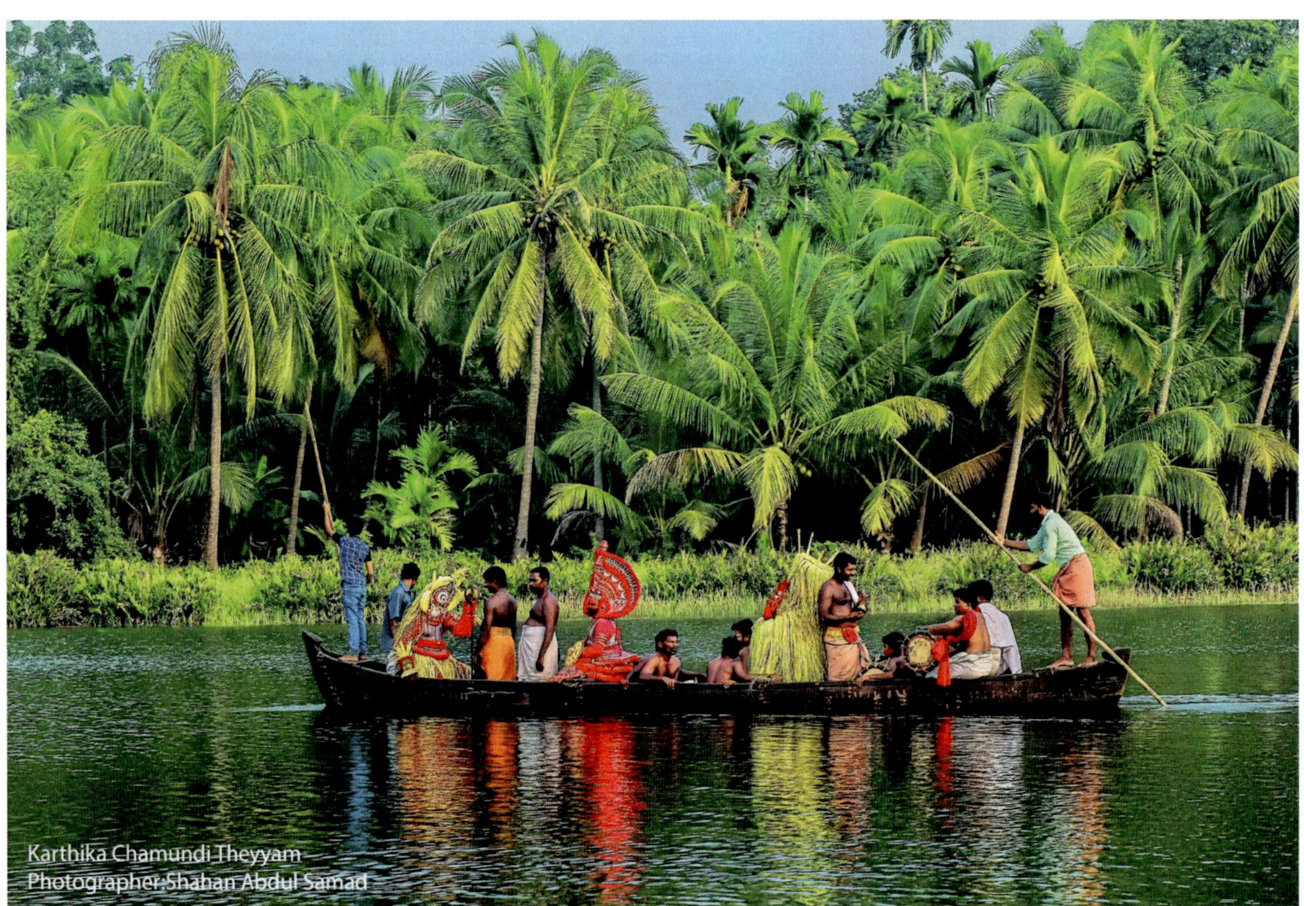
Karthika Chamundi Theyyam
Photographer:Shahan Abdul Samad

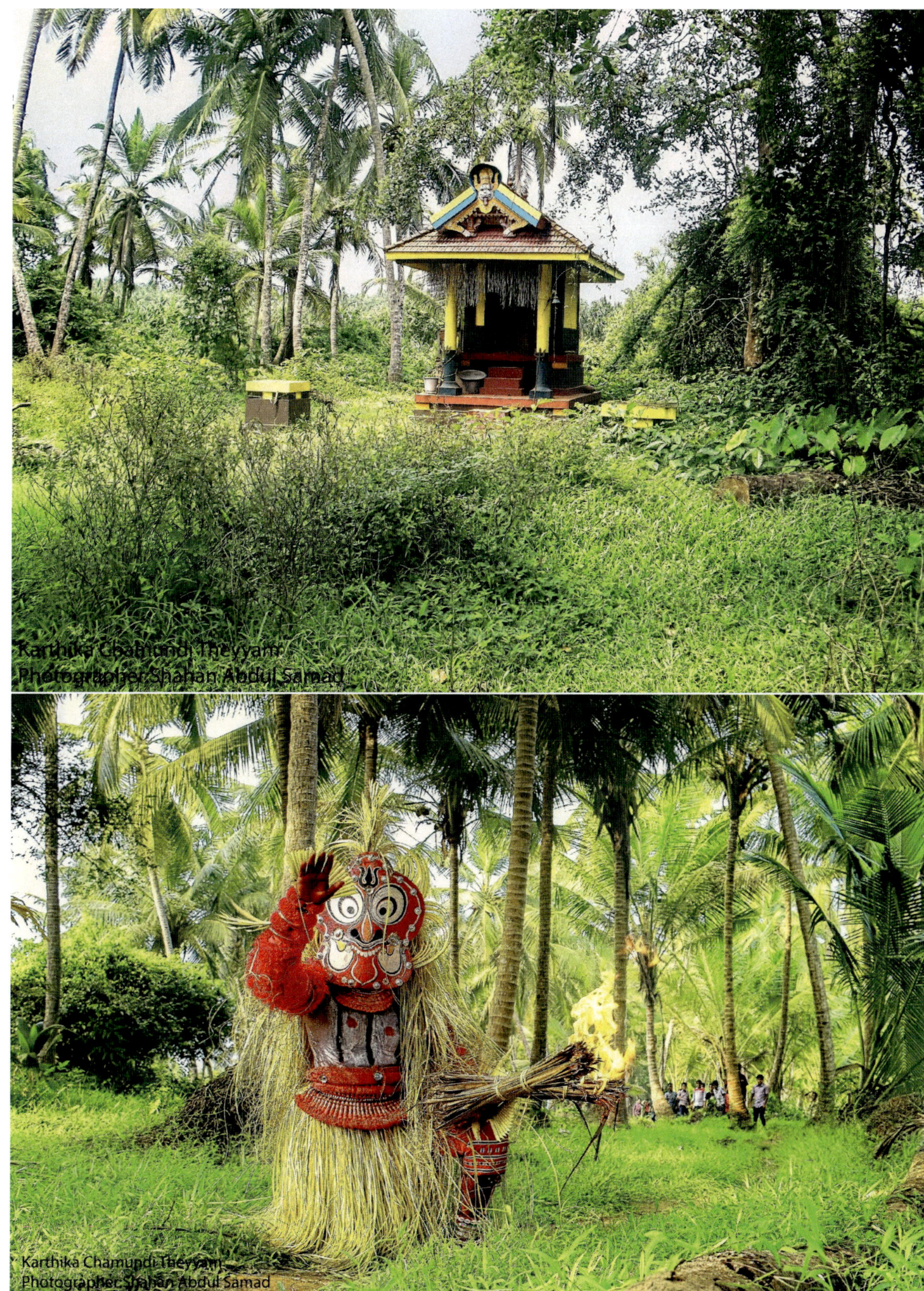

Karthika Chamundi Theyyam
Photographer Shahan Abdul Samad

Karthika Chamundi Theyyam
Photographer Shahan Abdul Samad

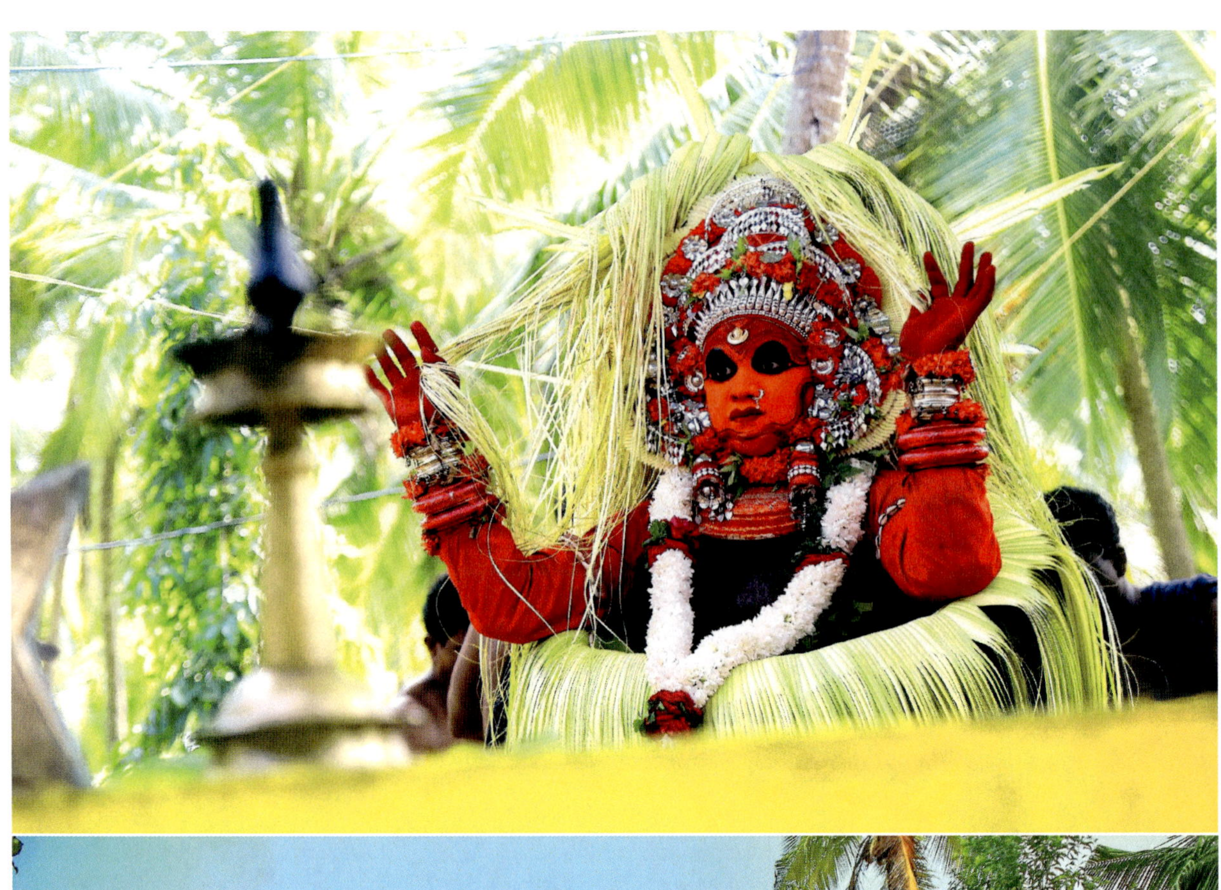

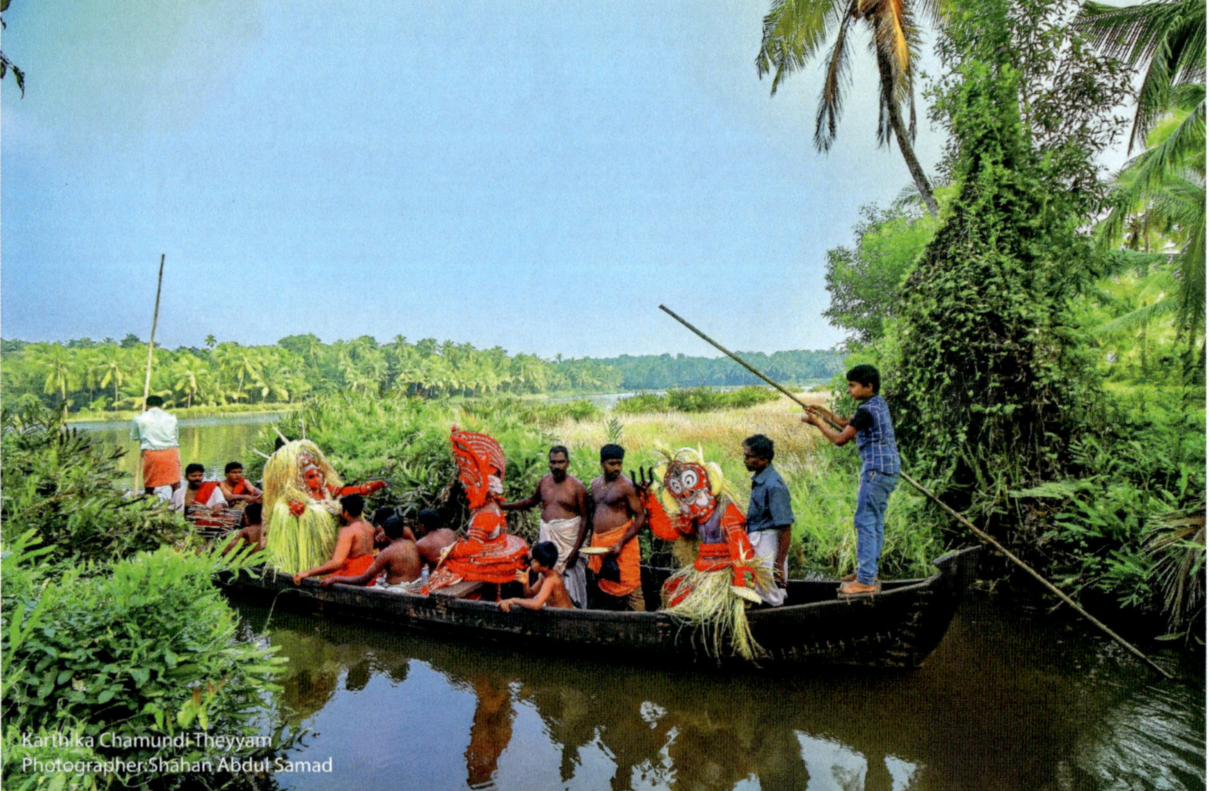

Karthika Chamundi Theyyam
Photographer:Shahan Abdul Samad

Paraliyamma Theyyam

Paraliyamma is a form of Goddess Parvati, and the Goddess is mute in this form. Here, others must utter for the Goddess.

The Goddess was the guard of Thiruvarkad Kaavu (shrine), and she happened to kill and eat a visiting Brahmin. Thiruvarkad Bhagavathi was so angry when she heard about the killing that she plucked out Parali's tongue and threw her away. The thrown tongue fell at Arippamba. That's where the abode of Parali is installed. This *Kola Swaroopam* is a forest Goddess performed by the Chinkathan community members. The same accusation was issued against Kammiyamma, too, and Thiruvarkad Bhagavathi also hurled her away. Legend says Kammiyamma fell at Eruvatty.

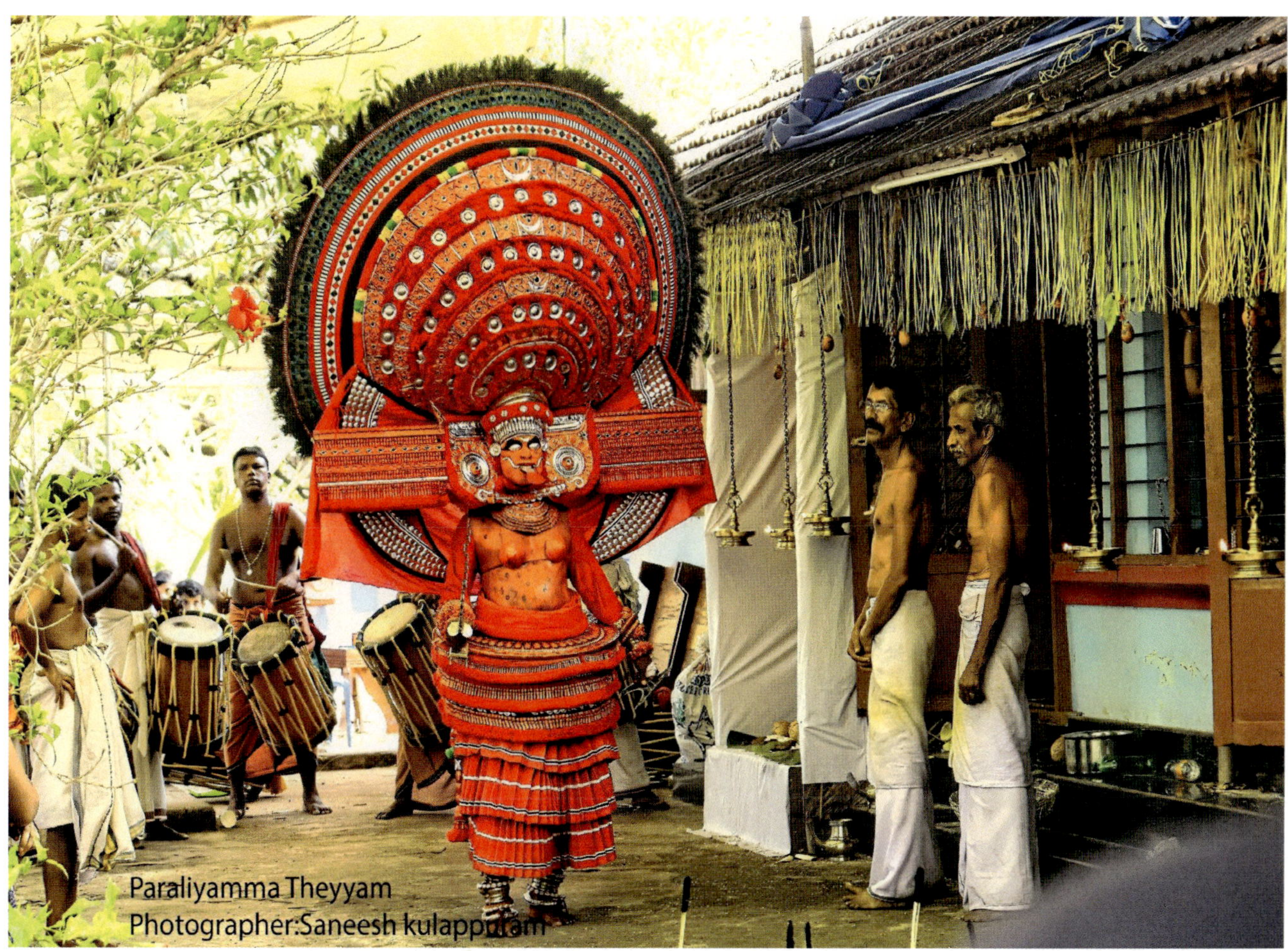

Paraliyamma Theyyam
Photographer:Saneesh kulappuram

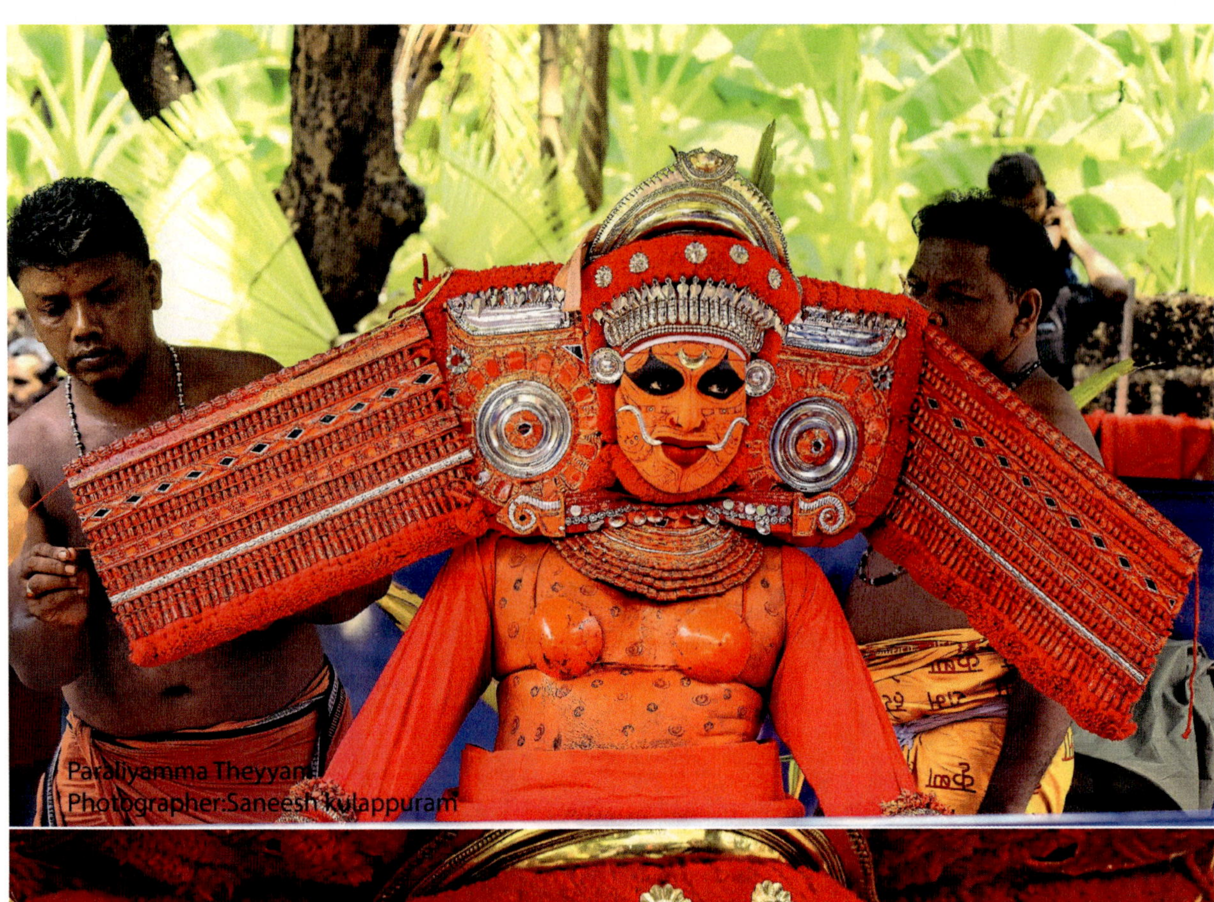
Paraliyamma Theyyam
Photographer:Saneesh kulappuram

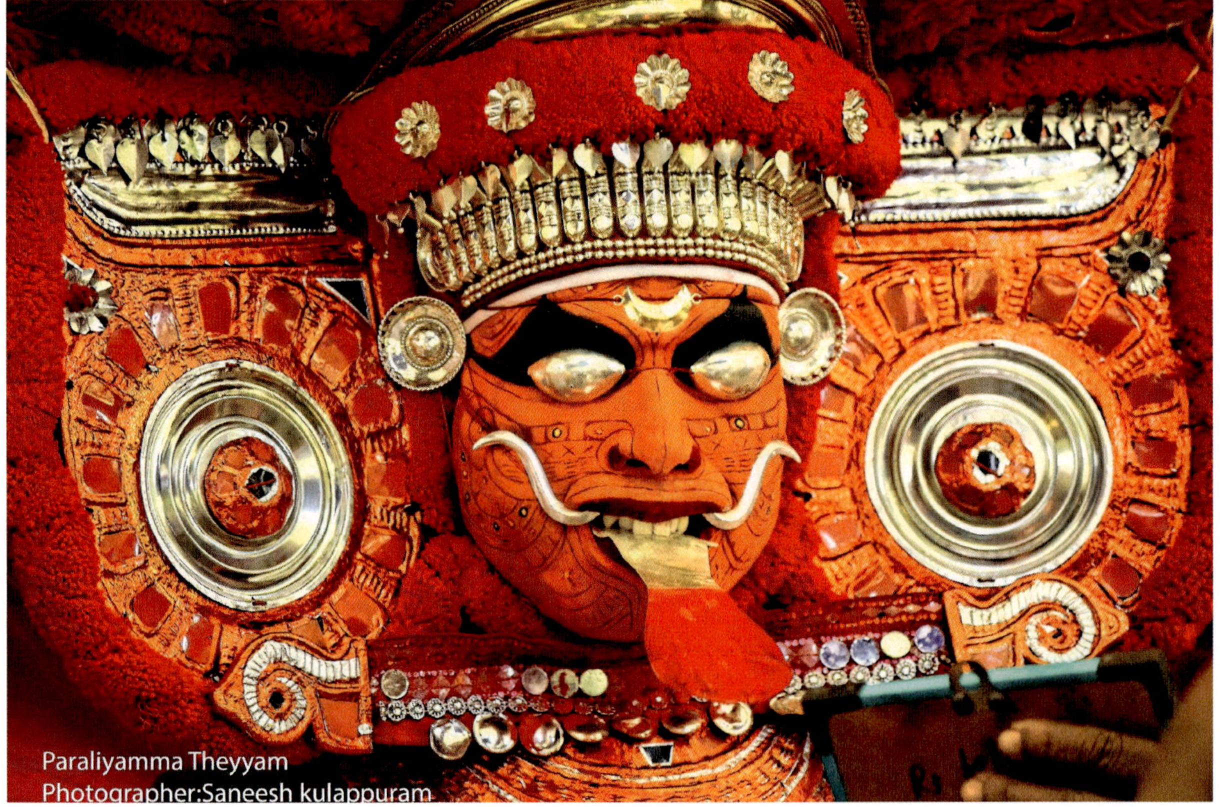
Paraliyamma Theyyam
Photographer:Saneesh kulappuram

Gulikan Theyyam

It is believed that *Gulikan* was born from the toe of Lord Shiva. Markandeyan, a human boy, was granted only sixteen years of life. He was an ardent devotee of Lord Shiva. When he turned sixteen, *Kaalan*, the God of death, came to take him to the afterlife. But Markandeyan hugged the *Shiva Lingam* (an abstract representation of Lord Shiva on stone) tightly and refused to let go. Thus, *Kaalan* took Markandeyan along with the *Shiva Lingam* to the afterlife. Lord Shiva came to know about this and became enraged. He killed Kaalan by opening his third eye.

With the death of Kaalan, there was no more death on earth. Fearing overpopulation, Mother Earth and the other Gods went to Lord Shiva to redress their grievance about the eternal lives of humans. On hearing their plea, Lord Shiva placed his toe on earth, and from which emerged *Gulikan*. *Gulikan* was assigned the duties of *Kaalan; hence, Gulikan* is the deity of death. Devotees believe worshipping Gulikan can extend their lifespan.

It is believed that there are many versions of *Gulikan*, like *Vadakkan Gulikan, Thekkan Gulikan, Mari Guilikan, Pula Gulikan, Japa Gulikan, Karim Gulikan, Kara Gulikan, Jataka Gulikan, Unmattha Gulikan, Chuvanna Gulikan*, etc.

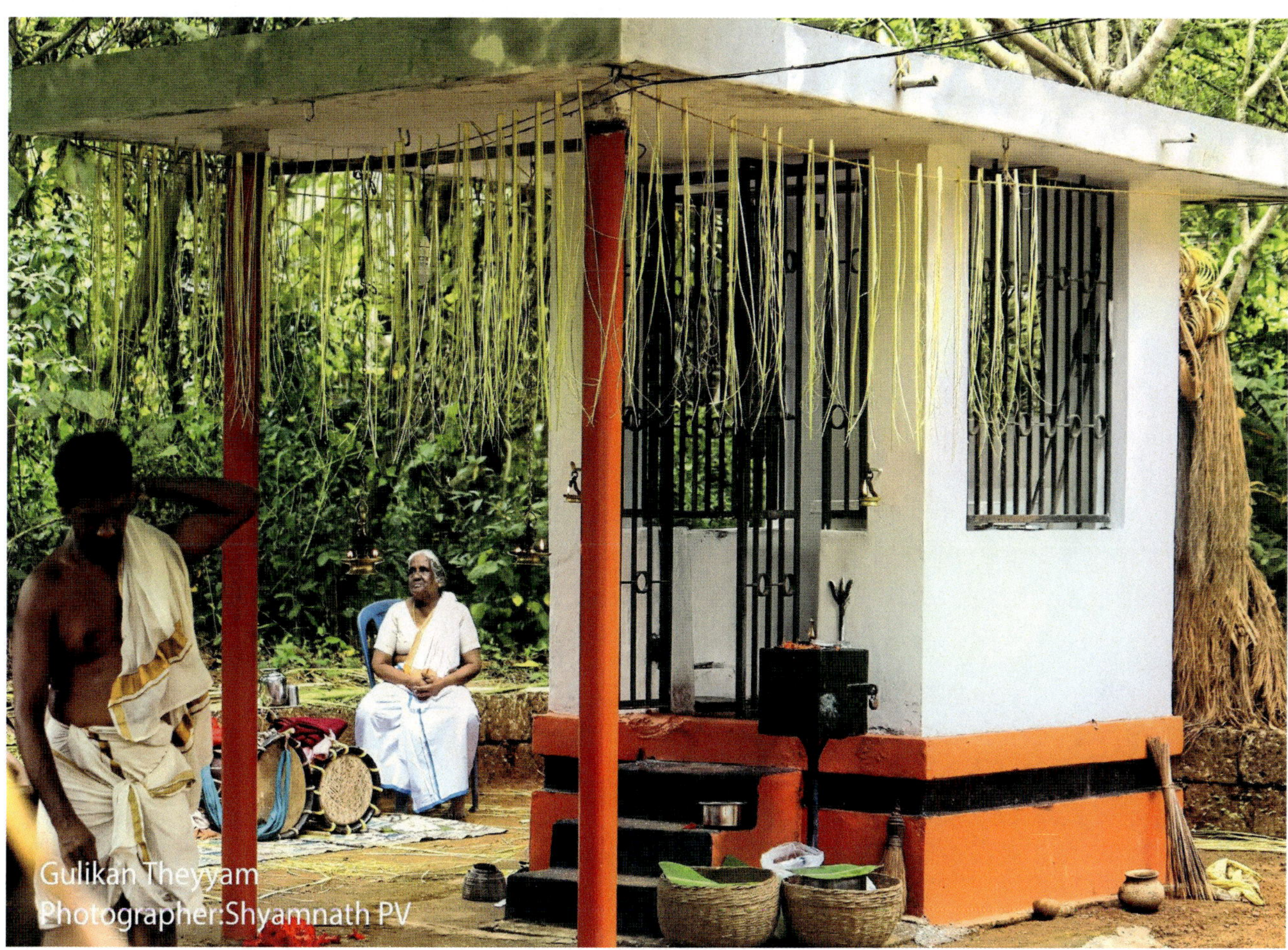
Gulikan Theyyam
Photographer:Shyamnath PV

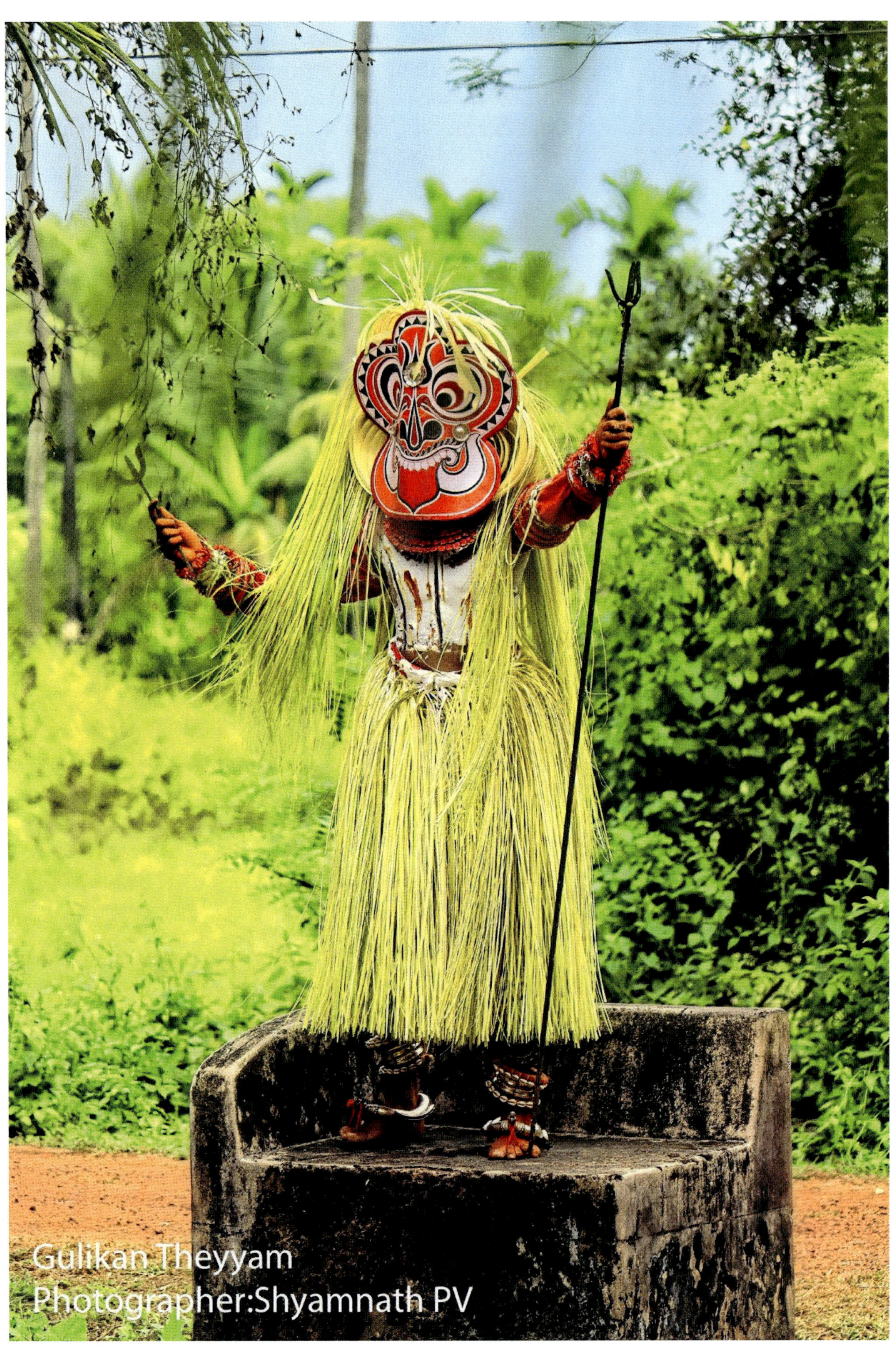
Gulikan Theyyam
Photographer:Shyamnath PV

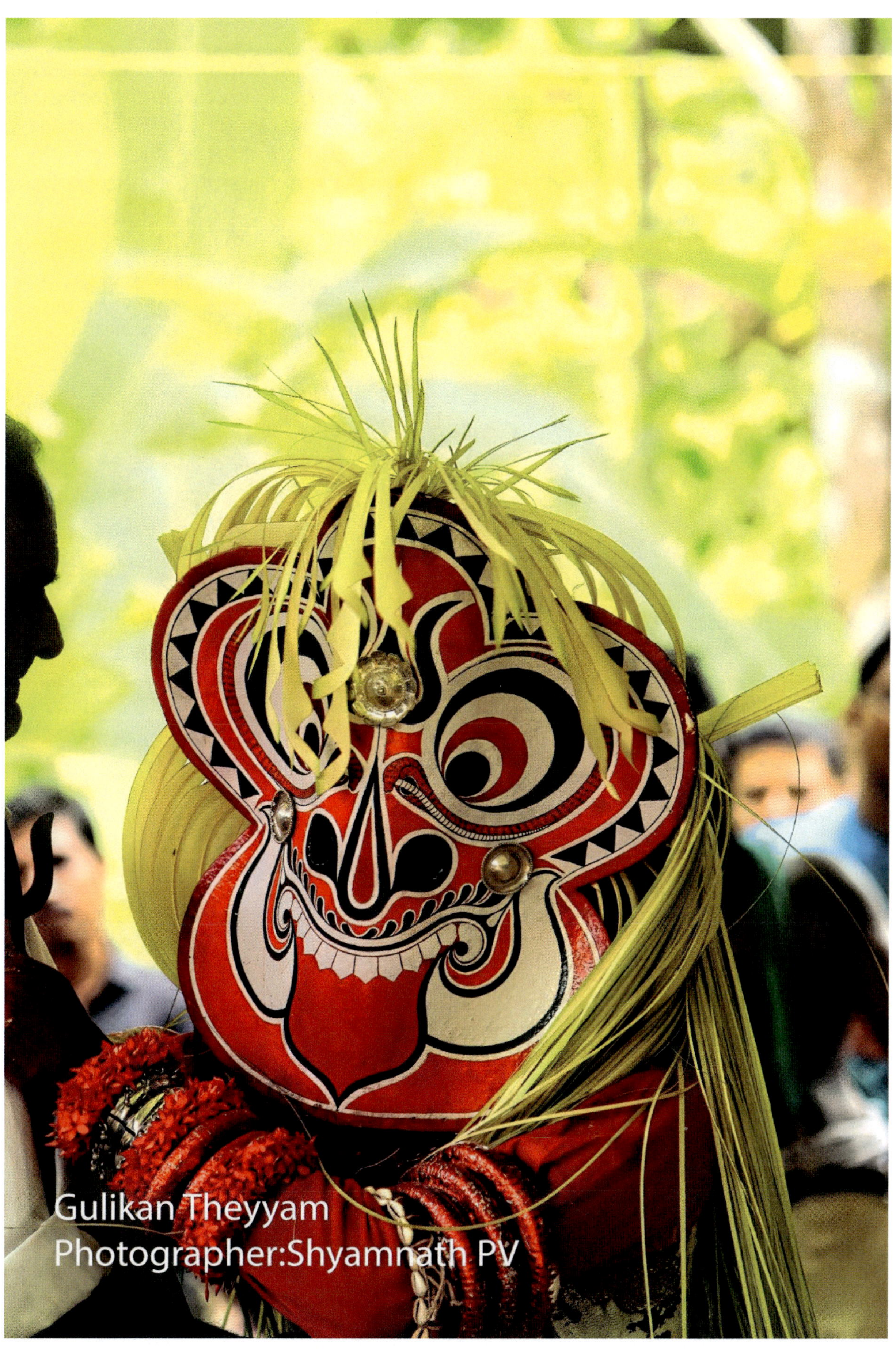

Gulikan Theyyam
Photographer:Shyamnath PV

Kutti Theyyam

Kutti Theyyam is performed at Perunthottam Neeliyar Kottam in Kannapuram, near Mottammal. The myth behind *Kutti Theyyam* is that it conspires naughty tricks to please *Neeliyar Bhagavathi (Goddess)*. This Theyyam comes to perform with little make-up or ornaments and spins around on its legs for about an hour. That is why it is named *Kutti Theyyam*. As the Theyyam spins around in circles, the sound of Chenda (a percussion instrument) intensifies, taking the performer to a trance state. This is a unique and exciting sight to watch. The people of the Anjoottan community perform this Theyyam.

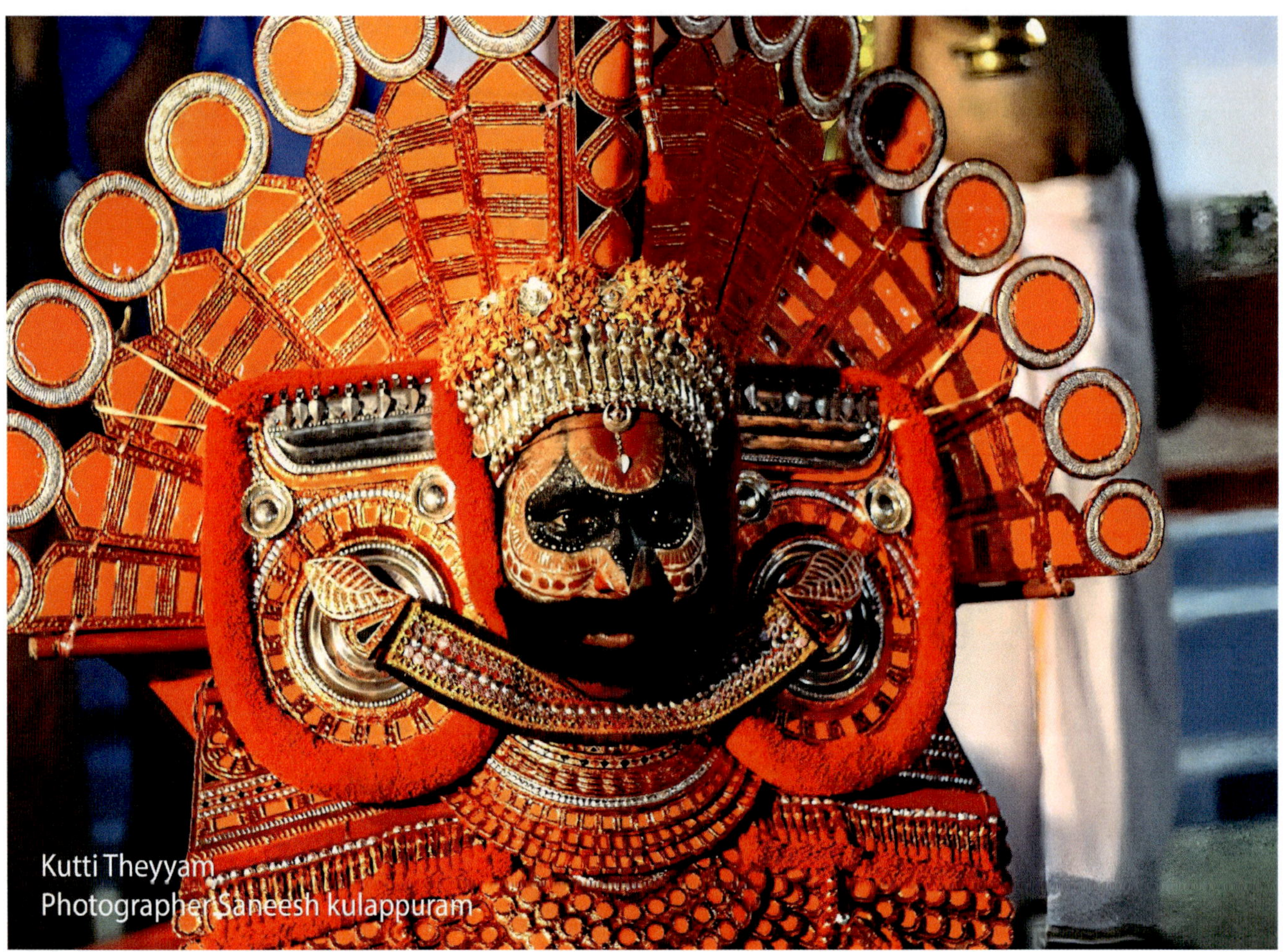

Kutti Theyyam
Photographer Saneesh kulappuram

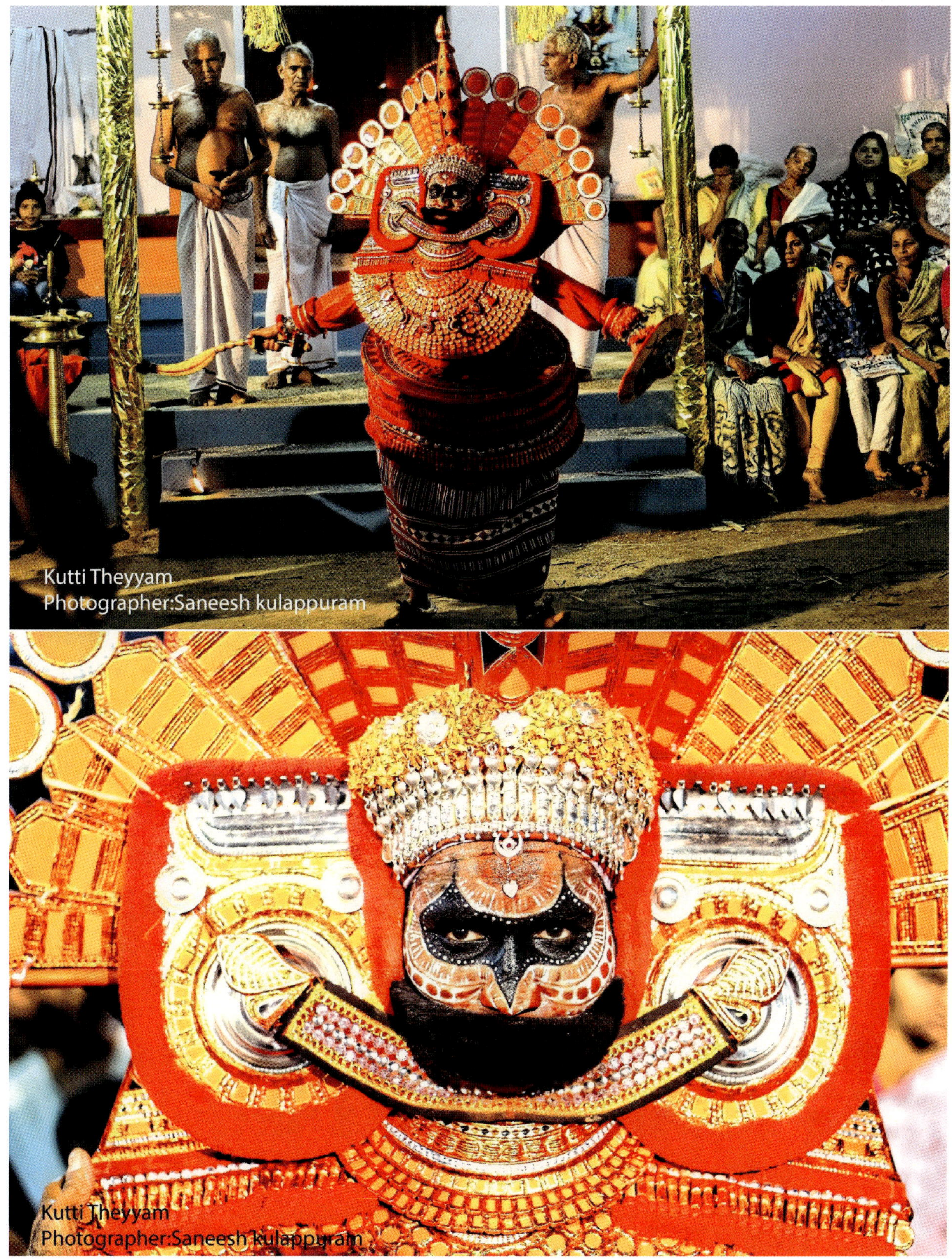

Kutti Theyyam
Photographer:Saneesh kulappuram

Kutti Theyyam
Photographer:Saneesh kulappuram

Karkkidaka (Adi) Theyyam & Vedan Theyyam

Karkkidakam is the fourth month of the Malayalam Calendar. The corresponding month in the Tamil calendar is called *Aadi*. The Gregorian calendar equivalent of both Karkkidakam and *Aadi* is the period from mid-July to mid-August. The Vedan Theyyam performs at the rural Tharavadus (prominent families) in North Kerala, while Karkkidaka (Aadi) Theyyam performs at various other places. Both these Theyyams as a group are called the Aadi-Veda Theyyams.

Vedan and Aadi are performed by the Malaya and Vannan community, respectively. They sing "Thottam Pattu" (a ballad) before the performance, accompanied by the percussion instrument, the Chenda. The Theyyam is believed to eradicate misfortunes and miseries. Adi Theyyam is based on Goddess Parvathy, the partner of Lord Shiva.

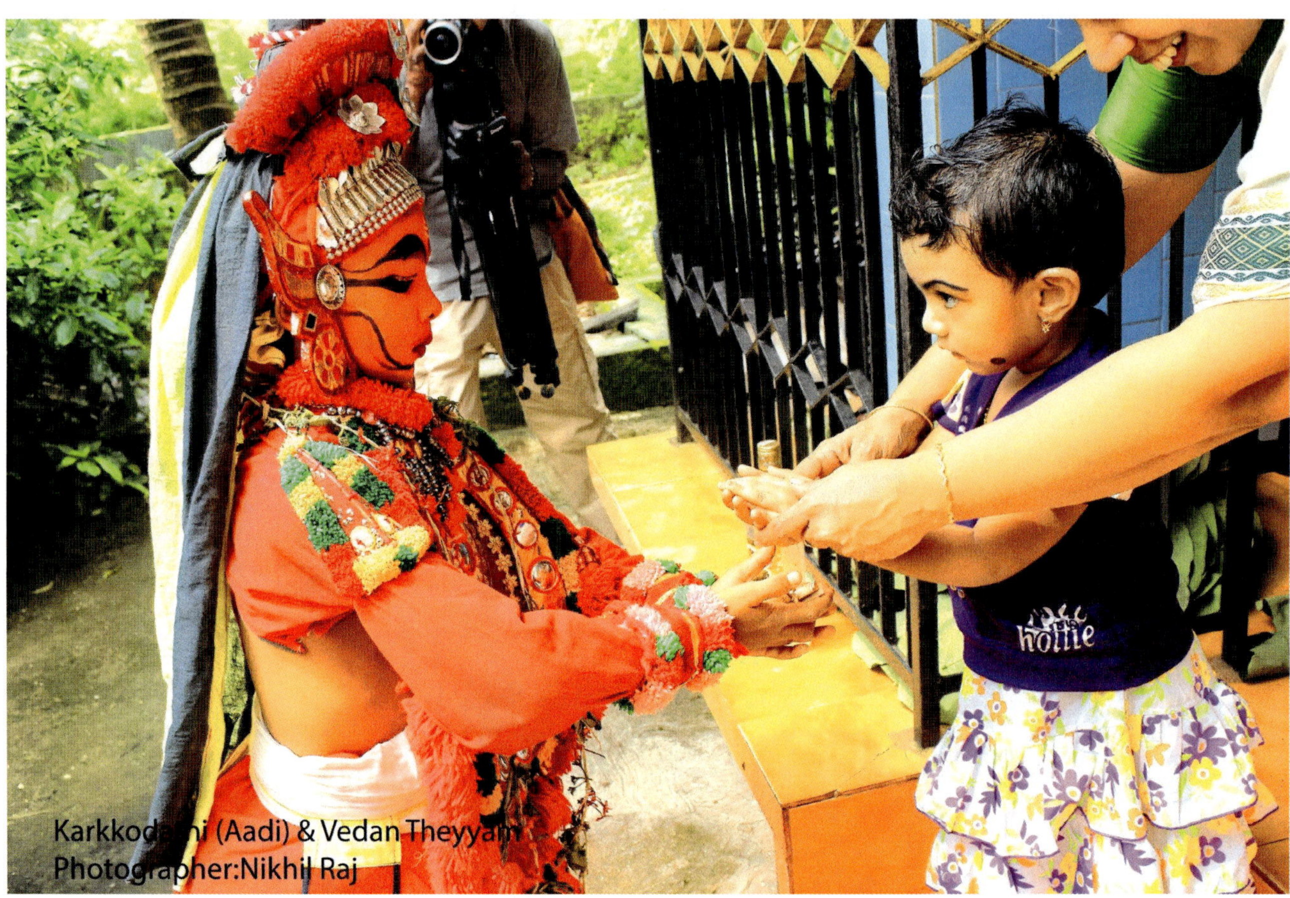

Karkkodami (Aadi) & Vedan Theyyam
Photographer:Nikhil Raj

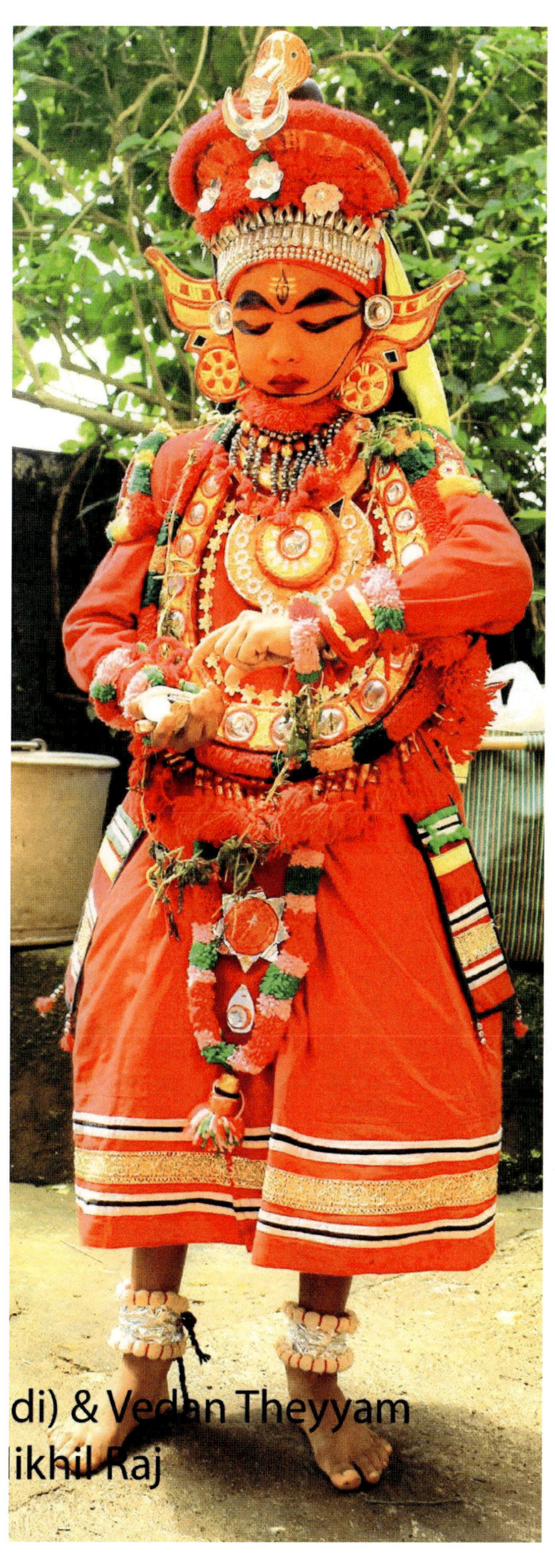

di) & Vedan Theyyam
likhil Raj

Kattu Pothi Theyyam

Kattu Pothi Theyyam shares the legend of Kadavath Bhagavathy in which *Kalakkatt*, an eminent *Tantri* (priest), was intensely focused on his tantra mantra (sacred rituals) practices when the cry of a child annoyed him. Instead of soothing the child, the Goddess he worshiped killed it. The infuriated Tantri discards the abode of the Goddess, which falls on the premises of Palayil Idamana Tantri, who installs the Goddess at his residence. The wooden planks of the Goddess discarded by the Tantri cross the Arayi river and come to the courtyards of Arayi Thiyya, a lower caste person. This Goddess came to be known as Kadavath Bhagavathy or Kattu Pothi Theyyam. The same Goddess is known as *Kanakkara Bhagavathy* in the Cheemeni Alanthatta region. The legend of the *Kanakkara Bhagavathy* is also similar. They performed mainly *Kadavath Bhagavathy or Kanakkara Bhagavathy Theyyam* at the Mundya shrine at *Arayi Erath* in Kanhangad.

The legend of Kanakkara Bhagavathy is also similar to this legend. Kadavath Bhagavathy or Kanakkara Bhagavathy Theyyam is performed mainly at Vellikunnummal Padarkulangara Bhagavathi Temple in Neeleswaram.

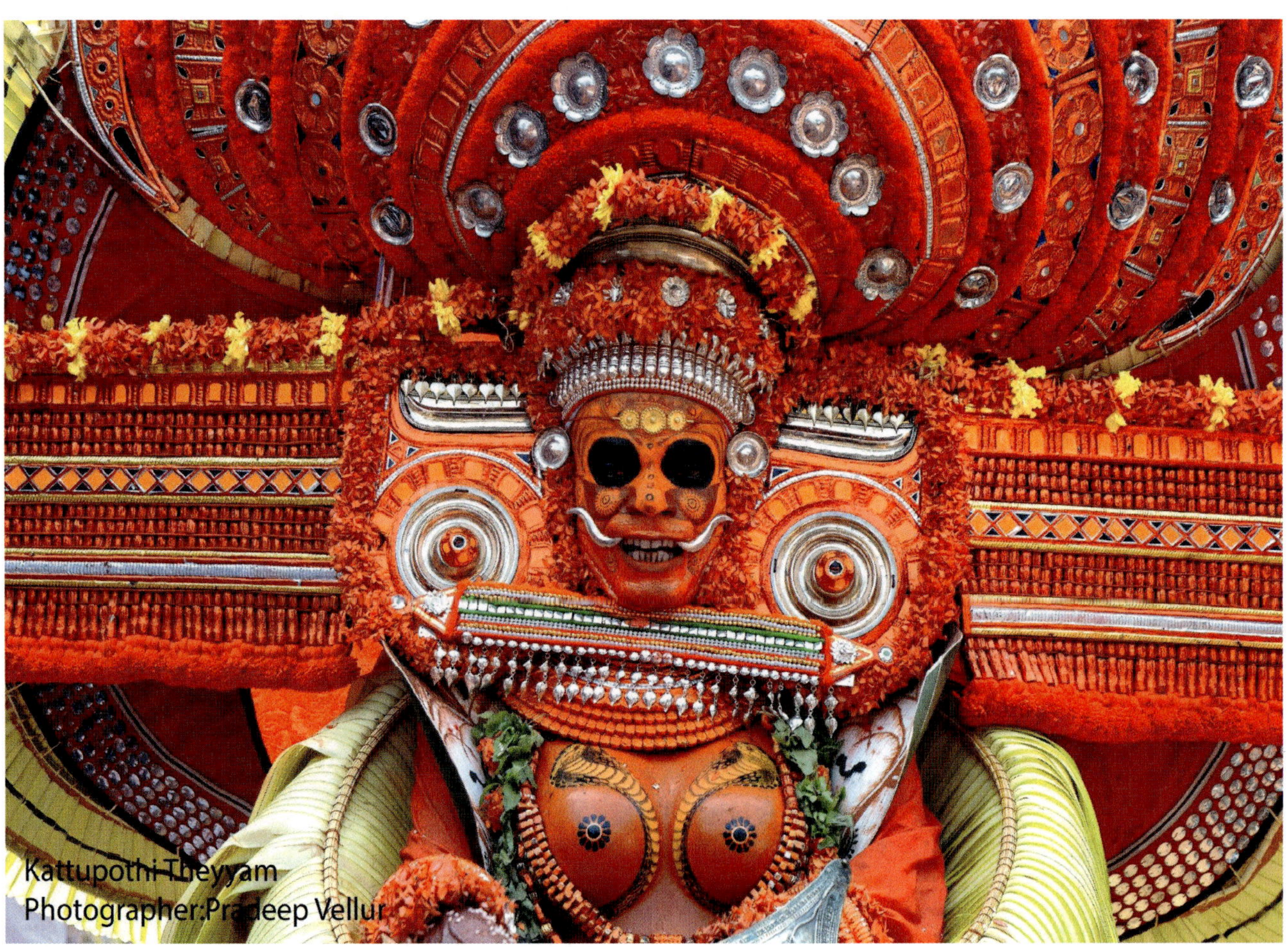

Kattupothi Theyyam
Photographer:Pradeep Vellur

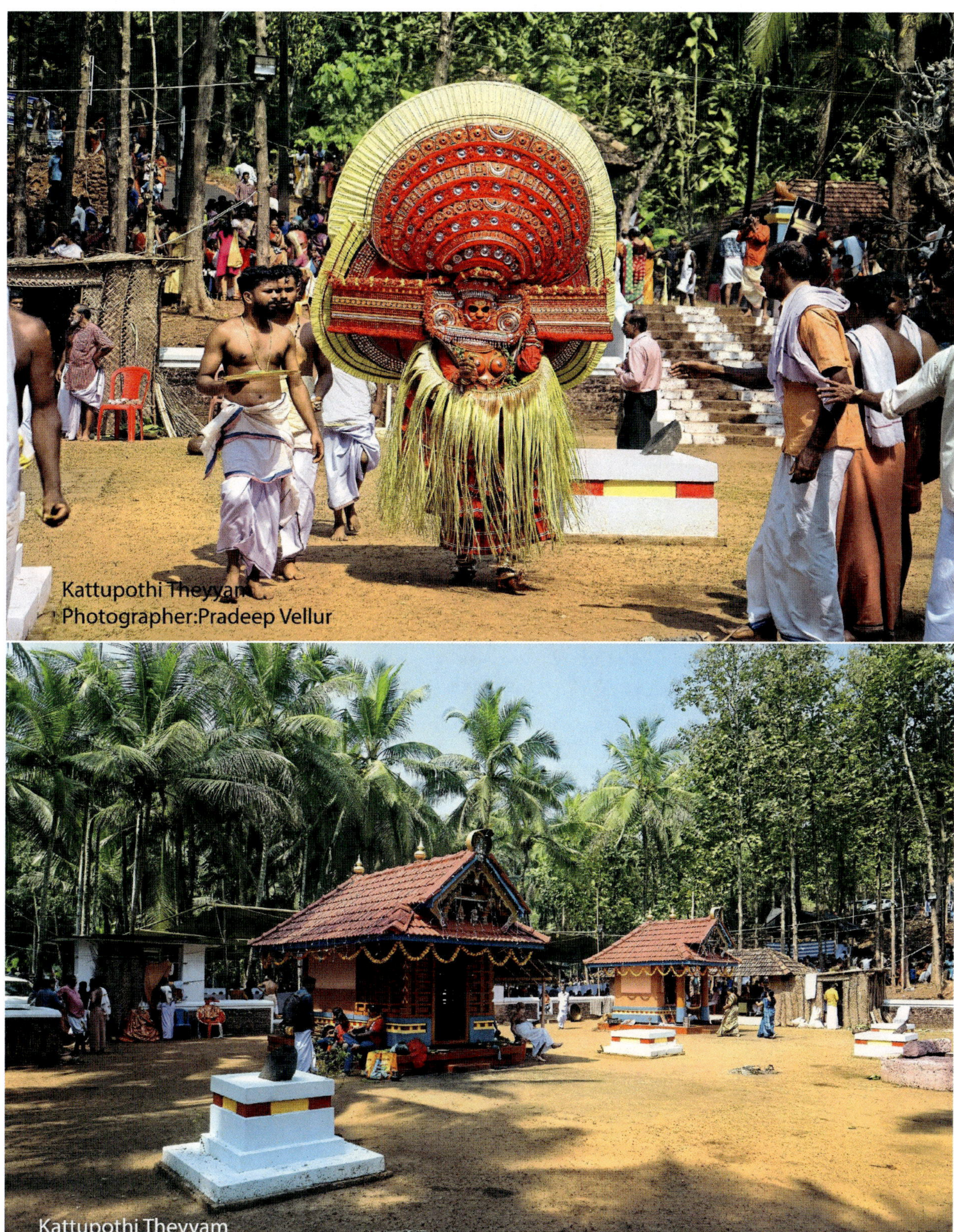

Kattupothi Theyyam
Photographer:Pradeep Vellur

Kattupothi Theyyam
Photographer:Pradeep Vellur

Aryakkara bhagavathy

It is believed that some gods and Goddesses came from Aryanadu (The land of Aryas), crossing the sea on a ship. Some of them are depicted as Theyyams. For example, *Arya Poonkanni, Arya Poomala, Aryakkara Bhagavthi, Aayitti Bhagavathi, Uchoolikkadavathu Bhagavthi, Sreeshoola Kumariyamma (Marakkalathamma), Chuzhali Bhagavthi, etc*. Some examples of male gods who came by ship are *Villapurathu Asuralan Daivam, Vadaken Kodiveeran, Poomaruthan,* and *Bappiriyan*.

Aryakkara Bhagavathi came to see *Kolathunadu* (Kerala) from *Aryarnadu*. The Goddess, who crossed the oceans, stopped at Kadinjikadavu when she was enamored by the beautiful smell of Champak flowers. She passed a test by the Allada (Neeleswaram) King to ordain her. She also cured smallpox of *Kanikkara Achan*. Thus, *Aryakkara Bhagavthi* became the Goddess beneath the Champak tree in Kadinjikadavu. She got her place in *Aryakkara* and *Anjootambalam Kavu*. Her favorite offerings are Champak Flowers. The Devi (Goddess) is placed so that she faces the sea in the west. People of the Vannan community perform this Theyyam.

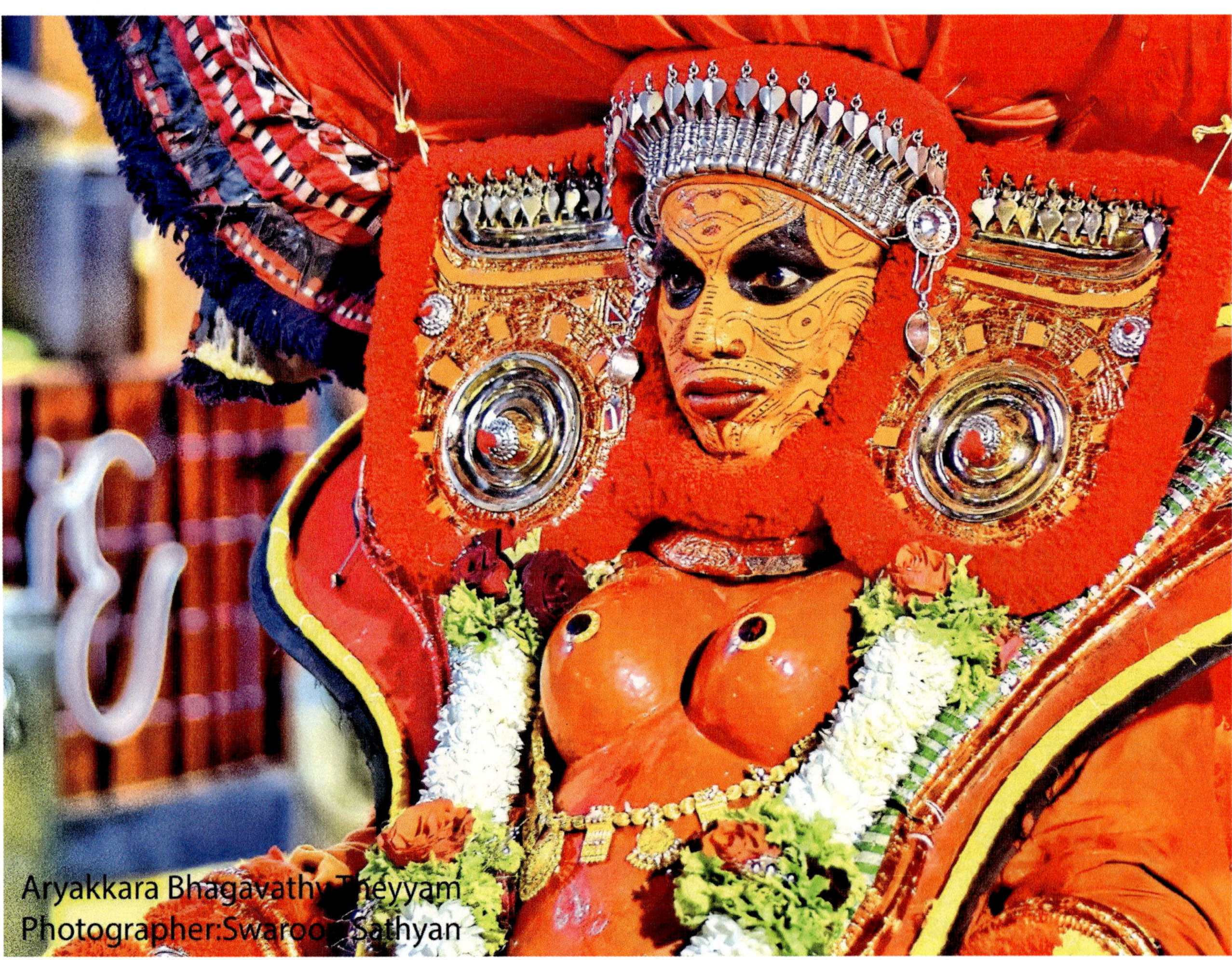

Aryakkara Bhagavathy Theyyam
Photographer:Swaroop Sathyan

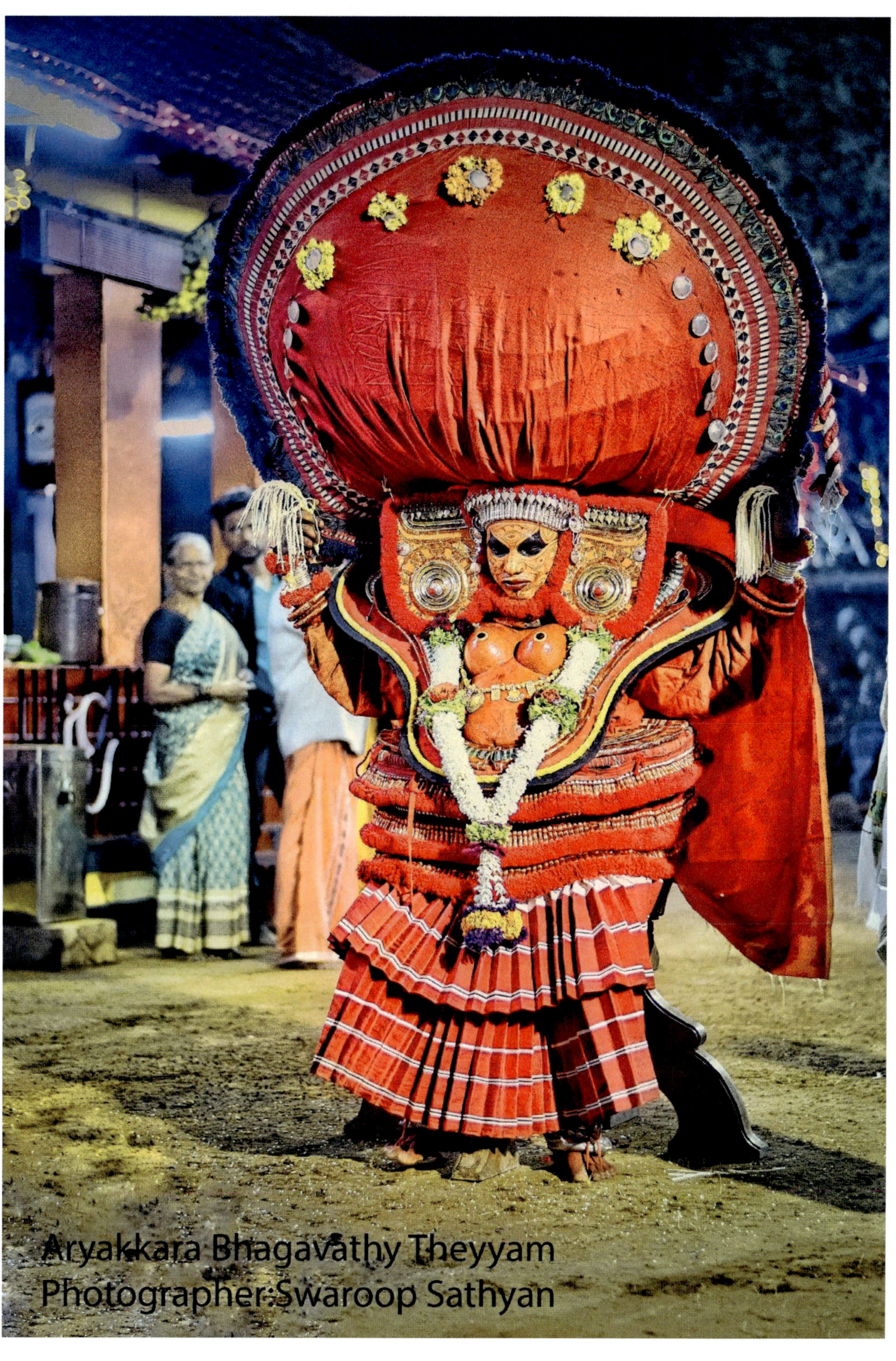

Aryakkara Bhagavathy Theyyam
Photographer:Swaroop Sathyan

Kanakkara Bhagavathy Theyyam

This Theyyam shares the legend of Kadavath Bhagavathy in which a desolated Goddess traveled by river to the premises of another Tantri and thereafter to the abode of a lower caste Thiyya. Although the legends are the same, Kanakkara Bhagavathy Theyyam has different attire and makeup than Kadavath Bhagavathy. These kinds of regional variations are found in different Theyyam classifications. This Theyyam is known as Kadavath Bhagavathy in the Arayi region in Kanhangad, and the same Goddess is known as Kaattu Pothi Theyyam at Vellikunnummal Padarkulangara Bhagavathy temple in Neeleswaram.

The Kanakkara Bhagavathy Theyyam is performed mainly at Cheemeni Alanthatta Puthiyadathara Devasthanam.

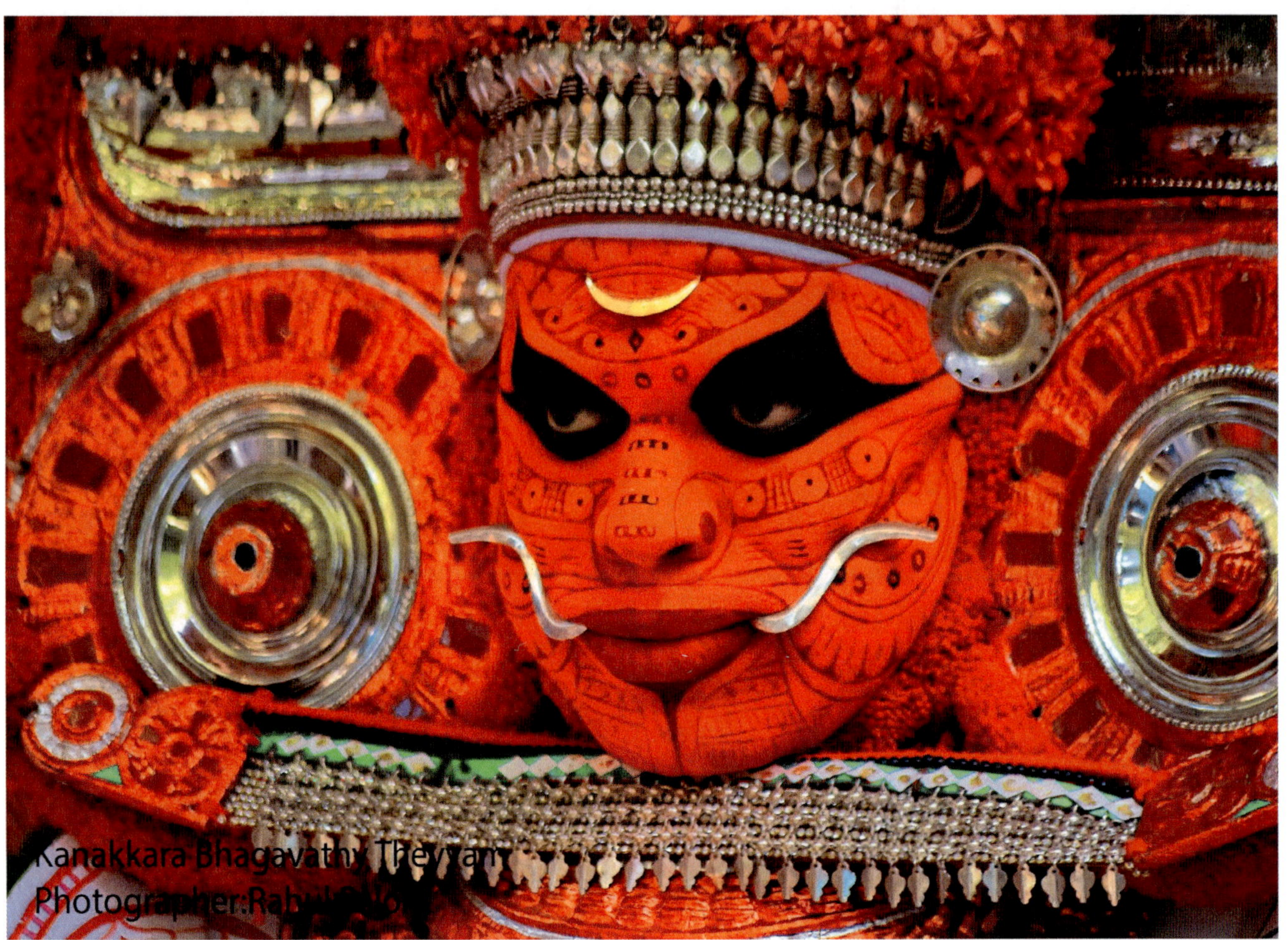

Kanakkara Bhagavathy Theyyam
Photographer:Rah[illegible]

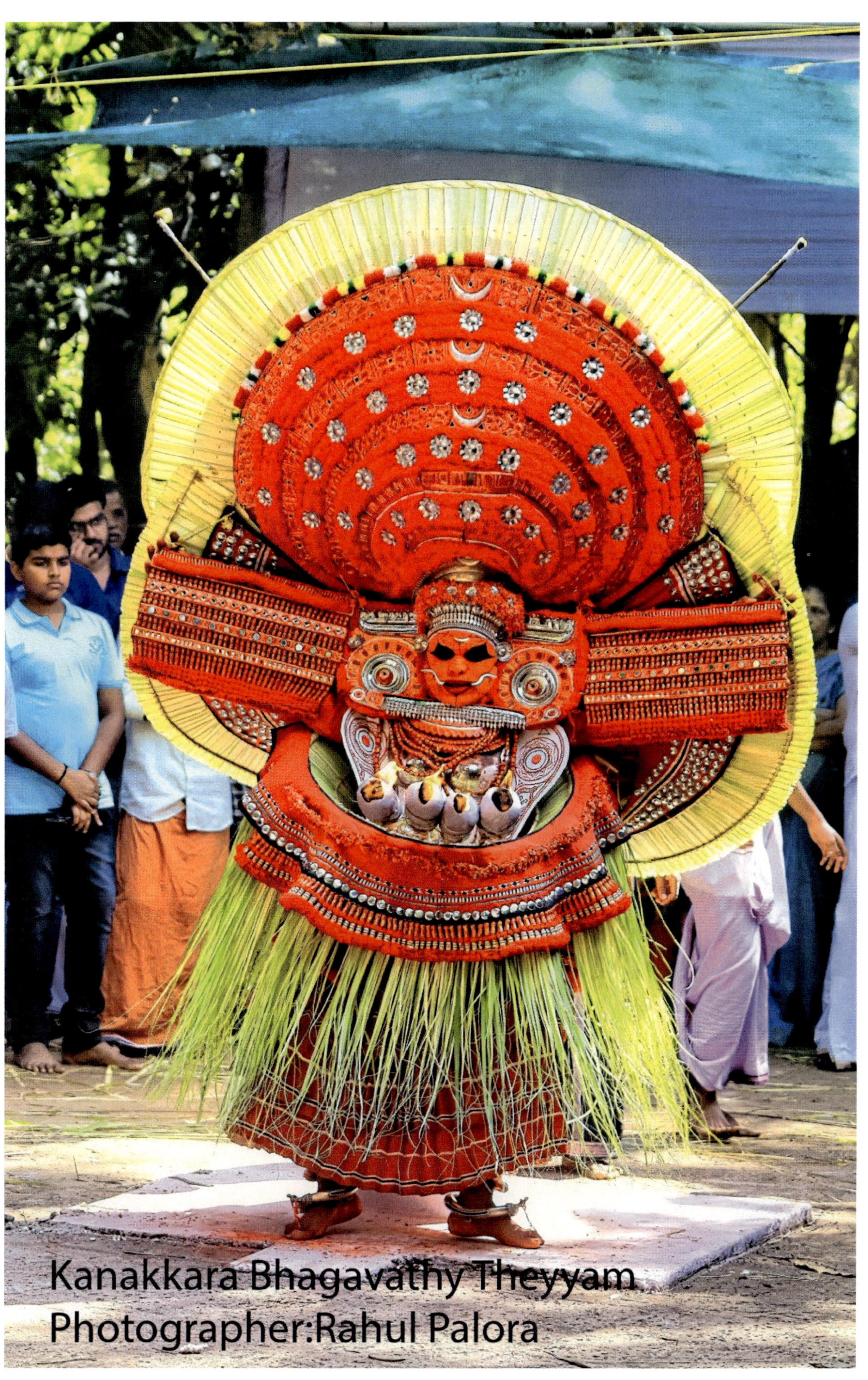

Kanakkara Bhagavathy Theyyam
Photographer:Rahul Palora

Padaveeran Theyyam

Born heroes who fought with superhuman abilities later became Theyyams following their martyrdom. The *Padaveeran Theyyam* tells a similar story about the son of martyr Achanthattu Kurumadathil Koppala Maniyani, who turned into *Padaveeran Theyyam*. *Padaveeran* was a polyglot who spoke several languages and was trained by his uncle. On his debut as a warrior, he defeated his uncle. Though defeated by his nephew and disciple, his uncle was delighted about Padaveeran's superhuman abilities and blessed him.

Once, when he was about to have supper, he heard the war cry of the army from Kodagu (Coorg). He decided it was wrong for a man to continue eating food when the enemy had issued a war cry. He rushed to the battlefield like a tempest and annihilated several soldiers. However, their army of Kodagu later deceived him, resulting in his death. The war hero *Padaveeran* thus came to be depicted as a Theyyam. This Theyyam, also known as Kathavannoor Veeran Theyyam in other regions, resembles the stories, attire, and makeup.

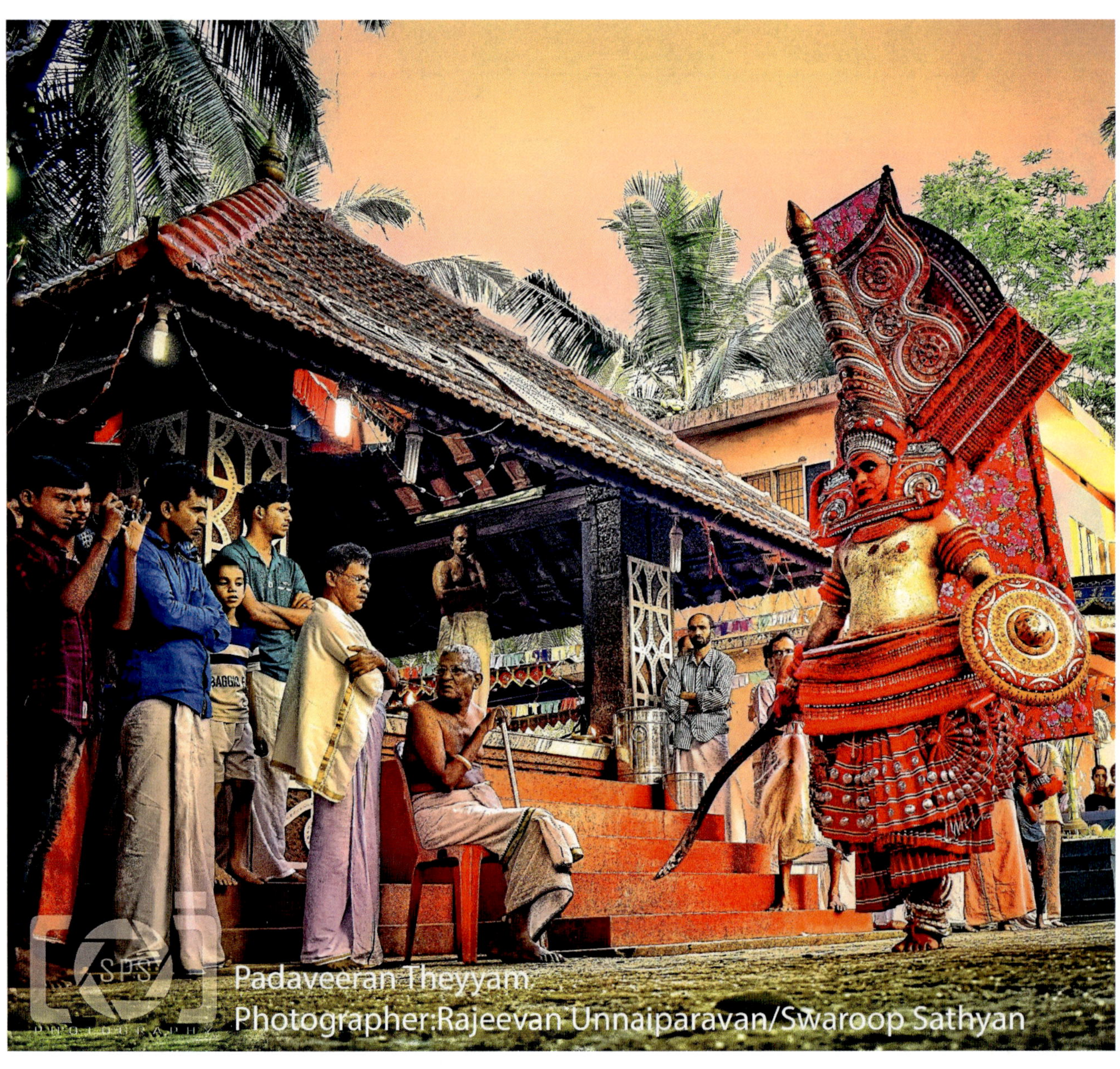

Padaveeran Theyyam
Photographer:Rajeevan Unnaiparavan/Swaroop Sathyan

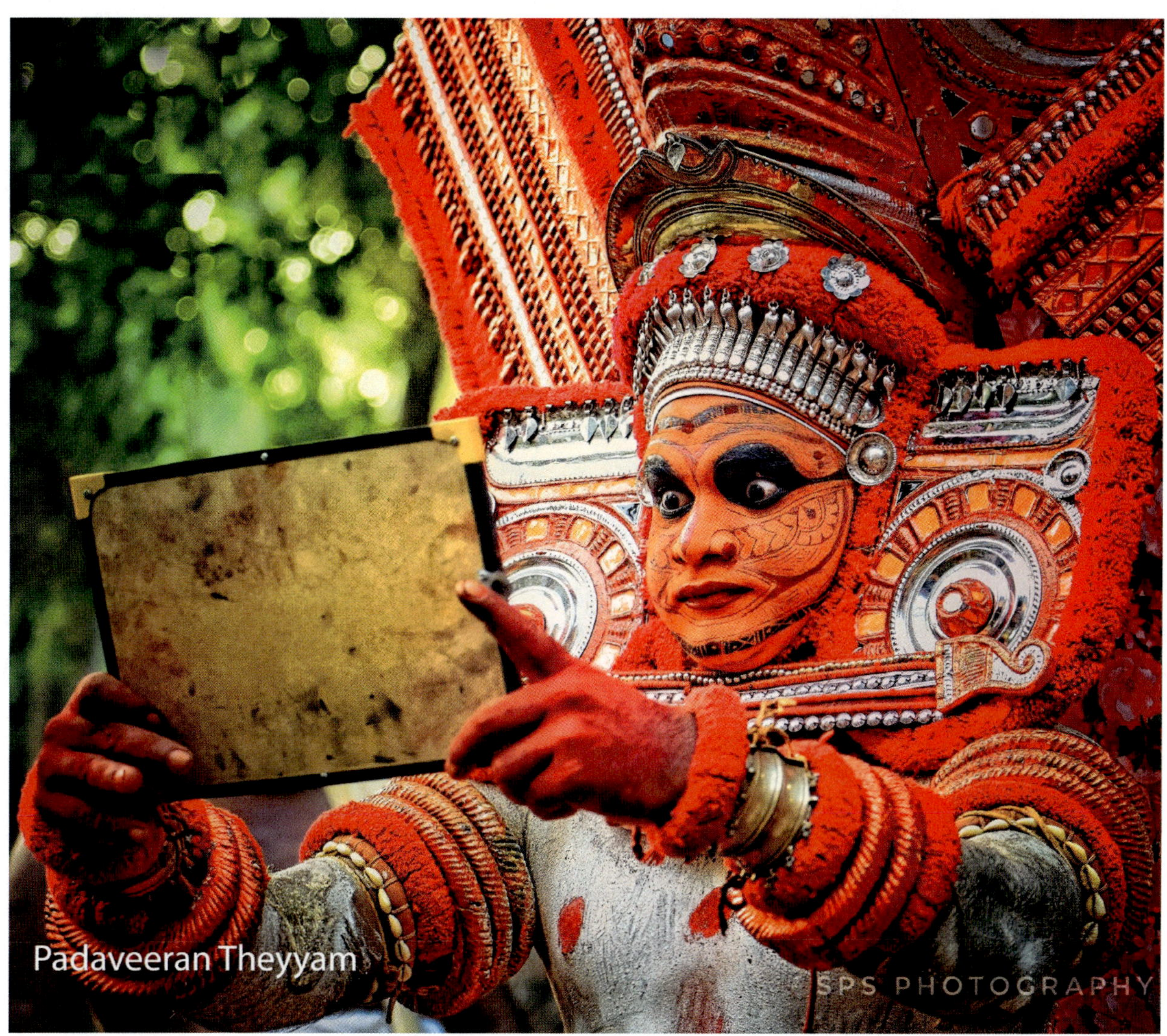

Padaveeran Theyyam

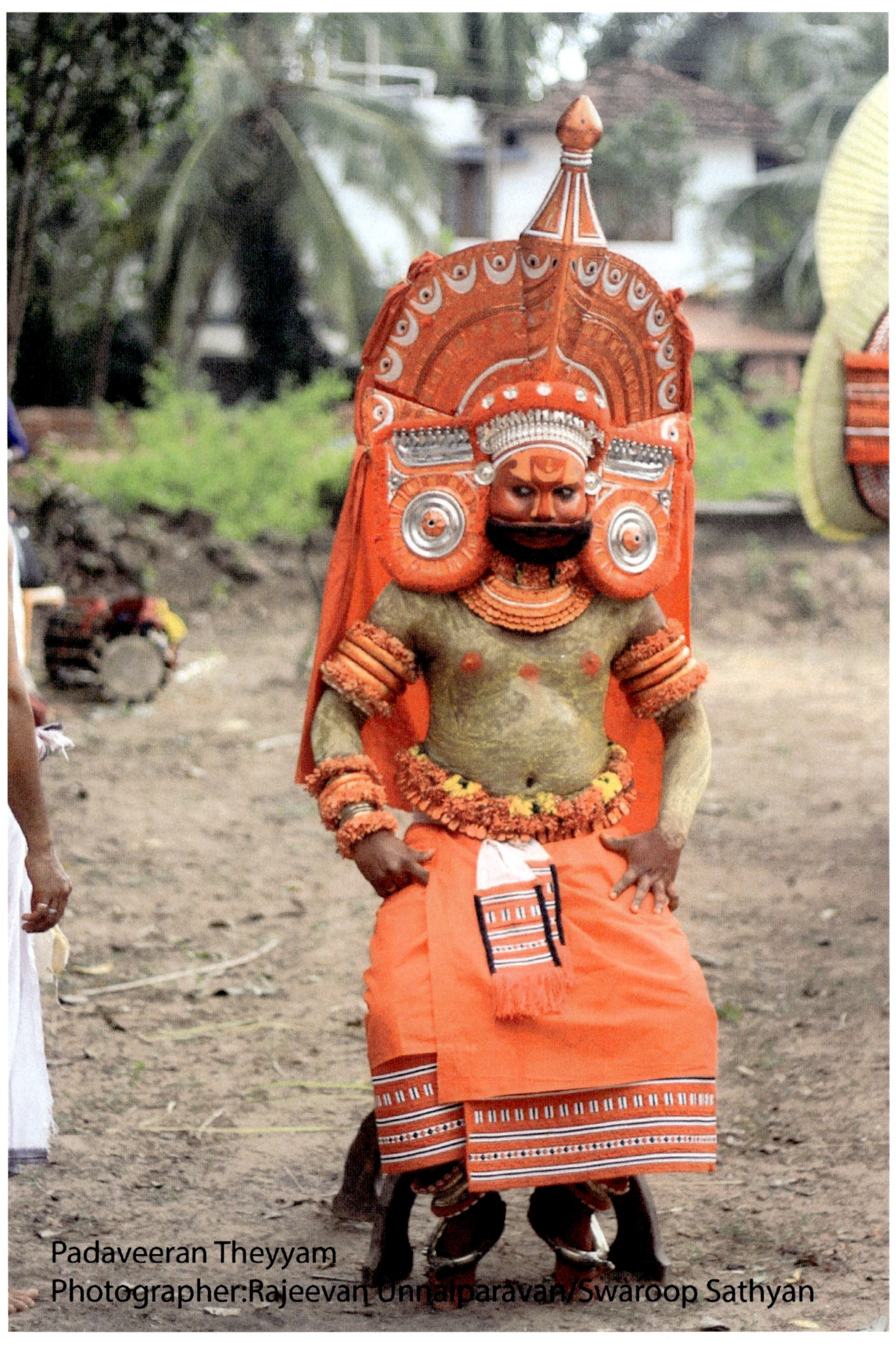

Padaveeran Theyyam
Photographer:Rajeevan Unnalparavan/Swaroop Sathyan

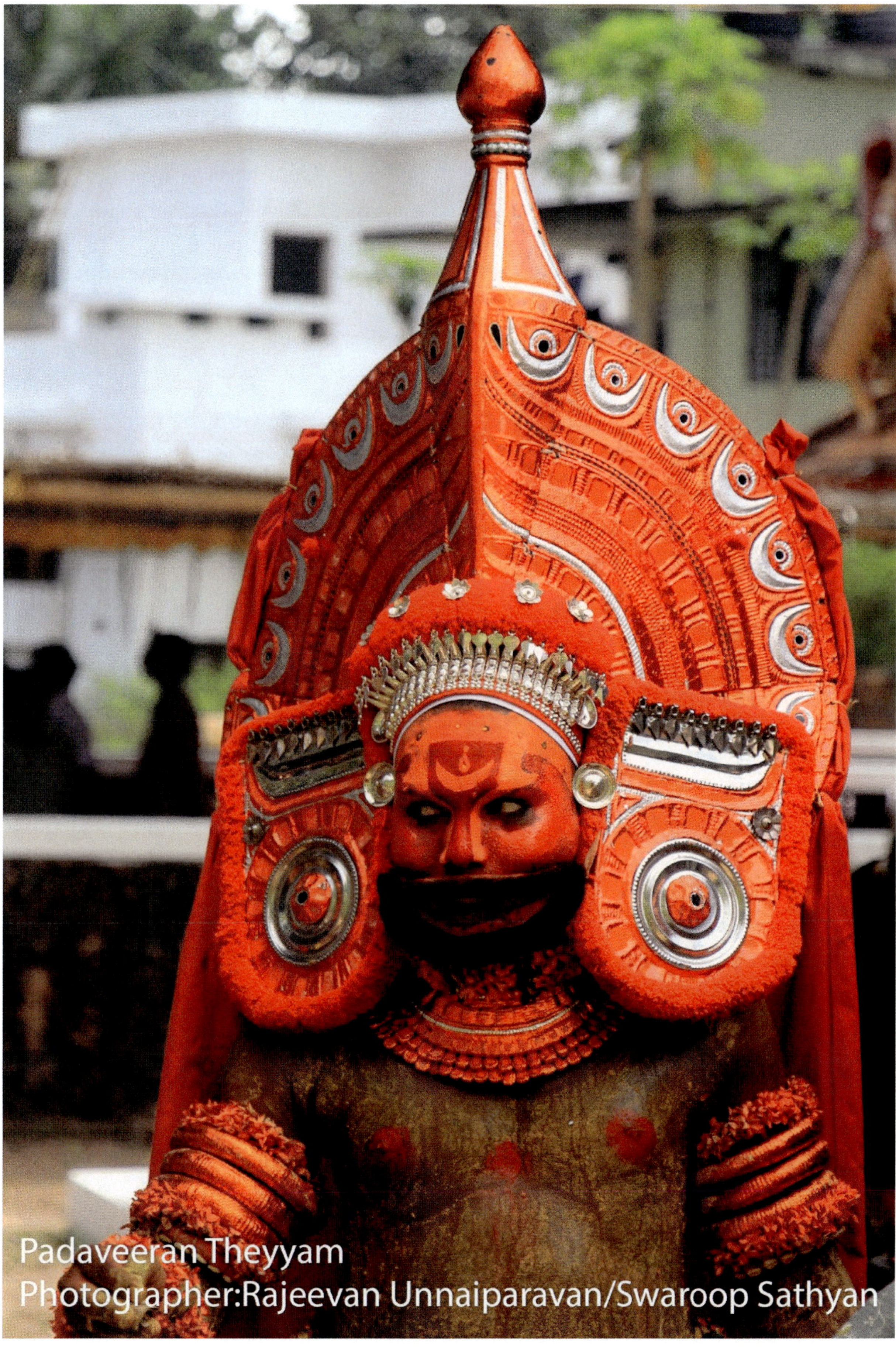

Padaveeran Theyyam
Photographer:Rajeevan Unnaiparavan/Swaroop Sathyan

Pazhassi Bhagavathy

Pazhassi Bhagavathy is considered the daughter of *Payyavoor Appan*. The *Manayani* community calls her *Pazassi Kannangatu Bhagavathy*, and the *Thiyya* community respectfully names her *Payatiyal Bhagavathy*. The tales claim she originated at the Paiyavur north gate as Yashoda's daughter who guided *Kannan* (or Lord Vishnu when he incarnated as Sri Krishna) to kill Kamsa.

Pazhassi Bhagvathy is a Goddess in the *Roudramoorthy* (roudra means anger) classification who is wild and ferocious. The deity is tied to a banyan tree until the end of *Ootutsavam* (festival with a feast) in Payayavur Shiva temple. On the very next day after the festival, Theyyam is performed.

This Theyyam is also tied at *Ramanthali Koithatta Tharavadu*.

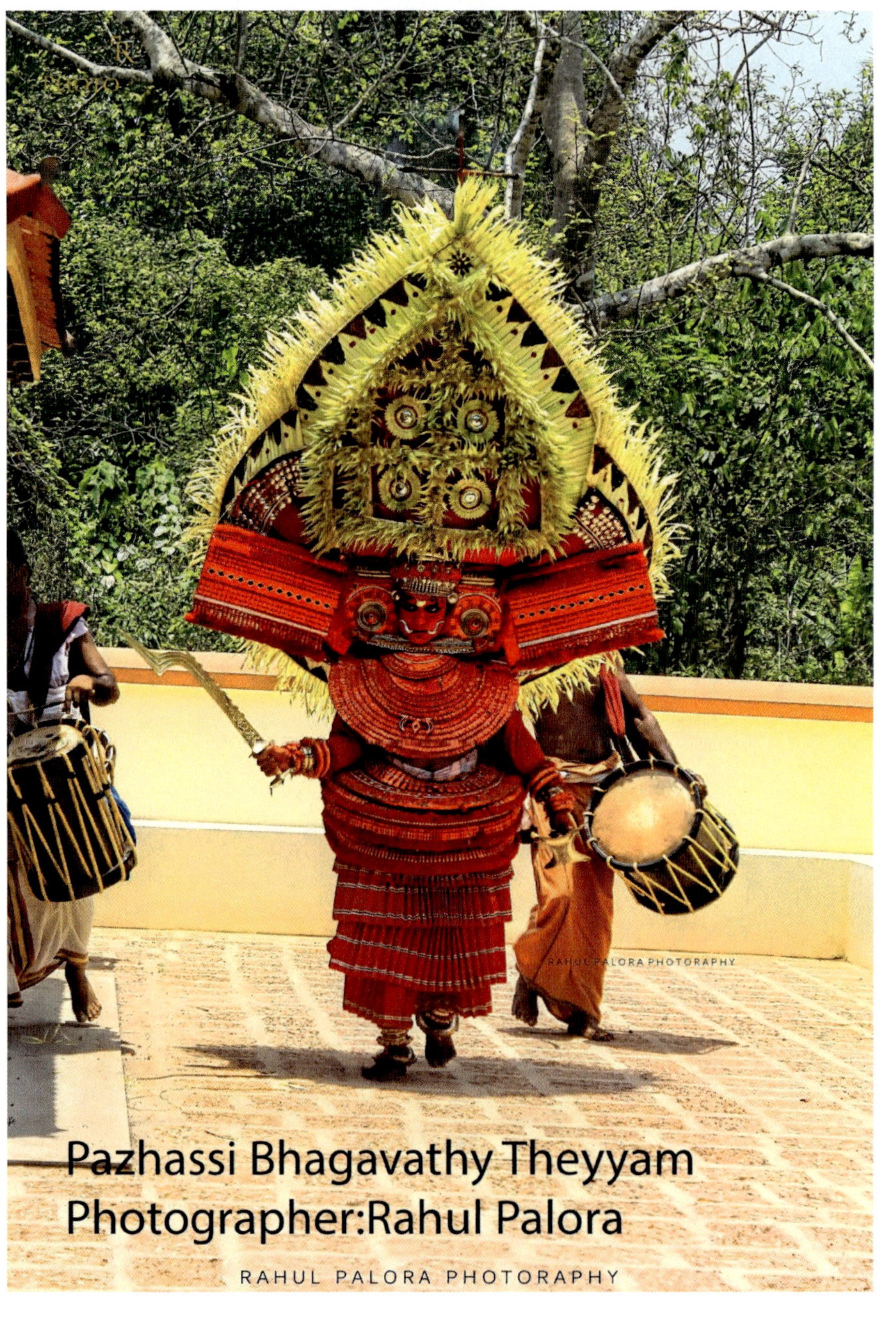

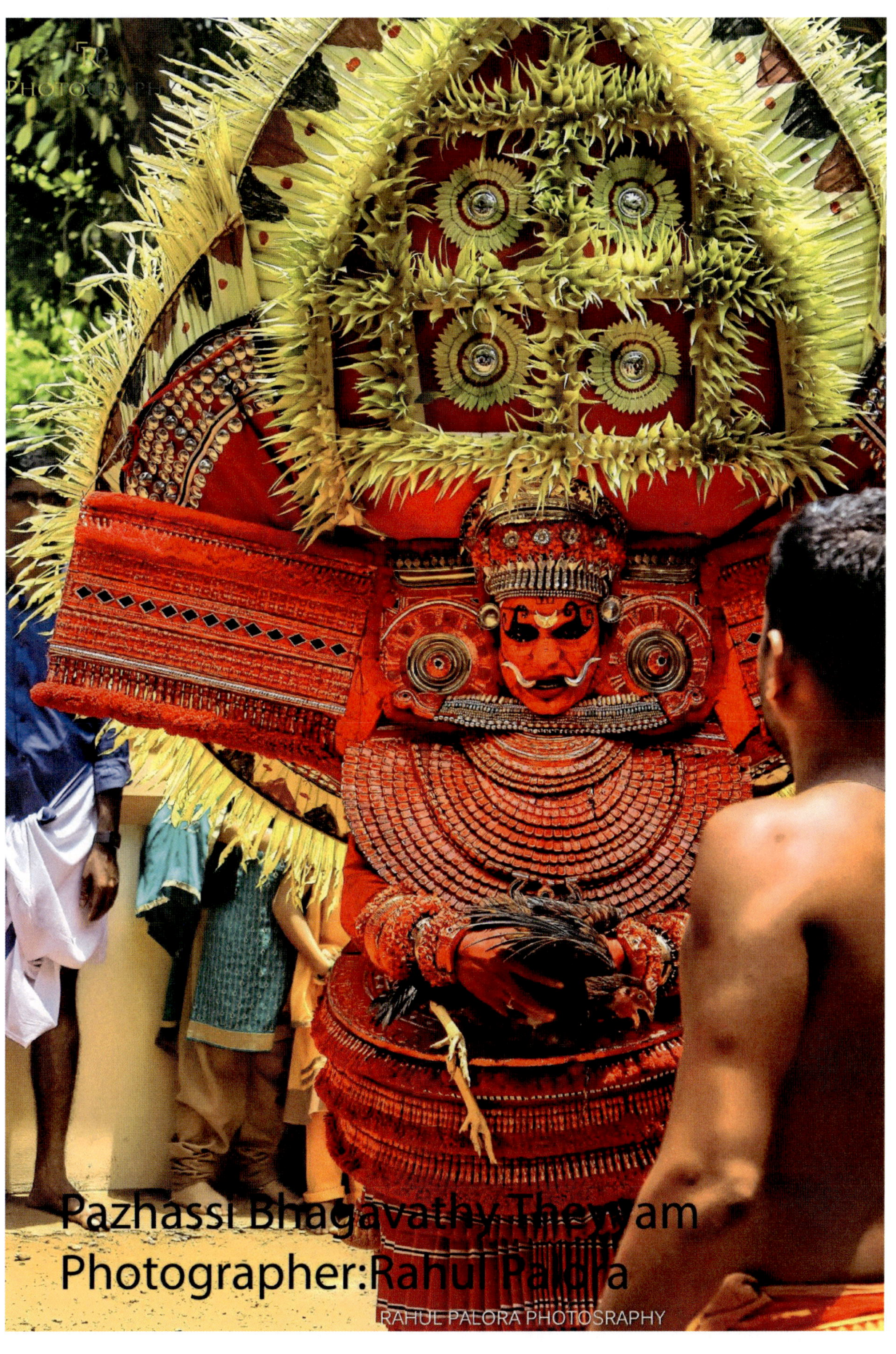

Pazhassi Bhagavathy Theyyam
Photographer:Rahul Palora

Karuval Bhagavathy

Karuval Bhagavathy is a form of Manthra Moorthy. This Goddess was born in the Karuval Mountains. According to the hymn called the Kattumadathinkal Karuval Bhagavathy, her first abode is said to be *Kattumadam Thanthri madom*. Besides this, she is revered and worshipped in 18 other Nampoothiri households like *Adiyeri*, *Pullanjeri*, *Kattumadom*, etc.

Goddess Parvathi and Lord Shiva lived on as tribal people and gave birth to a son, Kuttichathan. Karuval Bhagavathy is believed to be the sister of Kuttichathan.

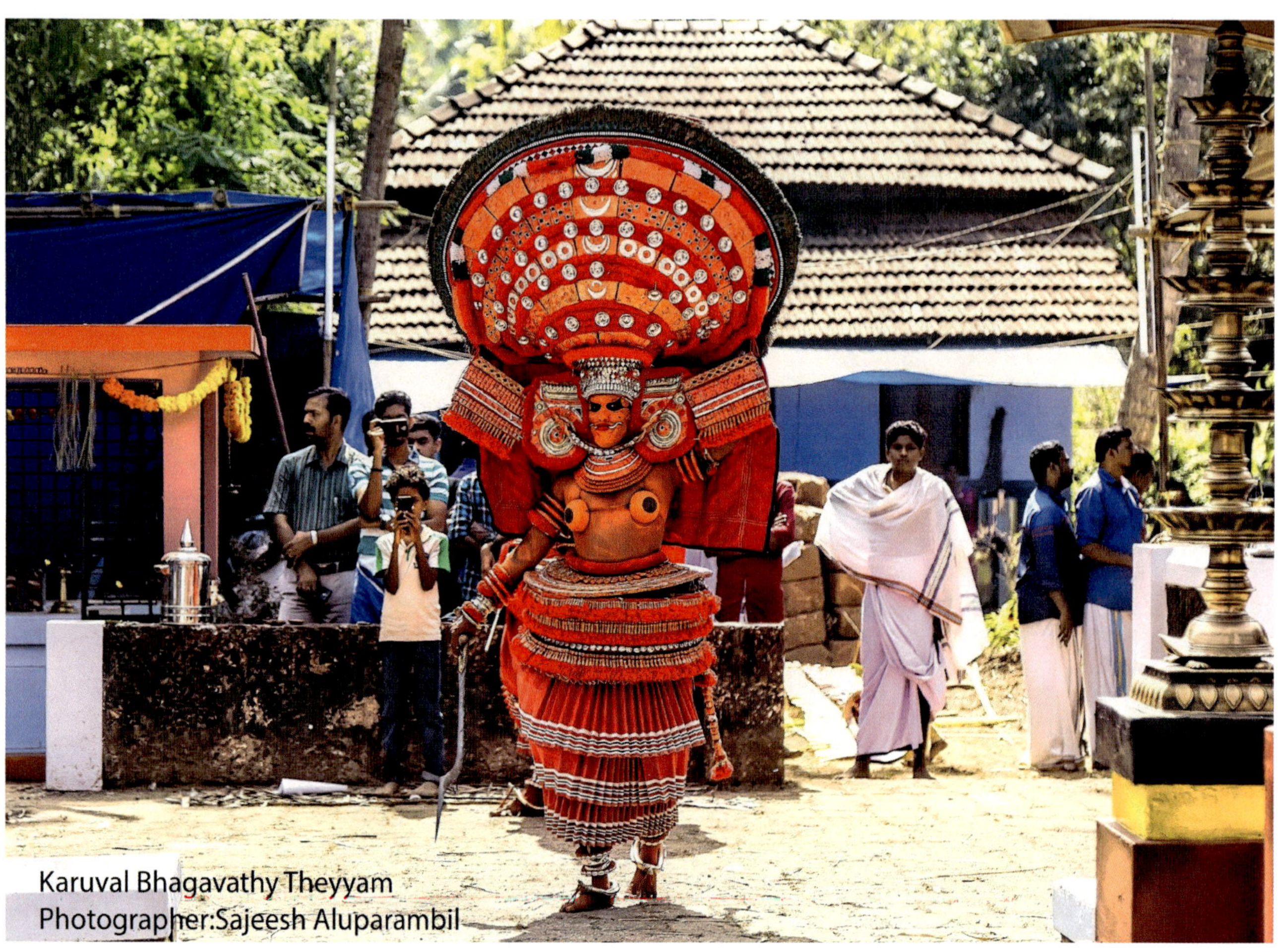

Karuval Bhagavathy Theyyam
Photographer:Sajeesh Aluparambil

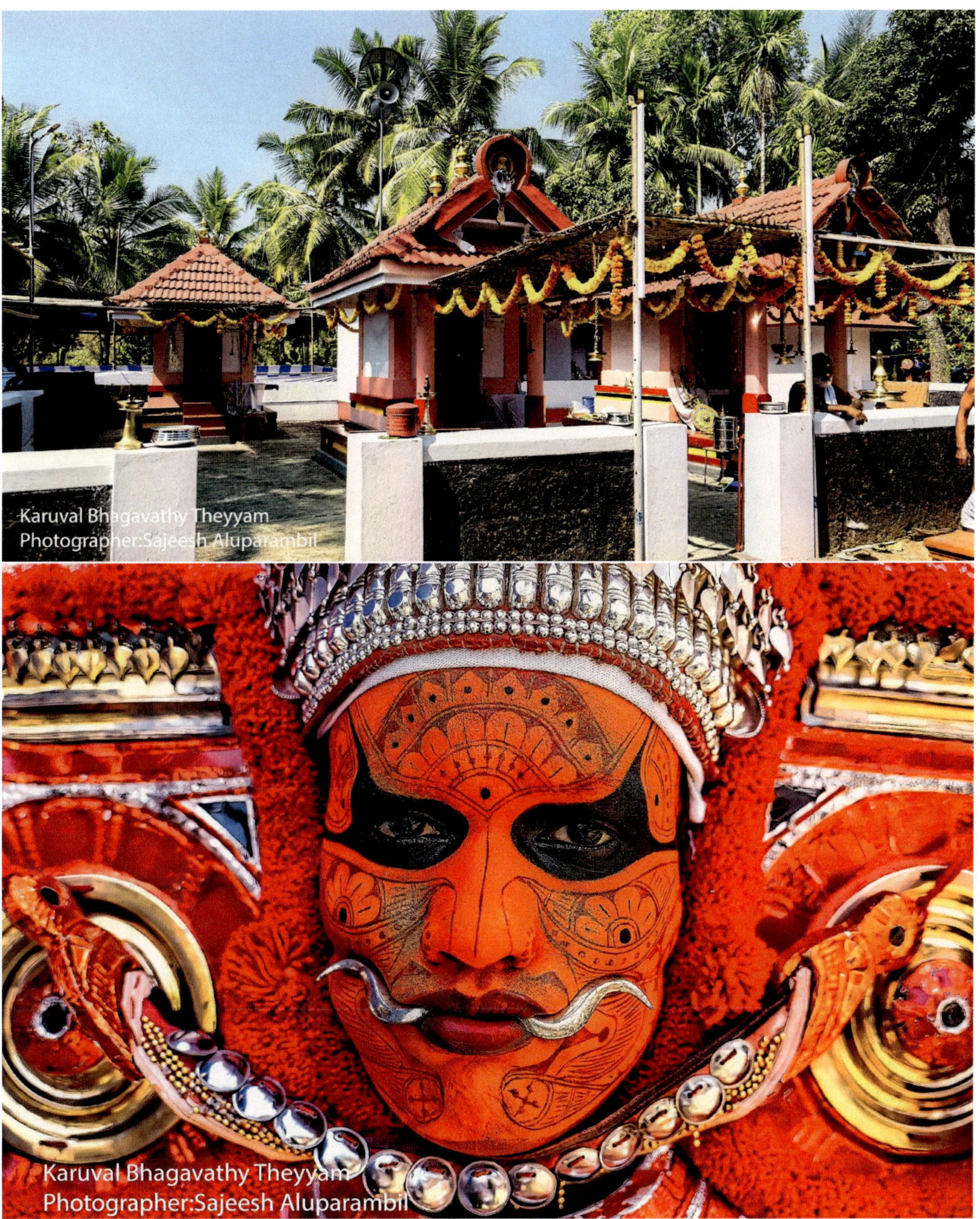

Karuval Bhagavathy Theyyam
Photographer:Sajeesh Aluparambil

Karuval Bhagavathy Theyyam
Photographer:Sajeesh Aluparambil

Mambally Bhagavathy

Mampally Bhagavathy, also known as Kakkara Bhagavathy, is a Bhadrakali figure. With the 'Bhadrachotta' face and fiery appearance, devotees stand in awe and fear watching her dance. Thottampattu describes her real name as Kalkkura Bhagavathy; her position as Kalkkurakkaavu or Kakkarakkaavu. Mambally Bhagavathy goes by different names in different regions. A popular variation of this Theyyam is Kadavath Bhagavathy Theyyam.

This deity has various names such as Mampalli Bhagavathy, Arumpalli Bhagavathy, Chekkicheri Bhagavathy, Karattu Bhagavathy, Kozhikulangara Bhagavathy, Dhooliyanga Bhagavathy, Kurumbilottu Bhagavathy, Kaya Bhagavathy, Kalkkura Bhagavathy and Poyil Bhagavathy in different lands. These Theyyams possess similarities in their face paintings and make-up.

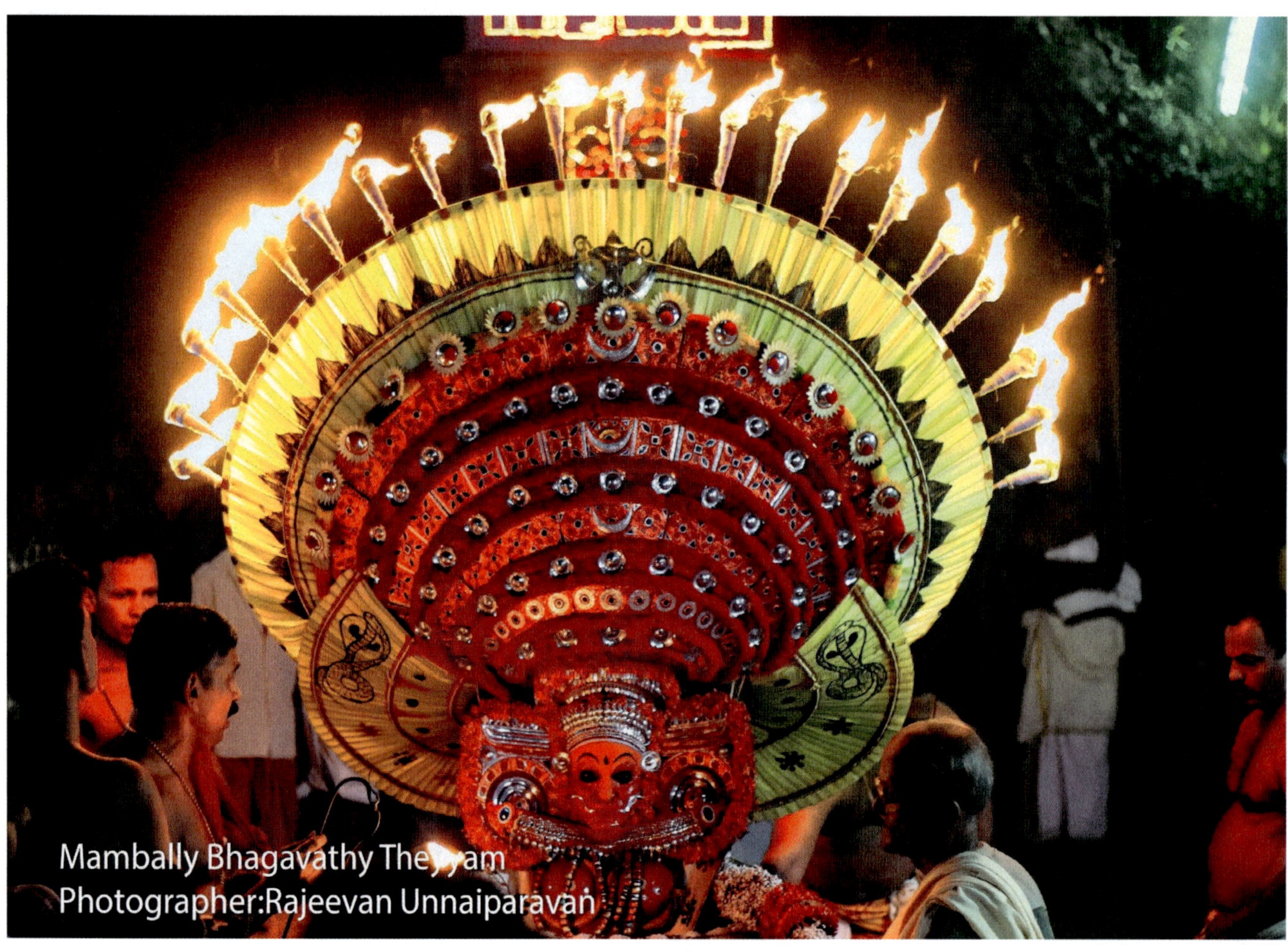

Mambally Bhagavathy Theyyam
Photographer:Rajeevan Unnaiparavan

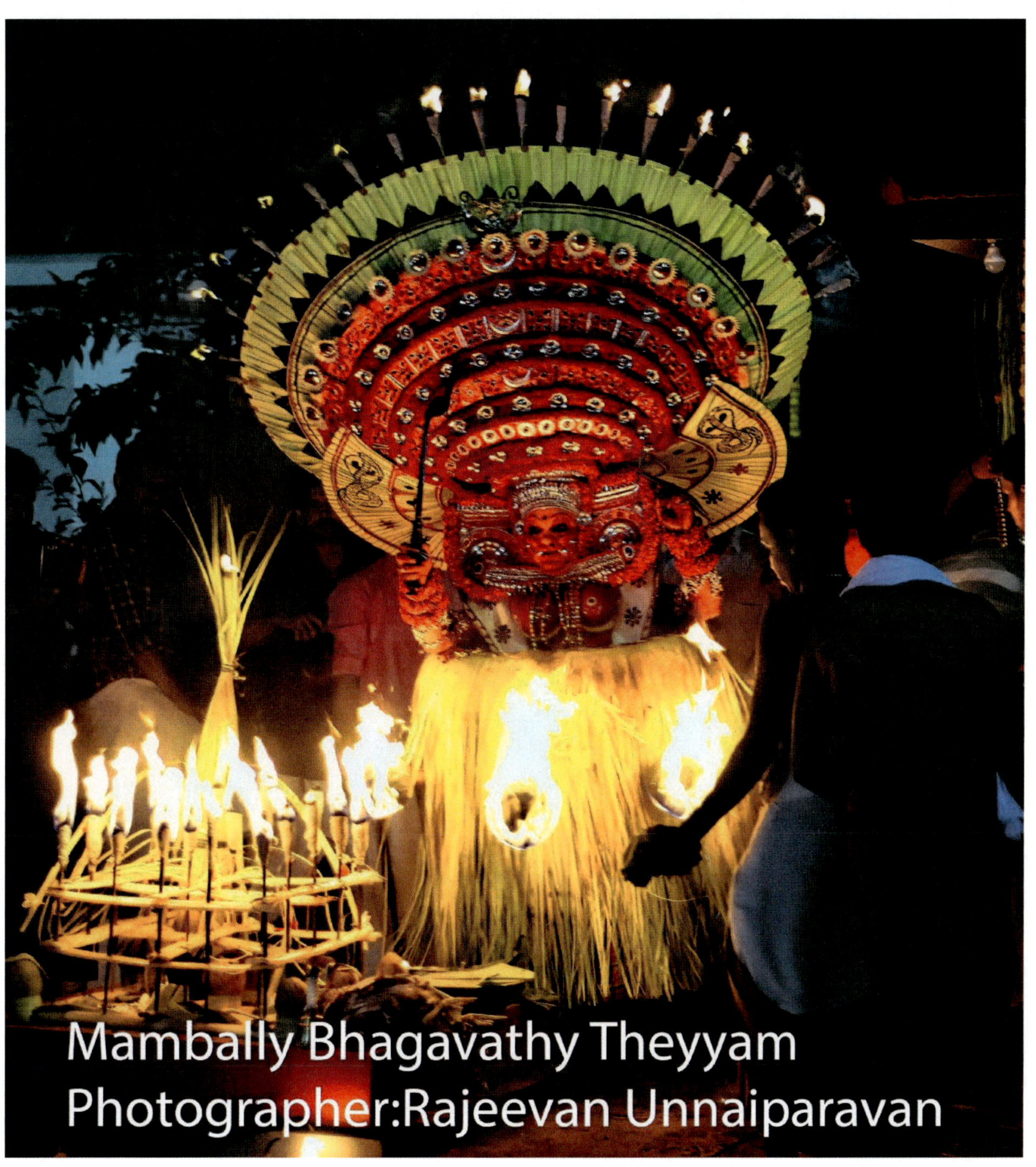

Mambally Bhagavathy Theyyam
Photographer:Rajeevan Unnaiparavan

Bhootham Theyyam

White, black, and red Bhoothams are Shivamshabhoothas. Ghosts who emerged as a result of unnatural deaths also fall under the category of Bhoothas. Anangu Bhootham, Kalar Bhootham, and Vattipootham are some of them. Demons such as Anchanangum Bhootham and Anthi urangum Bhootham are performed around the Kasaragod areas. Ghost worship is more common in Tulunadu, where these ghosts appear at night.

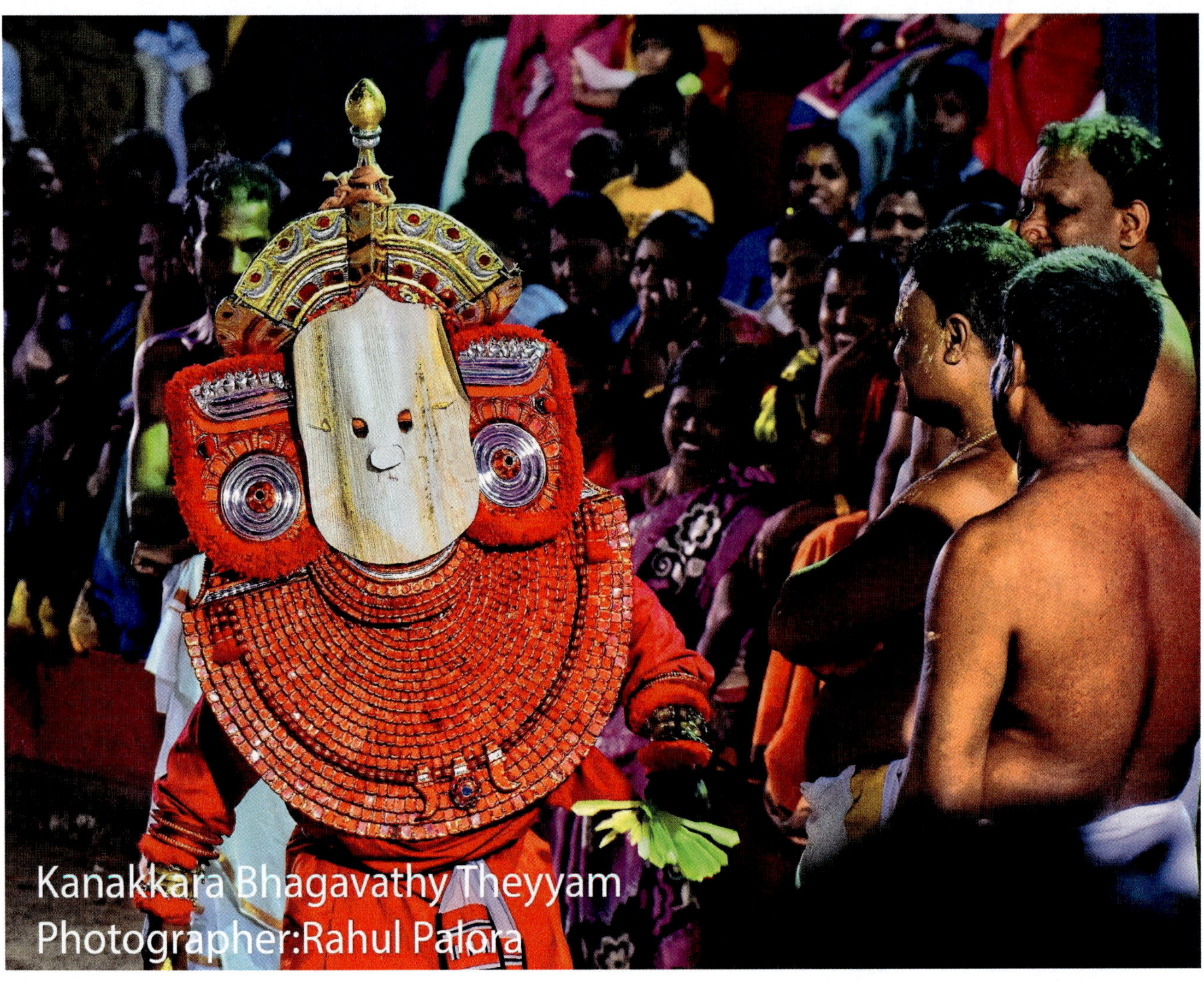
Kanakkara Bhagavathy Theyyam
Photographer:Rahul Palora

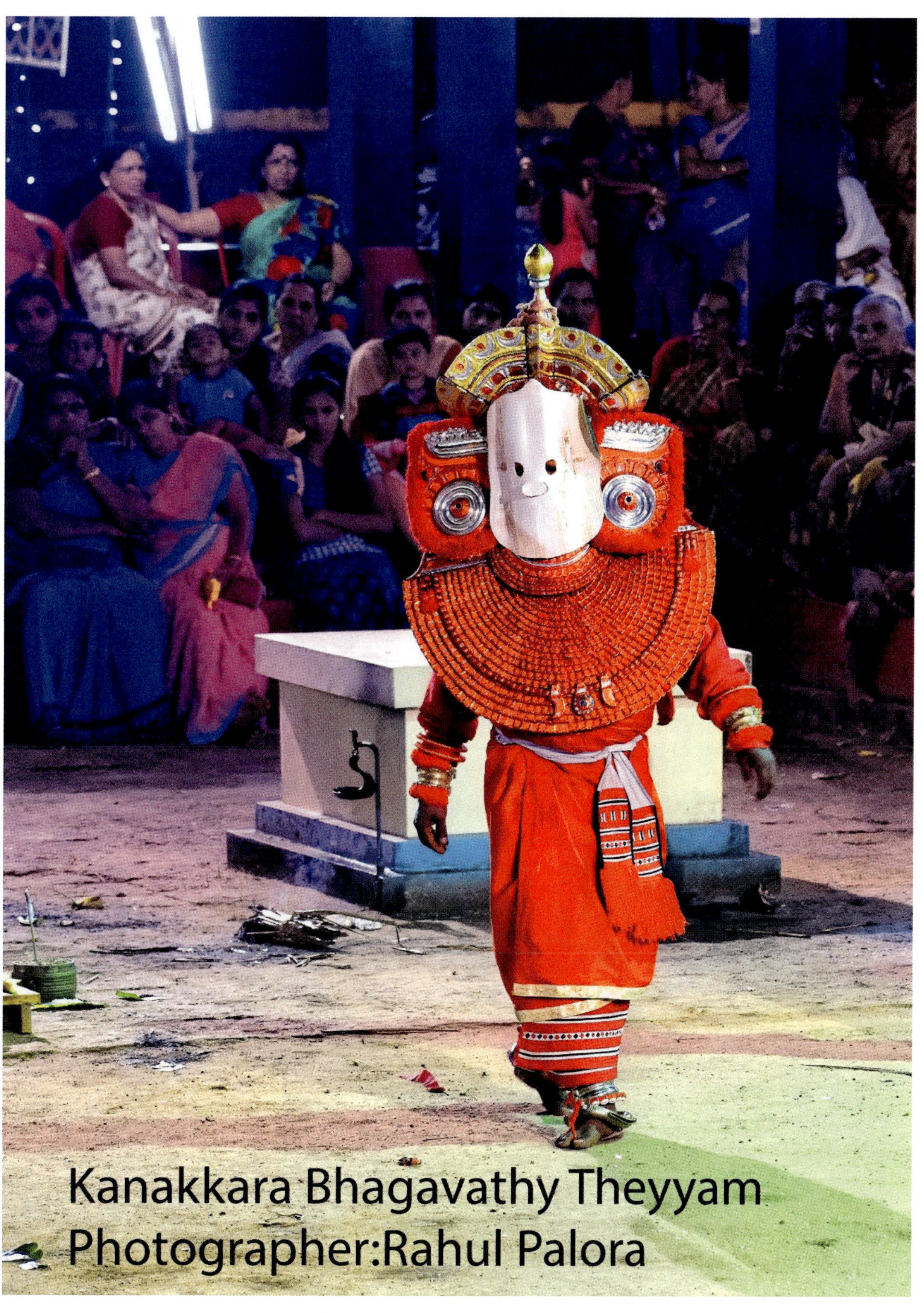
Kanakkara Bhagavathy Theyyam
Photographer:Rahul Palora

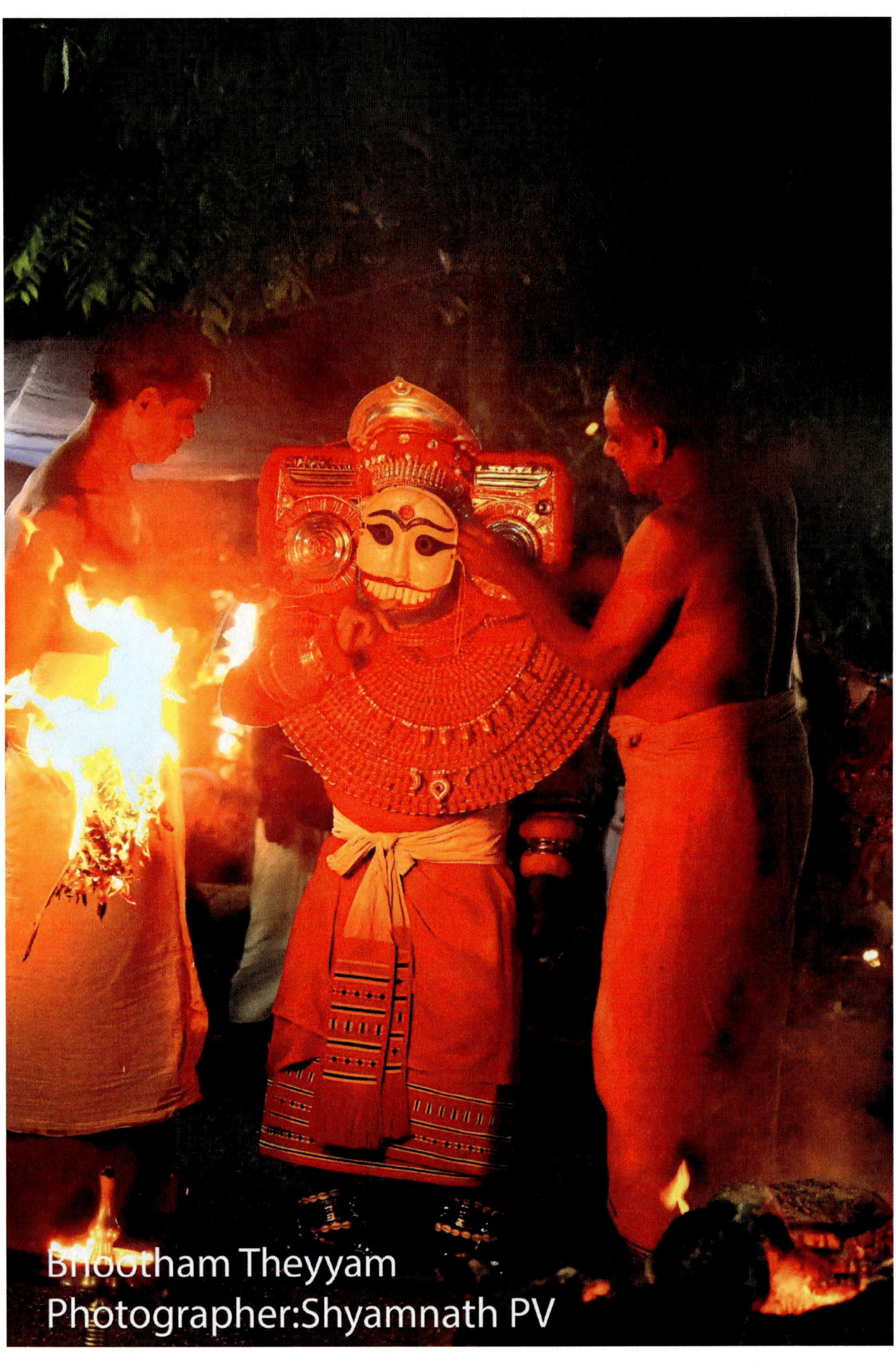
Bhootham Theyyam
Photographer:Shyamnath PV

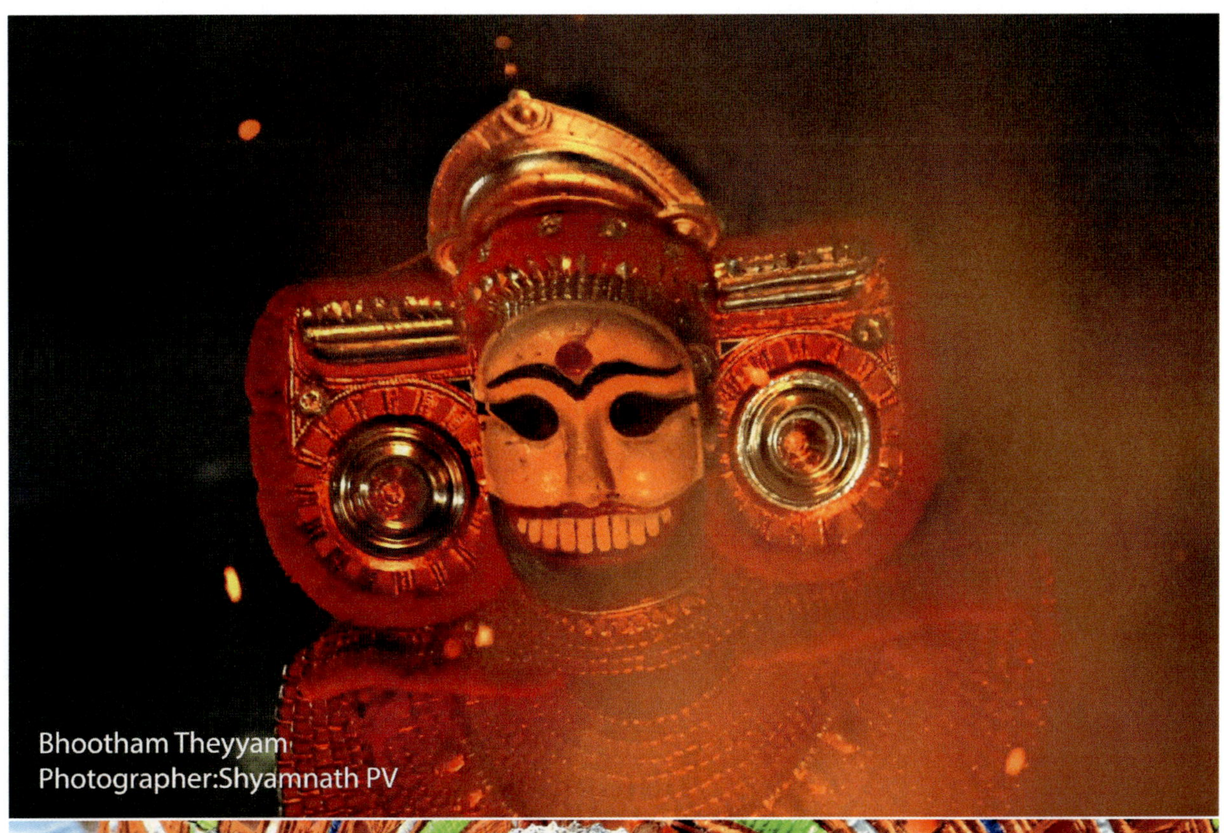

Bhootham Theyyam
Photographer:Shyamnath PV

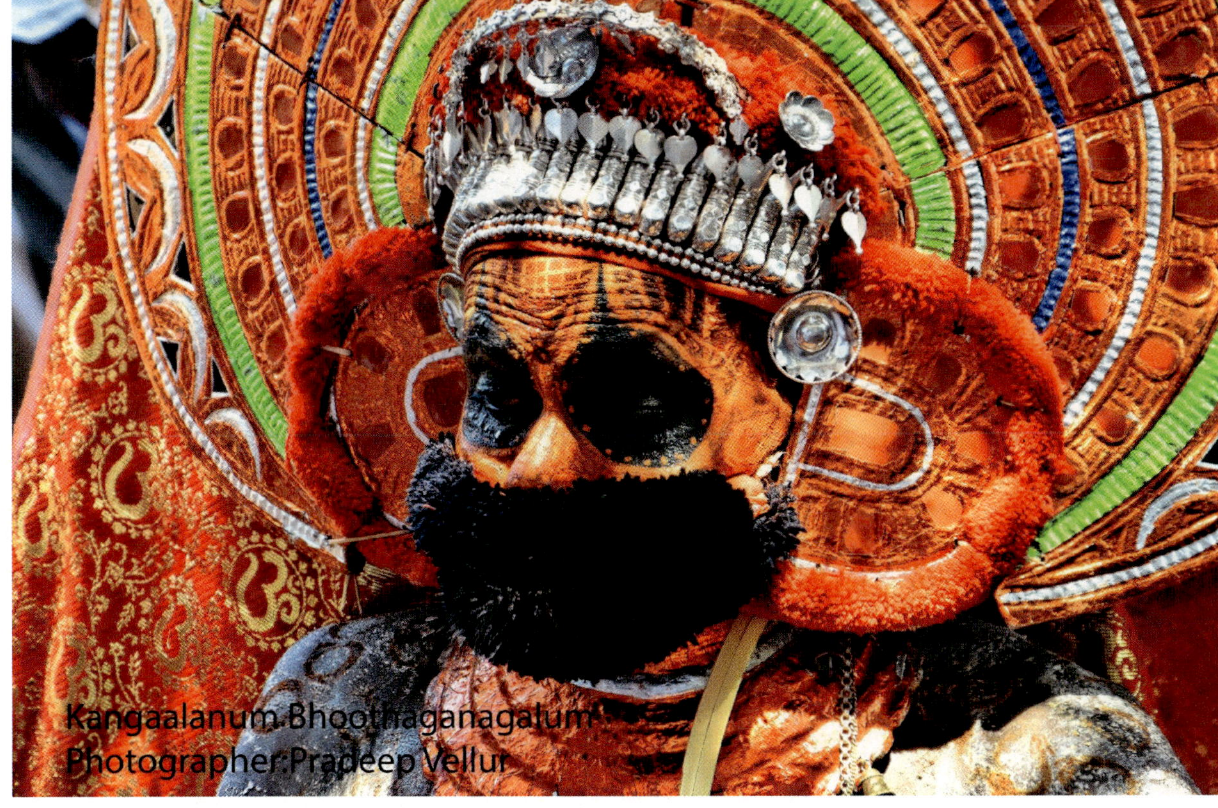

Kangaalanum Bhoothaganagalum
Photographer:Pradeep Vellur

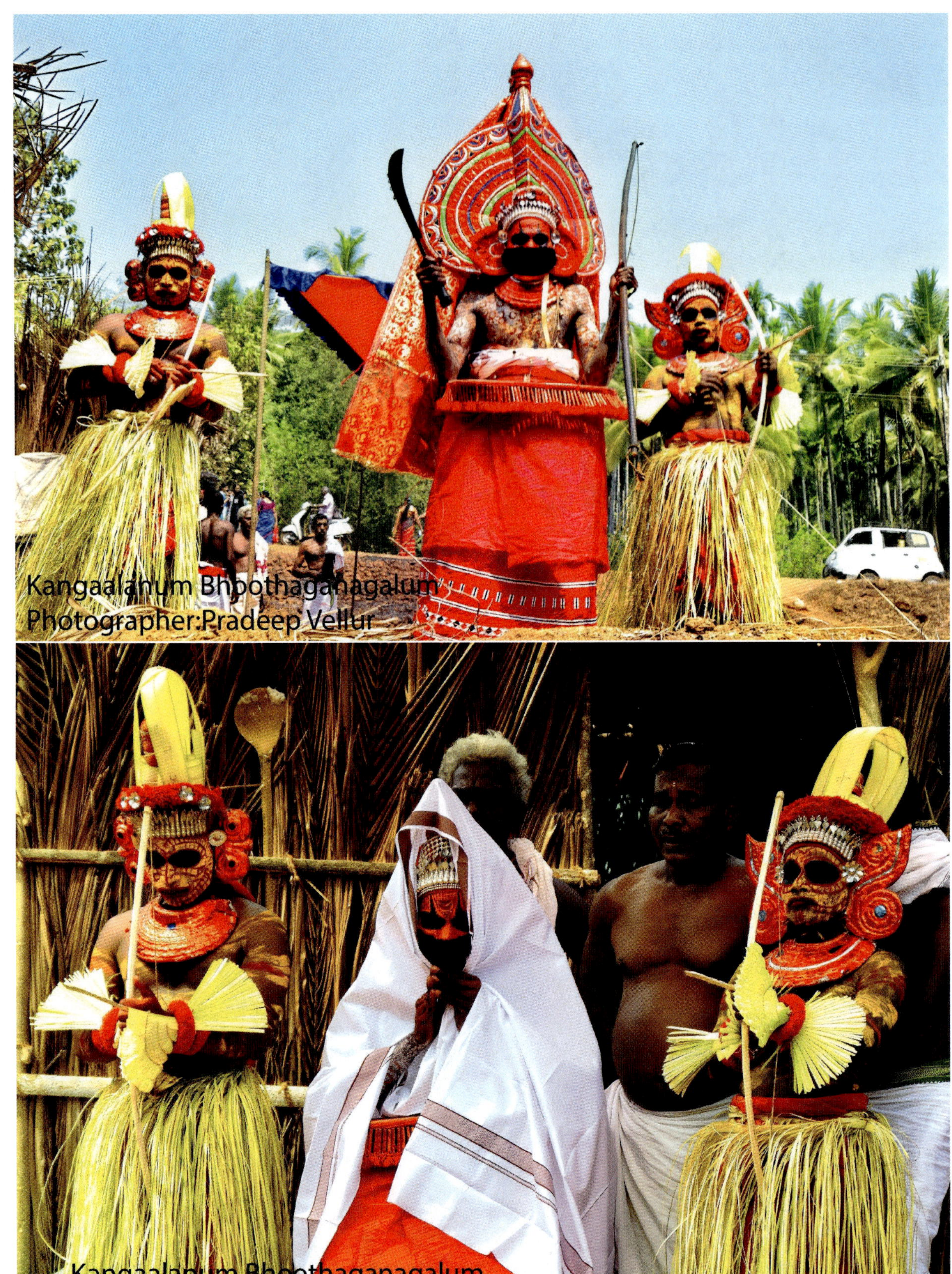
Kangaalanum Bhoothaganagalum
Photographer:Pradeep Vellur

Kangaalanum Bhoothaganagalum
Photographer:Pradeep Vellur

Chorakkattiyamma Theyyam

Chorakkattiyamma was the youngest of seven Goddesses and was dearly loved by her parents. So much so that her elder sisters envied her. Once, while traveling, she was thirsty, and her sisters pointed her to an abandoned well along the way. Unaware of her sister's plot, the innocent girl scooped water from the well with an areca sheath (a kind of palm) and drank it. Only then did the sisters reveal that the well belonged to a lower caste community. They also accused her of being tainted by her deed and told her to stay away from them. Saddened by this incident, Chorakkattiyamma left her sisters and met a Nampoothiri (higher caste person) of *Palorath Illam* (A prominent Namboothiri family) on the way, transforming herself into his white palm umbrella. Following this, the *Palorath Illam* witnessed several harmful incidents. Chorakkattiyamma believed this was an aftereffect of drinking water shared by the lower caste. The sorrowful and infuriated Chorakkattiyamma declared her intention to leave her caste and join the lower caste forever.

Legend says that she turned into the ferocious Moorthy of the *Vellakkudiyan* family (lower-caste people whose well she drank water from). Since the Goddess was incarnated through 40 days of *Agni Homam* (fire sacrifice) and *Vayu Homam* (air sacrifice), it is customary to conduct *Agni bhojanam* (eating fire symbolically) and *rudhira paanam* (drinking blood symbolically) while performing Chorakkattiyamma Theyyam. The vigorous dance looks horrific, with the hair woven by tender palm leaves and frightening *Mukhathezhuth* (facial make-up). This Goddess is worshipped as an exorcising deity. This Theyyam is one of the rarest performed and is conducted at *Keezhattur Madayi Idam Mayyil Bhagavathi Kavu*.

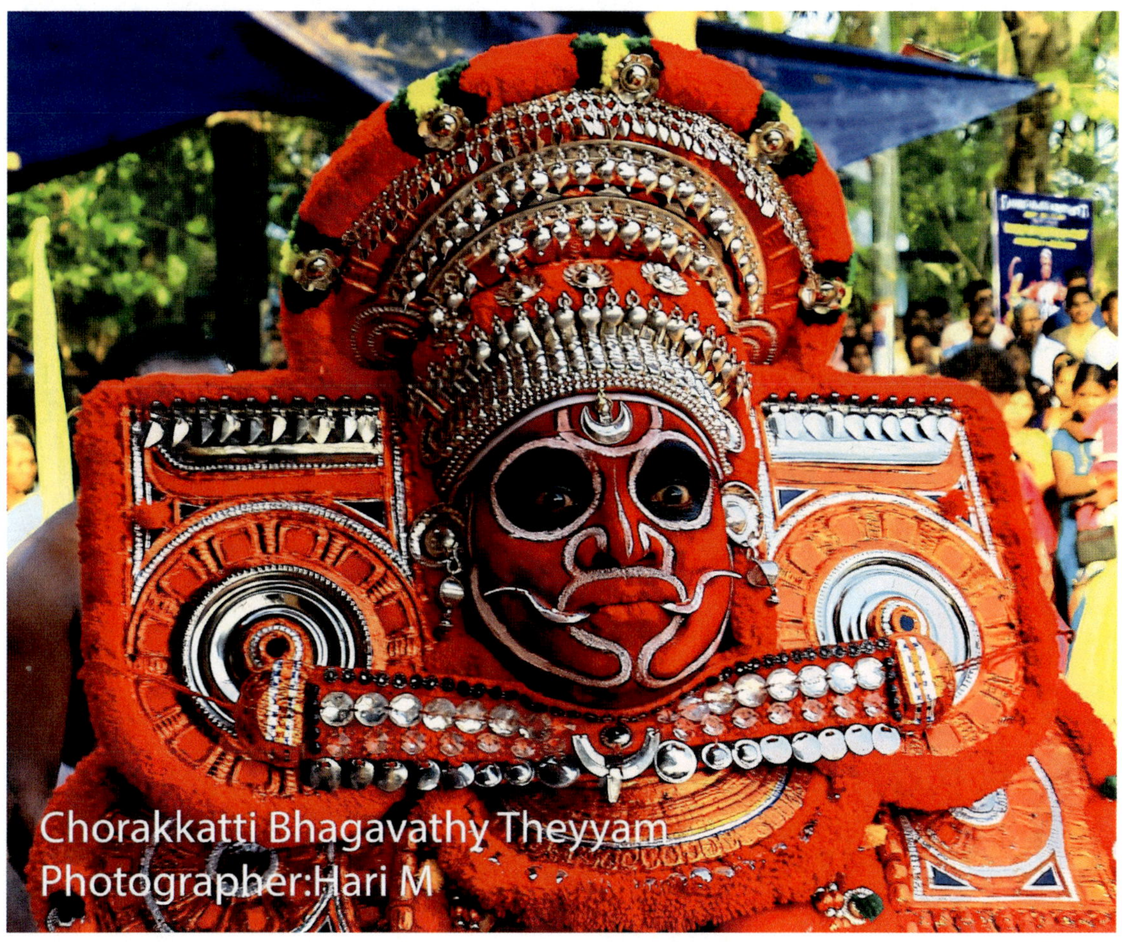

Chorakkatti Bhagavathy Theyyam
Photographer:Hari M

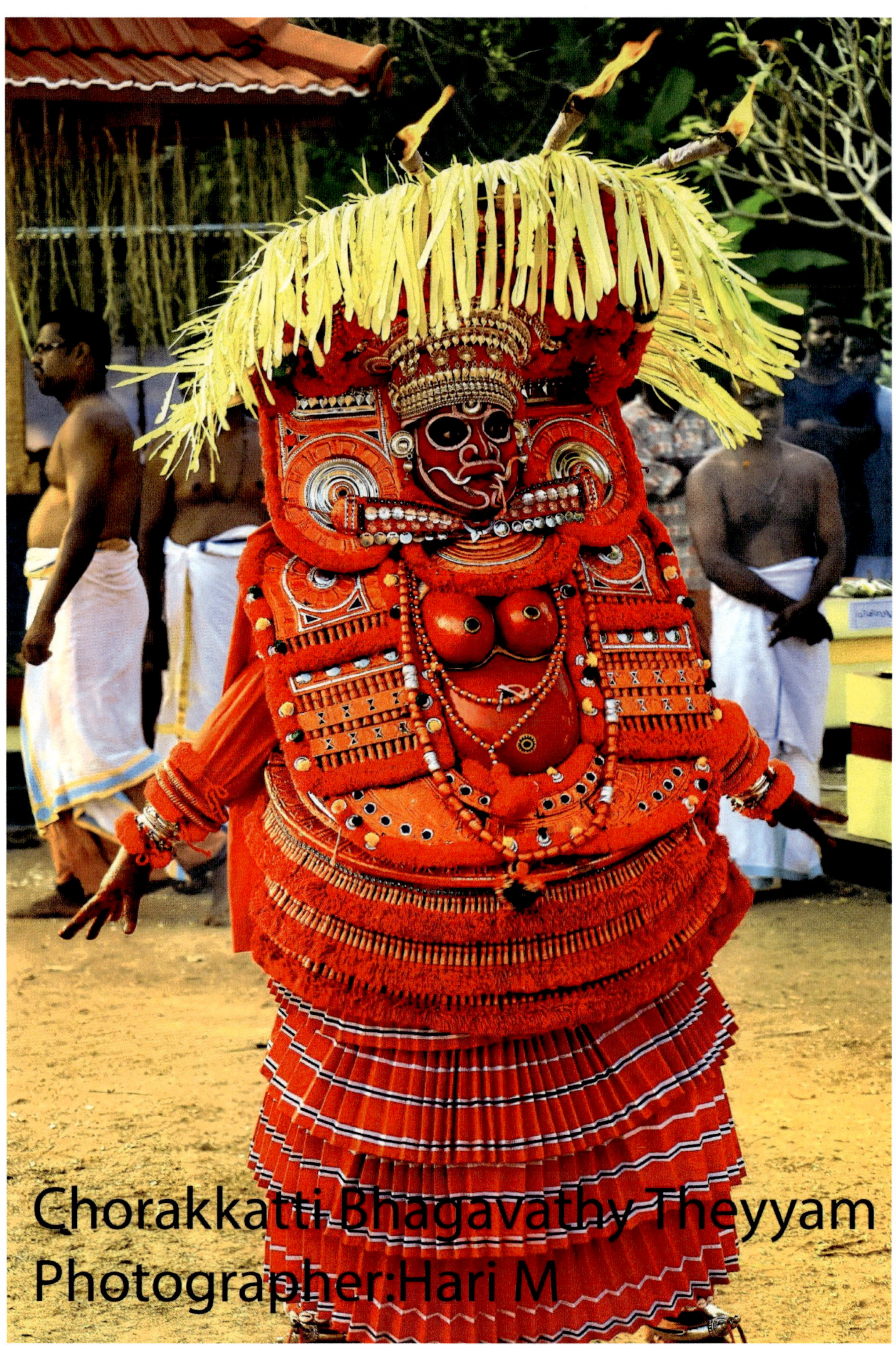

Chorakkatti Bhagavathy Theyyam
Photographer:Hari M

Mootha Bhagavathy

In ancient times, diseases were associated with Goddesses. Several such infecting and healing Goddesses can be found in Theyyam legends. These Theyyams are classified as disease-causing Goddesses and disease-healing Goddesses. Cheerumba Goddesses - Mootha Bhagavathi and Ilaya Bhagavathi (elder and younger Bhagavathis), *Dandadevan*, *Kandakarnan*, and *Vasoorimala* are considered the deities that create the diseases. *Puthiya Bhagavathi* is regarded as a Goddess who heals diseases. There are several other illness-related Goddesses, such as *Thoovakkali*, *Thoovakkaran,* and *Mari*.

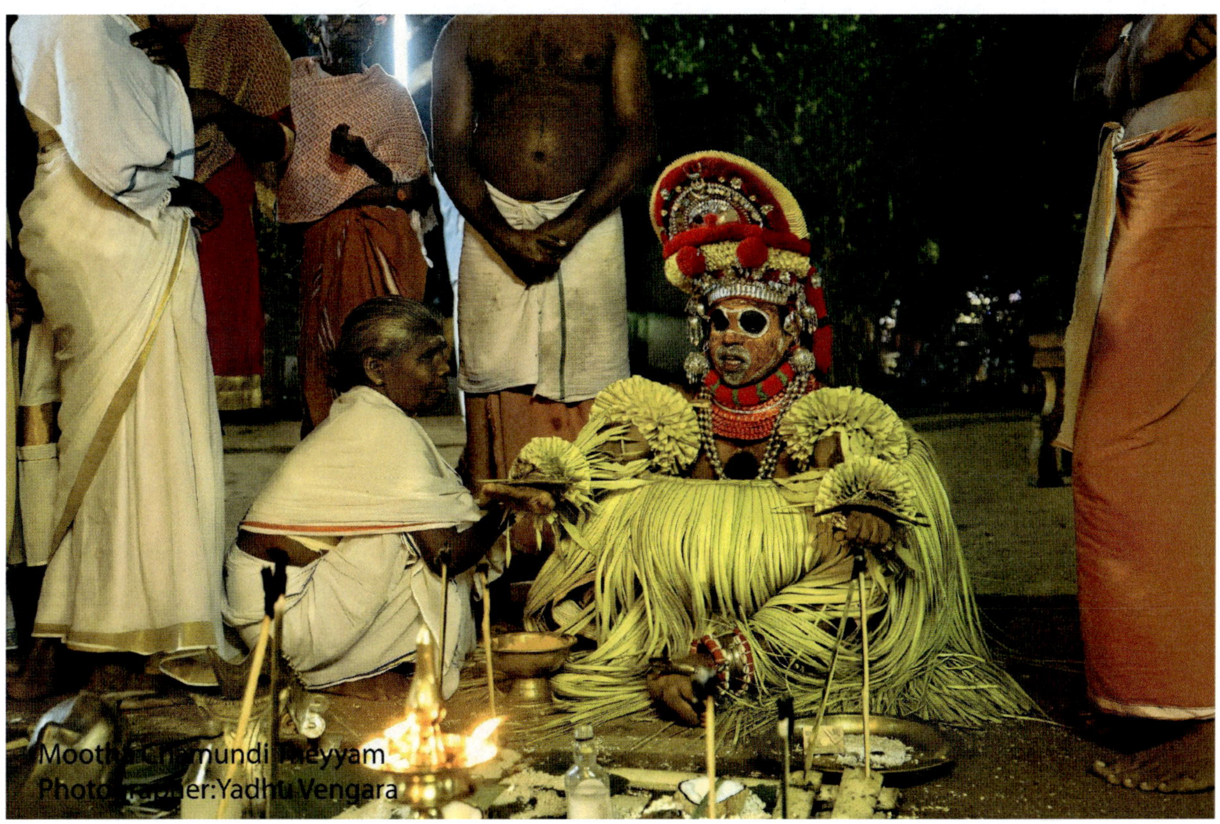

Mootha Chamundi Theyyam
Photographer:Yadhu Vengara

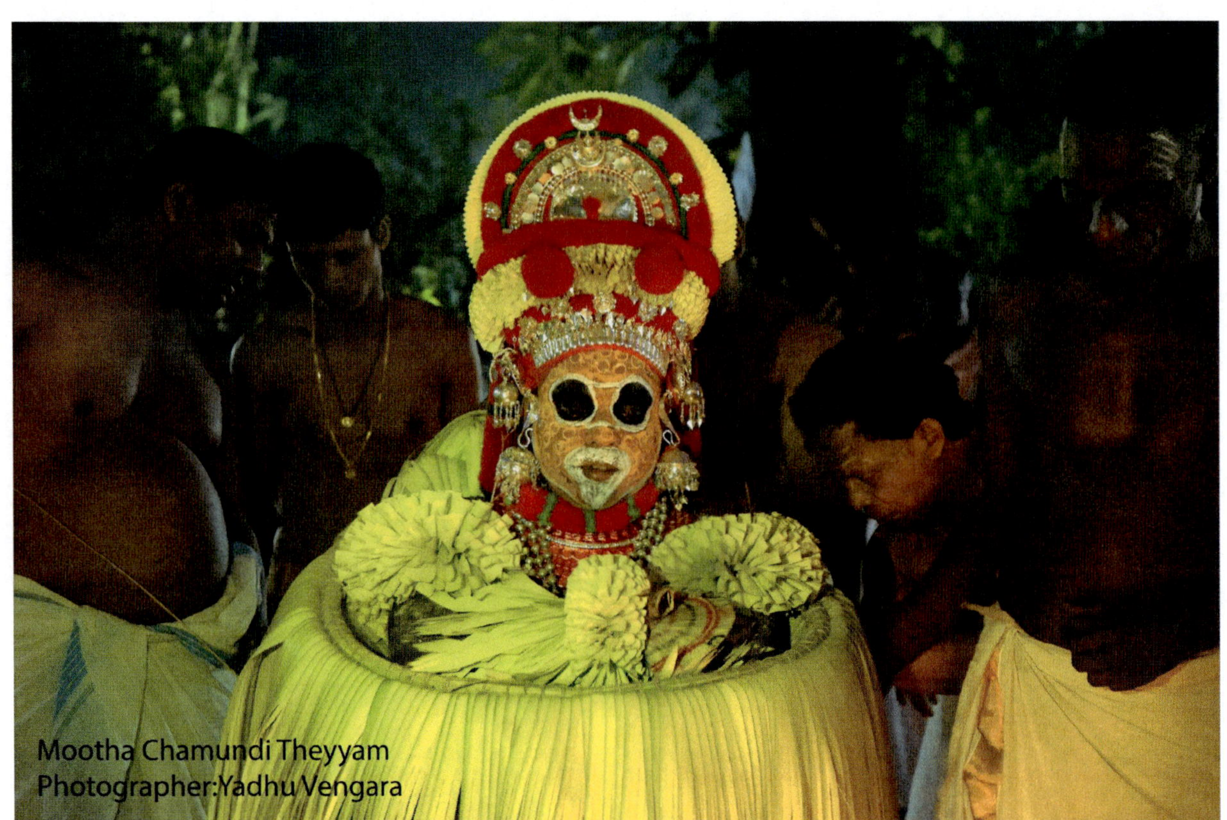

Mootha Chamundi Theyyam
Photographer:Yadhu Vengara

Manikya Bhagavathy

Manikkamma of *Chembaka Illam* was on a journey when she felt thirsty. Thankfully she soon reached a river bank on the way and stepped into the river to drink water. While drinking water, she bore the brunt of Goddess Chamundi's rage. This incident turned her into a Goddess.

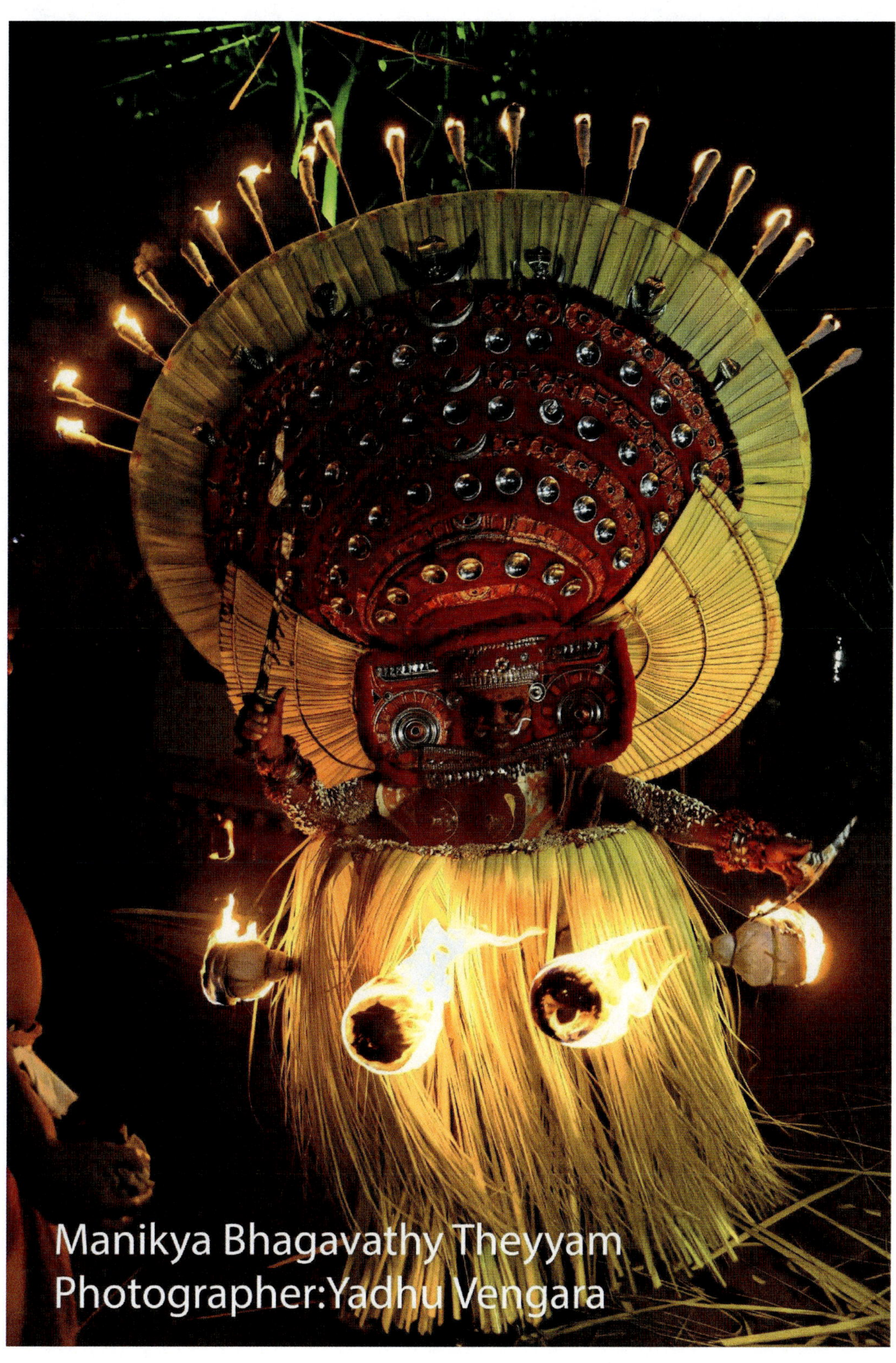

Manikya Bhagavathy Theyyam
Photographer:Yadhu Vengara

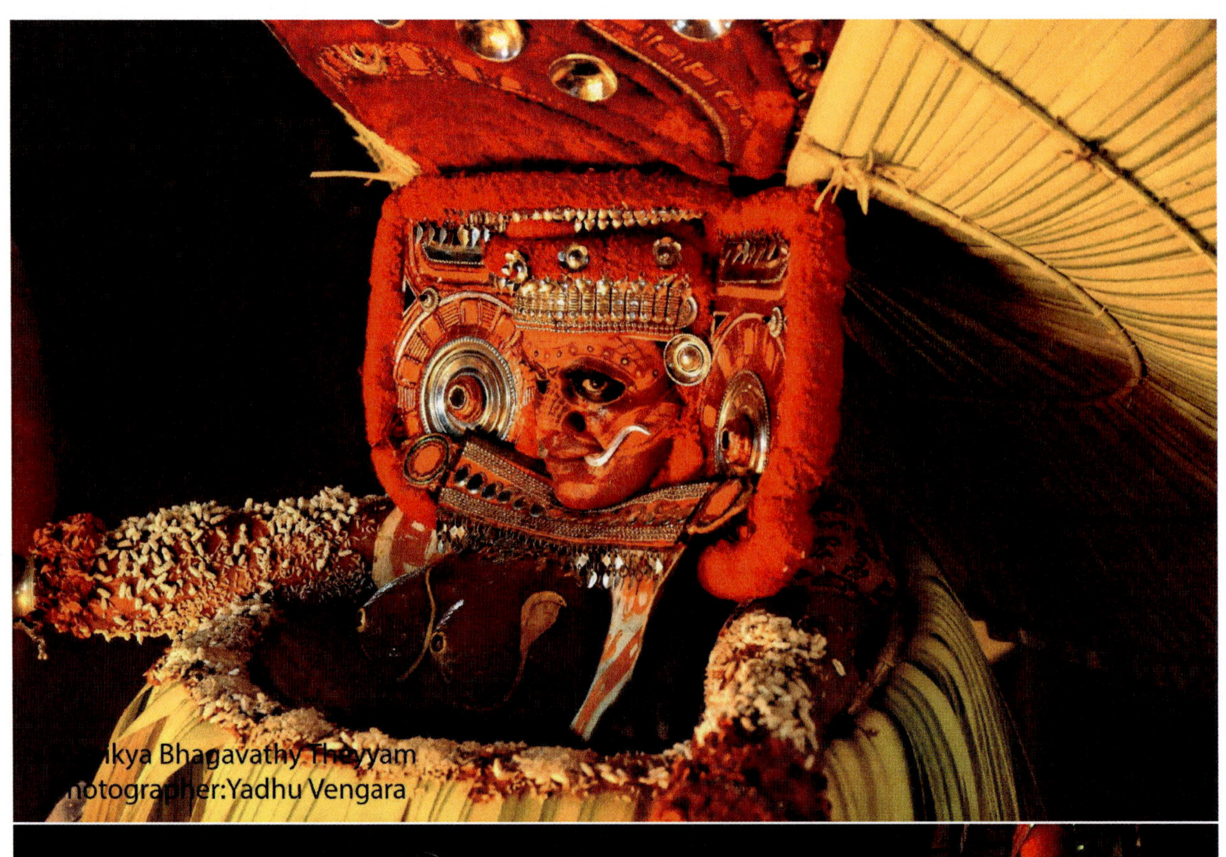

Manikya Bhagavathy Theyyam
Photographer:Yadhu Vengara

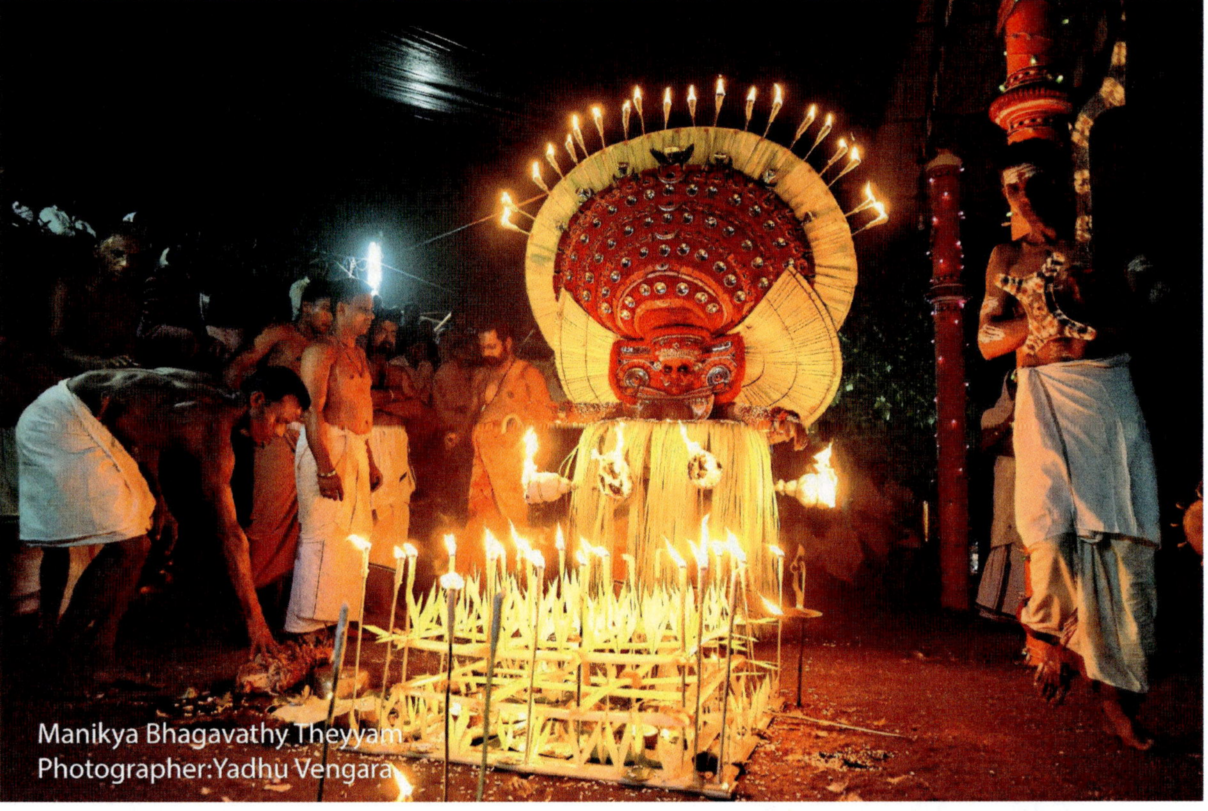

Manikya Bhagavathy Theyyam
Photographer:Yadhu Vengara

Angakkaran Theyyam

Angakkaran, an expert martial artist, won over his enemy, Kelu, in the Payyur mountains. Kelu fled the mountains and tried to hide from his enemy but failed. He was chased by Angakkaran and finally killed. This Theyyam is performed with an accompaniment representing Kelu, wearing red headwear and holding a sword. During the performance, Angakkaran Theyyam takes the sword from Kelu and pretends to kill him. This Theyyam is worshipped for specific reasons like winning legal battles, getting back lost ornaments, etc.

Angakkaran Theyyam, performed along with Andallur Theyyam, is the incarnation of Lakshmana from Ramayana. The mudi of this Theyyam is made in silver, and the face painting is in black, which emotes the anger in the Theyyam. Bappooran Theyyam, a form of Hanuman from Ramayana, is also performed with this. The Thiyya community worships Angakkaran Theyyam, and the fight between the Theyyam and its enemy is the specialty of Angakkaran, with the name itself denoting a warrior.

Chemminiyan Kavu of Kannur district of Kerala performs this Theyyam. Another Theyyam called *Palottu Dhaivam* is performed for similar purposes as Angakkaran Theyyam, with slight differences in the *Mukhathezhuth* (facial make-up).

Another Theyyam known by the same name is *Karivanchal Dhaivathar* of Cheraman Kettil. This is also in the memory of a warrior but is performed by the Vannan community.

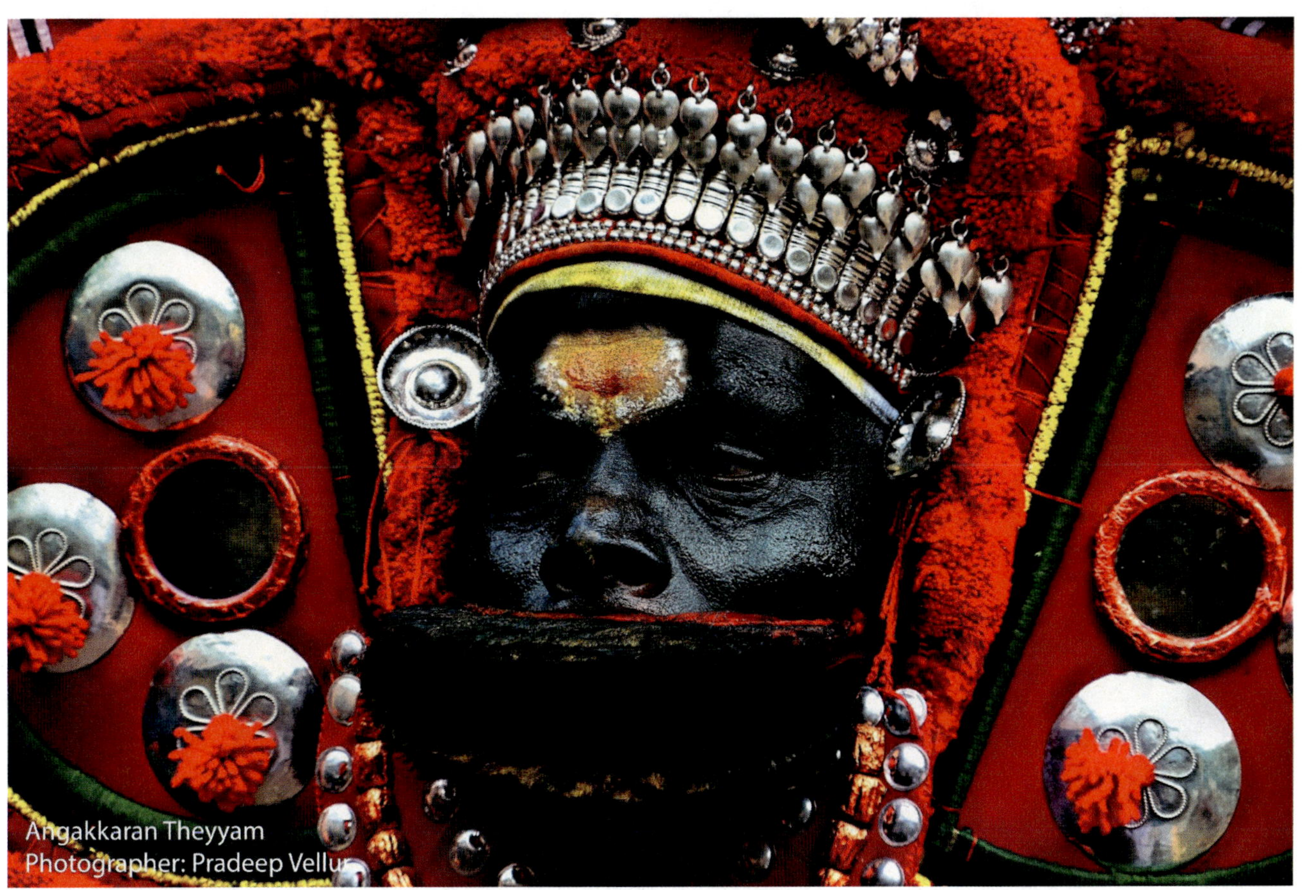

Angakkaran Theyyam
Photographer: Pradeep Vellur

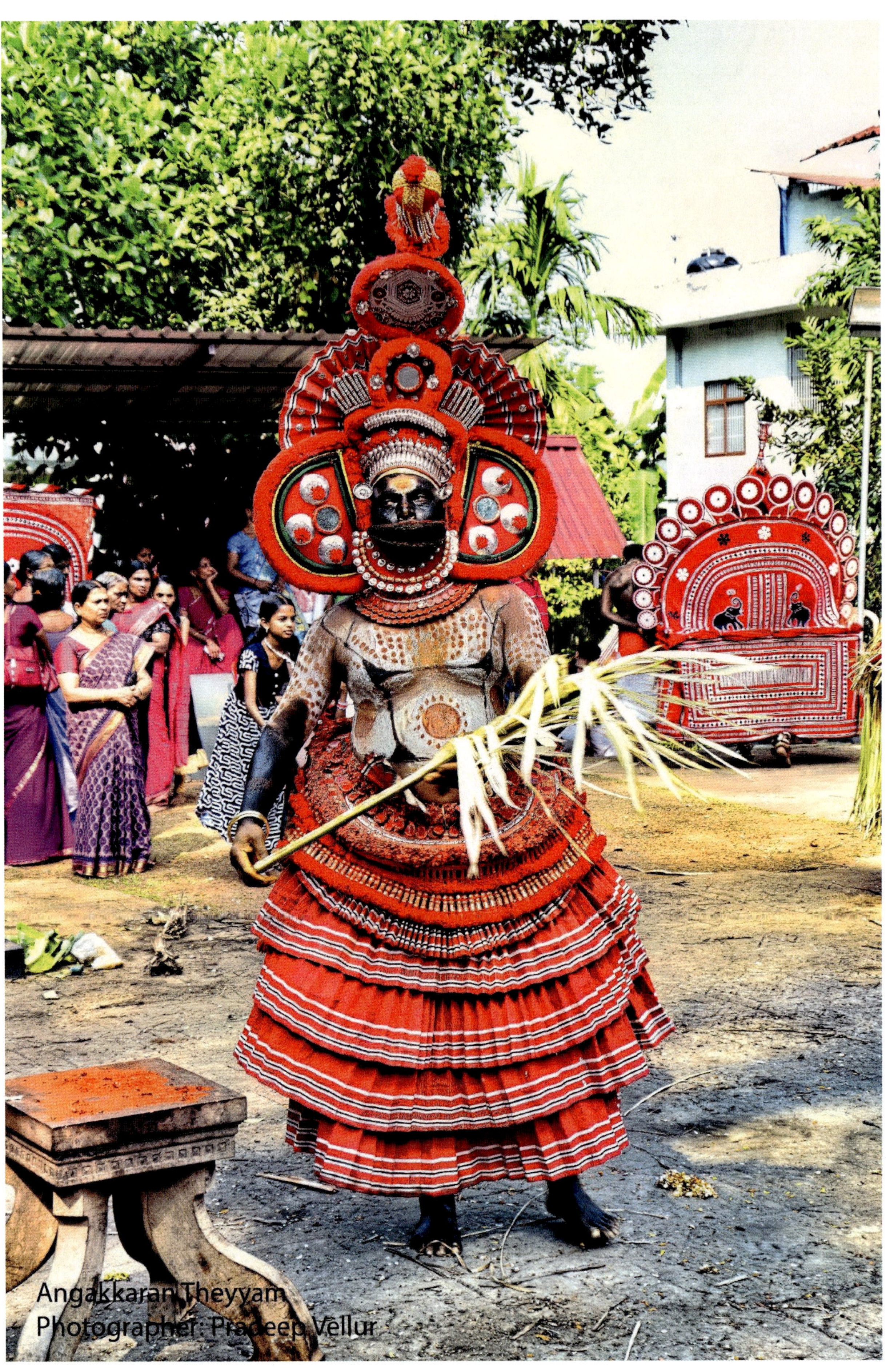

Angakkaran Theyyam
Photographer: Pradeep Vellur

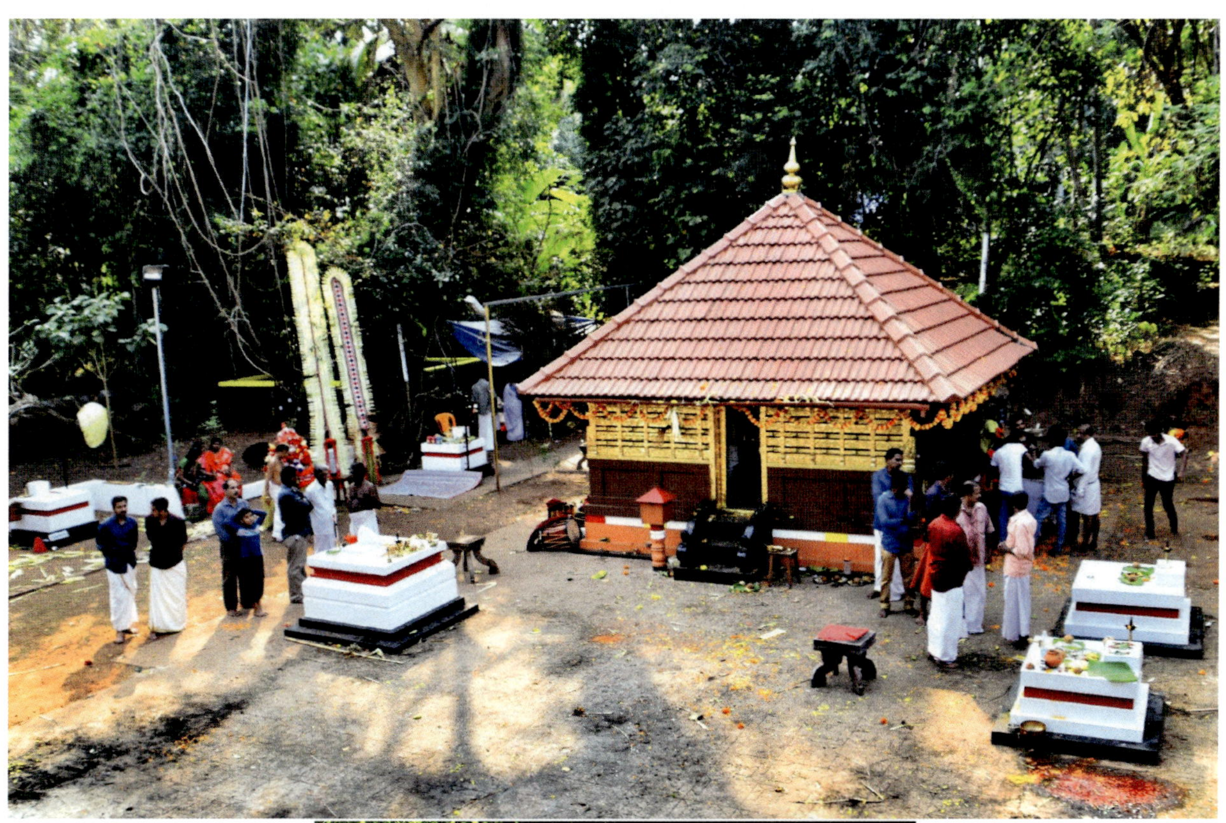

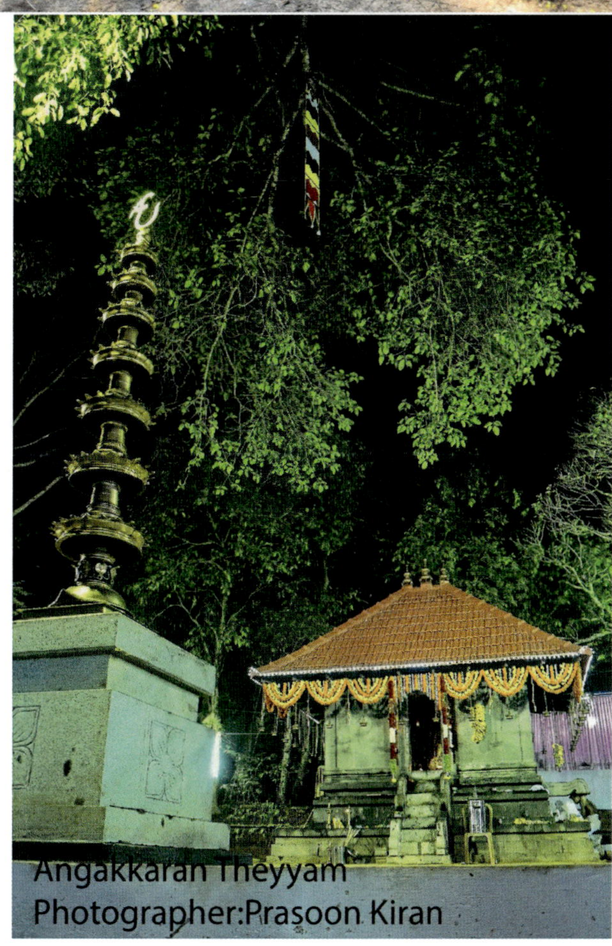

Angakkaran Theyyam
Photographer:Prasoon Kiran

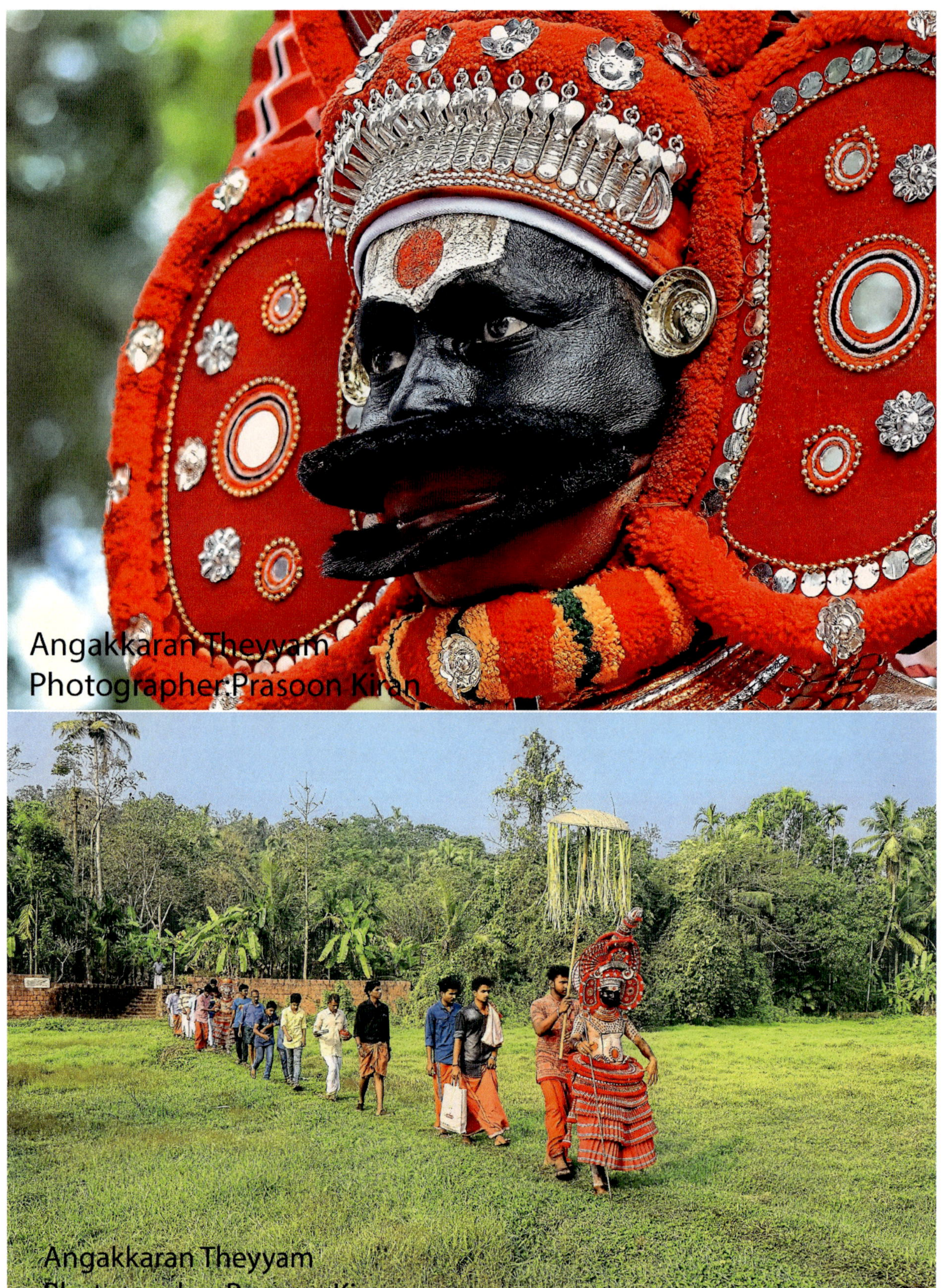

Angakkaran Theyyam
Photographer:Prasoon Kiran

Angakkaran Theyyam
Photographer:Prasoon Kiran

Kattuchirakkal Bhagavathy

Kattuchirakkal Bhagavathy is the clan deity of Chenicheri tharavadu (a prominent family) that belongs to the Nambiar community of Ezhom near Pazhayangadi, Kannur. When Nambiars of Chenicheri migrated to Ezhom from the Tulu forests, their clan deity Kattuchirakkal Bhagavathy is believed to have accompanied them. Kattuchirakkal Bhagavathy shares many characteristics of Puthiya Bhagavathy, but unlike the slow and poised pace of the Puthiya Bhagavathi Theyyam, Kattuchirakkal Bhagavathy is characterized by a fast-paced dance form.

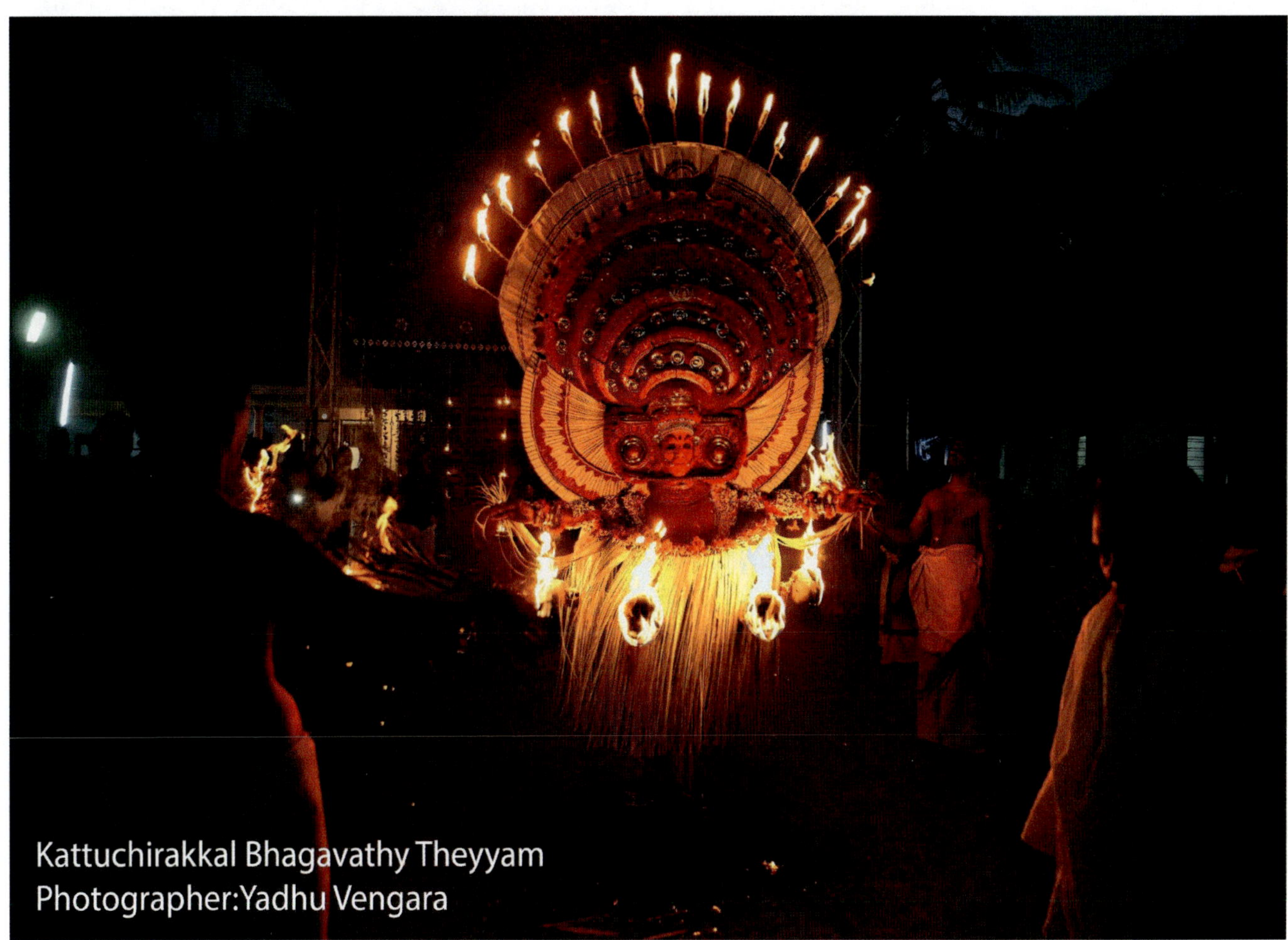

Kattuchirakkal Bhagavathy Theyyam
Photographer:Yadhu Vengara

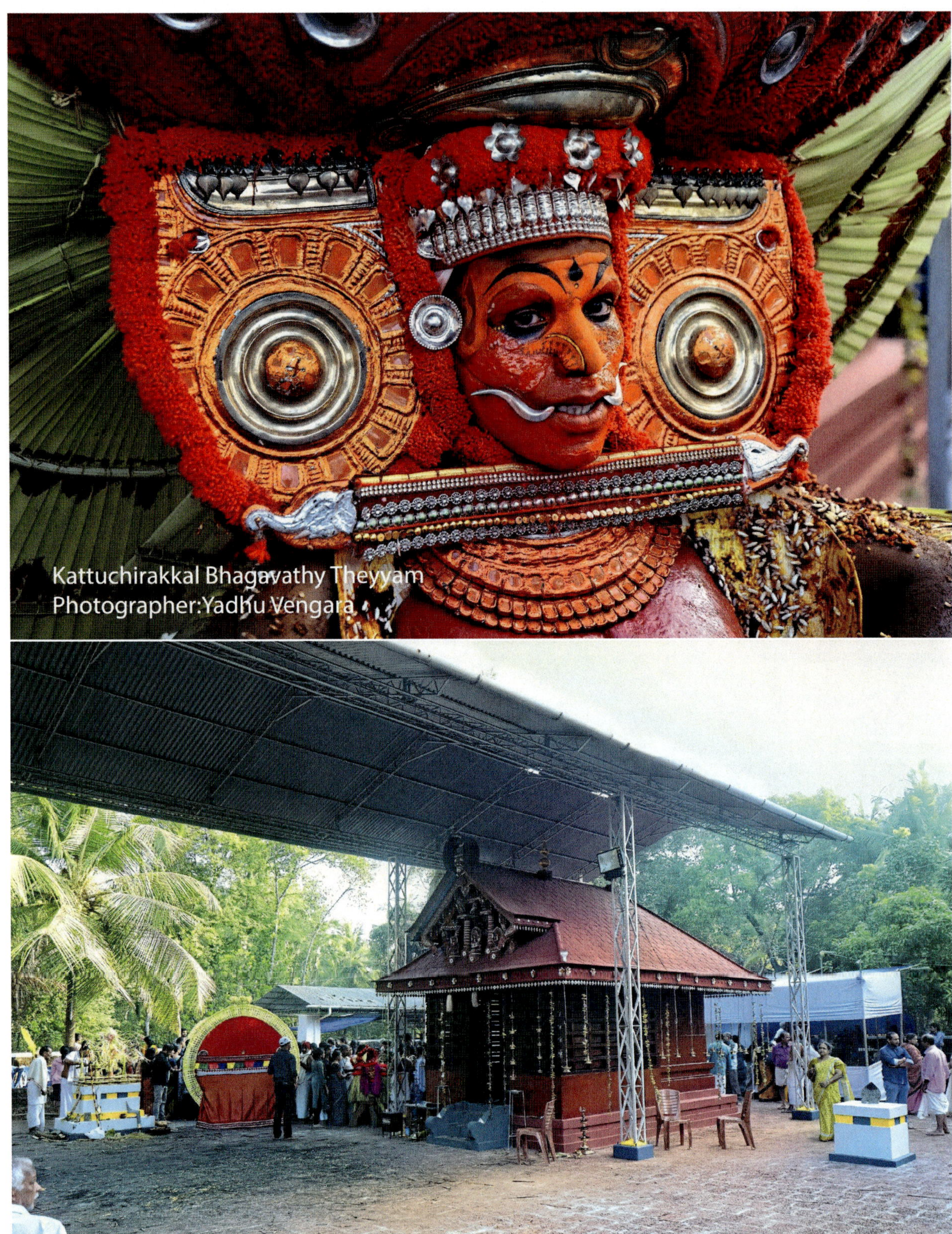

Kattuchirakkal Bhagavathy Theyyam
Photographer:Yadhu Vengara

Kuvalamthattil Bhagavathy Theyyam

Kuvalamthattil Bhagavathy is the incarnation of Goddess Mahakali, who killed the *Asura* (Demon) called Darikan. This Theyyam is also known as Pullanthattu Bhagavathy and Koolanthattu Bhagavathy.

The Goddess was on the way to Ashtamachal Bhagavathi Temple from Madayikkavu. On the way, she met Koothoor Maniyani (Maniyani is a caste name of the Yadava sub-caste, traditionally engaged in cattle-rearing), who was grazing cattle. He presented the Bhagavathy with milk in a piece of bamboo to quench her thirst. The Goddess was delighted and decided to stay at Maniyani's *Kannikottil* (a resilient room where the valuables are stored). This incident happened in Karalikara, where she occupied eleven sacred locations.

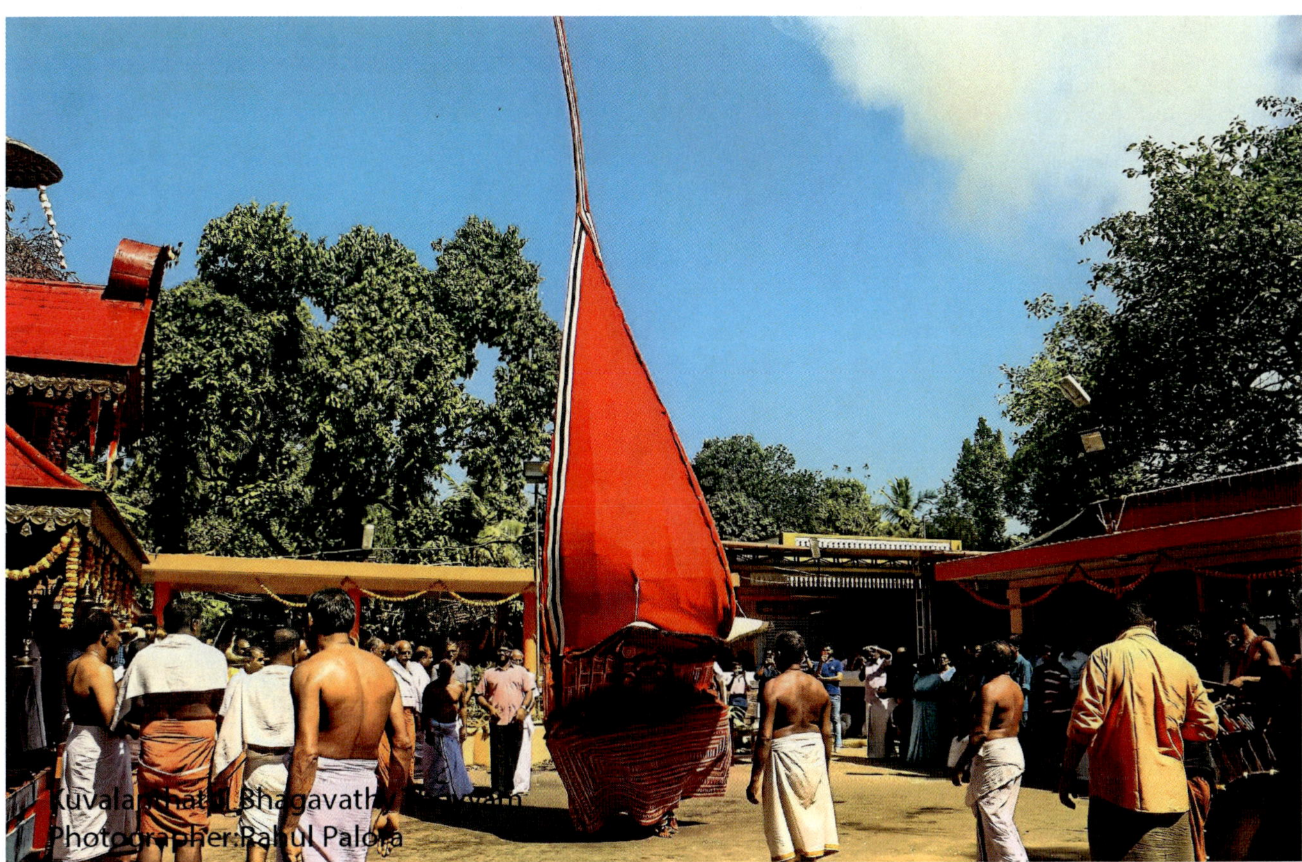

Kuvalamthattil Bhagavathy Theyyam
Photographer:Rahul Palora

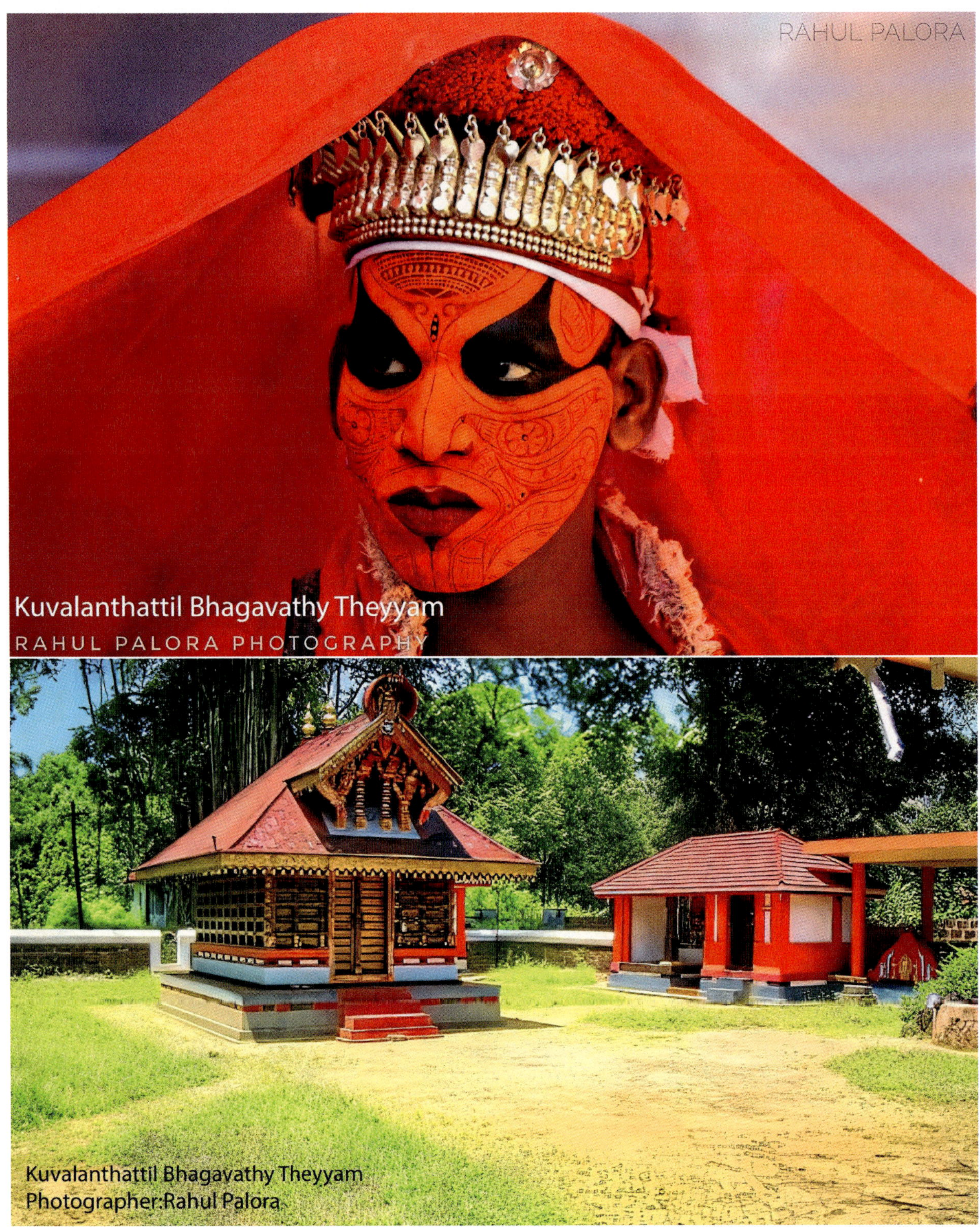
RAHUL PALORA
Kuvalanthattil Bhagavathy Theyyam
RAHUL PALORA PHOTOGRAPHY
Kuvalanthattil Bhagavathy Theyyam
Photographer:Rahul Palora

Panjuruli Theyyam

Panjuruli is a Theyyam based on the concept of *Varahi* or the boar. This represents the deity that gave darshan (to appear in front) to Ammina *Mavilan* on his way to hunt in the Kudaku mountains.

When the Goddess incarnated to defeat Sumbha Nisumbha *Asuras*, seven deities emerged from Maheswara's Homa Kunda (the fire altar) to assist her. Panjuruli, in the form of a boar, is one of these deities. The word "Panji " in Tulu means a boar or pig, and the word "*Panjiyurukaali* " evolved into Panjuruli later.

There is another myth where Kaali takes the form of a boar to kill the *Pancha Veeranmaar* (the five warriors) to sustain peace and prosperity on earth, hence the name *Panchuruli or Panjuruli*. Another popular legend says that the Goddess got a position in *Pattuvam Kadavu*, as promised by Devi Kuloor from Tulu land, to kill the *Asura* using her sacred spear and came to be known as Panjuruli.

This Moorthy is the embodiment of calmness and rage simultaneously. She starts dancing calmly and eventually steps into aggressive form. At her peak of expression, *Moorthy* runs towards her devotees, shouts at them, and beats them with her long hair. Towards the end, this Theyyam remains seated peacefully and blesses the devotees.

Malayan, Velan, Mavilan, Koppalan, and Pampathar are the different castes of people who perform this Theyyam. There are animal sacrifices in the name of this Goddess in some temples. Panjuruli's face paintings and make-up are known as "*Rudhra Minukk*." During the performance, Chamundi Theyyam forms such as *Madayil Chamundi, Kundora Chamundi, Karimanal Chamundi*, and *Chamundi* (*Vishnu Moorthi*) wear masks resembling the face of a pig. Manippana Theyyam is another Theyyam based on the concept of a boar.

Baali, Puli dhaivangal, and *Vishnu Moorthi* have a make-up known as *Thandaval*. This is a concept known as "the beast with a tail." Their movements are animalistic, while the ornaments and face paintings also reveal the respective animal embodiments. *Vishnu Moorthy* is a half lion and half human form (the embodiment of *Narasimha* or the sacred lion).

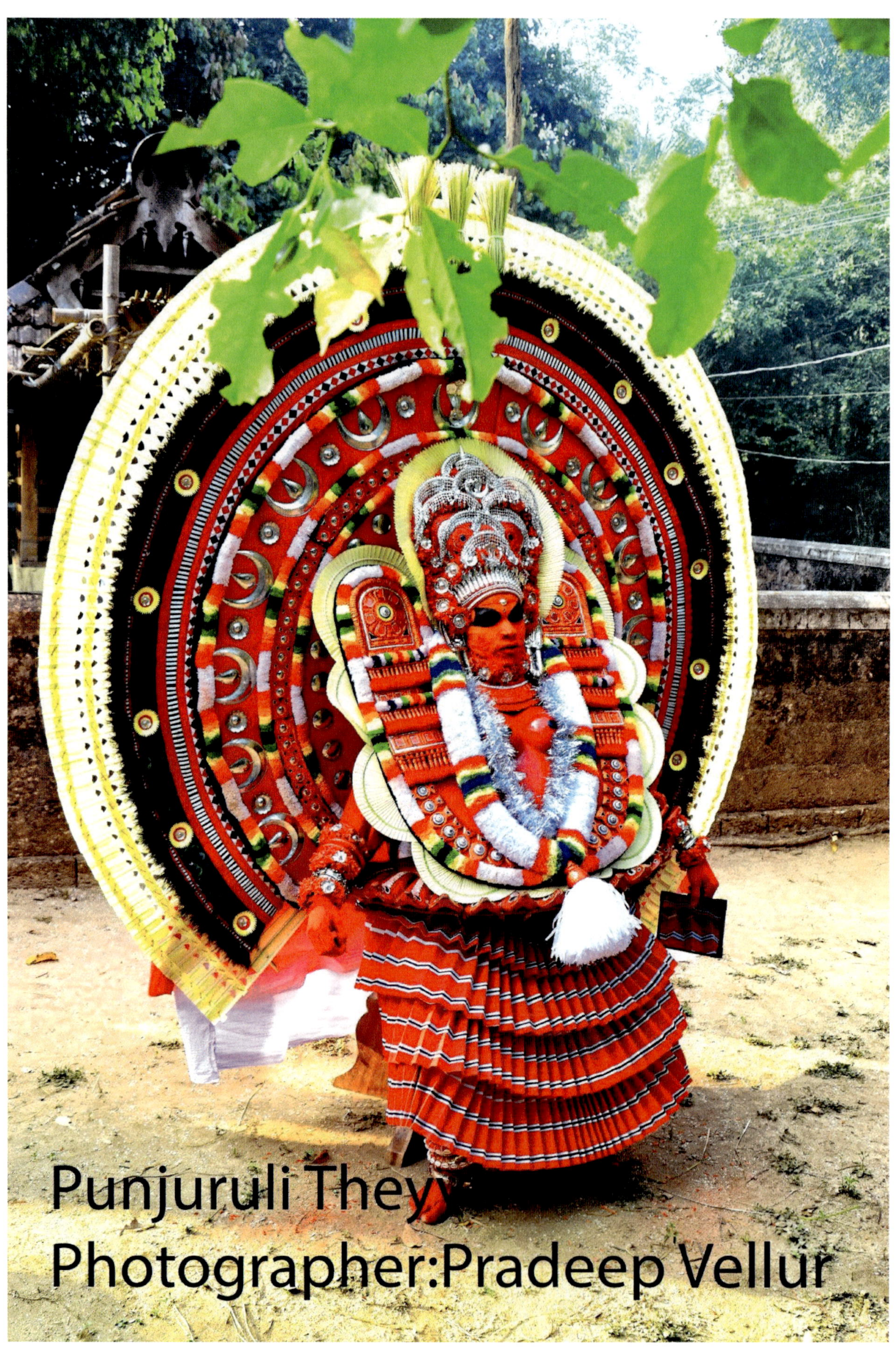

Punjuruli Theyy
Photographer:Pradeep Vellur

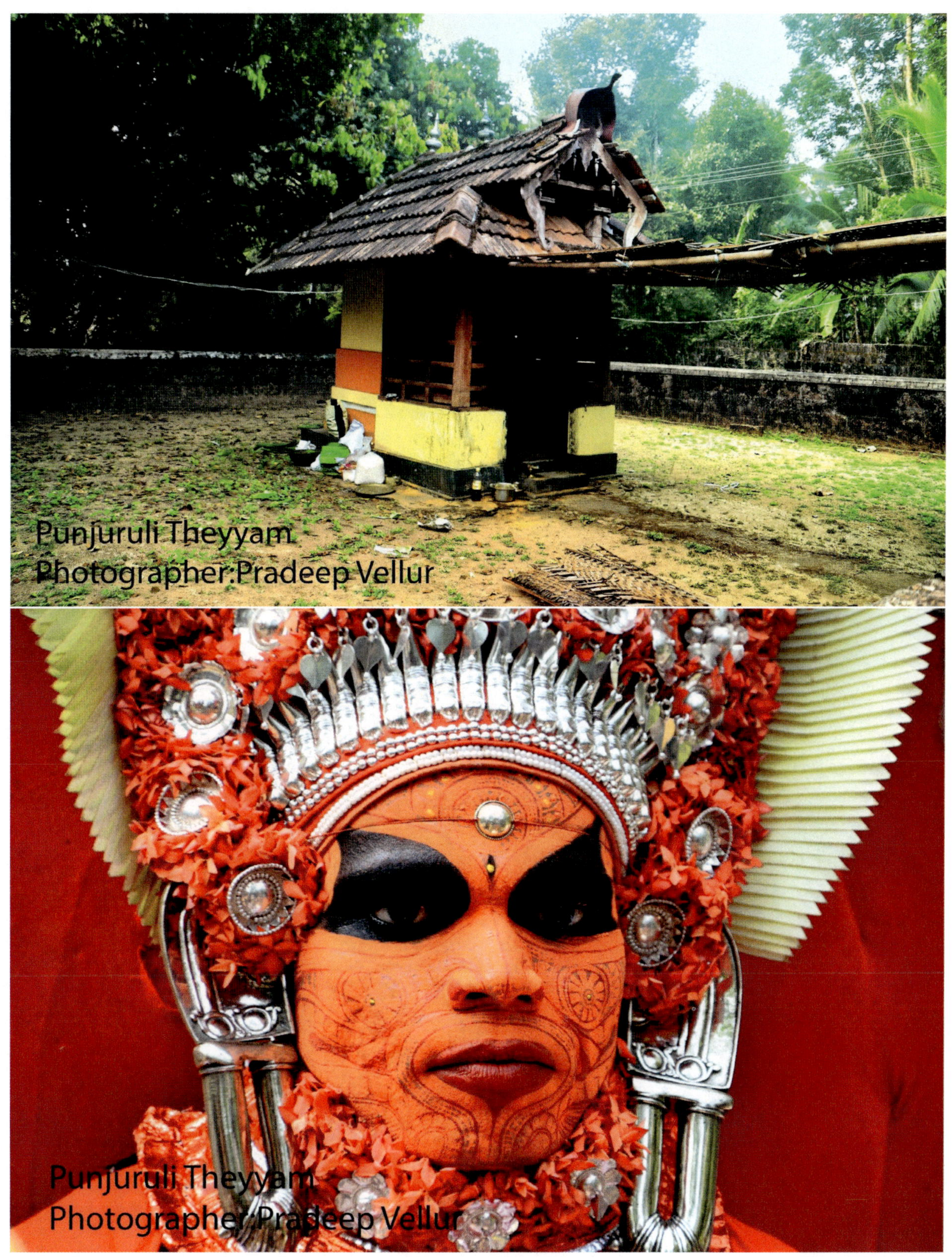
Punjuruli Theyyam
Photographer:Pradeep Vellur

Punjuruli Theyyam
Photographer:Pradeep Vellur

Pookkuttichathan

Kuttichathan Theyyam or Kuttishastan Theyyam is popular in the Northern parts of Kerala. Kuttichathan is a *Mantra Moorthi* worshipped by eighteen notable Brahmin families. Karimkutti, Pookkutti, Theekkutti, Parakkutti, and Uchakkutti are the most prominent Theyyams among the magical Theyyam Gods. Non-Brahmin families also worship Kuttichathan Theyyam.

It is said that Kuttichathan was born to Lord Shiva and Parvati Devi when they were disguised as *Valluva* and *Valluvathi* (the tribe that practices astrology and medicine). They gifted the child to the childless *Namboothiri* (Brahmin) of Kalakaattu *Illam* (Noble brahmin house) to raise as his own. From then, Kuttichathan, who reached the Kalakaattu *Illam*, rebelled against the Brahmins.

The story of Kuttichathan is that of a brilliant but defiant child who murders his teacher, attacks his mother, and eventually escapes the deathbed created by his father, only to emerge in multiple forms to take revenge on the Brahmin families of the village. He was later appeased and worshiped as a deity to escape his mischief.

The Malayans who weave the Theyyakkolams believe that Lord Vishnu was incarnated as Gridhraraja to balance the height of the Manthara Mountain. This incarnation is believed to be the Kuttichathan Theyyam.

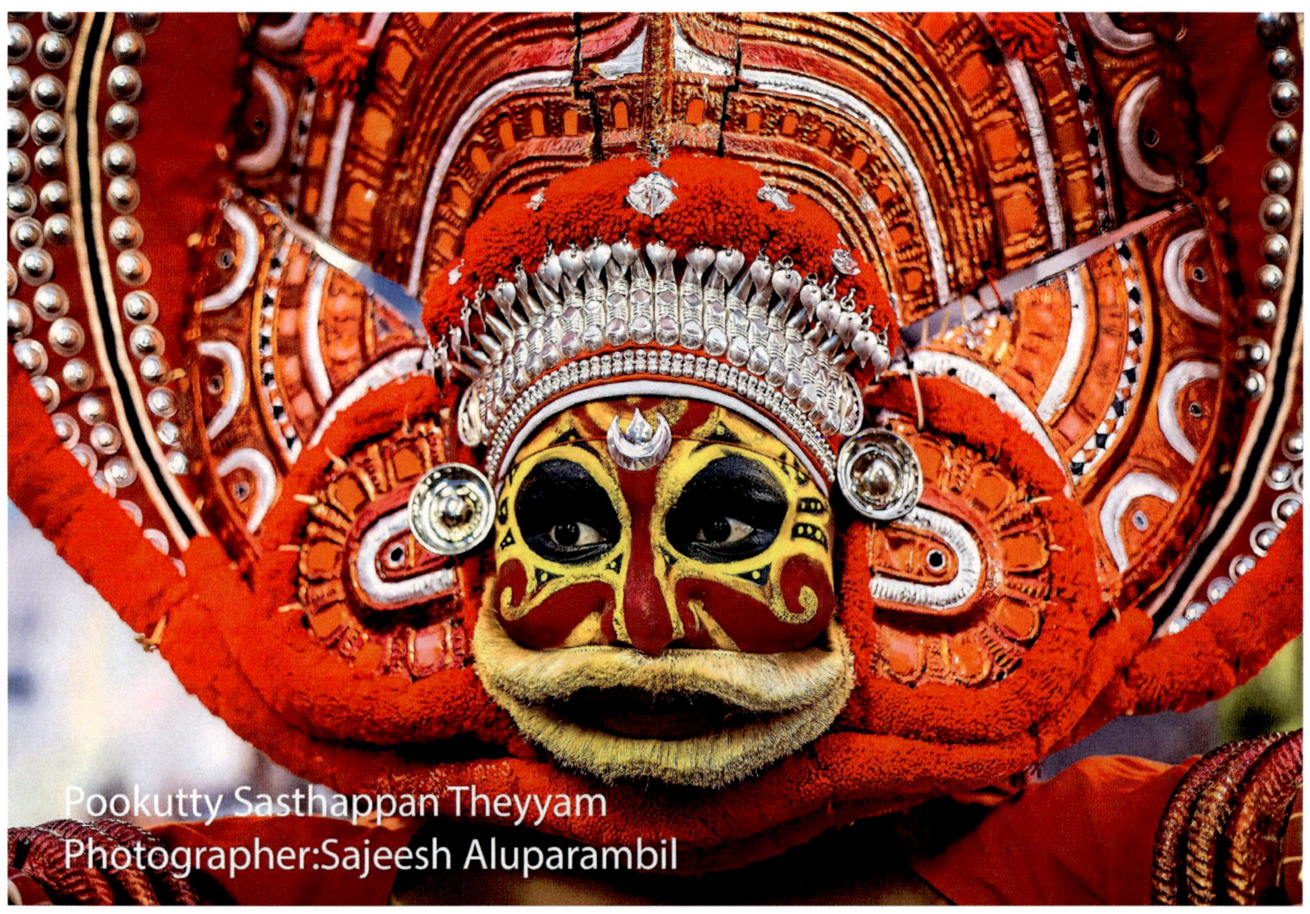
Pookutty Sasthappan Theyyam
Photographer:Sajeesh Aluparambil

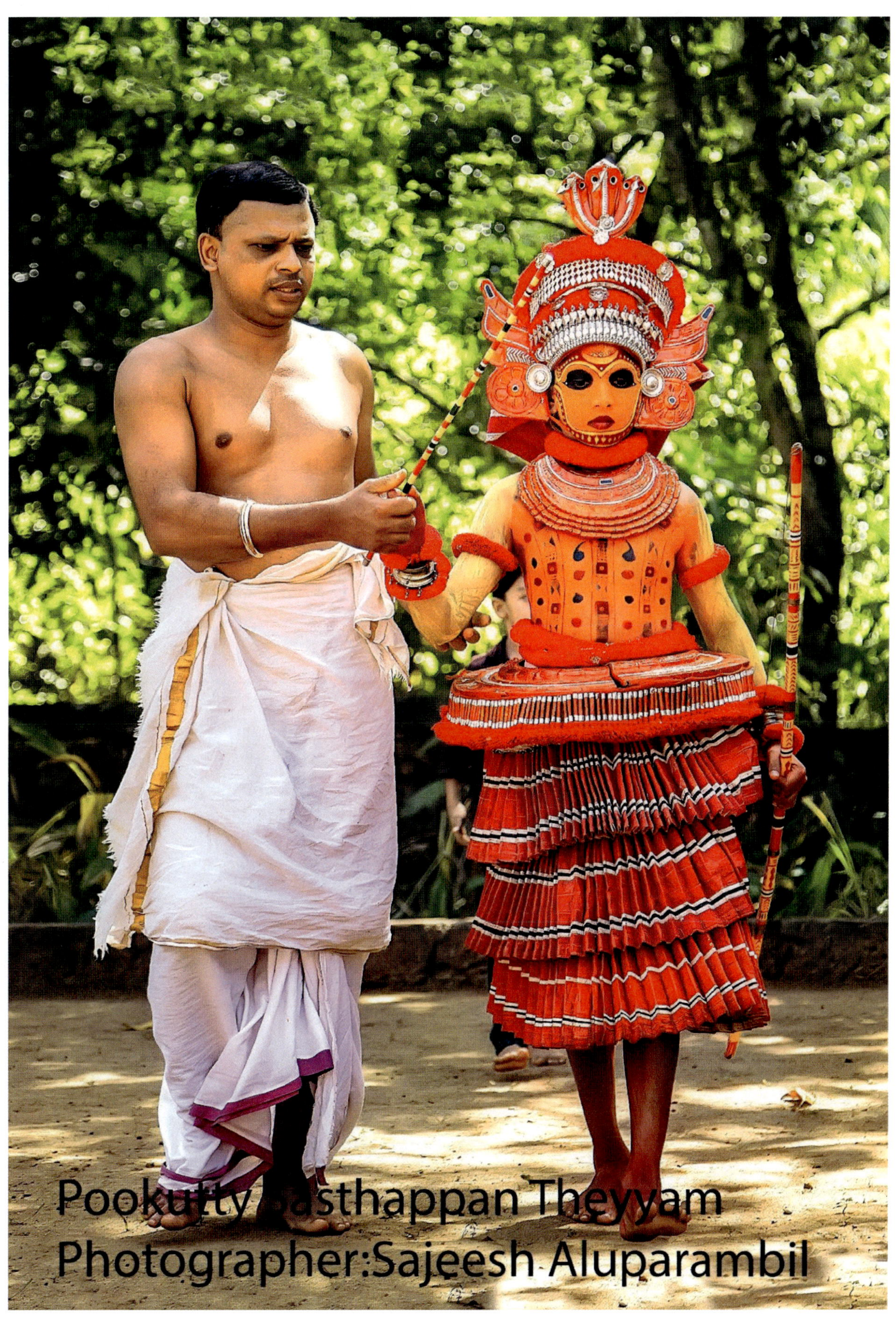

Pookutty Sasthappan Theyyam
Photographer:Sajeesh Aluparambil

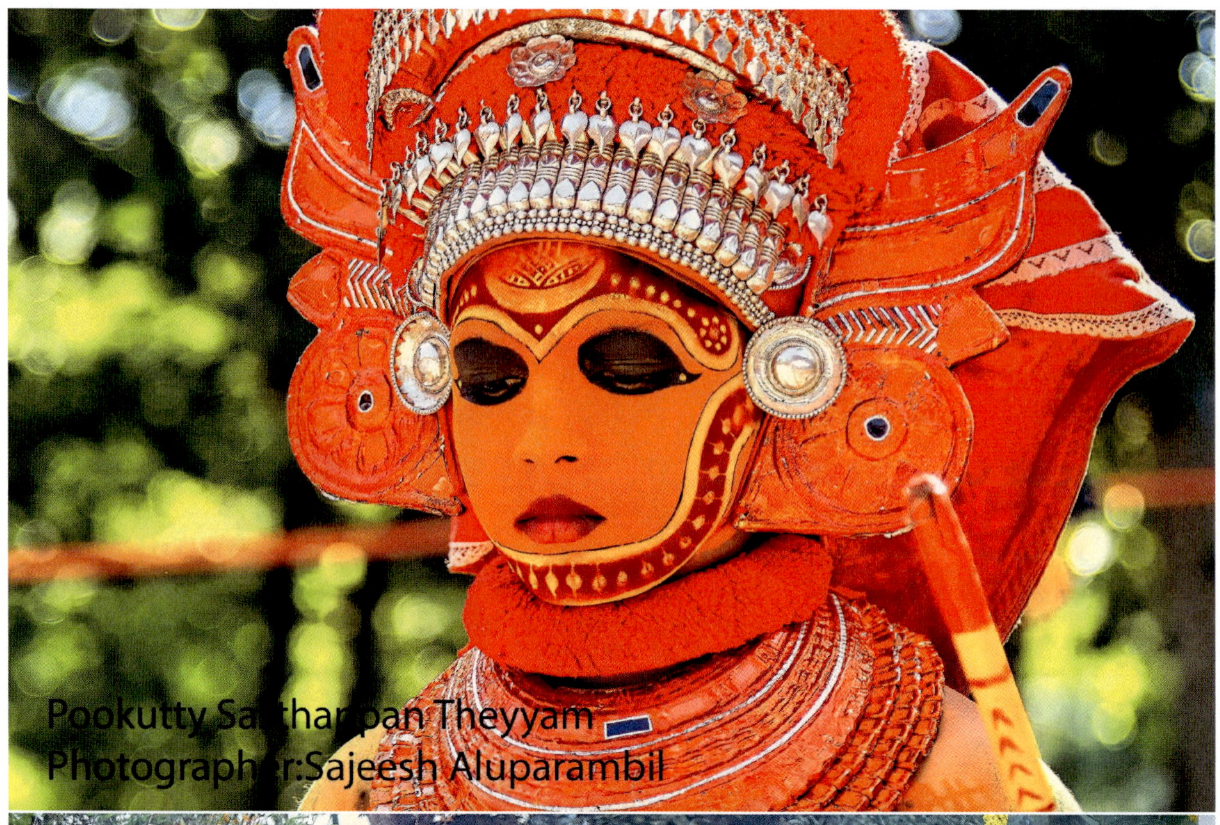

Pookutty Sasthappan Theyyam
Photographer:Sajeesh Aluparambil

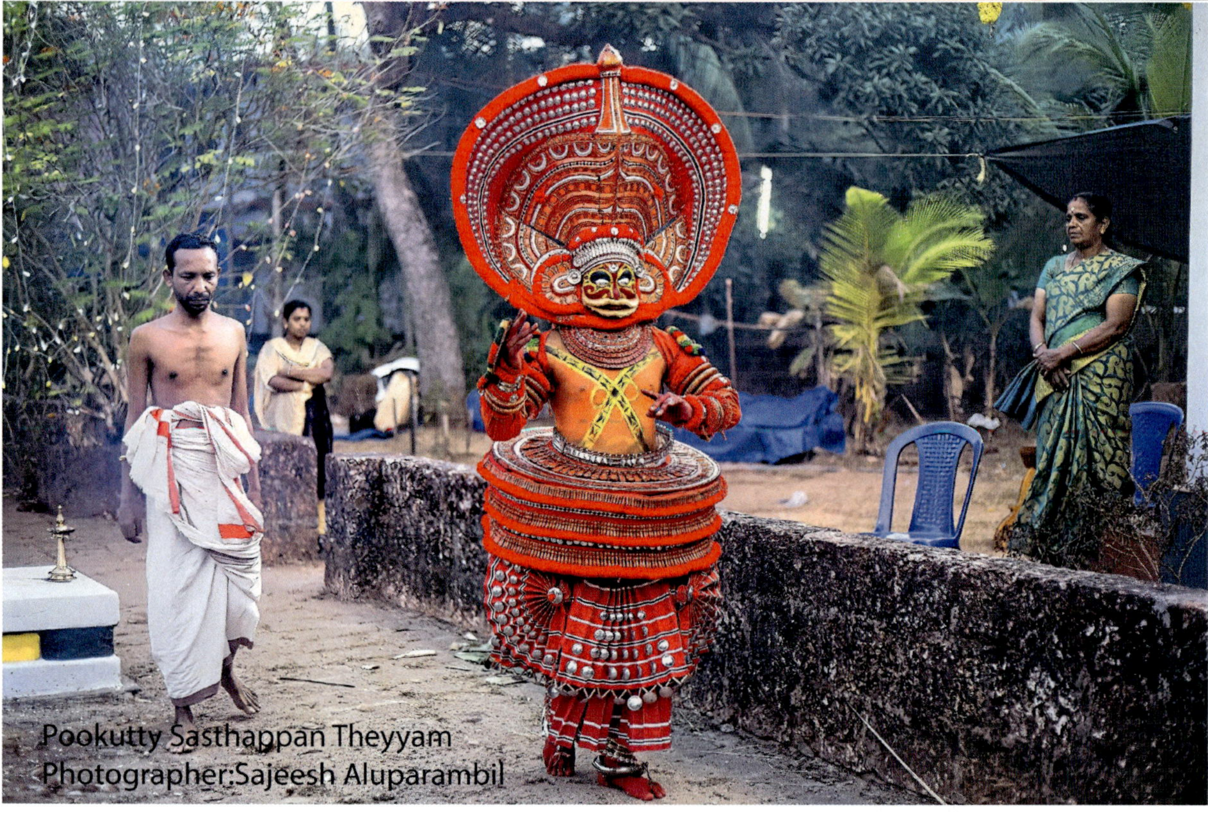

Pookutty Sasthappan Theyyam
Photographer:Sajeesh Aluparambil

Karimanal Chamundi

Karimanal Chamundi Theyyam has close resemblances with Madayil Chamundi Theyyam in the legend that they follow. Both the Theyyams depict the story of *Poduval (temple-dwelling caste in Kerala)* of *Vannad Tharavadu* (a noble family), who went hunting along with his assistant Kuruvadan Nair. Between hunting for wild goats, they disturbed Pathala Bhairavi, who killed the assistant, Kuruvadan Nair. The desperate Poduval sought the help of Goddess *Kanakkara Bhagavathi*.

The Goddess calmed down the enraged Pathala Bhairavi by assigning her an abode and installing her as Malayil Chamundi, also known as Karimanal Chamundi or *Alanthatta Madavathilkkal Bhagavathi* because she appeared from a cave in the forests in the *Alanthatta* area. This deity is also called *Pathala Moorthy* because she went to *Pathala* or the netherworld. Although the legends behind these Theyyams (Karimanal Chamundi and Malayil Chamundi) are the same, both are performed with different costumes and makeup to differentiate them.

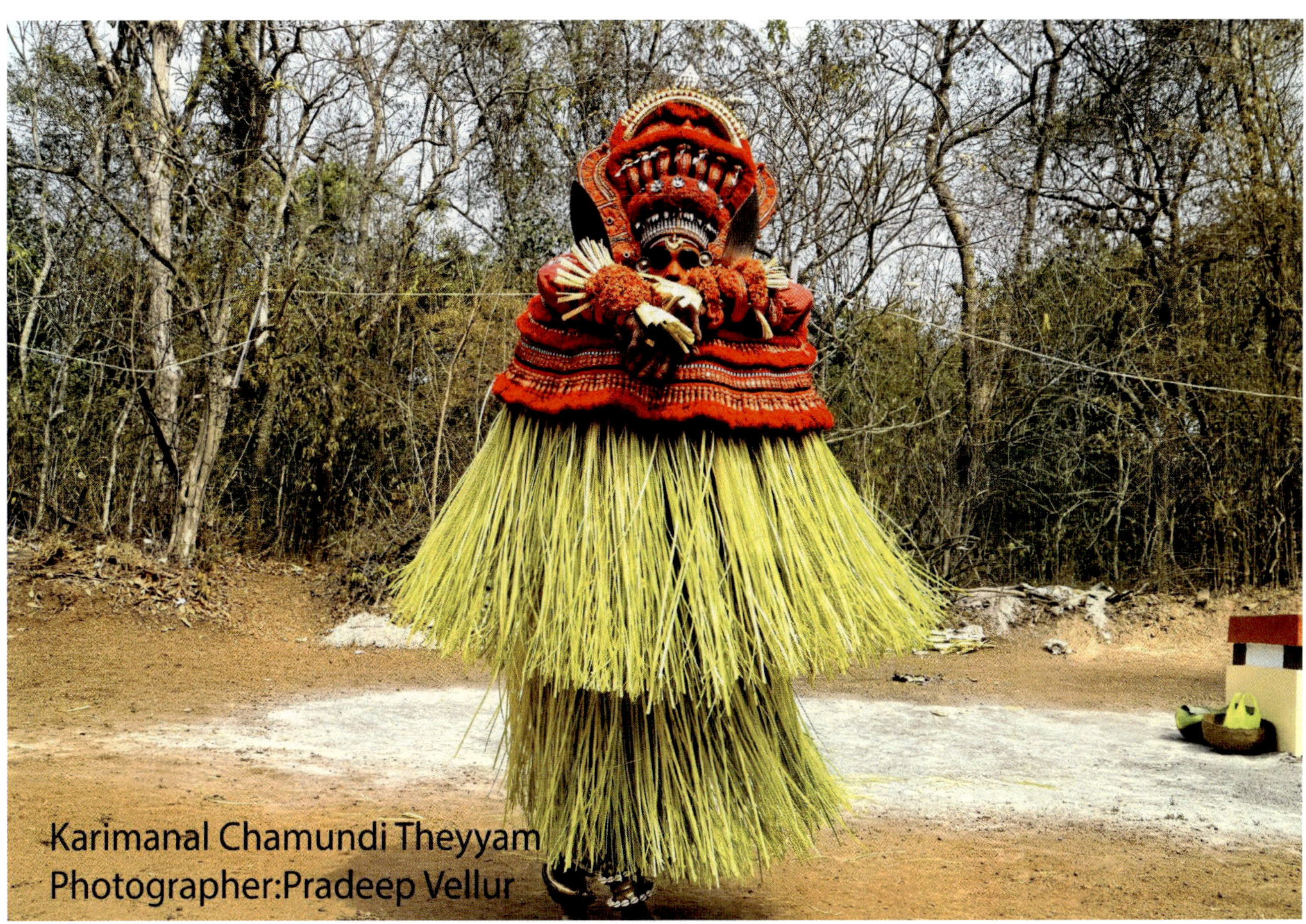

Karimanal Chamundi Theyyam
Photographer:Pradeep Vellur

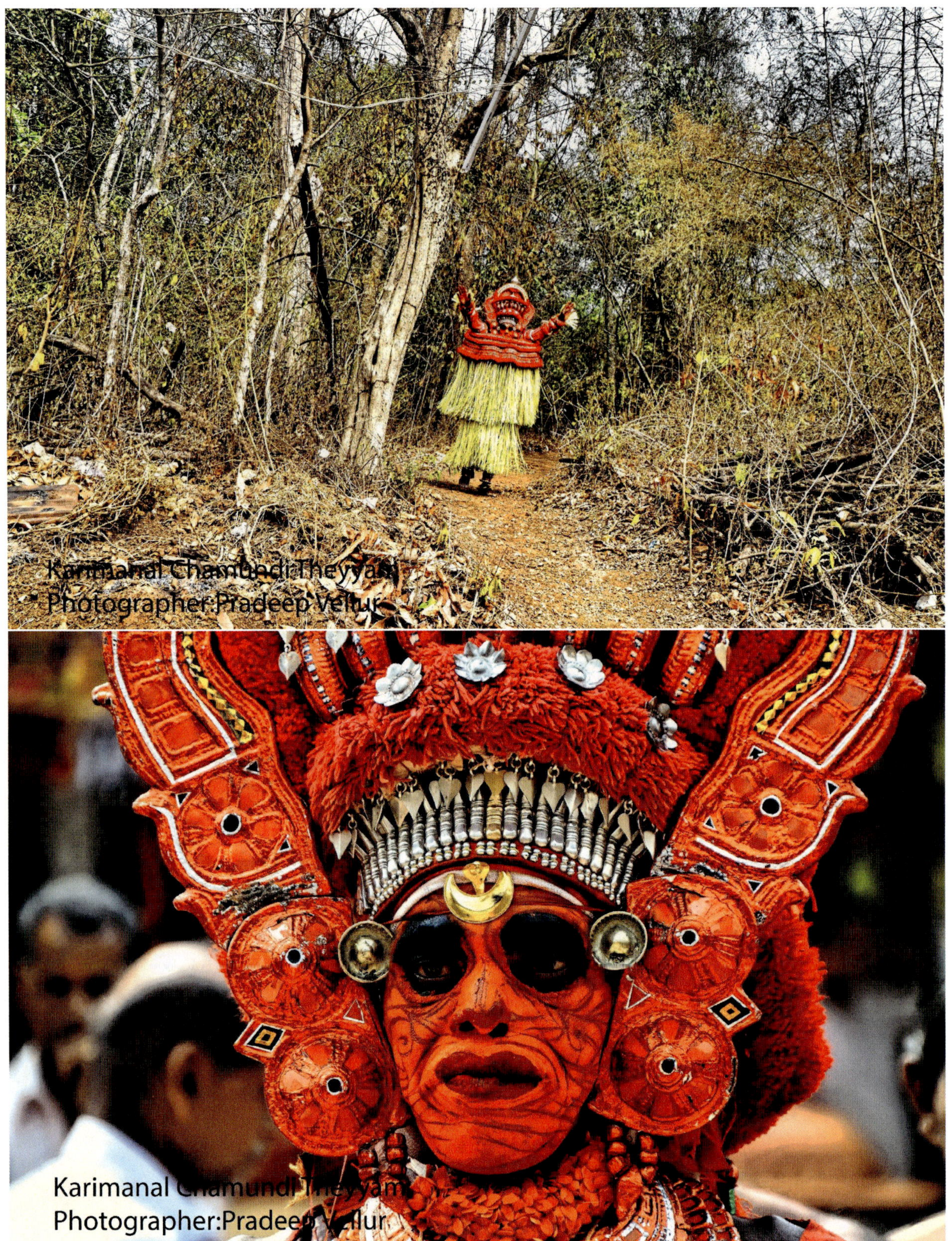

Karimanal Chamundi Theyyam
Photographer:Pradeep Vellur

Karimanal Chamundi Theyyam
Photographer:Pradeep Vellur

Ukkomil Chamundi

Ukkomil Chamundi is a version of the Raktha Chamundi Theyyam. Since the deity accompanied the senior caretaker of Ayiram Thengu Chamundi from the Ukkomil Tharavadu (a noble family) and hence resided there, she came to be known as Ukkomil Chamundi.

The legend is as follows. Rakthabeejasuran was the son of the Asura Krodhavathi. During the war against the *Asuras* (demons) Shumbha and Nishumbha, Rakthabeejasuran fought against *Chandika Devi*. From each drop of his blood, many Asuras took birth. The Goddess turned furious and, after failing to defeat Rakthabeejasura, a horrifying, dark-faced creature with a flailing tongue pierced and emerged from the Goddesses' forehead. This creature sucked every drop of Rakthabeejasura's blood, thus preventing the procreation of any more Asuras. Henceforth, the deity came to be known as Rakthabeejeswari or Raktha Chamundi Theyyam. This Goddess is the clan deity of the Moovari community and is performed by the *Malayan* society.

After a major flood hit the Kolathiri region and there was widespread famine, the people had only their King to seek refuge with. The Kolathiri King prayed hard to Goddess Annapoorneshwari for a way out of this turmoil. The Goddess and 16 other Goddesses traveled to the Kolathiri region on a vessel with seeds for sowing. They touched the shores of *Ayiram Thengu* and descended there. The king and his folks idolized and worshipped these Goddesses there. He offered tender coconuts to her, and once she quenched her thirst, she hurled the coconut husk away. She demanded a space for her on the spot where the husk rolled and finally settled there. Thus, the *Cherukunnil* Temple was formed by the Goddess Annapoorneshwari. The *Moovari* community collected flowers for the *poojas* (ceremonial offerings to God). Among the other Goddesses that came along with Goddess Annapoorneswari to Kolathunad, Raktha Chamundi was endeared by the *Moovari* community. They idolized her as their clan deity henceforth. She is also known as Ayiram Thengil Chamundi.

Since the Goddess gave immense importance to *Rudhiram* (Blood), she is also known as Rudhira Chamundi. Neelankai Chamundi, Raktheshwari Chamundi, Kuppola Chamundi, Aayiram Thengil Chamundi, Kuttikara Chamundi, Kizhakkera Chamundi, Rudhirakali, Periyatt Chamundi, Kaarel Chamundi, Chalayil Chamundi, Plavadukka Chamundi, Idappara Chamundi, Veera Chamundi are some of the other names by which she is known.

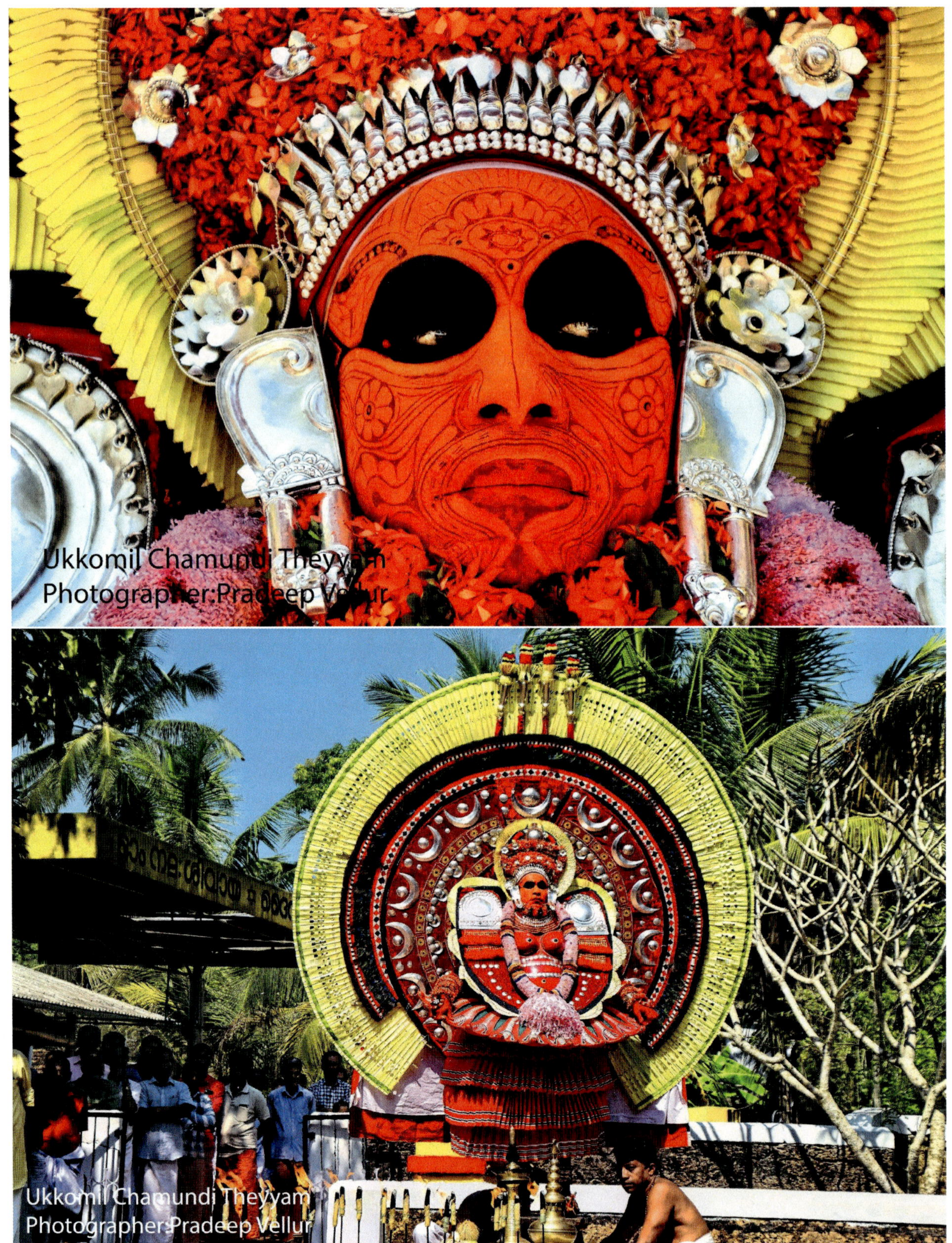

Ukkomil Chamundi Theyyam
Photographer:Pradeep Vellur

Ukkomil Chamundi Theyyam
Photographer:Pradeep Vellur

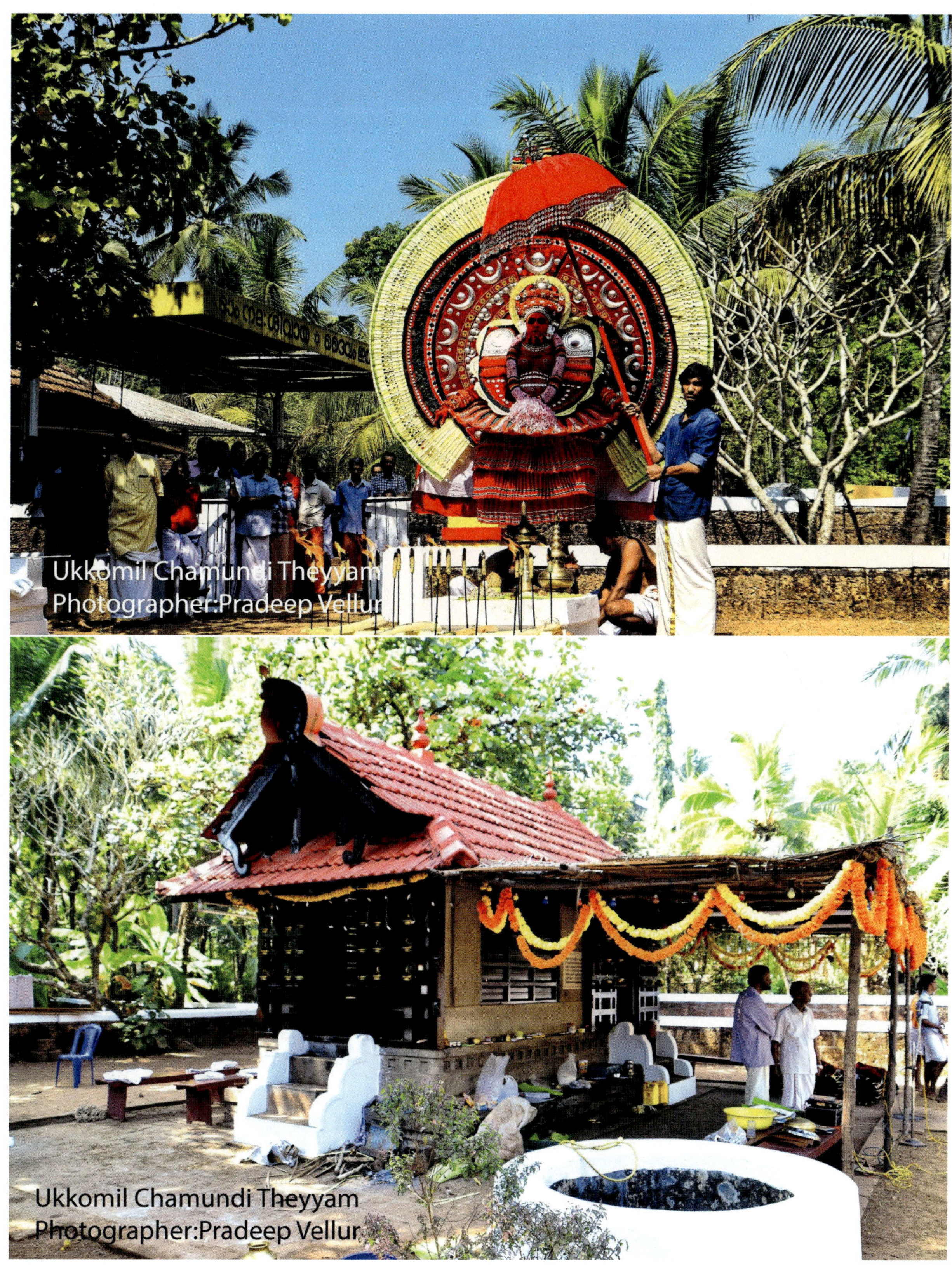

Ukkomil Chamundi Theyyam
Photographer:Pradeep Vellur

Ukkomil Chamundi Theyyam
Photographer:Pradeep Vellur

Konganichal Bhagavathy

Konginichal Bhagavathy Theyyam is a variation of the Narambil Bhagavathy Theyyam performed at the *Alakkad Konginichal Bhagavathykavu* (shrine) in the Kannur district of Kerala.

The Konginichal Bhagavathy is a manifestation of the warrior Goddesses. History states that she took shape from a pool of blood post-war to spread peace and good deeds worldwide. She came to be known as Narambil Bhagavathi as a Nair gave her a seat in the Narambil kavu (shrine). People from the *Vannan* community perform this Theyyam, which is similar to Puthiya Bhagavathy in its attire. Since four flaming torches are attached to the costume, this Theyyam also comes under the category of fire Theyyams.

Narambil Bhagavathy, seen as the sub deity of the Bhagavathy at Rayaramangalam, reached Udhinoor and joined with the Kodakkal Nair to secure a place in the Narambil area. Hence, she was referred to as Narambil Bhagavathy. Later, she was also given space at Peringoth Vettakorumakan Kottam, Alakkad Kalarikkal, Maavil Pathayapura, Puthoor Kuduvakulangara Kavu, Maniyara Poomalakavu, Kandothu Kuthur Tharavadu, Maavicheri Kavu, Kodakkal Tharavadu, and Kallettukadavu Narambil Bhagavathy Kavu.

Konothu Adiyodi, a patron of the Rayaramangalam temple, married a woman from the *Naramabil Tharavadu* (a noble family) and brought her to Pilikod. She faced mistreatment at her in-law's house and prayed hard to her ancestral Goddess, Narambil Bhagavathy. The infuriated Goddess immediately started her journey to the *Konothu Tharavadu*. Knowing this, the Goddess of Rayaramangalam appointed Muchilottu Bhagavathy to calm Narambil Bhagavathy down. Thus, Muchilottamma (Muchilottu Bhagavathy) persuaded Narambil Bhagavathy, took her to Karivellur Muchiloor, and placed her on her pedestal, thus uniting her altogether.

In Muchilottu Kavus, Narambil Bhagavathy has a fierce or angry demeanor. One can spot this in her songs and her costume as well. The face makeup of this Theyyam is called *Bhadra Chotta*. Waistbands, flaming torches, white fabrics, and a curled-up hairstyle are common features of the Theyyam. In other Kavus, the face makeup might vary from that of Muchilottu Kavus. Face makeup, known as *Kutti Shanku* and *Vaireedalam*, and slow and light footwork are other features of this Theyyam.

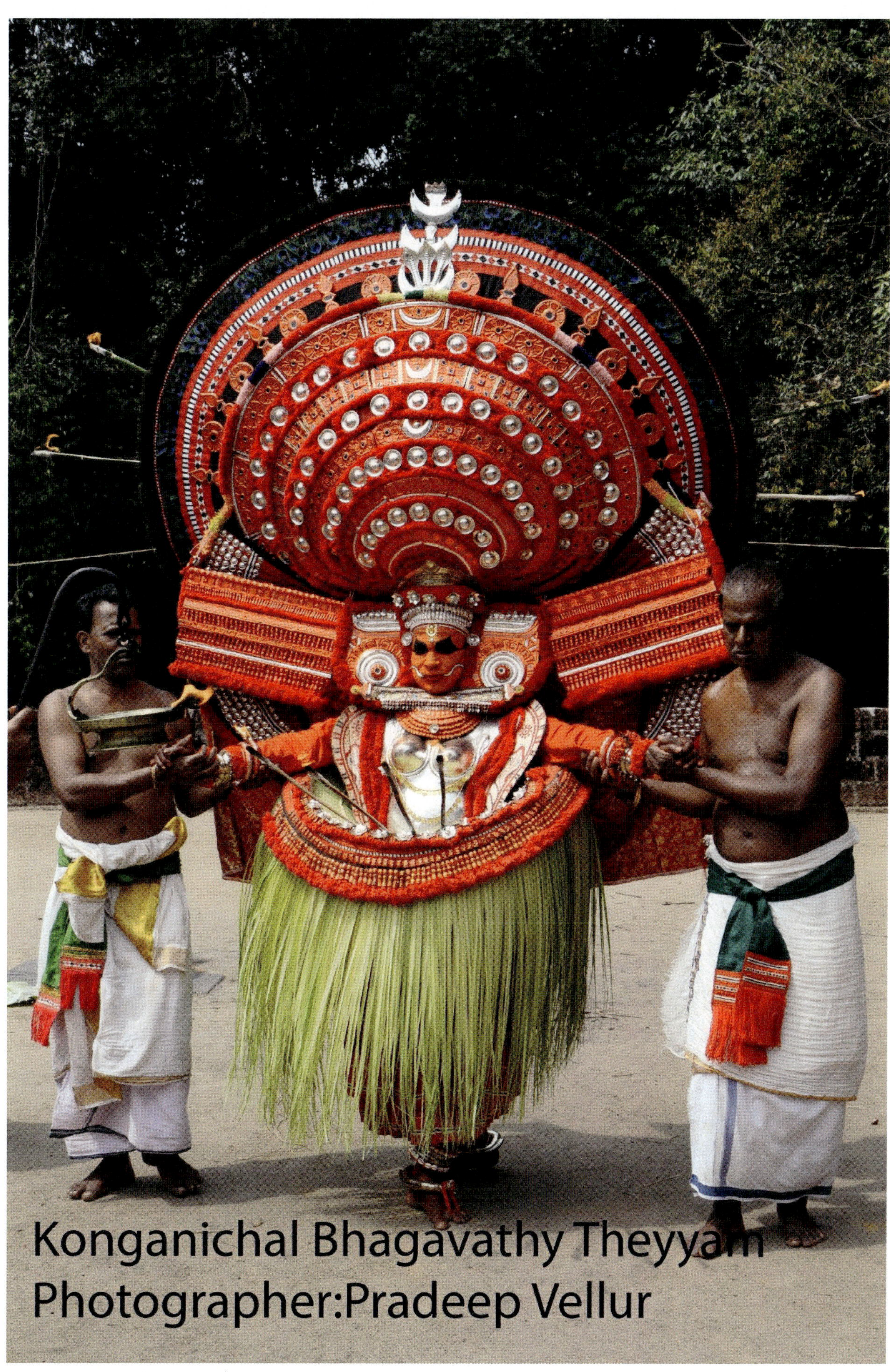

Konganichal Bhagavathy Theyyam
Photographer:Pradeep Vellur

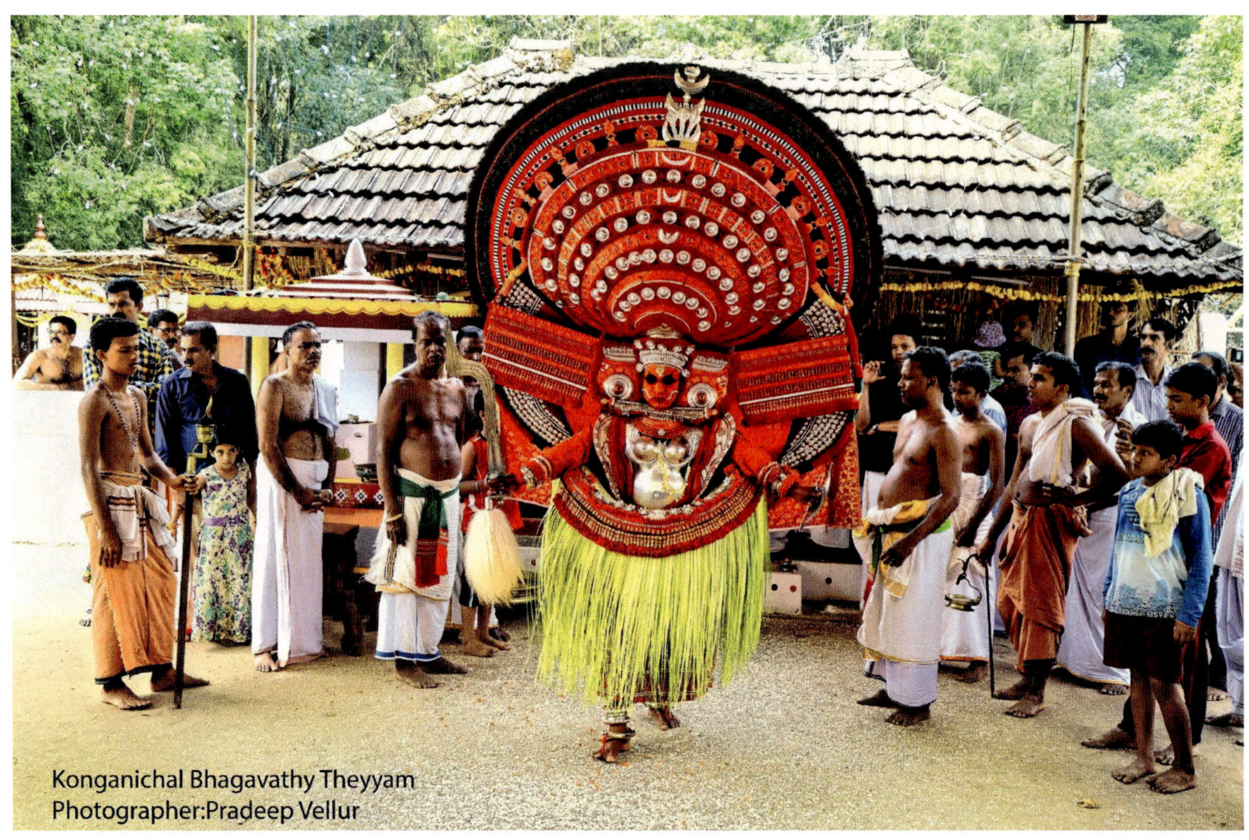

Konganichal Bhagavathy Theyyam
Photographer:Pradeep Vellur

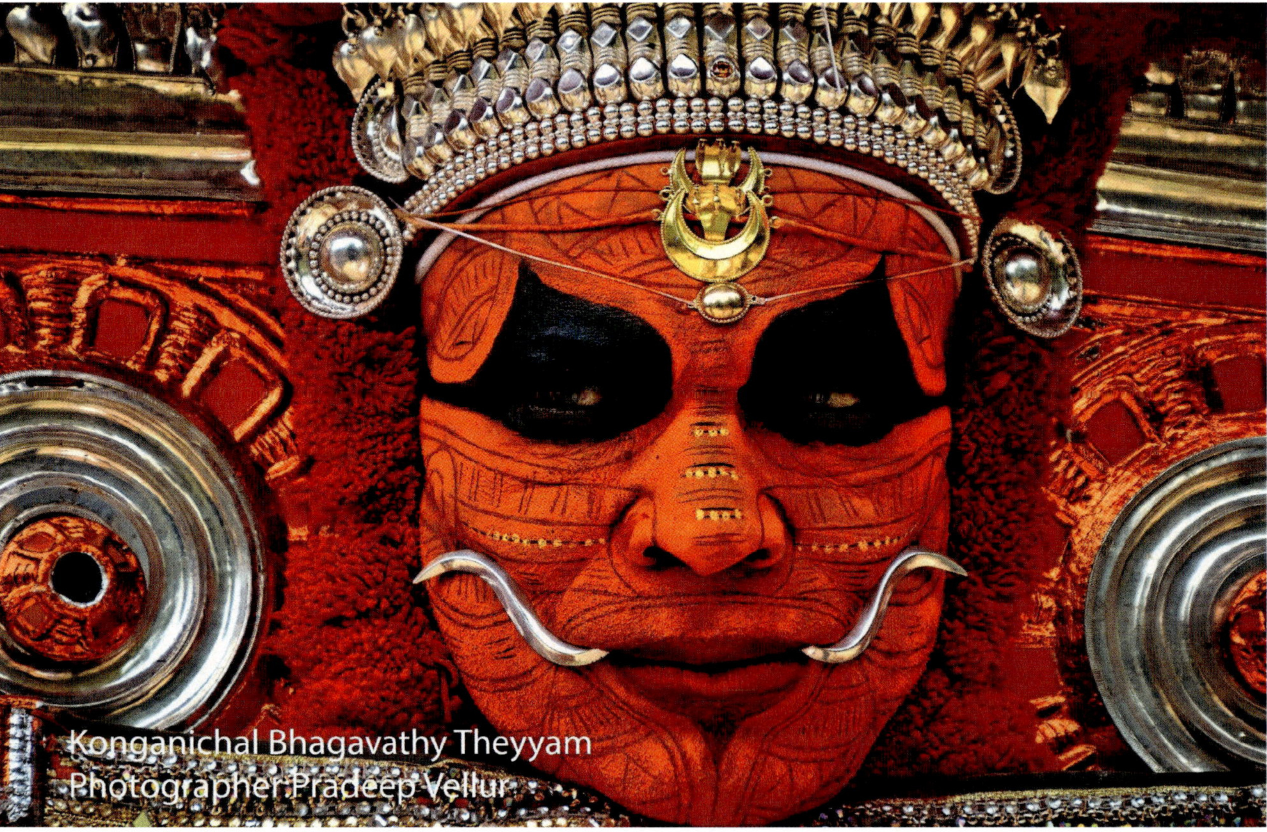

Konganichal Bhagavathy Theyyam
Photographer:Pradeep Vellur

Ardha Chamundi

Ardha Chamundi was born out of a sacred pyre carried out in the hail of Lord Shiva. People of the *Velan* and *Koppalan* communities perform this Theyyam. The major temples at which this Theyyam is performed are Kodallur Shri Vishwakarmadevasthanam, Ardha Chamundikavu, etc. In the battle against the demons, when there was no way out but to be subdued by them, Devi called out in loud prayers to her Lord Shiva. He fused the form of Shiva and Shakti into Devi's body. The Devi thus transformed into Ardha Chamundi. People usually conduct the performance of Ardha Chamundi Theyyam to fight against evil or ill forces that might affect them and for prosperity.

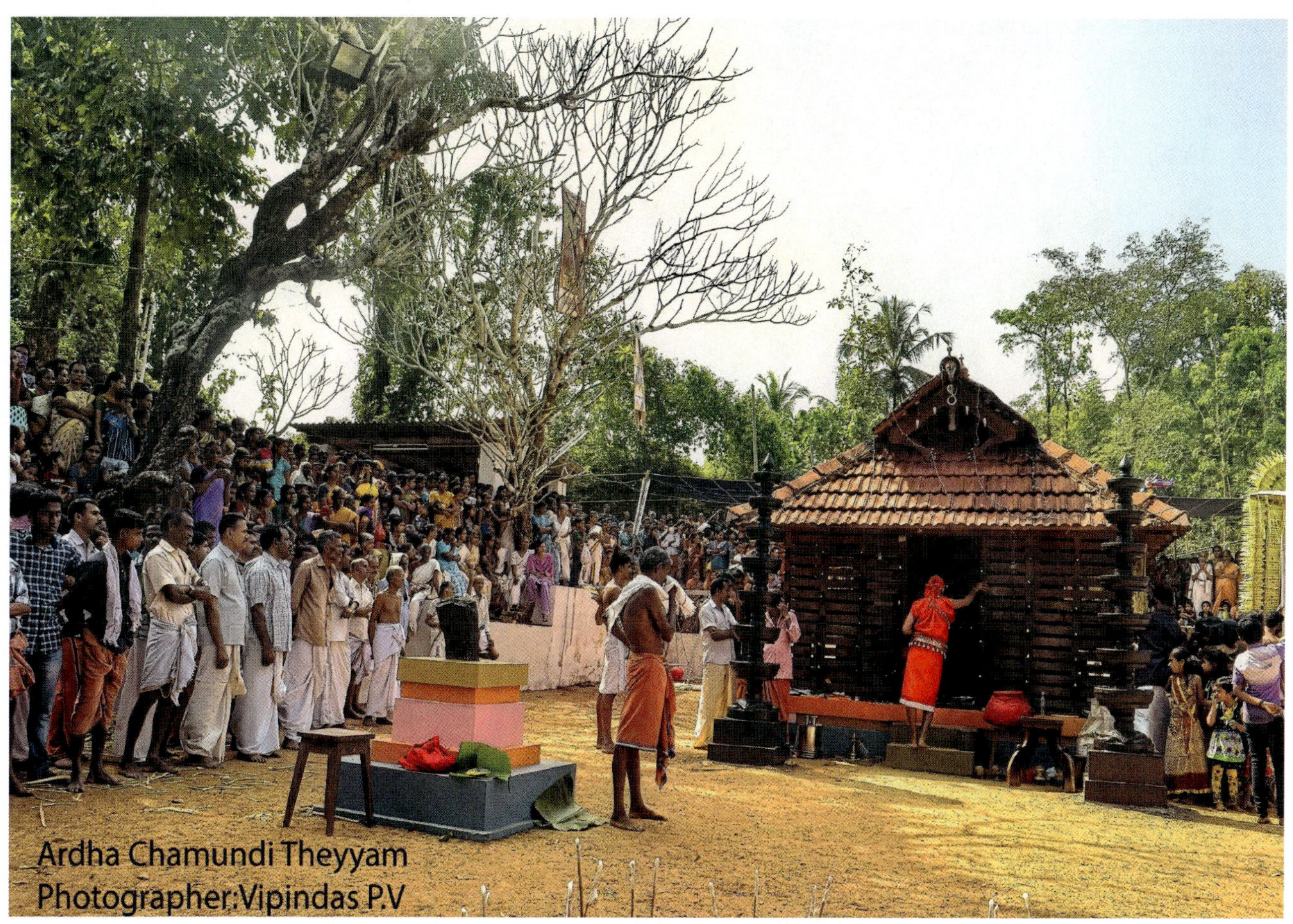

Ardha Chamundi Theyyam
Photographer:Vipindas P.V

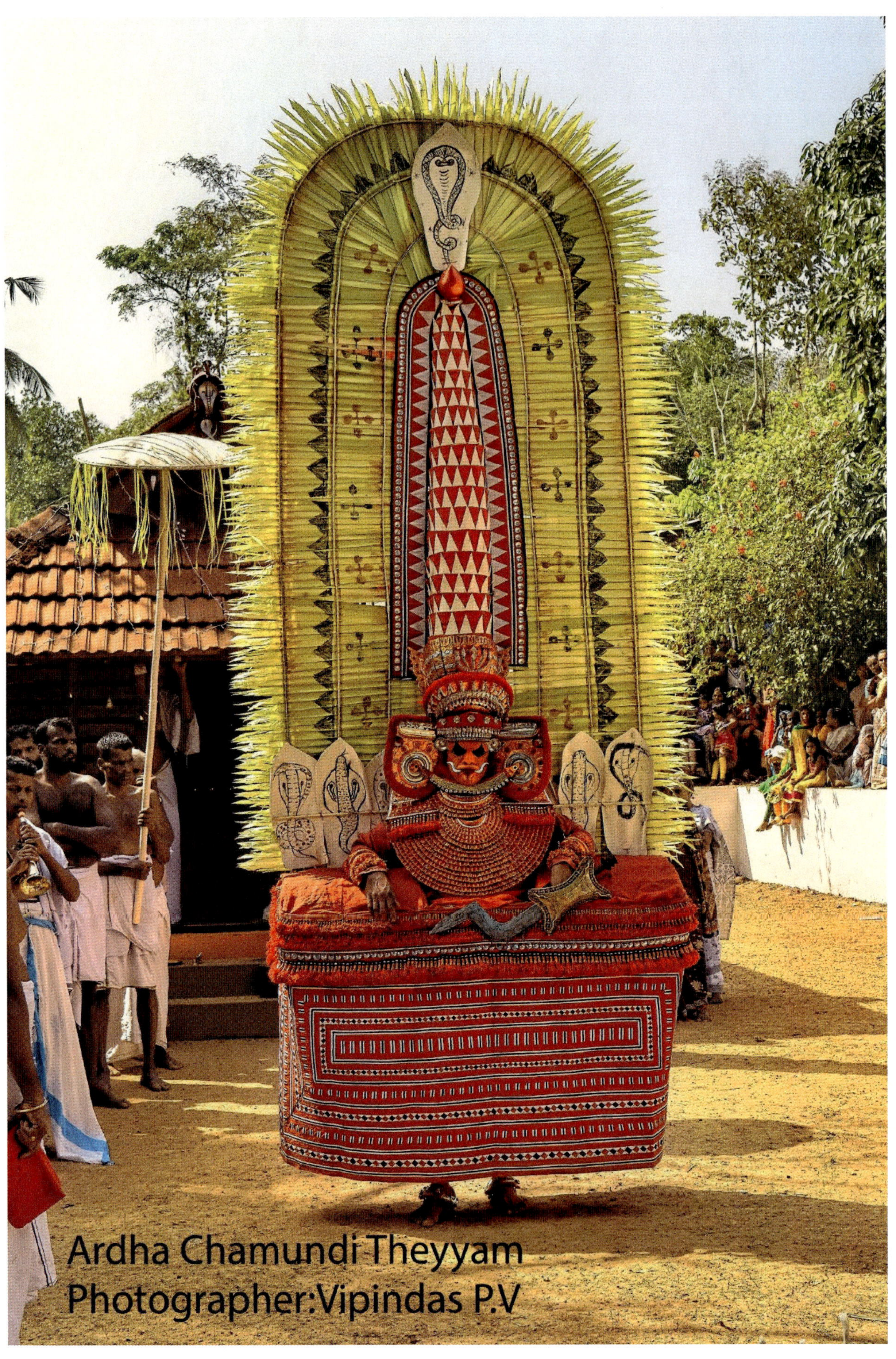
Ardha Chamundi Theyyam
Photographer:Vipindas P.V

Karuval Bhagavathy

Karuval Bhagavathy is a form of Manthra Moorthy. This Goddess took birth in the Karuval Mountains. According to the hymns, the first abode of Kattumadathinkal Karuval Bhagavathy is Kattumadam Thanthrimadom. Besides this, she is revered and worshipped in 18 other Namboothiri households like Adiyeri, Pullanjeri, Kattumadam, etc.

Goddess Parvathi and Lord Shiva lived on as tribal people and gave birth to a son Kuttichathan. Some also believe that Karuval Bhagavathy is the sister of Kuttichathan. This Goddess, worshipped by the *Pulaya* community, is believed to be an evil deity that possesses pregnant women. A curled-up hairdo and silver-plated accessories are traditional features of this Theyyam's costume.

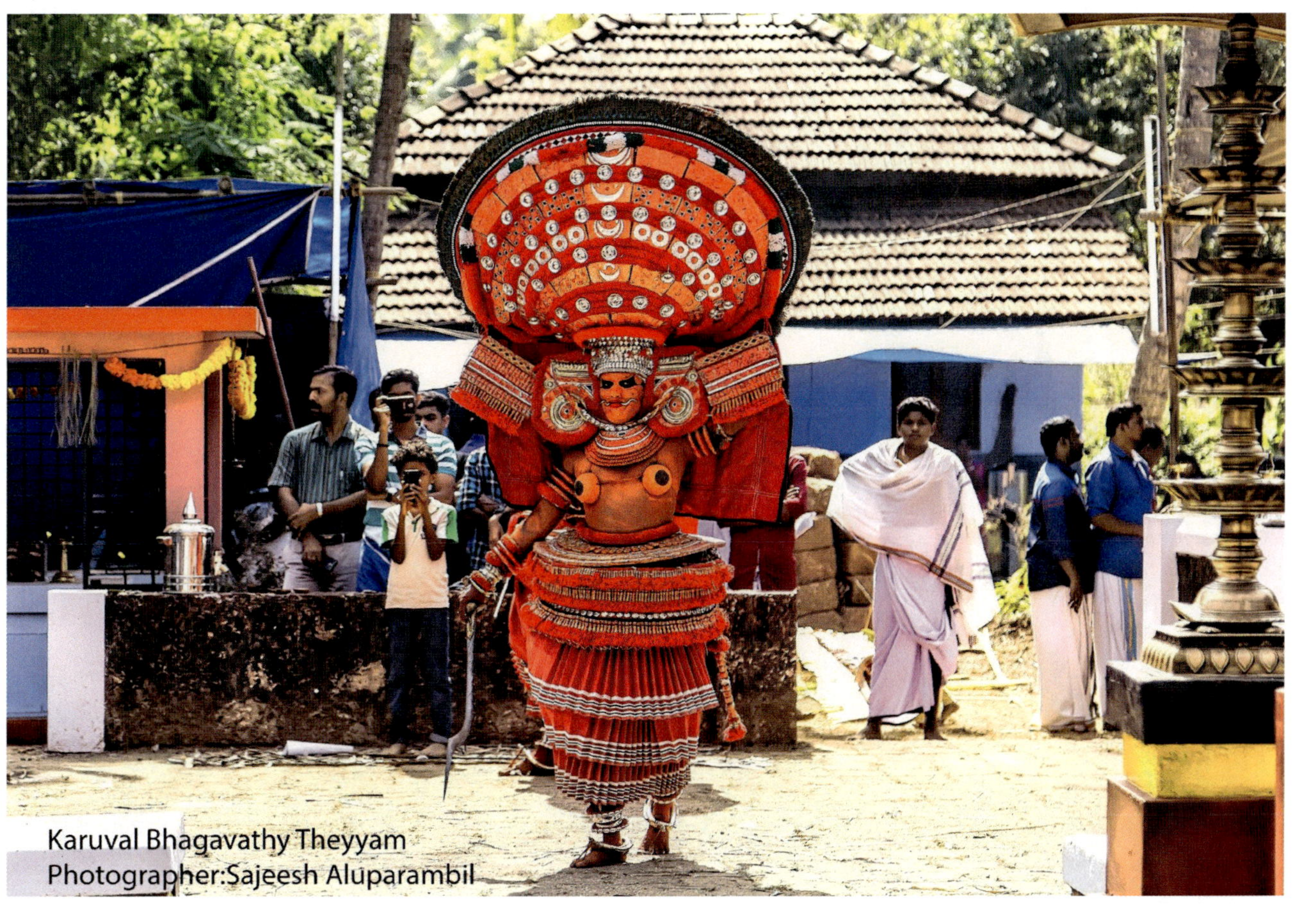

Karuval Bhagavathy Theyyam
Photographer:Sajeesh Aluparambil

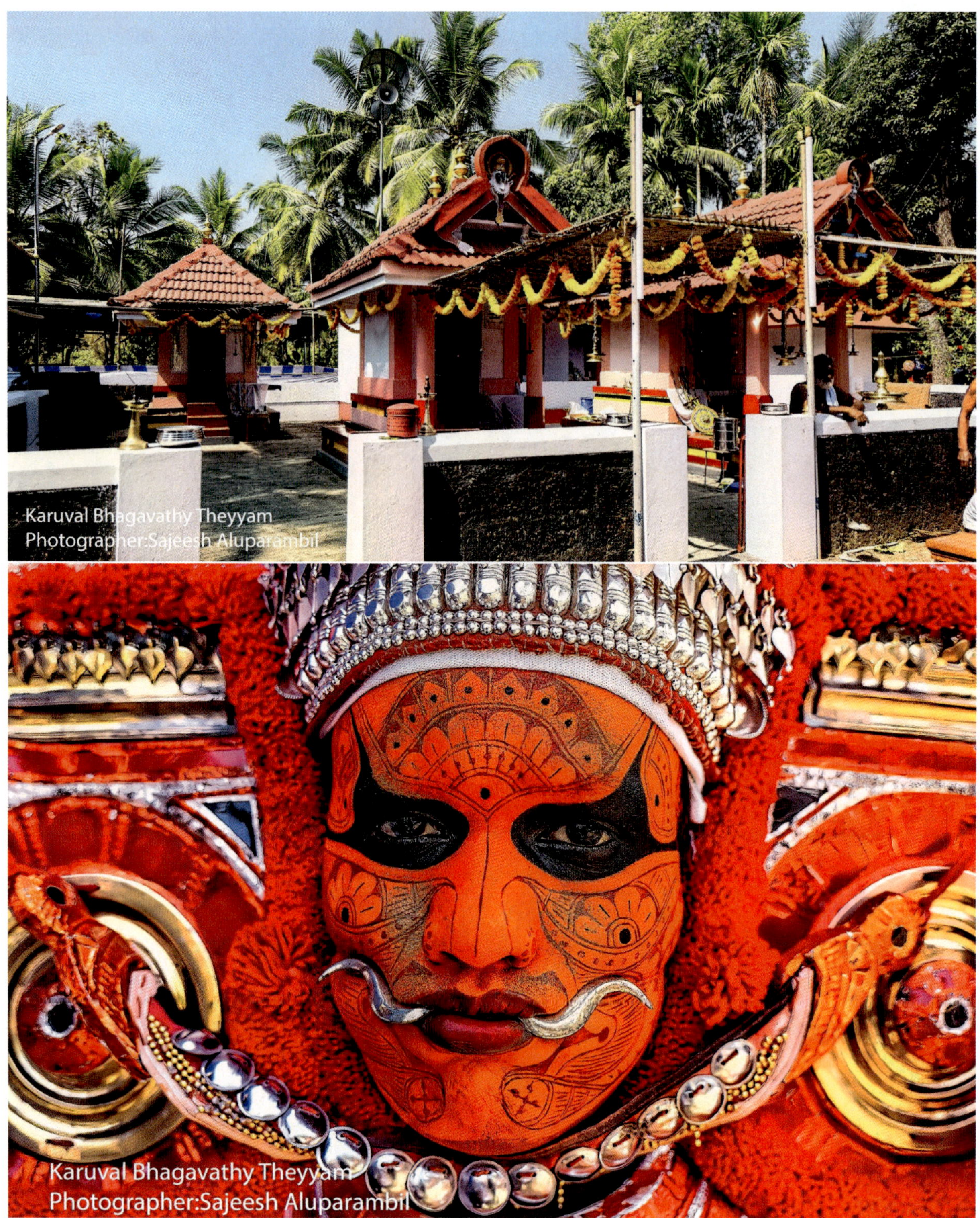

Karuval Bhagavathy Theyyam
Photographer:Sajeesh Aluparambil

Karuval Bhagavathy Theyyam
Photographer:Sajeesh Aluparambil

Rakthajathaneeswaran

Rakthajathan and Vairajathan are the incarnations of Lord Shiva. Lord Shiva incarnated as Rudra and did a frenzied dance in the hall where king Daksha was conducting a *Yaga* (ritualistic sacrifice). Rakthajathaneeswaran was born out of this ferocity of Rudra.

Daksha was the father of Sathi, the wife of Lord Shiva. Once, he decided to conduct a *Yaga* without inviting Shiva and Sathi since they had married against his will. Regardless, Sathi went to the *Yaga* hall, stating that no invitation was needed to attend a *Yaga* conducted by her father. Lord Shiva was against participating in the *Yaga and* warned Sathi about this. He also told her not to return to Kailasa if she went to the Yaga. Despite Shiva's warnings, Sathi went to take part in the Yaga. But to her disappointment, Daksha insulted her by saying she was participating without his invitation. Sathi became depressed and killed herself by jumping into the firepit of Yaga hall.

Lord Shiva became angry when he learned about this, pulling his matted hair and throwing it, which Veerabhadran was born out of. He is also known as Sri Vairajathaneeswaran, Rakthajathaneeswaran, etc. Following the orders of Lord Shiva, he went to the Yaga hall along with the soldiers of Shiva and killed everyone present there. Shiva was pleased and blessed him. Later, Shiva sent Veerabhadran to earth to help Kshethrapalakan and Vettakkorumakan.

According to another legend, *Alladaswaroopam* was the royal dynasty that ruled north Kerala. Eight landlords ruled under this dynasty but were a threat to the king. Kshethrapalakan, warrior and commander of the Samoothiri dynasty, was sent by the Samoothiri king to capture *Alladaswaroopam*. He successfully captured Alladaswaroopam and gave control to Samoothiri king Keralavarma. He later decided to stay with Mulavannor Bhagavathy. He was respected and given an abode and the title, Rakthajathaneeswaran.

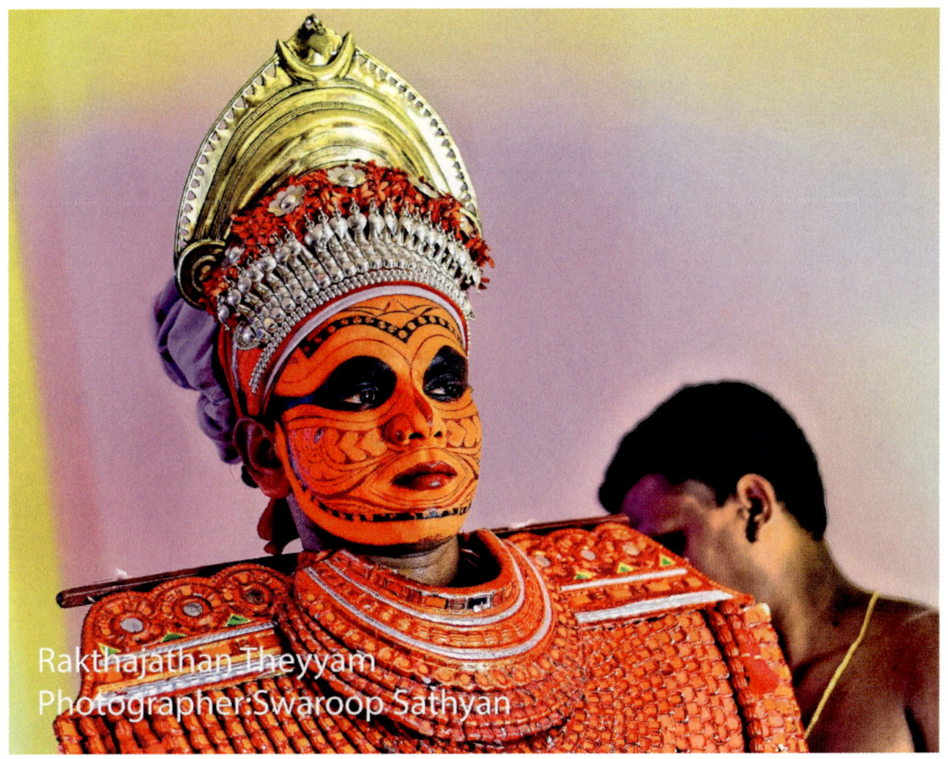
Rakthajathan Theyyam
Photographer:Swaroop Sathyan

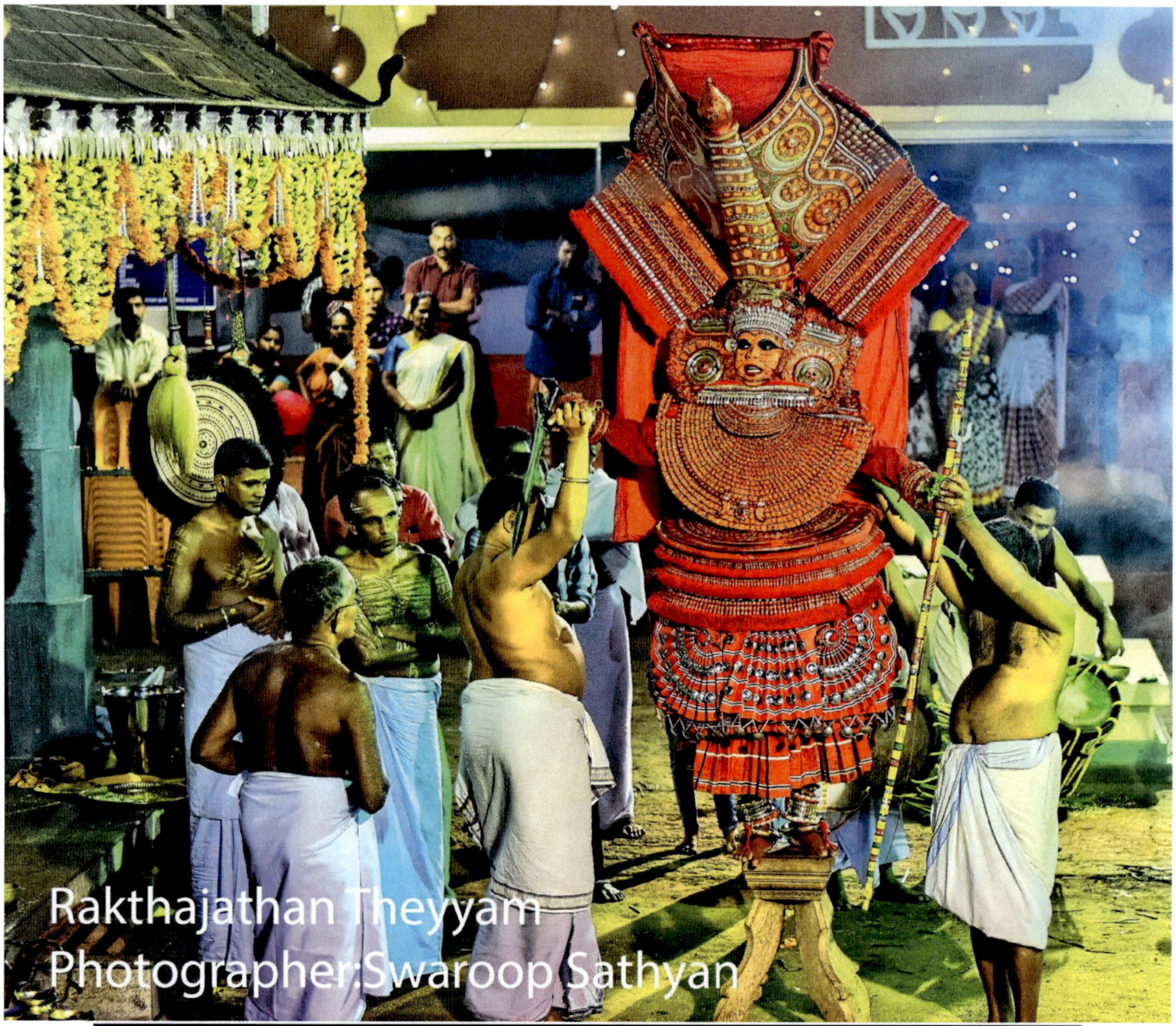

Rakthajathan Theyyam
Photographer:Swaroop Sathyan

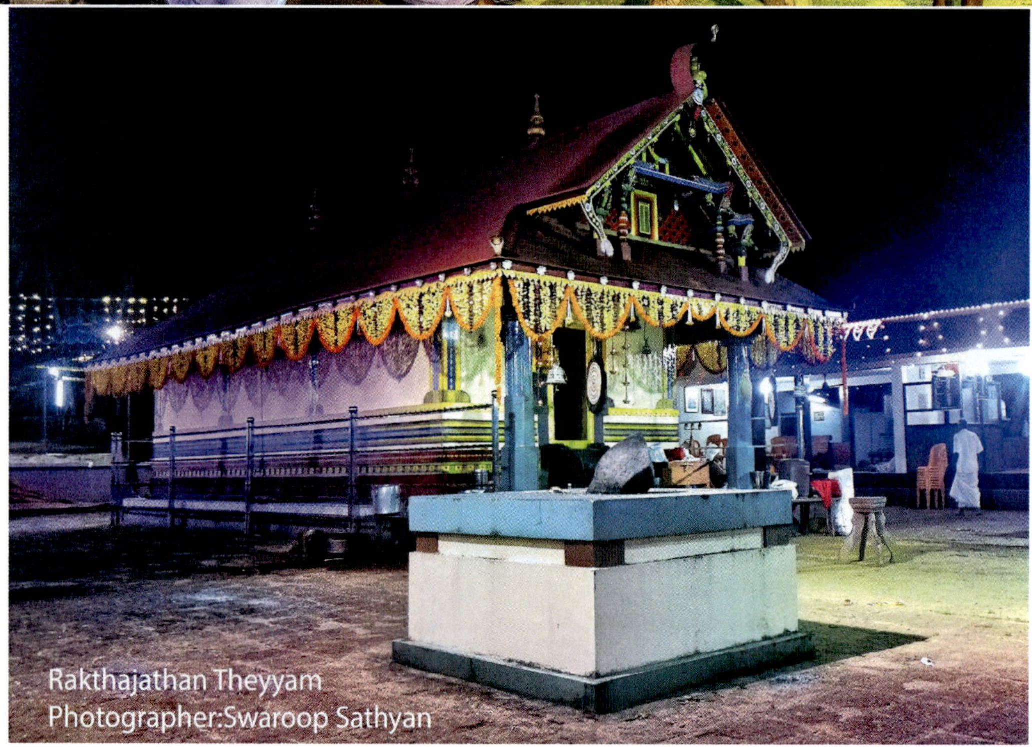

Rakthajathan Theyyam
Photographer:Swaroop Sathyan

Kannikkoru Makan

Kannikkoru Makan, or Manichery Dhaivam, is believed to be the incarnation of Dhanvanthari, who is the chief among physicians. Hence, he is a healer God. It should be noted that the devotees reach the peak of pleasure when the Theyyam says, 'I will be standing next to your right and left as the one hundred and eight medicines for the ninety-six epidemics and Dhanvanthari.'

Vakkathoor Akkam Thammassery was a virgin who belonged to the *Puthoorvadi kotta*. She had no heir. Once, she was kidnapped by thieves for her ornaments, but she escaped from them with the blessing of Lord Shiva and reached the mountains of Kodagu, where she lived alone. As a result of her monumental prayers, Lord Shiva blessed her with a son named Vakkathhoor Kelu. Although this child was the heir of the *Puthoorvadi kotta,* his uncle did not know this and believed that his sister was dead, so he ruled the region. Having been predicted at the time of birth as someone born to rule, *Vakkathoor Kelu* grew up as a warrior and a physician. At age twelve, he went to meet his uncle with a necklace given by his mother that would reveal his identity. But when the child reached *Puthoorvadi kotta,* he fought with his uncle, who failed to recognize his nephew. The kid defeated his uncle and revealed his relationship to him. His uncle then made him the king.

According to legends, sometime later, Kelu went to serve the people along with his friend Shasthav and was gifted with the powers of the three major Gods. Many years passed, and the chiefs of the *tharavdus* of *Idavalath Pakkam, Moovakkattu*, and *Manicheri* were once on their way back home from Wayanad. They found a diamond that contained the vigor of Kannikkoru Makan. The chiefs deposited the diamond in the attic of Manichery Tharavadu. However, the diamond leaped onto the nearby blackboard tree because of its power. The astrologer informed the chief of Manichery *tharavadu* that the reason for this movement was the vigor of God. Hence, they built a temple at the place where the diamond was found sitting. Kannikkorumakan is the Theyyam that depicts this legend.

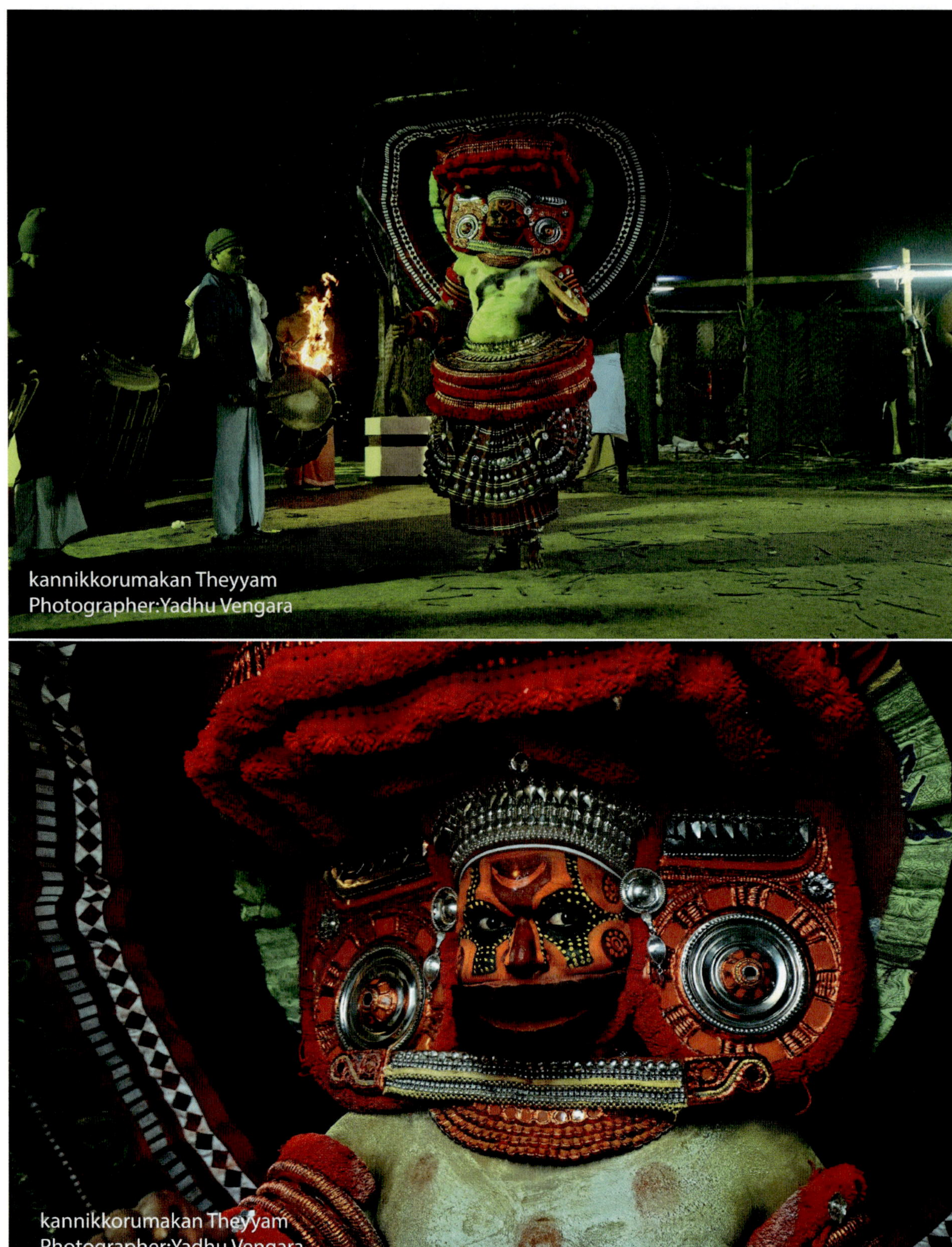

kannikkorumakan Theyyam
Photographer:Yadhu Vengara

kannikkorumakan Theyyam
Photographer:Yadhu Vengara

Bhairavan Theyyam

Once, Lord Brahma lied about seeing the universal form of Lord Shiva, which made Shiva angry since no one could see his universal form. The furious Shiva ripped off one of Lord Brahma's four heads and threw it away. Lord Brahma cursed him, and as a result, he had to go about begging on the earth with a skull in his hand. This Theyyam wears false eyes and uses a skull as a begging bowl. This form of Lord Shiva is known as Bhairavan Theyyam.

Another legend about Bhairavan Theyyam comes under the vaishnavite tradition. Usually, the *Panan* community is the one who performs this Theyyam. According to this community, Bhairavan is the child of a lady known as *Choyiyar Matathil Cheeralan*. She cut Bhairavan into pieces and cooked gravy with the bits to serve yogis. When they called "*Cheerala,*" the meat pieces in the sauce started moving. It is said that each piece turned into a form of Bhairavan.

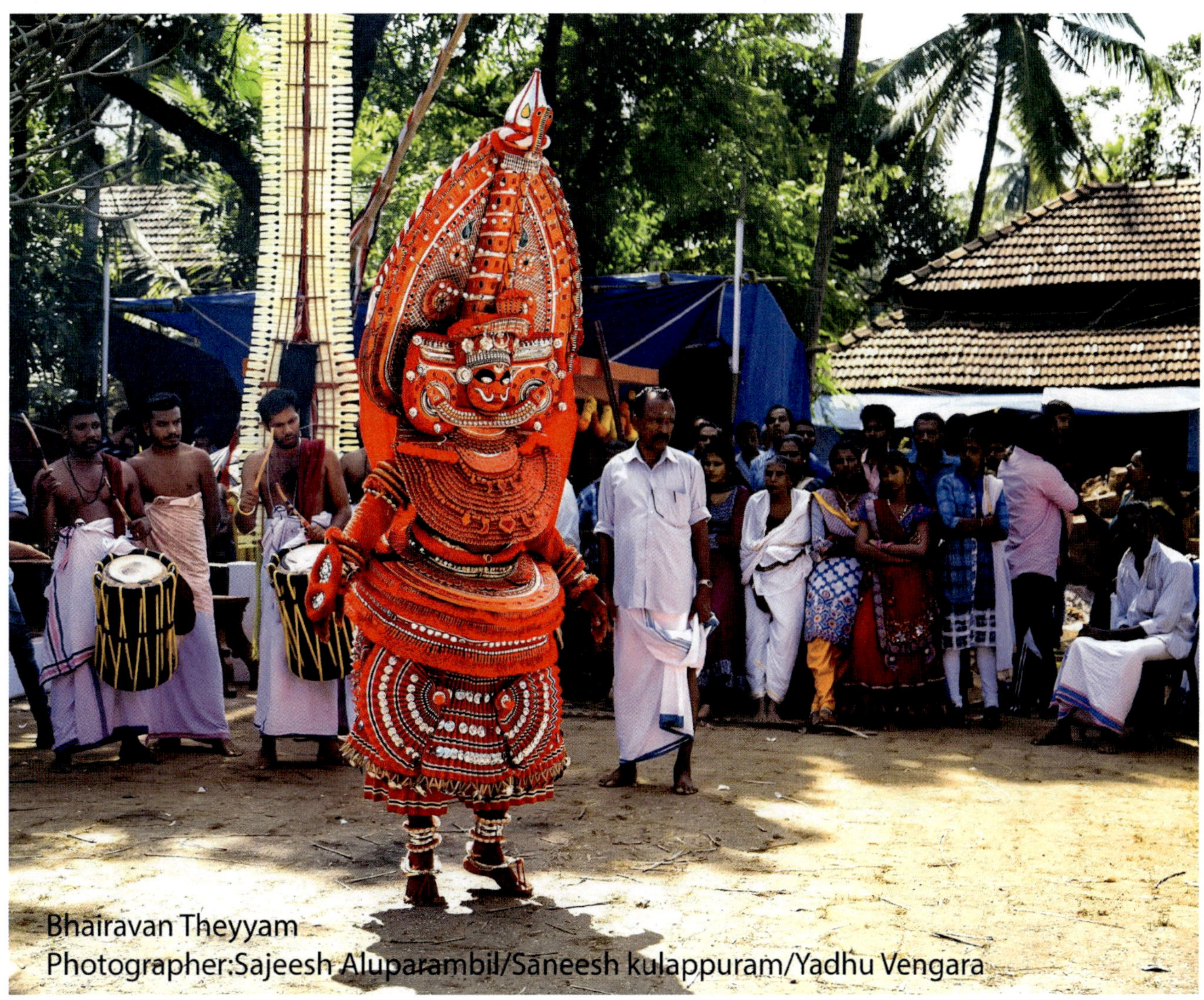

Bhairavan Theyyam
Photographer:Sajeesh Aluparambil/Saneesh kulappuram/Yadhu Vengara

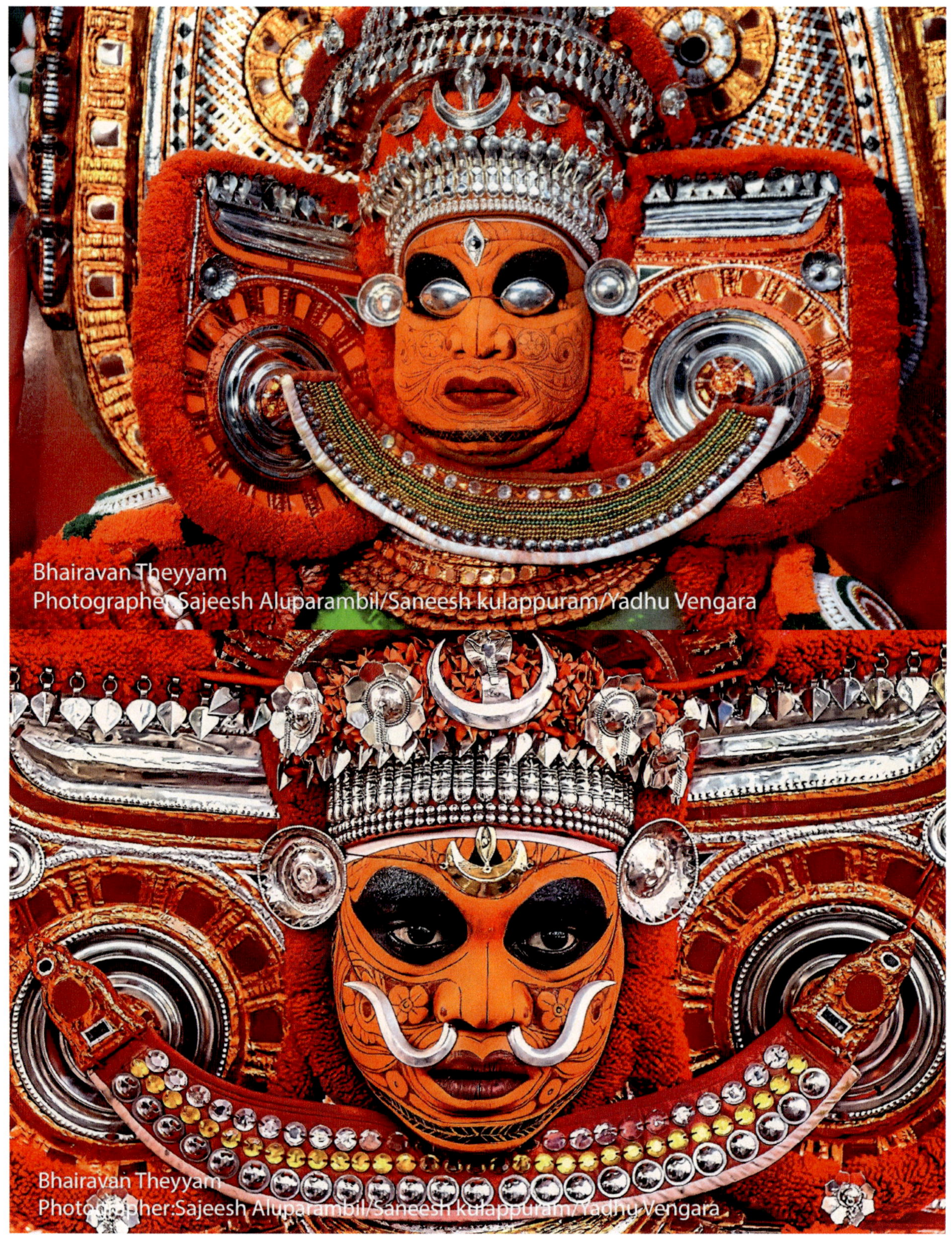
Bhairavan Theyyam
Photographer:Sajeesh Aluparambil/Saneesh kulappuram/Yadhu Vengara
Bhairavan Theyyam
Photographer:Sajeesh Aluparambil/Saneesh kulappuram/Yadhu Vengara

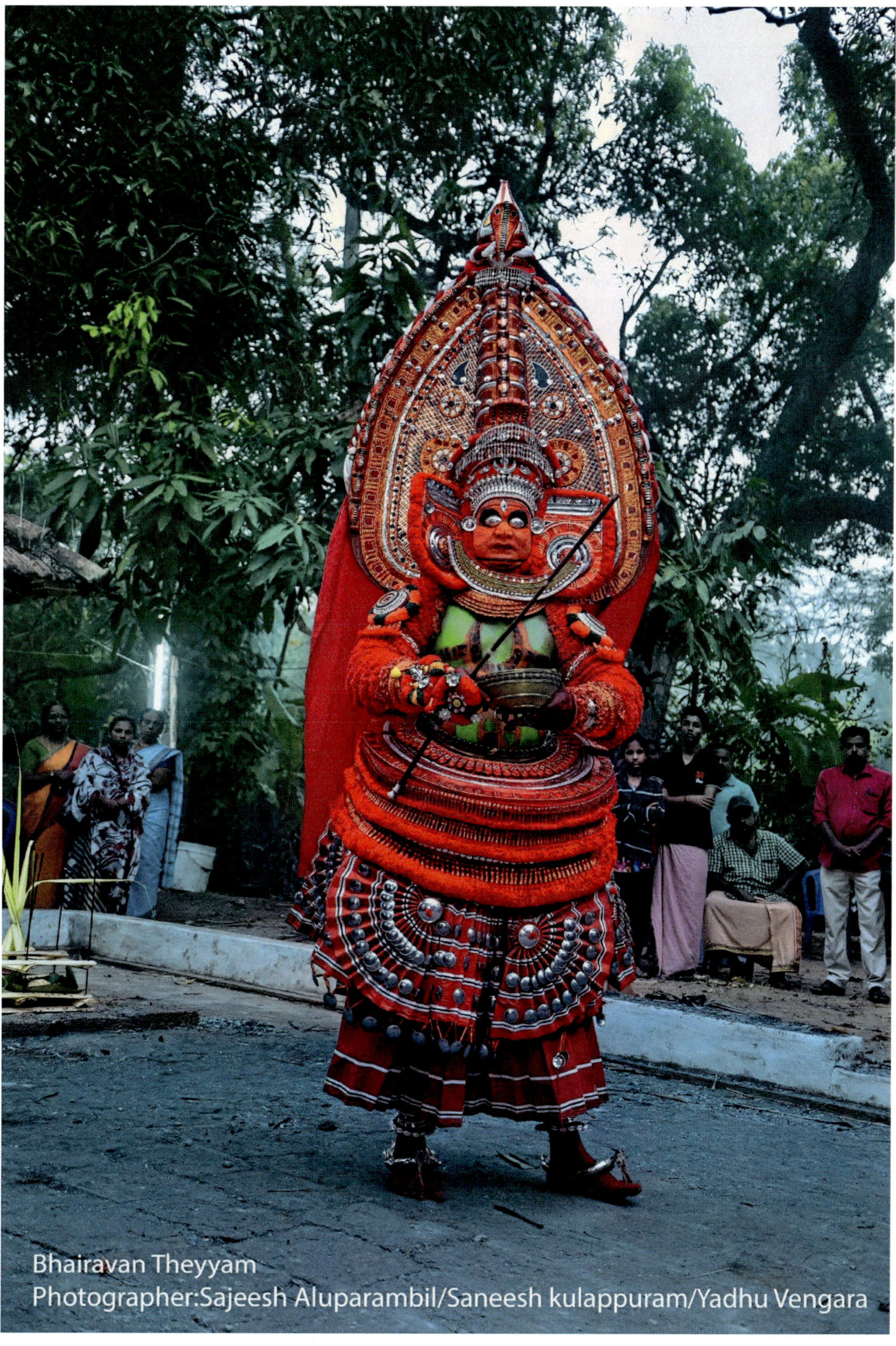
Bhairavan Theyyam
Photographer:Sajeesh Aluparambil/Saneesh kulappuram/Yadhu Vengara

Elladath Bhagavathy

Elladath Bhagavathy is a powerful Goddess. She is believed to wear two elephants in both of her ears. The Naga King Karkkodakan slithers around her neck like an ornament, while the bow serves as a sacred thread around her body.

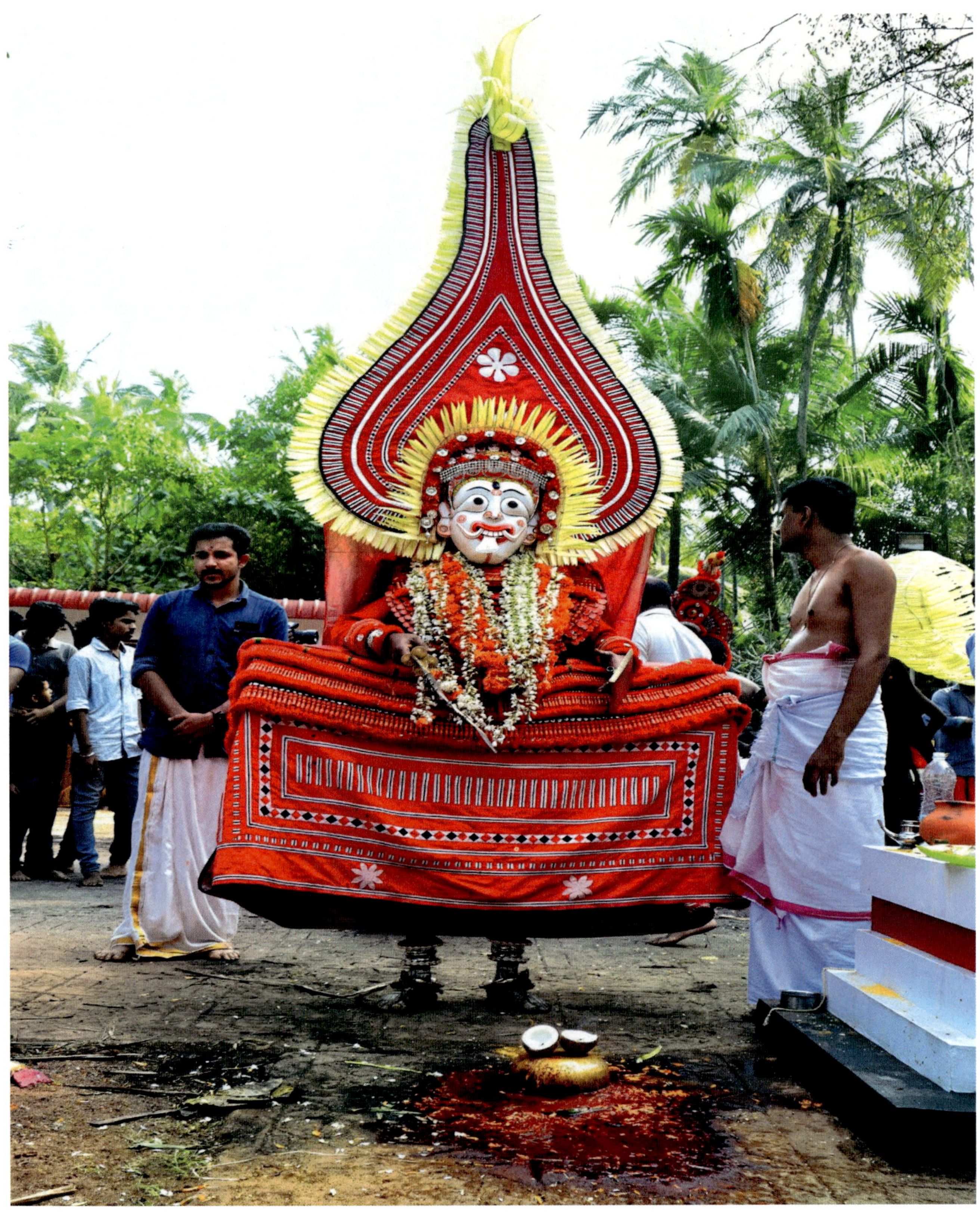

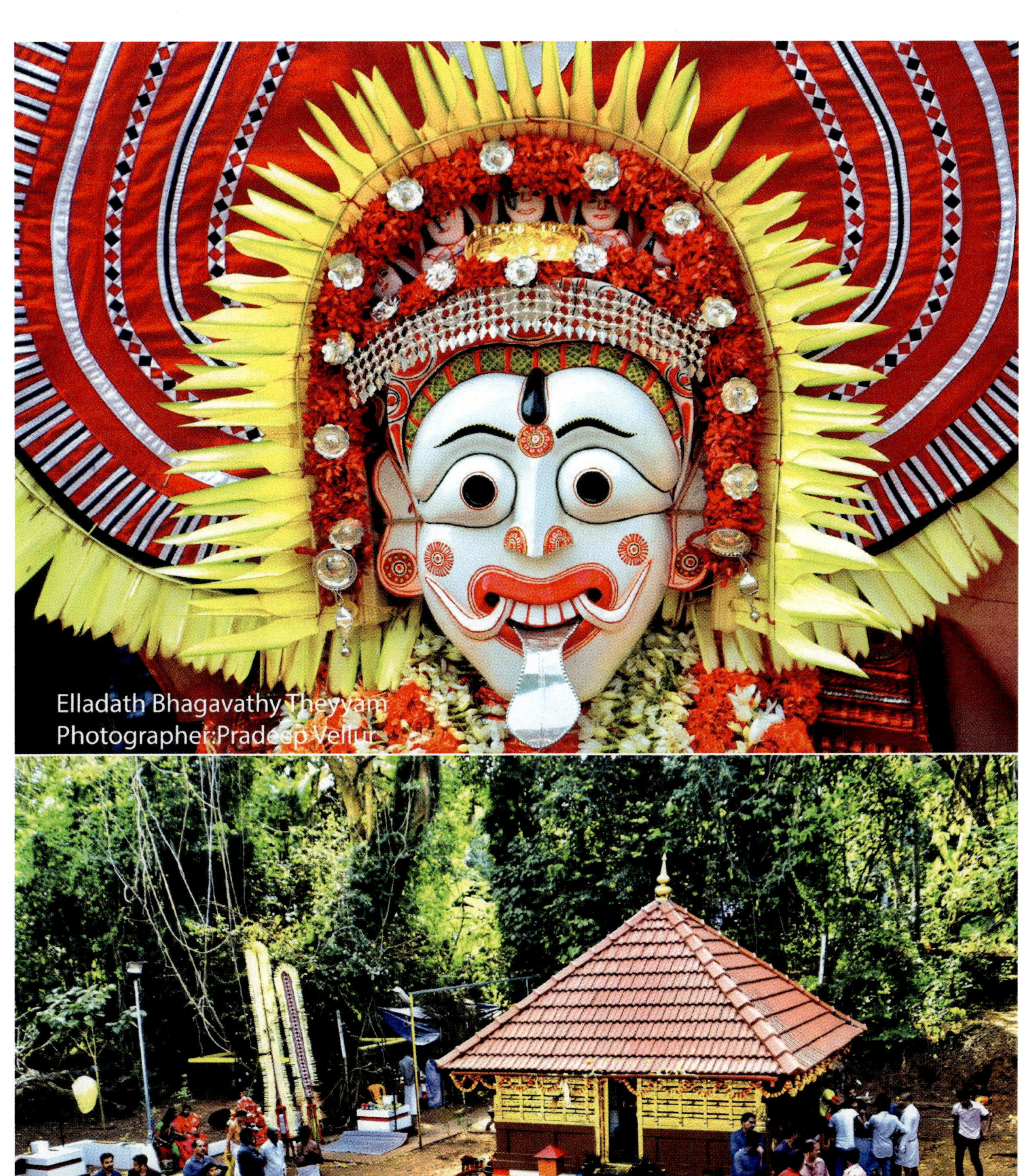

Elladath Bhagavathy Theyyam
Photographer:Pradeep Vellur

Elladath Bhagavathy Theyyam
Photographer:Pradeep Vellur

Puthiya Bhagavathy

Puthiya bhagavathy is a category of Theyyams considered healers. While smallpox was an epidemic on earth, Lord Shiva created her as a cure.

The legend talks about *Chirumbamar,* who originated from the third eye of Lord Shiva and intended to create happiness on earth and in heaven. Instead, Chirumba infected him and the world's people with smallpox, which disrupted the universe's equilibrium. Devas complained to lord Shiva about this, and a *Yaga* was conducted as a solution. Puthiya Bhagavathy originated from the *Homakunda* (sacred fire pit) on the forty-first day of the *Yaga*. She was ordered to heal everyone who was infected with smallpox. Puthiya bhagavathy was given a fowl as gurusi (sacred sacrifice) to quench her thirst, which pleased her. She cured the smallpox of Lord Shiva first and then of the other Gods. Following this, she was sent to earth along with the six sons of Lord Shiva, where she healed many people. During her travels worldwide, she encountered the Asura known as Karthaveeryan, and in a battle with him, all of the six sons who accompanied her were killed. An infuriated Puthiya Bhagavathy killed and burned the Asura.

Puthiya Bhagavathy then traveled to the north as a Goddess of vengeance and destroyed everything along the way. She also met her sister Chirumba Bhagavathy and expressed her rage. Puthiya Bhagavathy then traveled south, where she met the Maroth Veerarkali Amma. But since she had destroyed all the people on her way, Veerarkali refused to allow her beyond her temple's threshold. Puthiya Bhagavathy's grief and wrath made the noon appear like dusk, and Maroth Veerarkali Amma realized that the person who came to her was not an ordinary person but the daughter of Lord Shiva. She opened her threshold and gave the abode on her right side to Puthiya Bhagavathy. Puthiya Bhagavathy didn't settle there but continued traveling. She reached the *Moolachery Tharavadu* (a noble family of magicians), where the family recognized her and proclaimed their respect by giving her abode. The Chieftain of Kolathunadu, Chirakkal Raja, ordered the performance of this Theyyam following her appearance in his dreams. Puthiya Bhagavathy was presumed to be pleased with this honor, and she protected the Kolathunadu region from distress.

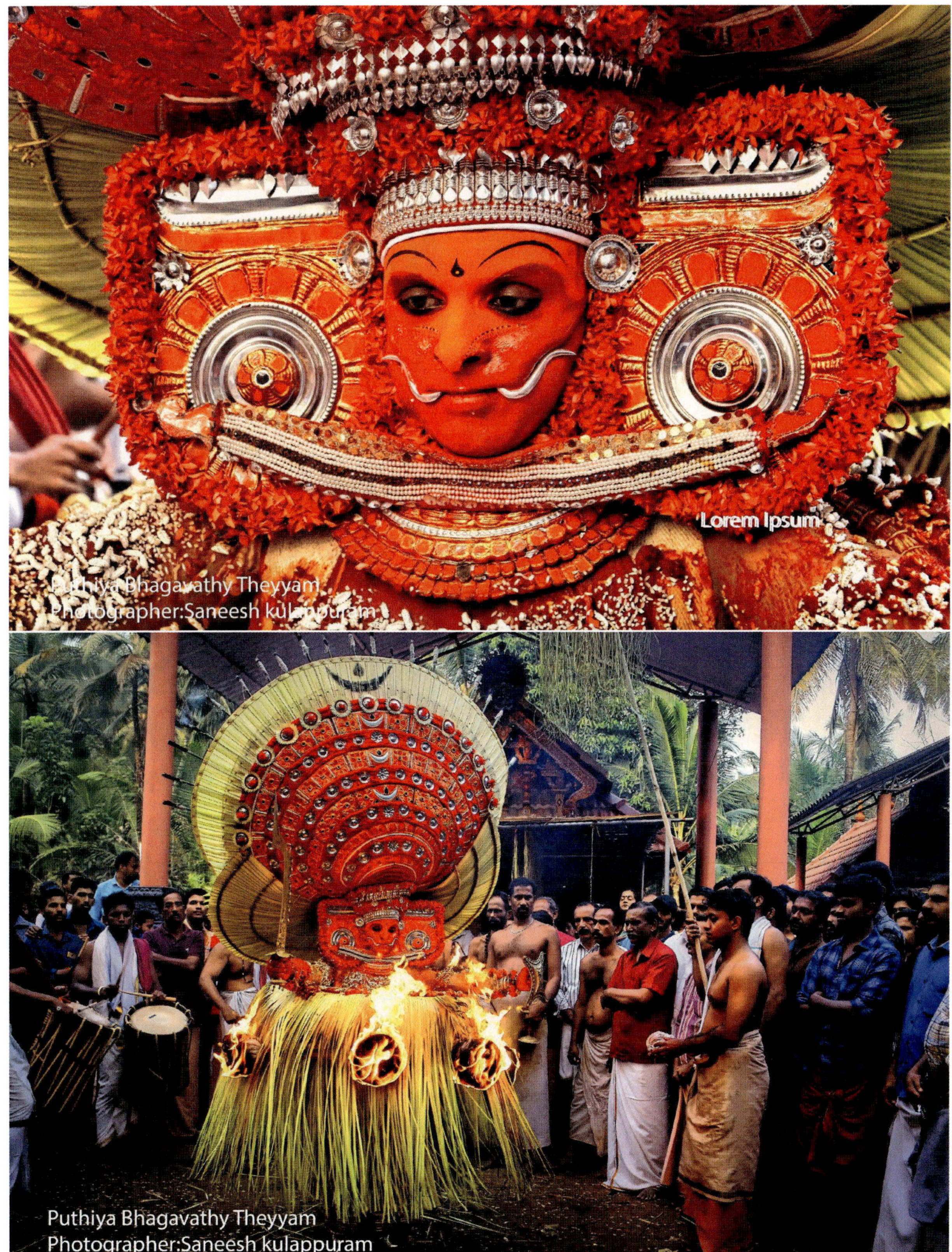

Puthiya Bhagavathy Theyyam
Photographer:Saneesh kulappuram

Puthiya Bhagavathy Theyyam
Photographer:Saneesh kulappuram

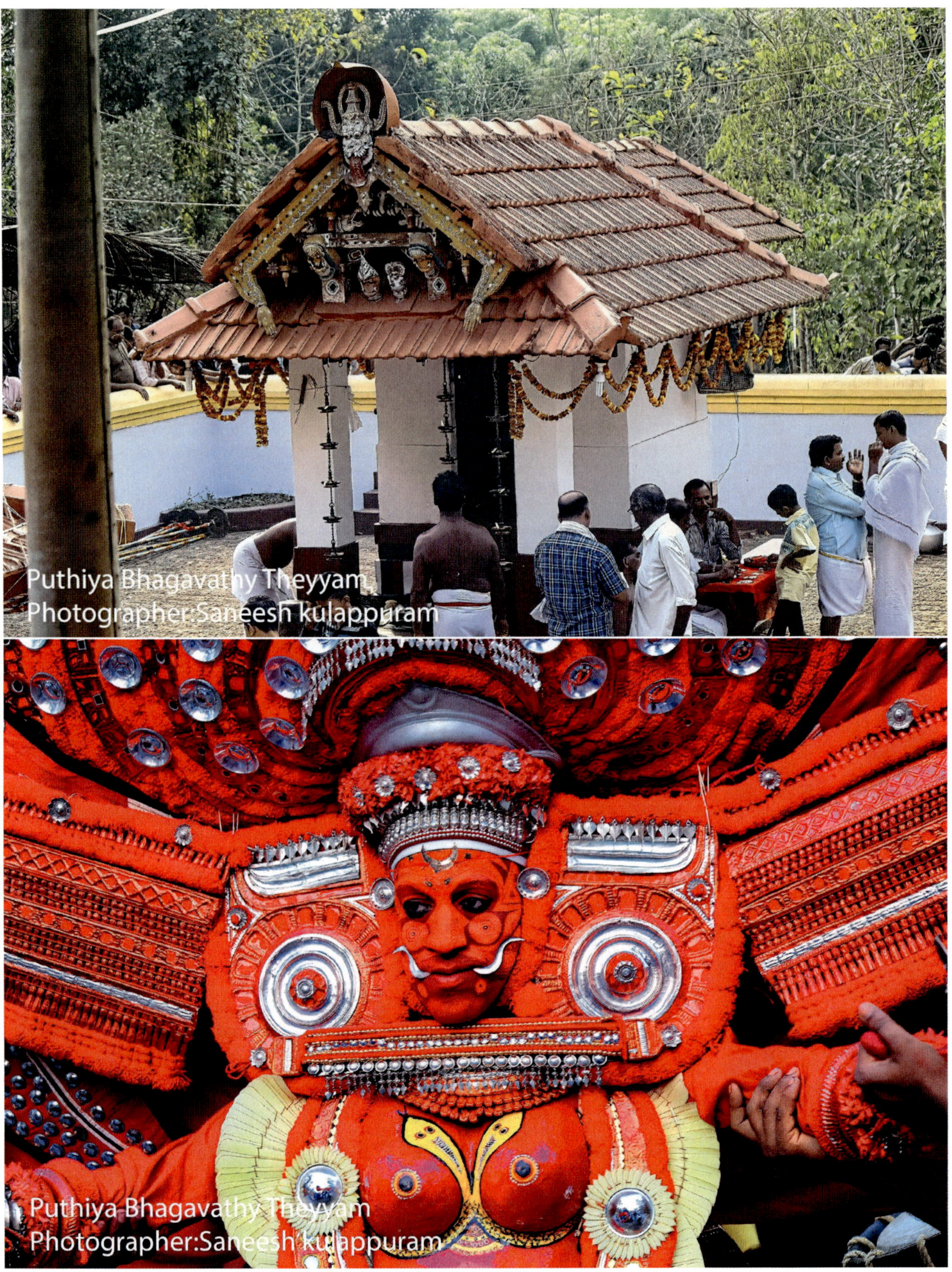

Puthiya Bhagavathy Theyyam
Photographer:Saneesh kulappuram

Puthiya Bhagavathy Theyyam
Photographer:Saneesh kulappuram

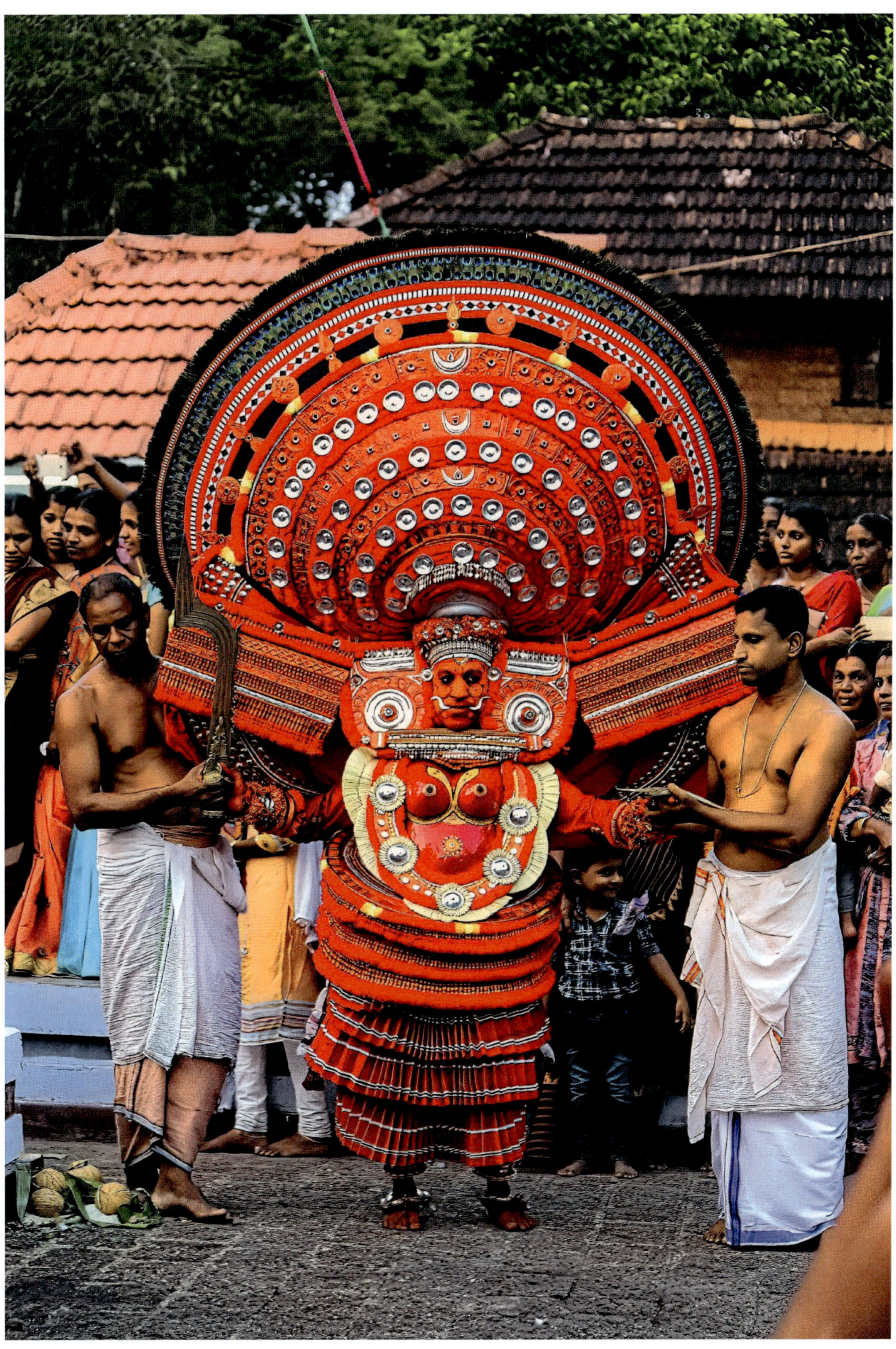

Acko Chamundi Theyyam

Acko Chamundi Theyyam is performed at *Kottayil Tharavadu* (a joint family system practiced by people in Kerala) of Kamballur village in Kasargod district. Acko Chamundi, a nymph from the orient, is the legend of this Theyyam and is believed to be the protector of Kamballur village. Hunter-gatherers perform this Theyyam Adivasi [16]Tribe called *Mavilan*.

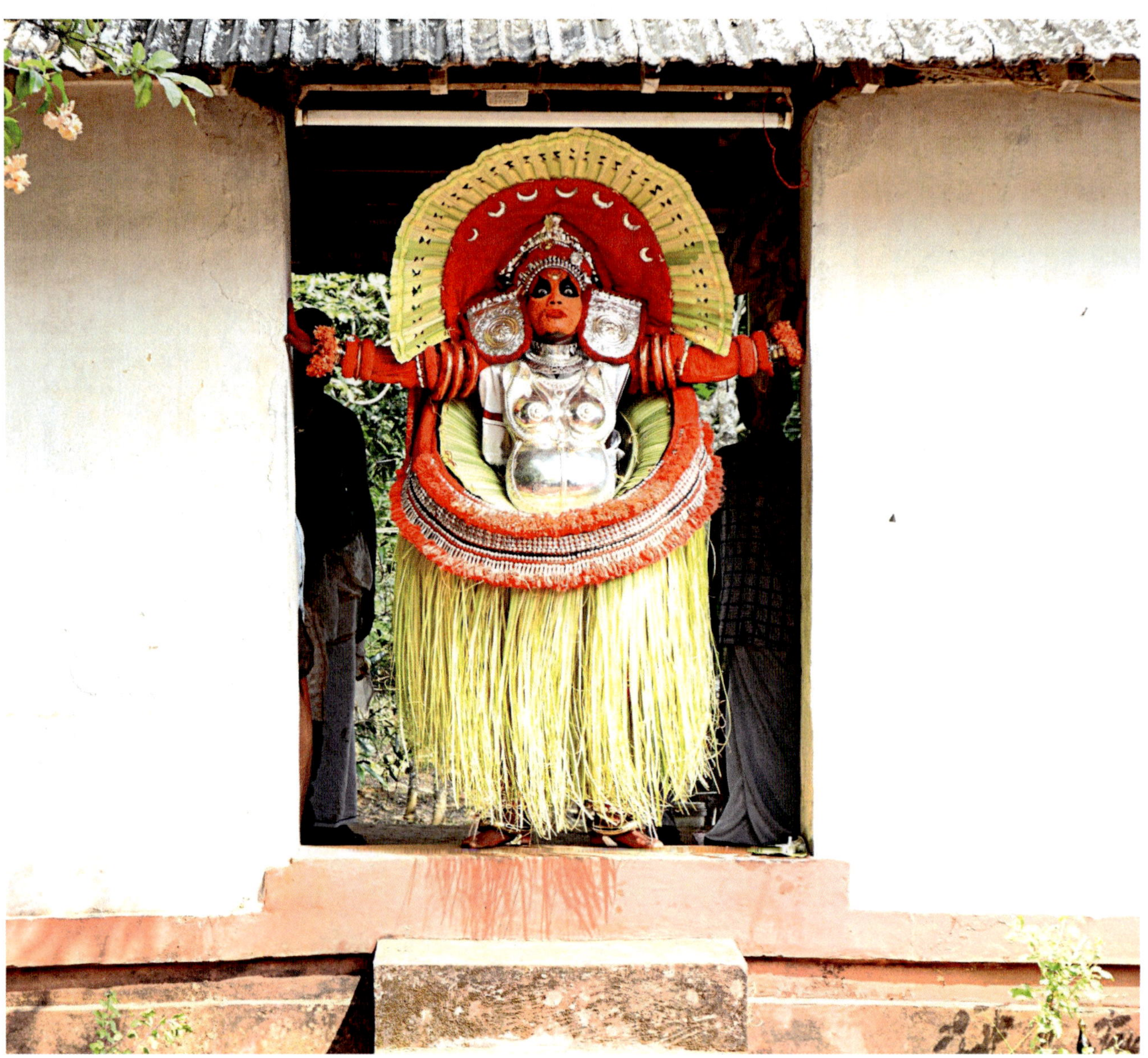

[16] The aboriginal tribal peoples living in India before the arrival of the Aryans in the second millennium BC.

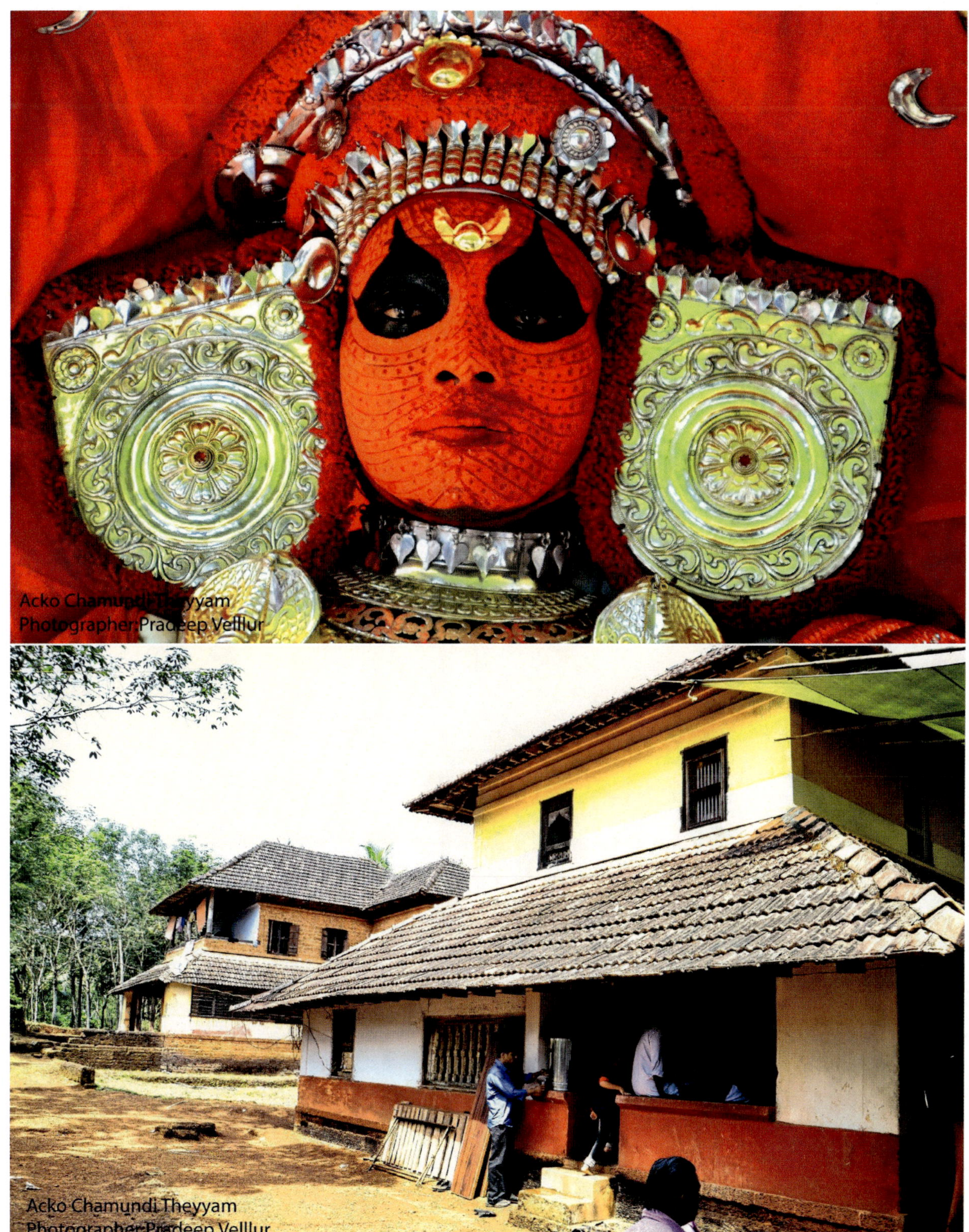

Acko Chamundi Theyyam
Photographer:Pradeep Velllur

Acko Chamundi Theyyam
Photographer:Pradeep Velllur

Dhooliyanga Bhagavathy

Dhooliyanga Bhagavathy emerged from the hundred-yardstick deep *Homakundam* (sacred fire pit for sacrifice) of the *Yaga* performed for Lord Shiva. She appeared along with *Haviss* (melted ghee used for sacrificial offering). Dhooliyanga Bhagavathy's name is derived from the word 'dhooli,' meaning dust or smoke. Usually, the *Vannan* community is the people who worship this Theyyam. She is also known as Guliyanka Bhagavathy, Kuliyanka Bhagavathy, etc.

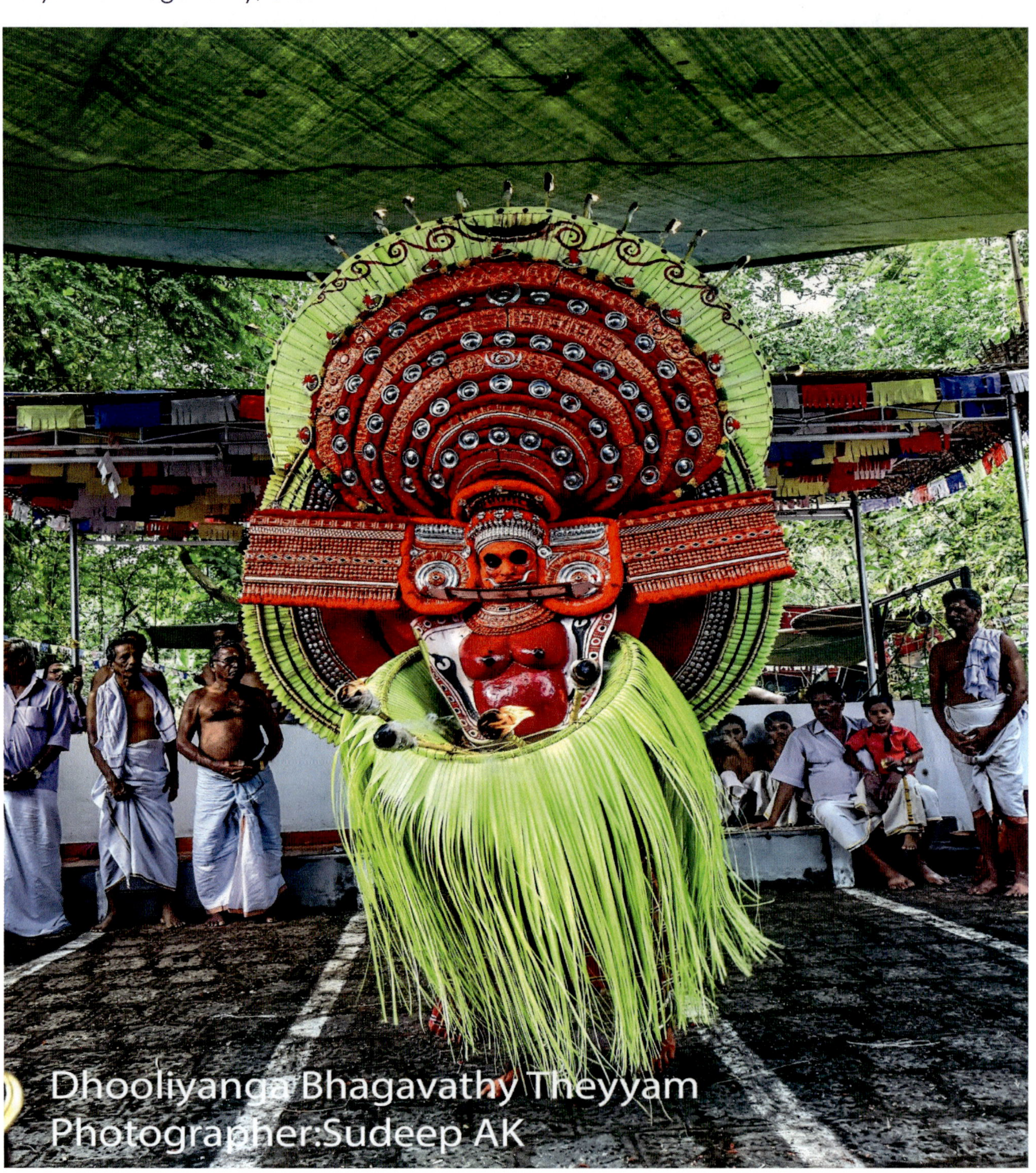
Dhooliyanga Bhagavathy Theyyam
Photographer:Sudeep AK

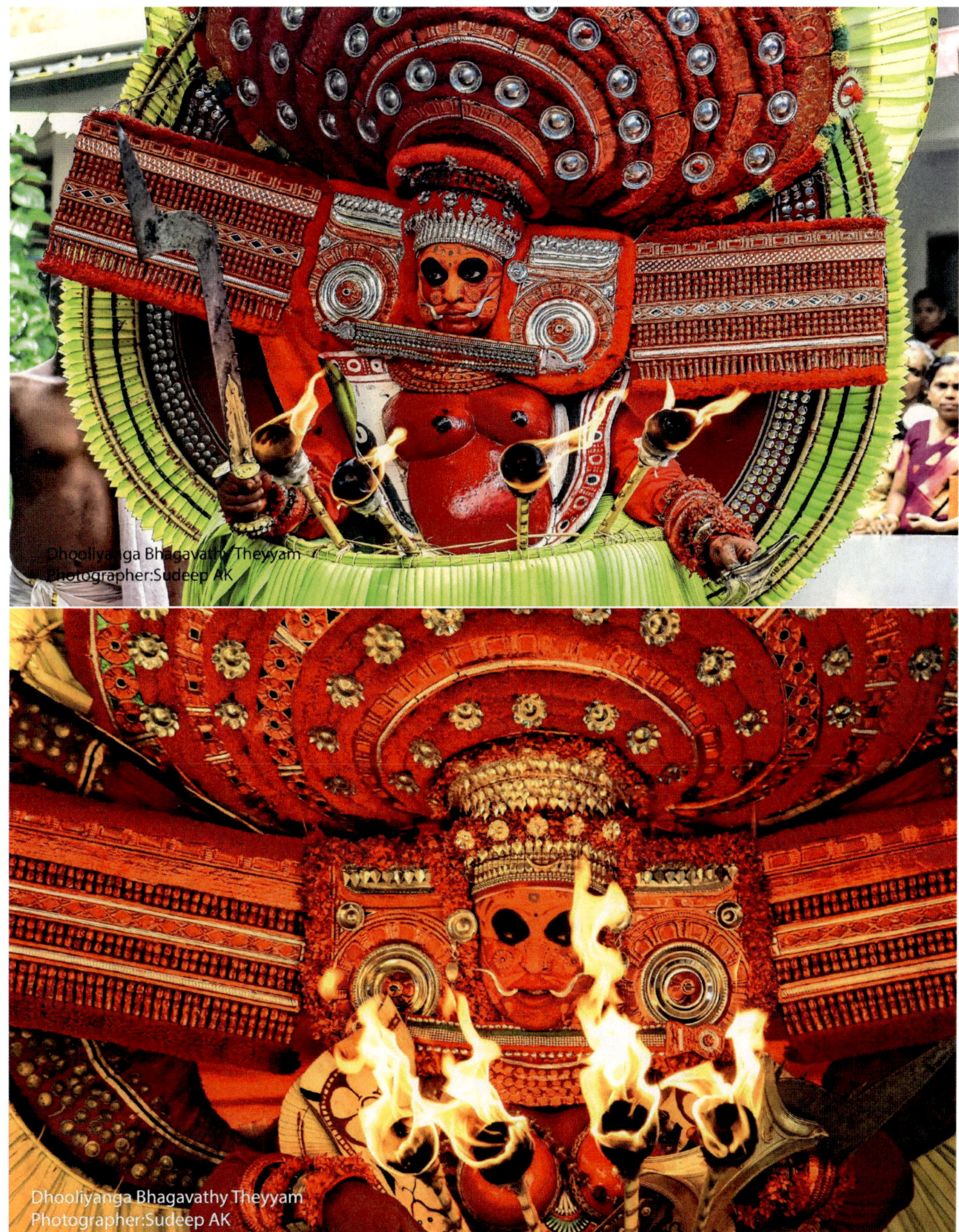
Dhooliyanga Bhagavathy Theyyam
Photographer:Sudeep AK
Dhooliyanga Bhagavathy Theyyam
Photographer:Sudeep AK

Brahmanjeri Bhagavathy

These Theyyams are performed by the *Vannan* community. According to the legends, this theyyam originated from the third eye of lord Shiva. Hence, she is considered his daughter. When she came to the planet earth, she took Puramancheri kavu as her abode at first. She is known as Puramancheri Bhagavathy for that reason. Later this name is changed from Pramanjeri to Brahmanjeri Bhagavathy through continuous use.

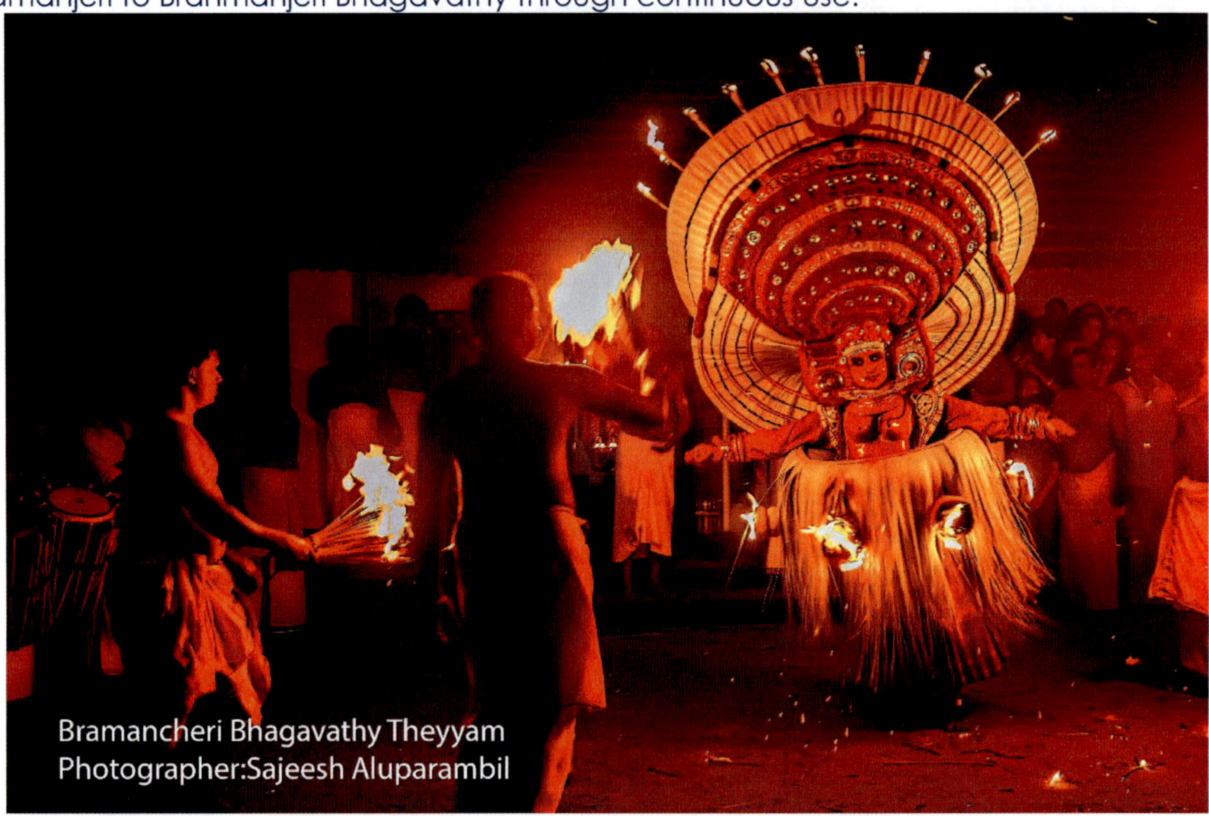

Bramancheri Bhagavathy Theyyam
Photographer:Sajeesh Aluparambil

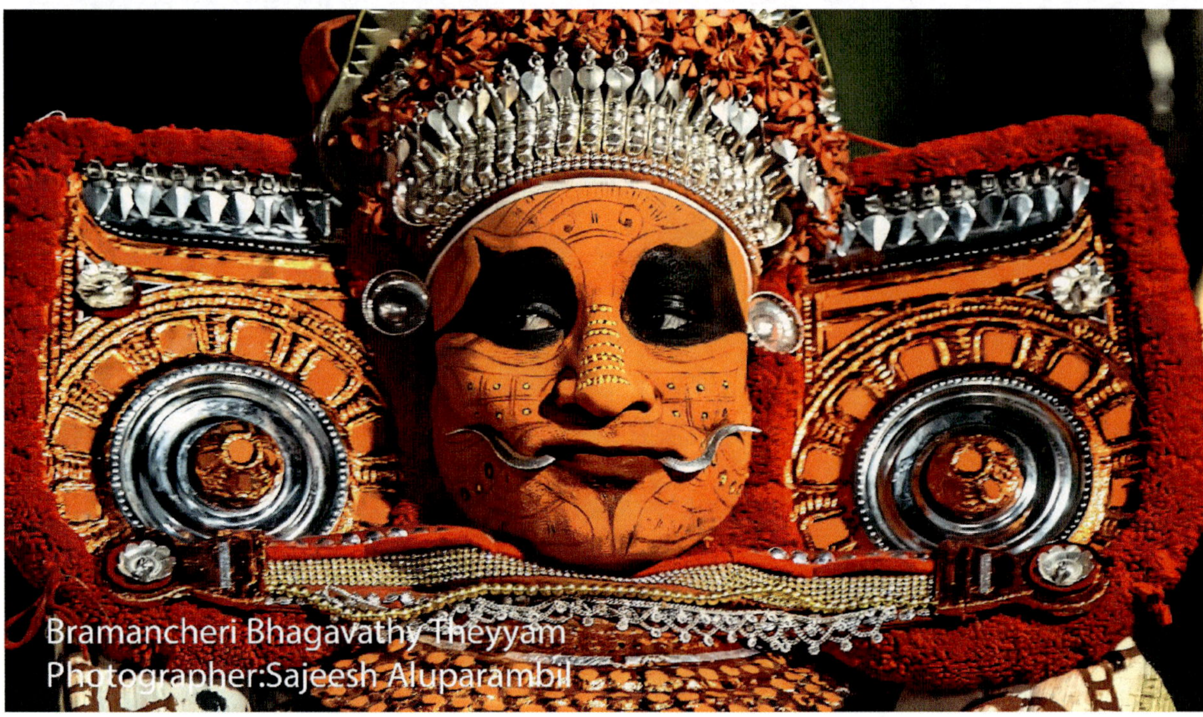

Bramancheri Bhagavathy Theyyam
Photographer:Sajeesh Aluparambil

Kallanthattu Bhagavathy

Kallanthattu Bhagavathy is considered the daughter of lord Shiva. She originated to destroy the Asuras (Demons). She is believed to be the protector of the people.

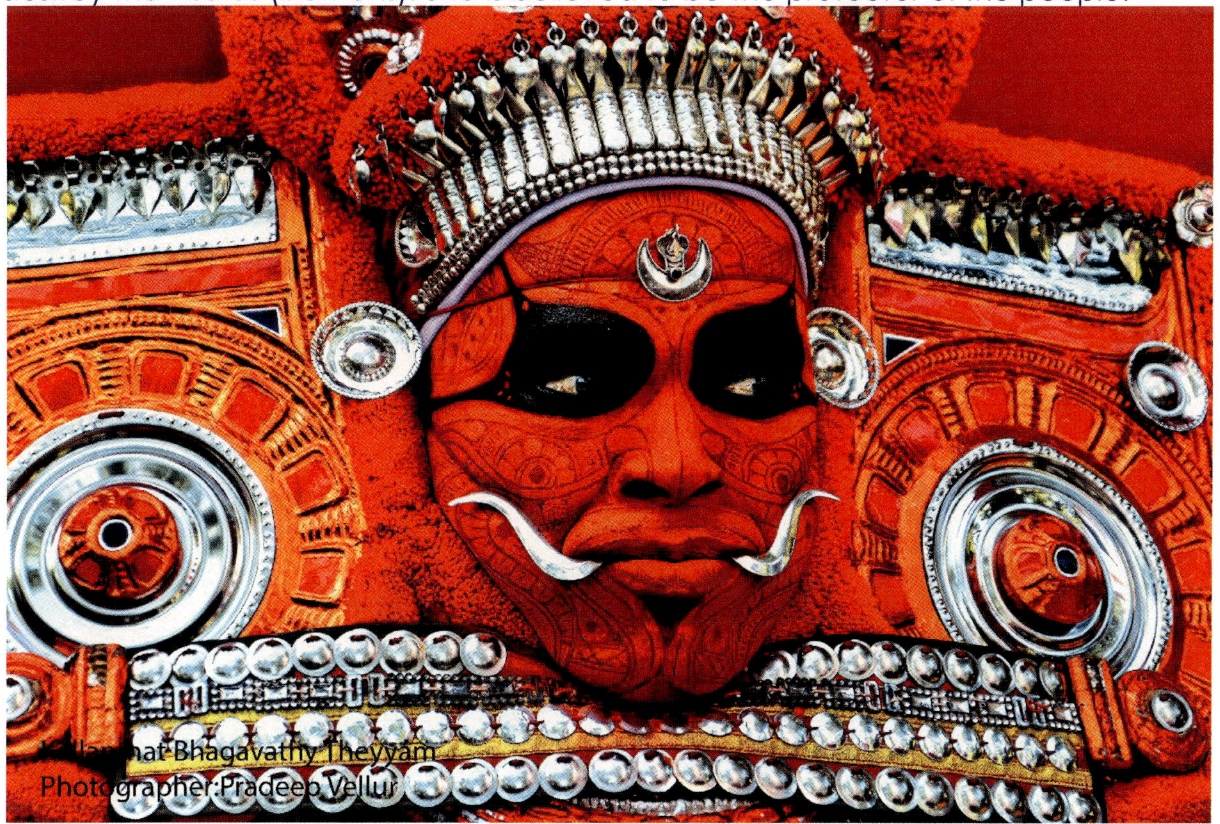

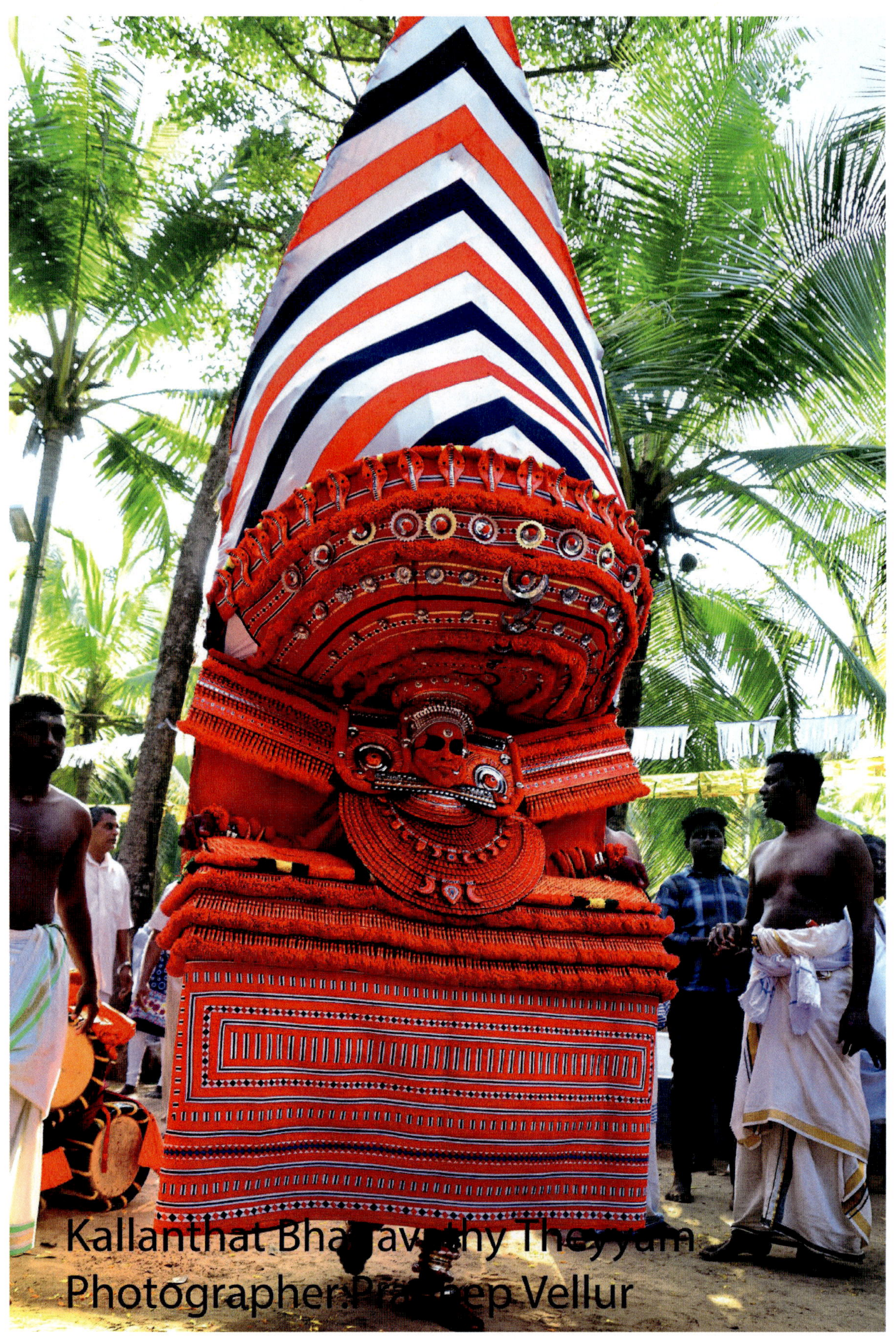

Kallanthat Bhagavathy Theyyam
Photographer:Pradeep Vellur

Vedan Theyyam

The five brothers known as Pandavas from the epic Mahabharata had to undergo forest-dwelling for a Vyazhavattam or a Jupiter cycle (the time taken by the planet Vyazham which is known as Jupiter in English, to revolve the sun once) since they failed in gambling. One among the brothers called Arjuna started a Pooja (ceremonial offering to God) to gain Pashupatasthra (a celestial weapon affiliated with Lord Shiva) during this time. Lord Shiva and Parvati, planning to test the devotee, came to that forest disguised as Kirata (A tribal hunter). While meditating, a wild boar caught Arjuna's attention, and he shot an arrow at it. Lord Shiva, disguised as Kirata, also shot an arrow in its head after Arjuna. The boar fell. Both of them initiate a fight over who owns the pig. The quarrel led to war. Adiveda's story is connected with this incident.

During the war, Arjuna became unconscious and fell to the ground after being struck by the arrow. He felt ashamed for being beaten by a Kirata. Arjuna decided to fight back and started Shiva Linga Pooja (Worshipping, a religious symbol in Hinduism that represents Lord Shiva) to attain strength from Lord Shiva. But all the flower petals he offered in the Shiva Linga began to fall on the Kirata. Arjuna realized that it was Lord Shiva himself who came in the form of Kirata to test him. He fell at their feet and offered homage. Pleased by his actions, The Ardhanareeswara (a form of Lord Shiva combined with his consort Parvati) presented Pasupatasthra to Arjun and returned to Kailasa Mountains. The Kirata form of Lord Shiva is the one who incarnates as Adivedan and visits houses.

When Theyyam comes home, people receive it by lighting the lamp in the west. After a dance with bells, the eldest ladies of the house carry the lamps and burn ashes in the fire. After the process of Gurusi (a method of worshiping various forms of Mother Goddess like Goddess Bhadrakali), the negative energy is supposed to leave the house and surroundings while prosperity enters. A certain amount of money, rice, and coconut are the offerings delivered. Theyyams go to the rest of the houses only after the visit of the temple authorities, people from Tharavadus, etc.

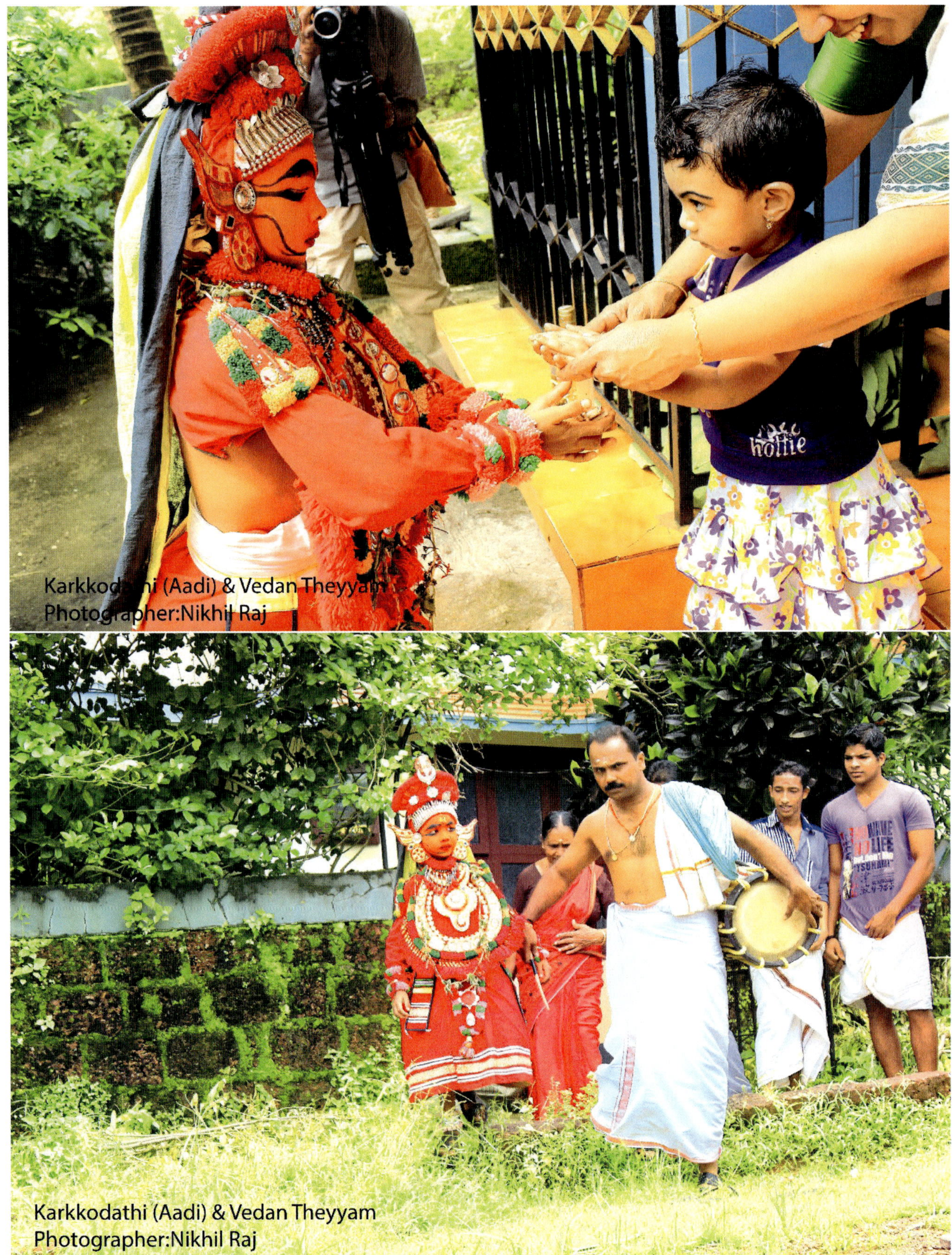

Karkkodathi (Aadi) & Vedan Theyyam
Photographer:Nikhil Raj

Karkkodathi (Aadi) & Vedan Theyyam
Photographer:Nikhil Raj

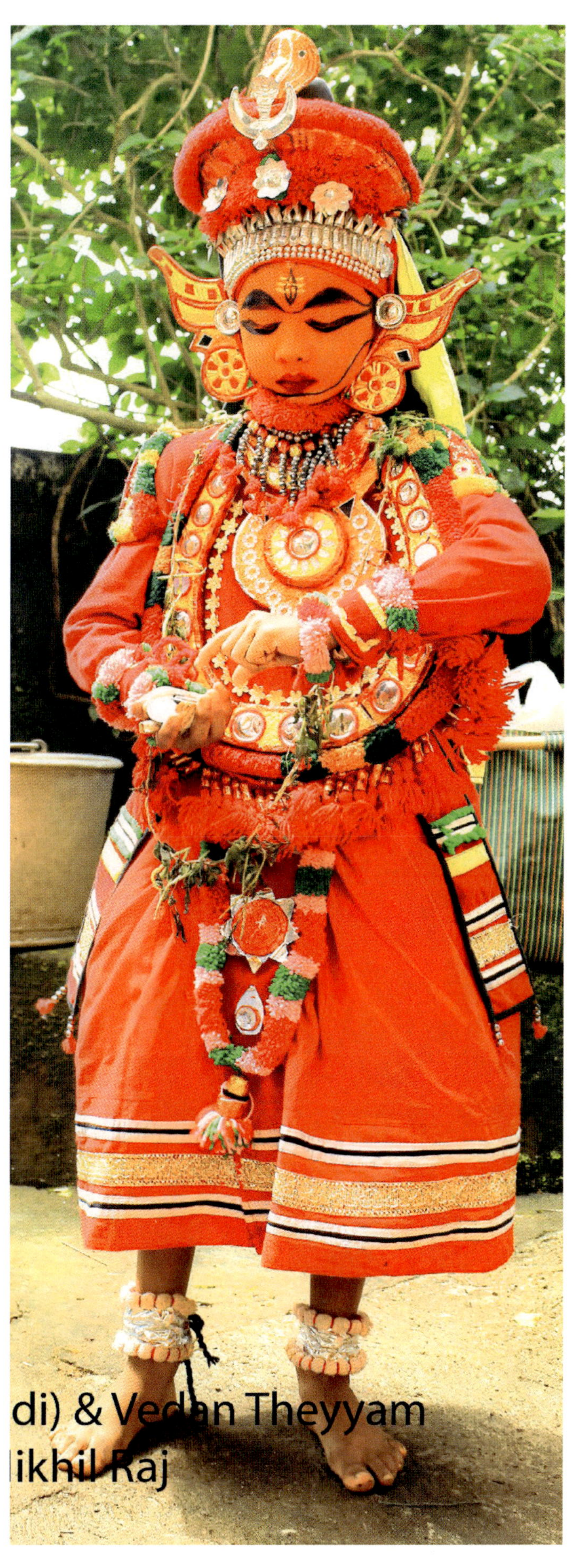

di) & Vedan Theyyam
ikhil Raj

CONTRIBUTORS

Content & Editorial

1. Saji Madapat
   Santhosh Vengara (Images & Source Stories)
2. Nandakumar Gopalan
3. Sachin Malayattil
4. Shwetha S Kumar
5. Poorna Krishnan
6. Aswathy Anitha
7. Sumeera Ashraf

Images

COVER IMAGE: Pulli Bhagavathy Theyyam by Vikas Kidakkat

1. Santhosh Vengara (Images & Source Stories)
2. Saji Madapat
3. Pradeep Vellur
4. Bijith K
5. Hari M
6. Jasin Aniyeri
7. Lijil Nallakandy
8. Nikhil Raj
9. Prasoon Kiran
10. Priyank preman
11. Rahul Palora
12. Rajeevan Unnaiparavan
13. Sajeesh Aluparambil
14. Saneesh kulappuram
15. Santhosh T P
16. Shahan Abdul Samad
17. Shyamnath PV
18. Subin Kothrone
19. Sudeep AK
20. Swaroop Sathyan
21. Vikas Kodakkat
22. Vipindas P.V
23. Yadhu Vengara
24. Ranjith M V

Humble Request to Review My Book

*I trust that you enjoyed reading this book. I'd like to hear from you and humbly request you take a few minutes to post a review on Amazon. Your feedback and support will significantly improve my writing craft for future books and make this book even more commendable. This is a living manuscript and will continuously evolve based on your constructive wisdom (**direct contact details @ https://www.epm-mavericks.com/sanctuary**). Thank you in advance!*

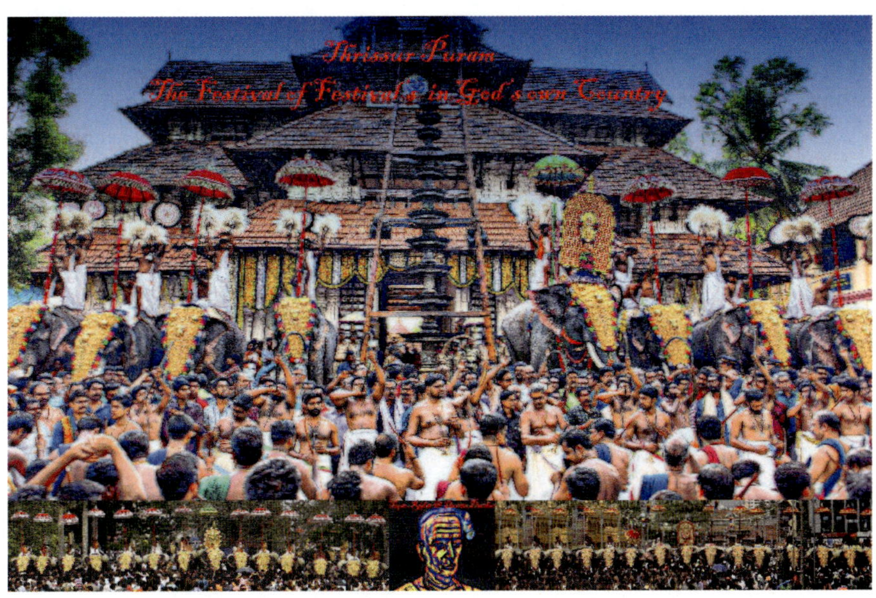

For a FREE Copy of my other books, please contact

@ https://www.epm-mavericks.com/sanctuary

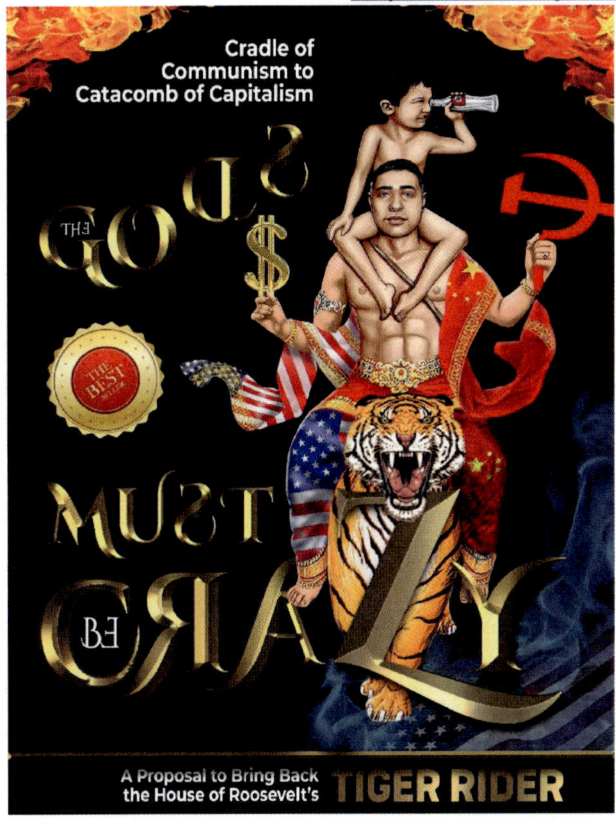

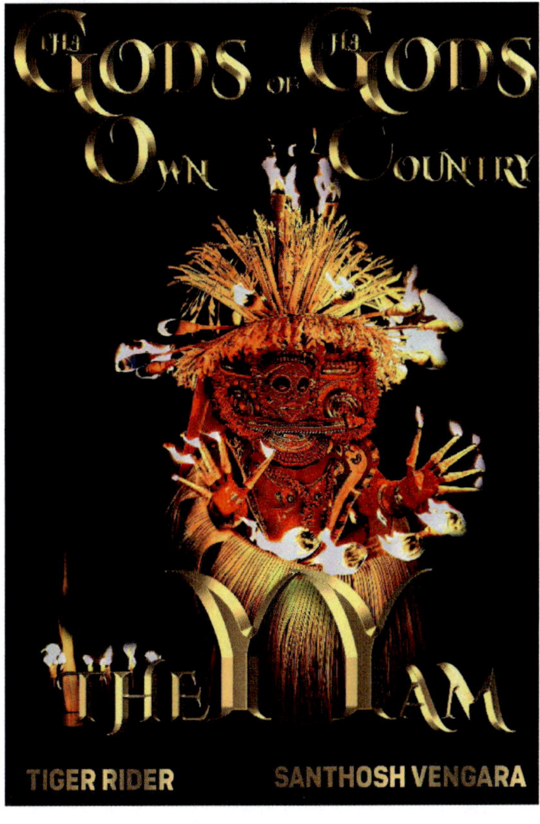

Made in the USA
Monee, IL
21 November 2022

3a31bb60-1ee3-450f-b121-90734f074287R01